Libraries
Read Learn Connect

THIS BOOK IS PART OF ISLINGTON READS BOOKSWAP SCHEME

Please take this book and either return it to a Bookswap site or replace with one of your own books that you would like to share.

If you enjoy this book, why not join your local Islington Library and borrow more like it for free?

Find out about our FREE e-book, e-audio, newspaper and magazine apps, activities for pre-school children and other services we have to offer at www.islington.gov.uk/libraries

ISLINGTON
For a more equal future

CONSTANTINOPOLIS / ISTANBUL

CONSTANTINOPOLIS / ISTANBUL

Cultural Encounter, Imperial Vision, and the Construction of the Ottoman Capital

Çiğdem Kafescioğlu

THE PENNSYLVANIA STATE UNIVERSITY PRESS

UNIVERSITY PARK, PENNSYLVANIA

Publication of this book has been aided by a grant from the Graham Foundation for Advanced Studies in the Fine Arts.

MM

Publication of this book has been aided by a grant from the Millard Meiss Publication Fund of the College Art Association.

Library of Congress Cataloging-in-Publication Data
Kafescioglu, Cigdem.
Constantinopolis/Istanbul : cultural encounter, imperial vision, and the construction of the Ottoman capital / Cigdem Kafescioglu.
        p.   cm.—(Buildings, landscapes, and societies)

Includes bibliographical references and index.
Summary: "Studies the reconstruction of Byzantine Constantinople as the capital city of the Ottoman empire following its capture in 1453, delineating the complex interplay of sociopolitical, architectural, visual, and literary processes that underlay the city's transformation"—Provided by publisher.
ISBN 978-0-271-02776-0 (cloth : alk. paper)

1. Architecture, Ottoman—Turkey—Istanbul.
2. Architecture, Islamic—Turkey—Istanbul.
3. Architecture and state—Turkey—Istanbul—History—15th century.
4. Architecture and state—Turkey—Istanbul—History—16th century.
5. Istanbul (Turkey)—Buildings, structures, etc.
6. Istanbul (Turkey)—In art.
I. Title.

NA1370.K34 2009
720.94961'8—dc22
2009002611

The Pennsylvania State University Press is a member of the Association of American University Presses.

It is the policy of The Pennsylvania State University Press to use acid-free paper. Publications on uncoated stock satisfy the minimum requirements of American National Standard for Information Sciences—Permanence of Paper for Printed Library Material, ANSI Z39.48–1992.

To *Ahmet* and *Mihri*

CONTENTS

Color Plates follow page 142

MAP 1
Major sites and constructions in Constantinople/Istanbul during the reign of Mehmed II.

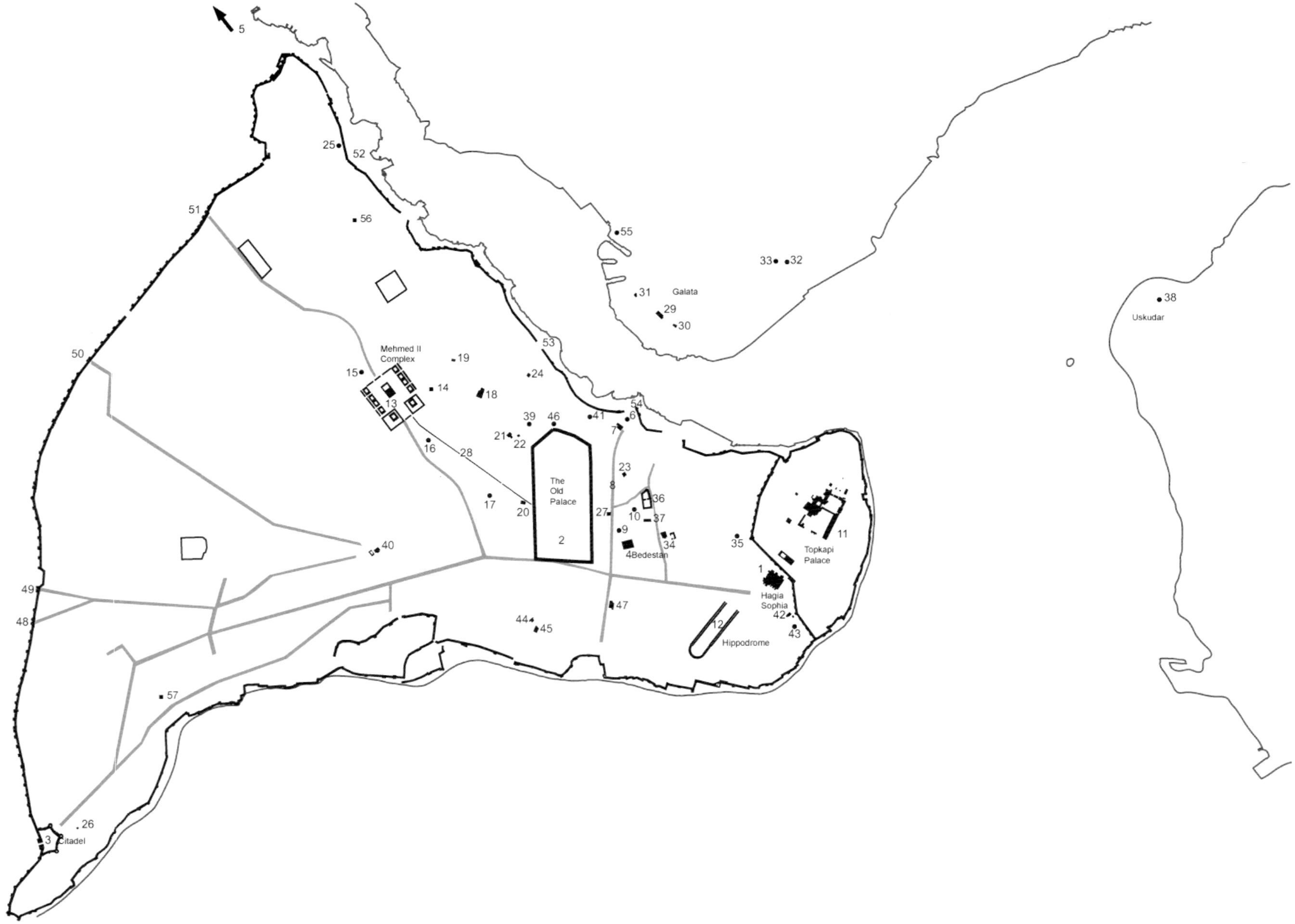

Topkapı Palace
Hagia Sophia
Hippodrome
The Old Palace
Bedesten
Mehmed II Complex
Galata
Üsküdar
Citadel

1. Hagia Sophia
2. Old Palace
3. Citadel (Seven Towers)
4. Bedestan and markets complex
5. Ayyub al-Ansari funerary complex
6. Hacı Halil masjid/Taht al-kalʿa market
7. Taht al-kalʿa bath
8. Makros Embolos/Uzunçarşı
9. Sultan caravanserai (hypothetical location)
10. Beglik caravanserai (hypothetical location)
11. Topkapı Palace
12. Hippodrome
13. Mosque complex of Mehmed II
14. Çukur bath
15. Sultan Bazarı markets
16. Sarrachane (saddlemakers) markets
17. Janissary barracks (hypothetical location)
18. Pantokrator monastery/Zeyrek madrasa and masjid
19. Eski İmaret soup kitchen and masjid
20. Kyriotissa church/Kalenderhane convent and masjid
21. Vefa convent
22. Vefa bath
23. Samanviran masjid
24. Yavuzer Sinan masjid
25. Balat bath
26. Citadel bath
27. Mercan Ağa masjid and Sırt bath
28. Aqueduct of Valens
29. St. Paolo church/Friday mosque of Galata (Arap Cami)
30. Bath in the quarter of the Friday mosque
31. Direklice bath
32. Tophane (cannon foundry)
33. Tophane bath
34. Mahmud Pasha convent-mosque and madrasa
35. Mahmud Pasha palace (hypothetical location)
36. Mahmud Pasha caravanserai
37. Mahmud Pasha bath
38. Rum Mehmed Pasha complex
39. Rum Mehmed Pasha palace (hypothetical location)
40. Has Murad Pasha complex
41. Has Murad Pasha caravanserai (hypothetical location)
42. İshak Pasha masjid and bath
43. İshak Pasha palace (hypothetical location)
44. Nişancı Mehmed Pasha masjid
45. Nişancı Mehmed Pasha bath
46. Nişancı Mehmed Pasha palace (hypothetical location)
47. Gedik Ahmed Pasha bath
48. Kalagru Gate
49. Silivri Gate
50. Cannon Gate
51. Edirne Gate
52. Balat Gate
53. Un Kapusı
54. Feslügen/Vasiliko Gate
55. Arsenal
56. Monastery of the Pammakaristos; Greek Orthodox patriarchate
57. Monastery of St. Mary Peribleptos (Sulu Manastır)

MAP 1 LEGEND   xix

Uskudar

Galata

Topkapi Palace

Hagia Sophia

Hippodrome

Bedestan

The Old Palace

Mehmed II Complex

Citadel

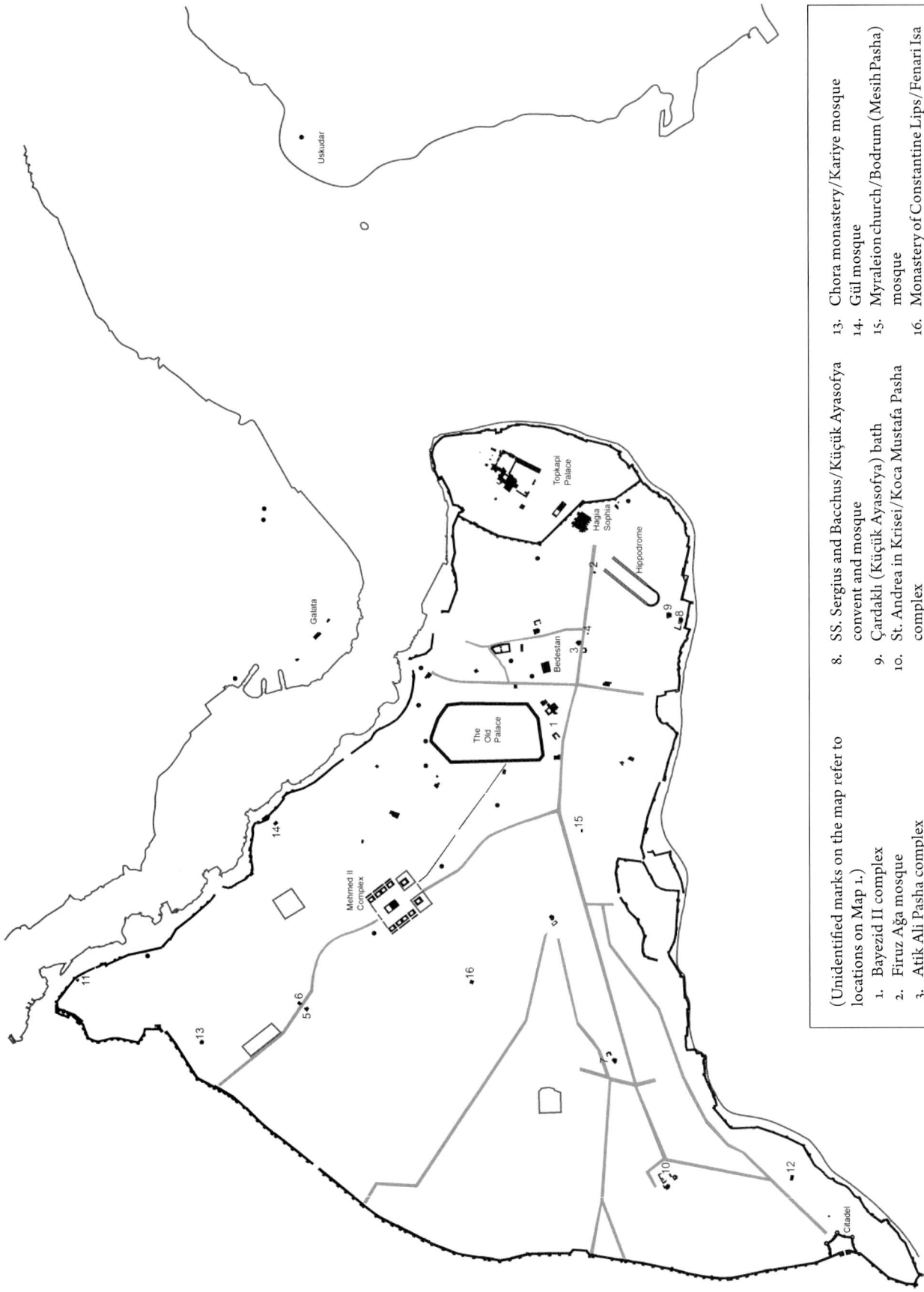

(Unidentified marks on the map refer to locations on Map 1.)

1. Bayezid II complex
2. Firuz Ağa mosque
3. Atik Ali Pasha complex
4. Elçi Hanı
5. Zincirlikuyu bath
6. Zincirlikuyu (Atik Ali Pasha) mosque
7. Davud Pasha complex

8. SS. Sergius and Bacchus/Küçük Ayasofya convent and mosque
9. Çardaklı (Küçük Ayasofya) bath
10. St. Andrea in Krisei/Koca Mustafa Pasha complex
11. St. Thekla (?) church/Atik Mustafa Pasha mosque
12. St. John Studius monastery/Imrahor mosque and convent

13. Chora monastery/Kariye mosque
14. Gül mosque
15. Myraleion church/Bodrum (Mesih Pasha) mosque
16. Monastery of Constantine Lips/Fenari Isa mosque

MAP 3

Quarters of Istanbul *intra muros*, 1453–1546 (legend follows, pages xxii–xxiii).

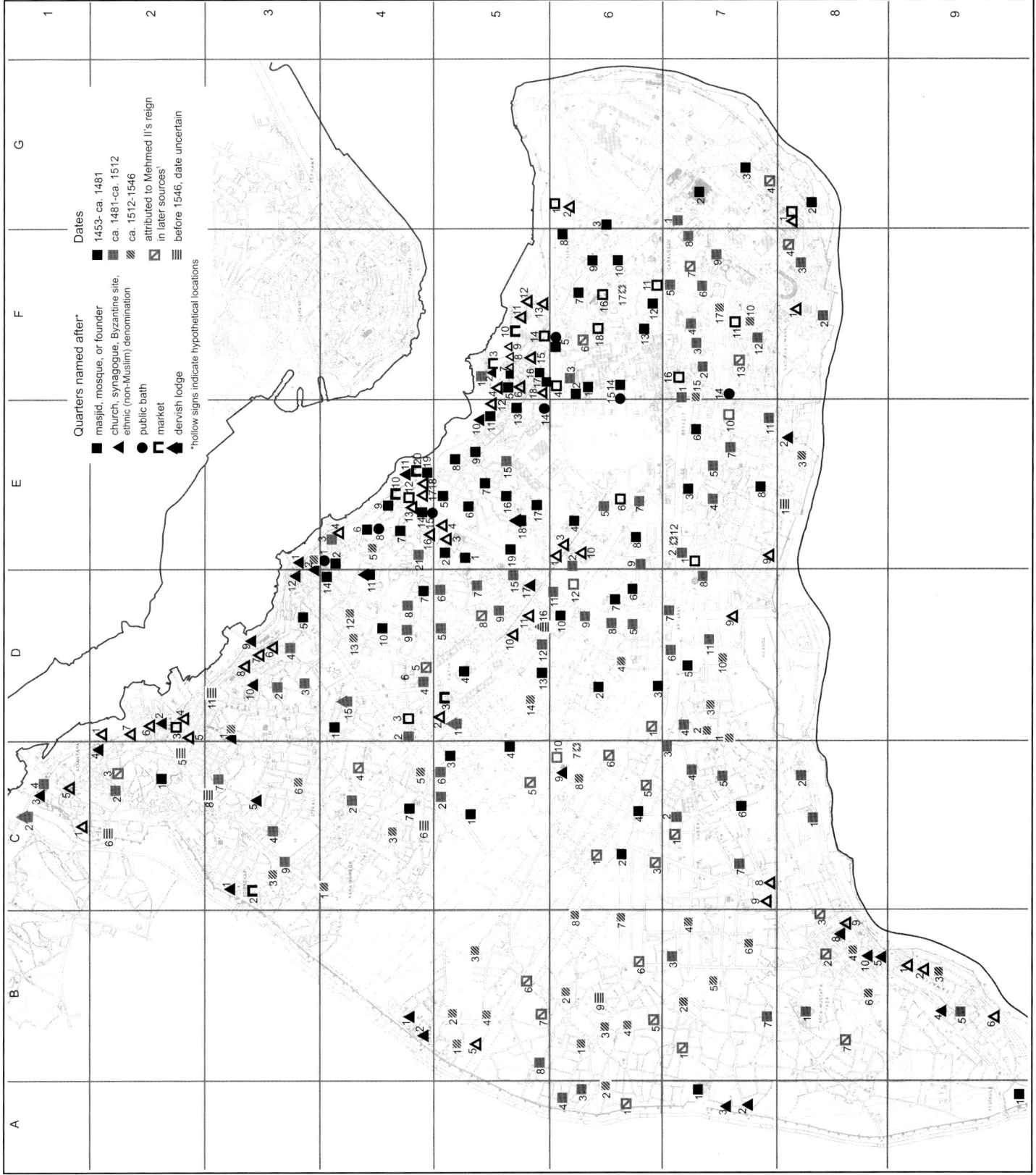

Quarters named after*

- ■ masjid, mosque, or founder
- ◀ church, synagogue, Byzantine site, ethnic (non-Muslim) denomination
- ● public bath
- □ market
- ◀ dervish lodge

*hollow signs indicate hypothetical locations

Dates

- ■ 1453– ca. 1481
- ■ ca. 1481–ca. 1512
- ▨ ca. 1512–1546
- ▢ attributed to Mehmed II's reign in later sources[1]
- ▤ before 1546, date uncertain

A6: 1. Tarsus masjid
2. Evliya masjid
3. Yazıcı Murad (Hasırcı) masjid
4. Melek Hatun (Karaağaç) masjid

A7: 1. Bala Süleyman Ağa masjid
2. Silivri Gate
3. Mahelle-i Yeni

A9: 1. Kulle (citadel) mosque

B4: 1. Topyıkuğı
2. Aya Romano Bab-ı Tob

B5: 1. İskender Beg masjid
2. Bayezid Ağa masjid
3. Katib Müslihüddin masjid
4. Kürkcibaşı masjid
5. Manastır
6. Ereglü (Şehremini) mosque
7. Sufiler masjid
8. Simkeş Hacı masjid

B6: 1. Mimar Acem masjid
2. Yusuf Fakih (Cafer Ağa) masjid
3. Hace Muhyiddin
4. Yayla (Aydın Kethüda) masjid
5. Uzun Yusuf masjid
6. Koruk Mahmud masjid and lodge
7. Macuncu Kasım masjid
8. Sarrac Doğan masjid
9. Çavuş Hacı İbrahim masjid

B7: 1. Kapucı Karagöz masjid
2. Zihgirci Kemal masjid
3. Seyyid Ömer masjid
4. Hacı Timur masjid
5. Arabacı Bayezid masjid
6. Katib Müslihüddin masjid
7. Canbaz Mustafa Beg masjid

B8: 1. Koca Mustafa Pasha mosque and lodge
2. Mirza Baba masjid
3. Sancakdar Hayrüddin masjid
4. Abdi Çelebi (Çilingirler) masjid
5. Samatya Gate
6. Hacı Kadın masjid
7. Ali Fakih masjid
8. Sulu Manastır
9. Argos
10. Kulikarpe (Hagias Menas)

B9: 1. İbn-i Marola
2. İbsomatya
3. Hacı Hüseyin masjid
4. Aya Kostandin church (Ermeniyan-ı Karaman)
5. İmrahor İlyas Bey mosque and lodge
6. Bab-ı İstemad

C1: 1. Vlaherna (Tekvur)
2. Yavedut
3. Eksiliporta
4. Tokludede masjid
5. Eleğuza ve Alagöz tabiꞋ Eksiliporta

C2: 1. Mevlana Aşki masjid
2. Hacı İlyas (Yatağan) masjid
3. Hace Ali masjid
4. Aya Dimitri church
5. Hacı İsa masjid
6. Çakırcıbaşı (Egrikapı) masjid

C3: 1. Edirne Gate
2. Çarşu-yı bab-ı Edirne (S. Dimitri)
3. Hace Muhyiddin masjid
4. Kasım Ağa masjid
5. Kefeluyan (S. Nikola and S. Maria)
6. Mimar Derviş Ali masjid
7. Hammami Muhyiddin masjid
8. Hacı Kasım masjid
9. Hadice Sultan masjid

C4: 1. Keçeci Piri masjid
2. Atik Ali Pasha mosque (Zincirlikuyu)
3. Muhtesib İskender masjid
4. Efdalzade masjid
5. Hasan Pasha (later Mesih Mehmed Pasha) mosque
6. Akşemseddin masjid
7. Akseki masjid

C5: 1. Mimar Sinan masjid
2. Mevlana Ahaveyn masjid
3. Hace Üveys masjid
4. KemalüꞋl Harrat (Sarıgez) masjid
5. Saru Nasuh masjid
6. Hacı İvaz bin Kassab masjid

C6: 1. Saru Nasuh
2. Nurlu Dede masjid
3. Mevlana Fenayi masjid
4. Mevlana Gürani masjid
5. Saru Musa masjid
6. Eğri Minare masjid
7. Tahta Minare masjid
8. Mevlana Şeref masjid
9. Libs Manastırı
10. Nukreci Bali masjid

C7: 1. Etmekcioğlu (Nevbahar) masjid
2. Başcı masjid
3. Şirmerd Çavuş masjid
4. Keyçi Hatun masjid
5. Canbaz Mustafa Beg masjid
6. Hubyar masjid
7. Davud Pasha mosque
8. İsa Kapu
9. Altımermer (Exi Marmara)

C8: 1. Bayezid-i Cedīd masjid
2. Kasap İlyas masjid

D2: 1. Günkoz Kapusı
2. Balat
3. Suk-ı Balat (Balat Bazarı)
4. Baryak
5. Ohri
6. Kenise-i Havr[a]

7. Kinkoz Eftalyanos ve Çarşu-yı Eftalyanos

D3: 1. Pammakaristos church/Fethiye mosque
2. Tacbegzade (Nişancı Cafer Çelebi) masjid
3. Cebecibaşı masjid
4. Mismarcı Hacı Şüca (Ekserci) masjid
5. Debbağ Yunus masjid
6. Batrik
7. Fanar Trabzon
8. Fanar Cinboz
9. Balat kapısı
10. Theotokos Mouchliotissa
11. Tahta Minare
12. Ayakapu

D4: 1. Begcügezoğlu masjid
2. Pirincci Sinan Ağa masjid
3. Kıztaşı
4. Ahi Çelebi
5. Kirmasti masjid
6. Şeyh Resmi masjid
7. Eski İmaret
8. Sinan Ağa masjid
9. Yarhisarzade masjid
10. Altı Boğaca masjid
11. Aşık Pasha (Sarı Saltık) lodge and masjid
12. Müfti Ali Çelebi masjid
13. Çerağcı Hamza masjid
14. Küçük Mustafa Pasha mosque
15. Kovacı Dede lodge and masjid

D5: 1. Emir Buhari lodge
2. Seyyidi Ali
3. Sultan Bazarı
4. The New [Mehmed II] Mosque
5. Haraccı masjid
6. Hacı Hasanzade masjid
7. Şeyh Süleyman Halife masjid
8. Demirciler masjid
9. Manisavi Mehmed Çelebi masjid
10. Can Alıcı church
11. Gürci
12. Dülgerzade masjid
13. Mustafa Beg masjid
14. İskender Pasha mosque
15. Sekbanbaşı İbrahim Beg masjid
16. Karaca Ahmed lodge
17. Kırkçeşme

D6: 1. Cerrah İshak Beg (later Kazgani Sadi) masjid
2. Mevlana Husrev (Sofular) masjid
3. Murad Pasha mosque
4. Kızıl Minare masjid
5. Oruçgazi masjid
6. Kemal Pasha mausoleum
7. Hacı Hoşkadem masjid

8. Baba Hasan masjid
9. Muhtesib Karagöz masjid
10. Mimar Ayas masjid
11. Firuz Ağa masjid
12. Haydarhane masjid

D7: 1. Kürkcibaşı masjid
2. Ahmed Kethüda masjid
3. Katib Müslihüddin masjid
4. Hacı Bayram Haftani masjid
5. Çakır Ağa masjid
6. Garib Yiğitler Ağası (Camcılar) masjid
7. Alemi Beg (Iğciler) masjid
8. Bodrum mosque
9. Langa (Ulanka)
10. Bostan masjid
11. Koğacı Dede (Baklalı) masjid

E3: 1. Aya Nikola church
2. Aya Kenisası/Gül mosque

E4: 1. Mustafa Pasha bath
2. Mevlana Husrev masjid
3. Sivrikoz masjid
4. Cübbe Ali
5. Şeyh Muhyiddin Kocavi (Karanlık) masjid
6. Çakır Ağa (Üsküblü) masjid
7. Babuccıoğlu (İbn-i Meddas) masjid
8. Haydar bath
9. Haraccı Kara Mehmed Beg masjid
10. Debbagin
11. İskele Gate
12. Saruhan masjid
13. Tatarlar
14. Sinan bin Elvan masjid
15. Azebler bath
16. Fil Damı
17. Sinan Halveti
18. Mustafa Ragıyfi
19. Yavuzer Sinan masjid
20. Un Kapanı
21. Bıçakcı Acem Ali masjid

E5: 1. Zeyrek madrasa masjid
2. Ali bin Hacı Demirhan masjid
3. Defterdar Sinan
4. Yusuf Seffad
5. Arabacılar masjid
6. Hızır Beg masjid
7. Mehmed Pasha masjid
8. Hace Hayrüddin masjid
9. Bodrum masjid
10. Odun Kapusı
11. Saru Timur masjid
12. Tabib Yakub
13. Hace Hamza masjid

14. Küçükpazar bath
15. Katib Şemsüddin (Cankurtaran) masjid
16. Saru Bayezid masjid
17. Kilise (Mevlana Gürani) madrasa
18. Şeyh Vefa lodge and masjid
19. Hace Teberrük masjid

E6: 1. Topcu Urban Evleri
2. Emin Nurüddin (Burmalı) masjid
3. Manastır (Kilisa-i Panaya)
4. Mevlana Husrev masjid
5. Kalenderhane
6. Dalgıç Ahmed
7. Camcı Kara Ali masjid
8. Balaban Ağa masjid
9. Mevlana Kestel masjid
10. Gedikci

E7: 1. Mimar Kemaloğlu masjid
2. Katib Bali (Kızıltaş) masjid
3. Sekbanbaşı Yakub Ağa masjid
4. Katib Sinan masjid
5. Soğan Ağa masjid
6. Emin Beg (Dibekli) masjid
7. Sarrac İshak masjid
8. Nişancı masjid
9. Kiramarte
10. Kemal Nahhas masjid
11. Çadırcı Ahmed masjid
12. Kuyumcu Bahşayiş

E8: 1. Cerrah İshak Beg (Kazgancı) masjid
2. Kumkapu
3. Tavaşi Süleyman Ağa masjid

F5: 1. Ahi Çelebi masjid
2. Vasiliko Gate
3. Taht al-kalᶜa
4. Musa Beg
5. Timurtaş masjid
6. Aslanlı Ev
7. Hace Keşkek
8. Yavaşca Şahin
9. Bezzaz-ı Cedīd
10. Acemoğlu
11. Halil Pasha Bergosu
12. Bozahaneler
13. Orya Gate
14. Balık Bazarı
15. Edirneli Yahudiler/Hacı Halil masjid
16. Saruca Pasha
17. Han-ı Gürani
18. Maruloğlu

F6: 1. Samanviran masjid
2. Merdivenli masjid

3. İbrahim Pasha mosque
4. Hubyar masjid
5. Alaca bath and Çelebioğlu masjid
6. Hacı Küçük masjid
7. Kara Şems
8. Hace Sinan bin Elvan masjid
9. Hace Üveys (Hoca Pasha) mosque
10. Nallı masjid
11. Şeref Ağa masjid
12. Servi masjid
13. Mahmud Pasha mosque
14. Mercan Ağa masjid
15. Sırt bath
16. Hace Sinan bin Hace Kasım
17. Sahhaf Süleyman
18. Daye Hatun

F7: 1. Hace Piri masjid
2. Mimar Hayrüddin masjid
3. Atik Ali Pasha mosque
4. Mevlana Fenari
5. Cezeri Kasım Pasha masjid
6. Hace Rüstem masjid
7. Çatalçeşme masjid
8. Üskübiye masjid
9. Firuz Ağa masjid
10. Dizdarzade masjid
11. Uzun Şüca masjid
12. Katib Sinan masjid
13. Emin Sinan masjid
14. Gedik Ahmed Pasha bath
15. Halıcı Hasan masjid
16. Divane Ali Bey
17. Sinan Ağa masjid

F8: 1. Limun-ı Kadırga
2. Küçük Ayasofya mosque and lodge
3. Nakılbend Hasan masjid
4. Kağnı masjid

G6: 1. Daye Hatun masjid
2. Nevbethane
3. Karakadi Hüseyin Çelebi masjid

G7: 1. Acem Ağa (Hayrüddin Beg) masjid
2. Ayasofya mosque
3. İshak Pasha mosque
4. Cankurtaran masjid

G8: 1. Güngörmez church/masjid
2. Akbıyık masjid

(Note: Attributions from Hafız Hüseyin al-Ayvansarayi2019s *Ḥadīḳatü*'l Cevāmiᶜ or from the 953/1546 survey of foundations to be supported by royal funds.)

MAP 3 LEGEND   xxiii

MAP 4

Map of Constantinople in Cristoforo Buondelmonti's *Liber Insularum Archipelagi,* ink drawing, ca. 1481 (fig. 111), with legend.

1. Byzantion (Topkapı Palace)
2. S. Elini
3. S. Maria
4. S. Paulus
5. S. Demetrius
6. Darsinale regium
7. Stabula regis
7a. Darsinale
8. Constantinopolis
9. S. Sophia
10. Theodosius (statue of Justinian in the Augustaion)
11. Palacium ruptum (remains of the Great Palace)
12. Ipodromus (Hippodrome)
13. Imarat Maomot Bassa (convent-mosque of Mahmud Pasha)
14. Dom. Boihardorum (house of Bocchiardi)
15. Aqueduct
16. Bisastanum (bedestan)
17. Columna S. Crucis (column of Constantine)
18. Claustrum regianum puelarum (Old Palace)
19. Taurus (column of Theodosius within the Old Palace grounds)
20. Sepulchrum Soltano Meometi (mausoleum of Mehmed II)
21. Imarat (complex of Mehmed II)
22. Locus cafensium
23. Balneum (double bath of the Mehmed II complex, Çukur Hamam)
24. H(ab)itacula iagitherorum (janissary barracks)
25. Palatium imperatorum
26. Ch(r)stus i(n) chora
27. Pantocratora i(n) q(u)a imp(era) tores sunt sepul(ti)
28. Fanarium
29. Turri di medio (tower of wheat)
30. Turri francorum
31. Arx.xea i(n) qua erarium reginum (castle, royal treasury)
32. Pelilefto
33. Studio
34. Blanga locus aquosus
35. Syvolofus (column of Arcadius)
36. (arch at Isakapı [?] and practicing archer)
37. Cosmidi (Eyüp complex)
38. Pons despine (sweet waters)
39. S. Galatini
40. Hedificium apappirorum (Kağıthane, paper factory)
41. Aque dulces
42. (Arsenal at the Golden Horn)
43. Pera
44. Sepulcra turcarum
45. Burgi filacora(?)/filatoria(?), burgi S. Antoni
46. Turris S. Crucis
47. Burgi d(e) lagirio
48. Fuxina bombardarum
49. Hic sunt vinee burgensium pere (vines of Pera)
50. . . . valis gonele
51. Columne (Diplokionion)
52. S. Angelus
53. (Rumeli Hisarı, Ottoman castle on the western shore of the Bosphorus)
54. Cazale burga
55. Mare ponticum
56. Grecia
57. Turchi(a)
58. (Anadolu Hisarı Ottoman castle on the eastern shore of the Bosphorus)
59. Scutari
60. (Rum Mehmed Pasha convent-mosque)
61. Turris arcla

(Note: The legend follows the transliterations and identifications by Arne Effenberger in Buondelmonti, *Liber Insularum Archipelagi,* ed. Siebert and Plassmann, with alterations and additions.)

MAP 4 LEGEND   XXV

MAP 5

Giovanni Andreas di Vavassore, *Byzantium sive Constantineopolis*, ca. 1530 (fig. 114), based on an original dating to ca. 1480, with legend.

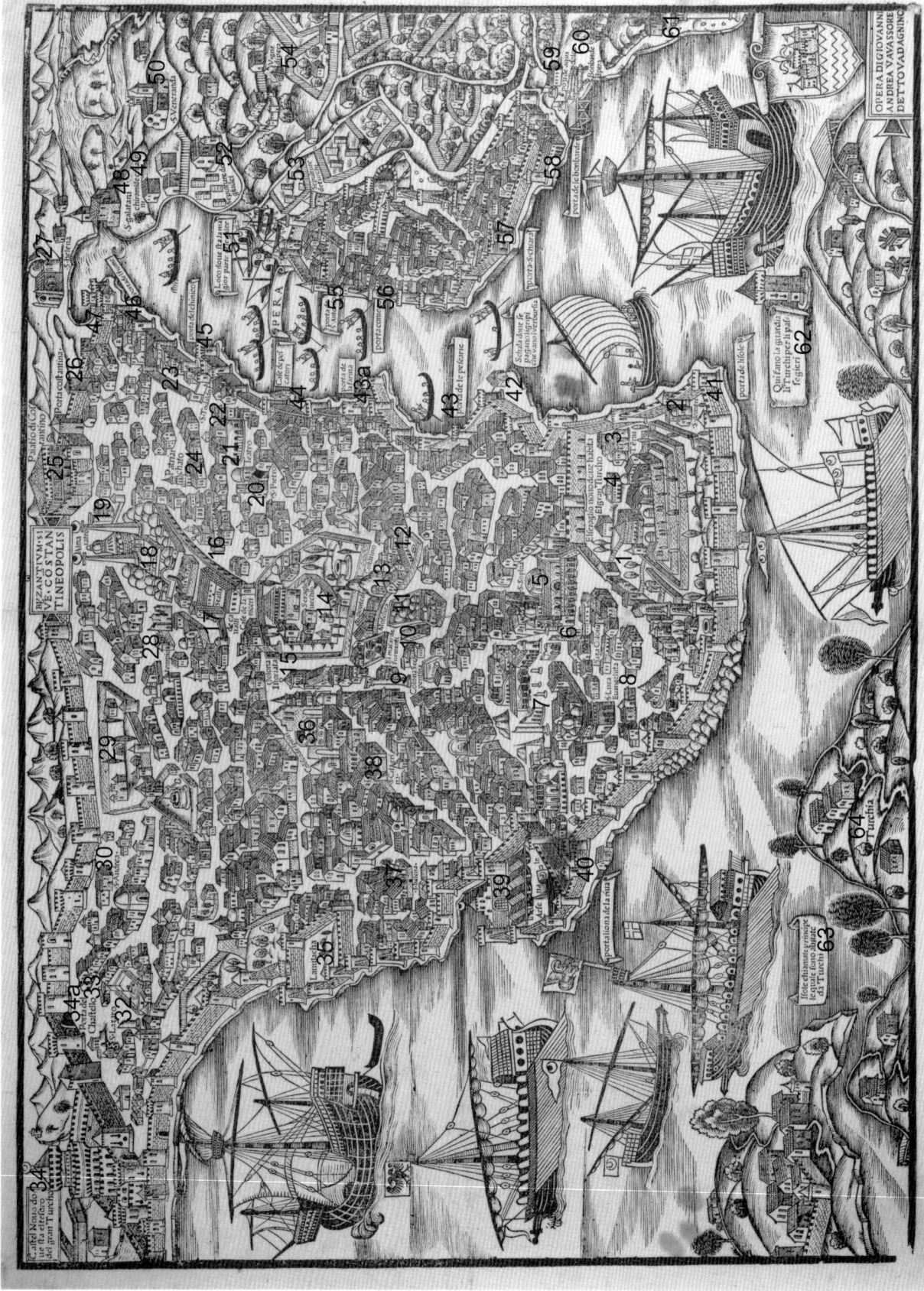

1. El seraglio novo dove habita El Gran Turco (the new palace where the Grand Turk lives)
2. S. Demitri
3. Tennu
4. (Tiled Pavilion)
5. S. Sophia
6. Piaza Colona (column of the Augustaion)
7. (Hippodrome)
8. S. Luca Evangelista
9. Colona Serpentina (column of Constantine)
10. El masar de formenti
11. Moschea (convent-mosque of Mahmud Pasha)
12. (Han and bath of Mahmud Pasha)
13. Monte di Costantino (mound of Constantine)
14. Seraglio vechio (Old Palace)
15. Colona Istoriata (column of Theodosius within the Old Palace enclosure)
16. (Aqueduct)
17. Stalla de cavalli (stables) and Case de Ianiceri (janissary barracks)
18. Almaratro, "imaret" (complex of Mehmed II)
19. Maiden2019s tower
20. S. Pietro
21. Teatro
22. S. Tadaldo
23. (Petrion)
24. Patriachato

25. Palatio di Costantino
26. Porta Costantina
27. S. Helena (Ayyub al-Ansari convent-mosque)
28. Tempio
29. (Mokios cistern)
30. S. Andrea
31. (Exakionion, near Isa Kapı)
32. (Arcadius column)
33. S. Lazaro
34. Castel novo dove sta el tesoro del Gran Turcho (the new castle where the Grand Turk2019s treasury is kept)
34a. Porta del Chastello (Castle Gate)
35. Lauulacha (Langa)
36. Coliseo de Spiriti (Myrelaion [later Bodrum mosque] and rotunda)
37. S. Helena
38. S. Caterina
39. Arsenale
40. Porta liona de la riva
41. Porta de l2019isole
42. Schala dove se pagano li gripi che vano in ver bursia (landing station to Bursa)
43. Porta de le pescarie (Fishmongers2019 Gate)
43a. Porta de la farina (Un Kapusı; Flour Gate)
44. Case de pescatori (Fishermen2019s house)
45. Porta del Chinico (Balat Gate)

46. Porta del fiume
47. (Blachernae Gate)
48. S. Galatani
49. Chiramide cinatroni
50. S. Veneranda
51. Loco dove sta la magior parte de le galee (where most galleys lie)
52. Sepulture de giudei (Jewish cemetery)
53. Sepulture de turchi (Turkish cemetery)
54. Vigne di Pera (Vines of Pera)
55. Porta de S. Antonio
56. Porta comego
57. Porta S. Chiara
58. Porta de le bonbarde (Tophane/ Cannon Foundry Gate)
59. Pozi de aqua dolce (wells of sweet water)
60. Bonbarde di Pera (Tophane/ cannon foundry)
61. (Diplokionion)
62. Qui fano la guardia li Turchi per li passegieri (where the Turks guard passage)
63. Isole chiamate principe le quale sono abitate da Turchi
64. Turchia

(Note: Identifications and transliterations largely follow those of Berger in "Zur sogenannten Stadtansicht des Vavassore," with some additions and alterations.)

MAP 5 LEGEND   xxvii

THROUGH THE LONG stretch of time between the conceptualization of this study and the publication of this book, I have had the good fortune of benefiting from the support and guidance of many individuals and institutions. It is a pleasure to thank them all here. *Constantinopolis/Istanbul* is substantially based on the doctoral dissertation of the same topic; I have broadly reworked and added to it, while retaining the conceptual framework and the basic outline of that work. The dissertation was completed at Harvard University, under the advisorship of Gülru Necipoğlu, who has, then and through the following years, been an unwavering source of support, knowledge, critical insight, and inspiration. Cemal Kafadar's erudition and enthusiastic and stimulating teaching and guidance have greatly enriched my own approaches. Oleg Grabar generously gave of his time and insights during my earlier wanderings through different facets of the urban history of the Middle East. I fondly acknowledge the encouragement of the late Aptullah Kuran, who introduced me to the study of Ottoman architecture, and who remained an always knowledgeable and supporting presence. I offer my heartfelt thanks to these scholars who have, personally and through their work, remained sources of wisdom and inspiration.

Several institutions have generously supported this project in different ways along the way. Harvard grants for research and writing enabled me to complete the first version of this work. Two post-doctoral grants, from the Getty Foundation and from the Aga Khan Program in Islamic Art and Architecture at Harvard University, enabled me to conduct new research and to prepare a final draft. During my year as a Getty post-doctoral fellow in the history of arts and the humanities, I enjoyed the kind hospitality and the resources of New York University's Department of Middle Eastern and Islamic Studies. The nurturing and stimulating academic environment of my home institution, Boğaziçi University at large and the History Department in particular, has added a lot to this study. I would particularly like to thank Ayşe Soysal, former dean of the Faculty of Arts and Sciences, and Selçuk Esenbel, former chair of the department, for facilitating my two leaves. I thank the Millard Meiss Publication Fund and the Graham Foundation for Advanced Studies in the Fine Arts for publication grants awarded to the Pennsylvania State University Press for this book. At Penn State Press, I am grateful to Sandy Thatcher, Eleanor

Goodman, Cali Buckley, Laura Reed-Morrisson, and Patricia Mitchell, who guided different stages of the publication and editing process with meticulous care. To Keith Monley's knowledgeable, thorough, and thoughtful copy editing, the book owes a lot. To his interest in this book, and to his patience and good humor, I owe special thanks.

I thank the directorates and staffs of the Topkapı Palace Archives and Library, the Prime Ministry Archives in Istanbul, the Archives of the Directorate of Pious Endowments in Ankara, Süleymaniye Library, Istanbul University Library, Nuruosmaniye Library, Istanbul Atatürk Library, Vatican Apostolic Library, and Bibliothéque nationale de France, where research for this book was conducted. Andras Riedlmayer and Jeff Spurr of the Fogg Library at Harvard were always generous sources of bibliographic and visual information during my years at Cambridge. Nuran Özgenler at the German Archaeological Institute at Istanbul was most helpful during my search for photographs in the Institute's visual archive. I warmly thank Filiz Çağman, formerly of the Topkapı Palace Museum, whose admirable knowledge and kind support made work there such a rich and pleasant experience.

It is not easy to adequately express my profound gratitude to Ahmet Ersoy, who has had to live with the various adventures and apparitions of this book over the past years, who has shared his deep knowledge, keenness of thought, and wonderful humor in discussing matters of all manner and significance regarding it. I extend a special thanks to Derin Terzioğlu, who read the final draft and discussed it with me, and whose extraordinary patience has never wavered in the face of my endless questions. I feel most fortunate to have had, over the years, the support, advice, insight, inspiration, companionship in libraries or site trips, and above all the friendship of Leslie Meral Schick and Arben Arapi, Shirine Hamadeh, and Selim Kuru.

I am grateful to Slobodan Ćurčić, Edhem Eldem, Suraiya Faroqhi, Halil İnalcık, Selma Özkoçak, and Christine Smith for reading the complete manuscript and for the kind encouragement, insightful comments and criticism they have offered from different vantage points. Halil İnalcık has led me to several archival documents I have used in this study. I have not been able to examine the earliest Ottoman survey of Istanbul, dated 1455, which was submitted for publication by Professor İnalcık when this book was in the last stages of the publication process. I thank him for informing me that my findings and conclusions are largely in line with the data in that document. I warmly thank Zeynep Çelik for the encouragement and suggestions she has provided in various instances. To Robert Ousterhout and to the anonymous reader for Penn State Press, I owe sincere thanks for the close reading, thoughtful commentary and criticism, and suggestions from which I have benefited. I am especially indebted to the late Stéphane Yerasimos, who, in characteristic thoroughness and generosity, gave me detailed and most constructive comments on one draft of this work, and shared archival documents on which he had been working. It is a pleasure to acknowledge the contributions of many friends and colleagues—Nebahat Avcıoğlu, Serpil Bağcı, Nicholas Bakos, May Farhat, Kate Fleet, Paolo Girardelli, Hayashi Kayoko, Dimitris Kastritsis, Dimitris Kyritses, Christoph Lüthy, Paul Magdalino, Julia Meisami, Nevra Necipoğlu, Karen Pinto, David Roxburgh, Ariel Salzmann, Haris Stavrides, Işık Tamdoğan, Baha Tanman, Lucienne Thys-Şenocak, and Zeynep Yürekli among them—who read parts of drafts, discussed aspects of the topic with me, offered criticism, answered questions, or opened vistas into other places, questions, and sources. I was fortunate to have had the guidance of the late Şinasi Tekin in my first encounters with some of the Ottoman documents used in this study. Wheeler Thackston helped with particular passages in Persian that I had difficulty with; May Farhat and Himmet Taşkömür provided guidance with some translations from Arabic. Christoph Lüthy guided me to the Vatican and the Basel University libraries and to several texts in Greek and Latin.

Parts of this work, in its different stages, were presented at the Istanbul branch of the American Resarch Institute in Turkey, at Boğaziçi University, at the Department of Art History at Cambridge University, at the French Archaeological Institute in Istanbul, and at the University of Texas at Austin (where Ian Manners graciously shared his copy and his views on a then unpublished map of Istanbul). Comments, questions, and discussions during those events, and during graduate seminars at Boğaziçi University, have helped me rethink some of the questions and to refine some of my interpretations. Needless to say, I remain responsible for any mistakes that may remain.

My heartfelt thanks go to Naz Koyunlu, who was a convivial companion during visits to many of the sites and who prepared, with meticulous care, the maps and the majority of the architectural drawings (the latter mostly based on drawings by Ekrem Hakkı Ayverdi, Wolfgang Müller-Wiener, and Aptullah Kuran). I thank Gülru Necipoğlu for permission to use nine drawings and a number of historical images from her *Age of Sinan*, and Zeynep Yürekli for making these available to me. I thank Reha Günay for generously opening his photographic archives and for permission to reproduce a number of images.

I am profoundly grateful to my parents, Ruhi Kafescioğlu and Sevgi Koyunlu, and the late Alpaslan Koyunlu, who remained sources of unfailing support and encouragement, and who were the ones, much earlier and in different ways, to direct my eyes to sites and stories that would found my love of and fascination with Istanbul. And in one sense, of course, this book is simply the response of one inhabitant to the city, to its past and to its present. I dedicate it to my closest co-habitants, Ahmet Ersoy and my daughter, Mihri Ersoy, for a thousand and one reasons that I will not begin to recount here.

A NOTE ON TRANSLITERATION

Standard forms in English have been used for Byzantine and Ottoman denominations of major sites and buildings (Constantinople, Hagia Sophia). Ottoman Turkish renderings of these names have been used when quoting or paraphrasing from Ottoman sources (Ayasofya, Kostantiniyye). Proper names and place names are rendered in modern Turkish orthography; terms and book titles in Arabic script have been transliterated according to the *İslam Ansiklopedisi* system. Turkish, Persian, and Arabic terms that have entered English-language dictionaries are used in their Anglicized forms.

Introduction

Asymbolic locus embodying and representing myriad meanings, the political center of the eastern Mediterranean, and one of the largest urban centers of the world, Constantinople/Istanbul has been the site of large-scale urban and architectural interventions several times in the course of its history. Changing visions, changing political, cultural, religious orientations of those who lived there and those who ruled from there, have been inscribed in its spaces, transforming it, lending it new meanings. This book is about such a period of change and remaking: the decades following the city's capture by the Ottomans in 1453, during which a grandly conceived urban project was implemented to reconstruct the capital of Eastern Rome as the capital of the Ottoman Empire. Through these decades, the construction of the city was fundamentally interlocked with the construction of empire. As the empire was built up around reorientations political and cultural, and the creation of a new concept of sovereignty and a new ruling elite, so the space and image of Constantinople, too, were constructed. The millennium-old center of the Eastern Roman Empire was not merely a setting for the profound changes that took place in the Ottoman realm in the latter half of the fifteenth century. Possession of the city was the primary catalyst in the transformation of the Ottoman polity into an empire; the city was the site that would accommodate, represent, and reproduce the new configuration of the Ottoman polity.

This study explores the dialectical relationship between the Ottoman urban project and the city's Byzantine layout and architecture, its historical legacy, and its inhabitants. It investigates the mechanisms and patterns of building, preserving, altering, and representing the urban environment during a formative period, and the meanings communicated through these acts. In short, this book attempts to explain the spatial and visual aspects of early Ottoman Istanbul as central components of a complex and fascinating urban process, that of the creation of a capital city through the interpretation and appropriation of another.

That creation was ultimately the product of the fall/conquest of the city, an event that led to the encounter of diverse cultural traditions on a site of immense significance and to profound transformations in the Ottoman political realm itself. The selective appropriation of the imperial legacy of Byzantine Constantinople

1

was central to the making of Ottoman Istanbul, as were Ottoman urban and architectural practices of the preconquest period. Through a set of connections between the Ottoman and Italian courts, Renaissance ideas of ordering the urban environment played a significant role in the conceptualization and realization of new projects. The tension between Mehmed II's imperial vision and the ethos of the frontiers found reflections in the first Ottoman undertakings in the new capital. Situated between the Byzantine, Latin, and Ottoman worlds, *ghazi* (Islamic frontier-warrior) and imperial ideologies, the city became a physical and symbolical site upon which contrasting visions and perceptions would be projected, where cultural meanings would be contested, negotiated, and remade.

This was a time, largely erased as it was from Istanbul's later histories and documents, when a marble relief of the Byzantine eagle marked the monumental portal of the newly built commercial center, when city views meant to represent either Byzantine or Ottoman Constantinople conspicuously displayed symbols of the other, when a man by the name of Mustafa son of Yanni lived in a quarter that was alternately called the neighborhood of Aya Kenisası ("Saints Church")[1] and the neighborhood of the Mevlana Husrev masjid. The image of Christ Pantokrator at the summit of Hagia Sophia's dome watched over the Muslim congregation in the great nave below. "El Gran Turco" read the caption of a kingly portrait in Mehmed II's collection of Italian prints; it was a likeness of John VIII Palaeologos, adapted to represent the Ottoman sultan as triumphant warrior. Hence Barthes's slash transposed to the space between Constantinopolis and Istanbul, where it will serve as the mirroring edge against which the city's many selves are defined, imagined, represented.[2] For if history and

topography render this a site whose multiple selves will perpetually face, mirror, confront, and define each other across time and across social and physical space, these attributes assume particular import through the period with which this book concerns itself.

1453 AND AFTER

It may not be wrong to assume that the huge army that laid siege to Constantinople in 1453 included the whole spectrum of Ottoman polity of the later fifteenth century: the empire builder in the person of the sultan, grandees of Balkan and Byzantine aristocratic origin, an army of converted Christian recruits, a landed aristocracy that had constituted the ruling elite of the state until and into the reign of Mehmed II, frontier warlords and their retinues of ghazis, dervishes, recent converts, and those uprooted in the tumultuous atmosphere of late medieval Anatolia and the Balkans. The two major factions within this wide spectrum were the builders of the sedentary state and the soldiers of the frontier, whose power and dynamism were based on the semi-independence of their political and military conduct. To the former, Constantinople was the natural locus of power; ruling from the city would make the House of Osman the foremost ghazis within the realm of Islam and simultaneously inheritors of the legacy of Eastern Rome. To the latter, Constantinople was no more than a particularly prestigious object of war and conquest; the significance of its takeover lay in the erasure of an inauspicious Byzantine presence in the midst of Muslim territory. Hence, Mehmed II's declaration, shortly after the conquest, that Constantinople was the seat of his throne, and his first measures in restoring and repopulating it, marked the first steps in the final resolution of the tension between state building and unrestrained military activity on the frontiers: the

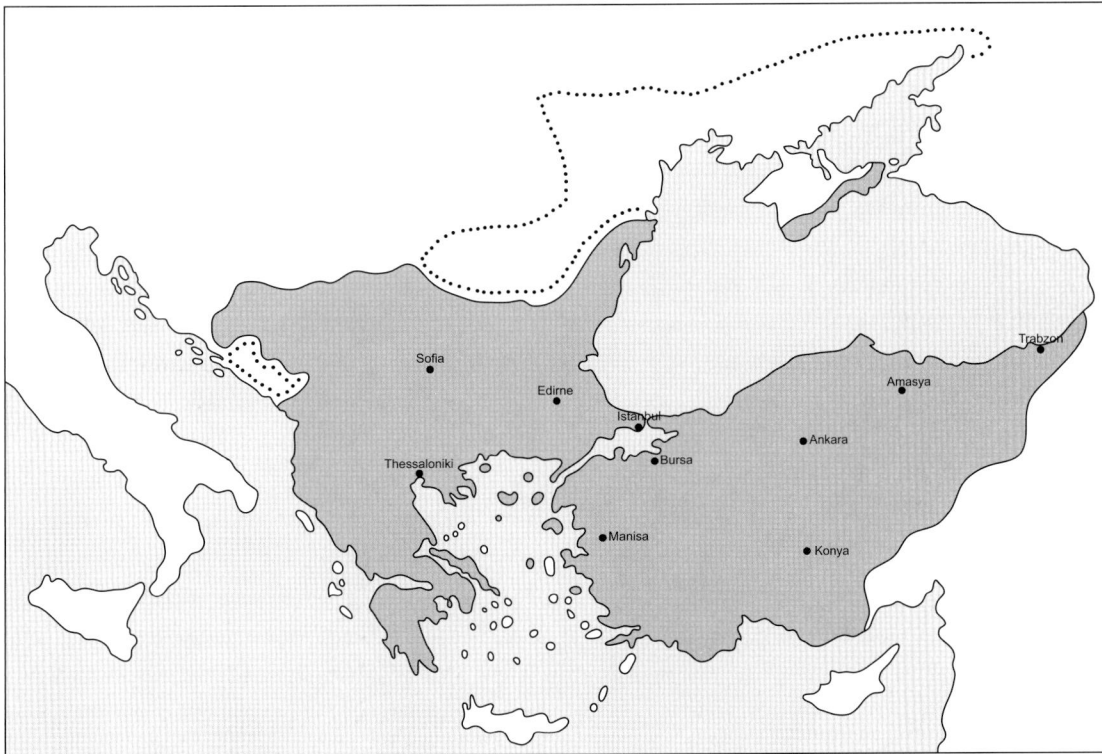

FIGURE 1
Map of the Ottoman territories
ca. 1480. The dotted line
indicates zones of influence.

Map labels: Sofia, Edirne, Istanbul, Thessaloniki, Bursa, Manisa, Ankara, Amasya, Trabzon, Konya

rebuilding of the city was constitutive of the building of empire. In the process, the frontier ethos and its propagators, a foundational component of the Ottoman polity since its modest beginnings as a tiny principality in Bithynia a century and a half before, would be marginalized within the Ottoman political spectrum, ceding to an increasingly pivotal center and its agents.[3]

The figure of Mehmed II (r. 1444–46, 1451–81) looms large over the Ottoman world of the fifteenth century. He was the motor force behind the cultural and political reorientations and transformations that took place in the Ottoman realm and the restructuring of the administrative apparatus that followed the conquest of Constantinople.[4] His realization of an ancient dream of the Islamic realm earned him the title *ebū'l-fetḥ*, "father of conquest." Further conquests in the Balkans and in Anatolia erased the last remnants of Byzantium and

of the post-Seljuk principalities in the region, diminished the hold of Genoese and Venetian trading establishments in the Aegean and the Black Sea, and brought under Ottoman unitary rule a region that had remained politically fragmented for nearly four centuries (fig. 1). The primary and persistent motive that shaped Mehmed II's rule was creation of a world empire governed from Constantinople by a centralized administrative apparatus. To that end, he diminished the power of the landed aristocracy and of the frontier lords, replacing them with a new military-administrative elite of *devşirme* (Christians conscripted for service in the palace or the army) origin and a larger janissary army. In an effort to centralize the learned establishment and to endow it with a hierarchical structure, he founded the Eight Colleges (*Ṣemāniye*) as part of his new mosque complex in the new capital; here ulema of the highest rank would be educated. Creation of a new style of rulership was central to the foundation of empire. Assuming royal titles of the highest order, *ḫünkār, ḫān,* sultan, caesar, and *ebū'l-fetḥ,* Mehmed II invented a new court ceremonial and conduct emphasizing his seclusion from his subjects, which highlighted his absolute authority and the sacredness of his person. The mode of rule articulated through his reign, based on Turco-Mongol, Irano-Islamic, and Byzantine notions of kingship and sovereignty and resonating with contemporary political currents in the Euro-Mediterranean sphere, was to shape the conduct of the Ottoman house, with transformations, through the following century and beyond. A *ḳānūnnāme* (law code), written after 1477 captured and encoded for subsequent generations of Ottomans the imperial ideology and practice that were elaborated throughout Mehmed II's reign; in particular, it defined and detailed the structure of the administrative, military, and religious hierarchies. It sanctioned imperial seclusion and the custom of royal fratricide.[5]

Imperial claims brought new notions of cultural patronage, through which the Ottoman world embraced the high cultural traditions with which it had come into contact.[6] Thus Mehmed's patronage extended beyond Ottoman domains, to the arts and sciences of the Iranian and the Italian worlds, as well as to Greek men of letters. He collected Byzantine relics and works of art and aspired to surpass that empire's glory and splendor. His imperial ambitions, set among other places on Italy, he closely followed the innovations in the arts, architecture, and military technology there. The wide scope of the sultan's cultural patronage reflected his self-image as world emperor (figs. 2, 3, 4). Conquest and consolidation effected cultural encounters, which in turn gave shape to the dynamic eclecticism

and inclusivism characteristic of the fifteenth-century Ottoman world in general and Ottoman court culture in particular.

The Byzantine capital was in a ruinous state at the time of its fall. Stripped of its hinterland by the Ottoman expansion of the previous century, impoverished by successive Ottoman sieges of the preceding decades, it is estimated to have housed forty to fifty thousand people in its vast expanse. Its reconstruction aimed, of course, to reverse its destitute state but also to re-create it as the locus of the Ottoman world. In this process, the imperial heritage of Byzantium was selectively appropriated or rejected, as is powerfully exemplified by the conversion of Hagia Sophia, the religious and political center of Eastern Christendom, into the royal mosque of the city and the subsequent demolition of the equestrian statue of Justinian that stood nearby. As Mehmed II's centralizing policies were enacted and his vision of empire and of himself as emperor crystallized in the later decades of his rule, the city was given shape to accommodate those changes and to embody and manifest that vision. His two major additions to the city, a palace and a mosque complex conceived in 1459 and built through the 1460s and 1470s, created the spaces in the city where his authority over the military and the religious elite became manifest. The building projects of the ruling elite—including religious and charitable institutions, commercial structures, palaces, and waterways—contributed to the revival of the city. At the same time, the architecture of these urban institutions, the buildings of the monarch and the ruling elite, reflected their new hierarchical structure; the formal hierarchies introduced into the cityscape bespoke the a new political and cultural order. A monumental format and a working infrastructure were thus created for a capital conceived at an enormous

FIGURE 2
Gentile Bellini, *Portrait of Mehmed II,* ca. 1480. National Gallery, London.

FIGURE 3
Portrait of Mehmed II, ca. 1478. Topkapı Palace Museum, H 2153, fol. 145v.

FIGURE 4
Costanza di Ferrara, portrait medal of Mehmed II, ca. 1481. National Gallery of Art, Washington, D.C., Samuel H. Kress collection, 1957.14.695.

scale. Reconstruction entailed repopulation: invitations to the city and grants of property, as well as forced resettlement of Muslim, Christian, and Jewish communities from other parts of the Ottoman realm, aimed at the creation of a thriving cosmopolitan capital.[7]

THE HISTORIOGRAPHY OF CONQUEST AND CONSTRUCTION

The fall/conquest of Constantinople added a new set of narratives to the rich constellation of histories, myths, and memories that have, over centuries, interpreted the city and its past, making them intelligible to a diverse spectrum of audiences. The political and cultural consequences of the final demise of the Byzantine Empire have rendered the city's "fall" or "conquest" an enormously charged topic in Byzantine, Ottoman, and Western cultural traditions alike. Texts originating in these milieus, in separate veins but at times merging with each other, have told and retold the stories of this important moment in the life of the city. Encapsulated in the emotional charge of the words "fall" and "conquest" and written into the histories and myths of Constantinople is a complex of perceptions and visions concerning the city and the realm to which it belongs.

Whether to lament the fall of the city or to celebrate its long-desired capture, historical accounts of this period focus largely on the momentous events of spring 1453, detailing episodes and moments of the siege, the capture, the sack.[8] Ottoman chronicles written from the later fifteenth century onward, whether narrating the history of the dynasty or events of the reign of Mehmed II, have summary or detailed sections on Mehmed's efforts to rebuild and repopulate Constantinople. They narrate the sultan's order to his grandees to undertake constructions of public and private buildings in Constantinople, and they report also on the grand vizier's constructions. These accounts, full of praise for the sultan's enormous endeavor, constitute the first examples of the Ottoman historical narrative that asserts that Istanbul owed its rebirth and its subsequent prosperity as the Ottoman capital to Mehmed II. The early-sixteenth-century historian Neşri presents this position succinctly: "In short, Sultan Mehmed Han built Istanbul, and he made it flourish in such a way that travelers today say 'there is no city like it in the universe.'"[9] Some decades later Saʿdüddin described how the city became an abode where innumerable people lived and worked comfortably under the peace-giving shadow of the sultan.[10] In the seventeenth century, Evliya Çelebi, when detailing the deportation of communities to the capital, wrote of Mehmed II's Constantinople as the wealthy, thriving city he was proud to inhabit.[11] Tracing these narratives through time reveals also the steps in the making of a myth: a century after Evliya Çelebi, Hafız Hüseyin al-Ayvansarayi, writing his Ḥadīḳatü'l Cevāmiʿ (Garden of Mosques), attributed a large number of quarter mosques to those who had partaken in the 1453 siege, thereby inscribing stories of the conquest onto the space of the city.[12] (Ayvansarayi's partly false attributions, in turn, figure prominently in most modern accounts of the early Ottoman city.)

The writings of contemporary and later authors no doubt attest to the grand enterprise of the sultan in the rebuilding and repopulation of the new capital. They are not, however, the only accounts dealing with the subject. Narratives originating from the milieu of frontier warriors, who were increasingly marginalized by the new state, tell a strongly contrasting tale of Constantinople's reconstruction. The authors and audiences of those texts understood only too well that the move from the former capital Edirne to Constantinople was part of a centralizing policy and that empire building was its corollary. Their strong opposition to both is clearly manifested in historical narratives such as the anonymous Tevārīḫ-i ʾĀl-i ʿOṣmān (chronicles of the House of Osman), which portray the sultan's attempts to restore and revitalize the city as markedly less successful than those depicted in narratives originating from the "center": "Even a sultan like Mehmed restored it with difficulty in three, four years, and so many parts of it are still in ruins."[13] The objection to the rebuilding itself is wonderfully demonstrated in a text completed ca. 1474, that is, after the most intense period of building activity in the new capital was already over. An imaginary conversation between Mehmed and his commanders prior to the siege of the city captures the sense of exasperation prompted by the sultan's urban venture. The commanders warn the ruler: "Because of adultery and sodomy and lewdness and debauchery, black waters emerged from its ground at night, and it remained ruinous. [. . .] If you rebuild this city, it will destroy the world, and you will be the cause of this destruction. It will never flourish. However many times you build it, it will fall back into ruin again."[14]

These narratives are of documentary as well as historiographic value. On the one hand, they provide insights into the contrasting and competing meanings of Constantinople within the fifteenth-century Ottoman world, meanings to which I return in the following chapters. On the other hand, they provide insights into the making of the city's Ottoman and, later, modern Turkish history. While the accounts that narrated the conquest and the subsequent restoration of the city as tales of glory remained central in the historiography of the dynasty and of the city, those which referred to Constantinople as the site of doom and destruction and voiced objections to its status as Ottoman capital were either marginalized or domesticated into mainstream accounts. These texts are reminders that Mehmed II's grand urban project was realized only with the estrangement and marginalization of many, at huge costs to Ottoman subjects and treasury alike. Not surprisingly, it was the former picture, not the latter, that survived the passage of time.

New images of the Conqueror and the Conquest were fabricated in the later nineteenth century, when Ottoman intellectuals revisited court chronicles and the complex of narratives on Mehmed II and his spiritual, political, and military companions in popular histories, hagiographies, and topographic accounts. At a time when (control over) imperial territory eroded, with the Ottoman elite compelled to respond to a rapidly changing political and ideological landscape, emergent modes of historicist thinking offered Ottoman intellectuals a new framework for imagining and representing the imperial past. In the writings of Namık Kemal, one of the prominent intellectuals of the Ottoman nineteenth century, the golden age of Ottoman rule, the "age of conquest" (*devr-i istīlā*), was re-created, its zenith marked by the conquest of Constantinople.[15] In articulating notions

of nationhood (*millet*) and fatherland (*vatan*) to become the building blocks of an emerging nationalist imagination tightly anchored to notions of dynastic continuity, Kemal endowed Mehmed II, who had occupied a central place in Ottoman historiography, with new significance. Now referred to as the Conqueror (*Fatih*), he became the ultimate symbol of an age of glory, a bygone era of conquests summoned to stand in stark contrast to a present of losses. More significantly, Istanbul, the city, and 1453, the date, provided spatial and temporal anchor points to the inchoate ethos of nationhood, since the conquest was now a chapter in the history of the Ottoman *millet,* and the city was the center of the territorial entity it inhabited. The conquest marked an honorable beginning, that of Ottoman ("national") history as history of empire.

"One rarely searches for beginnings unless the present matters a great deal," wrote Edward Said. An imaginative and emotional need for unity underlies the quest for beginnings, for the beginning provides sequential, moral, or logical order to an otherwise diffuse set of circumstances. The promise of unity and cohesiveness embodied in the idea of *the* beginning, in turn, works to fix and theologize knowledge, whereby the beginning, ceding its place to that which it gave rise to, assumes virtuality.[16] Said's "meditation on beginnings" may help explain the continued import of the Conqueror and the Conquest in modern Turkish historiography, once they were salvaged from the pages of manuscripts and rendered part of a "national" historical narrative. A large body of literature on the subject has been produced from the last decades of the nineteenth century onward, with significant additions around 1953, when the five hundredth anniversary of the conquest of Constantinople provided opportunity for celebration for those riding on an ascending wave of nationalism. The program of commemorations included publication of studies, as well as editions and facsimiles of numerous fifteenth-century literary and historical works. At the same time, the "celebrations" marked 1453 and its associations as an increasingly crucial, at times fetishized, symbol for strands of nationalism within the Turkish political spectrum. During the last decade of the twentieth century and the first decade of the twenty-first, the Conqueror and the Conquest have become subjects of contestation in a polarized political landscape whose diverse constituents have (mostly) different claims on the Ottoman past.[17] The debate has brought into sharper focus what are ostensibly contradictory aspects of the Conqueror's character and conduct. An anachronistic and exclusionary nationalism and religious zeal and an equally anachronistic progressivism are by turns attributed to Mehmed II: to some, the Conqueror is the foremost warrior of Islam, who captured and converted into a Muslim and Turkish city the heart of Eastern Christendom; to others, he is a Renaissance prince in Ottoman garb, an enlightened, progressive, European-oriented ruler.

What I broadly outline here is the process by which the conqueror and the conquest were constructed as *sites of memory* central to Ottoman and, later, modern Turkish historical consciousness.[18] That construction (and perhaps the Constantinople of the *fall* as a differently constructed site of memory to Greek historical imagination) should be a subject of scrutiny in itself. My sketch, however, has a different aim: to highlight the ways in which the process of construction following 1453 is represented in the modern historiography of the city. For the writing on this period and on its foremost figure has shaped and colored the ways in which modern scholarship has approached the city, as it has the ways in which modern urbanism and urban conservation have interpreted and

treated the remains of this period. While the majestic figure of the conqueror came to overshadow everything else in the fifteenth century, the image of his Istanbul as the glamorously built capital was reinforced. Little attention was given to other histories or to documents that would complicate the narratives of Istanbul's reconstruction, revealing (instead of overlooking) the complexities and the chaotic aspects of that process.

While this overview has focused on the historiography of conquest and reconstruction in Ottoman and modern Turkish scholarship, it should be noted that some of the premises of modern historiography, shaped in turn by orientalist and nationalist legacies, bear on Western scholarship on Byzantine as well as Ottoman cultural history in comparable ways. Turkish and Western scholarship alike have largely abided by widely accepted geographic (Middle Eastern versus Western), religio-cultural (Islamic versus Christian), and nominally dynastic but in effect ethno-religious (Ottoman versus Byzantine) divides, which have in turn tended to obfuscate connections across those categorizations or hindered the use of alternative frameworks.[19] In one of the fascinating spatiotemporal constructions of modern historiography (effected also, but not only, by a history of conflict and coexistence of two world religions in this complex cultural landscape), Constantinople, as it were, abandons its Roman (read Western) context on 29 May 1453 and becomes part of a different geography: the Islamic, or the Middle Eastern, world. This year has thus constituted a neat and precise dividing line in scholarship on the city, seldom crossed, incontrovertibly separating the "Byzantine" and the "Ottoman" domains. Questions regarding Ottoman uses of forms associated with Byzantine architectural culture have often fallen into the trap of a loaded debate of "influences," rendering it difficult, if not impossible, to understand the products of a complex cultural environment marked with interactions, fluidity, and hybridity.[20] Likewise, questions regarding connections between Ottoman and Byzantine urbanistic practice have seldom drawn interest. Recent cultural history has been altering this picture of insular fields and particularistic approaches, introducing important insights into shared histories and cultural contacts and interrelationships across the larger medieval and early modern worlds.

The fifteenth century figures prominently in several studies of Ottoman architectural history. The bibliography and references of the present study will make apparent the important ground covered by earlier scholarship on the topic.[21] The construal of Ottoman architecture of the later fifteenth century in these works once more evokes Said's observations in his *Beginnings.* Under the spell of Ottoman Istanbul's classical image, which largely took shape in the second half of the sixteenth century, modern scholarship has tended to understand the city's premodern urban and architectural history as a continuum, regarding the first Ottoman works in Istanbul, in terms of their conception and design, as the first steps in a linear and evolutionary scheme that culminated in the grand projects of a later era of magnificence. Despite a strong current of continuity in the Ottoman architectural tradition, a focus on the evolutionary dimension of that history obscures significant aspects of fifteenth-century Istanbul and its architecture that had more to do with the complex cultural dynamics of the era than with any future traditions to which they gave rise.

Within the framework of urban history—or, more precisely, the vaguely defined area within urban history that concerns itself with aspects of urban spatiality and visuality—Ottoman

Istanbul has often been lodged either on the "organic" or the "Islamic" side of dichotomous and mutually exclusive categorizations. The Islamic city model, a product of orientalist scholarship largely based on an essentialist understanding of Islam as the foremost determinant of urban culture in the Middle East, has been the subject of an extensive debate from the 1950s onward. The writing on urban history from the 1990s onward has covered considerable ground in historicizing the urban processes of particular periods and areas and hence problematizing the essentialist aspects of the model, if not doing away with it altogether.[22] Where Ottoman studies are concerned, a somewhat different picture emerges. Created and elaborated by scholars of the medieval Islamic world, the Islamic city paradigm (based in turn on Weberian urban theory, which relied heavily on definitions of the city in medieval Europe) could never embrace early modern Istanbul as comfortably as it did medieval Aleppo or Fez. Scholarship on Ottoman history, in its turn, has until recently proved itself rather disinterested in historical processes connecting, or dividing, the larger Islamic world. Tacit acceptance of received opinion, then, rather than attempts to create or apply models, has at times led scholars to the Islamic city model for interpreting the shape and the structures of the Ottoman capital.[23]

It might be useful to regard the organic and the Islamic city models together in terms of their bearing on the study of Ottoman urbanism, although these represent distinct lines of inquiry in urban history. For where spatial configurations are concerned, both models presume the absence of a geometric principle ordering the urban environment, a geometry regarded as a constitutive aspect of Western urbanism by virtue of the mark it has left on cities of the Greco-Roman, Renaissance, and post-Renaissance eras. The absence of a geometric principle shaping the city, in turn, has been read as an indicator of spontaneous development of urban structures, whereby builders possess neither the will nor the ability to premeditate on a grand scale the formal, functional, and symbolical implications of their interventions in the cityscape. Recent work has brought important changes to this picture. The organic city paradigm has been divorced from the presumption of spontaneity,[24] while work on Ottoman cities has explored alternate ways in which urban configurations took shape, acquired and manifested meaning.[25]

THIS STUDY

Alongside nationalist historiographies or equally rigid civilizational divides, the mere absence of an in-depth study on the topic, too, accounts for the obscurity of important aspects of Istanbul's first Ottoman decades. It is one of the objectives of this book to fill this gap, presenting a layered and multifarious picture of the city through this era, highlighting the complexity of the urban process that transformed Constantinople and the hybridity of its spaces and images. I construe the Ottoman capital city as the product of a range of encounters, dialogues, and oppositions between different actors within the Ottoman realm as well as between the Ottomans, Byzantium, and the West. Beyond that immediate locus, interconnections, parallelisms, and incongruities in the emerging early modern world (of which the Ottomans were part) constitute a parallel theme in my exploration of urbanistic trends in fifteenth-century Istanbul. Investigating aspects of urban spatiality and visuality beyond strict categorizations of planned and unplanned, and stepping outside of the geometric paradigm within or against which urbanism has often been evaluated, this study aims to reveal the urbanistic

notions at work in the ordering of Istanbul's urban environment during a formative period. The book delineates emerging urbanistic trends in Constantinople/Istanbul in their connections to the making of a new political structure, underscoring the ways in which the urban interventions of this era bear on the shape of Istanbul in later centuries. Equal emphasis, on the other hand, is placed on those aspects of the fifteenth-century city that were to be erased from its mainstream historiography.

This book focuses on the first three decades of Istanbul's Ottoman history. Three interrelated themes constitute its framework: monumentalization, representation, and inhabitation. Here, monumentalization refers to a building program that aimed to establish and communicate the city's new identity as the center of the Ottoman realm through the introduction of a new visual and spatial order to the urban environment. This new spatial and formal hierarchy, created through the construction of Ottoman monuments and the selective appropriation of Byzantine sites and monuments, in turn represented, accommodated, and engendered a new political and social order. Urban monuments, in this framework, were at once buildings intended to communicate a range of meanings to diverse audiences and sites that enabled their users to partake of the urban space and its practices.[26]

By portraying, surveying, accentuating, and at times silencing symbolically significant sites or consequential events, the city's images projected the visions and claims of their makers regarding those particular sites or events and the city at large. My exploration into modes and manners of representing the urban body extends to visual and literary images of Constantinople/Istanbul, as well as to archival documents such as imperial edicts or property surveys that offer insights into the cultural meanings bestowed on and projected by the city and its parts. A dialogic of representation is particularly pertinent to this subject: products of an era of political and cultural encounters and transformations, these images escape singular interpretations with clear and distinct meanings. Whether pictures, poems, chronicles, or epics, that is, whether iconic or narrative, they often convey a range of contrasting perceptions regarding their highly symbolic subject. My analysis aims to capture the plurality that constitutes the city's representations,[27] for this offers an entry into the plurality that constitutes the city at large.

The city's commercial and residential fabric were woven from political and cultural processes that gave shape to its monuments and images as much as from the workings of daily life. The formation of that fabric and its interrelationship with the city's monumental structure and image are integral to an understanding of the larger urban process with which this book concerns itself. By looking into the formation and use of residential and commercial patterns and into the social, political, and institutional processes underlying these patterns, I delineate aspects of the immediate material environment of the city's inhabitants.[28] At the same time, this inquiry into the formation of residential and commercial patterns reveals Ottoman notions of city and urbanity, informed by Islamic legal practices, on the one hand, and by newly articulated notions of spatial hierarchy, on the other.

I regard these the three main aspects of the making of the city, interrelated processes that reshaped its physical space and its image, investing both with new meanings. Inspired by Henri Lefebvre's triad of the conceived, the represented, and the lived, whose dialectical relationship underlies the production of space, this conceptual framework provides the means for a synchronic exploration of the multiple processes that informed the transformation of the capital of Eastern Rome into the capital of the Ottoman Empire.[29] While the main themes that underlie and structure my study—monumentalization, representation, inhabitation—broadly relate to Lefebvre's triad, the correspondence is neither literal nor complete. My inquiry into the dialectics of the physical, the mental, and the social mediates an entry into an exploration of emerging modes of spatiality and visuality operative in a particular urban setting.[30]

The primary sources of this study—histories, epics, hagiographies, poetry, archival documents, and visual images—constitute repositories of data pertaining to the material environment of the fifteenth-century city and the social, political, and institutional processes that shaped its urban environment. These documents are simultaneously analyzed in this book as representations of Constantinople, providing insights into the attitudes, perceptions, and claims of the makers of those documents with regard to the city.

It is surely not coincidental that the later fifteenth century marks the first significant outburst of Ottoman historical writing, concerning both the history of the Ottoman dynasty from its humble beginnings and the contemporary history of the period.[31] Cemal Kafadar, writing on the birth of an Ottoman historical consciousness in the era following the Timurid invasion of Anatolia, has suggested that the resolution of the interregnum subsequent to the Ottoman defeat and the emergence of a new configuration of power (whereby the Ottomans were relegated to vassal status by their Timurid adversaries) led the Ottomans to represent themselves in historical terms.[32] The formation of a new cultural and political configuration under the reign of Mehmed II encouraged further articulation of an Ottoman historical consciousness. Significantly, three works exclusively on the reign of Mehmed II, in Greek, Persian, and Turkish by the order of their publication, were written in the 1470s and 1480s. The chronicles of Kritovoulos of Imbros, Mu'ali, and Tursun Beg (the first two presented to the sultan and the latter to his successor) are detailed accounts of the period and constitute important sources of information on the events of the era as much as on the varied cultural and political attitudes and dispositions of those who partook in them. A more broadly scoped work on Ottoman history as a whole, *Chronicles of the Ottoman Sultans,* by Karamani Nişancı Mehmed Pasha, was completed in the final years of Mehmed II's rule.

The end of Mehmed II's reign, as separately observed by Stéphane Yerasimos and Cemal Kafadar, brought forth a new era of reckoning, as Bayezid II's policies made it possible to criticize Mehmed's often harsh measures aiming to build a centralized state.[33] Anonymous chronicles of the House of Osman, as well as those by Uruc, Aşıkpaşazade Derviş Ahmed, and Ruhi of Edirne, are products of this period, providing historical accounts of the Ottoman experience of the previous two centuries while simultaneously articulating and manifesting reactions to Mehmed's rule. The House of Osman, in turn, produced its own versions of the consequential events of these decades: works commissioned by Bayezid II, most notably İdris Bidlisi's *Heşt behişt,* in Persian ("Eight Paradises," referring to the rules of the eight Ottoman sultans up to Bayezid II), but also Kıvami's *Fetiḥnāme-i Sulṭān Meḥmed* (Book of Conquest of Sultan Mehmed), are histories dealing extensively with this period. A new historiographic line, represented by writings of the religious elite, also produced its first works in the early decades of the sixteenth century. The

Chronicles of the House of Osman by İbn Kemal and the *Cihannümā* by Mevlana Mehmed Neşri are the early examples of this genre. Not surprisingly, the rebuilding of Constantinople and the endeavors of the Ottoman ruling elite in this regard received particular attention from the authors of these chronicles.

Fifteenth- and early-sixteenth-century Greek historical writings, as exemplified by the chronicles of Doukas, Sphrantzes, and a number of anonymous authors, constitute important sources on the era and provide significant, if summary, information on the city subsequent to its fall. European visitors to and captives in the Ottoman court who wrote accounts of their stays following their return to the West—Giovan Maria Angiolello, Giovanni Antonio Menavino, Georgius of Hungary among them—offer important information and complementary views.

In the decades following the Ottoman conquest of Constantinople and the decision to make it the Ottoman capital, authors belonging to diverse segments of Ottoman society and with different attitudes toward the conquest and its aftermath produced a body of literature treating the city, its past, and its significant sites. The *Patria,* a collection of Greek texts on the history and monuments of Constantinople, was partially translated, upon a royal commission, into Persian (and eventually into Turkish). The city's myriad stories, translated, adapted, and appropriated to varying ends from medieval Greek and Arabic literature, figured in anonymous chronicles and in such compilations of late medieval lore as *Dürr-i Meknūn* and the *Ṣalṭuḳnāme* (an epic of Ottoman expansion in the Balkans compiled in the 1470s). Hagiographies of figures as diverse as the grand vizier Mahmud Pasha, the heterodox (and to Ottoman authorities highly troublesome) dervish Otman Baba, and the Sufi scholar

Akşemseddin (spiritual guide to Mehmed II during the siege of Constantinople) are other literary products in which the city figures as setting to a variety of narratives representing and interpreting newly emerging social and political configurations. During the same period the city and its spaces entered the realm of Ottoman poetry, in which are apparent the nascent themes and tropes through which Istanbul would be represented to its Ottoman audiences across the following centuries. Belonging to a different strand of literary production are the earliest biographical dictionaries of Ottoman poets and scholars: those by Latifi and Sehi Beg, as well as Taşköprizade's *Şaḳaiḳu'l-Nuʿmaniyye,* although works of the middle decades of the sixteenth century, are rich with information on the networks and settings of intellectual activity in fifteenth-century Istanbul.

The fifteenth century lacks the rich mines of archival documentation, such as court records and *mühimme* registers (compilations of imperial edicts and decrees), available to students of later Ottoman urban history. Among the available archival sources that deal with the builders, inhabitants, and buildings of the city during this period are unbound imperial edicts, surveys of urban property, sales and ownership documents, and the deeds and account books of pious endowments. The most voluminous among these are the documents related to pious endowments: individual waqfiyyas (endowment deeds) and citywide surveys of endowed property, which provide significant information on the city's physical and social makeup, on patronage patterns involved in the creation of monuments as well as in the making of residential and commercial areas. These documents make possible a partial mapping of the city's social and built fabric; they simultaneously provide valuable insights into notions shaping the conceptualization and organization of urban life.

Chapter 1 focuses on the first years following the conquest (1453–59). Although Constantinople was declared the capital of the Ottoman realm upon its capture, it was only in the 1460s that this decision was fully implemented. The initial Ottoman interventions in the cityscape following 1453 were responses to immediate concerns and needs, rather than parts of a larger project. Reflecting the sultan's decision to rebuild the city on a vast scale and endowing it with some of its powerful symbols, the projects of these years of orientation and reorientation simultaneously betray a lack of clarity regarding the status of the city and the possibilities offered by its topography. The conflict between the former Ottoman order, defined by largely centrifugal forces, and the newly emerging political configuration, shaped by a centralizing vision, found reflection in the first architectural projects in the city. I focus on the main Ottoman interventions in the Constantinopolitan cityscape through these years, highlighting at once the projects that were to be subsequently marginalized and those that were to leave a permanent mark on the city.

The second chapter, "Constructing the City," focuses on the monumentalization of urban space in its political, cultural, social, and visual dimensions. It takes as its starting point Mehmed's announcement in 1459 of a new campaign in rebuilding the capital and his order to members of the ruling elite to undertake constructions in the city alongside him. Three sections structure this discussion, the first devoted to the royal project, the second to the architectural patronage of the new ruling elite, and the third to an overall assessment of major Ottoman interventions in the cityscape. The architectural works of the period are evaluated in the context of the construction of empire, as a collective enterprise of the ruling body to create the imperial capital. Here, I delineate those aspects of the architectural projects that link them to each other and justify their study as parts of an urban project, considering them in terms of their functions, visual idiom, relationship to the urban environment, uses and reception, and their roles as centers of further urban development. Central to this discussion is the interaction between the Byzantine and Ottoman urban and architectural traditions, on the one hand, and the Renaissance ideas of ordering the urban environment, on the other.

The third chapter turns to representations of Constantinople/Istanbul. As the space of the city was transformed through a large-scale urban project that had its roots in Ottoman, Byzantine, and Italian urban practices, the city's image, too, was remade, to represent the Ottoman capital as it emerged at the end of Mehmed's rule. The views of the city in the numerous manuscripts of *Liber Insularum Archipelagi* of Cristoforo Buondelmonti, produced throughout the latter half of the fifteenth century, the Vavassore map, which is a copy of an earlier drawing dating from ca. 1480, and the image in Hartmann Schedel's *Liber Chronicarum* of 1493 are analyzed in the context of the changing cultural meaning of the city concomitant with its fall/conquest. Subsequently, literary images of the city in later-fifteenth-century Ottoman sources are analyzed as textual counterparts to the visual images. I discuss the intent and meaning of these representations, situating them in their cultural and political milieus of production and use. In light of the complexities of their representational modes and content, the ambiguity and polysemy they embody, I discuss transformations in the cultural identity and meaning of the city.

The fourth chapter explores another main theme of the study, urban space as inhabited. Here, I return to the physical space of the city, its buildings, and the primary sources treating them, now to map out a residential topography of the new capital and to delineate its relationship to the city's monumental order. I begin with a focus on the organizing principles of the archival documents relevant to the topic and the representational strategies manifest in them. Close reading of this documentation exposes ruptures between representations of the urban body and the practices that shaped it. This, in turn, sheds light at once on Ottoman concepts of urban structure and on modern interpretations of those concepts, informed by at times overly literal readings of the documents in question. Delineating patterns in the formation of new neighborhood centers and in the patronage mechanisms involved in this process, I propose a revised residential map of the city. At the same time, by tracing the first steps in the formation of the city's residential structure, I demonstrate that this was a less straightforward process than has generally been assumed. I turn finally to the physical fabric of the residential areas, to the uses of Byzantine structures and new constructions, to reach an understanding of the tangible mass that surrounded a newly configured monumental layout.

The epilogue turns to the reigns of two successors of Mehmed, Bayezid II (r. 1481–1512) and Selim I (r. 1512–20), providing an overview of Istanbul on the eve of a second major construction boom, led by Süleyman I, which endowed the city with its "classical" features. A celebrated image of Ottoman Istanbul, Matrakcı Nasuh's view of ca. 1537, mediates both a survey of the city at this time and a discussion of the imperial urban vision that shaped it, leading to an exploration into the interrelationships between urban representation and urbanistic practice in the Ottoman world. Comparing Matrakcı's image to earlier representations of the city discussed in the third chapter, I locate their differences in shifts in political and cultural orientations that marked the late fifteenth and early sixteenth centuries, and in concomitant changes in patronage patterns and sponsorship of urban institutions. This brief overview (of another little-studied era in the history of Istanbul) aims to buttress one of the theses of this study: through the first decades of Ottoman rule, the formal and conceptual foundations for Istanbul's later development were laid. But those decades also inscribed in the space of the city and in its images traces of the complex dynamics of an era when diverse cultural traditions encountered each other on a site of immense symbolic significance. By the time the Matrakcı view was created, traces of that former era were in part obscured, as a more univalent imperial vision of the capital city was articulated.

Between Edirne and Koṣtantiniyye

THE CITY'S FIRST OTTOMAN YEARS

CHAPTER 1

Bearing the traces of economic decline, political isolation, loss of its hinterland to Ottoman expansion in the previous century, Constantinople was destitute at the time of its fall. Its vast expanse housed some fifty thousand people, a large population by late medieval and early modern standards, but diminutive when compared to the city's more prosperous times. Travelers to the city in the early fifteenth century commented on its rural character: it was mostly empty; small villagelike settlements and monasteries were separated from each other by uninhabited areas, orchards and farmlands.[1] The sack that followed the conquest left the city bereft not only of its treasures but also of its inhabitants: many left, and those who survived the siege were enslaved.

"And the City was desolate, lying dead, naked, soundless, having neither form nor beauty," wrote the contemporary chronicler Doukas, ending his account of the siege and fall of Constantinople.[2] As much as the misfortunes of the city's inhabitants and the desecration of its religious monuments, Doukas lamented the death of empire. His powerful image is one among a host of narratives dating from these years that render visible the dismal state of the city following its siege and sack. The Ottoman interventions that followed, reflecting divers attitudes and dispositions, responded in their turn to the conditions Doukas depicted and to the ideological and spiritual associations of the city at large.

The chronicles of Tursun and Kritovoulos, two witnesses to these early years of Ottoman presence in Constantinople, leave no doubt that Mehmed planned, from early on, to make the city the seat of the Ottoman throne. Although his narrative is not strictly chronological, Tursun notes soon after his account of the conquest that Mehmed announced to his viziers, officials, and slaves that "from now on Istanbul is my throne."[3] Kritovoulos writes that Mehmed rode through the city shortly after its capture, planning "how to repopulate it, not merely as it formerly was but more completely, if possible, so that it should be a worthy capital for him, located as it was most favorably by land and by sea."[4] Mehmed would have to wait, however, to make this momentous move, not only because the city possessed few inhabitants and few of the amenities a functioning urban infrastructure would require but more particularly because not all who were part of the conquering army shared his desire to inhabit Constantinople.

Mehmed spent the following years mostly in Edirne, ancient Adrianople, a major seat of Ottoman power, alongside Bursa, and base for military expansion into the Balkans from its capture in the 1360s onward. Through these years after the fall of Constantinople Edirne continued to house the janissary army as well as the sultan's retinue. Fifteenth- and early-sixteenth-century chronicles note that Ottoman military campaigns departed from and returned to this city.[5] Only in Kritovoulos's history are we told of the winters of 1454 and 1455, parts of which the sultan spent in Istanbul, supervising its building and population. That the grand circumcision ceremony of Mehmed's sons in 1457 took place in Edirne (*dārü'l-mülk-i ḳadīm,* the old capital, according to the chronicler İbn Kemal), not in Istanbul, demonstrates the primacy of the former capital during these years. Not coincidentally, perhaps, this one week–long celebration, the most pompous event to be staged by the Ottomans in the 1450s, shortly followed the Ottoman defeat at Belgrade. According to Aşıkpaşazade, sumptuous feasts, festivities that began in the morning and continued through the night, and exchanges of gifts with guests of importance from within and beyond the Ottoman realm added up to "a complete and perfect demonstration of the sultan's greatness and majesty."[6]

While the prospect of Kostantiniyye's becoming the seat of the Ottoman throne attracted the severe reactions of many, one of the central policies in realizing this objective was in place soon after the conquest: the inhabitation of the city and its environs. Kritovoulos's chronicle entry narrating Mehmed's plans concerning the population of the city in the first days following the conquest is the earliest source underlining the conception of such a policy. The first measure to this effect was Mehmed's release of his share of war captives (one-fifth), perhaps a few thousand people, in order to resettle them in the city.[7] Some captives, Kritovoulos writes, were put to work in constructions in the city, so that they might earn their ransom and stay on. Those who came to settle there on their own were initially offered land and property.[8] Invitation and enticement notwithstanding, the primary method of populating the city was forced resettlement (mostly of non-Muslim and particularly Greek communities in the early years) from newly conquered territories. Contemporary Ottoman chroniclers and a host of narrators of various ethnic backgrounds witnessed and commented on the major reshuffling of populations in the effort to populate the city and its environs.

Attempts to populate the city, although subject to changes in procedure and method, remained a constant in Ottoman policies concerning Constantinople through the early decades of the sixteenth century. The same cannot be said for Ottoman interventions in the cityscape. Unlike the major architectural and other urban projects undertaken in the decades following 1458, which were products of an overarching vision concerning the shape and the image of the imperial capital, those tackled in the first years following the conquest were conceived as responses to immediate concerns and needs, whether of a symbolic or of a practical nature. In view of later developments and the comments of contemporary observers, it can be surmised that this relative lack of focus owed in large part to the diverse views of the city held by a divided political elite: To the monarch, it was the seat of empire; it would form, literally and figuratively, the grounds upon which an imperial ideology would be formulated and an imperial administrative apparatus put to work. To a considerable portion of Mehmed's political base, on the other hand, conquering and possessing the seat of Eastern Christendom and inhabiting it were different matters. Constantinople's all-too-tangible associations with imperial power and official Christianity made such inhabitation doubly undesirable. Hence the occasionally inchoate nature of initial urban interventions by the Ottomans: a series of projects responded to the tensions and reorientations revolving around the shape of Ottoman rule and the status of the city, their future to be

determined by the way those tensions would eventually be resolved. Five projects, of different natures and varying significance in the city's later history, come to the fore: the conversion of Hagia Sophia into a mosque, the construction of a palace and a citadel, the radical expansion of the city's commercial infrastructure, and finally the construction of a religious complex over the miraculously discovered grave of Abu Ayyub al-Ansari, a warrior saint who had been present in the Arab siege of Constantinople of ca. 667.

AYASOFYA

Contemporary histories agree that the very first act of Mehmed upon entering Constantinople was to visit Hagia Sophia, and that the conversion of the Great Church into a mosque was the first Ottoman intervention in the city (figs. 5, 6). The conversion of the monument realized

a dream whose history went back to the early centuries of Islam. Simultaneously, this act marked the initiation of a process central to the making of the Ottoman capital city, namely, the selective appropriation of symbolically significant aspects of Byzantine Constantinople.[9]

No other site in the city embodied and bespoke as clearly and as powerfully as the Great Church notions of imperial rule that shaped the history of Constantinople, and no other site represented as clearly as Hagia Sophia centuries-old Muslim aspirations to conquer the capital of Eastern Rome. Two contemporary sources highlight the central place this monument assumed in contrasting imaginings of the city. One of these authors is Tursun Beg, whose *History of Mehmed the Conqueror* includes a lengthy description of the building that underlines its paradisal qualities. That to this author and his patron the building's

heavenly beauty and imperial associations were intimately linked becomes clear in an image of the young Mehmed contemplating the ruinous state of the church's environs. Moved by the ruins before his eyes, Mehmed cites a couplet by the Persian poet Sadi:

> The spider serves as gatekeeper in the halls of Khosrou's dome
> The owl plays martial music in the palace of Afrasiyab

The image of Hagia Sophia as imperial locus did not appeal to all. In the ghazi legends compiled in the 1470s, Mehmed's begs, while discussing an attack on Constantinople, advised him to "build a wall around Ayasofya and destroy the rest." ("Let us conquer it first, and we will see to its destruction," was Mehmed's aloof answer.)[10]

Magnificent images of its legendary qualities and narratives of its miraculous construction had long located Ayasofya at the center of an Islamic lore of Kostantiniyye, as a site of high esteem and semiveneration.[11] Through the decades following the Ottoman conquest new narratives rewrote the story of Hagia Sophia's construction to endow it with a more particularly Ottoman Islamic past, rendering it the nexus and symbol of divers attitudes and dispositions concerning the city at large.[12] At the same time, Hagia Sophia, from its conversion by the Ottomans into one of the very first places of Muslim worship in the city until centuries later, remained a benchmark in the architectural culture of the wider Ottoman world, against which every construction enterprise of importance was measured. With two exceptions, all large-scale mosques and convent-mosques built in the city during the reign of Mehmed displayed iconic reference to Hagia Sophia: they featured either a single half dome or two that supported a central sanctuary dome.[13]

In part due to its immense symbolic significance, but also to predispositions regarding the Byzantine past particular to this era, the conversion of the building did not involve radical changes in its architecture or decorative program. The sanctuary, stripped of its relics, icons, and furnishings linked to Christian liturgy, was endowed with the most fundamental requirements of the Muslim congregation: a marble prayer niche and a pulpit. A number of Muslim relics and victory emblems were placed in the sanctuary, signifying its passage into an Islamic and Ottoman order: a prayer carpet associated with the prophet Muhammad hung near the mihrab, and banners commemorating the conquest of Constantinople were placed at its two sides.[14] Some of the figural mosaics (possibly those immediately within view of the Muslim congregation) were plastered over; but the majority remained intact, including such potent images of Christian worship as the Virgin and Christ over the apse and Christ Pantokrator at the summit of the main dome.[15] The earliest evidence for Arabic inscriptions in the sanctuary (excepting those on the mihrab) date from Bayezid's reign.[16] Images of Constantine and Justinian presenting models of city and church met the visitor to the building at its southern entrance; narrative images adorned the narthex.

Imagining the Hagia Sophia in later-fifteenth-century Istanbul is not easy today, as our image of the building is heavily influenced by its later Ottoman representations produced when traces of its Byzantine past had been obscured under layers of plaster, paint, additions, and increasingly more visible signs of Muslim ritual. Tracing the information on the visual structure of Hagia Sophia's interior in the later fifteenth century, one finds a highly hybrid space: emptied of all tools of Christian worship and liturgy and endowed with the basic Muslim ones, the building nevertheless preserved to a remarkable degree its Byzantine Christian identity. A similar coexistence of potent symbols marked the building's exterior. The cross atop its dome was removed, along with the bells of the belltower. The belfry itself remained intact into the seventeenth century, an immediately recognizable sign of the monument's Christian past and simultaneously a testimonial to Ottoman cultural attitudes that characterized the era immediately following the city's fall. The destruction of belfries and erection of minarets in conquered territories is a trope in all chronicles and ghazi legends of the era; for a considerable time, Hagia Sophia featured both: although the belfry emptied of its bells marked the entrance to the sanctuary, a wooden minaret was built atop a buttress at the southeast corner of the building. Soon afterward, possibly following the construction of the New Mosque, with its royal iconography of twin minarets, the Hagia Sophia was given another minaret, of ashlar masonry, to rise at the opposite corner of the qibla wall.[17] The two unequal minarets are visible in a partial view of Constantinople, with Hagia Sophia and Justinian's statue in the Augustaion, in Hartmann Schedel's *Liber Chronicarum* of 1493 (fig. 119; one of the minarets flanking the main dome is crowned by a composite symbol, a cross atop a crescent); the belfry is featured prominently in Scarella's drawing of ca. 1686 (fig. 7). The ease with which multiple identities were accepted and adopted into the Ottoman order, whether individuals and groups of diverse background or important sites and monuments, is also to be observed here. The image of Constantinople in one copy of the *Liber Insularum*, where Hagia Sophia is represented with a cross atop its dome and a crescent atop its minaret, is not completely off the mark (see fig. 111).

Unlike any other converted church in the city, the building's name remained unchanged.

Until the completion of the mosque of Mahmud Pasha in 867/1462–63, Hagia Sophia was the only congregational mosque in the city proper. And until the completion of Mehmed's New Mosque complex in 874/1469–70, it was the primary religious and educational institution in the city. A madrasa was built to the north of Hagia Sophia shortly after its conversion, and Mevlana Husrev appointed its first professor. The greater part of the city's Byzantine urban property, of which Mehmed II had declared himself the sole owner, was endowed for the mosque shortly after the conquest. Indecisions regarding the status of this property notwithstanding, it was in large part leased out to the inhabitants of Constantinople following a citywide survey and registration.[18] Apart from the mosque itself, the Ayasofya endowment supported the first religious and charitable institutions in the city.[19] Among these were a number of mosques outside of the walls of Constantinople proper: the Friday mosque of Galata, converted from the

FIGURE 7
Francesco Scarella, *Santa Sophia*, ink drawing, 1686. Austrian National Library, Picture Archives, Codex 8627.

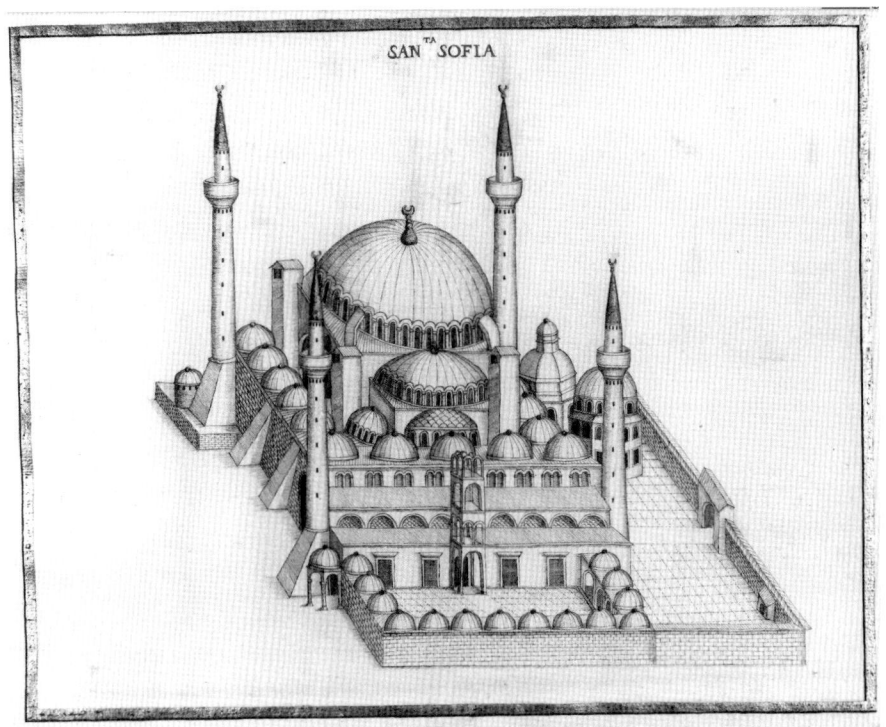

Dominican church of the Genoese colony (the later Arap Cami), the mosques of the two forts on the Bosphorus, and the mosque built within the new citadel at the Golden Gate. Four Byzantine churches were converted to serve purposes of education, accommodation, and health care. Significantly, these remained the only churches, other than the Great Church, converted for religious or charitable purposes within the walled city through the rule of Mehmed: The Zeyrek madrasa, named after its professor, Mevlana Zeyrek, was housed in the Pantokrator church and monastery,[20] while close by another Byzantine church (possibly the Pantepoptes monastery, later to be called the Eski İmaret—Old Hospice) served as the city's first hospice. Another Byzantine monastic church, the Kyriotissa to the west of Mehmed II's first palace, was made a convent referred to as the Kalenderhane.[21] An Aristo bīmārḫānesi served as the city's only hospital until the completion of the one attached to the New Mosque complex.[22]

Hagia Sophia's institutional primacy was short-lived, in striking contrast to its monarchical primacy, which it retained as Constantinople's royal mosque throughout its Ottoman history. With the completion of Mehmed's New Mosque complex, Ayasofya became the lesser-endowed sultanic foundation. Its madrasa was closed down (later to be reinstated by Bayezid II), while the Zeyrek madrasa, the first imaret, and the hospital were to lose their functions and reemerge as quarter mosques with the establishment of those institutions around the New Mosque in the 1470s.

THE FIRST PALACE AND THE CITADEL
Before leaving the city for Edirne less than a month after the conquest, Mehmed ordered the repair of the city walls that were damaged during the siege, the destruction of the walls surrounding Galata (it was still possible that the Genoese community would side with European allies in case of military conflict), and the construction of a palace. He chose "the finest and the best location in the city" for a vast enclosure that measured about a mile in circumference. The palace was situated between the Mese (the ceremonial artery of the Byzantine city that ran from the Hippodrome to the Golden Gate) and the slopes descending to the Golden Horn, the southern end of its enclosure overlapping part of the Byzantine Forum of Taurus. A star-shaped fortress was conceived and built against the Golden Gate, the ceremonial port of entry to the Byzantine city, during the same years (map 1; see also fig. 12).[23]

Little is known of the architecture of the first palace except that it housed numerous kiosks, gardens, and hunting preserves within a roughly rectangular walled enclosure.[24] The view by Vavassore, based on a late-fifteenth-century original, shows the column of Theodosius as a prominent feature within its walls, at the southwestern corner of the enclosure (fig. 8; see also fig. 9). The enclosure of the monumental narrative column within the palace grounds speaks powerfully of Mehmed II's keen interest in the city's Byzantine monuments. Copies of minute drawings of the narrative relief indicate that the monument was examined and recorded by one of the Italian artists who worked under Mehmed's patronage, perhaps Gentile Bellini. Mehmed's enthusiasm for the monument's preservation is brought into sharper focus against its fate during his successor's rule: Bayezid II had the column pulled down to open space for a bathhouse and used fragments of the reliefs as spolia for bold exhibition in the Ottoman building.[25]

A contemporary narrative of Mehmed's funeral, in 1481, suggests the relationship of the palatial enclosure to the forum on which it was placed. On its way to the New Mosque, near which the sultan was to be buried, the procession arrived at the *place de serragolio*. Here the sultan's many wives and concubines, dressed in black, appeared in a gallery, where they cried and wept until the procession was no longer visible (fig. 10).[26] The *place* was possibly the remaining section of the Forum of Taurus, which now constituted a forecourt to the palace; and the gallery was possibly the belvedere of a gate complex, modeled after ceremonial palace gatehouses that were part of Islamic as well as Roman and Byzantine palatial traditions.[27] Soon to acquire the name Sārāy-ı ʿAtīḳ, "Old Palace," this first palace never did become Mehmed's permanent residence. He used it in alternation with the Edirne palace during these years when he resided primarily in the former capital. Once the New Palace was completed and became the sultan's permanent residence and the locus of Ottoman rule, the vast enclosure on the Taurus was abandoned to the imperial harem.

Mehmed's first palace, surrounded by walls that isolated it from the city in whose midst it was located, was conceived as a *ḳalʿa,* or palace-citadel.[28] Such walled palatial enclosures situated at a prominent and often elevated location, central to the spatial configurations of cities in the post-Abbasid Islamic world, offered an urban model to the Ottomans. In their more immediate vicinity were the medieval citadels of politically significant urban centers such as Konya, Bursa, and Ankara (the latter two inhabited by them). But it was not only Islamic precedents that the Ottomans could turn to in this respect. Evidence for the palace-citadel as a widespread phenomenon of the late medieval world is, of course, to be found within Constantinople itself, in the Blachernae Palace, which housed the Byzantine administration from the later thirteenth century onward.[29] Unlike the Blachernae, where the security offered by location at the edge of the city was a prime factor in the choice of site—and unlike the Topkapı, at the city's opposite edge—Mehmed's first palace was boldly located at the very center of Constantinople and above the only densely inhabited area of the peninsula at the time, the shores and slopes along the Golden Horn. The name Taht al-kalʿa (literally, "under the citadel"; Tahtakale in modern Turkish), already in use during the first decades of Ottoman rule to

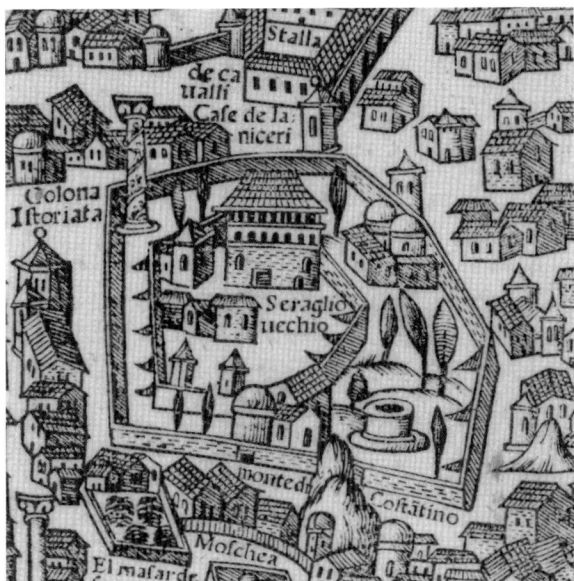

FIGURE 8
The Old Palace, detail from Giovanni Andreas di Vavassore's view of Istanbul, ca. 1520, based on an original dating to ca. 1480 (fig. 114). Harvard University, Houghton Library, 51-2570PF.

FIGURE 9
The Old Palace, detail from Nasuhü's-Silahi [Matrakcı], view of Istanbul in the *Beyān-ı menāzil-i sefer-i ʿIraḳeyn*, ca. 1537 (plate 7). Istanbul University Library, T.5964, fol. 8v.

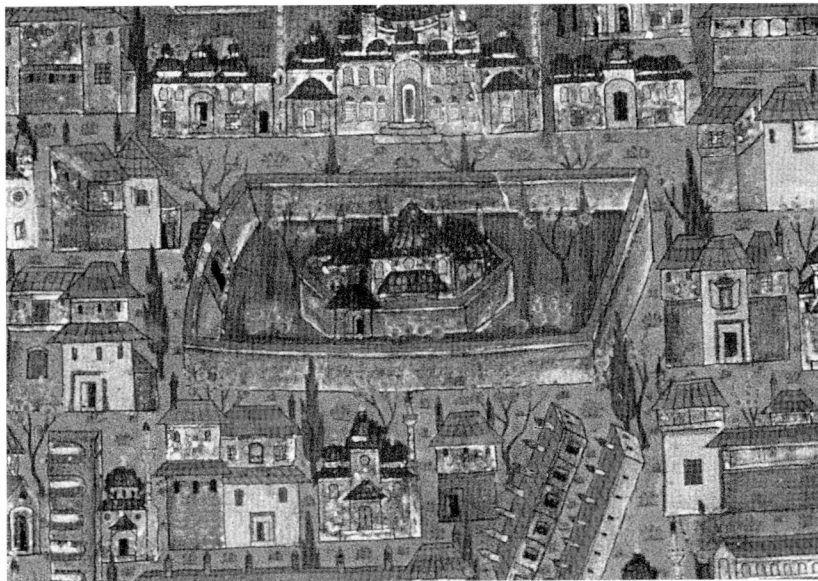

denote the commercial center on the Golden
Horn (a site also to be found in other Ottoman
cities), is indicative of the urban model that
shaped the decision concerning the location of
the first palace.

What, then, of a second citadel at the
Golden Gate, which blocked the ceremonial
gate of Byzantium and integrated it into its
pentagonal star-shaped enclosure (figs. 11, 12)?
A military counterpart to the palace vulnerably
situated at the center of the city, the citadel was
meant to serve as a refuge and a point of defense
in times of conflict. Papal campaigns for the
organization of a Crusade following the Ottoman conquest of Constantinople must have
had a role in the decision to construct a fortress
at the strategically important point where the
city's land walls met the sea. For if a Crusade

was ever launched, the Ottomans would have
had to secure the city against an Italian fleet
approaching from the Aegean and Austrian
and Hungarian troops approaching from the
Balkans.[30]

The earlier history of Ottoman and Byzantine relations, as well as Ottoman knowledge of
Byzantine history, might also have had a role in
the choice of site. The Porta Aurea was not only
the ceremonial entrance to Constantinople
for those arriving through the Via Egnatia but
also one of the military strongholds of the city.
Thanks to the four towers flanking the gate, this
was the strongest point of the land walls and
a safe refuge during the city's troubled times.
Reinforced by John VI Cantacuzenus in 1347,
it was expanded by John V Palaeologos and
succesfully protected him from attack by the
cannons and other firearms of his grandson
John VII in 1390. Bayezid I, in forcing John V
to dismantle the citadel in 1390–91, after taking custody of the emperor's son, exhibited
his awareness of the strategic value of the site.
Kritovoulos's account of Mehmed's ordering
"the construction of a strong fortress near the
Golden Gate where there had formerly been an
imperial castle"[31] likewise makes it clear that
the Ottomans appreciated this site as a valuable
point of defense in case of assault or internal
conflict. Ottoman knowledge of former uses
of the castle adjoining the Golden Gate may
also explain the location of the new citadel
inside, rather than outside, the city walls, and
the direction of its bastions toward the city.
Unlike their Byzantine predecessors, however,
the Ottoman rulers never had to take refuge in
the citadel. It housed the treasury (or part of
it) and prisoners of the highest order.[32] In the
early sixteenth century, Menavino described it
as a fortified and strongly guarded palace that
housed the treasury, the "third palace of the
Grand Turk."[33]

Although the strategic significance of the site might have been the primary factor in the decision to build a citadel there, the location and shape of this "third palace" are also indicative of Ottoman attitudes toward the Byzantine past. Building the citadel, the new authority blocked what had once been the city's ceremonial artery, the main branch of the Mese, which connected to the Via Egnatia beyond the gate.[34] In the same way the New Mosque was to replace the church of the Holy Apostles, the citadel replaced and rendered obsolete the ceremonial entrance to the Byzantine city. This gate, which Cyril Mango has noted resembled a Roman triumphal arch rising to some twelve meters and featuring a complex composition of spoliated antique and Byzantine figural reliefs,[35] became itself an immense piece of spolia incorporated into the Ottoman military structure, like so many other Byzantine relics integrated into Ottoman monuments within those decades (fig. 13).

The formal configuration of the Byzantine castle is not known with certainty. Bruno Meyer-Plath and Alfons Maria Schneider have reconstructed it as a rectangular structure attached to the exterior of the city walls.[36]

Although most scholarship follows this reconstruction, Mango has argued that it more likely flanked the inner side of the gate, forming a fort ("a little town" according to Doukas) that reached as far as the seashore.[37] Mehmed's castle, a sizable enclosure also built inside the city wall, measuring some 150 meters on the north-south axis and surrounded by towers 25 meters in height, was radically different in its scale and nature from the Byzantine structure.

The plan of Mehmed's citadel, soon to acquire the name Yedikule, or Seven Towers, is based on a six-pointed star overlapping the Golden Gate: three salient angles of the star face the city, while the Theodosian walls, making a westward turn south of the monumental gate and featuring two towers that mark the northern and southern limits of the enclosure, replace the remaining three angles of the ideal plan (fig. 14). The marble towers flanking the ceremonial gate are incorporated into the fortress, while on the east three towers rise at the salient angles of the star. The northeast and southeast towers are cylindrical, while the eastern tower, the one at the center, facing the now walled-in Golden Gate, is a dodecagonal structure, which introduces an axial dimension to the layout.

If awareness of this location's strategic value and symbolic significance was one factor that

shaped the choice of site, Italian inspiration seems to have been another. The ground plan, along with the site chosen for the enclosure, reveals an unmistakable relationship to architectural theories developed in the same decades by Leon Battista Alberti and Filarete.[38] The citadel at Constantinople's Golden Gate marks the first time a geometrical military or urban enclosure conceived in Italian architectural treatises was realized in stone and mortar. Projects for polygonal military and urban enclosures were elaborated by Filarete and later by Francesco di Georgio as ideal layouts that would at once bespeak the power and prestige of the monarch and protect him from military assault (figs. 14, 15). Before them, Alberti had considered the function and location of the citadel in his ideal cities. His statement (itself based on ancient tradition and medieval practice) that a tyrant's

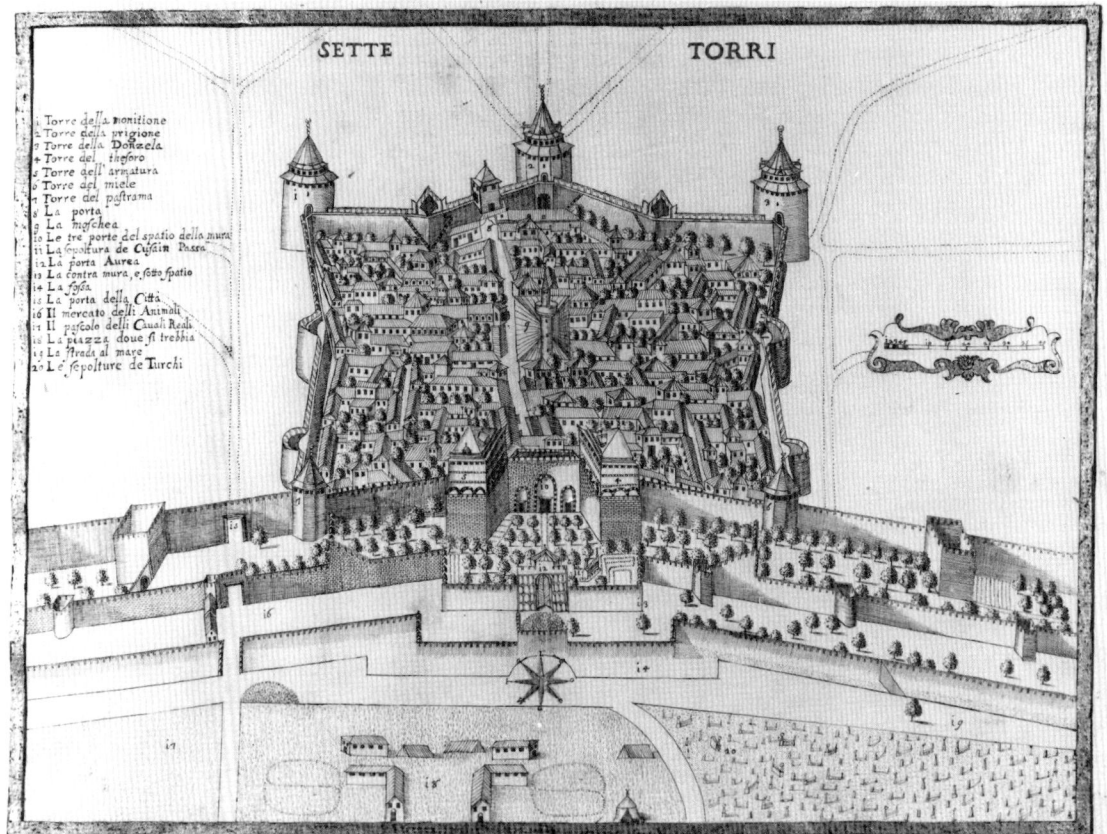

FIGURE 13
Francesco Scarella, *Sette Torre* [Seven Towers], depicting the golden gate and the citadel, ink drawing, 1686. Austrian National Library, Picture Archives, Codex 8627.

citadel should be at the edge of the city was in line with Mehmed's choice of site. Such a location, Alberti argued, would facilitate defense and recovery of control in case of foreign assault or civil unrest. The Ottoman monarch had reason to expect both in the years immediately following the city's conquest. How this plan, unmistakably a product of contemporary Italian architectural culture, reached Constantinople soon after the city's fall remains a matter of conjecture. It is, nevertheless, hardly unique as an instance of Ottoman use of Italian architectural ideas and design. The novel, idealized ground plan of the fortress and its medieval elevation, lacking provisions for artillery, have been related to those of Filarete's Sforzinda, the ideal city he designed for Count Sforza of Milan, whose octagonal enclosure displayed a similar idiosyncrasy.[39] Filarete's name, and his enigmatic role in royal projects in fifteenth-century Istanbul, will come to the fore again, about a decade later, in the design of Mehmed's New Mosque complex.

This first star-shaped fortress of Renaissance Europe remained, at the end of one of the main axes of the city, a rather marginal addition to Ottoman Constantinople. Unlike, for example, the citadel of Turin, which the duke of Savoy said was his most precious jewel and which, after his heir, he loved best, Yedikule was endowed neither with the status of an ideally planned Renaissance fort nor with its central location in the city.[40] The sheer size of Constantinople, which (unlike much smaller Italian cities) did not allow the citadel comparable formal and visual prominence, was doubtless a factor. The spatial organization of the capital city, including the location of the military within it, was another: the citadel of Istanbul was a refuge far removed from the city center and not the primary base of the military, as in most other premodern cities. Although referred to as

a "third palace" by one contemporary observer, Yedikule never became a central military or administrative space. It is telling that in contemporary Ottoman sources the enclosure was not called a *ķalʿa,* as a citadel in the Ottoman/Islamic tradition would have been, but was referred to as a *ķulle* (tower) (fig. 16).

According to Kritovoulos, the palace on the Forum of Taurus was completed in 1456. In 1458 Mehmed announced his decision to build a new palace at the northeastern tip of the Constantinopolitan peninsula. The haste with which the first palace and the citadel were completed and the former abandoned for a new one speaks to the sultan's yet uninformed acquaintance with the city's topography and his vacillating vision of the future shape of the imperial capital. Simultaneously, the peculiar (and short-lived) combination of two "citadels," one

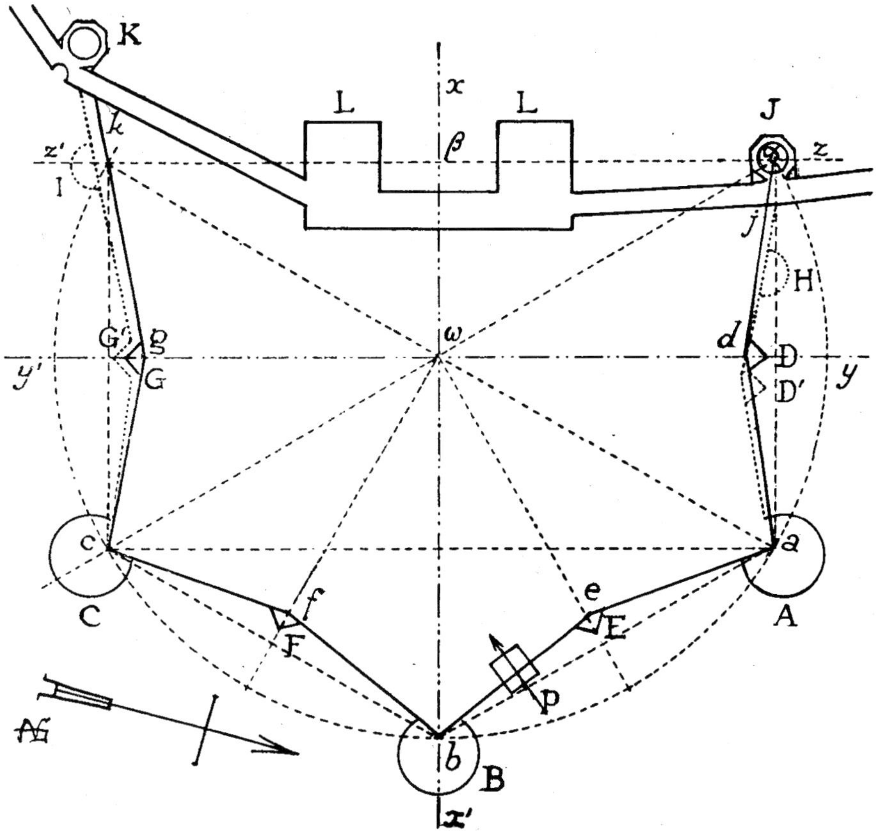

FIGURE 14
Albert Gabriel, geometric scheme of the star-shaped citadel.

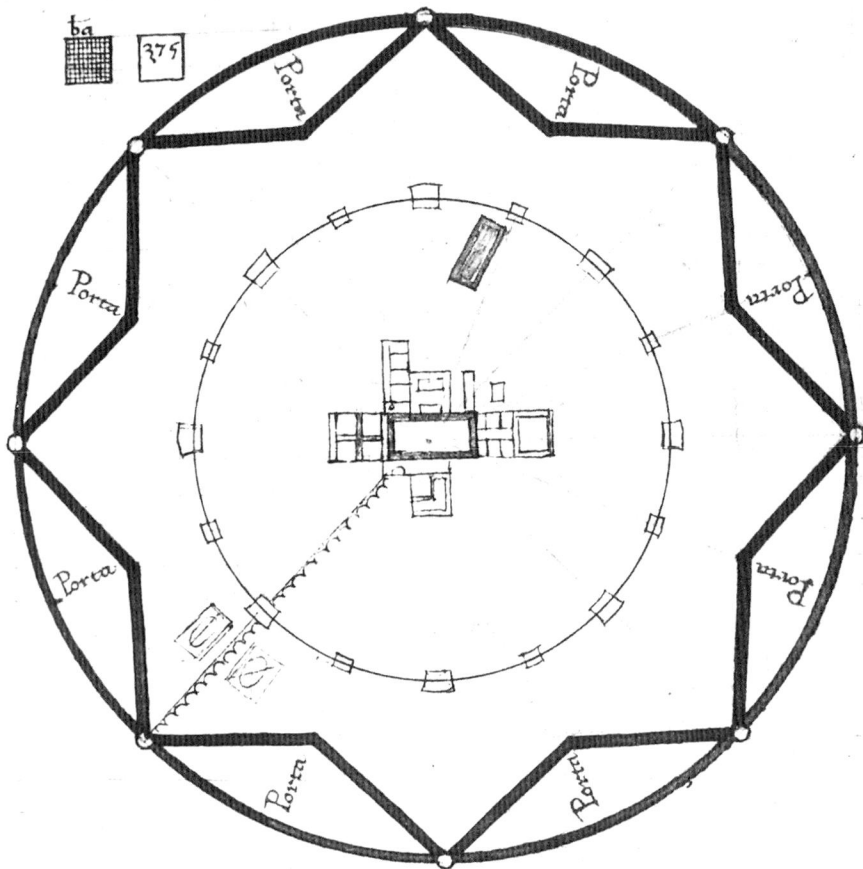

FIGURE 15
Antonio Averlino, called Filarete,
plan of Sforzinda from *Trattato
di Architettura*, ca. 1461–64.

of an Ottoman and the other of an Italian order, bespeaks the eclecticism and idiosyncrasy that characterized the Ottoman cultural environment through this period.

NEAR AND BELOW THE PALACE: ESTABLISHING THE INFRASTRUCTURE OF COMMERCE

Of the Ottoman interventions in the city immediately following the conquest, the most expansive were those that involved the establishment of a commercial infrastructure. This was realized through the reuse and revitalization of Byzantine structures and patterns as much as extensive new constructions.[41] New monumental loci marked both the former Byzantine and the newly created Ottoman fabric. The initial constructions in what were to remain the two core areas of Ottoman Istanbul's commercial district, the port and the bedestan, date to these years.[42]

Kritovoulos's chronicle offers a chronology for the initial endeavors concerning the commercial infrastructure while simultaneously providing insights into their broader context. These are the subject matter of a chapter of the *History* entitled "How the Sultan Took Care of the City," which describes Mehmed's arrival at Constantinople in the winter of 1455, where he found the palace and the castle at the Golden Gate completed and the city walls restored. The sultan then ordered overseers to repair bridges and roads that led to the city, to pave the roads at dangerous and difficult areas, and to build "caravanserais and halting places for travelers approaching the city." The construction of the bedestan ("a very beautiful and very large marketplace in the middle of the City, somewhere near the palace"), the building of "splendid and costly baths," and the restoration of the aqueducts that would bring the city an abundance of water were linked to the endeavors concerning the city's hinterland and its repopulation "with people of all nations but more especially Christians." "Many other such things he also ordered to be done for the building up and beautifying of the City, and for the benefit and needs and comfort of the inhabitants," writes Kritovoulos. "So profound was the passion that came into his soul for the City and its peopling, and for bringing it back to its former glory."[43] The Greek chronicler's passages mark the beginning, within the third year of Ottoman rule in Constantinople, of projects directed at reviving the city's commercial infrastructure. Revitalizing the economic life of the capital and reestablishing its links with the hinterland from which it had been cut off in the course of the Ottoman expansion of the previous century were the main motives behind the creation of an array of spaces of commerce, manufacturing, and financial exchange.

The natural and historical topography of the city doubtlessly informed trends of continuity between Byzantine and Ottoman spatial practices. The main consumption center of the eastern Mediterranean from the time of its conception as the capital of Eastern Rome, and with few natural resources in its immediate surroundings, Constantinople remained almost completely dependent on imports throughout its history.[44] Everything from staples to luxury items was imported, particularly via sea routes, rendering the ports, and the links between the ports and the rest of the city, central to the organization of urban space. The restoration of the city to its former glory, as imagined by Mehmed, meant the restoration of its former pattern of provisioning, with its components of transport, storage, and distribution.

Shaped by necessities that were part and parcel of the very existence of Constantinople, new projects nevertheless introduced to the cityscape aspects of Ottoman urban practice, which in turn merged with Byzantine and Italian structures and practices. The Ottoman commercial district had a bifocal layout: the port area on the Golden Horn, where a pre-existing urban structure was Ottomanized, and the newly created bedestan area close to Mehmed's first palace and to the Mese uphill. The establishments along the port were geared more heavily toward wholesale trade and artisanal activity; the uphill locale was a center of commerce in precious metals, textiles, and arms. The Uzunçarşı, the Makros Embolos of the Byzantine city, stretching between the port and the Mese, connected the two nuclei of the area (map 1).[45] Monumental buildings in an Ottoman architectural idiom, the bedestan in the new commercial center and the Taht al-kal'a bath in the port area, signified Ottoman

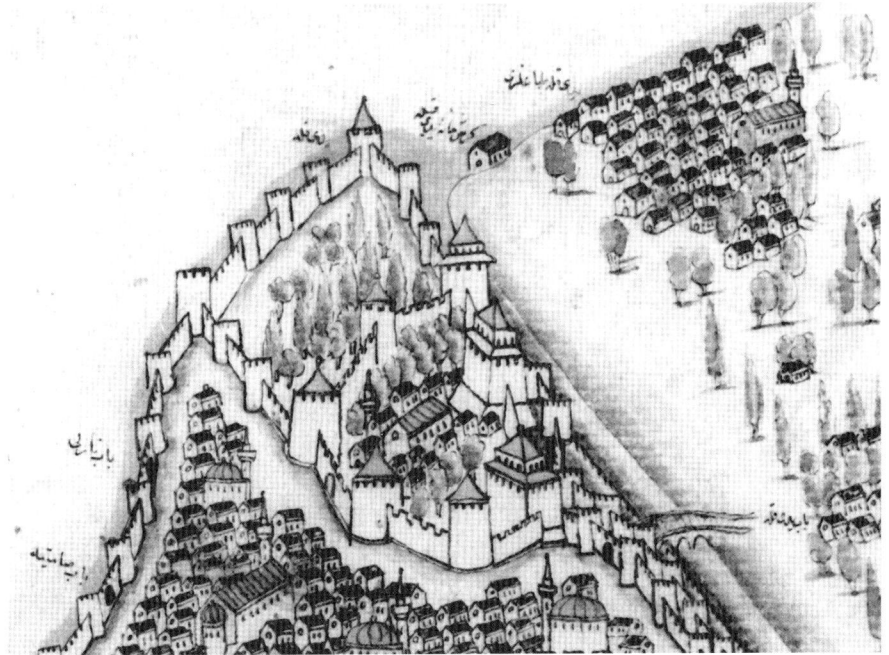

presence in districts most accessible and visible to the city's inhabitants of various backgrounds, as they were to foreign merchants and travelers. Along with the bedestan, a number of *khans* (urban caravanserais) constituted nodes within the commercial area. These focal sites and buildings were spaces not only for interactions revolving around imports but also for their regulation and the efficient collection of taxes. Frequent notes in imperial orders compiled in Mehmed II's book of laws specify the gates and ports of entry for particular goods and the spaces for their sale in the city.[46]

Perhaps the most striking aspect of the commercial establishment was its size. A comparison between the numbers and kinds of endowed commercial structures in Istanbul and those in Anatolian cities demonstrates that in the last decades of the fifteenth century Istanbul housed more commercial space than any major Anatolian city at the end of the next century.[47] This becomes all the more noteworthy if one remembers that Constantinople hardly had an urban character at the time initial and consequential decisions concerning commerce and its settings in the city were made. In part, the commercial structures were those of the Byzantine city, but more than half were new. Commercial spaces were newly created or restored for a projected urban population and volume of commerce rather than for those extant, a point that underlines the integrity of Mehmed's vision concerning the status of Constantinople as imperial capital.[48]

This grand-scale commercial undertaking, clearly oversized with respect to the city's current state, was concomitant with larger processes: the population growth of the city, on the one hand, and the transformation of the structure of Constantinopolitan trade, on the other. The radical increase of population from what must have been at the most slightly over ten thousand in 1453 to a minimum of fifty thousand in 1478 brought along not only a constant demand for supplies but also mercantile and artisanal activity. During this same interval commercial dominance of the Aegean and the Black Sea by the Italian city-states gave way to commercial dominance by the Ottoman state, driven by a network operated for the most part by Ottoman subjects based in Constantinople and Galata. By 1479, this process was largely complete, and Istanbul had, with respect to certain items, become the main commercial center of the Ottoman realm.[49]

The creation of the infrastructure for mercantile activity and crafts in Istanbul was concurrent with the formation of a populace of merchants and craftsmen who would inhabit that infrastructure. While many Italian merchants and Greek aristocratic/merchant families chose to remain in the city after its fall, particularly in Galata, the former Genoese colony across from the Golden Horn, and prevailed as prominent figures in international and long-distance trade, few remnants of the Venetian commercial establishment remained in Constantinople proper. In large part, merchants and artisans of Constantinople were members of deportee communities. That these communities included wealthy individuals, specifically artisans and craftsmen, is evident in contemporary and later chronicles.[50] Perhaps for this reason deportations often caused trouble, both for the communities and for the officials involved. Hadidi noted particularly that the deportees from Karaman were of the *ehl-i ṣanāyiʿ* and *ehl-i ḥiref* (men of crafts and men of arts). The ethnic background and wealth of those taken to Constantinople following the Karaman campaign were a source of conflict between two members of the imperial council, Mahmud Pasha and Rum Mehmed Pasha, resulting in the dismissal of the former and the abbreviated grand vizierate of the latter. A number of wealthy Bursa merchants did all they could to avoid leaving that commercial capital and moving to Istanbul, where possibilities for business (as well as an agreeable lifestyle) must have appeared very bleak from a Bursan point of view and where they would be under the close supervision of the state.[51]

The Port

Perfectly protected from natural and human interference, the ports along the Golden Horn were the main points of entry to the city at the time of the Ottoman takeover.[52] Here, along the eastern parts of Constantinople's Golden Horn shore, lay the city's main commercial quarters through the later fourteenth and fifteenth centuries; the stretch between the Neorion and the Platea Gates was the city's densest commercial area.[53] The Venetian trading colony was located at the center of this area, between the Neorion and the Drungarii Gates; to its east lay the Pisan, Anconan, and Amalfitan settlements.[54] As such a dense agglomeration of commercial and residential structures, in stark contrast to the rest of the walled city, this area figures in the Schedel view (plate 6). The intramural commercial establishments were connected to the stretch outside of the city walls, with its series of *skala,* or embarkation points, and the workshops and booths housing the functions linked to international trade.[55] Ottoman sources from the later decades of the fifteenth century (which frequently distinguish between pre-Ottoman and newly built structures) suggest that the slopes between the first two hills of the peninsula housed fewer commercial buildings in the late Byzantine period. The main feature of the slopes between the sea and the Mese was the Makros Embolos, the Ottoman Uzunçarşı, the artery that connected the two areas and served the distribution of goods to the city.

As the new regime did not change the manner of provisioning through ports along the Golden Horn, it was only natural that the Ottoman commercial establishment should occupy the same area and expand it. While the stretch between the Drungarii/Odun Gate and the Neorion/Orya Gate formed the core of the commercial district along the shore, further up the Golden Horn the Platea/Un Kapanı Gate, Balat, and the Gate of the Tanneries formed other, individual clusters. The principal *ḳapāns* (weighing stations for staples) of the city, several khans, as well as a large number of retail shops, were located in this area.[56] The majority of these were within city walls, while the weighing station and wholesale market for wheat, several groups of shops, and structures for storing and marketing goods occupied the narrow stretch between the walls and the sea.

It is difficult to determine exactly what percentage of the commercial properties in this area, which were endowed for the Ayasofya foundation, were Byzantine or Italian structures appropriated from the former regime, but frequent specifications in the endowment deeds and the surveys, such as *ḳadīm, 'atīḳ* (both words meaning "old"), or *kāfirī al-binā'* (infidel's building), suggest that these were numerous. The *kāfirī* commercial structures introduced a new feature to the vocabulary of Ottoman commercial architecture; these were two-story buildings whose ground floors were used for commercial purposes and upper floors as residences.[57] Though such a combination of functions, one over the other, was common to khans in Ottoman cities, individual shops, generally built as part of suks (marketplaces), were single-story structures. A comparison of the buildings constituting the commercial fabric of the port with the single-story shops newly built around the bedestan highlights the Veneto-Byzantine character of the port district.

As noted above, the commercial and residential fabric of this area, whether overtaken from the Italian trading establishments or newly created, was inhabited mostly by newcomers to the city rather than the area's former residents. Jews (from Edirne and elsewhere) and Muslims (from Bursa, Ankara, and other cities) constituted the majority of this population, and they lived and worked here in differing degrees of ethnic and religious isolation or mingling.[58] A Pontian Greek community was settled in the eastern sections of the Venetian settlement, where few Italian names were still encountered in the last decades of the fifteenth century. Documents dating from 1470s onward show the core of the Venetian colony, where the bailo's palace and the church of St. Mark were located, as inhabited by a largely Jewish community. Given that the Venetian bailo's residence was still in Constantinople proper, and not in Galata, as late as 1540,[59] and that a capitulation of 1454 had granted the Venetians settlement in the former Anconan quarter (which lay to the east of the Venetian quarter), the almost complete absence of Italians in the area is striking. Those Venetians who remained in the city might have chosen to move across the Golden Horn to Galata, as residence in the former colony must have allowed for freer conduct than an existence "below the palace" would.

While land surveys and endowment documents from the early 1470s onward suggest that the demographic makeup of the area had changed radically, specific buildings, as well as the fabric as a whole, preserved the city's Venetian and Byzantine heritage. Ibn Battuta had praised the paved streets of Constantinople's market area in the later fourteenth century; Arnold von Harff was taken to "long streets where the Jews lived" in the later sixteenth century.[60] The cartographic depiction of this area in the early decades of the 1800s is reminiscent of these older descriptions: densely lined streets parallel each other and the city walls, each, in the ordering of a premodern market district, designated to a different trade or craft (fig. 17). The earliest foundation deed of the Mehmed II waqf and its earliest extant survey suggest that these streets were in large part paved. Referred to as *zuḳāḳ* running between two rows of shops, this type of street is distinguished from the *ṭarīḳ al-ʿām* (throughway) and *ṭarīḳ al-ḫāṣ* (private lane or dead end) that formed the street network in the rest of the walled city.[61]

Ottoman rule kept these streets paved, at least in the early decades of its presence in the city. A document from ca. 1486 specifies four streets to be built or restored, two of them discernible in Istanbul today: the street running between the Sırt bath and Taht al-kalʿa, which was the main artery of the district, the Uzunçarşı/Makros Embolos; the street between the Drungarii/Odun and Balık Bazarı/Perama Gates; an unidentifiable road that ran between the bath of Mehmed Pasha and the house of a certain Salto; and, significantly, "the road along the wall where the sultan rode."[62]

Could this street traversed by the sultan have been the Constantinian *embolos* running along the sea walls, a road mentioned in the *Patria* and parts of which, it has been suggested, were extant in the twelfth century?[63]

To preexisting urban configurations the Ottomans often introduced their own forms and urban notions, as is best observed in the Taht al-kalʿa area beyond the city gate called alternately Bab-ı Vasiliko and Bab-ı Feslügen in fifteenth- and early-sixteenth-century sources (the first, an Ottoman rendering of the Greek name for the gate, Basilike; the second, a translation of the word "basil" into Turkish).[64] In former Ottoman cities as in present-day Istanbul, *tāḫt al-ḳalʿa* refers to a loosely defined area within the larger commercial district, characterized by a dense conglomeration of shops and khans, often marked by a monumental bathhouse.[65] Fifteenth-century documents, on the other hand, suggest that the Taht al-kalʿa of Istanbul referred simultaneously to a specific location within the commercial district and to a loosely defined space marking a main port of entry for people and goods into the city. The area is usually called a *mevżiʿ* (location), but once a *maḥalle* (quarter), in these documents; at its core was a large plot of land (*ṣaḥn*) fitting into the curve of the city wall to the two sides of the Basilike Gate, its southern limit defined by the Taht al-kalʿa bath and by the masjid of Hacı Halil. The same area, covered with large awnings, can be observed in the Lorichs panorama of 1559 (fig. 18). The 361 shops in the area housed "cooks, veterinarians, grocers, butchers, coppersmiths, and other men of various crafts."[66] A Taht al-kalʿa square is referred to at the end of the sixteenth century, in an edict ordering that encroachments of shops into the streets and the square be stopped and that shop owners respect former property boundaries.[67] The crowding of a large variety of trades

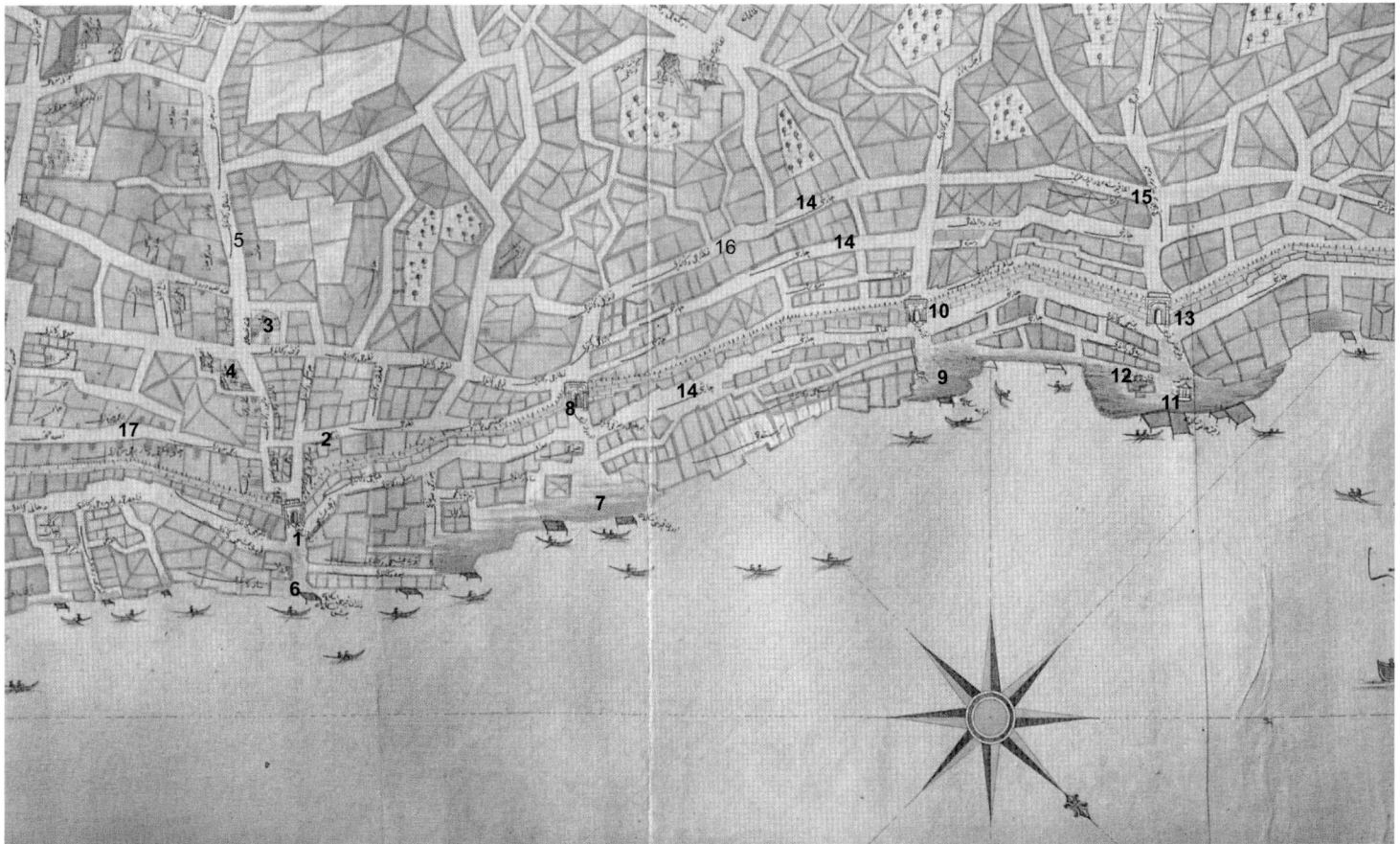

and crafts into and around a large courtyard suggests that the Taht al-kalʿa shops catered to newcomers to the city and the daily needs of those who lived and worked in this area, providing food and basic necessities at a main gate of entry.[68]

This Ottoman addition to Constantinople's Venetian quarter did not introduce new functions to the area. The ṣaḥn was situated at the very beginning of the Makros Embolos/ Uzunçarşı, the main artery that led to the bedestan and to the Mese (map 1). It has been suggested that the same area housed a market whose name echoed that of the gate, Basilike, in the fourteenth century, which might in turn have been a market for meat and other products as early as the fifth century.[69] Two buildings of importance in the late Byzantine city are

located at the eastern and western boundaries of the enclosure, underlining the centrality of this location. To the west, the Balkapan Hanı, judging by its dimensions and the architecture of its foundations, seems to have been a civil building of importance for the Venetian trading colony. A "House with the Lion" (Aslanlı Ev), most probably a public or palatial building within the Venetian settlement, featuring a prominent image of Saint Mark's lion, occupied a large plot of land to the east of the courtyard and market of the Taht al-kalʿa.[70] Some decades later the lion remained, while the house was no more, judging by a note on a "Garden with the Lion" in a land survey, in what appears to be the same location.[71] In the vicinity of the Vasiliko Gate was an abandoned church, in ruins in the early 1470s.[72]

FIGURE 17
The commercial district, detail from the map of the Bayezid II water-distribution system, 1812–13: (1) Zindan Gate (Vasiliko or Fesleğen Gate in early sources), (2) yarn sellers, (3) Taht al-kalʿa bath, (4) Rüstem Pasha mosque, site of Hacı Halil masjid, (5) Uzunçarşı, (6) Zindan Kapusı landing station, landing station for fruit, (7) landing station for timber, (8) Timber Gate, (9) Ayazma landing station, (10) Ayazma Gate, (11) landing station for flour, (12) weighing station for flour, Un Kapanı, (13) Flour Gate, (14) market, (15) road leading to the Ağa Gate, (16) weighers' shops, (17) rice merchants' shops and Asmaaltı (Under the Vine).

FIGURE 18

The Taht al-kalʿa area, detail from sheets 3 and 4 of the panorama of Istanbul by Melchior Lorichs, 1559, 1561–62. The double domes of the Taht al-kalʿa bath and the awnings of the market are visible behind the city walls, with the Basilike Gate at center right. The minareted building to the left of the bath might be the Hacı Halil masjid.

The starting point of a main artery and a core area of the commercial district, this was one of the first locations in Constantinople to be marked by Ottoman buildings: inside the gate the earliest known masjid of the Ottoman city, that of Hacı Halil, was endowed before 861/1456–57. It is not without significance either that this building, a converted church, was to be demolished by Süleyman's grand vizier Rüstem Pasha later in the sixteenth century, to clear space for a congregational mosque on a radically grander scale.[73] The Hacı Halil masjid was not a building of massive dimensions: it occupied a plot of land about one-third the size of the present Rüstem Pasha mosque.

The same cannot be said for the double bath of Taht al-kalʿa, which, with its stately domed apodyterium hall, in all likelihood featuring an elaborate muqarnas portal, constituted an unmistakably Ottoman landmark diagonally across from it, at the start of the street that would be traversed by all who entered the city through the Vasiliko Gate and headed for the bedestan (figs. 19, 20). The Lorichs panorama of 1559 captures the visual configuration of the area before the construction of the Rüstem Pasha mosque, which altered the visual priorities between bath and mosque (fig. 18).[74] A product of the campaign launched by Mehmed to restore the waterways of the city and build "splendid and costly" baths, this was to remain one of the largest bath structures in the Ottoman city through the following centuries. The discovery here of massive foundation walls of a former structure suggests that here stood an important building of Byzantine or Venetian origin.[75] What the function of this building was and in what degree of preservation the Ottomans found it unfortunately remain unknown. Its replacement by an Ottoman building, on the other hand, highlights the new administration's desire to introduce its own visual idiom to this central spot. That a monumental bath, rather than a mosque, was the means of marking this principal gate of entry to the city is significant for the architectural culture of this period (as I will elaborate in the following chapter).

The bath and the masjid marked the intersection of the Macros Embolos/Uzunçarşı with another long-term feature of the city's urban fabric, the Hasırcılar street, which, it has been suggested, was the Embolo Venetorum of the Byzantine city.[76] Running east-west within the city walls, this artery connected the neighborhoods and artisanal/commercial establishments lying along it to the core of the Taht al-kalʿa area. The high yearly income of the Taht al-kalʿa bath, 72,134 *akçe* in 1490, eclipsing the 5,000 to 39,000 *akçe* the other fourteen baths endowed for Mehmed's foundation yielded, suggests that this was a much frequented spot in the city.[77]

The gate and the market under the palace, then, provided passage into the city, retail trade catering to the daily needs of inhabitants, and a place where a resident or traveling merchant could find cooked food or the popular wheat drink *boza,* have a bath, and socialize. (It might not be coincidental that in less than a century Taht al-kalʿa was to house the first coffeehouse of Istanbul.) Here and in the streets of markets lying to the east and west along the Golden Horn were situated about a third of the city's artisanal industry, warehouses for storage, and inns for travelers. Close by were the weighing station and wholesale market for fruits and vegetables. For those working or residing in this commercial stretch along the sea, the Taht al-kalʿa constituted a core. Residents of the city's suburbs who disembarked at the Yemiş İskelesi and entered the city through the "Basil" gate and merchants who arrived from abroad would come into a vast but densely inhabited enclosure aligned and partly built-in by shops. The minaret of the masjid to the left and the bath further down to the right, distinguished by its monumental scale, its domes, and its ashlar masonry, in contrast to the mostly wooden one- or two-story buildings surrounding it, would be the principal foci of what was the most crowded area of Istanbul in the second half of the fifteenth century.

The Bedestan and Markets Complex

The Makros Embolos/Uzunçarşı, whose beginning was now marked by the Taht al-kalʿa market and bath and the masjid of Hacı Halil, led directly to the bedestan and its surrounding markets. The centerpiece here was a building of monumental scale and construction enclosing shops and a spacious hall, the locus of long-distance and interregional trade, modeled after similar structures in Ottoman cities. The Ottoman bedestan represented Ottoman accommodation and supervision of commercial activity at the city center. Its walls of ashlar masonry, lead covered domes, monumental gates, and

FIGURE 19
The Taht al-kalʿa area in the Goad insurance map, Charles Edward Goad, 1904–6: (114–21) the market area later occupied by shops, (122) site of the Hacı Halil masjid replaced by Rüstem Pasha mosque, (126) bath.

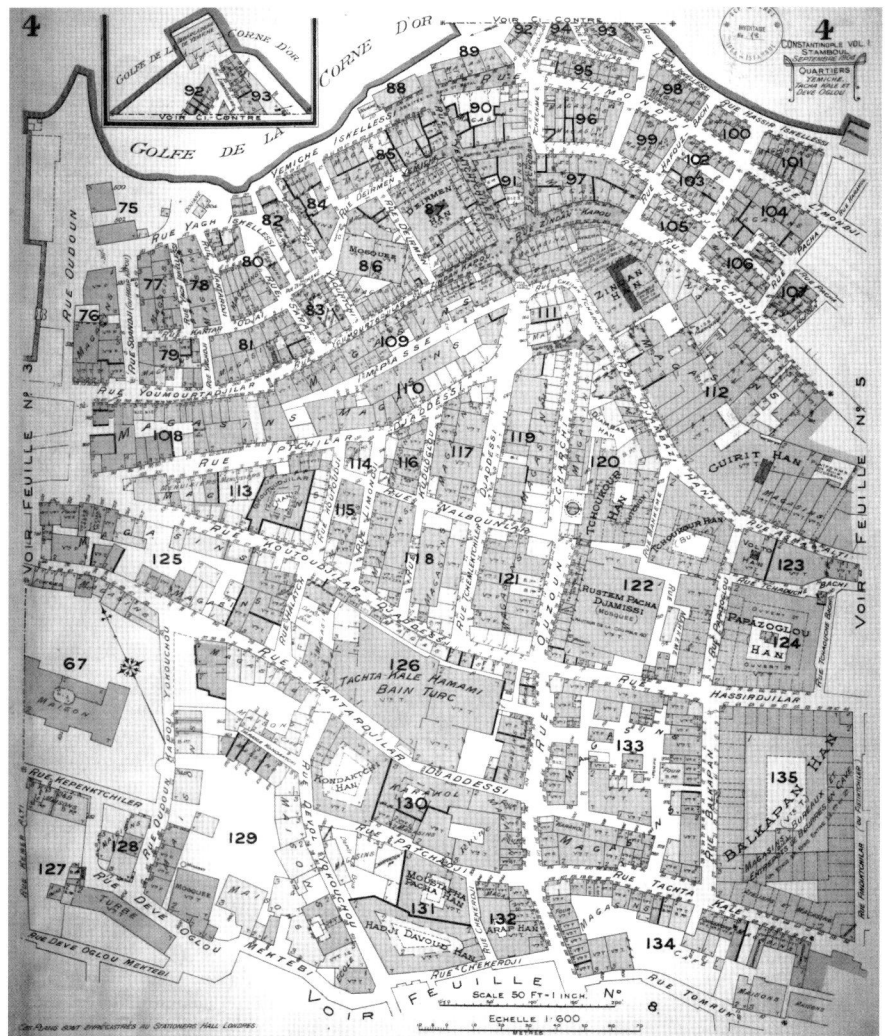

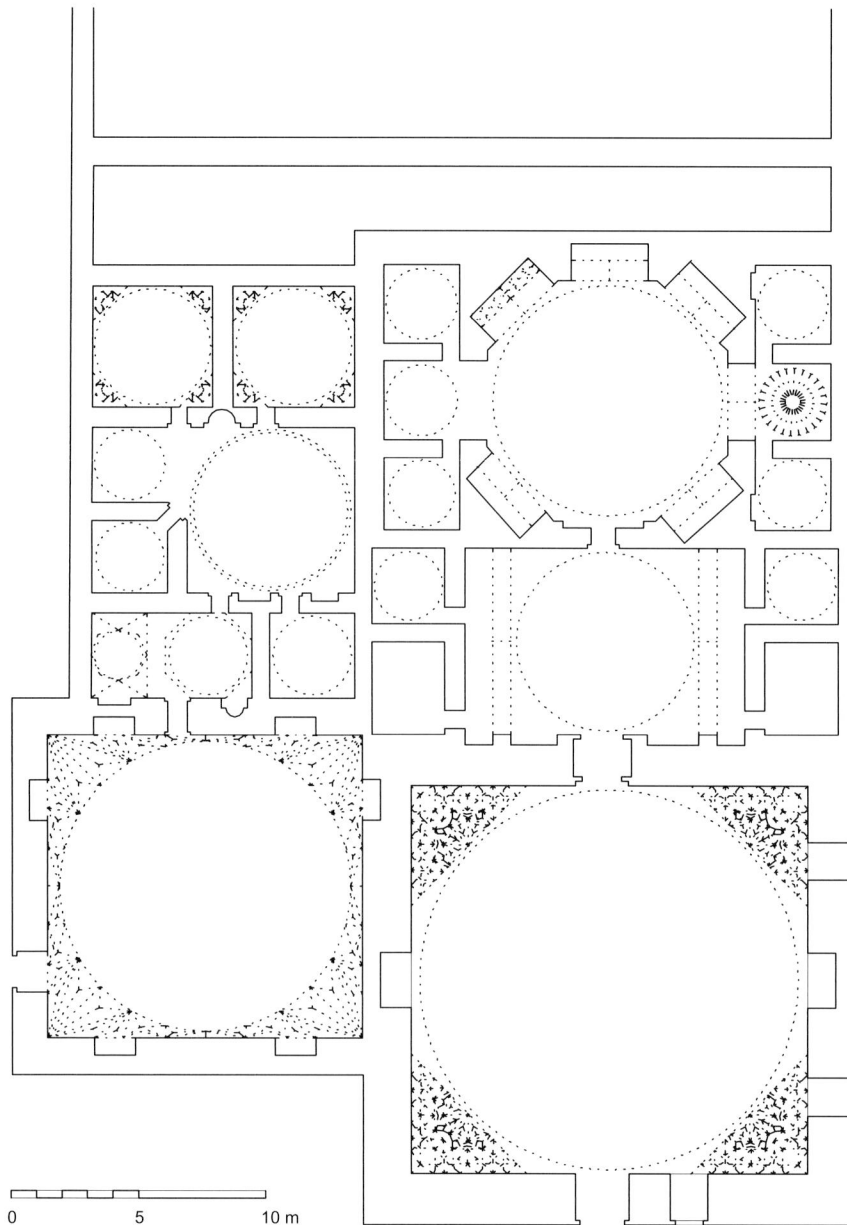

with functional and formal prototypes in the Islamic and the Greco-Roman worlds. It was an Ottoman adaptation of the *ḳaysariyya* (arabicized from Caesaria) of the medieval Middle East, itself derived from Roman commercial basilicas.[78] A number of European visitors to Istanbul in the sixteenth century portrayed the city's bedestans in ways that suggest their ancient pedigree as well as their impressive dimensions: Pierre Gilles described in detail the "two basilicas" that survived the fire that swept the bazaar area in 1546; Jean Chesneau likened Mehmed II's bedestan to a "grand temple."[79]

While following the conventions of Ottoman prototypes,[80] the first—and main—bedestan of Istanbul is architecturally and urbanistically a novel building. Unlike earlier bedestans, it was not an individually conceived and designed structure, and its spatial configuration differed substantially from earlier and contemporary examples. These were differences indicative of the introduction of a new, grander scale to the Ottoman urban landscape and of the deliberate planning of this central district of the city.

In their spatial configuration, the earlier Ottoman bedestans and the majority of those contemporaneous with or later than the Istanbul building resemble covered streets; they are oblong rectangles roofed by a series of double domes (see fig. 102, no. 9). The Istanbul bedestan, on the other hand, is a hypostyle hall rather than a throughway (figs. 21, 22). It is covered by fifteen domes, five along its length and three across. Its interior configuration and roof structure render the building interestingly like Ottoman congregational mosques of the fourteenth and early fifteenth centuries. Originally and through much of its history, the bedestan was furnished only with benches along the interior walls and around the piers, on which

iron doors fortified the enclosure, demonstrating the protection offered by the ruling elite for international commerce. Housing shops of the city's wealthiest merchants, the bedestan was a multifunctional structure: it provided space for financial transactions, trade in valuable imported goods, and storage of money and precious materials. It was a constituent of the urban legacy of the eastern Mediterranean, the merchants placed their storage boxes. In contrast to its disjunct spatial configuration today (with permanently built streets of shops within it), the interior constituted a contiguous whole.[81] Hans Dernschwam, who visited the market in the middle of the sixteenth century, noted that six people could comfortably walk in the lanes between the benches, which he said were one to one and a half cubits high and two cubits wide.[82] Could the inspiration for building in the shape of a hall rather than a throughway have lain in the loggias of the Italian trading establishments, meeting places that were among the primary constituents of the civil and commercial center of colonial settlements? The Venetian loggia, judging by the name of a quarter carrying its name mentioned in the earliest foundation deed of Mehmed's endowment, was near the church of San Marco and the bailo's palace in present-day Balık Bazarı. The loggia of the Genoese colony across from the Golden Horn in Galata possibly stood where the Galata bedestan was built in the later sixteenth century. This too is a hypostyle structure, covered by nine domes.[83]

It may be pure chance that the only surviving "inscription" on the Istanbul bedestan is a spoliated Byzantine eagle (fig. 23). But the survival of the imperial symbol of Byzantium over the eastern gate of the bedestan may also be telling in terms of the signifying practices of its builders. The earliest comment of modern scholarship on the bedestan eagle comes from a prolific scholar of Ottoman urban history, Osman Ergin. In an article on Ottoman bedestans published in 1949, Ergin argued that the Istanbul bedestan was a Byzantine building, as evidenced by the eagle image marking its entry. This assertion, initially accepted and unquestioned, became the subject of much criticism once Ottoman commercial structures were better studied and Istanbul's bedestan was

determined to be an Ottoman building.[84] The most zealous critic was Ayverdi, who noted that it was unlikely the Turks could have been unaware of the significance of this Byzantine symbol, and attributed the use of the image to their "love of bird images." He argued that the relief was put to use for a purely decorative purpose, and cited as support another spoliated Byzantine relief, featuring two peacocks, on a sixteenth-century fountain.[85]

Since the "Turks" must have been aware of the symbolic charge of the image, and since the bedestan was too central a building and the eagle too potent a symbol to make the decoration rationale convincing, it is likely that the image's connotative power was itself the reason for its use. As such, this would constitute an interesting case of appropriation in which an image with clear associations with imperial Byzantine rule, though not *the* Byzantine symbol as the Ottomans knew it, was used to mark one of the representational buildings of the city.[86] This is not unimaginable in the larger cultural context of the period. The sultan who styled himself the "Caesar of Rum" could have used an image reminiscent of the former Caesars of Rum to mark a monumental civic building inhabited or frequented by the wealthiest city merchants of all confessions, by merchants of Galata who conducted business there, and by long-distance traders. To some of the users of the bedestan at least, this image and its meaning would have been familiar, as it was to Osman Ergin five centuries later.[87]

Novel in its architecture and spatial configuration, the first bedestan of Istanbul also presents an urbanistic innovation. A portico covered by a vault supported by two rows of columns borders the building on three sides. (Perhaps it originally continued on the fourth side.) This tripartite vault covers side streets that range between 7.60 and 8.55 meters in width.[88]

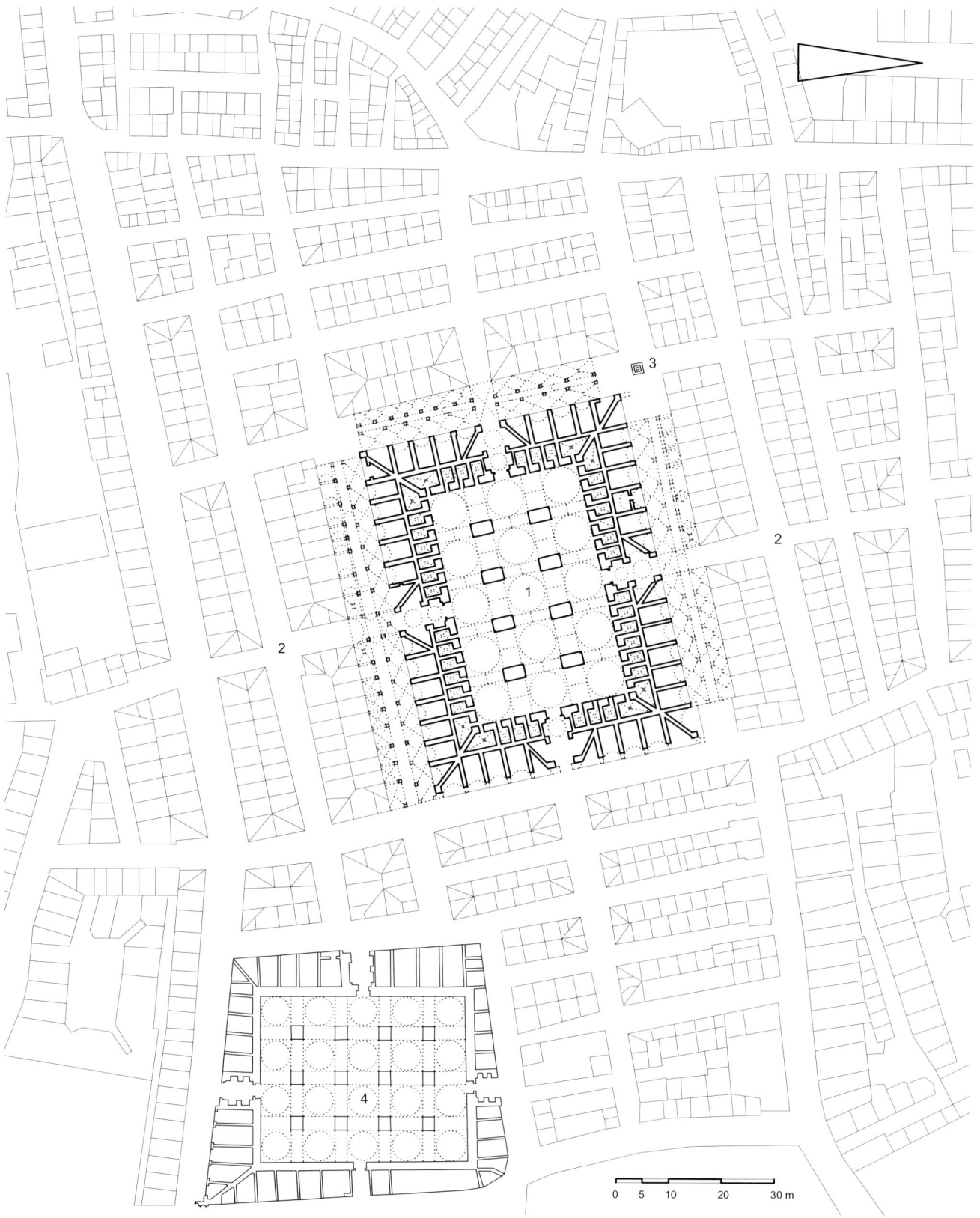

1

3

2

2

2

4

0 5 10   20   30 m

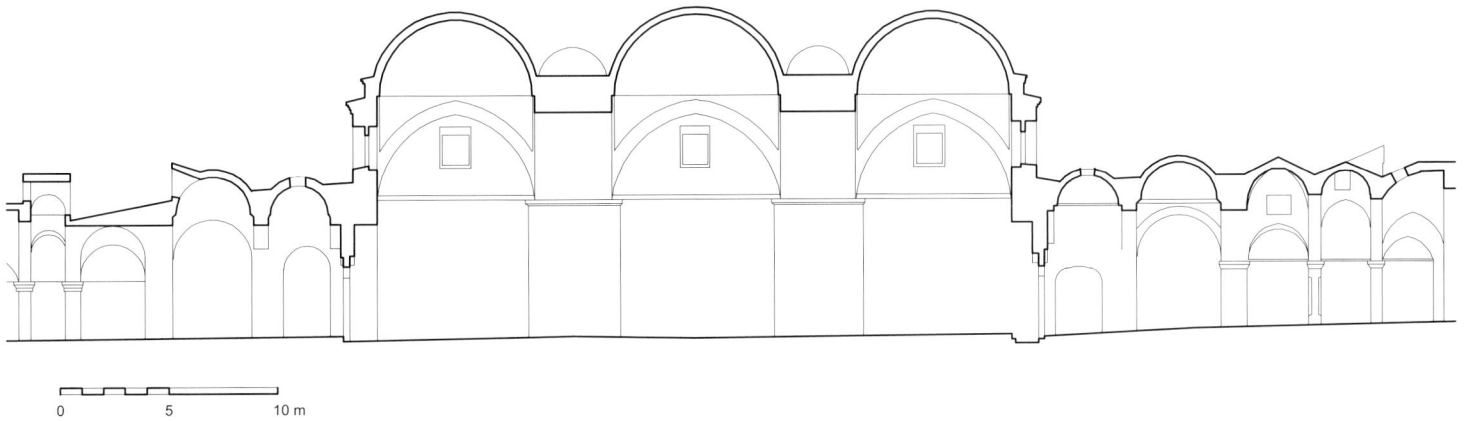

In an arrangement that remained unique in Ottoman practice, these covered streets flanked by shops constituted a transitional space between the core of the commercial area and the markets surrounding it, integrating the bedestan-markets area into a formally designed complex. The distinctiveness of this arrangement and the remarkable width of the streets surrounding the bedestan (the widest portion of the Mese/Divan Yolu measured six meters in the nineteenth century)[89] are noteworthy. Perhaps the colonnaded and porticoed streets of Constantinople, some of which were still extant around the eastern portion of the Mese and were used by the Ottomans for commercial purposes, provided inspiration to the builders of the new commercial center.[90] The land survey of 1489 records "shops called *kemer* [arches]" in the proximity of Hagia Sophia, possibly the last remnants of the porticoed city streets aligned with shops. These were either shop/stoa combinations, as described by Marlia Mundell-Mango, or former porticoes transformed into shops in the Ottoman era.[91] A public fountain, endowed by the grand vizier Mahmud Pasha, was placed at the bedestan's northwestern corner, at the point of intersection of two arcades: a charity to the users of the commercial center as much as a mark by the grand vizier on the sultan's building.[92]

The formal arrangement of the market area extended beyond the bedestan porticoes. Fifteenth- and early-sixteenth-century sources attest to the formal design and construction here of a complex of commercial streets, which in earlier and contemporary Ottoman cities were products of gradual growth around an initially freestanding building. This is also evident

FIGURE 21 (*opposite*)
Istanbul bedestan and surrounding markets, plan:
(1) bedestan, (2) shops, (3) fountain of Mahmud Pasha, (4) Sandal bedestan.

FIGURE 22
Istanbul bedestan, section.

FIGURE 23
East portal of the bedestan, with spoliated eagle relief.

in the present-day layout of the Istanbul bazaar: beyond the portico that surrounds the bedestan lie several blocks of shops on all four sides, following the orthogonal geometry established by the building in the center. The contrast between this initial core and the later development where streets do not follow a geometric order but the topography of the terrain and possibly the property divisions of later periods underlines the different stages in the expansion of the area (fig. 24).

The endowment deeds of the Mehmed II foundation and the surveys of property endowed to the Ayasofya waqf constitute the primary evidence on the design and construction of the bedestan and the surrounding retail markets, though they do not allow a complete reconstruction. The earliest surviving waqfiyya of the royal foundation, dating to ca. 877–78/1472–74, describes groups of adjacent shops occupying the area surrounding the bedestan. Twenty-nine of thirty-three such groups are surrounded by the suk on all four sides. The remaining four border the suk on three sides and either an empty lot or shops of other individuals on the fourth side. This suggests that the bedestan and the adjoining markets were built together as parts of the same project and that this plot was later bordered by shops that were the property of, or endowed by, other individuals. Another point worthy of note in this description is that it mentions only one street in this segment of the commercial area, a public thoroughway (ṭarīḳ al-ʿām al-shariʿ). Given that the several hundred shops mentioned could not have constituted a single block but must have been separated by streets, this particular street, mentioned as a boundary marker, was possibly a main artery, perhaps the Uzunçarşı leading to the Taht al-kalʿa and the ports beyond.

The evidence for an integrated bedestan-and-shops complex is supported also by later documents. The waqfiyya of ca. 883/1478–79 notes the "shops adjacent to [the bedestan] and the shops built around it, where cloth merchants, turban makers, and tailors reside, and the shops that are called the flea market [*Bit Bāzārı*]," counting a total of 849. The survey of the Ayasofya waqf of 895/1489–90 conveys a similar layout, dividing the 792 shops into streets aligned with the shopkeepers' craft (*ḥırfet*): goldsmiths and jewelers, merchants and craftsmen who dealt in various aspects of clothing, and bow makers are mentioned, along with a *Gelincik bāzārı*, a market for different types of fabric and ready-made clothing.[93] The flea market, a separate but adjacent group of shops close to the market of luxury goods, fulfilled a function integral to the everyday life of every premodern city, the exchange of used clothing.[94]

Two hans at a short distance from the bedestan area, the Sultan Hanı and the Bodrum Karbansarayı, both parts of Mehmed's endowment, were possibly built in the same years as the bedestan. The New Royal Khan (*ḥān al-sulṭān al-cedīd*) was also located near the bedestan; it was endowed together with ninety shops adjacent to and across the street from it.[95] The "*ḥān al-sulṭān* known as the Beglik Karbansarayı" is noted in the neighborhood of Daye Hatun. Close to the bath of Mahmud Pasha, this was a two-story building with 98 rooms and 42 shops adjacent to it.[96] The Bodrum Karbansarayı was a smaller two-story building, with 32 rooms, 14 shops attached to its exterior walls, and 9 rooms outside of it.[97] Imperial orders collected in the royal book of laws at the end of the fifteenth century reinforce the connection of these constructions to aspects of state supervision of commercial activity. Goods brought into the city had to be taken directly to khans and weighing stations, where they would be unloaded and weighed under the supervision of a broker [*simsār*],

FIGURE 24
Istanbul bedestans and surrounding markets, aerial view.

and only with due taxes paid would they then be distributed to shops, ateliers, or homes.[98] Hence, at least for the royal caravanserais in the city, the main function prior to storage, exchange, and accommodation was the supervision of imports and the collection of taxes.

The streets of shops composing the markets of the bedestan area were built of wood, or perhaps a combination of wood and mudbrick, unlike the solid stone masonry of their centerpiece. Wood, nails, *efrencī* (Frankish) roof tiles, and hinges and hooks are the main building materials whose purchase is noted in the accounts of the Ayasofya foundation, and carpenters, workers, and porters the only people whose payments are registered. The complete destruction of the market in the fire that allowed Pierre Gilles to study the "basilicas," otherwise concealed within a network of commercial streets, points in the same direction.[99] The need to construct the market quickly may have dictated the use of cheaper materials and simpler technology. This choice of materials may also have been dictated by earlier Ottoman practice, in which only the bedestan and some of the khans were built of ashlar or composite masonry. The early khans of Istanbul, on the other hand, were probably not built of durable materials, since the only extant one in Istanbul that dates from the fifteenth century is that of Mahmud Pasha.

As the locus of the city's commerce and wealth, the bedestan was a space of social interaction and at times a public forum for its inhabitants. Bertrandon de la Broquiere, in Bursa in 1432 or 1433, described the bedestan of this city as the meeting place of the city's notables; here he found the merchant who was his travel companion on a high stone seat along with others.[100] In the sixteenth century Hans Dernschwam portrayed the Istanbul bedestan as a place where valuable merchandise was displayed and sold and wealthy merchants of all communities sat on their benches, chatting, eating, drinking, and singing.[101] Narratives incorporated in sources dating from Mehmed's reign suggest that the building acquired this social function early on. Taşköprizade writes of one of the poets of the period, the *meyperest* (lover of wine) Mevlana Melihi, an inhabitant of the city since its conquest, who was in the habit of drinking wine in the bedestan. His biographer relates that the news of the *mevlana*'s drinking and misconduct in the marketplace reached Mehmed, who offered him a monthly wage on condition that he quit his habit.[102] The Vicenzan captive Angiolello relates the story of one dervish who from the top of a bench in the bedestan sang praises to Mehmed.[103] The sultan allegedly asked Gentile Bellini, in Constantinople upon a royal invitation, to paint a portrait of the man. This may be because Mehmed was in the habit of having the portraits of important men painted, as Angiolello notes, or because he wanted to study the mad look in the eyes of the dervish as captured by the painter, as he writes further down. The monarch, according to Angiolello, was not pleased with the dervish's performance, though we do not know what disturbed him, whether it was the public singing or the dervish's interpretation of his accomplishments or his conviction that the man was mad. He did question the Venetian painter regarding his opinion of the matter and learned, from a very hesitant Bellini, that it was quite common for Venetians to sing praises to their rulers in public places. Upon hearing this, Mehmed decided that he too was not against the practice, provided that the performer was sane. Whatever the degree of truth to Angiolello's amusing story is, it nevertheless suggests that by the end of Mehmed's rule the bedestan had become one of the public spaces in the city where Ottoman subjects, some discomfort notwithstanding, could sing their own renditions of their ruler's deeds.

The charismatic dervish Otman Baba was the protagonist of an episode staged elsewhere in the commercial area. His hagiography relates that one Ramadan day he and his two hundred dervishes arrived at the "wide road underneath the Old Palace, where all the people of God came and went."[104] This must have been the Uzunçarşı. They set up a feast here and started to eat and drink, celebrating the holidays of the passersby and forcing some to join them. In Otman Baba's hagiography, this story constitutes the introduction to one of the episodes that demonstrate, in the ambivalent discourse of its author, Küçük Abdal, the tensions between the court and the dervishes.[105] The setting to this striking act, on the other hand, was the Uzunçarşı, suggesting that the commercial area on the whole functioned as a space of social interaction already in the first decades of Ottoman rule in Constantinople. Without relating the rest of the long story, it is worth noting that the Ramadan episode unfolds in such a way as to posit an opposition between the market and the mosque (the Uzunçarşı and the New Mosque) as respective loci of dissent and authority.[106]

Authority, of course, was not absent from the marketplace. To the contrary, central authority was what founded, and to a large extent shaped, the social and spatial configuration of the commercial area. These and other narratives nevertheless attest to the formation of a public space concomitant with the formation of the commercial space, a global aspect, in fact, of premodern urban patterns. The commercial area was the space of daily interaction and simultaneously the stage where city dwellers might dramatize shared dispositions through symbolically charged acts, to communicate them to those who occupied the center of the newly configured state.

The two-centered commercial structure, with the bedestan situated on the second hill, the Taht al-kal'a at the heart of the port area, and the Uzunçarşı connecting the two, formed the core of all later developments of the commercial district. Already by the end of Mehmed's rule, a large number of smaller-scale foundations had been endowed near one or the other or along the main artery that connected them. Mahmud Pasha's foundation (to be considered in the following chapter) considerably expanded the commercial area eastward and revitalized another main artery between the port and the bedestan. A large market endowed by the grand vizier specialized in the sale of textiles.[107] In the vicinity of the mosque he built, the grand vizier's market possibly occupied the same plot on which the second bedestan of the city, the Sandal Bedestanı, was erected in the later decades.[108] Lesser members of the ruling elite, a significant number of them the very suppliers of the city and overseers of commercial activity, also endowed property in the bedestan area: 243 shops by Kürkcibaşı Şemsüddin, 56 shops by the city prefect Çakır Ağa, and some 150 shops by a prominent member of the ulema, Mevlana Husrev. The vizier Has Murad Pasha expanded the Ottoman foundations of the Taht al-kal'a area westward, with the construction of a khan and numerous shops in the adjoining coppersmiths market.[109]

Ottoman involvement with the material infrastructure of commerce in the suburb of Galata was distinctly different from that in Constantinople.[110] The measures taken concerning the population of Galata reveal a keen interest in continuing the commercial activity in what had been one of the most important trading colonies of the Genoese republic, while also replacing the Genoese with the Ottoman state and subjects as the prime beneficiaries of the lucrative Black Sea trade. Deportees and former residents who returned to the city upon invitation and with privileges granted by the sultan constituted the majority of its population. Some of those who chose to stay agreed to become Ottoman subjects of *ẕimmī* status, while others kept their status as "Franks," or foreign subjects. Whether they were subjects of the Ottoman or the Italian states, residents of Galata who returned were given property rights over their former residences, while they were asked to pay rent to the Hagia Sophia endowment for the land. The fate of the commercial property was similar. Concentrated in the neighborhood of Lonca (the former loggia of the Genoese colony) and dispersed also in the adjacent neighborhoods, shops and storage places were in large part endowed for the royal foundation and rented out to the merchants of the Maḥrūse-i Ġalaṭa.

These measures generally succeeded in reviving life and commerce in Galata.[111] It might be noted, however, that these were measures largely having to do with the legal status and rights of the city's inhabitants and with the regulation and taxing of goods. In striking contrast to projects realized in the city proper, no substantial additions were made to commercial space in Galata, and no commercial building of an official character was constructed.[112] The lack of architectural activity in an area with significant commercial endeavors and interests is in strong contrast to constructions in the city proper, which formed a spatial framework for commerce and artisanal production as well as its supervision. Extant commercial buildings might have been found sufficient for retail and wholesale commerce and its supervision. Still, the absence of a representational building of commerce newly built by the Ottoman government indicates a distinction between Galata and Constantinople whereby the former's social and cultural, if not legal, autonomy was tacitly granted.

Üsküdar, on the eastern shore of the Bosphorus, presents a still different case. A minor Ottoman settlement existed here from the later decades of the fourteenth century onward. The extent of Mehmed's interest in the township, which was to become an important port due to its links to Asian caravan trade, was to build a khan and a masjid there. Before the foundation endowed by Rum Mehmed Pasha in the 1470s, there was no other substantial building activity in the Anatolian suburb of the city, and until the first decades of the sixteenth century, relatively few commercial structures.[113]

Terrain, historical topography, and predicaments of premodern urban structure dictated a series of continuities between the earlier, Byzantine and Italian urban order and the newly established Ottoman one in the commercial area. The *ṣaḥn* of the Taht al-kalʿa, a central location within the Venetian settlement and a marketplace from earlier on, the spine that connected the port to the retail market and luxury shops uphill, and the assignment of particular streets to specific trades and crafts are the most salient aspects of continuities rooted in overlapping urban practices. Weighing stations, taxation and supervision procedures, and the infrastructure of storage and distribution along ports of entry were integral to the provisioning of the premodern city; it is not surprising to find that the new rule did not bring radical change to these basic procedures and the spaces that housed them. The specifically Ottoman feature of the commercial area, linking it to a wide spectrum of cities within the central lands of the Islamic world, was the bedestan and its adjoining complex of markets, with a specifically and exclusively commercial fabric, where accommodation was limited mostly to that provided to visitors to the city and to bachelors. The pattern established by this space was to determine the subsequent growth of the district, as it spread to areas surrounding the initial core, to become the Covered Bazaar of later centuries. The commercial sprawl that grew to occupy the peninsula's northeastern shores and slopes, thus, was shaped by Ottoman as well as by Veneto-Byzantine urban practices. Along the port was a district where commercial and industrial space coexisted with residential space in numerous multifunctional structures, part of the city's Veneto-Byzantine legacy that lived on through the earlier part of the sixteenth century.

A SHRINE AT THE CITY'S EDGE

While the initial Ottoman projects involving administrative and commercial loci were boldly directed at the city center, the first Ottoman building project of a religious nature was located on an extramural site. To the newcomers, it would seem, God resided not within but at the edge of a city. Likewise, in the conquerors' imagining of conquered territory, divine sanction and protection were offered not from within the impure core, which still belonged to the other (and where entrenched networks of power might still be intact), but from the uncontaminated (or vacant) edge.[114] The discovery of the grave of Abu Ayyub al-Ansari, a companion of the Prophet and warrior during the first Arab siege of Constantinople, on the Golden Horn at some distance from the city and the subsequent construction of a mausoleum and mosque complex there articulated a spatial and temporal distance to the sacred sites of the former rule (fig. 25).

The conversion and later history of Hagia Sophia clearly demonstrates that the Ottoman encounter with Constantinople was colored by a long history of encounters between the Byzantine and Islamic worlds. Arab traditions concerning the sieges of the city during the early centuries of Islam were part of this history and

were to have a bearing on the Ottomans' symbolic as well as physical inhabitation of Constantinople. Ayyub al-Ansari, leader of a naval expedition against Byzantium in A.D. 668–69, figures centrally in the chronicles of the ninth and tenth centuries and in a number of narratives that interpret aspects of cultural and

FIGURE 25
The Eyüp suburb, with the mausoleum and complex of Ayyub al-Ansari, detail from the panorama of Istanbul by Melchior Lorichs, 1559, 1561–62.

political relationships between the two realms. According to one version of his story, he died during this siege and was buried under the walls of the city. According to another version, the Byzantine emperor, promising to respect the warrior's tomb, built for Abu Ayyub a domed mausoleum, which became a site of veneration for Constantinopolitans.

While it is difficult to assess what portion (and which version) of these narratives was available to Ottomans during and after the siege of Constantinople, textual and architectural evidence reveals that Ayyub's story did resonate with Ottoman desires and aspirations. Several sixteenth-century texts tell of the miraculous discovery of Ayyub's grave at a difficult moment during the Ottoman siege of Constantinople. This discovery is attributed to the Sufi sheikh Akşemseddin, a prominent figure of the Bayramiye order and the spiritual guide of the ghazis who participated in the siege. Mehmed, in one narrative, asks the sheikh to locate the tomb, presumably in an attempt to boost the morale of his troops. Another narrative tells of a sort of sightseeing tour, in the environs of the walls, taken by the seventy-seven holy men in search of the relics of those Muslim warriors who had laid siege to the city during the time of the Prophet. The earliest biography of Akşemseddin, by Lamiʿi Çelebi, tells us that the blessed grave of Ayyub al-Ansari was *determined* by the sheikh, subtly privileging invention over fact.

Although it is not clear exactly when the holy grave was "discovered," these narratives suggest that the story of Ayyub was summoned either during or immediately following the city's conquest and that the site assumed the status of a holy sanctuary from early on. By 1457, a convent had been founded by the vizier Sinanü'd-din Yusuf Pasha on a plot of land near the designated grave. The endowment deed of the foundation, one of the earliest among such documents drawn up in the city, attests to the significance of the site in the eyes of the Ottoman elite: the land for the convent was a sultanic gift to the vizier; the undersigners of the deed were no less than the members of the imperial council, Mahmud and İshak Pasha among them.[115] Not long afterward Mehmed himself started construction here: in 1459 the mosque he founded near the grave was completed; presumably, the monumental tomb over the grave was built before or alongside the mosque. The chronology of constructions, however imprecise, nevertheless suggests that the decision to monumentalize this area was made early, but time had to be ripe for the construction of a royal monument within or near Constantinople. It may be remembered that no religious building of monumental scale was newly built by the Ottomans within the city during these early years; it may also be remembered that a considerable segment of the Ottoman political spectrum opposed settling in or near the city. Whether or not Mehmed was actually advised by his commanders to "build a wall around Ayasofya and destroy the rest [of Constantinople]," the political pressure captured in that suggestion was real.

Built shortly before Mehmed's definitive move to the city, the Ayyub foundation, through association with the prophet and his armies, aimed to legitimize the decision to inhabit the city.[116] It would turn out, however, that establishing (and using) that association was not the prerogative of the monarch only. Contemporary narrative sources incorporating the story of the warrior saint and the discovery of his grave reveal that the Ottoman invention of tradition involved a choice concerning the location of discovery. As Paul Wittek convincingly argued in 1951, two sites, not one, were venerated as the warrior's grave, the second site within the walled enclosure of the Blachernae Palace, at the point where the land walls met the sea. This is the Ottoman quarter of Ayvansaray, according to Wittek a corruption of the name Ayyub Ansari.[117] Wittek's main source was the anonymous history of Constantinople written in 1491. Another narrative, of the early sixteenth century, suggests that the matter remained unresolved: İdris Bidlisi wrote in his *Heşt behişt* that two different sites were venerated as the grave of Ayyub and that a mausoleum was built over the one outside the city walls.[118]

Medieval narratives of the first Arab siege place the warrior's grave either "under the city walls" or immediately within the fortifications; both versions make Ayvansaray the more plausible location for the grave of a sixth-century Arab warrior in or near Constantinople. The site discovered by Akşemseddin and his retinue, on the other hand, happened to be near the monastic church of SS. Cosmas and Damian, venerated for their healing powers through the Byzantine era. A set of conflations and continuities, in effect, continued to shape these spaces and their representations through the city's history: Ayvansaray, dotted with chapels and holy springs as much as graves of Arab warriors, could be a corruption of Ayyub Ansari as easily as of Aya Vassili; Eyüp, home to the mausoleum built by Mehmed, remained a site of Christian veneration as much as a Muslim one.[119] What, then, were the political or mental dispositions that informed the choice between an extramural and an intramural site for the saint's mausoleum? At one level, the duality has been interpreted as the spatial expression of the conflict between the ghazis and the sultan over his wish to make Constantinople the seat of his empire. An alternative to the imperially sanctioned grave, Yerasimos has argued, was indicative of the ghazi refusal to recognize the officially built house of worship in Eyüp.[120]

A number of narratives positing an opposition between the city proper and its environs offer clues to another set of attitudes toward the city and its inhabitation. According to biographies of Akşemseddin written in the sixteenth century, the Sufi sheikh credited with the discovery of Abu Ayyub's grave declined all favors and offers extended to him by the sultan and refused to reside in the newly built complex near the tomb. Crossing over to the Asian suburb of Üsküdar on his way to his hometown, Göynük, he told his son that he was finally able to breathe again and that the light of divine inspiration had left him while he was in the infidel's land. A similar attitude can be discerned in another Sufi sheikh, Mehmed Geylani, who in 858/1454 asked Mehmed for a plot of land and permission to build a convent *outside* of the city's sea walls, in present-day Eminönü.[121] The predilection for extramural sites, whether for the construction of a minor convent or for the discovery of a holy grave and the construction of a royal complex, is a manifestation, in spatial terms, of an unwillingness to inhabit the city itself. The site that sanctified the Ottoman conquest of and rule over the city remained outside, embodying the tensions between the ruler's centralizing, imperial vision, in which Constantinople represented the natural seat of power, and the ghazi vision, in which the city was no more than a target of conquest and expansion. The suburb that developed around this nucleus was the first predominantly Muslim settlement of Constantinople, a Muslim counterpart that was attached to—but not an integral part of—the still essentially Byzantine city.

The building complex constructed around the alleged grave is a monument in which a multiplicity of intentions converge.[122] This was a royal complex built, on the model of those in Bursa and Edirne, outside of the walled urban enclosure. With a mosque (most probably a convent-mosque), a public kitchen, hospice, madrasa, and bath, it replicated royal complexes in other Ottoman cities. Simultaneously, it was a willfully created Muslim shrine that responded to a site venerated by Christians before the conquest. Erection of the richly endowed complex around a monumental mausoleum, visits to the site, formation of a cemetery, and settlement of deportee communities in the area transformed the Christian shrine into one that celebrated a continuous Muslim presence at the edge of Byzantium, from the time of the prophet onward.[123] Angiolello, generally careful in his architectural descriptions, wrote that there was an antique church here, in which the Turks kept "san Giopo." Because of his devotion to this place, Mehmed had a large temple built here, leaving out the small church.[124] The Vicenzan captive's narrative suggests that parts of the former shrine might have been standing and put to use by the Ottomans at the time he wrote. While Ayyub's grave might initially have been related to the Byzantine church, the growing cult of the Arab saint was too important to the new administration not to be given its own funerary structure.

The account book of 896/1491 refers to the complex as "the foundation of the sacred mausoleum" (ʿimāret-i türbe-i muṭaḥḥara), suggesting that unlike typical Ottoman complexes, where a multipurpose convent-mosque was the functional and symbolic centerpiece, here the tomb was regarded the center.[125] This is the first funerary structure of monumental scale to be built in the city. A domed octagonal building of ashlar masonry, with proportions that emphasize the verticality of the mass and fine moldings that intensify the perpendicular accent on the façades, the mausoleum of Abu Ayyub occupies a stylistic midpoint between Bursan and later Istanbulite mausolea, where verticality in volume and surface treatment were subtly

compromised to achieve classical proportions. The building conveys a sense of monumentality akin to that of the series of dynastic mausolea to be built in the city in the following centuries (fig. 26). This is noteworthy because a building type reserved until then for recently deceased Ottomans was to accommodate a figure who preceded the builders of his grave by some eight hundred years. The elaborate monument over the "discovered" grave architecturally sealed the meaning attached to the site. Its distinctly Ottoman style linked the Arab warrior to the succession of Ottoman rulers buried in similar funerary structures. That link would be reinforced in the following centuries, during which Abu Ayyub became Eyüp *Sultan,* as Paul Wittek has noted.[126]

The mosque standing across from the mausoleum was the first house of worship to be built by the ruling body in Ottoman Istanbul. As this was one of the structures heavily damaged by the 1766 earthquake and was subsequently rebuilt, its original form must be gleaned from earlier historical sources. Aptullah Kuran, based on the seventeenth- and eighteenth-century descriptions of Evliya and Ayvansarayi, has suggested that the building featured a prayer hall covered by a single dome resting on squinches, expanded on the kibla side by a small niche housing the mihrab, roofed by a small half dome.[127] This core was flanked by convent rooms on two sides, and originally a single minaret rose to the right of the entrance portico. Kuran's proposal for a revised reconstruction is supported by Matrakcı's drawing of the mosque from ca. 1537, which shows the domed prayer hall flanked by convent rooms (plate 7; lower right corner of fol. 9r). Another possibility, also suggested by Kuran, is that the mosque had a layout resembling that of the Rum Mehmed Pasha mosque, with a full-size half dome on the qibla side.[128] In view of Evliya's mentioning "strong arches supporting the dome," which possibly refer to tympanum arches, this is also a plausible reconstruction. In either case, this "half dome, which is not so large," and the "strong arches supporting the dome," as described by Evliya, present the earliest instance of a trend that would mark Ottoman mosque architecture through the following centuries: references to and appropriations of elements in Hagia Sophia's domical structure.[129] The central dome rising over tympanum arches, and half domes expanding the domical superstructure to cover a larger part of the sanctuary, were to become integral devices in Ottoman mosque architecture, widely used in constructions of the ruling body through the early decades of the sixteenth century.[130]

A significant change was introduced to the mosque already during Mehmed's reign: it was given an additional minaret, marking the transformation of the building from convent-mosque into sultanic monument.[131] Possibly the completion of Mehmed's New Mosque (in 1463), with its royal iconography of twin minarets, prompted this addition to the sanctuary at Ayyub, taking the Arab saint one step closer to becoming part of Ottoman royal imagery. Hagia Sophia's second minaret, too, might date from the same construction campaign.

The complex surrounding the mausoleum today is a palimpsest of additions, alterations, restorations, and reconstructions carried on over the four and a half centuries of Eyüp's transformation into Istanbul's primary shrine. At the mausoleum Ottoman sultans received divine sanction upon their enthronement, and to it the city's population traveled on ventures of internal pilgrimage. Additions, repairs, and alterations in its spatial and visual configuration aimed not only to counter damages caused by time or natural disasters but also to accommodate changes in Ottoman ceremonial. Such additions and alterations

FIGURE 26
The mausoleum of Ayyub al-Ansari, exterior.

have obscured the original layout of the buildings,[132] disguising the unconventional spatial relations between the mausoleum, the mosque, and the madrasa. Alternative reconstructions have been suggested: Kuran places a U-shaped madrasa in front of the mosque, so that the former constitutes a forecourt to the latter, the earliest instance of a scheme frequently used through the later sixteenth century; Ayverdi suggests that the mosque and the mausoleum were located on the longitudinal sides of a rectangular courtyard, at either end of which were placed the madrasa rooms.[133] The earliest detailed description of the buildings, by Bidlisi, suggests that mosque, madrasa, and mausoleum were placed on a single axis as parts of a larger unit. Was the madrasa an afterthought and therefore lacking its own courtyard and classroom?[134] Or was the layout of the complex partly owed to that of the monastic establishment it might have replaced, as had been the case at the Pantokrator monastery turned into the Zeyrek madrasa?

It is not known with any certainty when royal visits to the tomb, marking and giving divine sanction to events of significance to the dynasty (such as the enthronement of a new ruler or the initiation and the end of military campaigns), began. Likewise, earlier stages in the articulation of the elaborate ceremonial of these visits remain unclear.[135] The ritual visits to the mausoleum, on the other hand, were possibly initiated by the founder of the "sacred mausoleum." Taşköprizade suggests that Mehmed visited the tomb with some frequency and that he followed a particular route during these visits, most likely the Mese/Divan Yolu, terminating at Edirnekapı, to give way to a suburban route that reached the new foundation.[136]

The foundation was not conceived only as a shrine commemorating the ancient hero and therefore establishing a relation between the former and current warriors of Islam who set out to conquer Constantinople. Simultaneously, and unlike major shrine complexes elsewhere within the Ottoman realm, it was conceived as the core of a district to be developed. Policies that were to inform inhabitation, and public services that would shape the city at large, were implemented here as well. Unlike Galata and Üsküdar, where inhabitation through mandatory settlements was not deemed of primary importance, this area was subject to the same policies of repopulation as the city proper: some years after the completion of the complex, Mehmed settled deportees from Bursa in its environs.[137] A central method of urban construction inherited by the Ottomans from former Turco-Mongol and Islamic polities, the delegation of public works to high-ranking state officials was already implemented here in 1457. At this time the vizier Sinanü'd-din Yusuf Pasha, with the donation of a plot of land by the sultan, founded an endowment for a convent near the tomb.[138] Contemporary narratives demonstrate Eyüp's rapidly acquiring a suburban character through such measures: according to Angiolello, by the later 1470s it had become a large and beautiful *borgo,* where many religious people appointed to the "church" lived and many others had built their houses and palaces.[139] Likewise, Bidlisi referred to the area as a township (*şehristān*), noting that through the foundations of the sultans it had become beautiful and prosperous.[140]

The sacred site created and sustained by the new rule soon added to its multiple roles that of a burying ground. A significant number of men, mostly members of the religious elite, were buried within the complex precinct, in the mosque graveyard. Among them were Ali Kuşcı, the famed mathematician and astronomer who had come from the Akkoyunlu court in Tabriz to teach in Istanbul, and the grand vizier Sinan Pasha, who had risen to the post after serving as *ḳāḍī ʿasker* (chief military judge) and had endowed the first convent near Abu Ayyub's tomb.[141] Bayezid II, Mehmed's pious successor, too had willed to be buried here, in a simple grave that would be covered by earth only. The monarch's will was not granted: tradition required that he be buried under the dome of a monumental mausoleum, and the city's emerging tradition located this at a highly visible site behind his Friday mosque on the Mese.[142]

While the Eyüp cemeteries were never to house a sultan until the dynasty's very late years, the graveyard near Abu Ayyub's mausoleum did become the core of a city of the dead, to coexist with the city of the living.

The monumental mausoleum built over the discovered grave was possibly completed before the mosque. It might not be coincidental that the completion of this mosque, in 1459, coincided with the sultan's launch of a series of extensive projects, which turned attention to the city proper and would result in the creation of a number of politically and urbanistically significant monuments within Constantinople. The completion of a sultanic mosque near the grave of the Arab warrior saint marked the consolidation of imperial claims over the site and consequently the first step in the remaking of the saint from Abu Ayyub to Eyüp Sultan. The imperialization of the site was to be a first step in the imperialization of the city itself.

The period between the conquest of the city and the completion of the first royal religious monument was marked by two diverse, if interrelated, dynamics. The division within the Ottoman political realm between the ideology and practices of the frontier state and those of the emerging imperial order must first be noted, as this conflicted process of radical reorientation affected decisions concerning the city. The dispositions of ghazis and their spiritual leaders, on the one hand, and of the emerging imperial order, on the other, left their marks on a series of urban interventions during these first years. Formulating a response to the sheer expanse of the city, its destitute state, and the distinct features of its geographical and man-made topography must have been as important as assimilating the symbolic weight Constantinople and its monuments bore. The city captured by the Ottomans was one of the largest urban enclosures of the premodern world, featuring the memories and in part the physical attributes of an imperial legacy celebrated in the Islamic world for its splendor and magnificence (and with which the Ottomans had been in different modes of contact for more than a century). A *reckoning with* the city, in the double sense of *coping with* and *thinking with,* as expounded by Donald Preziosi, is apparent in urban interventions and narrative sources of the period alike.[143] Hence the narratives of those authors who were personal witnesses to the period, Kritovoulos and Tursun, describing Mehmed's explorations in the city, his musings on its dilapidated state and on its past glory, his plans to populate it. Hence also the ambivalence that underlies initial Ottoman responses to nonreligious symbols of empire: the equestrian statue of Justinian in the Augustaion, near Hagia Sophia, which pointed eastward in a gesture that seemed rather threatening to some of the newcomers, survived at least the first years of Ottoman rule in the city; a story in which Mehmed threw his mace at the Serpent Column in the Hippodrome, only to be reprimanded and stopped by the patriarch Gennadios, found its way into the sixteenth-century *Hünernāme,* underlining a similar ambiguity (fig. 27). Urban nodes took their share of this ambivalence: the Golden Gate was forever blocked with the construction of the citadel, while the Forum of Taurus was, if temporarily, given a new definition as the forecourt of Mehmed's palace.

By accommodating, appropriating, and replacing aspects of Byzantine Constantinople, the first urban interventions responded to the city's immense symbolic significance and to its size and topography. When, six years after the conquest, Mehmed began a second and much more extensive campaign of rebuilding the capital, some of the powerful symbols of Ottoman Istanbul and a vast infrastructure of commerce

FIGURE 27
Mehmed II striking the Serpent
Column in the Hippodrome
with his mace and being
admonished by the patriarch
Gennadios, in Lokman bin
Seyyid Hüseyin, *Hünernāme,*
Topkapı Palace Museum, H 1523,
fol. 162v.

different sites venerated as the grave of Ayyub, as well as a state-of-the-art citadel, its presence owed to the antecedent Byzantine order and to expectations of a crusade in response to the city's fall. Since the former gradually lost its immediacy and the latter never materialized, the citadel soon became a marginal, if monumental, addition to the new capital.

Some of the "old" buildings mentioned here were late products of the former Ottoman order that accompanied Mehmed into the new capital, only to be marginalized through the increasingly articulate centralizing policies of the imperial state. The construction of the tomb of Ayyub outside the city proper demonstrates the prevalence—through these early years—of the ghazi mentality in its opposition to the rebuilding and the inhabitation of the city. The closing of the city's first madrasa and hospice and their conversion into masjids after the completion of the New Complex, on the other hand, mark a departure from the social and intellectual roots of the ghazi state. The abandonment of the first royal residence after the completion of the New Palace, too, marks a comparable rupture in the administrative style of the Ottoman state: the New Palace was carefully designed to manifest and perpetuate the imperial ambitions of the sultan and to accommodate his new notion of kingship. The abandonment of the vast enclosure that housed the first palace for the acropolis of Byzantium simultaneously underlines the Ottomans' changing understanding of the city's physical and symbolic topography.

were already in place. But the first six years of inhabiting new territory produced also a number of architectural and urban solutions that were soon found inadequate. A significant number of buildings or ensembles dating from these years, whose names carry the modifier *eski* or *ʿatīḳ* (old), were products of this period of orientation and reorientation and were soon replaced by others: the Old Palace, the Old Hospice, the Old (Zeyrek) Madrasa, two Old Horse Markets, an Old Flea Market, and an Old Bedestan are among these. At the edges of the city were two

Constructing the City

ARCHITECTURE AND ITS AUDIENCES

CHAPTER 2

PART 1

THE URBAN PROGRAM AND MEHMED II'S FOUNDATION

Under the year 1458, Kritovoulos entered the following in the chronicle he dedicated to Mehmed II:

> Command of the Sultan to all able persons, to build splendid and costly buildings inside the City
>
> Then he called together all the wealthy and the most able persons into his presence, those who enjoyed great wealth and prosperity, and ordered them to build grand houses in the City, wherever each chose to build. He also commanded them to build baths and inns and marketplaces, and very many and very beautiful workshops, to erect places of worship, and to adorn and embellish [order and glorify][1] the City with many other such buildings, sparing no expense, as each man had the means and the ability.
>
> The sultan himself selected the best site in the middle of the City, and commanded them to erect there a mosque, which in height, beauty, and size should vie with the largest and finest of the temples already existing there. He bade them select and prepare materials for this, the very best marbles and other costly polished stones as well as an abundance of columns of suitable size and beauty plus iron, copper, and lead in large quantities, and every other needed material.
>
> He also gave orders for the erection of a palace on the point of old Byzantium which stretches out into the sea—a palace that should outshine all and be more marvelous than the preceding palaces in looks, size, cost, and gracefulness.
>
> [. . .] Now it was his plan to make the City in every way the best supplied and strongest city, as it used to be long ago, in power and wealth, glory, learning, and trades, and in all the professions and all sorts of good things, as well as in public and private buildings and monuments.[2]

Earlier references of the Greek chronicler to the sultan's endeavors regarding the city, resettlements from newly conquered territories, and early building projects constitute brief entries dispersed between narratives of other events. This long passage stands apart from such summary notes in that it treats the city as an entity, as the object of an urban program. It rehearses the decision to make the city "as it used to be long ago" and captures the vision behind that decision.

It may not be coincidental that the passage is reminiscent of Arrian's narrative of the construction of Alexandria in his *Alexander legend*, a text regularly read by the sultan.[3] The presence of the same narrative, though in summary form, in the works of two contemporaries, Tursun and Muʿali, suggests that Kritovoulos's account was not merely a literary introduction to a history of Ottoman building activity in the city. Without mentioning a precise date, these authors, writing in Turkish and Persian respectively, note the sultan's order to his grandees to undertake constructions in the city.[4] The significance of these narratives lies not only in their representation of a series of urban ventures undertaken by the sultan but in their definitive demonstration that the locus of rule had moved from Edirne to Constantinople. It is not surprising that the winter of 1458–59 is the first that the sultan did not return to Edirne after supervising work in the city but instead spent all fall and winter in the new capital.

The chronology and the nature of large-scale construction in the new capital after 1458 indeed corroborates these narratives (map 1). In 1459, Mehmed began building a palace on the site of the ancient acropolis of Byzantium. The core of the New Palace, as it was called at the time, was completed by 1465, though construction continued through the 1470s. Between 1463 and 1470, the largest mosque complex yet to be built in the Ottoman realm rose on the hill marked until then by the church of the Holy Apostles, the imperial mausoleum of Byzantium until the eleventh century. As the New Palace and the New Mosque were being built, the grand vizier Mahmud Pasha initiated another large-scale building project. To the east of a complex of religious, charitable, and commercial structures, and adjacent to Mehmed's New Palace, Mahmud built his own palace. The centerpiece of this complex, the grand vizier's mosque, carries an inscription that dates it to the year 1463, while the construction of

the other buildings continued until 1473. A year after the completion of the second royal mosque in the city, the construction of two further large-scale congregational mosques were finalized—those of Murad Pasha in Aksaray, the former Forum Bovis, and of Rum Mehmed Pasha, across the Bosphorus in Üsküdar. Their dependencies, including charitable foundations and residences of the founders, followed. Within the span of twelve years the city witnessed the construction of five major building complexes that aimed to fulfill Mehmed's ambition to make the city "as it used to be long ago." A series of lesser projects realized during the last decade of Mehmed's rule, a number of baths and religious and charitable structures, marked the continuation of the trend set in 1458 by the sultan's command.

The building of new administrative and religious structures in an Ottoman idiom exhibited the urgency of reconstructing Constantinople in the image of an Ottoman city, to be rendered legible through its monuments. Hence the fate of the city's Byzantine buildings through this period: although the conversion of Constantinople's churches into mosques is a favorite theme of contemporary Ottoman authors,[5] the majority of these conversions in fact took place during the reign not of Mehmed but of his successors. None of the Byzantine palaces was used by the new administration. The building campaign initiated by Mehmed in 1458 instead aimed not only to provide services to a rapidly growing city but also, and equally importantly, to create and communicate the image of an Ottoman Constantinople.

The correspondence between the chroniclers' accounts and the chronology of construction after 1458 justifies a closer look at the passage quoted above, expressly indicative of a "plan" conceived by the sultan. For Kritovoulos represents the ruler's vision of his new capital, which provides insights into notions (urbanistic and political) that informed the rebuilding of the city. The text is striking in its treatment of the city as an entity that is to be ordered, adorned, and glorified through the construction of public and private buildings by the sultan and his grandees. Strands of medieval symbolism that objectified the city as receptacle of religious and political ideals or as apocalyptic locus were part of contemporary Ottoman literary culture, as they were of the larger late medieval world. But the city as the target of a project that aimed to order and glorify it was novel in the Ottoman literary/historiographic context. The theme of the city and its parts as objects representing and glorifying its builders, on the other hand, did exist in the Byzantine ekphrastic tradition. Part of the university curriculum through the late Byzantine period (architectural description was one of the fourteen literary subjects late Byzantine students studied in courses on rhetoric), this literary form had produced such celebrated texts as Cardinal Bessarion's description of Trebizond and Manuel Chrysoloras's "Comparison of Old and New Rome" in the early fifteenth century.[6] The latter, Christine Smith has observed, is the first text of the Renaissance to discuss a rational structuring of the urban environment. Although Kritovoulos's account does not offer descriptions of the city and its monuments as detailed as the ekphrases do, it is worth remembering that he was a product of the same educational system that accorded such centrality to architecture and the built environment, which, in turn, rendered architecture a yardstick against which ethical, cultural, and political achievement could be measured. Equally noteworthy is the coincidence of the writing of this passage with the emergence, in the Italian realm, of a discourse that conceived and represented the city as a formal entity to

be given shape in accordance with a political vision. It is not without significance that this emerging discourse was rooted, in part, in the home of the new Ottoman capital.[7]

Kritovoulos's *History* sheds light on several central aspects of Mehmed's plan and the political and architectural ideas on which it is grounded. The Ottoman ruler's desire to surpass the monuments of Byzantium is most immediately apparent among these: The height, beauty, and size of his temple (*naos*) should "vie with the largest and the finest of the temples already existing there." His palace should "outshine all and be more marvelous than the preceding palaces in looks, size, cost, and gracefulness." *His* buildings, in other words, should constitute the primary monuments of Constantinople. A notion of monumentality can be gleaned from the Greek historian's account: along with their usefulness to the public, their beauty, size, and prodigality were the desired qualities of the new "public and private buildings and monuments" of Constantinople. To Aşıkpaşazade, on the other hand, who wrote his history for a wider, rather than a strictly courtly, audience, charity was the sole virtue—if any—of the *āşār* (works) of sultans and grandees. Such a contrast between these views reflects the very diverse backgrounds of the two authors, the former no doubt influenced by the priorities of his patron.

Kritovoulos's account of Mehmed's order to his grandees to build grand houses, baths, inns, and marketplaces, beautiful workshops and places of worship, has often been noted in the context of the rebuilding of the city. Halil İnalcık surmises that the passage refers to a sultanic order to the grandees to choose sites where they would build complexes that would bear their names. These complexes, he notes, served to encourage settlement and prosperity and, along with a large number of smaller-scale foundations, more modest in size and function and humbler in materials and architectural style, constituted the cores of the first *nevāḥi* (sing. *nāḥiye;* larger urban units that comprised a number of residential neighborhoods) of Ottoman Istanbul.[8]

The symbolic import of the projects, as captured by the chronicler, is equally noteworthy. Asking his grandees "to build splendid and costly buildings" and "to adorn and embellish the City," and thus alluding to the spectacular aspect of the proposed constructions, Mehmed urged them to build, alongside him, the Ottoman *monuments* of Constantinople. The sultan's command and the responses to it provide evidence of the centralized administrative apparatus that he established in the city: the new military elite, whom he had situated directly under himself in a carefully designed administrative hierarchy and whose roles and conduct he was to articulate in his law code, were to be the major builders of symbolically significant sites of the capital, their works surpassed only by those of the sultan. Composed largely of converted soldiers who had risen in the military-administrative hierarchy (a significant number of them of aristocratic extraction), the new military elite was itself a product of the sultan's centralized imperial apparatus. Its members, through their agency in the foundation of urban institutions, were to partake in the creation of the imperial capital.[9] The establishment of the capital city's urban institutions, Edward Mitchell has argued, marked the construction of the city as the "site of state," for these establishments were central to the self-articulation of the state and the validation of its hierarchical structure.[10] The spaces that were to house those institutions and their visual configurations were integral to that hierarchy. Hence Mehmed's command that the structures to be built by his grandees be "splendid and costly";

hence his desire to surpass all existing monuments in the city.

What follows is an evaluation of Mehmed's urban program as a collective enterprise on the part of the ruling body, involving two overlapping processes: the creation of a network of administrative, commercial, military, religious, and educational loci, and the introduction to the cityscape of a new visual order and formal hierarchy that would in turn represent the new political and cultural order. The sources of that program were rooted in Ottoman, Byzantine, and European urban practices, on the one hand, and in the political configuration emerging in the Ottoman realm, on the other. The major architectural undertakings shaping later-fifteenth-century Istanbul were premeditated with regard to their wider urban context. Policies of the ruling body regarding the city, extant and emerging notions of architecture and urbanism, and the imprint and constraints of the city's extant layout were interrelated factors that informed the reordering of Constantinople's urban environment.

MOVING INTO BYZANTIUM: THE NEW PALACE

Mehmed's two major undertakings realized after 1458, the New Palace and the New Mosque, carved out two vast spaces from within the walled city (map 1). Both had been symbolically significant sites in Byzantine Constantinople: the palace was built at the eastern tip of the peninsula on the acropolis of ancient Byzantium; the mosque complex rose on the fourth hill, where once stood the church of the Holy Apostles. Both complexes radically altered the cityscape; both announced and accommodated radical changes in the Ottoman polity. Both, we learn from contemporaries such as Kritovoulos, Tursun, and Muʿali, were conceived in tandem, as sites that would frame and monumentalize newly reconfigured central institutions of the Ottoman state. Rooted in part in former Ottoman practices but departing from them significantly, both represented paradigmatic shifts in Ottoman palatial and religious architecture. The New Palace is the subject of an exhaustive study by Gülru Necipoğlu that provides an in-depth analysis and interpretation of the Topkapı's architecture and its uses and meanings at the time of its foundation. It therefore suffices here briefly to introduce the palace, in order to highlight the architectural, political, and urban themes that pervade the complex, and their links to the cultural and architectural trends of the era.[11]

The New Palace, or Topkapı, today is a palimpsest of architectural and decorative layers that over the course of more than half a millennium have accumulated atop and around the initial core founded by Mehmed (plate 1, fig. 28).[12] The relation of the palace as it stands today to its founder's conception and initial design is complex: although the palace preserves its original layout to a significant degree, major expansion, renovation, redecoration, and restoration programs have rendered the spatial and visual configuration of the original building difficult, and at times impossible, to reconstruct. An immediately visible cause of that difficulty is that the building's decorative skin has adapted to changing tastes of the Ottoman elite through the nearly four hundred years of its use as the primary imperial locus. The visual and spatial configuration of the fifteenth-century palace is further obscured because smaller-scale structures, some of which were built with lesser materials in an architectural idiom that belonged to the late medieval as much as to an emerging early modern world, were replaced, most notably in the sixteenth and seventeenth centuries, with grander versions that often occupied the same sites as their predecessors.

The fifteenth-century building was completed in phases: construction of the initial core began shortly following Mehmed's announcement of his urban project in 1458. It consisted of two adjoining courtyards, which would be flanked by another enclosure upon completion of an outer wall in 1478. The courtyard to the southwest housed service facilities (kitchens and stables) along the longer sides of the trapezoidal space, and these services were separated from the court by curtain walls; a core of administrative structures (the viziers' council hall, the public treasury, and the chancery) were grouped together at the court's northern corner and were marked with a tower. To the east of this grouping, in the middle of the trapezoidal court's shortest wall, was a domed vestibule leading to what was then the second courtyard, housing the sultan's private quarters and the palace school of recruited pages. Here, immediately beyond the monumental gate that marked the transition between the public and the private quarters of the palace, stood the sultan's audience hall.[13] At the two far corners of the second courtyard were two structures designed for the sultan's private use: to the north was the privy chamber, Mehmed's living quarters, comprising four domed square rooms arranged into a quadrangular plan. Colonnades lined both its courtyard and exterior façades. Opposite it, in the eastern corner, and behind another colonnade lay a treasury and bath complex, featuring a loggia that magnificently opened the building to seas and lands beyond through its lofty double arches to the north and east. Ashlar masonry, marble colonnades, and lead-covered pitched roofs and domes distinguished the inner court's royal buildings from the dormitories of the pages, who served various duties in the inner palace while receiving an education that would lead them to positions within the military/administrative hierarchy.

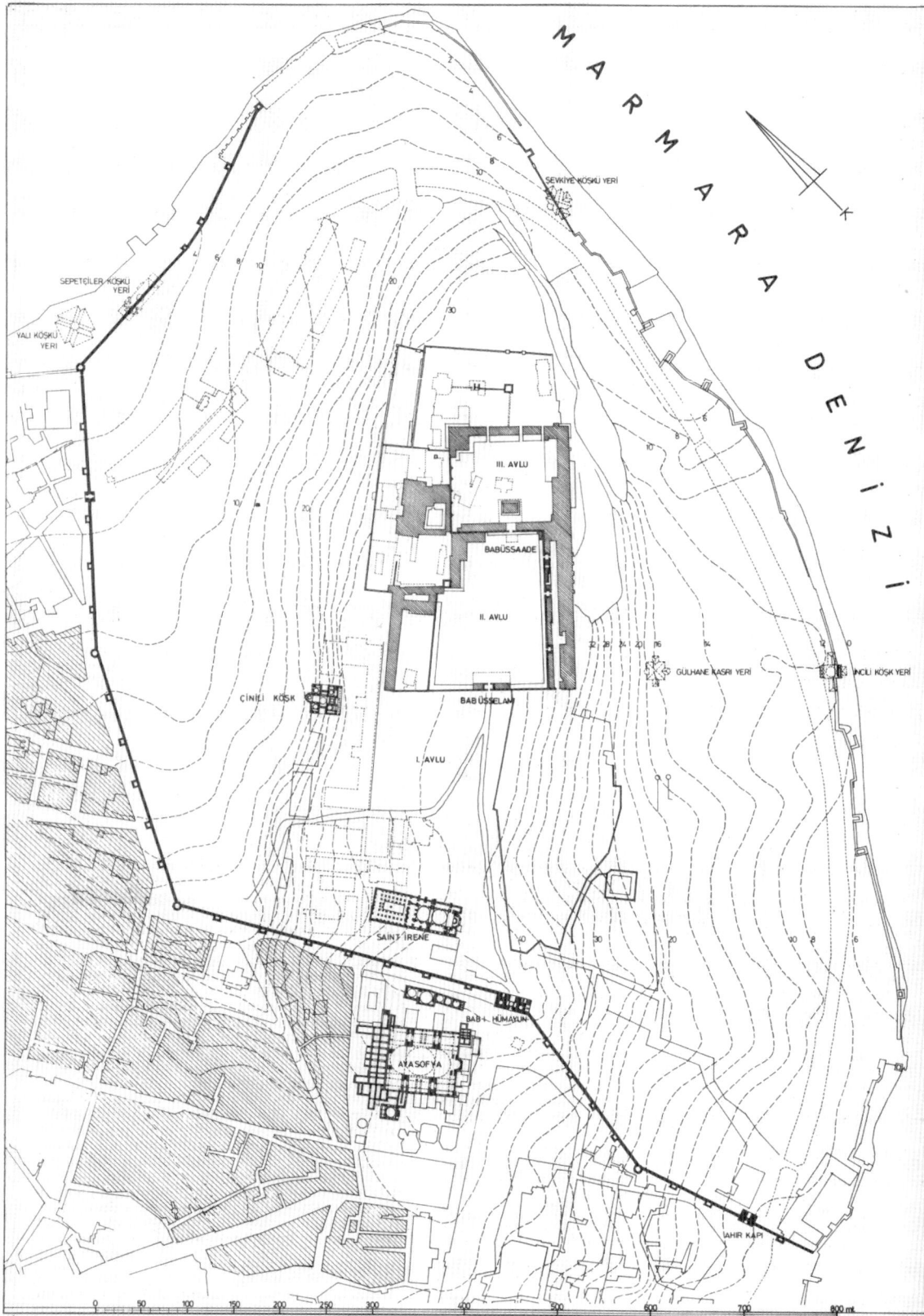

M A R M A R A   D E N İ Z İ

ŞEVKİYE KÖŞKÜ YERİ

SEPETÇİLER KÖŞKÜ YERİ

YALI KÖŞKÜ YERİ

III. AVLU

BABÜSSAADE

II. AVLU

ÇİNİLİ KÖŞK

GÜLHANE KASRI YERİ

İNCİLİ KÖŞK YERİ

BAB ÜSSELAM

I. AVLU

SAINT IRENE

BAB-I HÜMAYUN

AYA SOFYA

AHIR KAPI

0   50   100   150   200   250   300   400   500   600   700   800 mt.

To the west were the palace's harem quarters. Here, tucked into a corner of the palace's main core and enclosing a much smaller area, possibly centered around what later became the Courtyard of the Queen Mother, were the residences of the sultan's female consorts.[14] A hanging garden rising on vaulted structures and housing a marble terrace and pool, and adjacent to it a transparent pavilion constructed of fragments of crystal, extended the private section of the palace northeastward. Located at the northeastern end of the acropolis hill's highest terrace, the hanging garden was surrounded by a wall punctuated with belvedere towers.[15]

The second building phase endowed the palace with its outer wall, within which was now enclosed the entire promontory at the northeastern tip of the Constantinopolitan peninsula and the palace's three consecutive courtyards. The wall, completed in 1478, ran close to two and a half kilometers and was connected to the Byzantine sea walls along the Bosphorus and the Propontis shores. Beyond a new monumental gate to the newly expanded palace grounds stood an expansion of the palace's administrative and service facilities, the first courtyard. The surrounding area housed gardens, game preserves, and orchards. It was also after the enclosure of this vast area into the palace grounds that a number of kiosks and pavilions were built in the palace's outer gardens.

Through the site on which it was located, the New Palace reproduced the spatial configuration of the symbolic and actual center of the Byzantine city, where the loci of rule, faith, and urban ceremonial were embodied in the triad of the Great Palace, Hagia Sophia, and the Hippodrome. Choosing the ancient acropolis as the site of his New Palace, Mehmed took the first significant step toward the re-creation of that triad, now consisting of the New Palace, the Ayasofya mosque, and the Atmeydanı/

Hippodrome.[16] The location of the palace on the city's ancient acropolis, together with the Ottoman preoccupation with Constantinople's foundation myths, invites an analogy with the succession of palaces on Rome's Palatine Hill: the Constantinopolitan acropolis offered its Ottoman residents a locus of rule within the ancient city center, magnificent views of the urban landscape and the territories beyond, and, like the Palatine, a connection to the capital city's foundation myth.[17] Marking the move of the Ottoman house into the gravitational center of Byzantine Constantinople, the decision to construct the New Palace at the site of the ancient acropolis would in turn inform a series of subsequent decisions concerning the configuration and uses of urban space in Ottoman Constantinople.[18] The move to the northeastern tip of the peninsula initiated a long-term trend in the ceremonial use of urban space, as the first courtyard of the New Palace and its Imperial Gate near the Hagia Sophia were now the starting points of imperial processions that would traverse the Augustaion to proceed along the the Mese/Divan Yolu, tracing in part the itinerary and architectural markers of the Byzantine city's ceremonial route.

The palace on the ancient acropolis was also a site where fragments of the ancient Byzantine past were collected and exhibited. As Julian Raby has demonstrated, immediately past the second gate of the palace, one encountered four imperial Byzantine sarcophagi transported from two imperial foundations, the church of the Holy Apostles and the monastery of the Pantokrator.[19] Also within the second courtyard, where service facilities were located and the imperial council met, were numerous other fragments transported from the Hippodrome, the Augustaion, and the Pantokrator. Among these were a gigantic Corinthian capital and several drums (possibly fragments of one of the city's monumental columns) and the pedestals of a monument to Porphyrius the Charioteer erected by the emperor Arkadius on the spina of the Hippodrome. As late as the 1540s Pierre Gilles saw and measured "in the imperial precinct" the remains of Justinian's equestrian statue, which had stood in the Augustaion nearby and was taken down in or before 1456.[20] The site's Byzantine legacy was visible even to those who did not have the occasion or the privilege to enter the palace grounds: the Goth's column in the Topkapı's outer gardens immediately below the third court, housing the privy chamber, remained, like the column of Theodosius enclosed within the first Ottoman palace on the Mese, a prominent reminder of the site's Byzantine past. The column, according to Nikephorus Gregoras, who wrote in the early fourteenth century, once carried a statue of the city's legendary founder, Byzas.[21]

"They were all built," Kritovoulos wrote of the buildings of Mehmed's New Palace, "with a view to variety, beauty, size, magnificence; shining and scintillating with an abundance of gold and silver, within and without and with precious stones and marbles, with various ornaments and colors, all applied with a brilliance and smoothness and lightness most attractive and worked out with the finest and most complete skill, most ambitiously. Both in sculpture and in plastic work, as well as in painting, they were the finest and best of all."[22] Variety, foregrounded by Kritovoulos alongside other contemporary authors in their descriptions of the New Palace, was one of the themes that pervaded the complex and announced itself in every one of its significant buildings. The palace was as polyglot in its architectural language as the city's (and indeed the palace's) inhabitants in their spoken and written languages, another aspect of Mehmed II's Istanbul underlined by Kritovoulos. Each of the three successive

monumental portals that marked transitions into and within the palatial complex as thresholds between spaces variously conceived and used were conceptualized according to different contexts and functions; each portal, loaded with the symbolism attached to the sultan's gate, displayed a different architectural style and range of associations. The gate of the outer fortress (fig. 29), featuring an upper gallery, made a reference to the Chalke Gate of the Byzantine Great Palace nearby; the middle gate (fig. 30) boasted European-style polygonal towers with pyramidal roofs that made references to a newly emerging architectural language of power and authority; the domed vestibule of the third gate (its fifteenth-century configuration visible in the Düsseldorf view, fig. 31),[23] under which the sultan gave audience and whose marble colonnade may carry another memory, if not the actual remains, of the Byzantine Great Palace, referred simultaneously to the heavenly canopy framing the monarch and to the royal tent of the Turco-Mongol tradition.[24]

If variety informed a linear spatial experience in the traversal of the palace's expansive courtyards through its successive gates, it was also deployed synchronically in spaces that exhibited bold juxtapositions of diverse architectural and visual idioms. In the private third courtyard of the palace, the privy chamber and the treasury/bath complex stood across from each other, exhibiting distinctly Ottoman and Italianate/Byzantine architectural idioms, respectively (figs. 32, 33).[25] Here, the privy-chamber portico, with its pointed arches and muqarnas capitals, stood across from the mosaic-covered, round-arched portico of the treasury, with its composite Ionic columns. (The choice of these particular capitals by architect or patron may not be coincidental. John Onians notes that the imperial and triumphal associations of the distinctly Roman composite

FIGURE 29a
The outer wall of the Topkapı
Palace, including the Imperial
Gate, lithograph, looking
northeast.

FIGURE 29b
The outer wall of the Topkapı
Palace, including the Imperial
Gate, lithograph, looking east,
the İshak Pasha mosque and
bath at the far right.

capital was recognized by Renaissance architects from the fifteenth century onward.)[26] Behind the first lay the sultan's multidomed private quarters in a typically Ottoman idiom; behind the second lay his private treasury, with its lofty Italianate loggia, Byzantine mosaics, and Mamluk-style portal.

Beyond the initial core of the palace, in the outer gardens, pavilions in Timurid, Ottoman, and Byzantine idioms faced each other across a square (plate 2).[27] On the one hand, such eclecticism was a product of encounters and rapid transitions that marked the cultural environment of late medieval Anatolia and the Balkans, in which the Ottoman polity had emerged. This is perhaps why a similar predisposition toward variety and diversity of styles marked also late Byzantine palaces, as described by Manuel Chrysoloras.[28] At the same time, as Gülru Necipoğlu has convincingly argued, the "collection" and

exhibition of diverse visual idioms within the palace grounds was a metaphor for the universalism of the newly consolidated empire and a celebration of its subjugation of kingdoms that were represented here through their architecture.[29] Not only subjugated kingdoms but lands beyond the Ottoman frontiers were present in the palace in their visual idioms. Deliberate visual references in the palace to Byzantine, Timurid, Italian, and Mamluk worlds carried associations with the broad horizons of the Ottoman cultural world, newly visible from a Constantinopolitan vantage point. If the conquest of Constantinople brought the Ottomans into immediate contact with the Byzantine imperial legacy and simultaneously expanded their horizons to encompass the eastern Mediterranean and the Iranian worlds, this was nowhere more tangibly embodied than in Mehmed II's palace, his private residence and the locus of his rule.

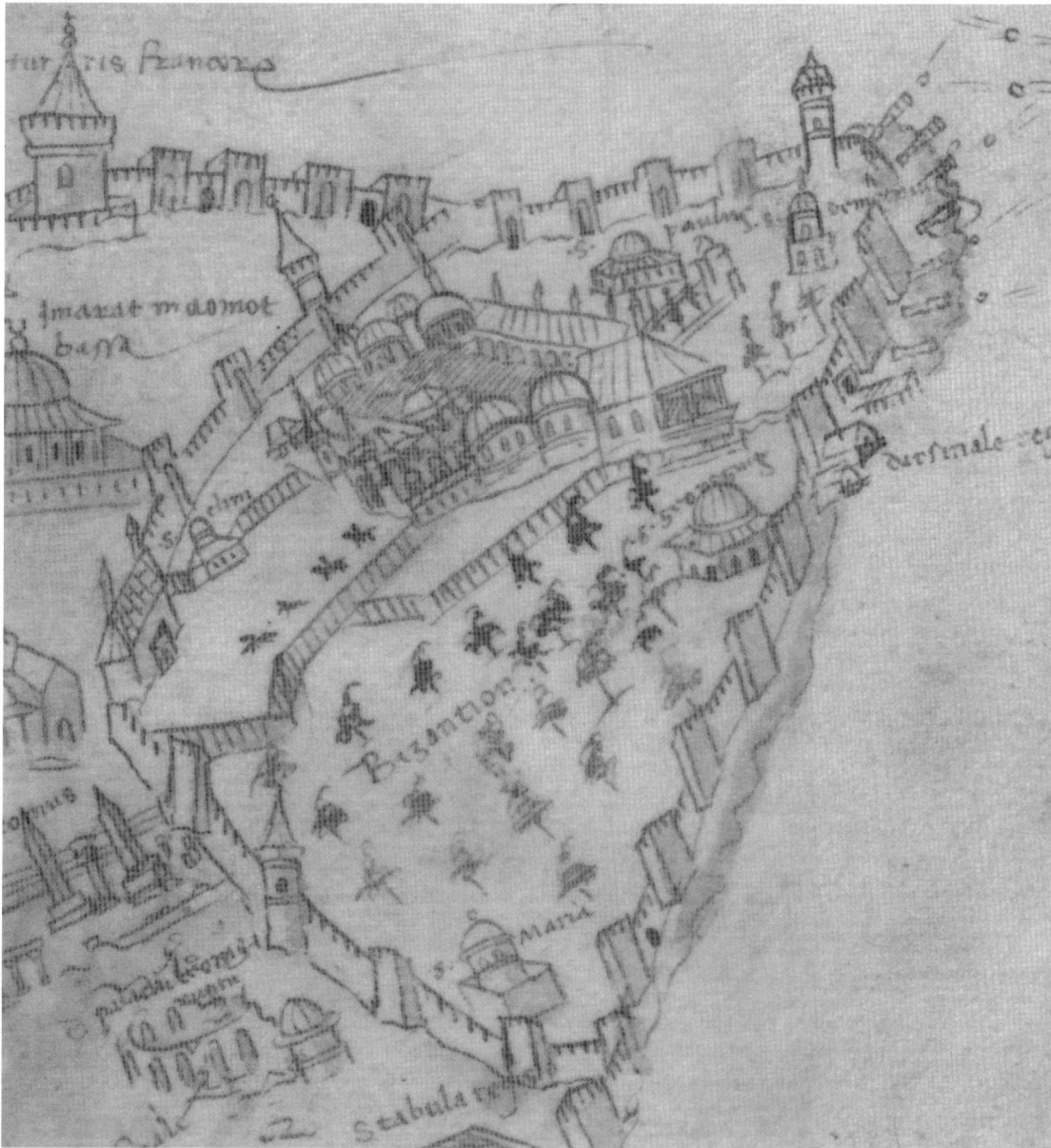

FIGURE 31
The Topkapı Palace, detail from
the map of Constantinople
in Cristoforo Buondelmonti's
Liber Insularum Archipelagi, ink
drawing, ca. 1481. Universitäts-
und Landesbibliothek,
Düsseldorf, MS G 13, fol. 54r
(fig. 111).

Like the New Mosque complex founded by the sultan in the same years, the New Palace was a complete newcomer to the Ottoman world. The novelty of the design, the hybridity of its conception, and its overriding themes of variety and appropriation linked the palace intimately to the broader political and cultural trends of the era. Unique in its unprecedented monumentality and in its visual idiom, it combined in one new configuration a variety of forms from a diverse range of sources. It replaced the loose spatial organization of early Ottoman palaces, which were each dotted with numerous pavilions and temporary structures and distinguished by a multifunctional royal tower, with a tightly organized (if not symmetrically or axially conceived) space where particular functions were distributed to a

ordered colonnade of precious marbles faced the second courtyard, suggests an inspiration from the Great Palace nearby, and an elaboration on the use of such a colonnade in Murad II's Edirne palace.[30] The multidomed, porticoed privy chamber for which no precedent remains in former Ottoman palaces suggests a transition from similarly planned urban structures into the private realm of the palace.

The making of such variety can be gleaned in the construction history of the privy chamber, whose massive foundations, it has been suggested, were laid out for the construction of a tower in the manner of the royal tower of the Edirne palace, completed by Mehmed II in 1452.[31] Significantly, in the Edirne palace, which had a spatial configuration very similar to the Topkapı's, the royal tower's location corresponded to that of the privy chamber in the Istanbul palace; and it was referred to as the Privy Chamber or the Privy Chamber Kiosk. If the privy chamber in Topkapı was indeed founded as a tower and the preference for a domed structure surrounded by porticoes followed later, then the building embodies in itself the abandonment of a medieval sensibility for an emerging new aesthetic. Such alteration in plans might also explain the novel conception of the treasury and bath complex across the court and the unusual location of the audience hall immediately behind the third gate: audience hall, residence, and treasury were now disconnected, and the latter was attached to a royal bathhouse. Concomitantly, the architectural aesthetic of a porticoed courtyard replaced one that highlighted the royal tower. The fifteenth-century palace did, of course, house one such tower, that of the outer treasury near the viziers' council hall.[32] Its presence evinces both the continued import of a treasury tower and a departure from earlier Ottoman practice, as the tower in the second courtyard no longer had a ceremonial or a residential function.

variety of newly designed structures. In the process, aspects of Ottoman public architecture and of Byzantine, Timurid, and Italian palatial idioms were transferred into the Ottoman palatial context, where they came to be associated with a new range of meanings. The architecture of the third gate complex, whose monumentally

Complex ties link the New Palace to late antique and medieval palatial traditions, through connections as immediate as the Constantinian Great Palace nearby and as distant as the Umayyad palaces of Syria. The palace's succession of courtyards progressing from public to private areas, its sumptuous displays of natural and material wealth, and its manipulation of landscape and architecture to provide commanding vistas of surrounding territories highlight its analogies to imperial palaces of the Roman realm, as well as to Abbasid and post-Abbasid palaces of the larger Islamic world. At the same time, the Topkapı displays organic links to Turco-Mongol and Persianate palatial traditions, with their loose arrangement of individual buildings within large garden enclosures, their uses of or architectural references to tent structures, and their complex symbolism of the gate.[33] The Topkapı, like the first Ottoman palace on the Forum of Taurus, was conceived as a citadel-palace, in conformity with a palatial paradigm of the late medieval Western and Middle Eastern worlds.[34] Its architecture thus resonated also with late medieval palatial traditions of the Balkans, as they were appropriated by the Ottoman ruling body from the earlier fifteenth century onward, an aspect of the complex most clearly visible in the multiple towers that marked the public treasury, the third court's enclosure wall, and the outer enclosure.[35] Through bold juxtaposition of diverse palatial traditions, in an expanse and monumentality that befitted the imperial ambitions of the monarch, this highly idiosyncratic ensemble embodied, reproduced, and represented the new configuration of the Ottoman polity.

The spatial, ceremonial, and visual links of the palace to the city and its suburbs across from the Golden Horn and the Bosphorus, too, were varied. The Topkapı was one of the main constituents of the larger symbolic and ceremonial locus of Constantinople and at the same time a highly isolated enclosure surrounded by a fortress wall that separated it from the city, setting in stone ideas of imperial seclusion that supported the divine and absolute authority of the sultan. Isolation, literally and metaphorically, was the primary motive in the enclosure of the palace within expansive gardens. Massive walls demarcated by towers and a monumental portal constituted its public face, turned to the city. To viewers across the Golden Horn and the Bosphorus, too, the tall exterior walls of the two inner courtyards rising vertically on the terraced promontory conveyed a fortresslike aspect.[36]

A corollary to the spatial isolation of the palace was its visual interrelationship with the city. As Gülru Necipoğlu has demonstrated, spatial and architectural configurations that literally and symbolically embodied the sultan's gaze over his dominion complemented the idea and the practice of imperial seclusion elaborated and codified through the later decades of Mehmed's rule.[37] At the northeastern end of the palace complex, situated on an elevation that projected out toward the sea, were two royal buildings that offered views of the city, its suburbs, and the seas and lands that lay beyond, constituting the loci of the monarch's gaze: the monumentally conceived loggia of the inner treasury and the porticoed terrace flanking the exterior of the privy chamber, semi-open, transitional spaces perched on the corners of the third courtyard's massive retaining walls, opened up the palace to its surroundings, simultaneously inviting gazes from across the bodies of water that surrounded the promontory (plate 1). The centrality of these buildings to the conceptualization of the palace is underlined by their prominence in the Dusseldorf view (one of the earliest eye-witness visual documents of the city, discussed in the following chapter), where the author particularly highlighted their monumentality and open nature. The treasury tower in the second courtyard and towers demarcating the third courtyard established further visual connections between the palace and its larger urban context. The belvedere above the palace's outer gate near the Hagia Sophia, and the polygonal towers marking the portion of the imperial fortress that stood between the palatial complex and the city, signified the monarch's gaze over his capital city, simultaneously providing spaces where he could literally look over processions taking place beyond the gates (fig. 29). Immediately across from two polygonal belvedere towers situated to the north and south of the palace's main gate were the foundations of two prominent members of the ruling elite, Mahmud Pasha and İshak Pasha.[38] Such architectural correspondence between sultan's and viziers' works signified extensions of the palace into the city. The visual and spatial links between palace and city were to be reinforced in royal processions that started in the outer courtyard of the palace and continued into the public space beyond the boundaries of the royal domain. "It was built on principles of justice and perfection / With it Istanbul became prosperous," wrote Tursun, underlining the profound interconnectedness of the construction of the palace and the construction of the capital city.[39]

THE NEW MOSQUE: RUPTURE AND CONTINUITY

"[T]he dynastic city is fixed for all time. This is what dynasties are all about. When there is a political upheaval and a new regime comes to power, it will have two options. It will either identify itself with the passing regime to establish legitimacy and continuity, or it will dramatize the break with the past by abandoning the dynastic city for one of its own."[40]

What took place in Constantinople in 1453 was more than a political upheaval, and its consequences outsized those of a change of dynasty, not an altogether seldom event in Byzantine history. Spiro Kostof's straightforward observation might still provide an appropriate introduction to a discussion of the mosque complex of Mehmed, who did see himself, among other things, as heir to Byzantine emperors. And while the reinstitution of patterns in the dynastic city was a key aspect of his urban program, it is the New Mosque, located on the site of the church of the Holy Apostles, that most clearly captures this continuum and the centrality of the image of the emperor Constantine to the Ottoman imagination of the fifteenth century.[41] Built by Constantine and rebuilt by Justinian as the imperial mausoleum, the church was given to the patriarch Gennadios as the seat of the Greek patriarchate, an event Kritovoulos dates to several months after the city's fall, January of 1454. No information remains regarding its state and use between the city's fall and its allocation to the patriarchate. It was deserted when Gennadios, not feeling secure in this uninhabited area, requested that his seat be moved to the monastery of the Pammakaristos.[42] Through Mehmed's decision to build a new complex here, the site that represented the millennial succession of Byzantine emperors became the site of the first sultanic mosque within the walled city. The Ottoman appropriation of the Byzantine site involved a selective use of the past: unlike the Hagia Sophia, which was completely absorbed by the city's new regime, the Holy Apostles was pulled down to open space for the sultan's ambitious building program. Several of the imperial sarcophagi were transported from the Holy Apostles to the New Palace as part of Mehmed's collection of Byzantine relics and antiquities; the monarch's own mausoleum was to rise behind the qibla wall of the New Mosque shortly after his death. No record survives of the monumental column supporting a large bronze statue group of the archangel Michael with the emperor Michael VIII at his feet offering a model of Constantinople. The column, erected by Michael VIII near the Holy Apostles, was visible to travelers to the city through the early decades of the fifteenth century and might have shared the fate of the church.[43] Monumental architecture and symbolic locus simultaneously represented rupture and continuity between two imperial orders.

Although Mehmed's initial allocation of the church to the patriarchate and his later decision to build the largest and institutionally most central public complex within the Ottoman realm on its site speaks for his awareness of the symbolic significance of the Holy Apostles, other factors must have played a role in this choice of site. One has to do with a new conception of the city, which Mehmed II announced would be his seat and which he declared would be made "as it used to be long ago." The New Mosque is the first major structure to be situated outside the Palaeologan city, shrunk, except for the Blachernae palace and monastic settlements, to the eastern shores and slopes along the Golden Horn. New structures sponsored by the sultan and his ruling elite would mark a breaking out of that medieval core and the emergence (or the revival, in terms of early Byzantine Constantinople) of a sense of grand urban scale and expanse.

Restoration of the city's ancient waterways made expansion outside the medieval core possible. The Holy Apostles was located on the branch of the system that carried water to the eastern sections of the city, near the western foot of the aqueduct that traversed the valley between the third and the fourth hills. This was one of the sections of the system restored

shortly after the conquest. Mehmed had marked this achievement also with the restoration of the Kırkçeşme (Forty Fountains), the water supply near the aqueduct, from which poured the waters of the restored canals. The presence of a restored water-distribution system in the area must have facilitated its choice as the site of a new complex, around which new commercial and residential areas were to develop (fig. 34).

The closeness of the Holy Apostles to the northern branch of the Mese was possibly another factor that made it a preferable site for a major Ottoman construction. Building his new, star-shaped citadel around the Golden Gate of the Byzantine city, Mehmed had in fact blocked the city's main ceremonial artery, the southern branch of the Mese, which connected to the Via Egnatia to reach Thrace and ultimately Rome. The northern branch of the artery was to gain importance instead, as the Charisios/Edirne Gate was now the point where the sultan entered and left the city on military campaigns and on trips to Edirne. More important perhaps is that the Edirne Gate led to the township of Eyüp, as the Golden Gate once led to Hebdemon, a suburb that had stood in a comparable relationship to the city. Although the articulation of Ottoman ceremonial to encompass the shrine on the Golden Horn would wait for another century, as would consolidation of a processional pattern in Istanbul, Mehmed II initiated courtly visits to the Abu Ayyub tomb. The New Complex constituted one of the monumental markers on that processional route, which ran to the north of the original track of the Mese, taking the walker through the outer courtyard of the complex.

This was the largest religious complex built by the Ottomans to date. Its superstructure bearing an unmistakable resemblance to that of the Hagia Sophia, the New Mosque stood at the core of a huge square plaza that measured 210 meters on each side. To the sides of the plaza were the mosque's dependencies, eight madrasas and eight preparatory madrasas, a hospice, a public kitchen, a hospital, and a Koran school for children (fig. 35, plate 3).[44] The foundation at large, comprising markets, baths, caravanserais, vast numbers of shops and residences endowed for it and for several other religious and charitable institutions, formed a network of patronage in the city.

The core of the complex was situated to the south of the Byzantine monument, whose ruins ("the place and a few fallen columns") were visible to Bidlisi in the first decade of the sixteenth century. The anonymous author of a Greek chronicle dating to the 1510s, too, wrote that "nowadays this church is the mosque of Sultan Mehmed in the southern part; sections of its buildings still stand."[45] The outer courtyard, around which the dependencies were situated in strict axial symmetry, was built on vaulted substructures (an adaptation and possibly an expansion of those built for the Holy Apostles)[46] that evened out the slope of the hill.

A monument to the new rule in the ancient city, designed to reproduce and represent a newly configured imperial order, the complex marked a turning point in the history of Ottoman architecture. Like so much in Mehmed's

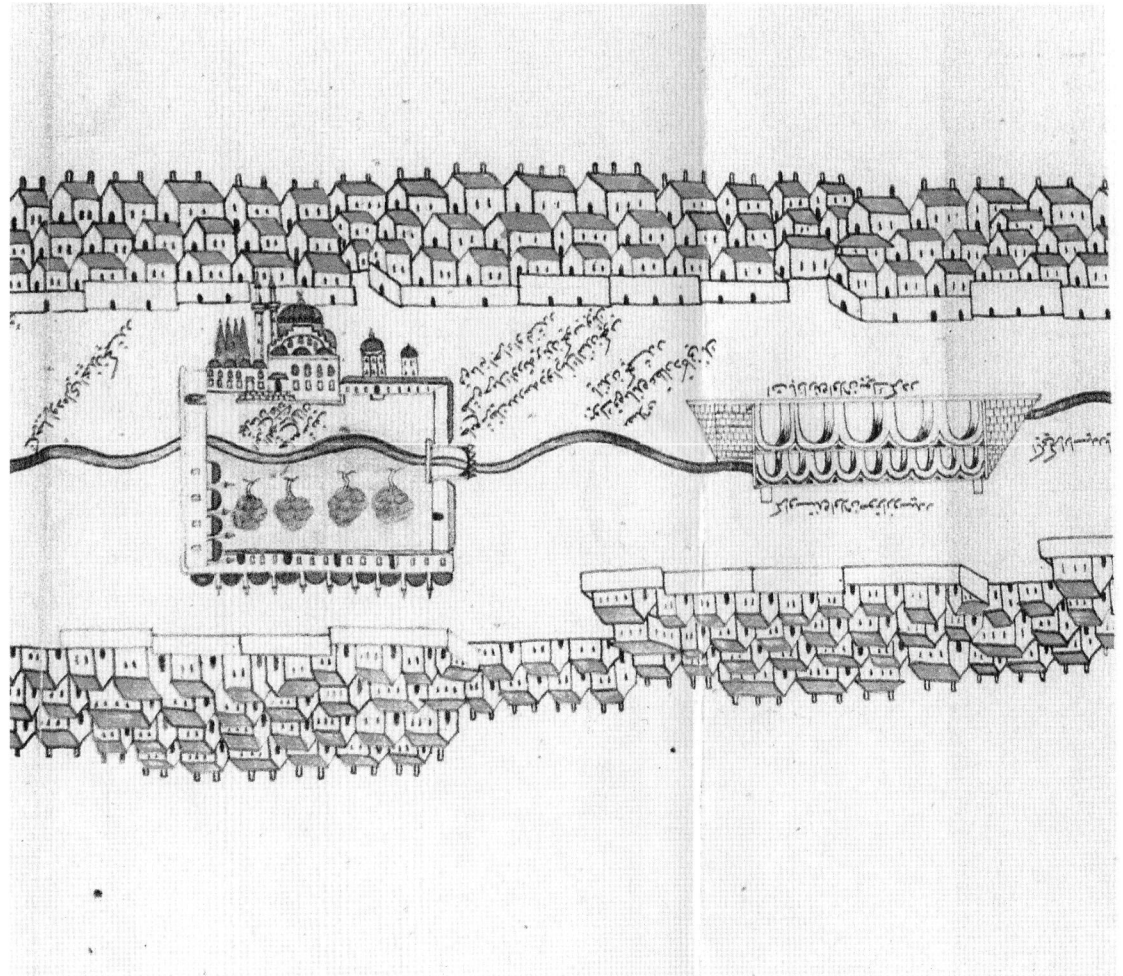

FIGURE 34
Mehmed II complex and the Valens aqueduct, detail from the Köprülü water-distribution map.

FIGURE 35 (*opposite*)
Mehmed II complex, plan:
(1) mosque, (2) mausolea of Mehmed II and Gülbahar Hatun, (3) garden, (4)≈madrasas, (5) preparatory madrasas, (6) hospital, (7) hospice, (8) stables, (9) kitchen, (10) elementary school, (11) library, (12) Börekci (Pastry Makers') Gate, (13) Çorba (Soup) Gate.

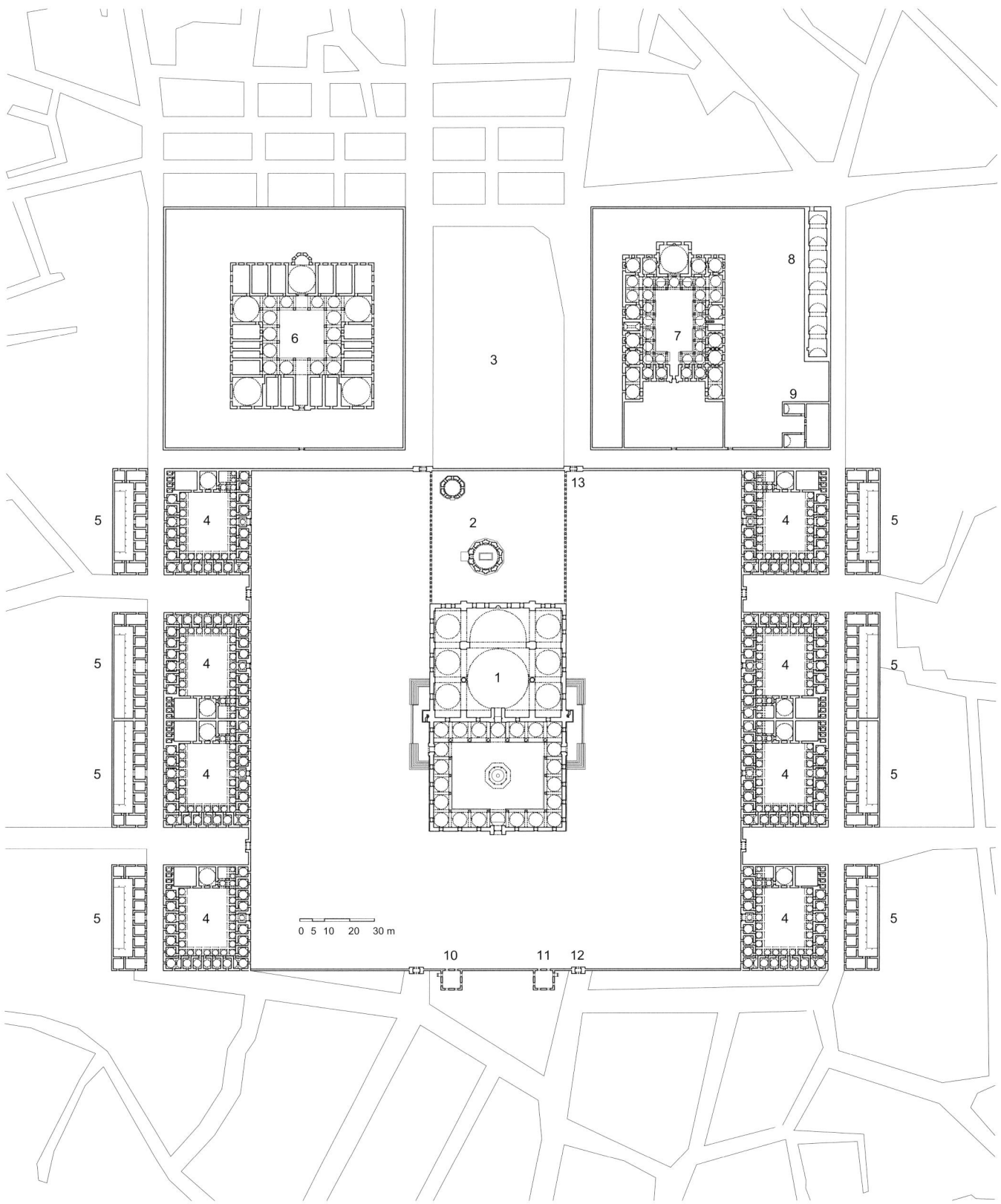

6

3

8

7

9

5 4   4 5

2

5 4   4 5

13

1

5 4   4 5

5 4   4 5

0 5 10   20   30 m

10   11   12

Istanbul, the cultural roots of the New Complex were multiple. As an Ottoman urban establishment, it drew together the congregational mosque, in earlier Ottoman cities a freestanding building at the center of the city, and the royal complex located at a distance from the city center. Starting with Orhan's buildings below the Bursa citadel, each Ottoman sultan had founded at least one socioreligious complex outside the walled enclosures of major Ottoman cities, featuring a madrasa, public kitchen, and public bath around a multifunctional convent-masjid that constituted the core of the ensemble. Starting with Murad I, royal complexes in Bursa assumed a funerary character: the founder's mausoleum was erected near the convent-masjid, often by the successor of the deceased. It was Murad, too, who chose a hilltop several miles to the south of the walled city for his royal complex, siting it in a manner that made utmost use of Bursa's hilly topopraphy to lend prominence and visibility to public buildings. Bayezid I and Mehmed I would follow this trend, founding complexes in what would become the symbolic and functional cores of Bursa's suburbs, simultaneously marking the slopes of mount Olympos with Ottoman buildings of a monumental order (figs. 36, 37). Novel to Ottoman architectural practice, such exploitation of topography harked back to precedents in ancient Anatolia, particularly to siting strategies that shaped the acropolises of several antique and late antique cities. The institutional framework as much as the modalities of siting and visuality of the royal complex was among Ottoman imports into the Constantinopolitan cityscape. Here these attributes would be transformed in a novel combination of building types, as the convent-masjid that centered all royal complexes until then would now be replaced with a mosque for congregational Friday prayer.[47] The vast New Mosque complex brought together four major functions: a congregational mosque, a dynastic monument, the premier educational institution of the empire, and the center of a newly developing residential and commercial area. This array of functions linked it closely both to earlier Ottoman architectural practice and to the church complex it replaced.

This was the first sultanic mosque complex in the new capital to serve as the funerary monument of the founder;[48] echoing the Holy Apostles, which had served as the dynastic mausoleum of Byzantine emperors until the beginning of the eleventh century, in a comparable combination of church and funerary monument.[49] A comparison between the New Complex and the Holy Apostles, made possible by Nikolaus Mesarites' detailed description of the Byzantine monument, composed ca. 1200, reveals that there is more to the functional affinity of the two houses of worship.[50] The complex of the Holy Apostles had housed the foremost educational institution of the Byzantine capital, with numerous colleges for grammar, arts, and sciences. Mesarites mentioned schools for grammar, music, arithmetic, rhetoric, and medicine arranged around colonnaded courtyards. Although the curriculum of the madrasas would have differed from that of their Christian predecessors, the unprecedented scale of the New Complex and of its educational component suggests that the remains of the Byzantine institution might have been an inspiration for it.[51]

In its program and functions, then, the New Complex exhibited novelties but was at the same time related to its predecessors in the Ottoman and the Byzantine realms. The same cannot be said for its layout. A glance at the site plans of Ottoman complexes built before the conquest, where the individual buildings follow the topography of the land rather than a geometrically

FIGURE 36
Bayezid I complex, Bursa.

FIGURE 37
Mehmed I (Green) complex,
Bursa.

ordered plan (fig. 38), suggests that one should look elsewhere to find the sources of the tight geometry that informs the layout of Mehmed's buildings. In this respect, the complex is a complete newcomer, not only to the Ottoman tradition but to the architecture of the early modern Mediterranean world as well.[52] The large plaza with the mosque at its center does have precedents in early Islamic architecture, such as the *haram* of the Kaba in Mecca and that of the Dome of the Rock in Jerusalem, a resemblance that was not lost on contemporary observers: Bidlisi, writing in the early sixteenth century, noted that the outer courtyard of Mehmed's mosque had been modeled after the *haram* of the Kaba.[53] While they were conceptually akin

to the Istanbul complex in their use of a large open space surrounding a highly significant building, the Mecca and Jerusalem enclosures lacked the tight geometry and the regularity of plan that characterized the layout of Mehmed's compound at large. A late antique model, the Library of Alexandria, suggests itself as another source of inspiration. Descriptions of the grand library, which stood on a raised platform and was enclosed by a temenos wall, were often reproduced in Greek ekhphrastic texts that may have been available in Mehmed's court.[54]

The monumental symmetry and axiality of the layout and the large open plaza that defines the siting of individual buildings testify to the impact of notions of and discourse on ideal

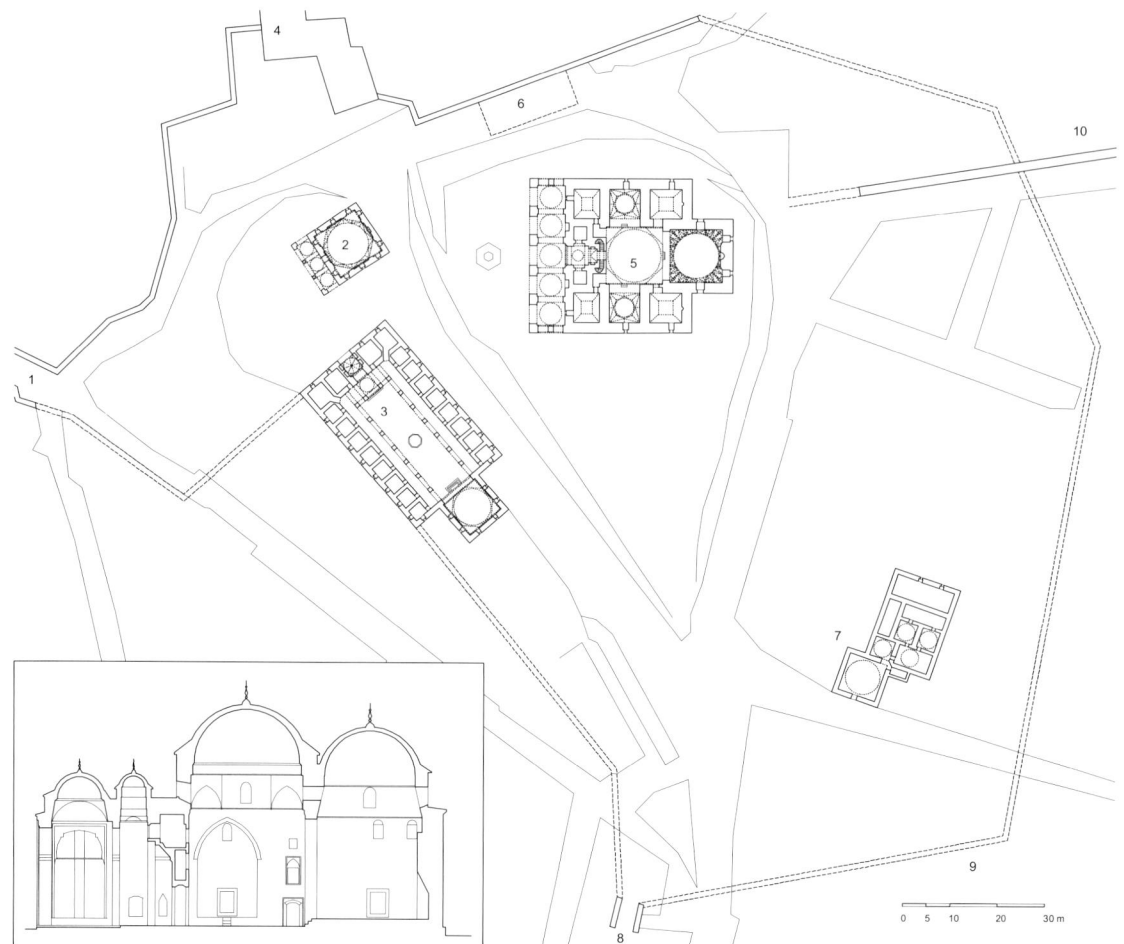

FIGURE 38
Bayezid I complex, plan, with inset section through the convent-masjid: (1) gate, (2) mausoleum, (3) madrasa, (4) site of royal garden palace, (5) convent-masjid, (6) hospice, (7) bathhouse, (8) gate, (9) reconstruction of precinct wall, (10) aqueduct.

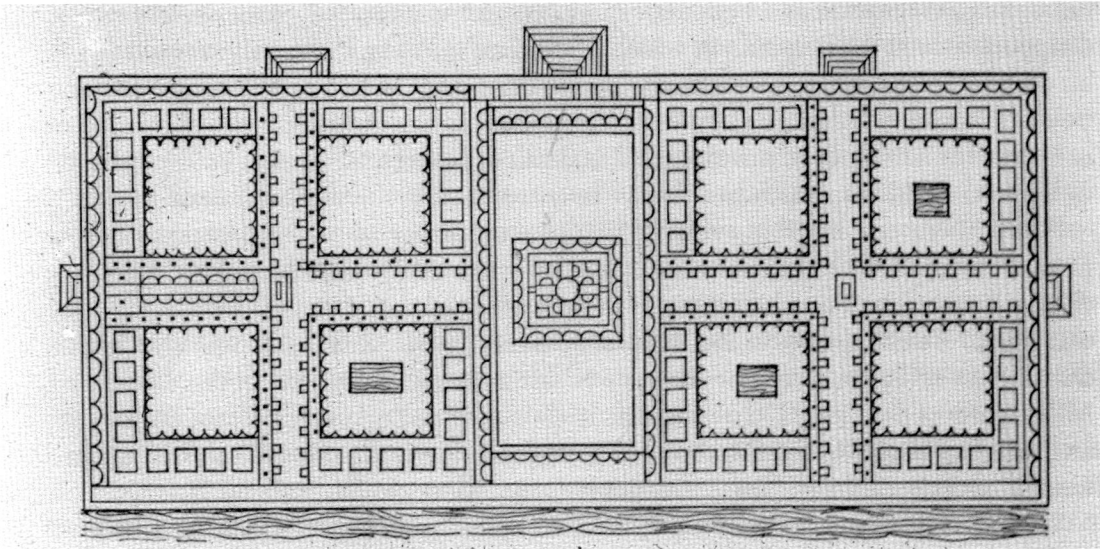

planning newly being elaborated in Renaissance Italy. The severe geometric order of the plan brings to mind Alberti's discussion of the connected nature of military and ecclesiastical activity. "But what of the priest?" he asks. "For him there is not only the temple but also that which serves him as a military camp; since it is the priest, and those under him in charge of administering the sacraments, who must wage that fierce and arduous war [. . .] of virtue against vice."[55] Several clues point to the hand of one of the earliest authors of Renaissance architectural theory, the Florentine Antonio Averlino: a medallist and goldsmith, "the most fantastic of fifteenth-century architects," in James Ackerman's words, who called himself Filarete, "lover of virtue."[56] No trace of Filarete's direct involvement with the design of Mehmed's complex remains, and he is not one of the architects whose names are associated with the construction of the building. The striking similarity between the plan of the Ospedale Maggiore he designed for Count Sforza of Milan and that of Mehmed's complex, on the other hand, has been noted.[57] Construction of the Ospedale Maggiore, which featured a large plaza centered on a church, and eight courtyard structures symmetrically flanking the plaza to house the hospital buildings, was begun in 1456 (figs. 39, 40). While this plan is noticeably similar to that of the Istanbul complex, the precepts of its layout, a piazza centered on a church and surrounded by courtyard structures, are to be found in other parts of Filarete's Sforzinda.[58]

Filarete planned a trip to Constantinople in 1465, and the last record of him before he mysteriously vanished is a letter of introduction written by a friend, the Hellenophile humanist Francesco Filelfo, to George Amirutzes, informing the latter of the architect's plan to make a visit to the city. Julian Raby has suggested that since the architect was in dire straits and in need of patronage at the time Filelfo wrote his letter of introduction (which does praise Filarete's talents as an artist), the reason for the planned trip to the Ottoman capital might have been the possibility of courtly patronage.[59] It has been argued that Filarete was involved in constructions in the city during this period: Marcell Restle, noting the similarity between the plans of the Ospedale Maggiore and Mehmed's complex, searched for Italian units of measurement in the dimensions of the latter and found them in the ground plans of the madrasas. He concluded that the plan of the complex might in part be a product of Filarete's personal participation in the project.[60] Julian Raby has noted that the personal supervision of the Florentine architect is not plausible, since the date of the planned visit postdates the beginning of the construction of the complex. Filarete may or may not have set foot in Constantinople during the construction of the New Mosque complex; although construction of the mosque started in 1463 and Filarete disappeared for good after 1465, planning and construction of the mosque's dependencies may have started later. But then, personal visits were not Mehmed's only means of access to European artists: throughout his career he used his Greek and Italian contacts, as well as Ottoman ambassadors to the Italian states, not only

to invite Italian artists and architects to work for him but also to acquire maps, prints, and manuscripts.[61] Preserved at the Topkapı Palace Archives, several fifteenth-century architectural plans that exhibit a conflation of Western and Islamic conventions of architectural drawing constitute palpable proof of relations between Ottoman and European (most probably Italian) architects during this period. One of these, a plan for a centrally organized sultanic mosque featuring a half dome on the qibla side preceded by an arcaded courtyard might in fact be an experimental project for the New Mosque (fig. 41).[62]

With the sources at hand, it is not possible to reconstruct the details of Filarete's (or any other Italian architect's) involvement in the design and the construction of the complex. What is significant about this involvement is the choice of a design, for the primary public monument of Ottoman Constantinople, that reflected a new way of conceptualizing the city. Central to the first two treatises on architecture written in the fifteenth century, those of Alberti and Filarete, is the city as an entity to be conceived and built as a whole. To both authors, political, social, and moral order bear directly on city form, which is in turn integral to architectural design.[63] Alberti's cities changed shape and content according to the character of the polity governing them; he suggested particular urban configurations to correspond to republican rule, the rule of a king, and that of a tyrant.[64] Similarly, Filarete created his Sforzinda solely to accommodate the political absolutism of Francesco Sforza of Milan. The representation of a central power through a hierarchical allotment of space to different segments of society was tightly worked into the layout of Filarete's Sforzinda and its individual buildings.

Given the nature of Mehmed's interest in contemporary Italy, as the object of his intellectual curiosity and the ultimate aim of his imperial ambitions, the appeal of an ideal city designed for a Lombard monarch could not have been due solely to the orderliness of the plan or Western "influence."[65] The hierarchized space that informed the tight geometry of Sforzinda and its ensembles resonated closely with the Ottoman ruler's conception of his capital city (and of the Ottoman polity at large). Filarete's plan was used in order to (and only as far as) it accommodated the absolutist aims of the Ottoman ruler.

John Onians has suggested that Francesco Filelfo, the humanist educated in Constantinople and related by marriage to Manuel Chrysoloras, was the main inspiration behind Filarete's treatise and his main provider of information on (ancient) Greek architecture and urbanism. Onians argues that Filelfo's desire to create a new Byzantium, in the face of the loss of the city to the barbarians, is visible in Filarete's preoccupation with the design and construction of Sforzinda.[66] Could it be that Filelfo, whose ambivalent attitude toward the new rulers of Byzantium has been captured in his correspondence, had a hand in carrying back to the city what had been formulated by his architect friend on the basis of Filelfo's particularly Constantinopolitan interpretation of "Greek" architecture and urbanism, to be used in a new Constantinople? Although his circle of contacts in the Ottoman, Greek, and Italian worlds does make this plausible, whether Filelfo did have a hand in the transportation of an Italian design (or designs) to Constantinople will have to remain, for the present, a matter of conjecture. Nevertheless, the layout of Mehmed's complex is in itself testimony to the interconnectedness of the fifteenth-century Italian and Ottoman worlds. The network of Ottoman, Greek, and Italian names associated with Mehmed's project, as much as the design itself, attests to the

movement of individuals, objects, and ideas across boundaries. Such movement in part owed to the vicissitudes of the fall of Byzantium and the rise of Ottoman power in its stead. But simultaneously, shared cultural and political dispositions in the Ottoman and Italian worlds rendered meaningful the cultural products that ostensibly belonged to the world of the other.

Using a scheme informed by the architectural language of authority and power, the New Complex set Mehmed's redefinition of

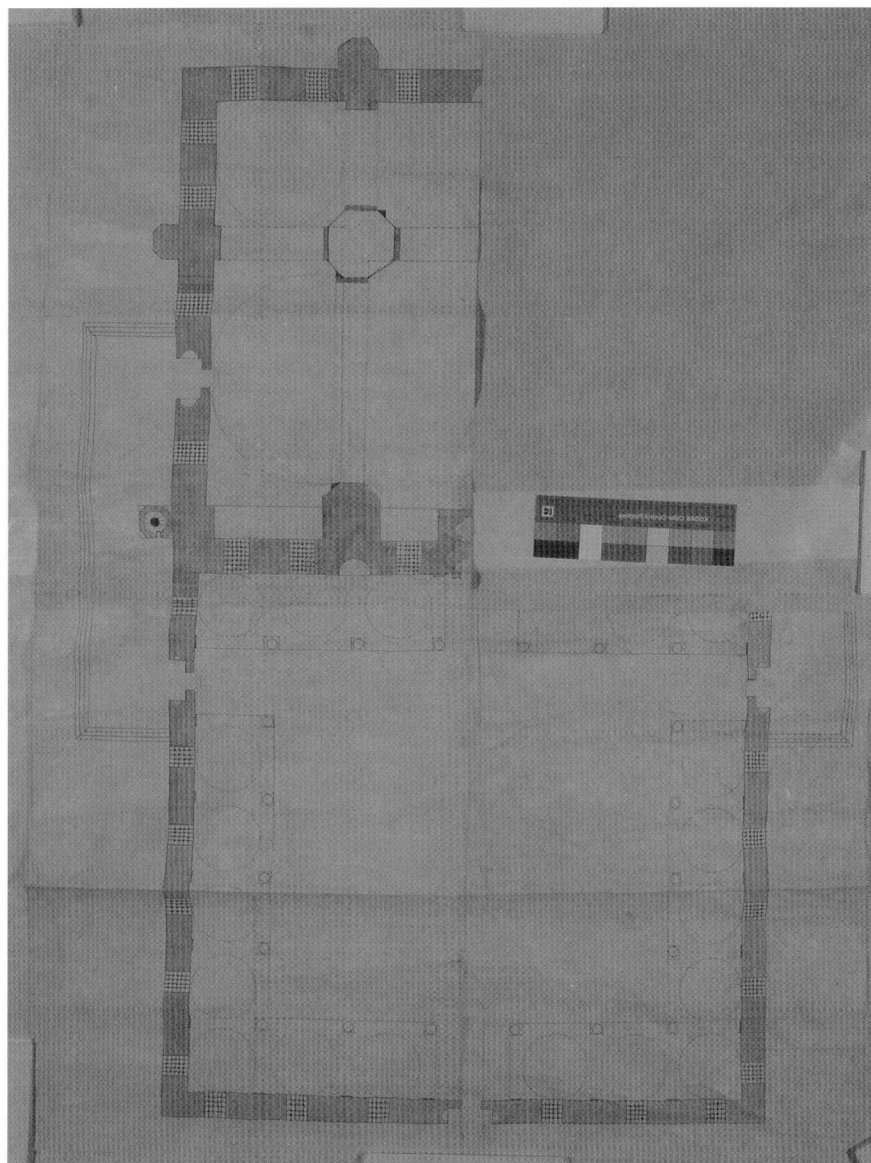

FIGURE 41
Fragment of a plan for an imperial mosque. Topkapı Palace Archives, E 9495-8.

religious hierarchies in stone. Lacking the convent for Sufi dervishes that was attached to all prior mosques in sultans' complexes, and isolated from its dependencies, the mosque had an iconic presence at the summit of the hill (fig. 42). The eight madrasas placed in rows of four on opposite sides of the plaza housed the highest-ranking religious schools within the Ottoman realm. This layout represented the newly designed hierarchy of the religious establishment within the newly reconfigured state: the religious elite, now part of the administrative hierarchy, were imbued with the power of the centralized state while simultaneously subordinated to the absolute authority of the sultan.[67] The ruler's religious space no longer accommodated the once celebrated Sufi dervishes. Instead of a convent, the complex included a hospice, which, according to the waqfiyya, would provide accommodation to

FIGURE 42
Mosque of Mehmed II, detail from the panorama of Istanbul by Melchior Lorichs, 1559, 1561–62. By permission of Leiden University Library.

SVL.^AN MEHEMED SECONDO

travelers and prestigious guests rather than house Sufi dervishes.

At the center of the Renaissance-style plaza, the mosque itself also exhibited a merging of traditions. Although it was severely damaged during the earthquake of 1766, its architecture has largely been reconstructed on the basis of the remaining sections and earlier visual and narrative sources.[68] Built of ashlar masonry on a platform that raised it above the level of the central plaza, the building was reached by marble staircases that led to its three public gates and the sultan's private entrance. The prayer hall, a laterally placed rectangle, followed a courtyard of the same size and shape. The dome covering it, twenty-six meters in width and forty-four meters in height, was raised over tympanum arches and buttressed by a half dome on the qibla side; three smaller domes covered the side spaces. Twin minarets, placed at opposite ends of the wall between the prayer hall and the courtyard, marked the building

as a sultanic monument. To the east, a private entrance provided direct access to the royal tribune, placed in the southeastern corner of the prayer hall (fig. 43).

With a large hemispherical dome covering the prayer hall, a ceremonial paved courtyard preceding it, and multiple minarets, the design of Mehmed's mosque was based on the Üç Şerefeli in Edirne built by Murad II some decades earlier (figs. 44, 45, 46). With its scale and proportions, its monumental dome and stone-covered courtyard, Murad's mosque was in turn the product of Ottoman encounters with the classical architecture of the Mediterranean, a tradition that had been absorbed into Ottoman architectural practices the previous century.[69] While following trends that had shaped the Edirne monument, the mosque in Istanbul simultaneously appropriated and revived the architecture of the Hagia Sophia, the primary imperial and religious symbol of the city, as can be observed most clearly in its

FIGURE 44
Üç Şerefeli Mosque, Edirne,
exterior.

superstructure (figs. 5, 47, 48, 49). The window-
pierced tympanum arches carrying the main
dome, and the half dome above the qibla wall,
which audaciously raised the already daringly
wide dome above the level of the walls, were
direct references to the architecture of the city's
main church. The emulation of the vaulting
structure of the Byzantine building marked a
definitive shift in the monumental expression
of Ottoman religious architecture: variations
on the Hagia Sophia theme were to remain cen-

tral to this school of architecture through the
following centuries.[70]

The later history of the building and the fate
of its architect, too, demonstrate how important to the design of the New Mosque emulation of Hagia Sophia was. It has been noted that
in scale and design the building was beyond
the means and skills of the Ottoman architectural establishment of the time. Although it did
not reach the heights of the Hagia Sophia, as
desired by the patron, the building was nonetheless unstable. It suffered from structural
problems prior to its final collapse during the
earthquake of 1766.[71] The architect Sinan, a
freed slave who, judging by his fairly large religious foundation near the New Complex, once
enjoyed the favors of the sultan, was executed
shortly after the completion of the mosque.
While chroniclers differ on the precise time
of and reason for his execution, the overriding theme in all sources is that the architect
attracted such wrath because he failed to fulfill
the patron's desire to match the Byzantine
monument in height and majesty.[72]

The courtyard, marked by a marble fountain and surrounded by a domed arcade, formally connected the New Mosque at once to
the Justinianic churches of Byzantium and
to the Üç Şerefeli in Edirne, the first Ottoman sultanic mosque to feature a ceremonial
courtyard. To its contemporaries, the fountain
symbolized *kawthar,* the source of water in
paradise to which allusion was also made in
the architecture of Hagia Sophia.[73] The four
cypresses that surrounded it demonstrate
how deliberate the emulation of the Byzantine
monument was: Şemsüddin Karamani, in
his translation of the *Patria,* wrote that eight
cypresses once surrounded the fountain in the
Hagia Sophia atrium; at the time when he was
writing, in 1480, two cypresses still adorned

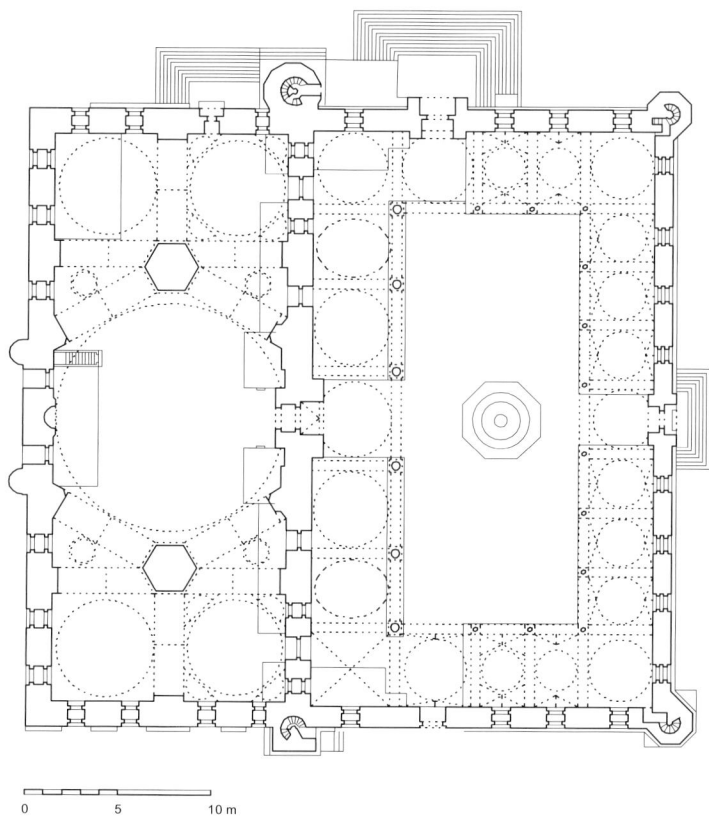

the courtyard.[74] Reproducing the atrium with cypresses in the city's new religious monument, the Ottomans were not only referring to the Justinianic church but also drawing on symbolism that had long imbued the royal monuments of the Near East with paradisal associations.

The royal entrance at the southeastern corner of the New Mosque and the sultan's elevated tribune decorated with gold and silverwork were novelties in the architecture of the Ottoman congregational mosque, marking a radical change in the Ottoman style of rulership, though such spaces had been integrated into major religious monuments of political import from early on. Hagia Sophia and the Great Mosque of Damascus, loci of Christian and Islamic polities of the early medieval Mediterranean world, both featured imperial enclosures. Mehmed I's convent-masjid in Bursa (1412–19),

an ambitious project commemorating the reconciliation of the Ottoman state following a period of interregnum, featured a lavishly decorated royal gallery above its entrance. The royal entry and tribune of the New Mosque were conceptually linked to such monuments and were perhaps inspired by Byzantine and early Ottoman models. Their incorporation into the sultan's mosque, however, appears more striking given the style of Mehmed's public appearances in the earlier part of his reign. According to Georgius de Hungaria, a captive in Istanbul in the 1450s, the sultan, on arriving at mosque, would conduct Friday prayer accompanied only by two pages and stood with the congregation; no spatial arrangement separated him from others and symbolized his status.[75] Spatial segregation, from the public as well as from his higher-ranking subjects, was a practice that

FIGURE 45
Üç Şerefeli Mosque, Edirne, plan.

FIGURE 46
Üç Şerefeli Mosque, Edirne, section.

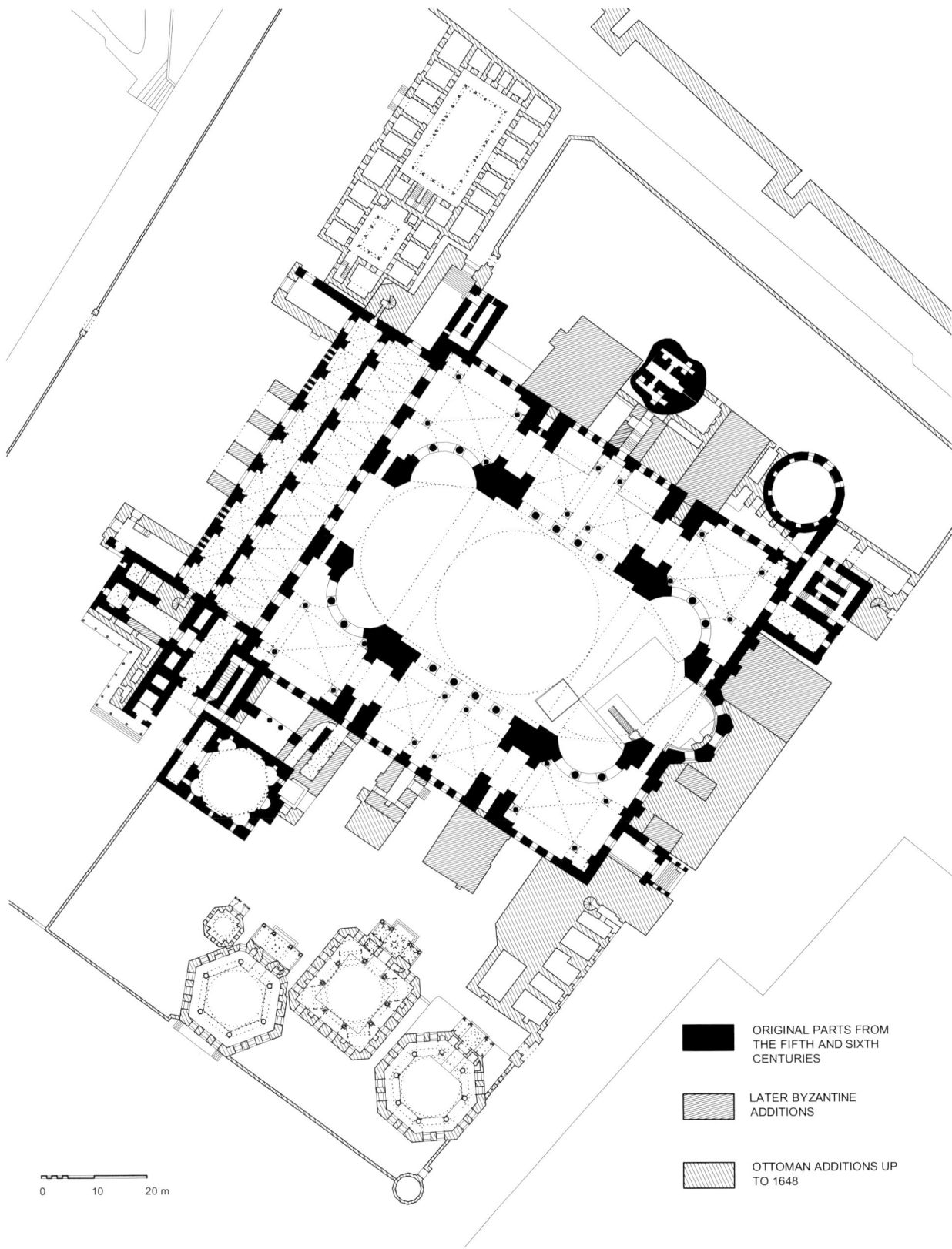

ORIGINAL PARTS FROM
THE FIFTH AND SIXTH
CENTURIES

LATER BYZANTINE
ADDITIONS

OTTOMAN ADDITIONS UP
TO 1648

0   10   20 m

characterized the later decades of Mehmed's rule. Notions of royal seclusion, underlining the sacredness of the monarch's person, had shaped the layout of the New Palace; likewise, they were to mark the architecture of the New Mosque.[76] Like other significant aspects of the architecture of the New Mosque, the royal entrance and the royal tribune remained integral elements of subsequent sultanic mosques.

Descriptions of the building before its destruction in 1766 suggest that decoration was concentrated in particular areas of the interior. Calligraphic and decorative roundels embellished the dome; lamps and ostrich eggs were suspended from golden chains. The floral ornaments and the muqarnas hood of the mihrab, the pure white marble of the minbar, and the calligraphic ornament on the wooden window shutters received the praise of contemporary and later commentators. Calligraphic panels of cuerda seca tiles within the window arches of the portico, floral and calligraphic marble engravings on the courtyard walls and Çorba Gate, are among the few remnants of the original decorative program of the building (figs. 50, 51).[77]

Situated behind the qibla wall of the mosque, the mausolea of Mehmed and his consort Gülbahar Hatun extended the longitudinal axis running through the center of the plaza southeastward.[78] Built by Bayezid II for his parents, most probably following the will of Mehmed, the funerary structures are located in an enclosed garden whose walls reproduced the dimensions of the mosque. It is not possible to know whether the enclosure housing the mausolea was conceived by the builder of the New Mosque or his son. Reaching the southeastern border of the outer courtyard, however, the funerary garden behind the mosque altered the main concept of design, that of the freestanding monument at the center of a paved plaza.

The eight colleges flanking the central plaza on two sides were built according to the conventions of the madrasa developed earlier in the Ottoman tradition. Each comprised a classroom, placed at the narrow end of a rectangular courtyard, and nineteen rooms for the students, lined along the remaining three sides. The red mortar, composite masonry of stone and brick, cut stone piers instead of marble columns to carry the courtyard arcades, and decorative brickwork over the window arches contrast with the white ashlar and marble of the mosque, lending the buildings something

FIGURE 47 (*opposite*)
Hagia Sophia, plan.

FIGURE 48
Hagia Sophia, section.

FIGURE 49
Mosque of Mehmed II, hypothetical section.

FIGURE 50
Mosque of Mehmed II,
calligraphic panel in entrance
portico.

FIGURE 51
Mehmed II complex, the Çorba
Gate.

foundation lay the remaining buildings of the complex. The hospice, public kitchen, and stables formed a compound within a walled enclosure.[80] The hospice, a courtyard structure with a large iwan and numerous guest rooms, was the most lavishly built part of this compound, exhibiting precious building materials and workmanship more like the architecture of the mosque than that of the other dependencies (figs. 53, 54). It was the model for other such hospices built as part of royal and dynastic foundations through the later Ottoman centuries. Little remains of the kitchen and the stables: of the kitchen, only an iwan and two flanking rooms are extant. The stables, no longer standing, consisted of a vaulted hall to the southwest of the courtyard. The hospital, also now demolished, was located in another walled enclosure at the eastern corner of the complex, across from the hospice–public kitchen compound. The waqfiyya mentions a bath near the complex; there can be little doubt that this was the Çukur Hamam situated to the west of the hospital, one of the monumental double baths of fifteenth-century Istanbul, its layout known to us only through drawings made by Charles Texier in the early nineteenth century (figs. 55, 56).

The New Complex marked a turning point in Ottoman religious architecture. Its site, its unprecedented scale, its architecture, the range of functions it encompassed, and its relation to both the Ottoman and the Byzantine past clearly announced the imperial claims of the state that now ruled from Constantinople. The foundation inscription of the mosque, too, announced the meaning of the complex as a monument to the conquest and to the dynasty (fig. 57). Inscribed in three panels, one above and one at each side of the portal to the prayer hall, it read:

of the architectural idiom of contemporary and earlier Bursa (figs. 36, 52). The contrast in the materials and architectural decoration between the mosque and its dependencies further visualized the hierarchical relationship between the institutions that were housed in them. Behind the madrasas on each side eight *tetimme,* or preparatory madrasas for lower-ranking students, possibly built of lesser materials, were paired with the main madrasas.[79]

To the southeast of the plaza/outer courtyard housing the mosque-madrasa core of the

> Praise be to God, the all-mighty and the
> all-knowing, the building of this Friday

FIGURE 52
Mehmed II complex, madrasa
courtyard.

FIGURE 53
Mehmed II complex, hospice
courtyard.

FIGURE 54
Mehmed II complex, column
within the hospice arcade.

of Orhan son of Osman; may the support of
God and his favors not cease, and may his
Sublime Porte never be without sons and
followers and auxiliaries, and may God pour
forth his forgiveness to his ancestors and
place them in the highest chambers of paradise. It is my prayer that God's mercy be on
his slave. He said with certainty in the holy
month of *Rajab* in the year 875, eight hundred and seventy-five, and its beginning was
in the *Jumādā'l-āḥir* of the year 868, eight
hundred and sixty-eight.

Above the first of these three panels, and thus
at its very beginning, is another, smaller plate
bearing the prophet's well-known saying on the
conquest of Constantinople: "They will conquer Kostantiniyye. Hail to the prince and the
army to whom this is given."[81]

The conquest, the exaltation of the city and
of its conqueror, and the restoration of knowledge and education in the city are the main
themes of the mosque's foundation inscription
and the hadith that introduces it. At the time,
this was the longest inscription to mark an
Ottoman royal foundation; its length and clear
thematic focus highlight the centrality of these
themes and the concern for communicating
them.[82] The intent of the project is made clear
at the entrance to the mosque: it is a foundation
for learning and knowledge, meant to make
visible in the Ottoman domains the works of
the ruling dynasty. The inclusion of Mehmed's
ancestors in his title and of his descendants and
his household in the prayer following it underscores the historicity of the House of Osman,
rendering the dynasty part of the act of conquest. This invocation may simultaneously be
another allusion to the Holy Apostles, for the
dynastic symbolism of the Byzantine monument was clearly not lost on Mehmed. His
interest in the sarcophagi housed in the church,

mosque, which brings life and restores
knowledge and learning, is completed, in
order that the pious foundations of the
House of Osman become visible in their
domains. And he is the greatest sultan
and the most magnificent *ḥāḳān;* he conquered with his sword this city whose like
has not been created, whose match has not
been built by the hands of the slaves [of
God], and which had not been conquered
by caliphs and sultans and emirs; he spent
every effort in the achievement of this goal.
And he is Sultan Mehmed Khan son of
Sultan Murad son of Sultan Mehmed son
of Sultan Bayezid son of Sultan Murad son

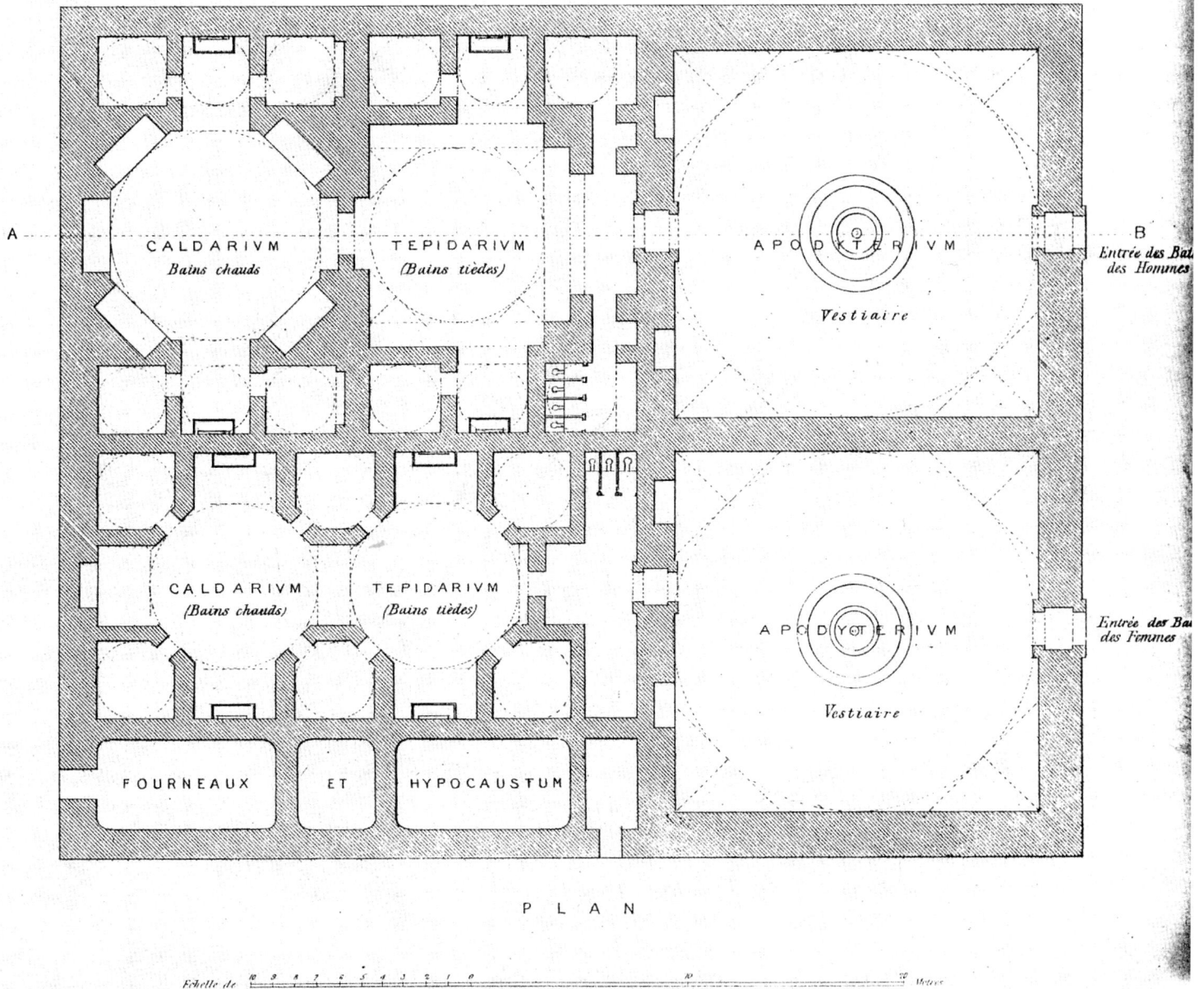

Text in the plan:

CALDARIVM
Bains chauds

TEPIDARIVM
(Bains tièdes)

APODYTERIVM

Vestiaire

Entrée des Bai...
des Hommes

CALDARIVM
(Bains chauds)

TEPIDARIVM
(Bains tièdes)

APODYTERIVM

Vestiaire

Entrée des Bai...
des Femmes

FOURNEAUX   ET   HYPOCAUSTUM

PLAN

Echelle de ... Metres

which were transferred to his new palace, shows Mehmed's awareness of the significance of the Holy Apostles as the dynastic mausoleum of Byzantium.[83]

Representations of the New Mosque

A public manifestation of a newly articulated imperial vision, Mehmed's New Mosque was the only building in fifteenth-century Istanbul to attract equal degrees of admiration and contempt from its contemporaries, from those who were differently positioned toward and differently affected by the new configuration of the Ottoman polity and by the transformations in the Ottoman political and cultural realm at large. The representations of the building

FIGURE 55
Mehmed II complex, the double bath (Çukur Hamam), plan (from Texier and Pullan, *L'architecture byzantine*, 1864).

FIGURE 56
Mehmed II complex, the
double bath (Çukur Hamam),
section (from Texier and Pullan,
L'architecture byzantine, 1864).

BAINS DE MAHOMET 2 À CONSTANTINOPLE.

COUPE SUR LA LIGNE A B.

complex in contemporary chronicles and literary works, and the narratives of its construction originating from different segments of Ottoman society, shed as much light on the architectural culture of the period as they do on its political dynamics. Authors close to court circles, many of them high-ranking court officials, highly praised Mehmed's buildings, dwelling on the beauty of the mosque, the importance of its educational function, and the extensive services it provided to the ulema, to travelers, and to the people of the city. These texts make it clear that the mosque's architectural allusion to the Hagia Sophia and its particular relationship to the Holy Apostles were intended and understood as such. The chronicles of Kritovoulos and Mu'ali, dedicated to Mehmed II in the 1470s, are among the earliest of these texts. Mu'ali, in the section of his *Hünkārnāme* entitled "Ṣaḥn der beyān-ı Ayaṣofya" (Section on the Description of Hagia Sophia), praises the wealth and the beauty of the building and writes that there is no likeness of it in the world. But in that same section he expends more words on the New Mosque than on the Byzantine monument. His description of the Hagia Sophia includes a comparison—

But the imaret of the shah is grander than it
They laid down an exalted building

—and a reference to the demolition of the Holy Apostles:

Before this they got rid of the mysteries
They built it on the foundation of Islam
Its gate and its ground and its space is vast
Thank God, after all this is a mosque.[84]

Kritovoulos, as already noted, underlines the sultan's ambition of creating a mosque more monumental than the Hagia Sophia and perhaps the Holy Apostles: he orders the construction of "a mosque which in height, beauty, and size should vie with the largest and finest of the temples already existing there."[85] Tursun Beg, writing his *Tārīḫ-i Ebū'l-Fetḥ* in the last years of the fifteenth century, notes that the New Mosque was built "in the likeness of Hagia Sophia." He explains that apart from encompassing all the arts of the latter, it was built according to the latest developments in a fresh new idiom and with immeasurable beauty, its miraculous splendor (clearly) visible.[86] Kemalpaşazade, following his account of Mehmed's restoration of the Hagia Sophia, writes: "In one part of the city he built a new mosque that was comparable to it in size and majesty and, as a likeness, matched it."[87]

With or without references to the Hagia Sophia, the height of the building is a recurring motif in this group of sources, a metaphor for its heavenly qualities as well as an indirect allusion to its rivalry with the Byzantine monument. Taci-zade Ca'fer Çelebi (d. 1514), the early-sixteenth-century state official and poet who devoted a long section of his *Heveşnāme* to the New Complex, writes:

> Its dome rose to the highest point of the heavens
> It touched the eye of the moon and the sun
> Growing in stature that eminent one of the times
> Its crown reached the roof of the heavens.[88]

İdris Bidlisi, who had arrived at the Ottoman capital from the Akkoyunlu court to serve in the military and to write his *Heşt behişt* (Eight Paradises, referring to the reigns of the eight Ottoman sultans from Osman to Bayezid II) in Persian for Bayezid II, was another author to dwell at length on Mehmed's complex. The lofty mosque, located in an elevated part of the city, he writes, was artfully built with wondrous architectural crafts. Referring to the tympanum arches that held the main dome, he notes that the arches on the two sides of the enclosure resembled the lesser spheres of the heavens visible from the ninth sphere. The arches of the iwans, in the midst of the heavens, were like the elevated rings of the spheres' luminous poles.[89]

Bidlisi's account stands apart from other writings on the mosque with its strong emphasis on the religious symbolism of the architecture.[90] It should be remembered that the *Heşt*

FIGURE 57
Mosque of Mehmed II, portal and foundation inscription.

behişt was commissioned by Bayezid II, who in his strong religious orientation differed considerably from his father. Like Ca'fer Çelebi, Bidlisi alludes to the age-old symbolism of the sanctuary dome as the dome of heaven. The height of the mosque, its sound construction with stone, marble, and granite, and its heavenly dome were to him metaphors for its strong foundation on Islam: "The arches of that enclosure have the proportions of the dome of heaven, and they have been built in the circumference of the zones of the zodiac. Its different levels, from the ground to the belvederes of the sky, are connected with solid lead; like the edifice of the faith of the community of the sincere, they were laid down and constructed firmly and solidly. And that heavenlike dome revolves side by side with Saturn, like the twin stars of Gemini."[91] The courtyard of the mosque, with its precious and colorful marble and granite columns, was also strongly and firmly built. With their resplendent and lustrous surfaces and their colors blossoming like spring flowers, these columns reminded Bidlisi of *cām-ı cihān,* the mythical mirror that reflected the world. They were the eyes of that place of faith; in them the faces of angels were visible. Describing the minarets, Bidlisi continues to imbue the mosque with religious symbolism. He likens the minarets of ashlar masonry to two candles that rose on the sides of the lofty dome. Without doubt, they were a metaphor for a pair of white flags of the shariʿa rising high in the dome of Islam; each was crowned with a crescent symbolizing the Light Verse (Nur [XXIV:35]). The four cypresses planted around the marble fountain of the courtyard were to Bidlisi four believers standing for prayer, four young angels assembling in that auspicious courtyard under the blue dome of heaven, and four green banners of Islam.

Like his contemporaries, Bidlisi makes no note of the Italian inspiration in the strict axial geometry of the complex and its use of a plaza in accord with the precepts of ideal Renaissance planning. He does nonetheless note the strict geometry in the layout of the complex: "Straddling the [central mosque/garden] enclosure

is a square measuring about a hundred cubits, and around it the madrasas are arranged in a geometric order; they are adjacent to each other, and four are across from the other four." Describing the madrasas, he returns to paradisal analogies, as realized in the larger domes of the classrooms and the smaller ones of the students' rooms, the rosy perfumes of their green courtyards. The eight madrasas were an allusion to *heşt behişt,* the eight levels of paradise mentioned in the Koran. Further down, he likens the high and lofty madrasas to the eight celestial spheres reaching the ninth sphere, the throne of God.[92]

The courtyard, with its marble fountain surrounded by cypresses, too was understood by most authors as a symbol of paradise, with its water source, *kawthar.* Bidlisi praises the pond artfully built with various multicolored stones, and the fountain at its center, with its *kawthar*-like eternal water. Caʿfer Çelebi writes of those who came to breathe the air of the paradise-like courtyard, with its beloved tall cypress trees, and to see its paradisal pond.[93]

As in the descriptions of the Hagia Sophia in the *Patria* of Constantinople, Persian and Ottoman translations of which were published in the last years of Mehmed's rule, the authors emphasize the use of precious building materials such as stone, marble, granite, and porphyry in Mehmed's mosque.[94] The masterful use of these materials was an important aspect of the monumentality of the building: they distinguished it from the surrounding buildings constructed with lesser materials and, through their sheer strength and durability, made it eternal. Sirozlu Saʿdi, after mentioning the sultan's mosque in an ode, alludes to the desire for perpetuity:

These imarets built of marble in this city
Will survive the day of judgment, although
the world is transitory.[95]

The strength and durability of the materials with which the mosque was built were not solely admirable qualities of the building itself. Rather, they signified the perpetuation of its builder's might and, later, of his memory. Bidlisi emphasizes the solidity of the mosque's architecture by directing attention to the use of stone, marble, and lead in its construction. In the introductory passages to his account of Mehmed's pious deeds, he elaborates on the two paths that made possible the sultan's stability in this transitory world and the continuity and perpetuity of his works (*āṣār*).[96] The first was the perpetuation of the self, which meant, Bidlisi explains, the strengthening of sultanic knowledge and the perpetuation of God's truths. The second path was the gain of rewards for good deeds and the efficacy of prayer through acts of piety. These two honorable masteries (*meleke-i kerīme*) would lead to the perpetuation of the self and of power (*'ömr ve devlet*). The continuous mention (by beneficiaries) of the sultan's good deeds would render his spiritual guidance and his favors eternal. The material strength and durability of his works would allow for the continuity of his good deeds; this would be his path to the perpetuation of his worldly power and also to divine benefaction.

While Bidlisi's account of the New Mosque emphasizes mostly the religious aspects of its symbolism and the political implications of the sultan's patronage, the writings of Mu'ali and Ca'fer Çelebi underline the spectacular aspects of the mosque's architecture. Mu'ali comments on the sultan's order for the decoration of the prayer hall and on the numerous craftsmen brought from Khurasan and elsewhere for this purpose, the painters and the calligraphers who rushed to finish the decoration.[97] After praising the loftiness of the heavenly dome, Ca'fer

Çelebi turns to the lavish decoration of the building in general:

> Its summit, its arches and arcades, are all
> ornamented
> Its gate and walls are ornate, its courtyard
> heart-attracting.

He describes the eye-dazzling brilliance of the roundels embellishing the dome and of the lamps that hung from it, the *ḫatāyī* and *rūmī* motifs adorning the window panes, the intricate patterns that completely cover the doors and windows. He praises the geometric ornaments (*girihkārī muḳarnes*) decorating the mihrab hood, the pure white marble of the minbar, and the wondrous gold and silver works of the royal tribune. Describing the mihrab area, he evokes the image of a beautiful garden. The calligraphy of the Koran manuscripts placed in front of the mihrab reminds him of the legendary calligrapher Ya'kut, and their illuminations resemble paradise-like gardens of roses and narcissi. The mihrab niche, too, is like a rose garden; the flanking candles are two young branches; the gold lamp hanging in front of it, an auspicious-looking narcissus.[98]

The paradisal associations of the building, the strength, durability, and value of its materials, and the artfulness of the articles and craftsmanship exhibited in its interior are tropes that shaped contemporary writing on the mosque. Directed at such conspicuous elements of the building as its dome, the courtyard, and the minarets, such focal points of the prayer hall as the mihrab, the minbar, and the royal tribune, they were in turn imbued with religious and royal significance.

These texts mark the emergence in Ottoman literature of a set of aesthetic and moral criteria with which religious monuments were evaluated.[99] They possibly drew on a medieval and Persianate (it should be remembered that two of the authors who wrote on the building, Muʻali and Bidlisi, hailed from the Iranian cultural sphere) understanding of architectural symbolism and aesthetics, but they nevertheless reflected the emerging architectural culture of the imperial capital. It is noteworthy that, with the exception of Bidlisi's description of the hospice, the dependencies of the mosque were not noted for formal qualities or the value of their materials and craftsmanship. Rather, they were esteemed only as the sultan's pious works and as educational and charitable institutions. This mirrors the architectural hierarchy of the complex, where the dependencies, located at the edges of the grand plaza, were built with lesser materials, in more modest dimensions, and, in all, were visibly secondary to the mosque. The differentiation between mosque and dependencies concretized notions of monumentality within the Ottoman cultural world. All the buildings of the complex were regarded the sultan's pious deeds and, as Bidlisi noted, were essential to the continuation of his worldly power and for securing his otherwordly existence. But the mosque, with the magnificence of its architecture and through its eye-dazzling decoration, collected in itself the attributes of a royal building.

In contrast to such authors as Muʻali, Kritovoulos, Tursun, and Bidlisi, who wrote for the ruling elite, Aşıkpaşazade, the dervish whose sympathies fluctuated between his own milieu and that of the sultans, appears completely uninterested in spectacular aspects of architecture. Nothing on the formal qualities of the buildings is to be found in his summary account of the sultan's works (*āṣār*) in his *Chronicles of the House of Osman*.[100] Aşıkpaşazade commends Mehmed for the abundance of his pious deeds (*ḫayr* and *ṣadaḳa*, charity and almsgiving): for building mosques, madrasas, and imarets in every city he conquered and, in particular, for building, when he conquered Istanbul, the "eight large madrasas with the large mosque in their middle and a large soup kitchen and a large hospital across from them." He praises the sultan for building other mosques and madrasas in Istanbul and for giving alms to the poor of all cities in his domain. Further down in his history, however, Aşıkpaşazade assumes a markedly critical tone:

Question: Hey dervish! This dynasty of the Ottomans has built large madrasas and large imarets; what is their desire, to make their domains prosperous, or to achieve prosperity in the afterlife?

Answer: To make prosperous the imarets of the afterlife.

Following this imagined dialogue is a discourse on the architectural patronage of sultans and their viziers, on the abuses of sultanic endowments by their supervisors, and on moneys that would find their way to the royal treasury through the latter's misconduct. The passage ends with a reiteration of the statement above: the pious deeds of the sultans were indeed for the hereafter.[101]

Artless and unblessed was Mehmed's monument in the eyes of its other audiences. If Aşıkpaşazade seemed at once appreciative of the sultan's undertaking and somewhat unconvinced of its piousness, the anonymous chronicles of the House of Osman, rooted in the margins of the Ottoman social spectrum as conceived by Mehmed, were much clearer in their stance toward this first major public monument of the imperial capital: they showed no trace of appreciation or sympathy for the sultan's grand architectural statement.[102] That the New Mosque announced, with unquestionable clarity, the marginalization of the ghazi-dervish segment of society (until the conquest of Constantinople a primary component of the Ottoman polity) is nowhere more apparent than in the chronicles' accounts of the building's construction.[103] Significantly, comments on Mehmed's mosque are found not at the end of the section on Mehmed's rule, as part of his *āṣār* (as was the case in Aşıkpaşazade and as would become the norm in later Ottoman chronicles), but within the section on the ancient history of Constantinople and Hagia Sophia. Here, Mehmed's mosque is not treated independently but within the context of, and in comparison to, the construction of Hagia Sophia by Justinian. Mehmed and his mosque suffer through this comparison. After describing the gifts given to the architect by the ruler who built Hagia Sophia, the author writes: "At that time builders were held in respect; in our times such respect and gifts are unheard-of." Further down he laments the fate of the architect. That "the architect Sinan, who had built the New Mosque and the eight madrasas and the soup kitchen and the hospital," should have been imprisoned and beaten to death was the surest sign of the utter lack of appreciation for masters and craftsmen.[104] The sultan's injustice and oppression are in fact the main themes of this account of the construction. In the idealized era when Hagia Sophia was constructed, "buildings were not constructed with oppression [*ẓulm*]. All [workers] were paid wages." "In the present time," on the other hand, those craftsmen and workers who toiled on constructions were forcibly deported from their hometowns and underpaid for their work. Mehmed's mosque consumed huge sums: "Only God knows what was spent on the transportation [of

the columns]," wrote the author; "and who can describe all that has been used up for the New Mosque in Istanbul?" What was "used up" was the unjustly collected taxes from the provinces, while not a penny was spent from the treasury. To the author, constructing a building in this manner, through oppression and with unjustly levied monies, was a deed impious and sinful: "Is it correct to expect God's reward for a building constructed in this way? Let us put aside the prospect of a good deed; rather, this is sinful and is nothing but impious."[105] The chronicles thus provide a rare insight into the reception of the building by a segment of society that deemed illegitimate the ruler's very act of legitimization.

The authors' perceptions of the building's beauty and artfulness (or lack thereof) were informed by their overall attitude toward the enterprise as a political and a pious act. This is best illustrated by comments on the formal properties of the building by the author of the anonymous chronicles. The architect, craftsmen, and workers whose mistreatment by Mehmed had earned his sympathies were not spared his critical remarks when he turned his attention from the patron to the building. Against the mastery and skillfulness of the architect and the craftsmen who built Hagia Sophia, and against the masterful organization of its work site, he presented a picture of numerous failures: The entirety of Hagia Sophia went up with great dispatch, even though every single stone used in the building was brought from a different clime, whereas the transportation of just two columns of the New Mosque dragged on and on. Far from reaching the highest spheres of the heavens, the building remained low: experts had declared the shortening of the columns a mistake.[106] A version of Oruç Beg's chronicle dating to ca. 1497, too, turned to the themes of skill and craftsmanship.[107] The precious and variegated columns and marbles of the mosque, which were the subject of so much praise by authors closer to the center of power and had been described as the eyes of the building and as mirrors of the world, seemed to this author to be lacking in sheen: they were the work of unskilled and ignorant craftsmen who did not know how to shape and polish stone properly. By impugning the craftsmanship of the complex, these authors by implication impugned the character of its patron. "An emperor who built badly did not commit merely an architectural error," writes Richard Sennet, "he broke his most important bond to the people."[108]

A shared architectural sensibility bore on the aesthetic judgments of authors from different segments of fifteenth- and early-sixteenth-century Ottoman society concerning Mehmed II's mosque complex. Touching upon similar themes, such as the height of the building, the value of its materials, the quality of its craftsmanship, they nonetheless produced radically contrasting evaluations of the monument. In their appraisals of the building, colored by political and cultural attitudes and dispositions, aesthetic judgments commingled with political and moral judgments.

These contrasting and competing images of the building were as much a product of this period of profound transformations as the building itself. Its celebration as a pious deed and a work of art and, alternatively, its condemnation as a sign of impiety artlessly constructed competed through the turn of the sixteenth century. Once the emerging Ottoman polity ceased to be a matter of debate, through the appeasement by Bayezid II of those opposed to it and through the final resolution, during the middle decades of the sixteenth century, of the tension between the builders of the imperial state and those against it, the building

that embodied and represented the new order, too, ceased to be a subject of criticism. Voices unsympathetic to Mehmed's act of patronage and unappreciative of the arts it encompassed were not to be heard in the later decades of the sixteenth century.

THE COMPLEX AND THE CITY

In terms of its elevation and its relationship to the urban fabric, the complex in Istanbul was far removed from its possible sibling in Milan. The Ospedale Maggiore, its monumental staircases aligned with the main axes of the plaza and the church that stood at its center, was planned to present finely sculpted and articulated façades to its surroundings (fig. 40). The New Mosque complex in Istanbul presented a walled precinct with a few unassuming entrances. The radical difference between these fronts is indicative of contrasting choices and attitudes concerning urban form in the Italian and Ottoman realms.

The Istanbul complex imposed strict geometry on the edges of the surrounding urban fabric. Built on vaulted substructures, the outer courtyard could be reached by flights of stairs on the southwestern and northeastern sides. To the world immediately outside, it presented the back walls of the madrasas (whose protection from graffiti writers the endowment deed had secured)[109] and window-pierced walls enclosing the outer courtyard on the southeastern and northwestern sides. An engraving by Melchior Lorichs and the rendering on the Istanbul map within the *Hünernāme,* though neither includes a fully accurate representation of the building, capture these aspects of the New Mosque complex (figs. 58, 59). In the first image the buildings rise behind high enclosure walls dotted with high windows; in the second, the outer walls of the madrasas form a clear boundary separating the complex from the surrounding dense and irregular fabric.

FIGURE 58
Melchior Lorichs, Mehmed II
complex, woodcut, 1570.

FIGURE 59
Mehmed II complex and the
surrounding urban fabric, detail
from view of Istanbul, 1584–85,
in Lokman bin Seyyid Hüseyin,
Hünernāme, Topkapı Palace
Museum, H 1523, fols. 158v–159r
(fig. 120).

Its formal isolation notwithstanding, the
complex was not designed as an enclosed entity
segregated from the rest of the city. Rather, it
was conceived as the center of a newly developing urban district. Completely uninhabited
at the time construction started, the area surrounding the New Mosque was soon occupied
by residential quarters and commercial establishments: a number of deportee communities
were resettled around it, in residential quarters
whose names memorialized their places of
origin (map 3). By the end of the fifteenth
century Büyük (Larger) Karaman lay to the
south of the complex, Küçük (Smaller) Karaman to its north; in the vicinity was a quarter
named Gürci (Georgians). The construction of
the commercial complexes, the Sulṭān Pāzārı
(Royal Market) and the Sarrāchāne (Saddlemakers' Market), close to the old course of the
Mese and flanking the religious buildings on
their eastern and western sides suggests that

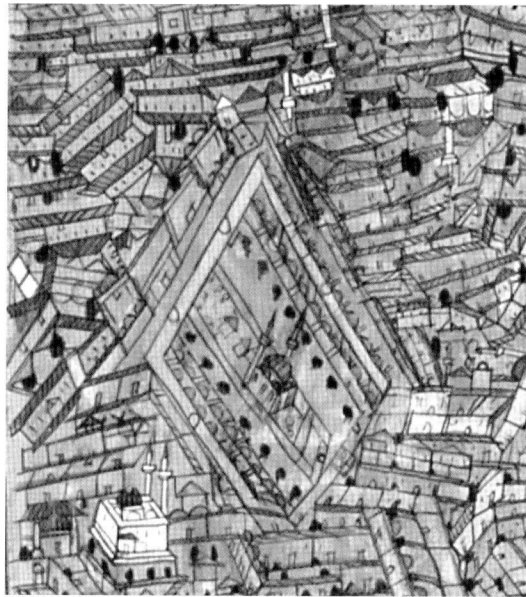

the New Complex was intended to function as a
congregational mosque at the center of the city
and simultaneously as an imaret at a distance
from the city center, juxtaposing the functions
of two different types of religious foundation

in earlier Ottoman practice. The foundation deed dating to 883/1478–79 lists 421 shops and thirty-two rooms in the markets around the New Complex: this was a sizable commercial establishment, spread out over an area about half the size of the markets surrounding the bedestan.[110] Angiolello described the markets, the bath, the mosque complex, and the janissary barracks as in a continuum, conveying the image of an urban district where a range of core buildings with a series of functions were surrounded by a commercial and residential fabric.[111]

Drawing together diverse architectural and urbanistic notions and practices, the building embodied contradictions best observed in the syncretistic relationship it had to its immediate environment, particularly to the ceremonial route on which it was located. While the Byzantine artery ran in a straight line to the south of the Holy Apostles to reach the Charisios Gate,[112] its Ottoman revitalization involved a shift in its course: it now had a slightly more northerly route, running through the outer courtyard/plaza of Mehmed's New Mosque. What remained of the northern branch of the Mese by the middle of the fifteenth century is not known with any degree of certainty. While Pierre Gilles refers to "the broad way that stretches along the top of the Promontory from the Church of St. Sophia to the Gate of Adrianople," his peculiar timeless prose, which often does not distinguish between ancient configurations and what was visible to him in the 1540s, makes it difficult to verify his statement.[113] The siting of several Ottoman public buildings dating from the later fifteenth century onward suggests that the straight course of the Mese was either lost by the second half of the fifteenth century or altered by new constructions, Mehmed's complex being the first.[114] Eighteenth- and

nineteenth-century maps show the northern branch of the Mese, then called the Divan Yolu, following a winding course, taking one directly into the outer courtyard of the New Complex from the Çorba Gate, then westward to the Edirne Gate on the land walls (fig. 60). An alternate route runs along the outer walls of the southwestern madrasas, turning northeastward at the western corner of the complex, then westward till it reaches one of the western entrances of the precinct, the Börekci Kapısı.

The passage of Istanbul's main ceremonial artery through the outer courtyard of the mosque would have compensated for the isolation of the monument induced by its architecture, as obligatory travel along this course would have increased the monument's visibility and rendered it more prominent within the city. The relation of the complex to its urban context is comparable to that of Byzantine fora to the Mese: a succession of monumental fora straddled the main artery, creating a contiguous space that traversed the city. While the inspiration for the Ottoman design might thus be sought in the city's Byzantine layout, the new configuration also had implications for the religious denomination of urban space in a multiconfessional environment. The Ottoman city's main artery traversed a major site of Muslim worship, in a spatial assertion of the politico-religious hegemony of the new rule. Nevertheless, this particular configuration suggests that restrictions concerning non-Muslim uses of Muslim religious spaces, which would appear in later centuries, were not operative at the time.[115]

Contemporary and later references to the plaza/outer courtyard connected to the main artery of the city are indicative of its hybrid conception and use. While Bidlisi alludes to the public function of this space by naming it *maydān* (square), to most authors this seems to have appeared more as an empty area surrounding the mosque: Angiolello, one of the earliest authors to describe the building, notes the outer courtyard embracing the mosque's forecourt, emphasizing its strikingly large dimensions. He indicates that it had a circumference of a mile and a half and housed "all the mass of the temple." To Gilles this was a spacious court around the mosque; to Mehmed Aşık it was two wide lots to the east and west of the mosque. To Evliya, also, it was a court (ḥarem) resembling a wide open plain (ṣaḥrā-yi 'aẓīm); to his contemporary Hezarfen Hüseyin it was the ṣaḥn, a large opening surrounding the sanctuary. These depictions convey at once the images of a square featuring a monument at its center and a negative space, a vast opening whose main function was to separate the mosque from the madrasas (fig. 61). The Süleymaniye, built a century later, must have informed the perceptions of Mehmed Aşık and Evliya, as Süleyman's complex featured an identical outer courtyard (a garden rather than a paved court), which did function mainly as a space setting the mosque apart from its dependencies, with no direct connection to the main arteries of the city.

The peculiar use of the piazza/outer courtyard around the New Mosque is indicative of Ottoman conceptions of urban space. Granting an Italian inspiration in the design of the complex, the relationship of the buildings to the street reveals the filters through which Italian theory and practice were domesticated within the Ottoman context. While the early Ottoman monuments in Constantinople betray a lack of interest in uniform street design and axial urban compositions, the location of the New Mosque, along with locations of the majority of monuments in early Ottoman Istanbul, suggests that each building's relationship to its main artery or square played a major role in the choice of site. At the same time, the Ottoman monuments were enclosed within walls, reminiscent of the Bursa and Edirne complexes that were situated outside the walled cities and therefore needed to be enveloped by walls of

FIGURE 60
Mehmed II complex in relation to the Divan Yolu and the surrounding urban fabric, in the map of the Bayezid II water-distribution system, 1812–13.

their own. The New Mosque's isolation from its immediate surroundings was compensated by its visual prominence within the walled city and across the Golden Horn from Galata. Mehmed's mosque was one of the building blocks of a new kind of relationship between monumental architecture and Istanbul's hilly topography that would shape the city's image through the following centuries. Prominently situated over an artificial platform atop one of the highest elevations of the peninsula, it, along with the Hagia Sophia and the Topkapı Palace, was one of the earliest constituents of the grand ensemble of monuments laid out along the city's hilltops. Its visual prominence was captured by authors of the city's panoramic views from the later sixteenth century onward, as the focus crowning the peninsula's fourth hill, dominating its surroundings (fig. 62).

THE ROYAL FOUNDATION AND THE CITY

A powerful symbol of the new order in the city and the changing religious politics of the Ottoman state, the New Mosque constituted the institutional center of a wide network of patronage within the city, through the property endowed to it and through its several hundred beneficiaries. Markets, baths, caravanserais, vast numbers of shops and houses, along with several religious and charitable structures that were part of the sultanic endowment, connected several thousand individuals and a range of activities to the monumental core of the foundation and, through it, to the person of the founder.

The sultanic endowment provided employment and benefits to a considerable portion of the urban population through its numerous religious, educational, charitable, and

FIGURE 61
Mehmed II complex, outer courtyard.

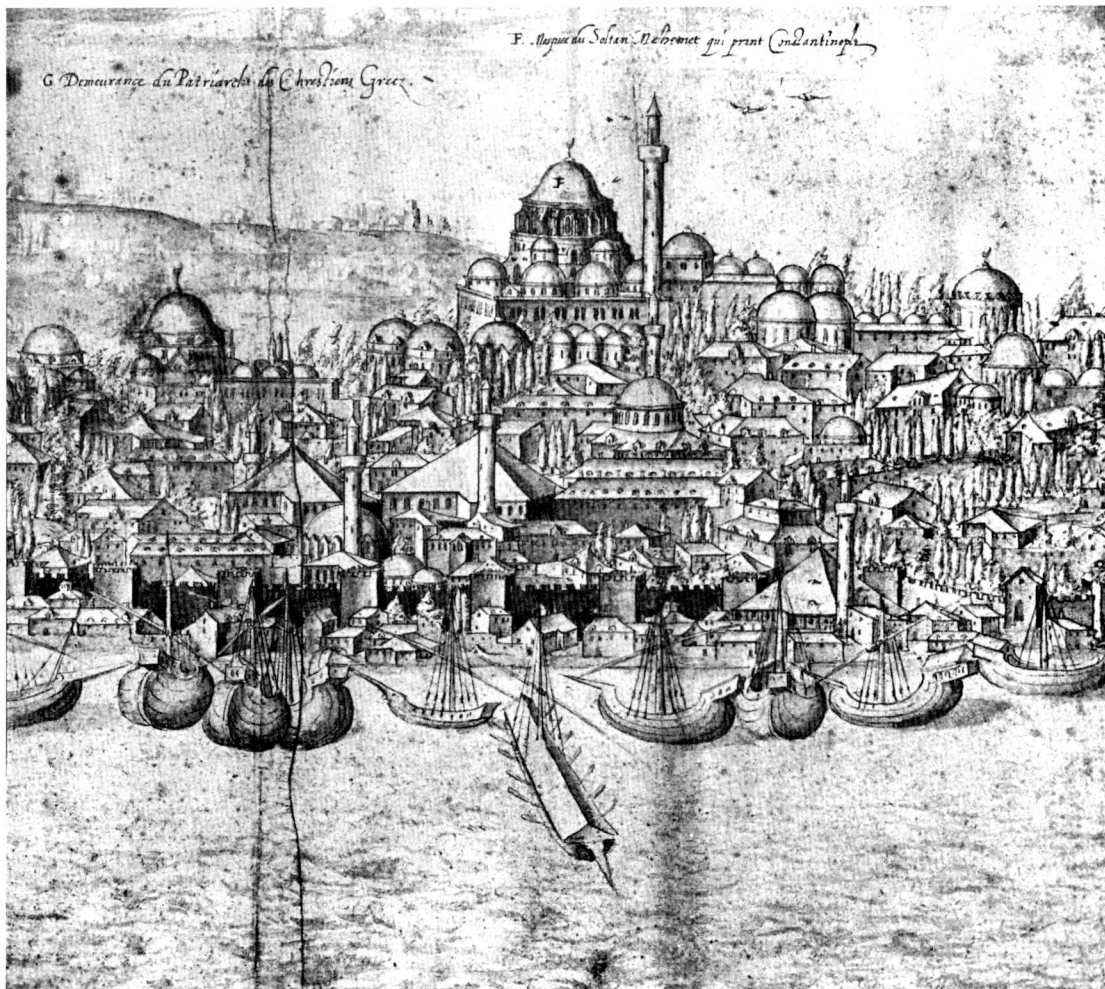

FIGURE 62
Mehmed II complex, with the
Zeyrek mosque and convent
(Pantokrator monastery)
downhill to its east (wrongly
marked as the Orthodox
Patriarchate), detail from a
panorama of Istanbul, ink
drawing on paper, ca. 1566–82.
Bibliothéque nationale de
France, Cabinet des estampes,
Res. B10.

commercial institutions, in a range of administrative, religious, educational, or manual activities. At the end of Mehmed's rule (1481), 435 people received wages from the foundations, 313 of whom were employed in the New Complex. In the years between 893 and 895/1489 and 1491, 558 people were employees or beneficiaries of the Ayasofya and the New Complex foundations, 337 of them employees of the New Complex. The increase is largely due to the architects, waterway builders, and restorers who are not mentioned in the foundation deeds, and to the numerous beneficiaries (zevā'idḫorān), many of whom received wages as a kind of pension. Among these were a retired (köhne) teacher of

the palace recruits, a retired chief tailor, and a retired chief gardener, numerous disabled janissaries, orphans and widows, poets and musicians, dervishes, and many relatives of men of importance, who received from Mehmed's foundation daily wages that ranged from one to twenty akçe.[116]

Including the endowed commercial and residential property, the network of physical spaces that constituted the royal endowment comprised around nineteen hundred shops and twelve hundred houses and rooms, either newly built or inherited from Byzantium, which were rented out as income-generating property of the royal foundation. A considerable portion of the city's population, then, partook in the relationships—administrative, educational, confessional, financial—that the foundation imposed at various levels between groups and individuals of diverse professions and venues. As one may glean from the apparent ease with which endowment deeds were rewritten to shuffle property and institutions between the New Mosque and the Ayasofya foundations, control of this network resided ultimately with the founder. Simultaneously, as one may glean from the debates that surrounded the workings of the foundation, such as the employment of individuals, imposition of rents, or uses of particular buildings, that network constituted one of the sites where the city's new social and political order was articulated, where, in Henri Lefebvre's terms, social space was produced.[117]

Significant among the numerous copies of the royal foundation's endowment deeds is a document preserved in the Topkapı Palace archives, the 1496 copy of an original possibly dating to the last years of Mehmed's reign.[118] A complete account of the sultan's public works in and around the city, it incorporates the Ayasofya endowment founded shortly after the conquest, itemizing the Byzantine churches converted through the first years of Ottoman presence in Constantinople, a number of mosques either converted from churches or newly built, convents, commercial buildings, and Byzantine residential and commercial structures endowed as income-generating property to the Ayasofya waqf. In short, apart from palatial and military spaces created by the Ottoman rule, it presents the sultan's involvement with the city as a whole.

The all-embracing nature of the endowment deed is striking. It is at once a legal document following the conventions of its type, a religious document attesting to the founder's piety, and a representation of the sultan's mark on the city

and the services he extended to its population. By displaying his urban interventions as a totality, it constitutes a conclusion to the process whose initiation Kritovoulos had described in his chronicle. By including the foundations predating the 1459 announcement, it renders them, too, part of the same project where the pride of place, as well as the highest number of employees and beneficiaries and highest expenses, belongs to the New Mosque complex.[119] The representational aspect of the document is supported by the fact that legally and administratively the Ayasofya endowment, including the bedestan with its surrounding markets and all appropriated Byzantine property, continued its separate existence.[120]

The preamble of the deed introduces this presentation by juxtaposing themes commonly encountered in waqf documents, such as *ḥayr* and *ṣadaḳa,* with subjects particular to the period: the conquest, the Alexandrian feat of Mehmed, his support of knowledge and learning (*ʿilm* and *ʿirfān*), and the institution of the shariʿa in the land of the infidel. It states that through (the act of) the sultan, God gave the city to the Muslims as *a new creation.* The hadith "he turned from the lesser war to the greatest endeavor" marks the end of the preamble:[121] what is presented in the remaining portion of the document, namely the religious, educational, and charitable institutions, the commercial and residential property endowed for their upkeep, the people employed and accommodated in them, was the product of the "greatest duty," that of building the city through the establishment of a pious foundation.

Mapping out on the city the particular buildings and institutions included in the deed yields a comprehensive picture of the sultan's urban interventions. Simultaneously, because some of these buildings changed functions between the time of their foundation and the time the deed was drawn, such an operation also presents aspects of the (not always straightforward) process that led to the picture of ca. 1480. Apart from the Hagia Sophia and the New Mosque, two congregational mosques are included in the endowment: the Dominican church in Galata, which was converted into the congregational mosque of the township and formed the center of a predominantly Muslim neighborhood, and the mosque in the the Golden Gate citadel. The bell tower of the Dominican church was put to use as a minaret, contrary to common practice, which would have entailed its demolition and replacement with an Ottoman-style tower (fig. 63). This was perhaps done in recognition of the predominantly non-Muslim character of the township, a demographic reality as much as a literary topos through the Ottoman history of Constantinople. The mosque in the citadel was a small structure; it owed its designation as a congregational mosque to the royal character of the citadel and to its remote location at the edge of the city. Scarella's drawing shows a building larger than, though architecturally not very different from, the surrounding houses (see no. 9, "La moschea," in fig. 13).[122] The monastic churches of the Pantokrator and the Pantepoptes, which had served as the chief madrasa and the chief hospice of the city before the construction of the New Complex, were endowed as masjids (figs. 64, 65). Their dependencies were rented out as residences. In the early sixteenth century, a lodge of the Nakshibendi order of dervishes occupied the dependencies of the Pantokrator monastery.[123] The masjids' names, however, continued to evoke their earlier uses: the rooms of the Pantokrator were referred to as Zeyrek Medresesi Odaları, "the Rooms of the Zeyrek Madrasa," while the latter masjid was referred to as "the Mosque of the Old Hospice," Eski İmaret Mescidi.

Among the religious structures endowed were two Sufi convents proximate to each other and to the first palace: the Kalenderhane and the mosque of Vefazade. The latter was built for the Zeyni sheikh Vefazade, a prominent figure of this Sunni-oriented order favored by the court during this period.[124] Mehmed's patronage of Vefazade is reminiscent of earlier Ottoman sultans' endowments for prominent Sufi personages. But at the same time, aspects of the foundation, as well as the architecture of the building endowed for the sheikh, are indicative of changes in the state's relation to the Sufi orders. The waqfiyya mentions a new mosque built for the sheikh and a bath built to bring income to it. But whereas stipulations are recorded in the deed for other endowed buildings, there are no specifications for the employees and expenses of the Vefa mosque. It was at the disposal of the sheikh for as long as he lived, and afterward would be added to the rest of the sultanic waqf as a Friday mosque.

FIGURE 63
Arap Cami (St. Paolo) from the east, with its bell tower converted into a minaret.

FIGURE 64
Church of the Pantokrator/
Zeyrek madrasa and mosque.

FIGURE 65
Church of the Pantepoptes/Eski
İmaret mosque.

Şeyh Vefazade himself built a public kitchen and hospice around the mosque (referred to as ʿimāret in the waqfiyya); he willed the supervision and income of these buildings to the dervishes.[125]

The setting provided to the Sufi sheikh, too, bespeaks changes in Ottoman architectural practice. This is one of the buildings of early Ottoman Istanbul in which the vaulting structure of the Hagia Sophia is adapted to a much smaller scale. A central dome of about ten meters in diameter with two flanking half domes covered a laterally placed rectangle, which was preceded by a five-bay portico (figs. 66–68). The rear of the mihrab niche, situated in a pentagonal apse, shared a wall with the sheikh's reclusion cell (çilehāne) and featured a door that provided access to it. The building was completed in 881/1476.[126] That we owe our only visual images of Şeyh Vefa's mosque to a nineteenth-century scholar who mistook the building for a Byzantine church is telling in terms of the architectural culture of the period.[127]

Earlier structures built by Ottoman sultans for Sufis were convents or convent-masjids; these were multifunctional buildings that provided spaces for ritual and accommodation as well as for prayer. The mosque built for Vefazade, on the other hand, consisted of a single hall that possibly functioned as the ritual space, culminating in the reclusion cell of the sheikh. Ayvansarayi, writing in the eighteenth century, notes that the mosque was referred to by its chronogram, *cāmiʿ ḫāḳāniyye* (sultanic mosque). The naming reflects the ambiguous designation of the building, a likeness of the city's primary religious monument, built by the sultan for a dervish, to be used as the latter's convent, and later to be converted into a Friday mosque.

From the sixteenth century onward, some authors refer to the Vefā meydānı, a square that faced the mosque, visible also in nineteenth-century maps of the city (fig. 69).[128] If the *meydān* predated or was contemporaneous with the mosque, a common urban and architectural theme of the period becomes salient in the Vefa foundation: the use of a square to lend prominence and visibility to significant buildings.

The other convent founded by Mehmed II, the Kalenderhane, was housed in one of the larger Byzantine churches in the city, identified as the monastic church of the Kyriotissa, situated very close to the western wall of the first palace (fig. 70).[129] In striking contrast to stipulations in the foundation deed for the Vefa convent, those for the Kalenderhane detail all the employees and the expenses of this foundation as well as the activities to take place in the building. Allotments are made for a sheikh, described as a pious and righteous ascetic withdrawn from passions and riches (of the world) ("ṣāḥibuʾl-mücāhede veʾl riyāże"), an overseer of the guests' dining, a *ḥāfıż* to recite the Koran during the gathering of the dervishes on Fridays, following the reading of poetry, two reciters of

FIGURE 66
Convent-mosque of Sheikh Vefa, interior (southwestern end of the prayer hall, beneath the half dome) (from Gurlitt, *Die Baukunst Konstantinopels*, 1907).

poetry, and four musicians. Money is allotted for the food to be offered to guests, who are specified as the ulema, the wealthy and the poor, and dervishes; part of the allotment was to be given to orphans as alms.[130] The name Kalenderhane, which has remained in use through its Ottoman and modern Turkish history, has led to the conviction that the building was given to the Kalenderis, the popular and marginal Sufi groups that played an important role through the early Ottoman territorial expansions and during the siege and conquest of Constantinople. The Kalenderis, on the other hand, were not known for strict and formal observance of ritual or accommodation of the ulema for which the waqfiyya had specifications and allotments (although such discrepancy between sufi practice and stipulations in foundation deeds of sufi establishments was not uncommon).[131] The name Kalenderhane may also point to its use by

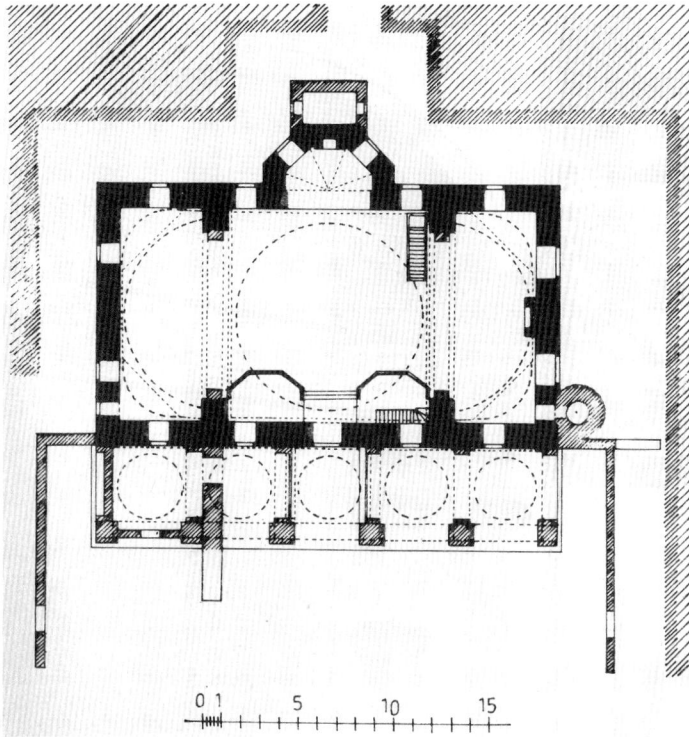

an order with Kalenderi leanings but with closer ties to central authority.[132]

Whether it was originally given to Sufis of more or less heterodox inclination, the building's life as a convent was not lengthy. Documents from the end of the century make no mention of the convent, whereas account books of the Ayasofya foundation mention the Kalenderhane Medresesi, with a court-yard and garden. How the Byzantine building functioned during this period is not clear; it was possibly used as the classroom of the madrasa and simultaneously as a masjid, for the registers for the school include the wages of an imam. By the middle of the sixteenth century, the Byzantine church was function-ing as a congregational mosque. The fate of the Kalenderhane, it has been suggested, may be linked to the establishment of a Mevlevihane in Galata, whose first sheikh was noted for his Hurufi-Kalenderi leanings. The location of the new lodge founded in the final years of the fifteenth century, within vineyards and orchards uphill from the Galata tower, implies a preference for a site distant from the city cen-ter, in stark contrast to the central location of the Kalenderhane.[133]

The story of the Kalenderhane follows the stories of a number of religious buildings in the city that owed their existence to an earlier religious and political order in which popu-lar Sufi sects played a central role, buildings whose functions changed soon after changes in the religious politics of the state. The con-version of the city's first sultanic hospice and first madrasa into quarter mosques following the construction of the New Mosque complex are shifts in the same vein. The intellectual "contest" between Mevlana Zeyrek and Mev-lana Hocazade related in engaging detail by Taşköprizade seems also to underline the cen-ter's changing attitude toward particular sects. Zeyrek and Hocazade were teachers in the city's old and new madrasas respectively. The former, a follower of the popular Bayramiyye order of dervishes, lost the debate, in the presence of the sultan, on an aspect of religious law. Humiliated, he moved back to his native Bursa. Possibly Mevlana Zeyrek, who "did not busy himself with scholarly works and compositions" and whose writings, according to Taşköprizade, were limited to marginalia, was not welcome in Mehmed's new educational establishment.[134]

THE REBIRTH OF THE PUBLIC BATH

The representational nature of the endowment deeds, and the desire to present the sultan's mark on the city in its totality, had a role in the inclusion of the commercial establishment and Byzantine residential structures in the later copies of Mehmed's endowment deed. Practically, these were income-generating properties of the Ayasofya foundation. Belonging exclusively to the new foundation, on the other hand, were fourteen baths, eleven of them located within the walled city and the remaining three in Galata. Public baths constitute a conspicuous group of buildings in Mehmed's Istanbul: a total of twenty-six were built during his reign, by him and by members of the ruling elite, a number of them possibly incorporating parts of extant bathing structures (fig. 71). A closer scrutiny of these buildings, therefore, may reveal aspects of the emerging architectural and urban order in Ottoman Istanbul.

The public bath as an urban building type had precedents in the cultures with which the Ottomans had come into contact from early on: in the Roman, the Byzantine, and the medieval Islamic worlds, the bath had been an integral part of urban life and consequently of the cityscape. The monumental Roman and early Byzantine baths, from which early Islamic dynasties drew inspiration, were, however, not reproduced in the later medieval era, either in the Byzantine or in the Islamic world. The

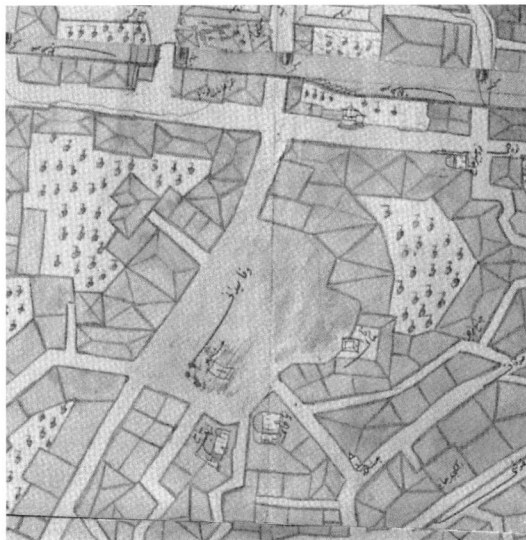

FIGURE 69
Vefa square, detail from the map of the Bayezid II water-distribution system, 1812–13.

FIGURE 70
Kalenderhane, from the south.

active baths encountered by the Ottomans in Anatolia and the Balkans, whether Seljuk or Byzantine structures, were in large part modestly scaled buildings.[135] It is therefore noteworthy of early Ottoman architectural and urban practice that baths assumed monumental form from the later decades of the fourteenth century onward, drawing inspiration from the Roman and early Byzantine models, as well as from

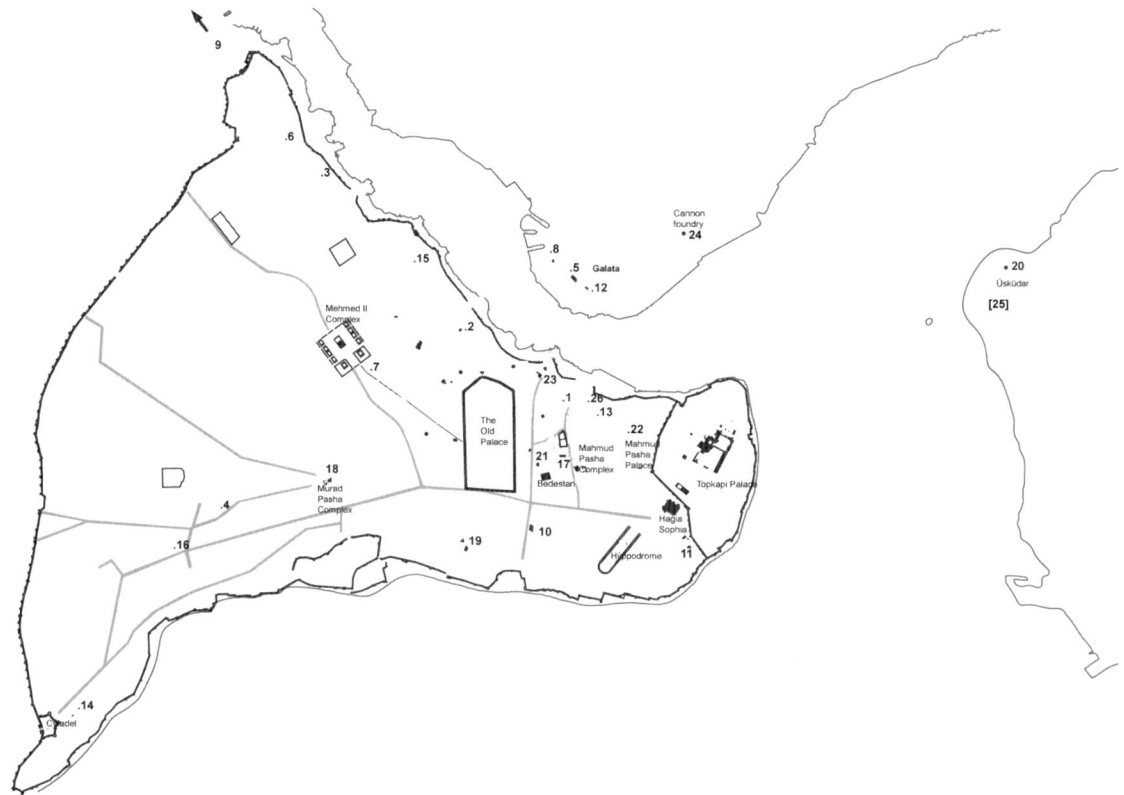

FIGURE 71

Public baths built during the reign of Mehmed II: (1) Alaca bath, (2) Azebler bath, (3) Balat Kapusı bath, (4) Bostan bath, (5) Galata Cami bath, (6) Çavuşbaşı bath, (7) Çukur (Mehmed II complex) bath, (8) Direklüce bath, (9) Eyüp complex bath, (10) Gedik Ahmed Pasha bath, (11) İshak Pasha bath, (12) Galata Karaköy bath, (13) Kazasker bath, (14) Kulle (citadel) bath, (15) Küçük Mustafa Pasha bath, (16) Küçük bath in Altımermer, (17) Mahmud Pasha bath, (18) Murad Pasha bath, (19) Nişancı Mehmed Pasha bath, (20) Rum Mehmed Pasha bath, (21) Sırt bath, (22) Sinan Pasha (Hoca Pasha) bath, (23) Taht al-kalʿa bath, (24) Tophane bath, (25) Üsküdar Mehmed II bath (hypothetical location), (26) Yahudiyyin bath.

extant bath structures.[136] An instance of such a relationship to the Byzantine past is preserved in Bursa, in the Eski Kaplıca bath, built by Murad I down the hill from his convent-masjid-madrasa. With its large caldarium/*sıcaklık* pool, its wealth of structural and sculptural spolia, and its wide rectangular apodyterium/*cāmekān* hall, the Eski Kaplıca bath clearly preserves memories and perhaps the actual remnants of a Byzantine bath (figs. 72–74).[137] Bayezid I's no longer extant Çukur Hamam within the walled city of Edirne, noted by the eighteenth-century author Hıbri to be a *kāfīrī* (i.e., Byzantine) building, presents another such instance. A later example, from Istanbul, is the public bath of the Küçük Ayasofya convent-mosque (converted from the SS. Sergius and Bacchus), whose circular and cruciform caldarium halls and wealth of spolia have suggested that it incorporates sections of a Byzantine bath.[138]

Baths were among the major types of public buildings sponsored by the Ottomans from early on: Orhan's complex in Bursa featured a double bath, and every subsequently founded socioreligious establishment neighbored one. As the Üç Şerefeli Mosque in Edirne marked a shift in monumental expression in Ottoman architecture, bringing it conceptually and formally closer to the Roman/Byzantine tradition, so did the baths built by Murad II in Bursa and Edirne.[139] Particularly the double bath in Edirne's *taḥt al-ḳalʿa* area, with its entrance hall carrying a sixteen-meter-wide dome and its elaborate interior arrangement, hints at the prominence these buildings were to acquire in the new capital. Here the parallels between Umayyad and Ottoman architectural culture, as each developed through encounters with the material environment of the late antique world, are evident. For just as the palatial bath assumed a rather short-lived monumentality and ceremonial centrality in the Umayyad world, the urban bathhouse assumed a monumentality in the early Ottoman centuries that would seldom be matched in the "classical" period and later.[140]

The Istanbul baths were built according to conventions that had taken shape through the previous century in Bithynia and Thrace, which were largely based on the conventions of the late antique baths of Anatolia and Syria.[141] A large entrance hall, corresponding to the apodyterium/ceremonial hall of the Roman bath, was followed by the *soğukluk* and the *sıcaklık,* corresponding to the tepidarium and the caldarium of a Roman bath respectively. The latter room, a square or octagonal hall to which smaller private rooms opened, at times in a cruciform scheme, constituted the main bathing space (figs. 75, 76). The same layout was repeated for both sections of a double bath, the women's section in most baths being slightly smaller in dimension. The most conspicuous and, for our interests, most striking feature of

the Ottoman public bath was the entrance hall. Called *ṣoyunmalıḳ, cāmegāh,* or *cāmekān,* this was a large square hall covered with a hemispherical dome and often featuring a pool or

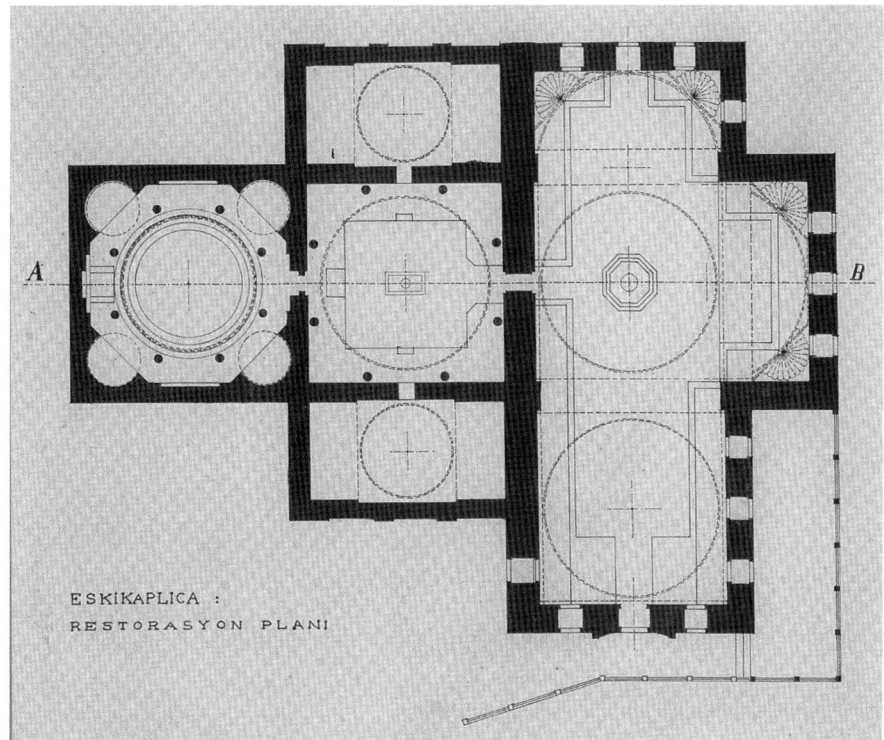

ESKIKAPLICA :
RESTORASYON PLANI

FIGURE 72
Eski Kaplıca bath, Bursa, plan.

FIGURE 73
Eski Kaplıca bath, Bursa, section.

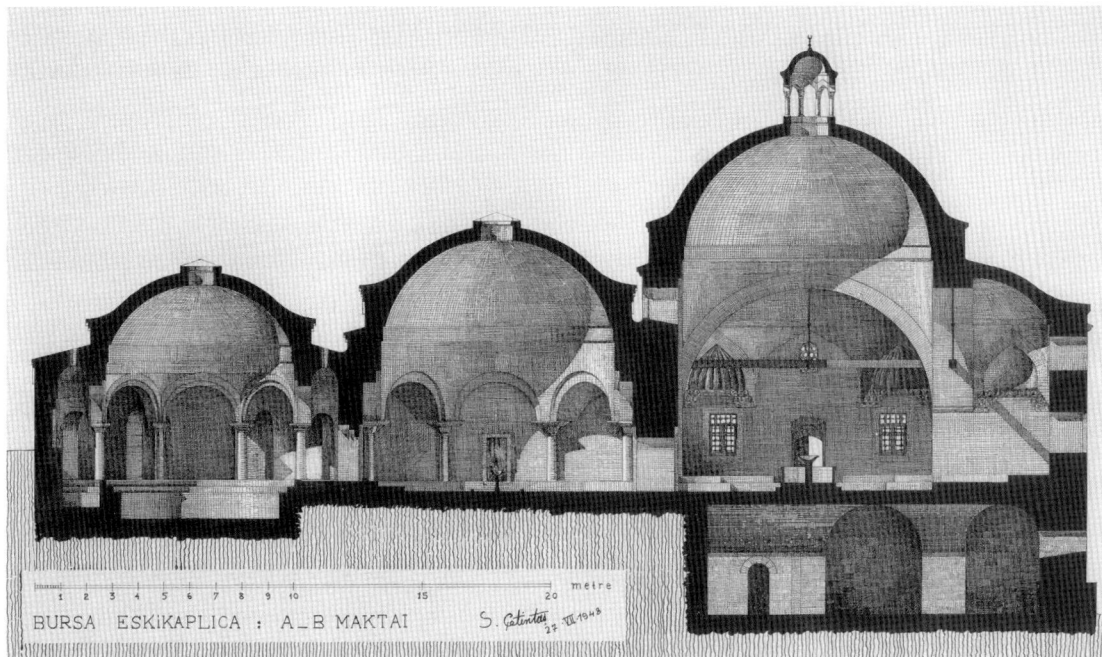

BURSA ESKIKAPLICA : A_B MAKTAI

a water spout at its center. Adopting the function of the much grander apodyteria of late antique baths, this was a space for social gathering before or after bathing, and the primary monumental feature of the building. This large domed hall, often marked with a high portal, would face the street and be directly accessible from it, unlike the majority of monumental religious structures enclosed within walls (fig. 84). With *cāmekān* domes measuring between ten and eighteen meters in diameter, the public baths of early Ottoman Istanbul competed with and often surpassed mosques in dimension, monumentality, and visibility within the urban fabric (figs. 98, 99). Of the fourteen baths included in the royal foundation, nine were such large-scale structures, comprising separate men's and women's sections.[142]

The construction of baths was made possible by a project realized in the early years of Ottoman rule in Constantinople: the restoration of the waterways bringing water to the city from the Thracian peninsula. Having no natural water resources of its own, the city had always been dependent on these waterways, which had fallen into disrepair in the later

Byzantine period. An entry in Kritovoulos under the year 1456 notes Mehmed's order to "bring into the City from the countryside an abundance of water." This was the system later to be referred to as the Kırkçeşme (Forty Fountains), after the line of fountains built inside one of the arches of the Valens aqueduct, also put to use during the same restoration campaign.[143] The Kırkçeşme waterways provided water to the two palaces, the New Mosque, as well as to the majority of vizierial mosques and baths and a number of neighborhood mosques. It is difficult to determine the original layout and the course of this system, as it was restored and expanded several times in the later sixteenth century and continuously thereafter. What is clear, however, is that the area serviced by the water-distribution system comprised the entire Constantinopolitan peninsula, for it took water to such distant locations as the citadel at the Golden Gate, the Ayyub complex at the far end of the Golden Horn, and the Topkapı Palace at the tip of the peninsula.

The spectacular appearance of the baths, as much as their utility, is underlined in the writings of contemporary chroniclers. In the bath near the New Mosque, according to İbn Kemal, were collected arts of all varieties; it was a rarity of the day, and its like had neither been seen nor heard of.[144] Kritovoulos writes of the sultan's order for the construction of "splendid and costly baths" in the context of the restoration of the waterways; these, he notes, were among the things Mehmed "ordered to be done for the building up and beautifying of the City, and for the benefit and needs and comfort of the inhabitants."[145] Among the fifteenth-century poet Hamidi's few eulogies to particular buildings are those written for the Taht al-kalʿa and Mahmud Pasha baths; he praises their lofty domes, precious materials, and intricate ornamentation.[146] In contrast to the late medieval world, where public bath buildings had been mostly utilitarian and humble structures, the early Ottoman culture emphasized splendor, beauty, and expense, reminiscent of Roman architectural culture and its continued legacy in the larger late antique world. The restoration of waterways and construction of baths was itself a neo-Roman venture: as Cyril Mango reminds us, the construction of costly aqueduct systems to bring water to cities all over the imperial Roman world was intimately connected to the centrality of public baths in Roman urban culture.[147]

Behind the proliferation and prominence of baths in the first decades of Ottoman rule in Constantinople were several factors. The most obvious among these was the necessity of providing water to urban dwellers and spaces for ritual bathing to Muslims—this latter, in fact, the reason why baths remained among the indispensable public structures in cities of the Muslim world from early periods onward. By the same token, the bath, alongside the masjid, often constituted the public core of a residential quarter.[148] Authors writing on public bathhouses in the Islamic world have often focused exclusively on the Muslim concern for ritual and actual cleanliness as the reason for the continued centrality of these structures in Middle Eastern cities.[149] This, however, is not sufficient to explain their monumental dimensions and elaborate architecture, particularly in comparison to the mostly modest dimensions of public baths elsewhere in the Muslim world. Neither does an explanation based solely on the necessity of ritual cleanliness explain the prominence of monumentally built and richly decorated bathhouses in the chronicles and poetry of the period. Baths were among the income-generating properties of charitable foundations. However, the proceeds from the fourteen baths endowed for the New Mosque foundation, considerably lower

FIGURE 75
Mahmud Pasha bath, caldarium.

than other revenues tied up for the waqf, suggest that their construction was not motivated solely by financial concerns either.[150]

Their construction and use made possible only by the Herculean restoration of the city's ancient water-distribution system, baths may also have been conceived as monuments to that restoration.[151] Patterns in the siting of baths, on the other hand, reveal other possible motives behind these constructions. Strikingly, the majority were built in commercial areas and those districts that were inhabited by a predominantly non-Muslim or a religiously mixed population.[152] Two were parts of larger establishments: one was part of the New Complex and was situated to the east of the main group of buildings; another was near the citadel of Seven Towers. The construction of a large-scale double bath in the Taht al-kal'a area followed a pattern established in Bursa and Edirne, both towns featuring their own baths in the commercial center. The Sırt Hammamı, situated on the Uzunçarşı, connecting the Taht al-kal'a

FIGURE 76
Mahmud Pasha bath, section.

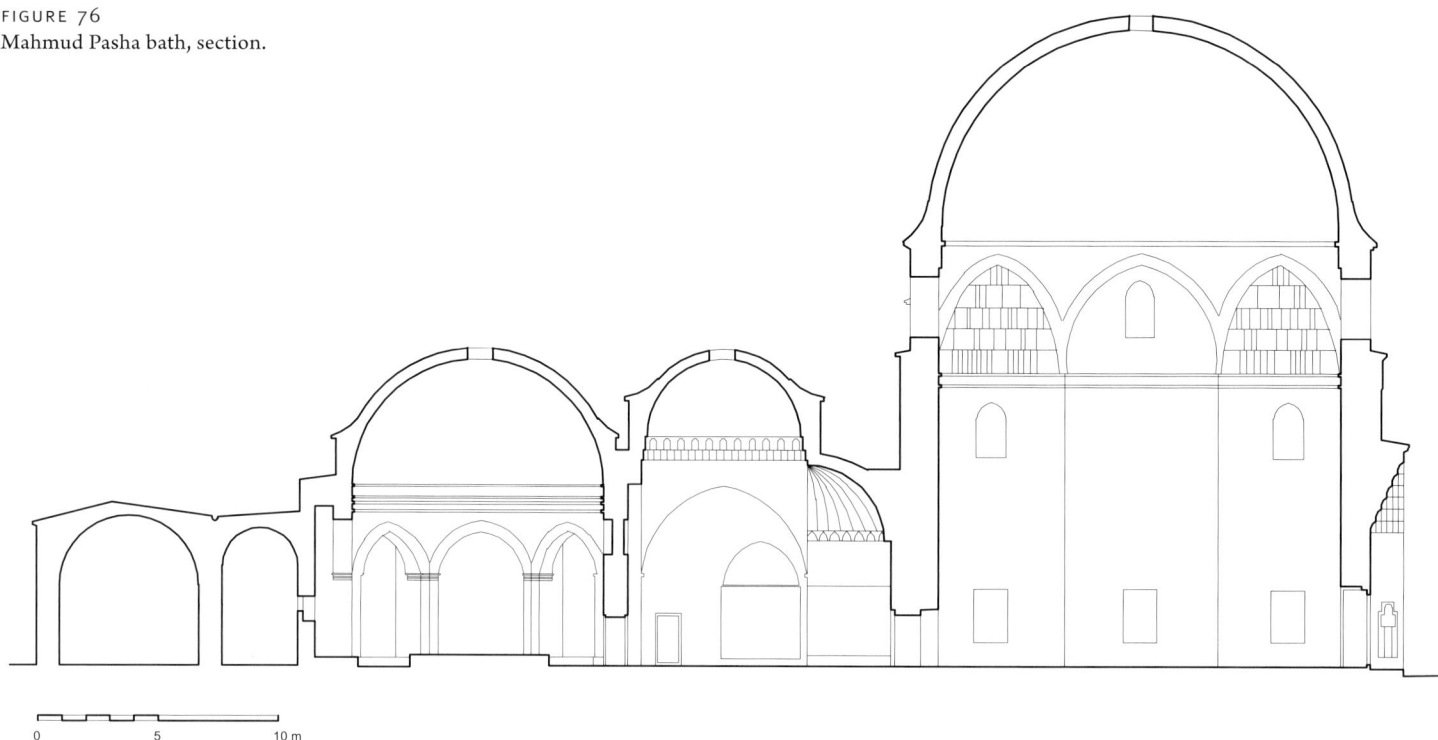

0   5   10 m

to the bedestan area, also follows the same pattern. Three were built in Galata; one was a double bath near the congregational mosque of the township. The remaining baths were in the Jewish and Greek neighborhoods along the Golden Horn. A map of fifteenth-century baths of Istanbul, including those built by the viziers along with the sultan's constructions, presents a network of Ottoman public monuments that only sometimes overlaps the network of religious monuments.[153]

Baths constituted nonconfessional urban foci that were nevertheless linked to the locus of rule, extending the patronage and the charity of the founders to all religious groups. Nonconfessional centers of social interaction, they were public spaces in which all could partake.[154] The baths of early Ottoman Istanbul, sharing the architectural language of the religious buildings, can be interpreted as elements in the monumentalization of a capital city that was deliberately populated, according

to Kritovoulos, with "people of all nations, but more especially of Christians."[155] Larger baths such as that of the New Complex (also named the Çukur Hamam), the Taht al-kal'a bath, or the Mahmud Pasha bath dominated the urban environment with their entrance halls opening onto the street (and not enclosed in walled precincts, as were the religious complexes) and their domes looming larger than the domes of most religious monuments. This was characteristic mostly of Istanbul's first Ottoman decades: the public baths newly built during consolidation of a more Sunni-oriented polity in the later sixteenth century no longer boasted the monumental dimensions and central locations of earlier ones. The demise of the monumental public bath in fact paralleled the demise of another legacy of early Ottoman architectural culture that had made its way to Ottoman Istanbul, the multifunctional convent-mosque. A later-sixteenth-century intervention in the Taht al-kal'a area, which radically altered the spatial and visual configuration of this commercial center, vividly captures the transformation in notions of self-representation and architectural patronage of the Ottoman ruling body: in the 1560s, the small church that had been converted into the Hacı Halil masjid across from the Taht al-kalʿa bath was taken down for the construction of a memorial mosque for the deceased grand vizier Rüstem Pasha, commissioned to Sinan. The bath that had until then been the visual node of the Taht al-kalʿa area was relegated to secondary status (and size), as Rüstem's new mosque, a celebrated monument of the sixteenth century, rose near it.

PART 2
THE PATRONAGE OF THE NEW RULING ELITE

Both Kritovoulos and Muʿali continued their narratives of Mehmed's order with an account of the works of the grand vizier Mahmud Pasha. Muʿali's title for this section is telling: "The Order of the *Ḥünkār* for the Construction of Imarets, and First the Buildings of Mahmud Pasha." Elaborating on the vizier's architectural patronage through themes such as the fame, justice, and generosity of the builder, and noting the uniqueness of the imaret embellished with a thousand beautiful forms, Muʿali also wrote that upon the order of the sultan the illustrious members of the court endeavored to build imarets. During the rule of Mehmed, he noted, Kostantiniyye became a big city (*Mısr*, also an allusion to Cairo), the like of which would not be found in the world.

The participation of the ruling elite in the building program was integral to Mehmed's plans for the city's restoration, on the one hand, and his conception of the structure of Ottoman rule, on the other. The announcement of his order evinced a shift in patronage patterns, which in turn reflected the transformation that took place in the makeup of the ruling body following the capture of Constantinople. Mehmed II's law code, sanctioning imperial seclusion as a means of articulating the divine and absolute authority of the sultan,

concomitantly marked the delegation of power to court officials, particularly the grand vizier, whose post was given the new definition of "absolute deputy [of the sultan] in all matters."[156] The agency of imperial council members, with few exceptions all of *devşirme* origin, in the foundation of urban institutions and in the creation of their architectural settings in the new capital was one of the manifestations of the unprecedented power, authority, and resources with which these individuals were vested in the new configuration of the administrative apparatus. Often, the inauguration of a project corresponded to the founder's term as grand vizier. The cultural and institutional patronage of viziers, instrumental in the formation of new social networks in the capital, was an important dimension of the new configuration of power. Through public and private building enterprises the new ruling elite partook in the formation of urban patterns that would be inscribed in the city's long-term history.

SHIFT IN PATRONAGE PATTERNS: THE BUILDINGS OF MAHMUD PASHA
"Precisely according to the wish of the Sultan . . . [Mahmud] beautified the City at his own expense and cost with buildings and monuments useful to the public," wrote Kritovoulos

in a section of the *History* entitled "Describing the Fine Structures of Mahmud."[157] These were the first public buildings of monumental scale to rise within the walled city, after the construction of commercial structures by Mehmed II. Grand vizier for thirteen years and the most central figure of the fifteenth-century Ottoman realm after (and at times alongside) Mehmed II, the patron was a member of an aristocratic Byzantine family based in Serbia. He was the first grand vizier of the Ottoman state to rise to the post from non-Muslim origins.[158] Mahmud held the grand vizierate between 1456 and 1468 and again in 1472–73, before his final dismissal and subsequent execution. One of the principal figures in the building of the imperial Ottoman state, Mahmud was the single most influential official in the political and military arenas through this period and, after Mehmed, the foremost patron of architecture and literary activity.[159]

Although no precise date is available, it may be surmised, judging by the narratives of contemporary historians and by the completion date of the mosque (867/1463), that Mahmud Pasha started to build his Istanbul complex at the same time Mehmed began constructing the New Palace. Mahmud's buildings were near the commercial area and the Forum of Constantine, between the city's two focal points at the time, the first palace and Hagia Sophia. Spread around an extensive area on the slope between the royal residence and the royal mosque, Mahmud's buildings consisted of a congregational mosque, his mausoleum, a madrasa, a Koran school, a public kitchen, two masjids, a bath, a caravanserai, his palace (with a private bath and a large garden), and a large number of houses, shops, and rooms (fig. 77).[160]

Curiously, three sources postdating the construction and separated from each other by centuries—the anonymous *Menāḳıb*

of Mahmud Pasha written in the 1530s, the eighteenth-century *Ḥadīḳatü'l-Cevāmi'*, and the nineteenth-century *Constantiniade* by the Greek patriarch Konstantios—relate that a church had previously occupied the site of the mosque, the *Constantiniade* specifying that it was dedicated to the archangel Michael.[161] Muʿali's account, written shortly after the completion of the mosque, also seems to suggest that a church, or the ruins of one, had existed on the site of the mosque.[162] Given that the dimensions and the proportions of the building are in line with Ottoman mosques of the same type, it is more likely that only the larger platform on which the church had stood was used, as was the case in several of the city's Ottoman buildings, including Mehmed's mosque.[163] Built of ashlar masonry on a platform that evened out the slope and at the same time made it more prominent within the urban fabric, the mosque constituted a visual focus in the area (figs. 78–80).[164] At the same time, it was a locus of social intercourse in the proximity of the commercial center: Bidlisi described Mahmud Pasha's *masjid-e jāmi'* as a place of comfort for rich and poor alike, with the open space fronting the entrance centered by a fountain and surrounded by lofty trees.[165]

The centerpiece of the foundation is a late and variant example of the multifunctional convent-masjid, one of the major types of monumental religious buildings in the Ottoman world through the fourteenth and early fifteenth centuries (as exemplified by the building in fig. 38). Featuring an iwan on the qibla side that served as prayer space, side iwans, and convent rooms surrounding a domed central hall in a cross-axial arrangement, the convent-masjid was a product of the cultural and political milieu of late medieval Anatolia and the Balkans, where individuals and groups were often on the move. It incorporated a masjid

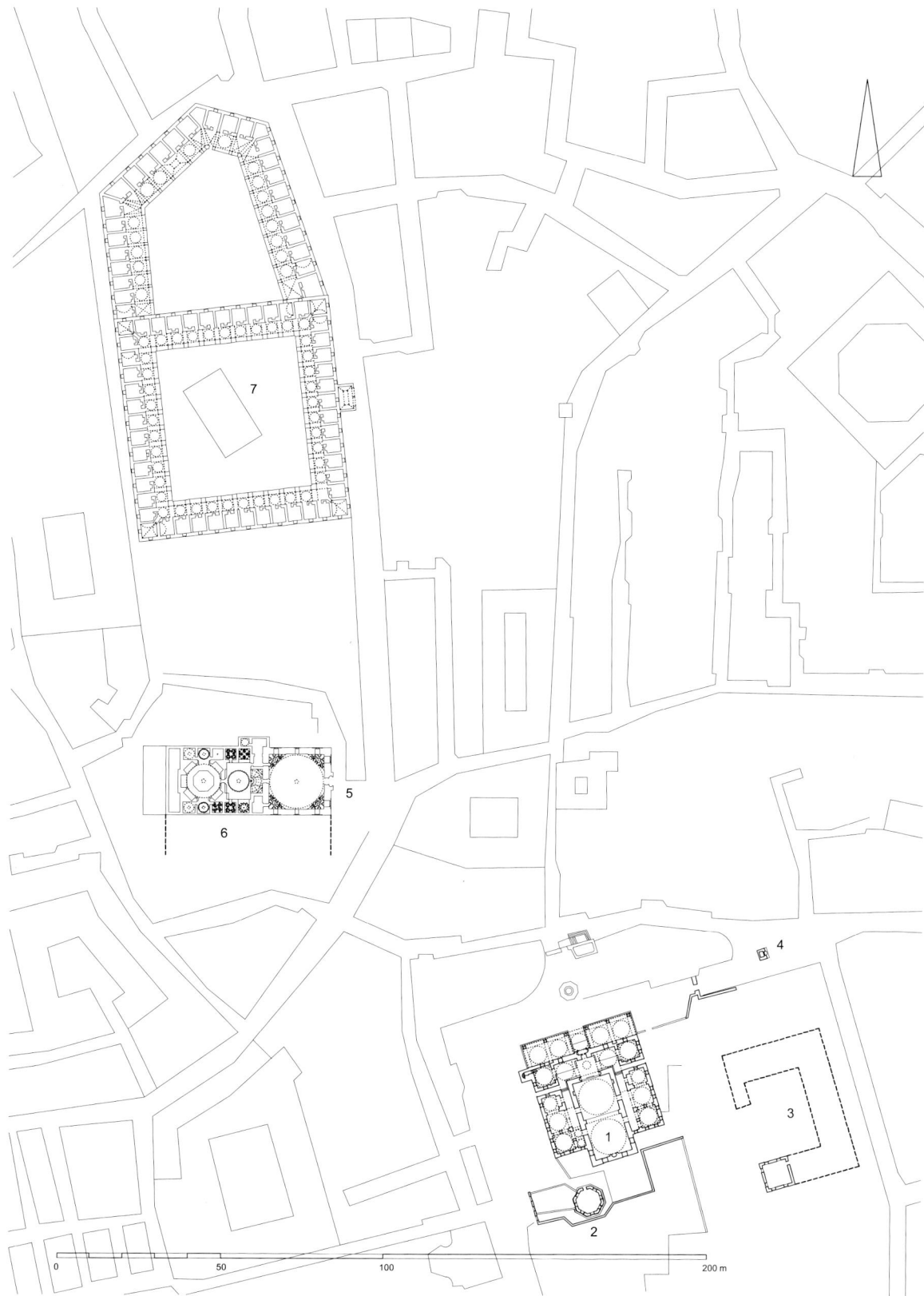

7

5

6

1

2

3

4

0   50   100   200 m

FIGURE 78
Mahmud Pasha convent-mosque
from the west.

FIGURE 79
Mahmud Pasha convent-mosque,
section.

while also providing accommodation and social spaces to dervishes and travelers.[166] Although this type of building survived the relative sedentarization of Ottoman culture in the later fifteenth and sixteenth centuries, the plans of later structures of this layout reflect the tension between their design as multipurpose buildings and the new use to which they were put as congregational mosques. In addition to the qibla iwan, the central hall under the main dome became part of the prayer area; the side iwans were eliminated in some buildings; the convent rooms were relegated to a lesser status through their diminutive size and the configuration of the interior. Side entrances provided alternate entry into the convent sections, diminishing the connection between the now enlarged prayer space and the convent rooms.

Sharing the features of most convent-mosques built by the Ottomans subsequent to the capture of Constantinople, Mahmud Pasha's mosque also incorporated aspects of

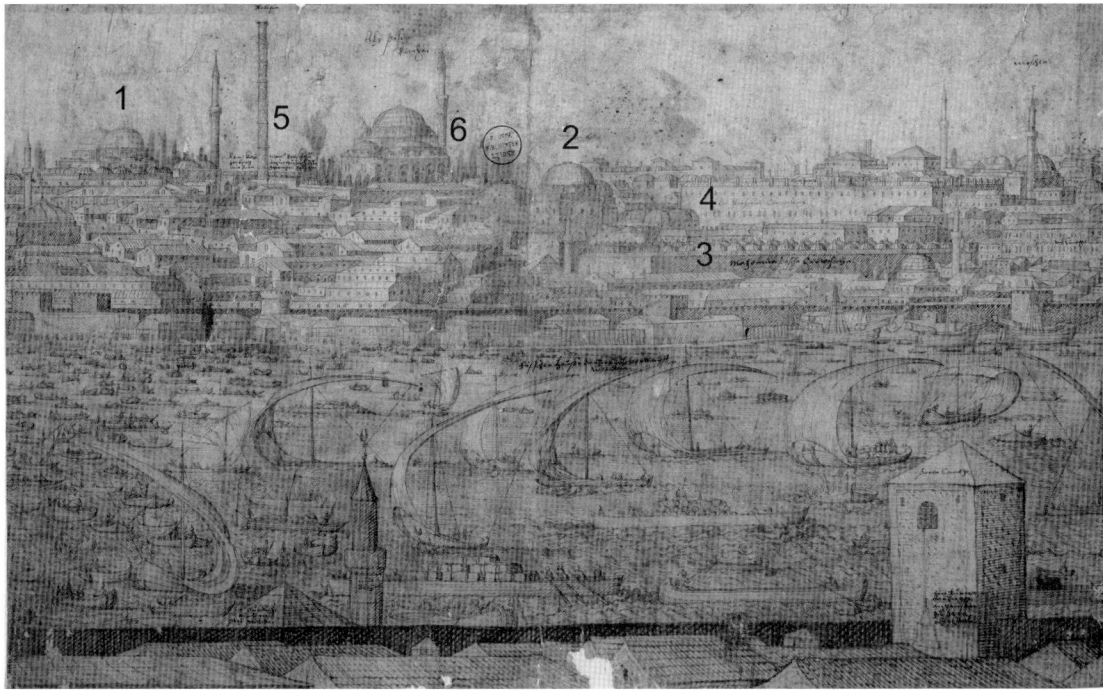

FIGURE 80
The Mahmud Pasha complex,
the commercial district, and
the Golden Horn, detail from
the panorama of Istanbul by
Melchior Lorichs, 1559, 1561–62:
(1) convent-mosque, (2)
bath, (3) khan, (4) royal khan,
(5) column of Constantine,
(6) Atik Ali Pasha mosque.

Constantinopolitan architecture. Here, the
prayer area constitutes the central core of the
building and is set apart from the surrounding
iwans and convent rooms by a U-shaped corridor that resembles the ambulatories of several
middle and late Byzantine churches. A narthex
forms a transitional space between the entrance
and the central hall.[167] Later additions to two
Constantinopolitan churches with ambulatories, the Constantine Lips and the Pammakaristos, had transformed the corridors, formally
speaking, into transitional spaces between the
naos and the later extensions (figs. 81, 82). Such
an arrangement would have appealed to the
builders of the Mahmud Pasha mosque, who
preferred to segregate the main prayer area
(now functioning as a congregational mosque)
from the lateral spaces of the convent, which
had their separate entrances on the two sides of
the building. This interpretation of the unique
ground plan of the grand vizier's mosque disregards the original function of the ambulatory in
Byzantine churches as a funerary space for the

founder (and his successors) near the naos.[168]
However, the funerary function of the ambulatory may have lacked significance for Muslim
users, which supports its interpretation as a
transitional space between the nave and surrounding areas.

Two contemporaries of Mahmud Pasha,
Mu'ali and Enveri, referred to the grand vizier's
building as an 'imāret, the term used at that
time for multifunctional convent-masjids built
by the Ottomans, as well as the larger compounds comprising the dependencies of these
buildings. Both authors praised the vizier for
his accommodation of guests. In this context,
Enveri also used the term ḥānḳāh (Sufi lodge)
for the building. Its foundation inscription,
too, designates the building as an 'imāret. The
distinction between 'imāret, as multifunctional building, and cāmi', as mosque, becomes
clearer in a comparison of the first two sultanic
mosques built in the city: while the inscription
plate of Mehmed's mosque refers to it as cāmi',
Bayezid II's mosque, built some decades later

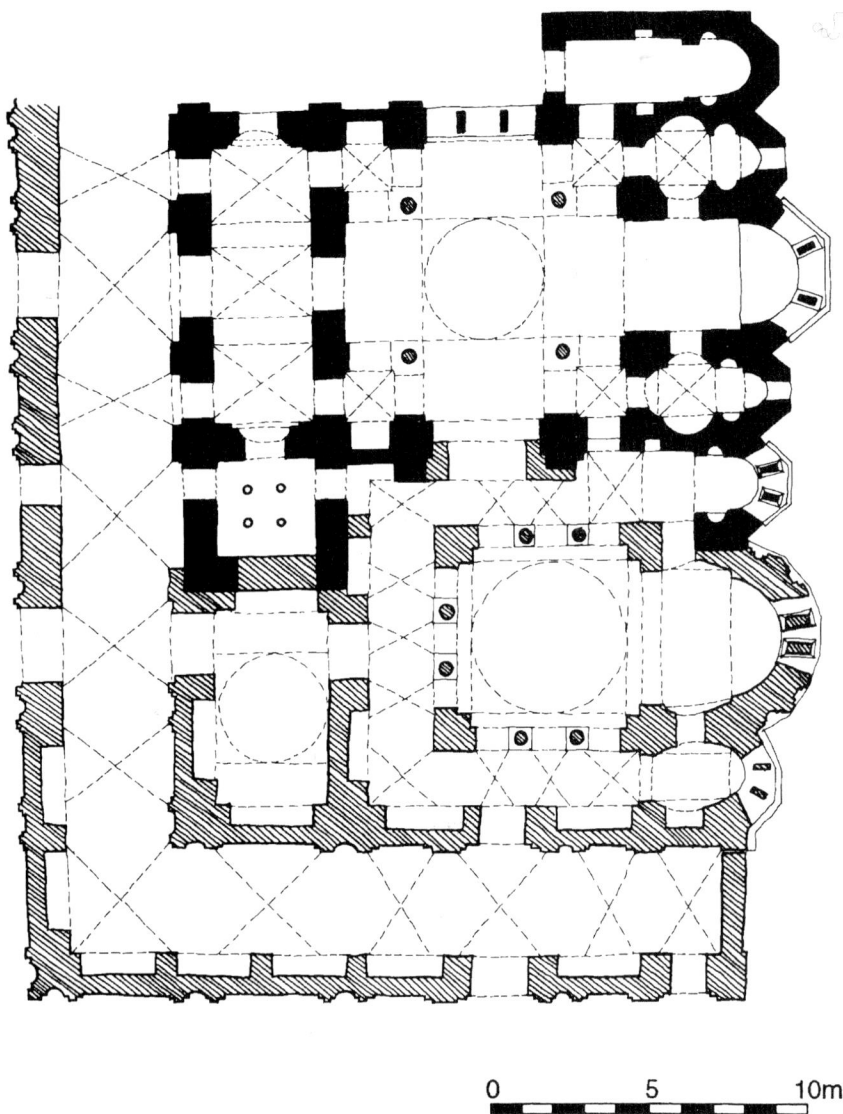

FIGURE 81
Church of Constantine Lips,
plan.

and featuring two sets of convent rooms in a striking combination of the convent-masjid with the congregational mosque as formulated by Mehmed II's architects, is designated in its foundation inscription an 'imāret.

Mahmud Pasha's mausoleum, unique in Istanbul, with the blue and turquoise tiles that adorn its exterior, conflates Timurid and Ottoman architectural idioms. It is an octagonal structure built of ashlar masonry, situated behind the mosque at its southern corner (plate 4). Moldings that frame its two levels of

windows emphasize its verticality, while the upper sections of the walls are decorated with tiles of dark blue and turquoise in Timurid-style geometric patterns. With these features, the mausoleum introduced to the urban environment of Ottoman Constantinople something of the Persianate architectural idiom that was otherwise secluded within the sultan's and possibly within Mahmud Pasha's palaces. The only other extant building in Istanbul with comparable tile work and façade treatment is the Tiled Pavilion of the Topkapı Palace (plate 2), possibly built by a team of Karamanid craftsmen and completed in 1472, in the wake of the victory over the Karamanid dynasty, in which Mahmud Pasha had played a central role.[169] Built before his fall from favor, the mausoleum demonstrates his access to craftsmen who worked for the palace.[170]

The prominence of the mausoleum attests to the prestige of the patron and his desire to communicate this architecturally within the space of the city. He achieved this: as his remarkable popularity rendered the executed vizier a saint (velī), his mausoleum became something of a shrine to which those who had palace-related wishes would first turn; before applying to the palace for new jobs, dismissed state officials would leave their petitions overnight in Mahmud Pasha's mausoleum, to obtain the approval of the perpetual grand vizier first.[171] Although the building thus became one of the loci of Ottoman Istanbul, its architecture, like the layout of Mahmud's mosque, remained unique.

The public kitchen was functioning in 953/1546 when the stipulations of its endowment were registered in a citywide survey. In addition to funds allocated for the daily provision of beneficiaries, the kitchen had funds for large feasts to be prepared for guests. The madrasa was situated near the mosque; these, the public kitchen and the children's school (referred to as *mekteb* or *muʿallimḫāne*), constituted the religious/charitable core of the complex.[172] The wages allocated to the madrasa professors, fifty *akçe* daily, were equal to wages paid to the teachers in Mehmed's new madrasas. This is striking, given that the instructor's wage was the principal indicator of the rank of a madrasa in the newly structured educational system and that Mehmed's eight madrasas surrounding his New Mosque were conceived as the primary educational institutions of the empire.[173] Was the rank of his madrasa, the only one to be founded by a member of the imperial council in the city at this date, another indicator of the grand vizier's exceptionally high standing within the newly configured hierarchy, a position that eventually led to his fall?

Another unique and equally intriguing element of Mahmud Pasha's complex is a free-standing fountain situated to the north of the mosque and the madrasa (fig. 83). This cubic structure, whose restoration inscription carries the date 1014/1605–6 and an attribution to Mahmud Pasha,[174] may have been the earliest example of a type of building that was to make its imprint on the city two and a half centuries later: the *meydan çeşmesi,* or the freestanding fountain. The building points to the presence of a small square near the religious and charitable buildings founded by Mahmud Pasha, significant in terms of emerging notions of urban space in Ottoman Constantinople. This constitutes another piece of evidence to counter the widely accepted notion that the Ottoman city lacked open public spaces. The fountain, an urban node in a dense urban fabric, prefigures a host of such foci in the city and its suburbs in later centuries. Questions regarding the inspiration behind this structure and why it remained unique for more than two centuries cannot be answered with our present knowledge. The

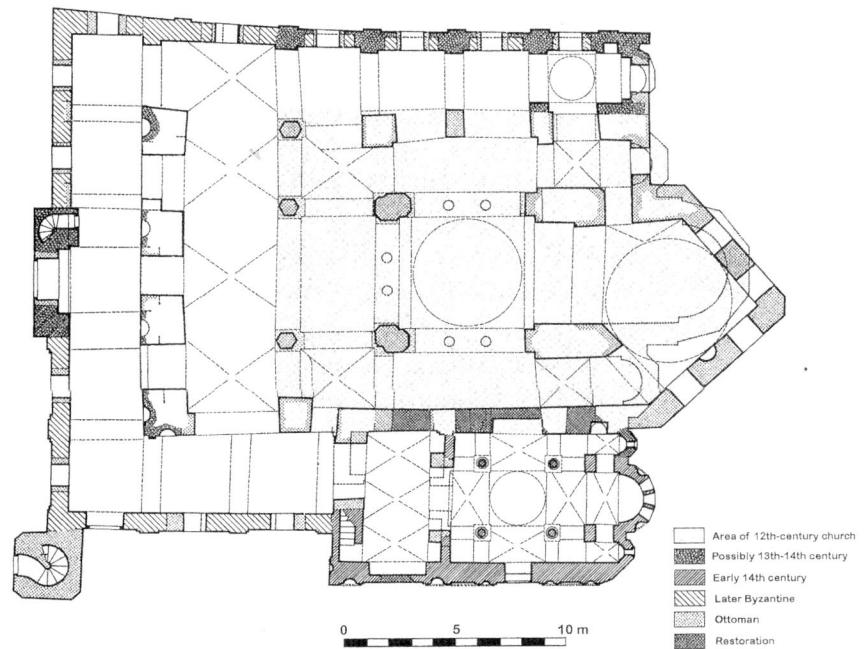

FIGURE 82
Pammakaristos, plan.

FIGURE 83
Mahmud Pasha fountain.

inclusion of the fountain in Matrakcı Nasuh's view of Istanbul painted in the 1530s, an image exclusively of public buildings and residences of significance, suggests that it was considered an important and visually prominent public structure (plate 7, right).[175]

With the exception of the foundation of Mahmud Pasha and that of Davud Pasha, completed in the first years of Bayezid II's reign, all vizierial foundations and baths of this period used water from the Kırkçeşme system restored and expanded by Mehmed. The restoration of the city's waterways did not mean that water was abundantly available to all: a number of individuals, the prominent scholar Mevlana Gürani among them, were denied permission to use water from the system for public buildings they founded. Mahmud's fountain thus attests and monumentalizes not only his charity but also his remarkable wealth and power. Moreover, the grand vizier placed a public fountain across from the northeastern corner of the bedestan, another construction that marked the prestige of the patron and simultaneously his proximity to the sultan.

Two small masjids located to the east of the main religious buildings belonged to the waqf. The Servi masjid and the Şeref Ağa masjid were allotted a prayer leader and a müezzin each in the waqfiyya of the founder and are recorded in the later surveys of the city as neighborhood masjids.[176] The Servi masjid, close to the the vizier's palace, was possibly built to serve his household. The Şeref Ağa masjid might have constituted a smaller focus in the less built-up segment of the area allotted to the founder, the section that lay between the palace and the religious core of his complex.

Contemporary authors praised Mahmud Pasha's buildings in terms similar to those they used to describe the buildings of the sultan, highlighting once more the unprecedented status and prestige of the grand vizier in the new configuration of power. Remarks by later Ottoman authors suggest that Mahmud Pasha's endeavor was not overshadowed by

the intensive building activity of the following centuries. The sixteenth-century historian Sa'düddin recognized the shift that took place in the patronage patterns of the Ottoman ruling body, as evidenced in Mahmud's buildings, noting that, until these were built, none of the viziers of the Ottoman state had undertaken such beautiful edifices. To Evliya Çelebi, who described the monuments of the densely built-up capital of the seventeenth century, Mahmud Pasha's was the only vizier's mosque that resembled a sultanic one.[177] Given the host of large-scale mosques built in the following centuries that were before Evliya's eyes, many carrying the names of Mahmud's successors in the grand vizierate, Evliya's remark underscores the builder's distinction rather than that of the building.

"Besides, he built grand houses for himself," wrote Kritovoulos, "rich and beautiful, and he planted gardens with trees bearing all sorts of fruit for the delectation and happiness and use of many, and gave them an abundant water supply."[178] These make up Mahmud's palace, located at the eastern end of the large plot on which the grand vizier's constructions were scattered, close to Hagia Sophia and Mehmed's New Palace. No information on the layout of the palace remains.[179] Judging from the locations of the palace bath, the masjid that possibly served the vizier's household, and other contemporary structures in the area, however, it is possible to suggest the boundaries of the palace and its extensive gardens. Its western boundary possibly lay between the Servi masjid and the madrasa of the religious complex, while its southern boundary ran slightly to the south of the palace bath, since the fifteenth-century mosque of Acem Ağa is situated less than a hundred meters away from that building.

The location of the palace is significant. Its grounds lay beyond the outer walls of the Topkapı Palace, across from the Kiosk of Processions (Alay Köşkü), the dodecagonal belvedere tower placed at a turn of the palace's outer wall (map 1). Thus the palace occupied the site of the present-day Bab-ı Ali, the prime ministry of the nineteenth century, and, before that, home to numerous grand viziers of the Ottoman state. Possibly the palace gate, like the nineteenth-century Bab-ı Ali Gate, was situated across from the kiosk. The location of Mahmud Pasha's palace not only points to continuity in the location of the prime ministry through much of the city's Ottoman history[180] but also reveals once more the premeditated nature of the city's development and the creation of its significant sites. The tower, an architectural link between the palace and the city, and a sign of the sultan's gaze over his realm, may well have been placed at this particular point as a response to the constructions of the vizier, who was "in charge of all the affairs of the government."[181] A similar arrangement is observed in the siting of İshak Pasha's masjid and bath (possibly his residence as well) across from the octagonal tower to the south of the palace's Imperial Gate. The high monumental towers that overlooked the vizierial buildings were signifiers of the sultan's supremacy over his officials. Spatial and architectural correspondences between the royal palace and the residences of the highest state officials thus symbolized the link between the sultan and his viziers, established visual and spatial dialogues between them, while simultaneously hierarchizing that relationship.

The only extant buildings belonging to the urban property endowed for the foundation are the caravanserai and the bath.[182] Both buildings, situated on the street known today by the name of the founder, the Mahmud Pasha Yokuşu, one of the main arteries connecting the bedestan with the harbor, provide insights into the use of urban space in this densely built-up area of the city. The monumental bath, marking the upper part of the street, was one of the most spectacular buildings of the fifteenth-century city. It presented to this street and to the one perpendicular to it a high, elaborately designed muqarnas portal. Behind it, the apodyterium, built in cut stone, carried one of the largest domes of Ottoman Constantinople before the construction of Mehmed's mosque (fig. 84).

The 113-meter-long exterior wall of Mahmud Pasha's double-courtyard han further defined this main artery. While the larger courtyard had a regular rectangular layout, the second one, situated below it on the sloped street, was given an irregular form in order to fit the intersection of two streets, one leading to the bedestan and the other joining the artery that ran along the eastern wall of the first palace, marked by a monumental gate (fig. 77).[183] The siting of the building in this particular spot and the lack of an orthogonal geometry in its second courtyard suggest a concern with displaying the building on these two busy streets. The no longer extant portal of the lower courtyard faced the intersection: to those walking up the hill toward the bedestan or toward the eastern gate of Mehmed's first palace, Mahmud Pasha presented the entrance of his huge khan (fig. 85).[184]

Two large clusters of commercial and residential property were gathered around the commercial and charitable buildings of Mahmud. Flanking and facing the khan were the "shops of Mahmud Pasha," over two hundred of them along the commercial artery that still carries the name of the grand vizier.[185] Some 135 houses, rooms, and shops were scattered mostly around the madrasa and the public kitchen. The exact number and locations of these buildings remain unclear, largely due to the complicated history of the Mahmud Pasha waqf, which

FIGURE 84
Mahmud Pasha bath from the
east, *cāmekān*/apodyterium
exterior and portal (from Gurlitt,
Die Baukunst Konstantinopels,
1907).

was incorporated into the sultanic foundation upon the vizier's execution, and subsequently restored, though it is not clear whether with the same property or not.[186] Perhaps the restoration of his foundation paralleled the post-Mehmed restoration of the grand vizier's prestige, along with that of a number of grandees who had fallen out of the monarch's favor.[187] By 1546, the date of the earliest surviving citywide survey of charitable foundations, the foundation was richly endowed again. Whatever its original size (though probably it was not much smaller), Mahmud Pasha's was the biggest nonroyal foundation in mid-sixteenth-century Istanbul, with the largest number of employees and beneficiaries and vast kitchen expenses. The agency of the vizier in the formation of a new spatial configuration and new social networks in the capital city is manifest in the range of spaces, occupations, and services provided by the foundation, and the expansive urban property endowed and rented out for it. The making and perpetuation of Mahmud Pasha's saintly reputation, too, must owe, in part at least, to his continued charity.

While the foundation lacked the strict symmetry and axiality of the sultan's complex on the fourth hill, there was little spontaneity involved in the selection of its site and in its layout in general. It was situated between the city's political and religious loci, the first palace (at the time Mahmud's complex was conceived, the sole Ottoman palace in the city) and the Hagia Sophia (the only congregational mosque in the city at the time); its proximity to the newly established bedestan and surrounding markets made it a focal point in the area. In one of the most densely inhabited districts of the city, the buildings of Mahmud Pasha not only adapted to the urban fabric but also transformed it, through the establishment of functional and visual foci. Conspicuous display, apparent in the monumental scale, extravagant building materials, and masterful craftsmanship, marks this act of transformation. The elaborately decorated muqarnas portal of the bath, its ashlar masonry (contrasting with the brick and wood of the buildings surrounding it), the variegated marble columns of the mosque's portico, and the colorful tile-patterned exterior of the mausoleum were elements new to the urban environment of Istanbul. The large scale of almost all of the buildings, the prominence of the bath's façade and dome, the collocation of the khan's façade and a good part of an important artery, the placement of portals at points that provide the largest possible angle of vision, the projection of the khan's surviving portal iwan into the street attest to the use of the urban environment in a manner at once adaptive and manipulative. In contrast to Mehmed's complex, whose idealized plan isolated it from its immediate surroundings by means of a walled enclosure, the complex of Mahmud Pasha spread out to mark and dominate a large district of the city and its street pattern.

AN OTTOMAN MONUMENT
ON THE ASIAN SHORE

Although various sources refer to an Ottoman presence in Üsküdar, on the Asian shore of the Bosphorus, from the early decades of the fifteenth century onward, this was not an urban space; neither was it marked by a significant work of architecture. The sultan himself founded no more than what the port across from Constantinople immediately required: the earliest surviving copy of Mehmed's foundation, dated to ca. 1472, includes a masjid, a bath, and a caravanserai in Üsküdar; these seem to have represented the extent of the sultan's architectural activity here.[188] The convent-mosque, soup kitchen, bath, caravanserai, and shops built by Rum Mehmed Pasha, therefore, not only constituted a sizable addition to public buildings here; they also are the earliest indication of Üsküdar's being conceptualized as Constantinople's Asian suburb, an integral part of a tripartite topographical layout embracing a triad of suburbs.[189]

The foundation inscription of Rum Mehmed's mosque carries the date 875/1471,

13,a KÜRKDSCHILER HAN HINTERER HOF

which corresponds to his term as grand vizier in 1471–72.[190] Contemporary chroniclers agree that Rum, or Greek, Mehmed was a native of Istanbul and was among those captured during the conquest.[191] Like Mahmud and Has Murad, he might have been of aristocratic Byzantine descent. Unlike them, he was a highly unpopular figure in the eyes of contemporary Ottoman chroniclers. Rum Mehmed Pasha played an important role in the Karaman campaigns and the deportations from Karaman to Istanbul; his harsh treatment of the Muslim population of Karaman and his destruction of the towns of Larende and Ereğli are recounted in chronicles of the period. He figures again in the context of state confiscation of freehold land and waqfs, another highly unpopular attempt by Mehmed's administration to increase state revenues. Aşıkpaşazade, himself a victim of changes in the status of urban property, wrote with considerable animosity that Rum Mehmed's father had been "a friend of the Greeks of Istanbul." Rum Mehmed Pasha was dismissed in 879/1474 and executed, possibly because of a conflict with another high-ranking official of the period, Karamani Mehmed Pasha.

FIGURE 85
Mahmud Pasha khan, second courtyard entrance, at the north (from Gurlitt, *Die Baukunst Konstantinopels*, 1907).

The siting of the buildings is indicative of the patron's motives, both of providing services to the small settlement here and of marking and monumentalizing the city's Asian shore in an Ottoman idiom. While the commercial and residential structures belonging to the foundation were located close to the port in Üsküdar, the mosque was situated on the slope of the hill to the south.[192] Like Mahmud Pasha's complex on the city's second hill, it occupied an elevated site that allowed it to dominate its surroundings (fig. 86). This suggests that the visual prominence of the Ottoman building on the shore across from the Constantinopolitan peninsula

FIGURE 86
Rum Mehmed Pasha convent-mosque from the northeast.

was a major concern in the conception of the project. The elevation of the main dome on tympanum arches rising above the level of the five-domed portico and the lateral rooms made this the highest among viziers' mosques in that period (figs. 87, 88). To those who climbed up the hill and the steps to the lofty portico, on the other hand, the mosque offered a view of the Constantinopolitan peninsula and the Bosphorus comparable to the vistas from Mehmed's New Palace.

Formally, the mosque of Rum Mehmed Pasha presents a striking juxtaposition of early and late Byzantine architectural idioms with early and contemporary Ottoman architectural idioms (figs. 88, 89). Like the mosque of Mahmud Pasha, it, too, is a variation on the convent-mosque type. The central hall is covered by a dome rising over tympanum arches, and is flanked on the mihrab side by an oblong space covered with a half dome. On each side of the central hall are two convent rooms. Several features distinguish the building from conventional examples of the type, and in these one can read something of the builder's intent. The most glaring difference, which prompted one Turkish art historian to follow the line of Aşıkpaşazade in the critique of Rum Mehmed Pasha, is the decisively Byzantine look of the building's superstructure (figs. 86, 90).[193] The tympanum arches rising above the cornices of the main hall, the arches of the dome windows forming an undulating cornice to the drum, the use of brick to delineate arches and window frames, and the composite masonry of brick and stone in the superstructure give the mosque something of the ornate exteriors of late Byzantine churches of Constantinople, with their dynamic surface and mass treatment. The window-pierced high tympanum arches carrying the main dome, and the half dome covering the qibla iwan, simultaneously constitute another set of equally interesting elements that distinguish this mosque. These features relate the building unmistakably to Mehmed's New Mosque, completed only about a year earlier, and through it to Justinian's Great Church (fig. 91).

As Aptullah Kuran has suggested, the late Byzantine features of the mosque may have been an expression of the Constantinopolitan patron's taste, or perhaps they are, as Robert Ousterhout has suggested, a sign of continuity in Byzantine workshop practices and hence of Rum Mehmed's patronage of Greek crafts-men.[194] But additional differences that connect the building to Mehmed's New Mosque and through it to Hagia Sophia render insufficient any interpretation based solely on practical or personal factors, whether the availability of craftsmen or the vizier's desire to emphasize his aristocratic Greek background. Emulating the features of Hagia Sophia's newly revived

architecture, Mehmed's vizier partook of the imperial architectural program of the ruler. With its siting and its architecture, the mosque of Rum Mehmed Pasha extended visual correlations between the city's focal points to the land across the Bosphorus. The building remained, well into the sixteenth century, the only Ottoman monumental mosque to imprint an Ottoman presence in the Asian suburb, and the only large-scale socioreligious complex there (fig. 92).

Mehmed Pasha's mausoleum, a domed octagonal building of ashlar masonry that does not share the Byzantine features of the mosque, is situated behind the mihrab wall of the mosque. The bath and the public kitchen were located lower on the slope of the hill. While the sixteenth-century waqfiyya summary shows a well-endowed public kitchen and a seemingly busy bath (with a yearly income of 23,000 *akçe*),[195] a few remains alone indicate the original location of the buildings today.

That the foundation, unlike the majority of large-scale foundations of the period, was

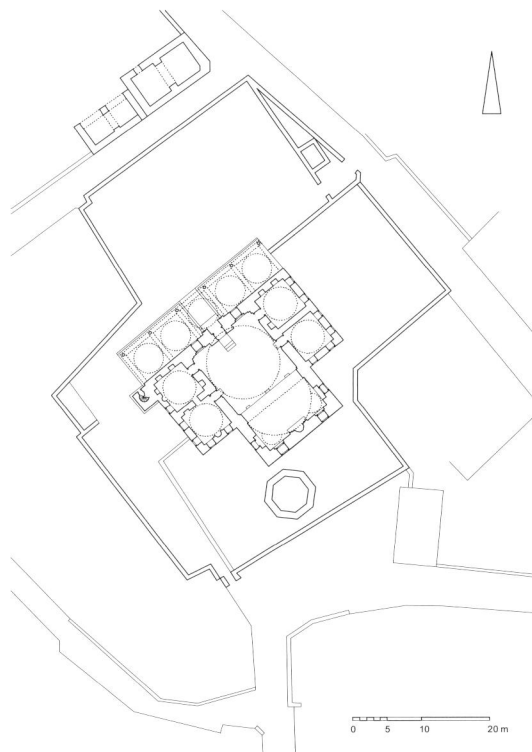

FIGURE 87
Rum Mehmed Pasha convent-mosque, plan.

FIGURE 88
Rum Mehmed Pasha convent-mosque, section.

isolated from the vizier's residence in the city proper underlines the period concern with creating an Ottoman locus in the Asian suburb, which would extend Ottoman presence visually and physically to the Asian shore. Rum Mehmed's residence was in the neighborhood of Hace Hayrüddin, to the northwest of Mehmed's first palace. The waqfiyya summary indicates that the *sārāy* consisted of a courtyard, family quarters (*ḥarem*), and rooms, for a total of thirty-seven *bāb* (rooms or sections).[196] In the 953/1546 register, in which the residence now appears as the palace of Mustafa Pasha belonging to the waqf of Rum Mehmed Pasha, the building is described as a complex of numerous single- and double-story structures and a private bath. A number of rooms and shops in this neighborhood and in the neighborhood of Katib Şemsüddin nearby belonged to the endowment.[197]

DEPORTATION AND CONSTRUCTION: THE FOUNDATION OF HAS MURAD PASHA

The third major vizierial project to be realized following Mehmed's order was the complex of Has Murad Pasha. Unlike the founders of the two other nonsultanic monumental complexes in Istanbul, Has Murad did not hold the post of grand vizier. He was, as were the other two founders, a Byzantine aristocrat recruited to palace service. A member of the house of the Palaeologi, he was, according to Angiolello, a nephew of the last Byzantine emperor. He attained the highly prestigious post of governor of Rumelia at a young age; in this post and during the campaign against Uzun Hasan in 1472–73, he drowned in the Euphrates as his army was defeated by the Akkoyunlu chief. Angiolello and Ottoman chroniclers agree that he was a favorite of the sultan, hence his title *ḫāṣ*.[198] The loss of this favorite, Ottoman chroniclers suggest, had a role in the sultan's final dismissal

of Mahmud Pasha from the grand vizierate in 1473.[199]

Has Murad's complex must have been built in the same years as that of Rum Mehmed Pasha, as their mosques were completed within the same year, 876/1471–72. The bath and the public kitchen were probably completed shortly after the mosque. The widely accepted argument that the main motive behind the construction of socioreligious complexes in postconquest Istanbul was the formation of urban cores that would encourage further settlement certainly holds true for this project. The deportation of several hundred households from the town of Aksaray to the area around Murad Pasha's complex in 875/1470–71 closely corresponds to the mosque's completion date.[200] Hadidi, who wrote a history of the House of Osman in verse, recognized the centrality of these deportations for the creation of an urban community, noting that the people brought from Aksaray were the well-to-do and the craftsmen of the town and that the sultan gave them orchards, where they built houses and bazaars.[201] The correspondence of the dates suggests that the construction and the settlement of deportees in the area were closely linked; to this day the district carries the name Aksaray. Maintaining control over the religiopolitical affiliations of the deported community might have been a factor behind state-sponsored building activity in this area, as suggested by the presence here of a number dervish lodges belonging to orders having troubled relations with the state.[202] A state-sponsored charity might have been deemed necessary in a district newly settled by large numbers of Muslim deportees and already inhabited by popular sects.

Like Rum Mehmed's foundation, the Aksaray complex did not originally have an educational building attached to it. Some years after the founder's death, Has Murad's brother Mesih, another recruit from the Palaeologan dynasty to become a member of the imperial council, expanded the waqf by the addition of a madrasa. A number of shops and rooms were constructed near these buildings, while commercial property was endowed also in the Taht al-kal'a area.[203]

Occupying a site on the southern branch of the Mese, Murad Pasha's mosque was built just to the north of a monumental arch, whose fragments were discovered in 1956 within the

FIGURE 89 (*opposite, top*)
Rum Mehmed Pasha convent-mosque, from the north.

FIGURE 90 (*opposite, bottom*)
Rum Mehmed Pasha convent-mosque, from the south.

FIGURE 91
Rum Mehmed Pasha convent-mosque and mausoleum, aerial view.

FIGURE 92
Rum Mehmed Pasha convent-mosque, represented uphill from the later-sixteenth-century Şemsi Ahmed Pasha mosque, detail from a map of Istanbul in Piri Reis's *Kitāb-ı Baḥriye,* second half of the seventeenth century, Staatsbibliothek zu Berlin, Preußischer Kulturbesitz, Orientabteilung, Diez A. Foliant 57, fol. 28, quarter b (fig. 121).

enclosure wall of the complex.[204] The same excavation uncovered fragments of a colossal figure of a river god, which Manuel Chrysoloras in 1411 had described as "a statue made of white stone or marble, which seems to rest on its elbow," on "the same road and just above the source of water that runs through the city."[205] This monumentally defined spot, situated at the intersection of the Mese and the river Lycus, has been identified alternately as the area of the Forum Bovis and that of the Forum Amastrianum.[206] Murad Pasha's complex, situated to the north-northwest of the forum area, presents the first instance of a trend that would continue into the sixteenth century: the construction of religious complexes on the fora of Byzantine Constantinople. Bayezid II's grand vizier Atik Ali Pasha was to build on the Forum of Constantine; the sultan himself was to choose the Forum of Taurus for the large complex he founded in 1500.

Scholarship on Ottoman architectural and urbanistic practices has generally interpreted these choices of sites as resulting from an incompatibility between large open urban spaces and Ottoman/Islamic notions of urbanism.[207] Ottomans, according to this interpretation of their urban practices, cluttered up the Byzantine fora with a host of public and private structures, for public squares in the Western sense were alien to Ottoman urban life, and social life in cities was centered around religious complexes only. Other reasons for these choices, however, suggest themselves. That remains of the forum's architectural and sculptural furnishings lay to the south-southeast of the Murad Pasha mosque implies that building up open space was not a particular concern for the Ottoman builders. The choice of the forum for Murad Pasha's buildings, on the other hand, demonstrates once more the concern with establishing monumental Ottoman foci in

central locations throughout the city. Sparsely populated and peppered with undeveloped areas, gardens, and orchards, fifteenth-century Constantinople would not have presented the builders with any difficulty in finding available construction sites other than the Byzantine forum.[208] The use of the forum area, on the other hand, would enhance the visibility of the buildings, both through the space it provided around the complex and through its siting on one of the main arteries of the city, leading to the recently completed citadel.

A note in Pierre Gilles's description of Constantinople suggests a further reason for such choices of site. He reports having been told by an "ancient native of Constantinople" that Mehmed had given the grounds of the Forum of Taurus to those who would build on it, because, like the Hippodrome, it was full of wild and uncultivated trees and was only a shelter for thieves and robbers.[209] The image of Constantinople in Hartmann Schedel's *Liber Chronicarum* (plate 6), where trees grow in ruined buildings, conveys the same impression. It was not the incompatibility between an urban ideal and what Constantinople offered its new inhabitants that determined the fate of the Byzantine fora, then, but the city's current state and a complex of symbolic and utilitarian choices regarding the use of its former layout.

The centerpiece of Murad Pasha's complex (fig. 93), too, is a convent-mosque. It closely follows the preconquest conventions of this type of building, excepting the side entrances to its convent rooms, a feature that is also found in the Mahmud Pasha convent-mosque, suggesting a growing need to separate its divers functions. A reminiscence of the original form of the convent-masjid, the domed unit on the qibla side has a higher floor level than the central hall, a distinction that is echoed in the different systems of transition to the dome in the two rooms (figs. 94, 95). For example, triangular panels connect the walls to the dome of the central hall, while the dome on the qibla side rises on muqarnas-covered pendentives. These formally distinct spaces, however, functionally constituted a contiguous unit. The unusual height of the main domes (twenty-one meters), hitherto evaluated in terms of the creation of a unified interior space,[210] alters the exterior configuration of the building. The mass of the main prayer hall dwarfs the side spaces, bespeaking a preoccupation with height in the early religious monuments of the capital (fig. 96).

The double bath built by Murad Pasha near the convent-mosque was sacrificed to a Haussmannian campaign in the 1950s, which involved significant destruction in the walled city (fig. 97). The plan that remains in Glück's *Die*

Bader Konstantinopolis shows it situated longitudinally to the east of the mosque, presenting to the remaining portion of the Forum Bovis large apoditeria measuring 14.50 meters on each side. The bath's domes surpassed those of the nearby mosque, partaking of a trend established in the early decades of Ottoman rule in Constantinople.

SMALLER FOUNDATIONS AND THE LATER YEARS OF MEHMED'S RULE

A number of projects realized by the military/administrative elite through the last years of Mehmed's rule underscore the prominence of monumental public baths in the urban environment of postconquest Istanbul, a salient aspect of the city's reconstruction discussed in the first part of this chapter. The patronage

FIGURE 93
Has Murad Pasha complex, plan.

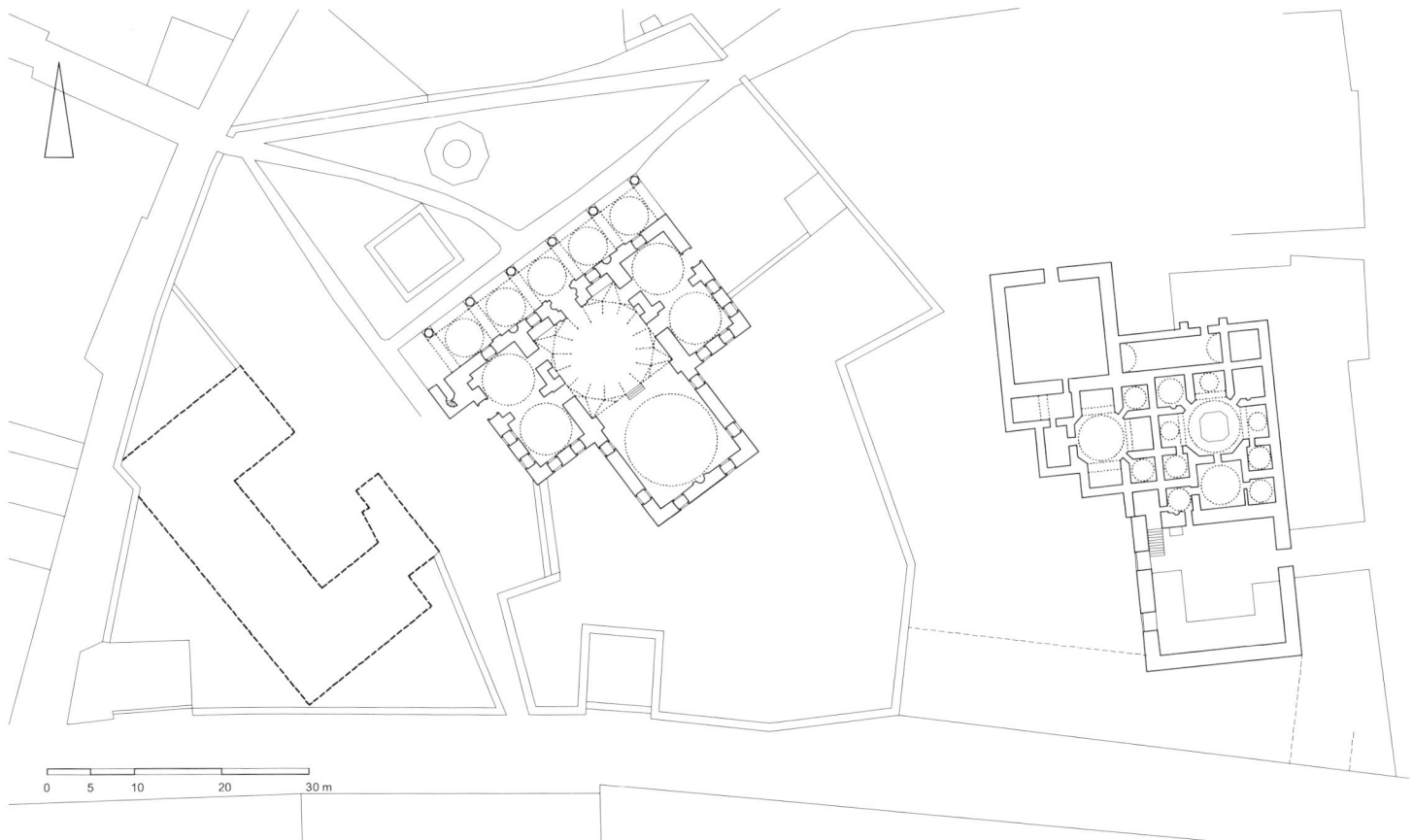

0   5   10   20   30 m

FIGURE 94
Has Murad Pasha convent-
mosque, section.

FIGURE 95
Has Murad Pasha convent-
mosque, interior, facing south.

FIGURE 96
Has Murad Pasha convent-
mosque, from the north.

of three builders who started construction of public works in the city in the later 1470s, all prominent members of the imperial council who held the post of grand vizier, focused on monumental bathhouses. Such a bathhouse, dwarfing the mosque built by the same founder, is today visible in the foundation of İshak Pasha near the Topkapı Palace. The second vizier and governor of Bosnia, grand vizier between 1468 and 1471, was given land across from the octagonal tower marking the southern section of the Topkapı Palace's outer walls, possibly the site of a ruined Byzantine building (figs. 98, 99; see also fig. 29b).[211] The location echoes that of the Mahmud Pasha palace, across from a palace-wall tower to the north, both sites participants in the visual and spatial dialogue between monuments of the monarch and those of the ruling elite. Another such assembly, with the same hierarchy of buildings, was built by Nişancı Mehmed Pasha (grand vizier from 1476 until his execution in the aftermath of

Mehmed's demise) in largely Greek and Armenian Kumkapı (and some fifty meters from the church of Surp Asdvadzadzin, house of the Armenian patriarchate from 1641 onward). As early as 1480, the Surp Asdvadzadzin was serving an Armenian community, possibly those Armenians brought to the city from Karaman in 1479.[212] A massive structure built of coarse stone masonry, the bath was well used by the inhabitants of the area. The mosque, although richly endowed, was the less stable structure: it is one of the many fifteenth-century buildings in the city that preserves nothing of its original structure.[213] Up the hill and to the south of the Mese/Divan Yolu was the bath of Gedik Ahmed Pasha, Nişancı's predecessor in the grand vizierate. One of the largest baths of the Ottoman city, it constituted the only Ottoman public building of monumental size in the area at the time it was built, in 1474–75 (fig. 100).[214]

These foundations were parts of larger endowments centered elsewhere: Gedik

FIGURE 97
Has Murad Pasha bath and convent-mosque, during the demolition of the bath, ca. 1955.

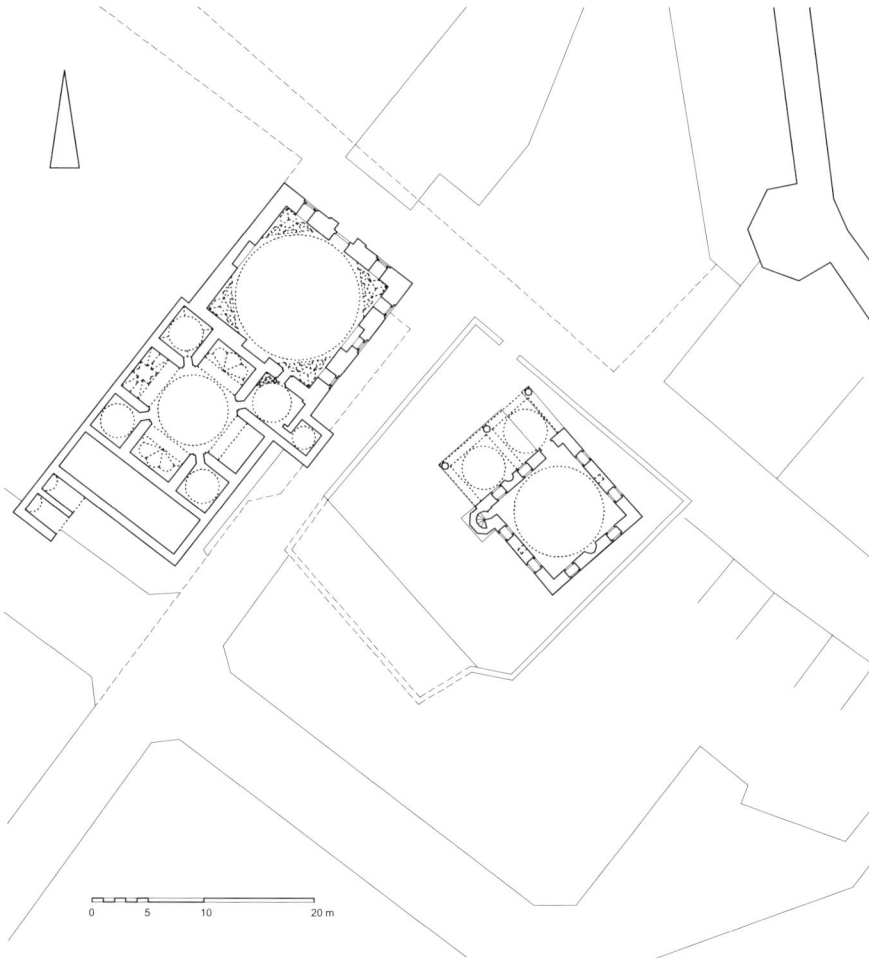

Ahmed's in the inner Aegean town of Afyon, İshak's in his hometown İnegöl. Unlike founders of larger complexes of the fifteenth and sixteenth centuries, whose palaces were often built near their public works, İshak, Gedik Ahmed, and Nişancı Mehmed located their residences at some remove from their public works, the latter two close to the Old Palace.[215] Nişancı's palace was built within successive courtyards and, like Mahmud's near Topkapı, included a private masjid.[216]

The relatively small sizes and limited functions of these later foundations suggest that the larger complexes completed in the early 1470s were deemed sufficient to answer the needs for public structures in the capital at this time. The next major building phase was to take place some decades later, in the latter part of Bayezid II's rule. The earlier structures founded by viziers, on the other hand, reveal a shift in patronage patterns related to larger political dynamics of the period. It is not their rank within the Ottoman administrative hierarchy (two were grand viziers, while one served as the governor-general of Rumelia) but their descent from the Byzantine aristocracy that links the three founders to each other. Given that only an allotment of property made the establishment of a pious foundation possible, the fact that the largest foundations of this period were realized by converted soldiers of aristocratic extraction points to a deliberate policy on the part of the sultan. The foundation of a building complex with religious, charitable, and commercial functions was in turn a step in the creation of a power base, as it would lead to the formation of a network of patronage in which the founder, employees, and beneficiaries would partake to different degrees. Through the 1460s and early 1470s, prominent members of the new ruling elite were expected to, and chose to, build primarily in the new capital, although they also undertook prestigious projects elsewhere. Their power bases were thus created in the capital, in contrast to the foundations of at least two later viziers who built large complexes elsewhere, İshak Pasha and Gedik Ahmed Pasha.

The shift in patronage patterns of the ruling elite becomes immediately visible when comparing the postconquest constructions with Ottoman architectural undertakings in the earlier part of the fifteenth century. Through the century and a half before the capture of Constantinople, the higher-ranking Ottoman emirs and ulema alongside sultans, had been the builders of public structures in Ottoman lands. Mostly of ulema origin, viziers of Mehmed I and Murad II built masjids and madrasas in the capital cities, while they undertook more ambitious projects in their towns of origin.[217] Military commanders, İsa Bey and Gazi Mihal among them, built convents or convent-masjids rather than congregational mosques and masjids; these structures served the ghazis and dervishes who constituted their power bases. Excepting the unusual case of Umur Bey, who built a congregational mosque in Bursa, no such religious establishment was founded by a high-ranking

FIGURE 98 (*opposite, top*) İshak Pasha mosque and bath, with the Topkapı Palace wall in the background, the octagonal tower on the far right.

FIGURE 99 (*opposite, bottom*) İshak Pasha mosque and bath, plan.

FIGURE 100 Gedik Ahmed Pasha bath, domes.

official in the preconquest period. Nor did the viziers and commanders of earlier Ottoman sultans build large urban complexes comprising a wide range of buildings serving religious, educational, and charitable purposes, as their postconquest successors did in Istanbul.[218] Their foundations, while central to the settlement and institutionalization of newly acquired territories, were for the most part individual structures rather than ensembles, with an impact on the institutional, spatial, and visual configurations of Ottoman cities lesser than that of sultanic projects. In function, scale, and formal features, the first vizierial complexes in Istanbul, as Evliya Çelebi observed, looking at Mahmud Pasha's mosque, were more like the sultanic complexes of former Ottoman capitals. This shift in the pattern of viziers' patronage of socioreligious foundations, in turn, reflected changes in the structure of the administrative hierarchy.

PART 3
MEMORY, SPACE, AND VISION IN CONSTRUCTIONS OF THE OTTOMAN CAPITAL CITY

The building projects surveyed here were parts of a program, a collective enterprise of the ruling elite to create the imperial capital. That creation was not conceived solely in terms of restoring the city's infrastructure and providing settings to institutions of the new rule. It entailed the monumentalization of the city in an Ottoman idiom, through the creation of a network of significant buildings and sites that would propose a range of meanings to a diverse set of users and audiences, providing a means of partaking simultaneously in the urban space and in its practices.[219] The conception of the city as an entity that was to be reshaped, to become receptacle and signifier of a new political and cultural order, was central to this program. To borrow a term Manfredo Tafuri used for the Rome of Nicholas V, the *resignification* of Constantinople was, in part, what the Ottoman project entailed.[220]

In the scale and expanse of the projects realized by the Ottoman ruling elite, it is possible to locate an emerging trend that was to reshape the capital cities of the early modern world, particularly from the fifteenth century onward. Fernand Braudel formulated this as a pact between the territorial state and the capital city: the capital city was created by an imperial or national unit, and the city, in turn, created that imperial or national unit.[221] A new conception of the capital as the seat of the centralizing monarch and as the site that would represent the polity was to leave its mark on a number of cities of the early modern era; concomitantly a new sense of urban scale and urban expanse was introduced to the cityscapes. The examples of Rome (exceptional in its territorial constitution but nevertheless partaking in the dynamics of the period) and, looking forward to the sixteenth and early seventeenth centuries, Isfahan and Paris would fall in the list of capital cities to be transformed and expanded through grand projects conceived and realized by centralizing regimes. Precisely in the years following the definitive move of the throne from Edirne, Constantinople expanded out of its late medieval core, through projects that encompassed the whole expanse of the walled city.

The intense building activity of these years created spatial and visual configurations that do not immediately fall into standard urban-historiographic frameworks such as "planned" or "organic." Multiplicity and juxtaposition, rather than recourse to a singular and homogeneous method, characterized Ottoman attitudes toward and manners of shaping the city. A syncretistic imperial vision appropriated and juxtaposed, to its own ends, a multiplicity of urban practices and modes of thinking about the city. Ottoman cities that had taken shape before the capture of Constantinople provided Istanbulite patrons and architects with models for the city, in part or in its totality, models that shaped and organized aspects of urban life. Architectural projects of the ruling body articulated responses to the past and the present of Constantinople. The complex interplay of rejection and appropriation that informed Ottoman attitudes toward and uses of the Byzantine past became salient in the space of the city, as did the interplay of utilitarian and symbolistic attitudes toward extant structures and configurations. Parallel political dynamics, engendering similar tendencies and sensibilities, rendered meaningful the notions of urban order contemporaneously emerging in Renaissance Italy.

To turn to Ottoman models first. A city center marked by a congregational mosque and a central commercial establishment, complemented by religious-charitable complexes built around convent-masjids, often at considerable distance from that center, characterized the urban layouts of Bursa and Edirne, the two primary cities of the Ottoman realm through the fourteenth and early fifteenth centuries. Both had developed outside the walled Byzantine enclosures; Bursa's citadel housed the Ottoman ruler's residence, while in Edirne the palaces of Murad I and Murad II were both situated outside of, and at a distance from, the old city (figs. 101–3).

Parallels to the institutional and spatial organization of the city center, and to the spatial relations established between the locus of rule and the inhabited city, may be found—with different degrees of exactitude—elsewhere in the Islamic and the Mediterranean worlds. The building complex centered around a convent-masjid and constituting an urban node in its turn, on the other hand, is a typically Ottoman urban model to which the builders of Constantinople had recourse.[222] While the urbanistic concept of the complex was adopted whole by patrons building in the new capital, an important change took place in its institutional framework and subsequently in its architecture: changes in the religious politics of the state effected changes in the architectural settings of socioreligious activity. The centerpiece of the royal compound was no longer a multifunctional convent, home to a set of socioreligious activities, but a congregational mosque, space of orthodox religion. Viziers founded convent-mosques, which, like the centerpiece of the royal compound, functioned as Friday mosques. As in other Ottoman cities, public kitchens, hospices, and baths were the primary dependencies of the city's mosques. The monumental hospice and public kitchen of Mehmed's foundation or of the vizierial complexes give form to the continuing import of a long-held Ottoman ideal, hospitality and generosity expressed through the offering of food and shelter: practices of high symbolic value integral to an ethos founded on the vicissitudes of a highly mobile society.[223] While the continuing patronage of public kitchens and hospices may be attributed to a well-established notion of political leadership, the specific conditions of the new capital must also have rendered them beneficial to a considerable number of people. In a city of deportees and of former members of the conquest army who had stayed on, many among

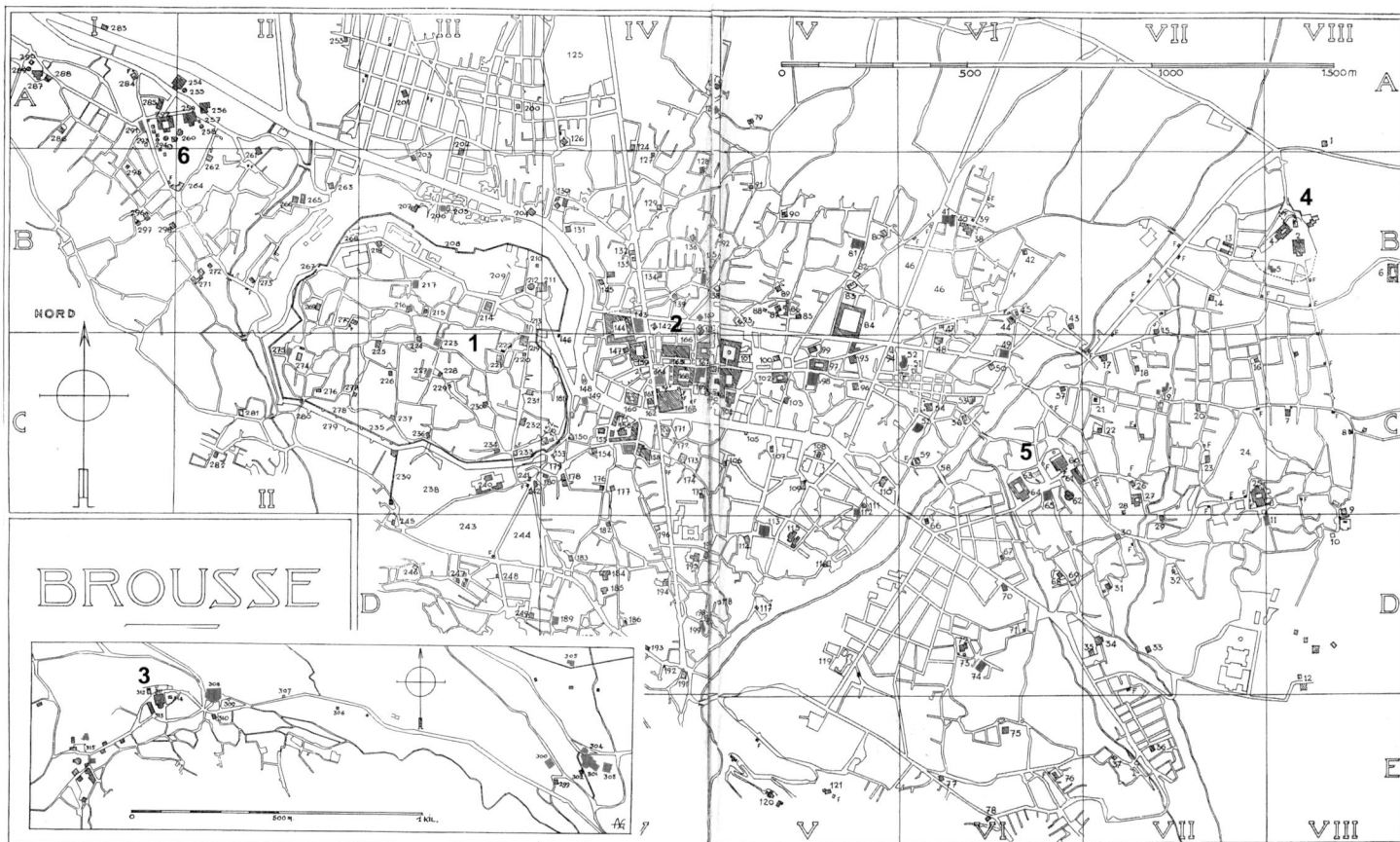

FIGURE 101
Map of Bursa: (1) citadel,
(2) city center, (3) complex
of Murad I, (4) complex of
Bayezid I, (5) complex of
Mehmed I, (6) complex of
Murad II.

whom must have become poorer, if not home-less, in the confusion of policy changes regard-ing the status of urban property, these institu-tions possibly answered immediate needs of the population.

Unlike the city's congregational mosques, which continued to occupy the spatial and insti-tutional centers of urban complexes through the Ottoman centuries, the postconquest constitution of their dependencies remained particular to those decades. Public baths were to lose their monumental dimensions and archi-tectural grandeur in the later decades of the sixteenth century, while hospices and public kitchens ceased to be part of vizierial building complexes. The madrasa, which was to become an integral element of most major and minor establishments from the early sixteenth century

onward, seems to have been a less visible insti-tution in the city at this time. While Mehmed's eight madrasas surrounding his mosque consti-tuted the central institution for religious edu-cation within the Ottoman realm, the viziers' complexes, resembling sultanic complexes of Bursa and Edirne in scale and function, did not all feature madrasas.[224] The significant excep-tion was the foundation of Mahmud Pasha, which paid the same wages to the madrasa teachers and students as the sultanic founda-tion. The sponsorship of education in the capi-tal, we may surmise, was the prerogative of the monarch and his highest-ranking official.[225]

The creation of the commercial district of the Taht al-kalʿa, or a market area established "below the citadel," was an Ottoman urban practice established before the capture of

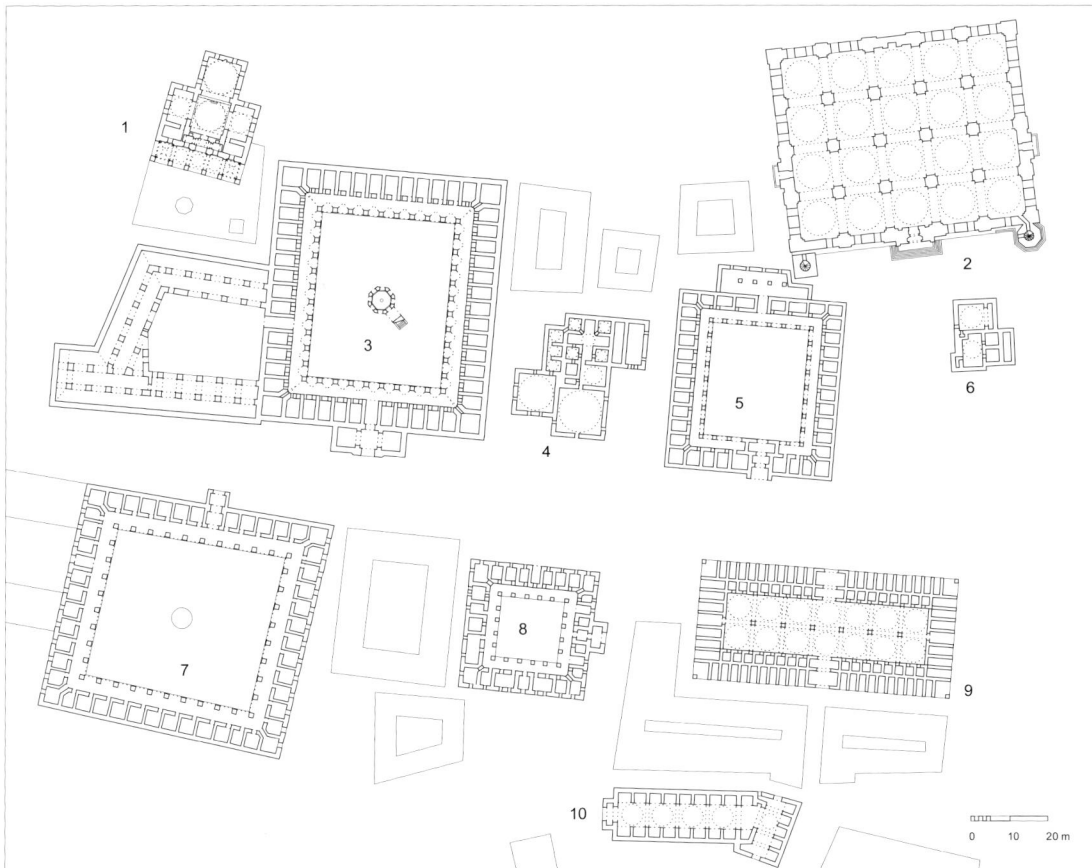

FIGURE 102
Bursa city center: (1) convent-masjid of Orhan, (2) Friday mosque of Bayezid I, (3) Koza Han, (4) public bath of Orhan, (5) Emir Han, (6) Şengül public bath, (7) Fidan Han, (8) Geyve Han, (9) bedestan, (10) Sipahiler bazaar.

Constantinople. The construction of the first palace at the center of the walled city and the establishment/revitalization of the commercial district nearby reproduced not only former Ottoman models but also the urban configuration of a number of medieval cities of the eastern Mediterranean. The siting of administrative loci at the edges of the city—the New Palace at the northeastern tip of the peninsula, the citadel at the Golden Gate—too, while choices that had a direct relation to the Byzantine topography of Constantinople, simultaneously reproduced a characteristic feature of premodern cities widely, if not globally, observed. Alberti himself—in a historical account of kings', as opposed to tyrants', uses of citadels—suggested that a ruler's palace and citadel be placed at the periphery of the city.[226]

This particular correspondence between Renaissance theory and Ottoman practice owes to their common roots in premodern urban practices. Architectural layouts used exclusively in sultanic projects (the star-shaped citadel blocking the Golden Gate, the ideally geometrical layout of the New Complex, the "Frankish-style" octagonal towers and the classicizing details of the New Palace) point to architectural and urban ideas newly formulated in fifteenth-century Italy.

Mehmed's contacts with Italy suggest parallels between Istanbul and contemporary Buda, where King Matthias Corvinus, another peripheral enthusiast of Renaissance ideas, owned copies of the treatises of Alberti and Filarete and where the work of a host of Italian artists and craftsmen in royal architectural projects is

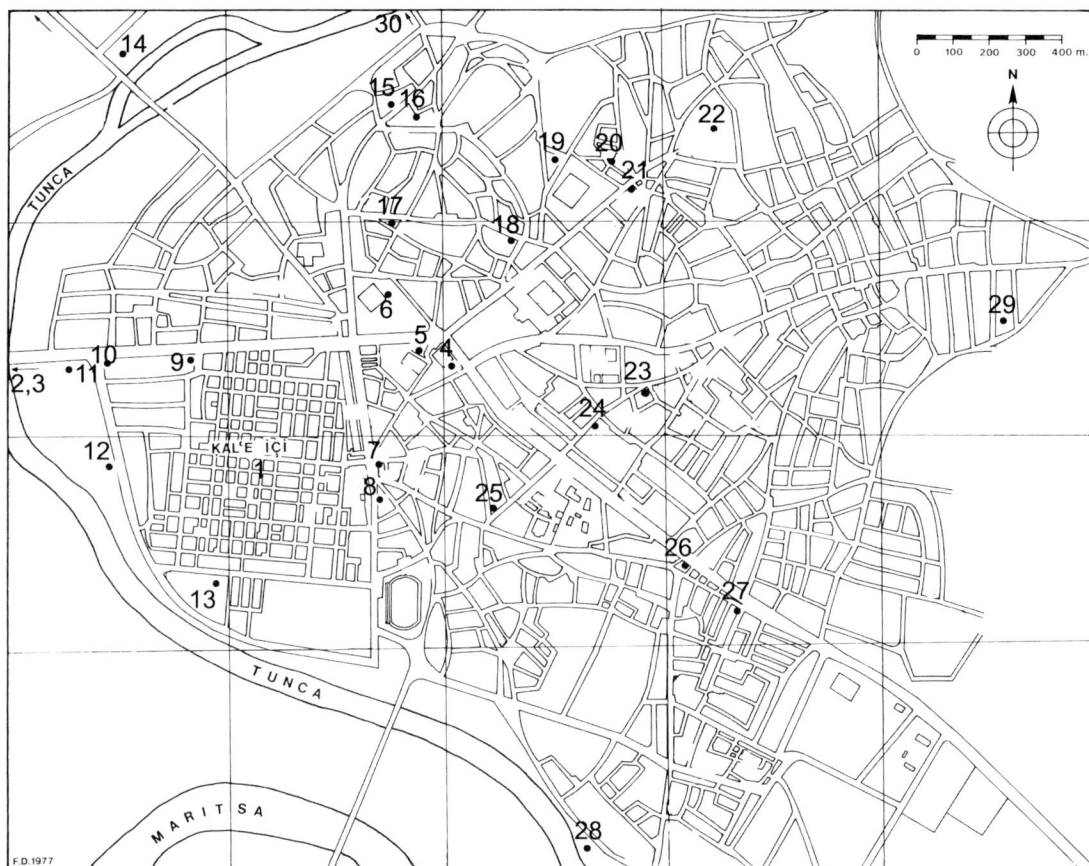

well documented.[227] Students of Ottoman cultural history have been less fortunate regarding
such documentation: while Mehmed's artistic
and cultural contacts with the Italian world
are well known, no record survives to help us
reconstruct the exact circumstances of the
exchanges through which particular architectural projects were conceived and realized. New
approaches to the Renaissance, on the other
hand, conceptualizing it as a cultural movement
taking place in diverse centers and peripheries,
where new ideas were filtered through extant
structures, juxtaposed to traditional forms, and
at times rejected, prove useful in evaluating
Ottoman uses of Italian theory and forms.[228]

Seen in this light, the emerging Ottoman
polity functioned as a filter through which late
medieval urbanistic practices of the Islamic

and the Byzantine worlds, along with emergent
urban concepts in the Italian realm, were selectively screened and syncretistically combined.
The selective nature of Ottoman receptivity
must be underlined: while the Ottoman urban
institutions that had taken shape in the preconquest period underwent transformations
in Istanbul, and while the imperial legacy of
Byzantium was selectively appropriated, the
Ottomans also proved receptive to aspects
of Italian architectural and urban thought,
particularly where it allowed them to accommodate and represent reconfigurations in the
political sphere. Hence the stamp of architectural and urban ideas newly formulated in Italy
on representational spaces of the new rule, the
citadel and the New Complex; hence the use of
classical and Italianate forms in the New Palace.

I noted above that certain correspondences between Renaissance theory and Ottoman practice can be traced to their shared roots in premodern urbanistic practices. In the case of royal Ottoman projects that conspicuously refer to contemporary Italian models, another dimension of cultural interrelationship across the Mediterranean becomes manifest: parallels in cultural and political dispositions particular to an emerging early modern world account for the enthusiastic reception of Renaissance ideas in Ottoman Istanbul. For the trend toward centralizing polities marking the larger Mediterranean world, and the concomitant concern with spatial representation in newly consolidated regimes, rendered fifteenth-century Italian formulations of a new spatiality appealing to patrons beyond the Italian realm.

Two projects carrying the stamp of Italian architectural thinking have been discussed in some detail in the previous sections of this book. A central aspect of the new mode of architectural and urban design that was consistently overlooked by Ottoman patrons and architects must also be noted: the ordering of streets and squares. Building on practices and notions of street and façade construction emerging in the late medieval period,[229] Renaissance theoreticians laid considerable emphasis on the orderly layout and uniform appearance of streets. To Alberti, the layout of streets and squares, along with the design of public edifices, was the principle ornament of a city; without order, he wrote, nothing handsome, convenient, or pleasing could be created. Comparable to a church or a senate house, a square was a particular type of building rather than a space surrounded by buildings.[230] To Filarete, division into streets and piazzas was the first step in the plotting of his Sforzinda, where streets ran from the gates to the center to meet a complex of piazzas aligned with

buildings housing the major urban and administrative institutions.[231] In stark contrast to Italian Renaissance theoreticians and patrons, who emphasized the street as an entity and therefore its ordered and uniform structure, those who shaped the Ottoman city remained conspicuously (and notoriously) uninterested in the uniform appearance of streets and squares.

Ottoman disinterest in geometrically conceived street layouts has led in turn to commensurate scholarly disinterest in the role main streets and squares did play in newly emerging urban configurations. If this lack of interest is largely rooted in paradigms of Greco-Roman and Baroque urbanism against which Ottoman spatial configurations lack form, then stepping outside these paradigms may reveal ways in which the main arteries and fora of Constantinople shaped Ottoman interventions in the cityscape and were themselves transformed in the process.[232] The conversion of the Hagia Sophia, the construction of the first palace on an area that encompassed part of the Forum of Taurus, and the construction of the citadel at the Golden Gate situated a number of Ottoman focal points on the ceremonial artery of the Byzantine city in the first years after the conquest. Two socioreligious complexes constructed in the decade that followed were located on the two branches of the thoroughfare. Mehmed's royal complex occupied the site of the church of the Holy Apostles, close to the northern branch of the Mese. Flanking the artery were two commercial complexes, the Sulṭān Bāzārı and the Sarrāchāne, while the janissary barracks were situated along the same artery further to the east. The complex of Murad Pasha, on the southern branch of the artery, most probably occupying part of the Forum Bovis, and Mahmud Pasha's buildings located along one of the main arteries that connected the bedestan to the harbor area underline the same pattern of siting. The Mese and the Uzunçarşı became, from early on, central elements in the daily and the ceremonial life of the city. The presence of minor squares, such as those flanking the Vefa foundation and surrounding the Mahmud Pasha fountain, suggests that concern for streets and squares was not limited solely to uses of formerly existing sites.

What remained of the ceremonial arteries of Byzantine Constantinople at the time the Ottomans captured the city is not known precisely (fig. 104). What is known suggests that fragments and traces of a former monumental layout remained, rather than an intact complex of streets and fora. In his "Comparison of Old and New Rome," which he wrote in Rome in 1411, Manuel Chrysoloras, referring to the Golden Gate and the southern branch of the Mese, mentions the "former city gate which is on the same road." His emphasis, however, is on what remained of the city's monumental columns, statues and pedestals "wallowing in mud and mire, having fallen into ruin," rather than the urban spaces that bore these.[233] Early Ottoman land surveys suggest that colonnaded porticoes were partly standing on the eastern portion of the Mese. The "shops called *kemer* (arch)" near Hagia Sophia, recorded in 1489, were possibly the last remnants of the porticoed city streets aligned with shops. These were either shop/stoa combinations, as described by Marlia Mundell-Mango, or former porticoes transformed into shops by the Ottomans.[234] Ceremonial use of the arteries had similarly declined. In a study of imperial and ecclesiastical processions in Byzantium, Albrecht Berger has noted that urban ceremonial in the last centuries of Byzantium used only fragments of the city's former ceremonial map. Rather than traverse the whole expanse of the Mese, later Byzantine emperors, in their increasingly infrequent visits to the city center, more often used a sea route from the Blachernae to the Seraglio Point and only there disembarked for a land-bound procession to the Hagia Sophia or the Hippodrome.[235] Accounts such as Gilles's description of the Hippodrome as overgrown with trees at the time of the conquest and Ottoman concerns with security in these spaces point in the same direction.

Sparse yet significant information on the Hippodrome through the early years of Ottoman rule in Constantinople survives. In the image by Vavassore published around 1530, based on an original dating to the late fifteenth century, the sphendone and the entrance complex, the latter to be spoliated in the construction of the Süleymaniye mosque and complex in the 1550s, are still intact. A hagiography completed in 1484, the *Velāyetnāme-i Otman Baba,* indicates that the open space of the Hippodrome—or, in its translated name, the Atmeydanı—was already a central spot in the city by the end of Mehmed's rule. In this account, the heretic dervish Otman Baba and his followers rather narrowly escape being brought here to meet their end at the stakes and hooks awaiting them.[236] An opposition between the city's center and edge, a metaphor also for proximity and distance vis-à-vis the state, is articulated here through narration of the steps taken to convey the dervishes to a convent near the Silivrikapı/Pege Gate along the land walls, and not to the Hippodrome. The *Velāyetnāme,* by an author at the margins of the emerging Ottoman order, does not grant a more precise view into the events regarding the dervish's trial. It does nevertheless provide a glimpse of the Hippodrome as one of the sites where the conflict between the heretic leader and the palace was acted out within the capital city, foreshadowing its centuries-long use as the stage where palace and city would meet for the administration of justice, state

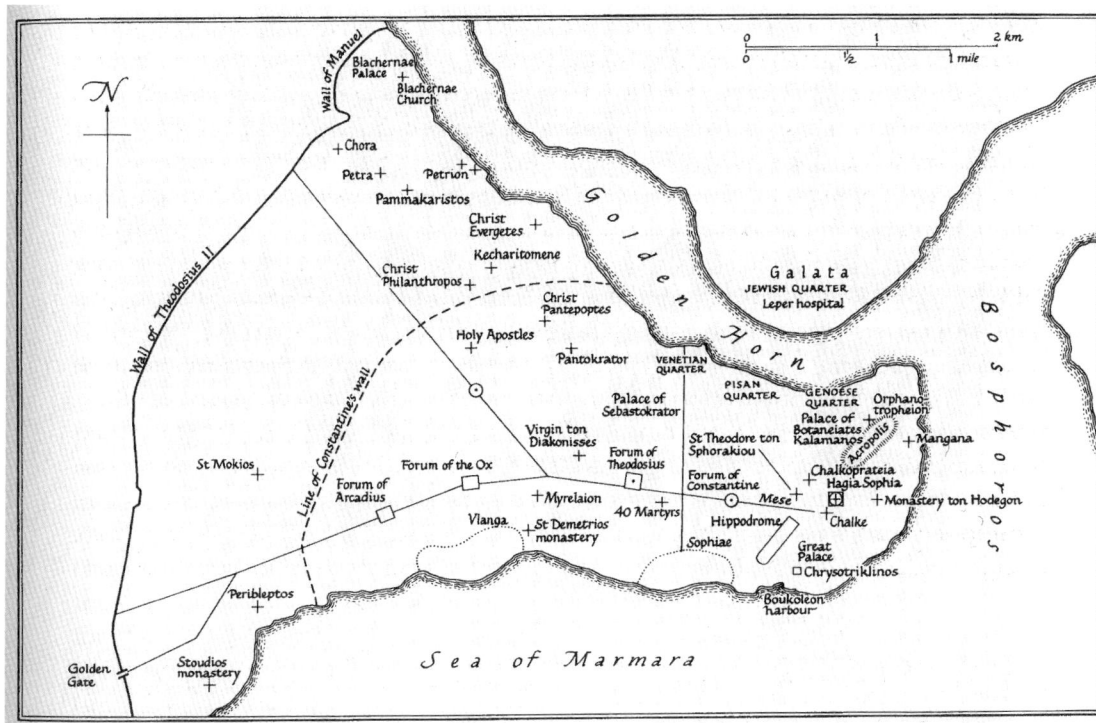

FIGURE 104
Komnenian Constantinople.

ceremonial, urban festivities, and expressions of popular dissent.

Major Ottoman constructions were conspicuously located on sites of former grandeur (map 1, fig. 104). The Ottoman inhabitation of the city's Byzantine layout entailed not only the use and transformation of an extant urban order but simultaneously the revival of an ancient one. Just as Rome expanded out of its medieval core through papal projects that redefined notions of monumentality and architecture, Constantinople within the same decades expanded out of its late medieval core through projects that encompassed the whole expanse of the walled city, creating new foci along its ancient routes. By appropriating, recontextualizing, and replacing elements of the Byzantine city, the buildings situated on these streets introduced a new visual order to the urban environment. At the end of Mehmed's rule, Ottoman monuments had substantially altered the iconography of Constantinople's ceremonial arteries, reviving a pattern in

the city's long-term history and reinscribing it in its urban spaces in a new visual idiom. Unlike the city of Constantine, whose monumental façade faced the Propontis, the late medieval Constantinople encountered by the Ottomans in the fourteenth century was inhabited and dotted with monuments mainly in the northern section. Hence the revival of the Constantinian layout also entailed a reversal in the ancient city's monumental order. Importance shifted from the southern branch of the Mese, which connected to the suburb of Hebdomon and through the Via Egnatia ultimately to Rome, to the northern branch, which passed through the New Mosque to lead to Eyüp and finally connected to the road to the old capital at Edirne. Corresponding to the Zoodochos Pege, the Byzantine city's sacred, protective shrine outside the walled enclosure at the south, was the Eyüp shrine at the north.

Whether they were informed by Byzantine urban structures or were products of earlier

Ottoman and Islamic urbanistic practices, Ottoman interventions in the Constantinopolitan cityscape were shaped by an awareness of the past grandeur of the city and a desire to recreate that grandeur. This is legible in, among other sources, narratives of Mehmed II's first encounters with Constantinople and his subsequent plans regarding it. Kritovoulos, among his contemporaries the author of the lengthiest accounts of the Ottoman ruler's plans regarding Constantinople, locates these always within the framework of a temporal comparison with the city's immediate or ancient past. In 1453, narrating the monarch's first tour of the city, he writes: "first he planned how to repopulate it, not merely as it formerly was but more completely, if possible, so that it should be a worthy capital for him, situated, as it was, most favorably by land and by sea." In 1456: "So profound was the passion that came into his soul for the City and its peopling, and for bringing it back to its former prosperity." In 1459: "Now it was his plan to make the City in every way the best supplied and strongest city, as it used to be long ago, in power and wealth, glory, learning, and trades, and in all the professions and all sorts of good things, as well as in public and private buildings and monuments."[237] The founder of Eastern Rome, Constantine, emerges as a topos in texts on or written for Mehmed II, highlighting the centrality of the emperor's image for the city's new ruler. "Hence, to the degree that Constantine's glory outshone that of all others, so too will your glory outshine his, just as the sun outshines the moon," wrote George of Trebizond in a treatise addressed to the monarch.[238] It was not only Mehmed's eulogists but also his critics who wrote of the sultan's involvement with the city in terms of past grandeur. In a highly negative assessment of Mehmed's building projects and his attempts to revive the city, the anonymous authors of the chronicles of the House of Osman compared the Ottoman monarch, unfavorably, to none other than Constantine (whose funerary monument, we may remember, was demolished to open space for that of Mehmed).[239]

The treatment of particular Byzantine sites and buildings, along with new Ottoman projects, echoes these various narratives in their articulation of a range of responses to the memory of Byzantium. At the end of Mehmed II's rule, the city housed a set of monuments that juxtaposed, at times in a single building, late Roman, late Byzantine, and Ottoman visual orders. Its monumental urban layout, in large part obscured at the time of its fall, was revived in an Ottoman idiom. The architectural discourse and practice of these decades were heavily implicated in the larger project of constructing the capital city of an emerging imperial polity. The conspicuous presence of Constantinopolitan memory in Ottoman urban narratives as well as in urban interventions can be understood within this context, the creation of empire *on* the locus of empire. Ottoman responses to the Byzantine past, whether textual or visual, also have broader implications regarding an as yet little explored topic: representations of the ancient past and its remains in the Ottoman world. The rising Ottoman awareness of Constantinople's past, manifested in new narrative and monumental forms, recent work suggests, resonates with the articulation of new notions of the past in the larger Renaissance world. In various loci within the contemporary Euro-Mediterranean realm, distinct aesthetic discourses were articulated, negotiating novel visual idioms with antique legacies. In all cases these discourses were grounded, to different degrees, in familiarity, utility, and political agendas.[240]

Diverse modes of planning, rooted in this complex of practices and cultural dispositions, were simultaneously operative in the siting of the primary monuments of the new capital. These I call, for the sake of convenience, ideal and adaptive. Mahmud Pasha's complex, where buildings spread over a large plot without a geometric order, constitutes an example of the latter mode. In one sense, this layout followed the model of earlier sultanic complexes of Bursa and Edirne located outside the walled cities, adapting to and marking the topography of otherwise uninhabited territory. Constructing within the walled city of Constantinople, with the salient motives of using and monumentalizing an extant layout, transformed this mode of building. The builders adapted their building sites to the extant street pattern, while also manipulating that pattern in ways that would make the buildings' presence more pronounced. In stark contrast to Mahmud Pasha's buildings was Mehmed's mosque complex, which imposed its strict ideal geometry and axiality and its highly centralized scheme on the urban environment. Although such uncompromising geometry was never to shape another Ottoman monument until the modern era, symmetry and axiality did become operative concepts in the design of religious complexes during the following centuries.

Whether through principles of ideal design or adaptation, urban spaces were used to lend the Ottoman monuments prominence and visibility, lending, in turn, new meaning to those spaces. What determined the fate of the city's squares and arteries was not an "Islamic" rejection of nonreligious public spaces. Rather, an earlier mode of planning, product of a specific topographic sensibility that held the relationship between landscape and monuments central, was transformed into one laying equal emphasis on the relationship of monuments to the extant street layout. A new urban image thus unfolded along the ceremonial arteries of

the city, along with one bound up with its tripartite topography.

This new urban image was not founded on perspectival and geometric configurations that imposed order and unity on extensive segments of the urban space. An emphasis on the privileged view and visual interrelationships between monuments and focal points in the city constituted an alternative to the geometric visualization of the urban body.[241] Several fifteenth-century projects share this emphasis on visual interrelationships within the larger urban context. The buildings situated on the hilltops of the northern part of the peninsula, Mehmed's two palaces, his Friday mosque, and the complex of Mahmud Pasha,[242] are notable in this respect, as is Rum Mehmed Pasha's in Üsküdar: from their elevated locations, these buildings offered views of the city and of other monuments while at the same time offering themselves up for view from within and outside the city. A number of studies have addressed the topic of views and visuality in the urban context of Ottoman Istanbul. In her study of the Topkapı Palace, Gülru Necipoğlu has demonstrated that the vistas of Istanbul and its suburbs offered by the site of the palatial complex were central to its design. Ceremonial windows, loggias, and belvedere towers literally and metaphorically framed the sultan's gaze over his subjects and his dominions, becoming elemental in the manifestation of the monarch's domination of the lands and seas before his eyes.[243] Writing on later centuries and turning his attention to the domain of the subjects rather than that of the monarch, Robert Mantran has suggested that a desire for a lookout to the sea shaped the architecture of Istanbul, as each building tried to surpass its neighbor to achieve a view. Enrico Guidoni has drawn attention to an opposite perspective, arguing that Ottoman Istanbul's urban façade, with the sultan's mosques constituting the primary monumental elements, had been constructed as an image to be viewed from the largely non-Muslim and partly European Galata; this consciously crafted representation, which achieved completion through the works of Sinan, was directed toward a principal viewpoint on the Galata waterfront.[244] In 1911, Le Corbusier, in Istanbul during his easterly journey, addressed the same issue visually. With masterful economy, his sketches of what he called the trinity of Pera, Stamboul, and Scutari capture the diversity of vistas and points of view the Istanbul skyline, punctuated with monuments, offers its viewers (figs. 105, 106).

These series of interpretations, focusing on a range of visual experiences of the urban sphere, underline the multiplicity of vistas and meaningful points of view the city presents to those looking at it from within or without. The topography of greater Istanbul, with its hilly land masses and tripartite layout separated by bodies of water, lends itself to the exaltation and the exploitation of the visual. And to Ottomans, whose primary acquaintance with Constantinople until 1453 had been from across the waters of the Golden Horn or the Bosphorus, the visual possibilities the city offered must have been apparent. Marked with major medieval monuments of the Byzantine city, the northern sections of the peninsula were where the majority of Ottoman monuments would be built in the following centuries. Here they would be subject to the gazes not only of the monarch but also of the inhabitants of the city proper and its suburbs across the waters of the Bosphorus and the Golden Horn.

Several early and contemporary accounts hint at this particular relationship with the city: a Byzantine source that narrates Bayezid I's siege of Constantinople notes how the sultan studied the churches of the city from the shore across, planning to distribute them to his sons and dignitaries, reserving Hagia Sophia for himself.[245] According to his hagiographer, Küçük Abdal, Otman Baba lay on a hilltop across from Constantinople and gazed at the city and its churches for forty days, contemplating the conquest.[246] The word Küçük Abdal uses to denote the mystic's gaze, *naẓar,* carries clear connotations of power and destruction (and through the course of his hagiography Otman Baba's gaze causes significant damage to rulers, palaces, and cities alike). The legendary Saru Saltuk, at a time of peaceful relations with the Byzantine *tekvur* (prince), asks him for permission to visit Constantinople and to stay in the Maiden's Tower, because "his blessed heart wishes to look at Islambol."[247] Although implicit in the narrative of Saltuk's visit is the desire to possess the city, his longing to watch it is captured in a word of a more peaceful nature, *seyr,* which implies a spectacle to be watched. Passages that refer to these two ways of looking, captured in the words *seyr* and *naẓar,* are narrated by Tursun in his *History of Mehmed the Conqueror:* describing Galata, he writes of how one could watch (*seyr*) the land of the Frank (i.e., Galata) from Rumelia (Istanbul), and Rumelia from the land of the Frank. Further down, he describes Mehmed looking at the city with the gaze of admonition (*naẓar-ı ʿibret*).[248] This, according to the author, reveals to the monarch a city in a ruined and confused state occupying a setting of heart-attracting beauty. A couplet by Muʿali in his description of the New Mosque is also revealing in this respect: (the mosque was) a locus of the gaze (*naẓargāh*) from every direction, the locus of the gaze of the pious and the clear-sighted.[249] Ottoman literary writing of the following centuries, abounding in descriptions of views toward and from within significant sites and buildings in the city, attests to the persistent centrality of the theme and its variations.[250]

These accounts and the urban configuration to which they refer mark the emergence of a modality and a poetics of vision that informed the conceptualization and representation of architecture in Ottoman Istanbul from early on.[251] Visual interrelationships were worked into the architecture of the city at a variety of levels, underlining the power and possession embodied in the monarch's gaze, urging the diverse viewers/audiences of the city into a set of correlations, establishing links between the politico-religious loci of the city, partaking in the formation of a representational language that aimed to manifest the established coherence of the space one inhabited or else contemplated as an outsider. This specific mode of visuality was founded on the interrelationships of topography and architecture as much as on the ever present oppositions in the imperial capital between ruler and ruled, Ottoman rule and its European onlookers, the city and its suburbs, each differently imagined and inhabited.

While new notions of urban spatiality and monumentality mark the buildings of the ruling elite, the particularities of their layout, siting, formal features, and functions present divers modes of spatial configuration and signification at work in the city. Thematic unity, evident in the re-creation of aspects of Hagia Sophia's architecture in sultanic and vizierial mosques, and diversity, evident in the contrast between the layout of the sultan's complex and those of the viziers, coexist. Although the buildings of late-fifteenth-century Istanbul are shaped by

FIGURE 105
Le Corbusier, the walled city and Pera viewed from the western end of the Golden Horn. © 2007 Artists Rights Society (ARS), New York/ADAGP, Paris/Fondation Le Corbusier

FIGURE 106
Le Corbusier, panorama of Istanbul with mosques of Süleyman and Mehmed II. © 2007 Artists Rights Society (ARS), New York/ADAGP, Paris/Fondation Le Corbusier.

shared sensibilities and concerns, they do not display the stylistic unity that characterized the architecture of fifteenth-century Bursa or the Ottoman visual domain through the later sixteenth and seventeenth centuries. A multiplicity of sign systems that parallel the multiplicity of spatial configurations are visible when one turns from large-scale projects to the inscriptions and emblems used on these buildings: while an inscription at the entry to Mehmed's mosque celebrates in eloquent Arabic prose the historicity and the expected perpetuity of the dynasty that now ruled Constantinople, over the portal of the bedestan hangs the spoliated relief of a Byzantine eagle, its meaning clear to its builders as well as to the international and multiethnic community of merchants and customers who used that building.

PLATE 1
The Topkapı Palace, aerial view
from the northeast.

PLATE 2
The Topkapı Palace, the Tiled
Pavilion.

PLATE 3
Mehmed II complex, aerial view.

PLATE 4
Mausoleum of Mahmud Pasha,
from the west.

Master of the Vienna Passion,
El Gran Turco, engraving with
watercolor, ca. 1470. Topkapı
Palace Museum, H 2153, fol. 144r.

PLATE 6
View of Constantinople in
Hartmann Schedel's *Liber
Chronicarum,* engraving with
watercolor.

PLATES 7 & 8
Nasuhü's-Silahi [Matrakcı],
view of Istanbul in the *Beyān-ı*
menāzil-i sefer-i ʿIraḳeyn, ca. 1537.
Istanbul University Library,
T.5964, fols. 8v–9r.

Representing the City

CONSTANTINOPLE AND ITS IMAGES

Ambiguity is the pictorial image of dialectics, the law of dialectics seen at a standstill.
—WALTER BENJAMIN, *REFLECTIONS*

CHAPTER 3

If architecture was part and parcel of the making of the imperial state and the site from which it ruled, simultaneously entailing the appropriation and the demolition of the Byzantine past, so too the construction of a new image of Constantinople was an essential aspect of the making of the imperial capital. The crafting of literary and visual images of Ottoman Constantinople in the last decade of Mehmed's rule attests to the recognition of the power of myth and of the visual image (a newly emerging type of visual image—the city view) in asserting the presence of a new order that ruled from the heart of Byzantium. As far as the message was concerned, however, constructing an Ottoman city through state-sponsored buildings proved a less complicated task than constructing visual and literary images with a clear and distinct meaning. The space of the city, especially in the beginning of Ottoman rule, was largely under the control of the palace and could often be easily manipulated by it. One may remember in this context Mehmed's assertion in the first days after the conquest that the land and the buildings of the city belonged to him only. The image of the city was situated in a conceptual space, or rather in the conceptual spaces of its contenders, by nature more difficult to manipulate than physical space.

For the European world that lost it to the "Turk," and for the "Turk" as well, Constantinople was symbolic landscape[1] standing for a multiplicity of political and religious ideals. While it may seem possible to construe Western and Ottoman attitudes concerning Constantinople as contrasting with each other, various strands of thought coexisted within both worlds. In the West, lament for the fall of the city and calls for a crusade led by the papacy found voice alongside apparent acceptance of the new order and willingness to establish and maintain favorable relations with it. Ottoman attitudes toward and perceptions of the city, likewise, were far from monolithic. The city and its loaded history meant different things to the builders of the centralized empire and to the propagators of ghazi ideals. Constantinople thus became a site upon which a constellation of ideas and ideals were projected, where these would be contrasted, contested, conflated. This was a debate, carried on by a range of actors in the Western and Ottoman realms alike, on the cultural meaning of Constantinople. The city's images crafted during this period partook in that debate.

THE VISUAL IMAGE: BYZANTIUM OR CONSTANTINOPOLIS?

Many of the earliest cartographic representations of Constantinople date to the decades following its fall, demonstrating the centrality the city acquired in European and Ottoman political and cultural consciousness at that time. That the interest in Constantinople found a visual expression had, however, to do also with the Western world's expanding interest in cartographic images of cities and a concern for realistic representations of the urban environment. This trend, integral to transformations in modes of representation that marked the European world in the fifteenth century, culminated in such celebrated images as Alessandro Strozzi's map of Rome and Jacopo de' Barbari's monumental bird's-eye view of Venice. Cycles of city views, not as settings or backgrounds to narratives with political and/or religious subject matter (whatever the significance of those settings may have been), but as independent images, for the first time decorated palatial interiors.[2] Geographical and historical works, in manuscript or print form, boasted series of elaborately rendered city views: fifteenth-century manuscript copies of Ptolemy's *Geography* for the first time featured images of the cities of the Greco-Roman *oikoumene;* the first world history in print, Hartmann Schedel's *Liber Chronicarum,* of 1493, included several hundred city views. Whether they were what Pierre Lavedan has termed "urban ideograms" or images that exhibited some degree of topographic and spatial accuracy, representations of cities had been intermediaries for the communication of political, religious, and intellectual ideas from the early medieval era onward.[3] Through the fifteenth century, the interest in the city as a spatial entity housing ancient and contemporary monuments merged with this age-old tradition of the urban image as representative of political and religious ideals. Concomitantly, the visual image was transformed, as it was filtered through the artistic ideals of the Renaissance, notably the focus on realistic representation. Political, religious, intellectual,

and artistic ideals converged in urban images that illustrated manuscripts or printed books, appeared as individual prints, or decorated palatial interiors.

Foucauldian readings of this imagery have often interpreted them as proclaimers of identity, territorial possession, power, or claims thereto. A corollary to the stress on power in the interpretation of topographic knowledge and representation, on the other hand, has been the assumption that the message of the topographic image is clear. Through the cartographic process, it has been argued, "power is enforced, reproduced, reinforced, and stereotyped."[4] The interpretation that follows takes an alternative route: granting that the makers' claim to power was no doubt integral to the intentionality of the cartographic image, I offer a dialogic reading of fifteenth-century views of Constantinople that highlights their polysemous nature.[5] For multiplicity and juxtaposition, not coincidentally but by default, defined and shaped fifteenth-century representations of the city. Symbols of diverse political and cultural orders that had claims on the past and the present of Constantinople coexisted in its images. Produced at a time when the city and the constellation of meanings attached to it were being remade, open to various readings in the diverse contexts in which they circulated, these images embodied multiple and interacting discourses. They were not irrefutable proclaimers of power and identity; rather, they constituted the very site of a debate on the symbolic possession of territory.

The City in a Book of Islands

It is perhaps not surprising that Cristoforo Buondelmonti, author of the highly popular *Liber Insularum Archipelagi,* included in his book a description of Constantinople and a topographical map of the Bosphorus. Although

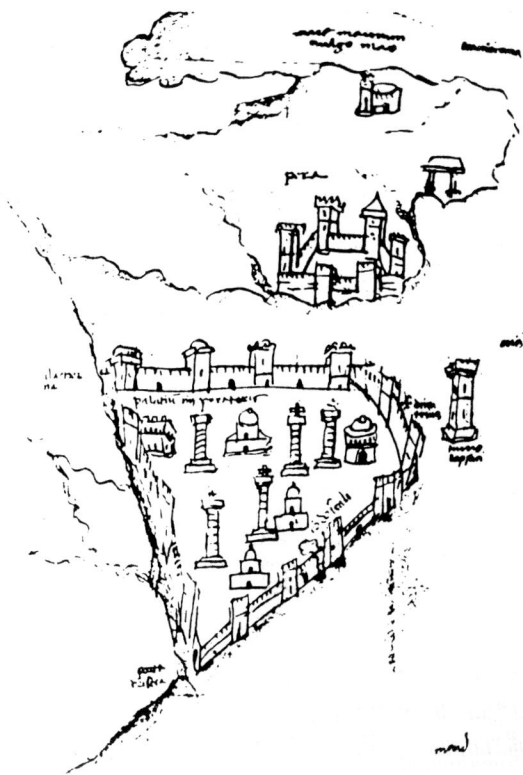

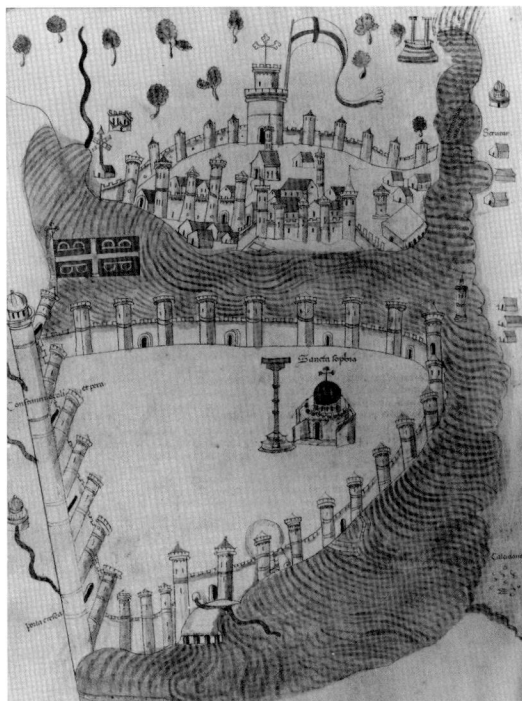

Buondelmonti himself felt the need to comment on the presence of the Byzantine capital city in his book of islands[6] (for the city, after all, was neither an island in itself nor the capital of an island), Constantinople had been from the start one of the centers of antiquity he had set forth to describe and where he had planned to end his travels in the Aegean. Buondelmonti completed his description of the Aegean islands before 1420 and presented it to Cardinal Giordano Orsini, but the majority of the manuscripts date from the 1460s to the 1480s.[7] As the original text was significantly altered and expanded in later copies, its topographic images became increasingly more elaborate, partaking in new developments in cartographic representation. In the process, the views of Constantinople, too, were elaborated. The view of the city in the earliest extant manuscript of the *Isolario* shows the walled peninsula within which rise four columns and four churches, Hagia Sophia

hardly recognizable among them (fig. 107). The following view, dated to 1429 and copied several times in later manuscripts, features only Hagia Sophia and a single column, presumably that of the Augustaion, within an otherwise empty walled enclosure (fig. 108). This is an iconic image of Byzantium in which the city is reduced to its two most potent symbols. That iconic image is to be encountered in different contexts in later decades and centuries. In contrast, Galata is represented as a densely built-up city, marked with a prominently displayed Genoese flag. The majority of the later views share the conventions of the earliest image and other contemporary city views in the same idiom: they show a walled enclosure and a number of monuments within. These later representations, however, are on the whole much more detailed than the earliest view (fig. 109).

The views of Constantinople in the *Isolario* share the conventions of Italian city views such as Strozzi's plan of the antiquities of Rome or the views that originated from Pietro del

PE RA

Massaio's Florentine workshop, among them several illustrated manuscripts of Ptolemy's *Geography*.[8] Technically, these were "bird's-eye views," a term that has been used in relation to city views to designate a wide range of images with related but different techniques and conventions and often fundamentally different visual effects. The earlier "bird's-eye views" depicted the boundaries of the city as if in plan but rendered the walls themselves in elevation, placing a number of—vastly oversized—monuments and landmarks within the walls, in elevation or in bird's-eye view.[9] The popularity of texts like the *Geography* and the *Isolario,* combined with the growing interest in the city image, resulted in the production of a large number of such views through the fifteenth century. During the same period, medieval conventions of urban representation were evolving to meet a newly emerging interest in realism. The medieval bird's-eye view was thus transformed through the fifteenth century; the outlines of the cities came to be drawn with more accuracy than they had been in the earlier diagrams, and the monuments within were rendered with greater concern for their spatial relations to each other and to the boundaries of the city. Some views even featured streets and vernacular buildings (fig. 110). But by and large, these were cities composed of monuments and significant sites, as the contrast with printed images produced from the later decades of the fifteenth century onward makes clear.

In the light of the new dating of the manuscripts of Buondelmonti's work, Ian Manners has suggested a new reading of the views of Constantinople included in those versions of the *Isolario* postdating the fall of the city.[10] Drawing attention to the apparent accuracy and precision of the content of the views, he has argued that the more detailed views of the city exhibit firsthand knowledge of the city's

topography and monuments. Some of the manuscripts can in fact be traced to the island of Chios, which was a refuge for Constantinopolitan exiles following the city's fall. Firsthand knowledge, however, was used to represent more than a neutral truth. With one remarkable exception, these representations of Constantinople are consistently silent on a rather significant fact: the fall of the city and its aftermath. Manners interprets this silence and the emphasis on the Christian heritage of the city— through their exaggeration of the size of Hagia Sophia and their inclusion of a large number of churches—as indicative of a reappropriation of the city by the West. The city as depicted is not lost to the Christian world but is still contested property. These views of Constantinople represent the Byzantine city, visually claiming the continuation of an epoch whose tumultuous termination some of their makers, at least, must have witnessed.

FIGURE 109 (*opposite*)
Map of Constantinople in Cristoforo Buondelmonti's *Liber Insularum Archipelagi,* ink and colors, ca. 1480. Vatican Apostolic Library, Vat. Lat. 5699, fol. 127v.

FIGURE 110
Map of Constantinople in Cristoforo Buondelmonti's *Liber Insularum Archipelagi,* ink and colors on parchment. Biblioteca nazionale Marciana, Venice, MS Cod. Marc. Lat. xiv, 25=4595, p. 123.

The makers of the Buondelmonti views were not alone in their chosen silence on the fall of the city. Similarly disposed were Jean Molinet, chronicler for the dukes of Bourgogne, who dealt at length with the history of the holy cities of Jerusalem, Constantinople, and Rome in his writings of the 1490s, and those of his contemporaries who in poetry and prose accommodated their patrons' belated interest in the fallen city. They portrayed Constantinople as a martyr, as the beautiful and chaste Penelope of Ulysses, and they situated it in antique Greece rather than in contemporary "Turkey." They lamented its loss but never directly acknowledged the Ottoman conquest or dwelt at length on its consequences for the city.[11]

Although the *Isolario* was one of the most popular books of the fifteenth century (it has been noted that its sixty-four extant copies are only thirteen fewer than Marco Polo's *Travels*),[12] little is known about the particular audience they addressed or the individual patrons or commissioners of the later manuscripts. In the increasingly more elaborate copies of the book, it is possible to discern converging interests in the past and the present of the Aegean archipelago: alongside the ruins of the Greco-Roman world to be found there, the Florentine explorer and his later copiers treated the islands' contemporary state, their inhabitants, and their material environment.[13] Likewise, an interest in and claims on the city of Constantinople prompted a desire for increasingly more elaborate representations of the city and its recent history.[14]

While the identity of particular patrons and commissioners of the later manuscripts is not known with any certainty, there can be little doubt that these were products of the Italian cultural sphere. Two other images of the city produced around 1480 support this contention. One of these is a view illustrating a Buondelmonti manuscript held at Düsseldorf's

university library and recently brought to light by Ian Manners; the other is the well-known "Vavassore map" printed in the 1530s. Of the two, the latter, certainly, and the former, possibly, are not "originals." Although the circumstances of their creation and the nature of the mediation that gave them their final shape remain obscure, their contents leave no doubt regarding their dating and strongly suggest the involvement of Ottoman patrons in their production. With an unmistakable emphasis on the Ottoman interventions in the cityscape, these two representations of Constantinople demonstrate that the Ottomans partook in the making of the city's new cartographic image.

Conceptually and thematically, the Düsseldorf map is related to earlier and contemporaneous Buondelmonti views depicting the Byzantine city, suggesting that an illustrated copy of the *Isolario* was available to the maker (fig. 111).[15] But the similarity ends there. The architectural environment depicted within this geographical setting presents a wonderfully lucid lesson on the uses of topographical images. Emphasizing as it does the Ottoman identity of Constantinople, this image tells the exact opposite of the story told by the other Buondelmonti views produced since the fall of the city. Using the very same setting and the same cartographic conventions, the maker of this view fills the city with the monuments of its new rulers. Unlike the "Byzantine" views, however, which ignore the Ottoman presence in Constantinople, the Düsseldorf image does not completely deny the presence of another, earlier order.

The map covers a larger area than the majority of the Buondelmonti views, as it shows the complete course of the Bosphorus up to the opening into the Black Sea, a composition largely necessitated by its narrative content.[16] The rendition of the boundaries of

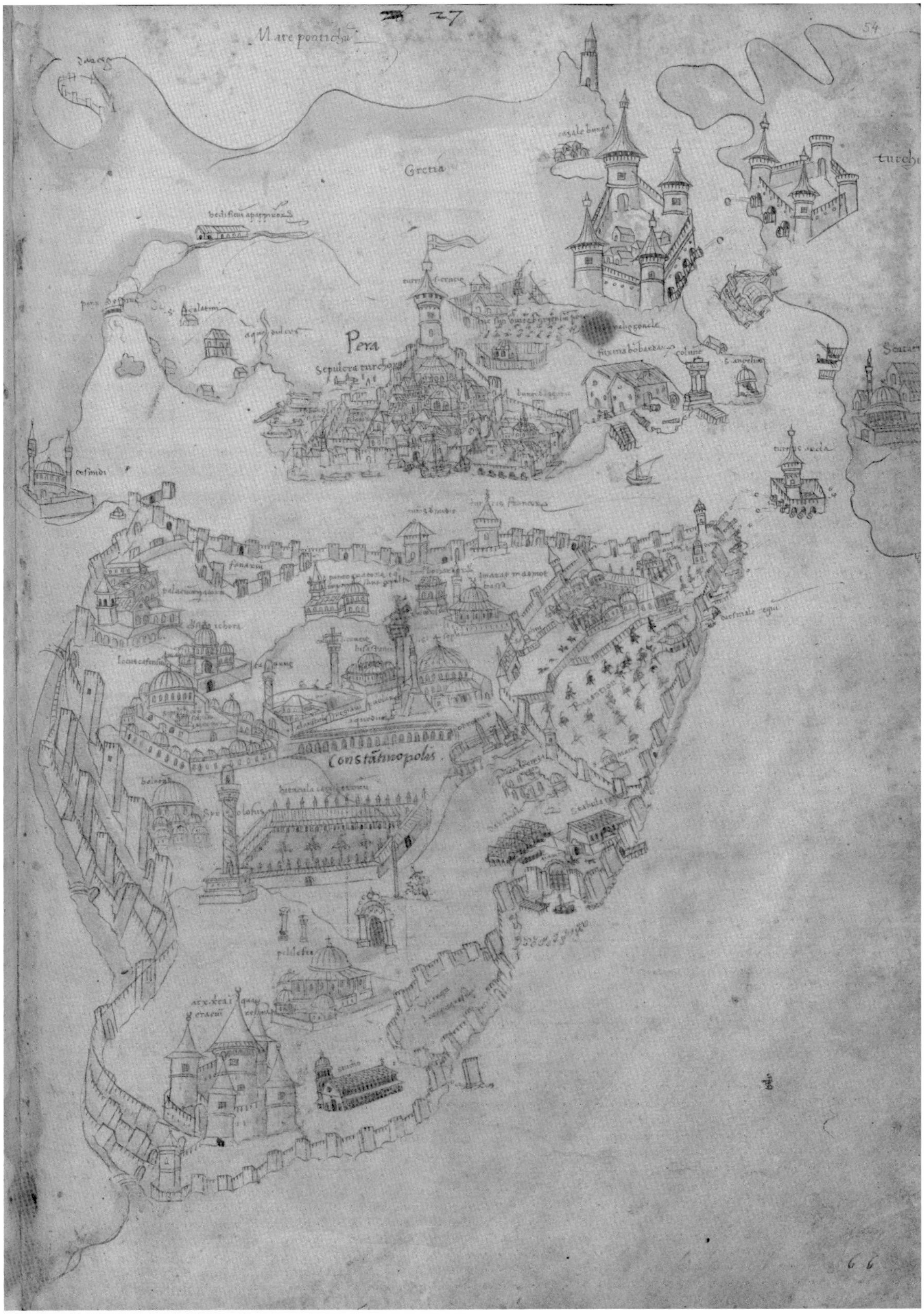
Gretia
Pera
Constātinopolis

the peninsula and of the land walls of Constantinople are significantly more accurate than in any of the other Buondelmonti views, where the land walls follow a straight line and the peninsula is rendered in the shape of a triangle or a semicircle. The Düsseldorf view, on the other hand, suggests that it might be the product of a new survey of the city's boundaries.[17]

Prominently featuring all the major architectural undertakings of Mehmed and his viziers, this is without doubt a visual testament to the monumentalization of the city by the Ottomans. The vastly oversized rendering of the castles of the Bosphorus, one of which was built by Mehmed and was functional in the final siege of the city, and the citadel at the Golden Gate, a strategic point from which control could be regained in case of assault or internal conflict, indicates that Constantinople was now completely under the command of its new rulers. The depiction of busily shooting cannons from the two Bosphorus castles, from outside the sea walls at the eastern end of the peninsula, and from the Leander's Tower suggests that the vessel sailing up the Bosphorus can do so only at their mercy.

The most significant among the civil undertakings of Mehmed, the New Palace occupies a particularly prominent position at the tip of the peninsula and includes several courtyards, the kiosks in its outer gardens, and gates flanked by towers (map 4 [1]). The intimate relationship of the palace to two other important centers of the city, Hagia Sophia and the Hippodrome, is effectively, if inaccurately, rendered. The first palace Mehmed built, on the Forum Tauri, its walls enclosing the monumental column of Theodosius, is discernible; next to it is the bedestan, the functional and monumental core of the commercial district, rendered as a multi-domed building (map 4 [18, 16]). A conspicuous structure of Byzantine Constantinople that

does not feature in any other Buondelmonti view, the aqueduct of Valens, traverses the whole area between the Hippodrome and Mehmed's mosque, bespeaking the restoration of the city's waterways (map 4 [15]). Below it, a large quadrangular courtyard building, with multiple chimneys and doors opening onto the courtyard, represents the janissary barracks (map 4 [24]). Carrying the legend "h[ab] itacula iagitherorum," the building is flanked by a column at which a mounted archer shoots. The arsenal at Kadırga and the dockyard on the northern shore of the Golden Horn (map 4 [7a, 42]) mark Mehmed's naval undertakings, while another vastly oversized building, the cannon foundry to the north of Pera (map 4 [48]), again speaks of the city's defenses.

Religious structures are also prominently indicated on the map. Hagia Sophia (map 4 [9]), situated between the Topkapı Palace and the bedestan, is flanked by its new minaret. Mehmed's New Complex (map 4 [21]), at the western end of the line of monuments that traverses the northern part of the peninsula, occupies a large area comparable to the space occupied by the New Palace. In front of the mosque, within a walled enclosure, stands Mehmed's mausoleum, marked with the legend "Sepulchrum Sultano Meometi,"[18] The vastness of the building complex is conveyed through the walled enclosure surrounding the mosque and mausoleum, which is aligned with domed buildings that stand for the dependencies of the mosque: the madrasas, the public kitchen, the hospice, and the hospital. The public bath of the compound, marked "balneum," is represented as a sizable domed building situated below the main enclosure (map 4 [23]). The other monumental religious building founded by Mehmed, the mosque built near the grave of Ayyub al-Ansari, "discovered" during the siege of the city, is also shown within a walled enclosure. It carries the legend "Cosmidi," referring to the church of SS. Cosmas and Damian that had formerly stood nearby (map 4 [37]). Notably, this is also the city's first representation to include projects of the ruling elite. Convent-mosques built by Mehmed's viziers—those of Mahmud Pasha and Rum Mehmed Pasha—feature prominently in the view, underlining the patrons' role in the Ottoman monumentalization of the city (map 4 [13, 60]).

Although these religious structures are marked with legends indicating their names, and some with crescents atop their domes, their rendition does not distinguish them radically from the city's Byzantine churches. Buildings with large domes over relatively high drums indicate religious structures, imbuing the image with a sense of uniformity and at the same time signifying the interchangeability of the two visual orders coexisting within the city. The representation of Byzantine and Ottoman presences in the city bespeaks a similar attitude: although the view privileges Ottoman additions to the cityscape of Constantinople, several of the symbolically significant monuments of Byzantium are also included. The Tekfur Saray, or the Palace of the Porphyrogenitus, visible in all other Buondelmonti manuscripts, is also included in the Düsseldorf view, at the northern end of the Theodosian Walls, as are the ruins of the Great Palace of Constantine, which, unlike the Tekfur Saray, are not found in other Buondelmonti views (map 4 [25, 11]). A number of churches are represented: the Chora (map 4 [26]); the abbey of St. Mary Peribleptos (map 4 [32]), near the citadel at the Golden Gate (later Sulu Manastır, the Armenian patriarchate that features in other Buondelmonti views); and the basilica of St. John Studius (map 4 [33]). These structures were not converted into mosques during the reign of Mehmed; some continued to function as churches. The monastery of the

Pantokrator, dynastic mausoleum of the last Byzantine emperors, is among those buildings that bear a cross (map 4 [27]). The Pantokrator monastery, it will be remembered, had been converted into the first madrasa of the city following the conquest, and into a masjid upon the completion of the eight madrasas flanking Mehmed's New Mosque. At the time the image was drawn, it carried the name of its first professor, Mevlana Zeyrek.

This anachronism may be explained by the presence of the Pantokrator in other Buondelmonti views depicting the Byzantine city, copies of which were certainly available to the maker of the Düsseldorf image. But it would be incorrect to regard this flaw as a mere mistake on the part of the draftsman. For this image presents the viewer with a multiplicity of "mistakes," anachronisms, and conflations of Byzantine and Ottoman symbols. The legend reading "Byzantion" on the outer courtyard of the New Palace, marking the ancient site and name of the city, is another such conflation of the past and the present of the city. On the whole, these mistakes and conflations constitute a discourse of ambiguity, as this representation of Ottoman Constantinople is marked with the persisting reminiscences of its former self.

The representation of the monumental columns in the Düsseldorf view demonstrates this point succinctly. As in other Buondelmonti images, the monumental columns that marked the fora of Constantinople are prominent features here. More familiar with the city's topography and keener on producing an accurate representation of it, the artist of the Düsseldorf image placed them in a correct spatial relationship to the neighboring monuments. Thus the column of Theodosius is located within the walls of the first palace, while the column of Arcadius, rendered proportionately larger than the others, is placed at the summit of a

FIGURE 112
Statue of Justinian in a fifteenth-century manuscript, ink drawing. Budapest University Library, MS 35, fol. 144v.

hill, possibly designating the Arcadian Forum (map 4 [35]). Highly significant are the representations of the column of Constantine and of the Forum Augustaion, flanking the Hagia Sophia. Located between the first palace and the bedestan, the column of Constantine bears its huge cross, which had been taken down more than two decades before the making of the view (map 4 [17]).[19] More striking is the rendering of the column of the Augustaion, from the top of which the equestrian statue of Justinian continues to threaten the "Turks," in the gesture of his right hand pointing toward Asia (map 4 [10]).

The equestrian statue of Justinian marking the Forum Augustaion was one of the most potent imperial symbols of Byzantium.[20] The representation of the emperor on a galloping horse, "clad like Achilles," holding a gilded orb in one hand, and pointing east with the other, stood for world dominion and the empire's expansion toward the east (fig. 112). The emperor's hand, extended toward the east, "[commanded] the barbarians that dwell there

to remain at home and not to advance any further."[21] Fifteenth-century and later Ottoman sources reveal that the meaning of the statue was clear to them, too, for with slight variations, they tell of the orb and the eastward gesture of the emperor.[22] A symbol of the city comparable only to Hagia Sophia and the Holy Apostles, with such a clear meaning for its viewers on both sides of the Bosphorus, the statue did not remain long in its place after the conquest. It shared the fate of the latter church, which the Ottoman order was not willing to accommodate. "Intriguers" (ġammāzlar), said Şemsüddin Karamani (not without a tone of lament), "astrologers," said Angiolello, persuaded Mehmed that it was a Christian talisman against the Muslims.[23] Whatever the sultan's personal attitude toward the awe-inspiring statue, he submitted to those who would rather have it removed from the city's skyline. It was taken down before the Belgrade campaign of 860/1455–56, in which at least parts of it partook in the shape of cannons.[24]

The presence of the huge cross crowning the column of Constantine and of the equestrian statue of Justinian flanking Hagia Sophia, more than two decades after their removal, is the most telling sign of the image's polysemous nature. The cross of the Constantinian column is the largest among the many crosses and crescents that mark the domes of religious buildings within the walled city. Justinian's equestrian statue occupies the exact center of the image; he stands in the midst of an Ottomanized Constantinople marked by the products of two and a half decades of intense building activity, his gesture reminiscent of a former Constantinople and its world of symbols.

This is not an image embodying technical novelties in the mode of its representation. Cartographically akin to the views illustrating the rest of the Buondelmonti manuscripts, the

Düsseldorf image presents the viewer with a city of monuments (and a highly selective set at that), rather than one of urban spaces. None of the city's humbler buildings can be seen here. Absent is the large commercial establishment surrounding the bedestan and the port area, as are the markets that flanked the New Mosque complex; likewise, the palaces of the viziers (of which at least that of Mahmud Pasha is known to have been sizable) are not included. The layout of streets, the open and built-up areas, and the residential quarters of the city are not a subject of representation to the maker of the image. The few scattered houses that feature in a number of the Buondelmonti views, and the rows of buildings that possibly denote the commercial area along the Golden Horn in some of them, are lacking here. What the Düsseldorf shares with most of the other views is the depiction of Pera as a densely built urban enclosure marked by its Genoese flag. In contrast to the representation of Constantinople, this rendition conveys the sense of a city rather than a collection of monuments in an otherwise empty enclosure. And this may well be a reflection of the contrast between Constantinople and Pera, one a vast and scarcely populated enclosure full of gardens, orchards, undeveloped areas, and deserted structures, the other a thriving commercial colony.

In this Constantinople of monuments mostly Ottoman, the maker conveyed the significance of buildings through their size, laying emphasis on the spatial relationships between them. Thus the monuments that by the end of Mehmed's reign occupied the hills of the northern segment of the peninsula, that is, the Topkapı Palace, the Hagia Sophia, the bedestan, the first palace, the New Mosque and its dependencies, and the columns of the Byzantine fora between them, are aligned, while the aqueduct of Valens, its length vastly exaggerated, runs in front. This monumental alignment and the relative importance of the buildings appear to have been the main concerns of the artist: he miniaturized the Old Palace and crammed it between Mehmed's mosque and the bedestan. The first palace in fact occupied an area comparable to that of the Topkapı, an area much larger than either building flanking it in the view. Similarly, the spatial relationship between the Topkapı Palace, the Hippodrome, and the Hagia Sophia is suggested, if not correctly rendered.

In terms of its representational conventions, then, the Düsseldorf image belongs to a tradition by then well established in the Italian realm.[25] What makes it novel and interesting (at present actually unique) is its content, that is, its choice of particular buildings and its manner of representing these. Its emphasis on the Ottoman character of Constantinople through a focus on Ottoman monuments clearly reflects not only a firsthand knowledge of the city but also an awareness of the grand-scale architectural undertakings of the previous decades, which had aimed to impose a new monumental format on the cityscape. These features suggest that the anonymous cartographer of the view was one with close links to the Ottoman ruling body and that the involvement of an Ottoman patron shaped some aspects of the image. The view itself betrays firsthand knowledge of the Topkapı Palace; particularly the detailed rendering of the private third courtyard—housing the audience hall, Mehmed's residence, bath, and treasury, and the pages' dormitories—evinces the close connection of the draftsman to the ruling body. Copies of the *Isolario* did circulate in Ottoman hands: within the manuscript collection of Mehmed housed in the Topkapı Palace Library is a copy of Buondelmonti's book, without illustrations.[26] The image of Constantinople in another copy, now in the Bibliothèque nationale, is captioned in Arabic cursive script

FIGURE 113
Map of Constantinople in Cristoforo Buondelmonti's *Liber Insularum Archipelagi.* Bibliothèque nationale de France, NAL 2383. Legends in Ottoman Turkish have been added to the map of Constantinople and other topographic images in the manuscript.

FIGURE 114 (*opposite*)
Giovanni Andreas di Vavassore, *Byzantium sive Constantineopolis,* ca. 1530, based on an original dating to ca. 1480. Harvard University, Houghton Library, 51-2570PF.

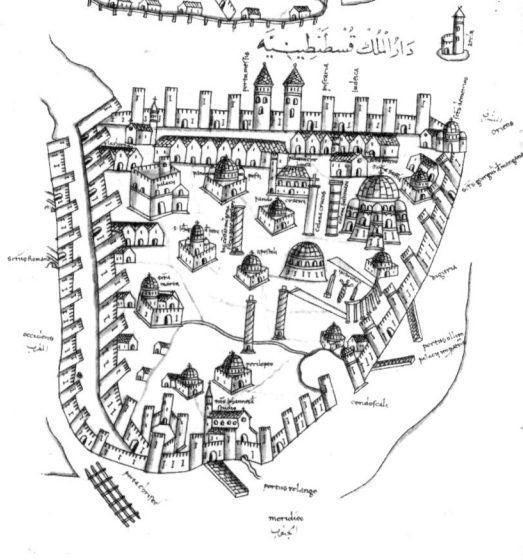

Picturing an Early Modern Capital City: Vavassore's *Byzantium sive Constantineopolis*

The bird's-eye view of Constantinople published by the Venetian cartographer Giovanni Andreas di Vavassore possibly in the 1530s, one of the earliest printed images of the city, has a striking history (fig. 114).[30] A copy of an original dating to ca. 1480, hence showing the city as it stood at the end of Mehmed II's rule, this image fitted in remarkably well in the corpus of city views that were products of the late-fifteenth- and sixteenth-century cartographic achievement in Europe: it remained *the* topographic image of Constantinople through the sixteenth century, its copies representing the city in numerous collections. Most notably, the Vavassore image represented the Ottoman capital in Braun and Hogenberg's *Civitates Orbis Terrarum,* the widely popular atlas of cities whose compilers, in their stress on the fidelity and precision of the topographic images they published, privileged perspective views and plans over more archaic forms of urban imagery. Long after the building boom that marked the reign of Süleyman (1520–66) transformed the city once more, endowing it with its famed silhouette, later editions of Vavassore's woodcut of Mehmed II's capital continued to represent Ottoman Constantinople in the Western world.

Behind the remarkable longevity of this image, I hope to demonstrate, lies its connections to emerging notions of the city and of urban representation that mark the early modern world. Relevant to these connections, then, are the circumstances of its making and the manner of its representation. Entitled *Byzantium sive Constantineopolis,* Vavassore's woodcut features all major Ottoman monuments built during the reign of Mehmed; it has therefore generally been agreed that the Venetian cartographer's source was an earlier drawing or print dating to around 1480. The apparent time

"Dārü'l-Mülk Ḳosṭanṭiniyye" and "Ġalaṭā," suggesting that it had once belonged to an Ottoman library (fig. 113).[27] It would not be far-fetched to assume that a member of the Ottoman elite who had access to such a manuscript featuring a view of Byzantine Constantinople conceived of an "Ottoman" version of it. The stress on the Byzantine heritage of the city and on viziers' buildings suggests that the patron might have been one of the grandees with Greek origins.[28] The ambivalence toward the Byzantine past and the particular juxtaposition of Ottoman and Byzantine symbols may also point to the identity of the cartographer. George Amirutzes' sons, who had captioned the Ptolemaic world map drawn by their father upon a commission by the sultan and had prepared a translation of the *Geography* (still preserved in the Topkapı Palace Library), come to mind.[29]

BYZANTIVM·SI·VE·COSTAN·TINEOPOLIS

PERA

OPERA DI GIOVANNI ANDREA VAVASSORE DETTO VADAGNINO

Turchia

difference between the production of the lost original and its earliest extant printed version has prompted questions concerning the originality of the image. Ian Manners has evaluated the view as derivative of an image in the Buondelmonti tradition, possibly the Düsseldorf view, since unlike other Buondelmonti images it includes Ottoman landmarks. Using this type of an image as his source, Vavassore, Manners asserts, "filled in" the rest of the urban space with an imaginary urban layout.[31] Albrecht Berger, too, has discussed the implications of the time difference between the creation of the view and its publication. He directs attention to the accuracy of the image and to the possibility that the walls of the city and the monuments within might have been drawn in perspective from different points of view. Particularly the accuracy of the contours of the peninsula, traceable on a modern map of the city, suggests that the draftsman patched together drawings made from various vantage points. Contrary to Manners's assumption, Berger suggests that the original, dating to between 1480 and 1490, might have been a more elaborate and accurate drawing than the surviving image. In support of this view, it is worth noting that in the 1530s Vavassore also produced a copy of Jacopo de' Barbari's view of Venice, a print much smaller and much cruder than its highly elaborate model.[32]

The contents and the representational idiom of Vavassore's lost source of ca. 1480 pose questions of some significance. The portrayal of some major monuments, impressionistic in some cases and fantastic in others, suggests that the original was altered between the time of its making and its publication. The huge tower at the Golden Gate, a likeness of Rome's Castel Sant'Angelo rather than Istanbul's Seven Towers, the dome of Hagia Sophia, piercing a pitched roof, and the fantastic architecture

of Mehmed's mosque imply that Vavassore, unfamiliar with the city and its architecture, interpreted and misinterpreted the major monuments in the process of copying the print he had at hand. The image nevertheless depicts major monuments in a convincing relation to the surrounding urban fabric and in an accurate spatial relation to other nodes within the city. Although buildings are magnified in relation to the overall area of the city, there is a sense of proportion in the scale of monuments and the fabric surrounding them that is lacking in the views included in the manuscripts of the *Isolario* and the *Geography*. The street layout, too, is largely accurate. The line of royal structures marking the northern part of the peninsula follow the course of the northern branch of the Mese, while the main arteries of the southern branch are suggested through depictions of adjacent buildings reaching the land walls. It would have been impossible to make such a view on the basis of an *Isolario*-type image, representing the city as a collection of monuments dispersed within a walled enclosure. The manner of conceptualizing and depicting urban space in the original Vavassore had at hand, then, must have been similar to that in the engraver's later rendition. It was, in other words, an image that partook in the emergence of a new idiom in topographic representation, which culminated in the type of view that Lucia Nuti has termed the "perspective plan."[33]

The perspective plan, perhaps due to the disappearance of others like it, appears to have made a spectacular entry into the world of images with the celebrated view of Venice attributed to Jacopo de' Barbari. But its appearance was doubtlessly related to other experiments in urban representation through the last decades of the fifteenth century, notably by the Florentine miniaturist, cartographer, and engraver Francesco Rosselli. Two views by

Rosselli that have survived in later copies, of Florence and Rome, mediate direct observation from an elevated viewpoint with a perspective system and betray the use of measuring instruments by the artist.[34] In light of the widespread use of aerial perspective in northern European painting and prints, such as the illustrations to Breydenbach's *Peregrinatio* and Schedel's *Liber Chronicarum,* a northern inspiration to the Rosselli and de' Barbari views has often been suggested. These elaborate images merged measuring techniques belonging to the realm of the Italian Renaissance, preoccupied as it was with accurate spatial depiction, with the oblique, or bird's-eye, view, which had, without "scientific" accuracy, shaped countless depictions of cities and landscapes produced north of the Alps. What Lucia Nuti has termed the "perspective plan" was thus the product of many fifteenth-century developments converging in the pictorial arts. Typically, in the production of such an image, the ichnographic plan of the city was laid out and its three-dimensional form superimposed. In his use of aerial perspective, the draftsman determined the angle of view, drawing the buildings and the urban layout from various viewpoints in space. Naturally, the precision of such a plan depended largely on the nature and amount of information available on the represented city. Where the city plan was well established through numerous former surveys, as in the case of Venice, such a view could possess a high degree of accuracy. When the precise layout of the city was not known, the artist, suggesting an actual point of view somewhere above the city, had to invent an urban layout.[35] In both cases, the resulting oblique view represented the city through interrelations of developed and undeveloped areas, streets and squares. In stark contrast to bird's-eye views illustrating copies of the *Isolario* or Ptolemy's *Geography,* major monuments were not isolated objects floating in an enclosed void, but emerged, however magnified, from within an urban fabric.[36]

It is most probable that the now lost view of Constantinople in six copper plates, listed in an inventory of Rosselli's work, was also such an image, and perhaps even the same one Vavassore copied in the 1530s.[37] While questions of authorship of the Vavassore view remain unanswered, the works by Rosselli and de' Barbari demonstrate that the printed city view was the medium for a radically novel mode of conceptualizing urban representation. The central role printing and printmakers played in the development and dispersion of newly developing techniques of topographic representation is therefore worth pursuing here.[38] It will be remembered that although some of the Buondelmonti views of Constantinople represented a street layout and included some residential buildings scattered within the urban enclosure, none before the end of the fifteenth century attempted to represent the city in the form of blocks of developed areas, streets and open spaces, as would be seen by an imaginary viewer situated at a point above it. One later Buondelmonti manuscript, however, features a view of Constantinople that does just this, though crudely and fictitiously. This manuscript is dated to ca. 1500; possibly its maker was familiar with the newly emerging city views in print and translated the new mode of representation into the manuscript medium (fig. 115).

Both Lucia Nuti and Juergen Schulz have drawn attention to the relation between the suggested and the actual precision of such images. This is a point pertinent to our image. The perspective view, drawn from a standpoint unattainable for a human being in 1500, suggests an imaginary precision and truthfulness. It is an illusionistic representation from an impossible viewpoint that nevertheless has a keen claim on its own truth. The claimed authority rooted in the apparent realism of the image only helps embolden its message.[39] At the time of its emergence, the perspective view did not only reflect an interest in realistic visual representation. The sense of totality conveyed by these images, it has been suggested, bespoke a novel conceptualization of what a city stood for. In his analysis of views of Paris as utopic constructions embodying emerging dynamics of political, social, and intellectual configurations, Louis Marin observes: "From the portrait of Venice by Jacopo Barbari to that of Paris at the end of the eighteenth century [. . .] a wholly new genre comes to the fore: utopia of the city. At the same time utopia and the city are proposed in their most perfect likenesses; the city is given visibly, as it appears, and not as its idea would have it, according to a geometrical perspective from a viewpoint. Here the viewpoint gives a complete, total, and final image."[40]

Looking at the Vavassore view with these observations on contemporary or near contemporary city views in mind, one can note that this first modern representation of Constantinople aiming to convey a realistic image of the Ottoman capital, too, represents a totality. What adds to its significance is the incongruity between the representational idiom of totality and completeness and the object of representation: a city whose cultural meaning was in flux and whose physical space was in the process of being remade.

The Vavassore view, then, is a copy of one of the earliest examples of a novel mode of urban representation, created around the year 1480. Unless new documentation comes to light, the author of the original view will remain anonymous. Gentile Bellini and George Amirutzes have been suggested;[41] the former, author of numerous paintings with meticulously detailed perpective urban backgrounds, was in the city in the years the image was created. Although no similar city view by Bellini is extant, he is known to have been commissioned by Mehmed to paint a view of Venice in the sultan's New Palace, and by Francesco II Gonzaga of Mantua to provide models for the murals of the *Camera della citta* in the marquis's villa, where Constantinople was represented along with Rome, Naples, Florence, Venice, Cairo, and Genoa.[42]

Mehmed's well-documented interest in cartography and in the newly emerging medium of the print makes him a likely patron of the view.

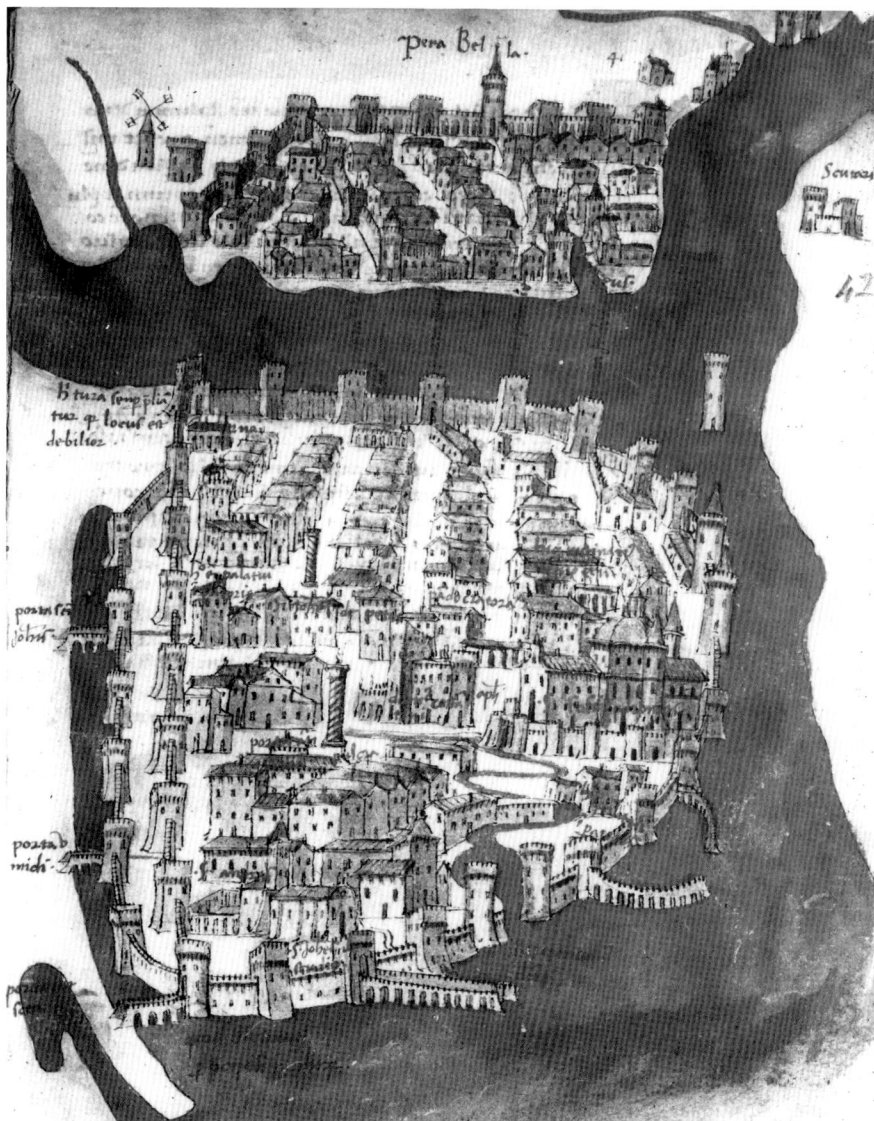

FIGURE 115
Map of Constantinople in Cristoforo Buondelmonti's *Liber Insularum Archipelagi.* Vatican Apostolic Library, Cod. Urb. Lat. 458.

From Sigismondo Malatesta's failed attempt to present him with a copy of Valturio's *De re militari* (including maps of Italy) in 1461, George of Trebizond's dedication to Mehmed II of several geographic works and treatises, and Francesco Berlinghieri's belated presentation in 1482 of the first printed geographic treatise based on Ptolemy, references that attest to his interest in cartographic material are numerous throughout his reign.[43] The collection of cartographic and geographic material still housed in the Topkapı Palace Library reflects an enthusiasm for geography, and particularly for modern translations and reworkings of Ptolemaic texts and maps, that the Ottoman ruler shared with his Italian contemporaries. As Jerry Brotton has argued, Berlinghieri's choice to dedicate his geographic treatise to Mehmed as the patron may be the most telling sign of the ruler's keen interest in recent developments in geography, as well as his Italian contemporaries' awareness of that interest.[44] At the same time, Ottoman military interests in Europe, and particularly in Italy, seems to have led to demands for cartographic material for practical purposes: such must be the reason for the representation of the Venetian *terraferma* within Mehmed's collection of maps and for the map of Europe said to be owned by the sultan.[45] This interest in geography and in cartographic material, however, did not express itself only in the shape of acquisitions of European material. Mehmed commissioned to George Amirutzes of Trebizond, at the Ottoman court from 1461 until his death in 1475, a large-scale map of the world to be compiled from the regional maps in Ptolemy's *Geography,* to George's son Basileos Amirutzes an Arabic translation of the same text, and, as noted already, to Gentile Bellini a view of Venice to decorate a palace room.[46] The collection of Greek and Arabic works on geography held at the New Palace, used by George Amirutzes

and his sons in their works, further underlines Mehmed's active patronage of geography.

A collection of sixteen prints attached to the so-called Fatih Album in the Topkapı Palace indicates that Mehmed's interest in the artistic innovations of the Western world also embraced this newly emerging medium.[47] In their subject matter, the Topkapı prints have nothing to do with city imagery. The disjunct nature of the collection, ranging from biblical to mythological themes, and including a scroll interweaving putti and penises, suggests that the prints were not diplomatic gifts but were instead acquired by Mehmed from the Florentine merchants of Pera. The representational possibilities of print as a medium could not have been lost on Mehmed: belonging to the same collection is a ca. 1470 portrait carrying the caption "El Gran Turco," the title Mehmed had acquired in the Italian world. The image, however, betrays a striking resemblance to portraits of John VIII Palaeologos, except for the fantastic headgear featuring a dragon, a symbol of Mehmed II as triumphant warrior (plate 5).[48] This is yet another picture with an ambiguous identity collapsing the images of the "Turk" and the Byzantine in a more tangible way than do the city views, and we cannot know with what degree of humor, curiosity, or fascination the Ottoman monarch might have viewed it. The portrait's presence in the palace collection, on the other hand, suggests an awareness on the part of the collector of the possibilities offered by the printed image, which would circulate in multiple copies. Mehmed, as is well known, had in fact assured the circulation of far more accurate images of himself in the European world as one of the earliest and most enthused patrons of the Italian portrait medal, another demonstration of his deliberate use of visual images to propagate his claims to power and to the imperial legacy of Byzantium (see fig. 4).[49]

If circumstantial evidence points to Mehmed as a likely patron of the Vavassore view, the image itself suggests that it could have been drawn only with official sanction. Berger has demonstrated that it was the product of on-site studies and drawings.[50] The boundaries of the peninsula have been drawn from high points within the city and from Pera: the Golden Horn shore of the peninsula from the Galata tower, the southern shores of the peninsula and of Pera possibly from the minaret of Hagia Sophia. Similar to the Florentine *Map with the Chain,* the ca. 1510 copy of an original by Francesco Rosselli dating to ca. 1482, some of the individual buildings have been drawn from points of view different from that of the image itself.[51] This suggests that, at least for a number of buildings, on-site drawings were made. In fact, the minute drawings of the reliefs of the Theodosius column within the Old Palace (uncertainly attributed to Gentile Bellini) may well be a product of such a process of recording monuments (fig. 116).[52] The main streets, developed and undeveloped parts of the city, and the denser area of settlement and construction in the eastern end of the peninsula are accurately represented.[53] The land walls, which in the earlier views (with the exception of the Düsseldorf view) were rendered as running in a straight line between the Propontis and the Golden Horn, are depicted with a high degree of precision. Clearly, the maker of the image worked in Constantinople for a considerable length of time, climbing elevated points within the city and in Pera, making drawings of individual buildings and such strategically important sites as the walls and the arsenal.

This manner of collecting information in a city of strategic importance would not have been possible without official consent in the early modern world, particularly for a foreigner. Topographic information was jealously guarded, as it could easily be put to political or military use by potential enemies.[54] The lengthy discourse of complaints on the difficulties of studying and measuring the ancient buildings and monuments of the city, which Pierre Gilles appended to his book on the antiquities of Constantinople, is worth remembering here.[55] The maker of the Vavassore view must have been someone to whom permission was given for studying the city's topography freely. And given Mehmed's well-documented interest in the pictorial arts of the West, in cartography, and in the newly emerging medium of the print, it would not be far-fetched to assume that the source of this permission, and perhaps of a commission for the creation of a printed view of the city, was none other than the sultan.

Noting that the Islamic character of the city is not emphasized in the Vavassore view, and drawing attention to the legends for numerous churches and other Byzantine landmarks, Albrect Berger and Ian Manners have both dismissed the possibility of an Ottoman involvement in its production. Their independently reached conclusion is based on a shared assumption: that the Ottoman administration aimed at the creation of an exclusively Islamic order in Istanbul. Cosmopolitanism, however, and an imperial vision that sought to embrace and include the other rather than transform it into the "Islamic" in a monolithic manner, I have argued in this book, defined the cultural disposition of the Ottoman ruling body through this period. Hence, the inclusion of Byzantine monuments, and a lesser emphasis on "Islamic" landmarks, do not exclude the possibility of an Ottoman involvement in the production of the image. To the contrary, such a picture is in complete accord with Mehmed's vision of the Ottoman imperial capital.

Revealing in this respect are the image's inclusion or exclusion of particular sites and its manner of representation. Revealing, too, is the point of view chosen to depict the city: the Buondelmonti views all depict Constantinople and Galata from the south, possibly a residue of Christoforo Buondelmonti's first description of the city: he dealt at length with the monumental columns that lined the southern branch of the Mese, but did not exhibit much interest in the religious buildings of Constantinople. The images illustrating his text show the city from

the south, depicting its monumental Byzantine façade as understood and described by the author. Two extant fifteenth-century images of Constantinople make use of a southeasterly point of view, that illustrating a copy of the *Notitia Dignitatum* made in Basel in 1436 and the Schedel view, to which I will turn shortly (fig. 117, and plate 6). Privileging the eastern end of the peninsula, both images render the Hagia Sophia and the column of the Augustaion the two most prominent sites. The conspiciousness of the city's main church flanked by the statue of Justinian in both images suggests that the choice of this viewpoint had to do with a desire to represent the city's most majestic prospect. This was also the point of view that would most visibly highlight the city's talisman against assault, the statue of Justinian, threatening the "Turk." Cyriacus of Ancona's drawing of the statue of Justinian, Patricia Brown has suggested, might have played a role in the making of the Basel image;[56] this would also explain the prominence of the statue in the view.

The Vavassore view depicts the city from the east but has very little to do with these two images. The use of new cartographic conventions whereby monuments are placed in an accurate relation to the rest of the city results in an image where Mehmed's New Palace, instead of the Byzantine landmarks, is highlighted. Thus the use of "new cartography" makes the image contrast strongly with those views, drawn from the east, in which Hagia Sophia holds the pride of place, and replaces the primary Byzantine monuments of the city with newly built Ottoman ones. Unlike any other image of the city produced in the course of the fifteenth century, the Vavassore image relegates Hagia Sophia to secondary status, situated as it is to the southwest of the palace (map 5 [1, 5]). Its size, too, is accurately proportioned to the size of the palace: another use of precision in the service of the image's intent.

Overall, the image is marked with an unmistakable emphasis on royal interventions in the cityscape. Along with the New Palace, the image features all of Mehmed's major projects. Following the northern branch of the Mese are the bedestan, the first palace (enclosed in walls), and the New Complex (with the adjacent establishments, the janissary barracks and the stables, the adjoining market). As in the Düsseldorf view, the Valens aqueduct is present, running between the first palace and the New Mosque (map 5 [14–19]). On the southern shore, the arsenal and Mehmed's citadel at the Golden Gate, both marked with crescents, form other focal points highly visible thanks to their size (map 5 [39, 34]). At the western end of the

Golden Horn, the mosque of Ayyub is marked "S. Helena" (map 5 [27]). On the northern side of the Golden Horn, to the west of Pera, appears another arsenal, also marked by crescents, while to the south, the cannon foundry is visible (map 5 [51, 60]). A legend next to the Leander's Tower reads "Qui fano la guardia li Turchi per li passegieri" (map 5 [62]), underlining Ottoman military control over the Bosphorus, if not the city, as had the Düsseldorf map.

Although the view privileges royal undertakings in the city, a large number of buildings distinguished from the rest of the urban fabric by their size or by their domes are possibly other monumental structures built by the ruling elite. Since new legends were added and some old ones omitted in the later reproductions of the print, these buildings, too, might have lost their legends sometime between the making of the original drawing and Vavassore's reproduction.[57] Among these are structures surrounded by a wall situated to the east of the bedestan; the domed building and the large courtyard here can be none other than Mahmud Pasha's mosque and its dependencies, his double bath and large han (map 5 [11, 12]).

Vavassore's Golden Horn is full of caiques busily carrying people from one shore to the other. The waters of the Bosphorus and the Propontis, too, are teeming with activity, though of another nature. Vessels of different types and sizes surround the peninsula. These caiques and trading vessels, which inhabit the seas as the monuments, markets, and houses inhabit the land, no doubt advertise the new Constantinople: no longer the scarcely populated and politically isolated Byzantium, and no longer the sacked and ruined city of the fall, but a densely built-up and inhabited city rich with international trade. But these vessels are at the same time a key to the representation of the city's multiple identities. For the flags of the vessels carry the Ottoman crescent, the winged lion of Venice, and the double-headed eagle of Byzantium, symbols of the political entities that had claims on the past and the present of the city.

Reentering the city with this multiplicity of symbols in mind, one encounters a similar multiplicity of presences in legends marking buildings. Along with the legends marking Mehmed's new structures and the city's defenses, a large number identify churches, in most cases with Italianized renditions of their Greek names.[58] As has been noted, these are those churches in the city that had not been converted into mosques at the time the view was drawn. The Tekfur Saray is also included, marked with the legend "Palatio di Costantino" (map 5 [25]).

The antiquities of Constantinople are prominently displayed in the Vavassore image. The remains of the Hippodrome and the adjoining buildings are carefully rendered, as well as the monumental columns marking the city's fora, devoid of the sculptures or crosses that once adorned them (map 5 [7]). A "coliseo di spiriti," possibly referring to the ruins of the monastery of the Myrelaion (built in the tenth century over a vast rotunda of unknown intent), stands prominently to the south of the Mese (map 5 [36]).[59] An unidentified ruin to the left of Mehmed's mosque is marked "tempio" (map 5 [28]), while a "teatro," possibly the structure to the northwest of the Süleymaniye mosque, whose remains Alfons Maria Schneider recorded in the 1930s, is situated between Mehmed's mosque and the Golden Horn (map 5 [21]).[60] Arcades and arched structures, particularly in the environs of the Hippodrome, must be other remnants of ancient Constantinople that were still standing at the time.

Thus the image represents a lot more than Ottoman additions to the cityscape of Constantinople. It presents the city as setting to an active Christian life and home to many remains of Byzantium. The coexistence of the signs of the former with those of the new political order in the image is key to its meaning. One can construe this as a re-presentation of the city to the West, an image that intentionally emphasizes the civic and religious monuments of its new, Ottoman rulers. At the same time this is a prospering trade center, home to a highly visible Christian community, a city that boasts, as did Rome in its contemporary images, antiquities of past ages.

Granting that re-presenting to the West the new image of Constantinople is the most likely motive behind the creation of the print, it displays the same ambiguity in terms of the city's identity, the fluidity of meaning, that informed other contemporary representations of the city. The double-headed eagle prominently displayed in the flag of a vessel, the many churches marked with names of saints, and the name of Constantine—wrongly—marking the Tekfur Saray and the adjoining city gate become elements in the peculiar discourse of the image, situating the city at once within the realm of the Turk, that of Byzantium, and that of the Christian West. The title of the view, placed atop the minarets of Mehmed's mosque and to one side of the "Palatio Costantino," *Byzantium sive Constantineopolis,* "Byzantium *or* Constantinopolis," is another sign of this ambiguity. Byzantium was the name that evoked the past of the city, its ancient as well as its immediate past. Constantinopolis, on the other hand, was the name that denoted the city for Christians and Muslims alike; its arabicized form, Kostantiniyye, had been and continued to be used by the Ottomans as the city's official name. Although one cannot know the degree of intentionality in its use (for the title conformed to a cartographic convention of the era), the conjunctive "or" in the title is an explicit indicator of the fluidity of the city's identity, the multiple realms to which it belonged, and the very name that should denote it. It is equally telling that Braun and Hogenberg, when they reproduced Vavassore's print for their immensely popular *Civitates Orbis Terrarum* of 1572, did not only remove the Byzantine eagle and the Venetian lion; they changed the view's title to *Byzantium Nunc Constantinopolis:* "Byzantium, *Now* Constantinople" (fig. 118). By the latter half of the sixteenth century it was clear that Byzantium belonged to the realm of history and that Constantinople, firmly in Ottoman hands, was the only name that could denote the city.

Schedel's Constantinople

The final images of Constantinople produced in the fifteenth century are those in Hartmann Schedel's *Liber Chronicarum,* published in 1493. They accompany a narrative of the building of the city by Constantine, and another section narrating the great storm of the year 1490, which blew up the Güngörmez Kilisesi, a former church used at that time as a gunpowder depot.[61] The latter is illustrated by a smaller and simplified version of the image accompanying the narrative of the city's foundation, and an engraving representing the terrible storm, with a partial view of the Hippodrome and its surroundings (fig. 119). A simplified copy of the imaginary portrait of Mehmed attached to the Fatih Album also adorns this section.[62]

The first, more elaborate and frequently reproduced image is a double-page bird's-eye view whose representational idiom reflects the late-fifteenth-century concern for topographic realism (plate 6).[63] The image is similar to several city images in Breydenbach's *Peregrinatio* that make use of aerial perspective to produce an oblique view. Not products of precise measurement techniques, as were printed Italian

FIGURE 118
Copy of the Vavassore view (fig. 114), in Georg Braun and Franz Hogenberg, *Civitates Orbis Terrarum* (Cologne, 1586).

views, these images nevertheless reflect contemporary developments in cartography. The maker of the Schedel view chose a viewpoint from across the Bosphorus. Foreshortening the city's triangular layout, or slanting the profile he would have seen from the Asian shore, he rendered the urban enclosure in the form of an oval. Paying some attention to the spatial relations between buildings but being extremely selective in his choice of what would be included, he placed structures and something of a street layout within that enclosure. In technique and conventions, this is thus a more innovative image than usually assumed, and interesting in that it presents a merging of the northern use of aerial perspective with the Italian concern with cartographic precision. Schedel notes that he consulted Venetian merchants trading in Constantinople for this view; the accuracy of certain features in the image suggests that he might have used his commercial connections to commission a drawing on which to base the print.[64] The inclusion of a simplified version of the portrait of Mehmed captioned "El Gran Turco" suggests an Italian connection in the creation of these images.[65]

The majority of the city views in the *Liber Chronicarum* are in some way inaccurate, a large number are imaginary representations, and a considerable number are used several times over as illustrations of different cities. The view of Constantinople is one of the few "real" urban images among the several hundred that this world history boasts. In this respect, Schedel's assertion that he consulted an authority for this view is striking. While the reader is asked to lend credence to what he sees under the caption "Constantinopolis," the picture tells a number of very different stories at the same time. Constantinople is depicted as an enclosure heavily guarded by strong walls, its walls and gates marked by crosses and double-headed eagles.

One of the major defenses of the city throughout the centuries, the heavy chains that sealed the Golden Horn at times of military threat and that Ottomans could only overcome by transporting vessels over the hills of Galata, is still in place. The most prominent feature in the image is the Hagia Sophia, flanked by the column of the Augustaion, with Justinian's east-pointing equestrian statue prominently displayed on it. The two most potent symbols of Byzantium, the first having served as the sultanic mosque of the Ottoman capital for nearly four decades at the time the view was drawn, and the second long since removed and employed in Mehmed's military ventures in the shape of cannons, are here still in place. Disregarding their fate, the maker of the image used the two structures to

FIGURE 119
Partial view of Constantinople in Hartmann Schedel's *Liber Chronicarum*, with Hagia Sophia, the column of Justinian, and the Topkapi Palace.

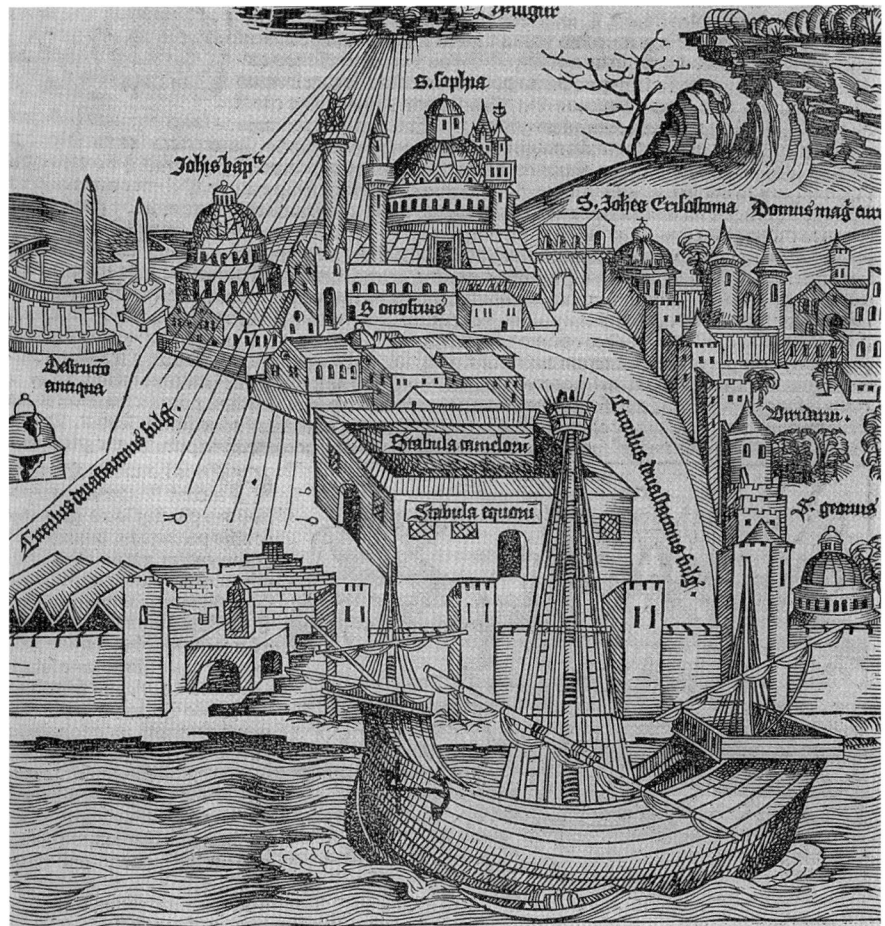

present a powerful and awesome façade of the city. The prominence of the images of Hagia Sophia and the statue of Justinian underline the iconic aspect of the view, reminiscent of other representations in which the two are the distinguishing marks of the city and the symbols of its religious and political significance. The Tekfur Saray, close to the northern end of the land walls, and a church whose five domes are marked with crosses are other prominent buildings within the walled city. At first sight, then, this is an image of the Byzantine city.

But other narratives are embedded in this image. At its center, between the Tekfur Saray and the church is a group of domed buildings flanked by four towers and surrounded by a wall. This can only be Mehmed's New Mosque and its complex, its two minarets inflated to four and exoticized into curiously crowned towers. Another building flanked by the same type of tower is in the foreground, close to the statue of Justinian. Although not marked by legends, as is the Hagia Sophia, the "minareted" buildings are silent but unmistakable signs of another visual order that has—mysteriously—made its way into the city. Two small edifices enclosed within walls may also be speaking of an Ottoman presence in the city, for this is just how the first palace and the janissary barracks are represented in the Düsseldorf view. Thus, in this city heavily guarded by massive walls and the miraculous chain sealing off the Golden Horn, there is also a "Turkish" presence.

The coexistence of Byzantine and Ottoman orders and the ease with which their symbols were juxtaposed are best seen in the partial view illustrating the eventful storm of July 1490. This image represents the southern end of the peninsula in its contemporary state, including the Byzantine monuments in the area, the outer walls of the Topkapı Palace, and its first and second courtyards, with the monumental

double-towered gate separating them. If the presence of the Topkapı leads us to perceive this as a representation of the Ottoman city, the representation of Hagia Sophia at once takes us back into the realm of flux and indeterminacy, as one of its minarets features a composite symbol made of the crescent and the cross. Close by is the equestrian statue of Justinian atop its column, seemingly not yet hit by the storm that, according to the text, caused its destruction.

The theme of ruin and destruction is a subtext underlying the main view of the city in the *Liber Chronicarum* as well. Doing something no other medieval and early modern visual image of Constantinople (and, to the best of my knowledge, no other visual city image of the period) does, it visually captures what was verbally described by numerous inhabitants of and visitors to the city through the fourteenth and fifteenth centuries: its destitute and ruinous state. Unlike the Buondelmonti images, which render the city as one of churches and monumental columns only (and standing ones at that), and unlike the Düsseldorf and Vavassore maps, which convey the image of a densely built-up and prosperous Ottoman Constantinople, the Schedel view shows the city in ruins. In the foreground and almost as large as the Hagia Sophia are torn-down walls, possibly of the Byzantine Great Palace, with trees growing in them. In the background, close to the land walls, stand more tree-growing ruins. Added to the general emptiness of the walled enclosure, which houses but few buildings, the representation of decaying structures strengthens the sense of the city, whether in the Byzantine or the Ottoman phase of its existence, as a deserted and destitute place. The contrast between the peninsula and the city of Galata across the Golden Horn reinforces this impression. Facing deserted Constantinople, Galata stands densely built-up, its buildings all intact.

Whether this was a statement on the destruction brought forth by the Ottoman conquest (Schedel's admiration of Aeneas Silvius Piccolomini, one of the most adamant actors of the period in the attempts to organize a crusade against the Ottomans, suggests the possibility of such an attitude on the part of the author) or a disinterested observation on the destitute state of the city in its late Byzantine and early Ottoman times, the emphasis on ruin and destruction is significant. In this sense the Schedel view has less in common with visual images than with the literary representations of the city, which freely allowed the description of destitution. While authors close to the locus of Ottoman power had uniformly asserted that Istanbul was rebuilt and became prosperous under the rule of Mehmed, outsiders of different sorts—travelers to the city, the anonymous authors of the chronicles of the House of Osman, and the Greek patriarch Gennadios— wrote about its ruinous and destitute state in the era preceding or following the city's capture by the Ottomans. The silence of the majority of visual representations of Constantinople on this rather important but perhaps not easily acceptable fact attests to the power of the visual image in shaping opinions and asserting a reality.

Representing the city and its recent tumultuous history, this series of late fifteenth-century images variously partook in the topographic realism that shaped city views through these decades. They situated the symbolic images of Constantinople within what claimed, with increasing authority, to be the actual landscape of the city. They were the products of a period in which the cultural meaning of Constantinople was a central concern for Western and Ottoman realms alike and in which that meaning was in flux, in the process of being remade. Thus the realism the makers of the views employed in

rendering the city and its buildings produced images that were radically different from each other. The messages they asserted through their suggested and actual topographic precision were not neutral; rather, they communicated the constructed truth of their subjective narratives. Often they conflated diverse narratives, speaking at once of the past and the present, displaying side by side some of the most powerful symbols of Byzantine and Ottoman Constantinople. Their messages were not singular but blurred in the polyphony of their multiple discourses.

Only later in the sixteenth century, when the actual and symbolic possession of the city was no longer a matter of debate for the West, when the imperial Byzantine past had lost its immediacy and perhaps some of its relevance for Constantinople's new rulers, and when the cultural boundaries between the Ottoman and the Western worlds had become more clearly defined than they were in the previous era, was the image of the city divested of its multiple meanings. As has been noted earlier, it was Vavassore's print, copied and reproduced several times, that represented Constantinople in numerous city atlases of the sixteenth century. But in these new prints the memory of Byzantium was silenced, the legends marking churches made less visible, the double-headed eagle of Byzantium and the winged lion of Venice removed. In the most widespread and popular of these atlases, Braun and Hogenberg's *Civitates Orbis Terrarum,* the center foreground of the image was now occupied by another, unmistakably Ottoman narrative: an equestrian portrait of the Ottoman sultan accompanied by attendants. To either side of this group, in a series of portraits within roundels, the whole Ottoman dynasty, from its founder down to Murad III, was present, announcing that this was the dynastic capital of the House of Osman. Above the horizon, the map's new title,

"Byzantium, Now Constantinople," affirmed this statement (fig. 118).

While Vavassore's bird's-eye view continued to be a model for later representations of the city, panoramic views drawn from Galata grew in popularity through the later sixteenth century. The creation of monumental panoramas of the Ottoman capital such as the one by Melchior Lorichs or the anonymous Paris and Vienna panoramas coincided with the perfection of the city's monumental prospect, marked with cascades of domes and a multiplicity of minarets.[66] These vastly sized and remarkably precise images defy the limitations of the panorama, as opposed to the plan, in their attempts to display and identify in exact detail all significant features of the capital city, including its ancient and modern monuments. And unlike the perspective view, the panorama format allows for an accent on the congregational mosques and their dependencies, which were the defining elements of the city's imperial and Islamic identity. If the building boom of the sixteenth century recast the shape of the Ottoman capital with a new emphasis on religious structures, the panoramas created contemporaneously by European artists, highlighting these same monuments, reflected the West's changing conception of Istanbul as the capital of the foremost Islamic power.

The Ottoman views produced through the sixteenth century take no share of the ambiguity that had shaped Istanbul's earlier images. Matrakçı Nasuh's celebrated view, to which I turn in the epilogue, represents the Ottoman capital with a stress on its dynastic and Islamic identity (plate 7). Of the monuments of Byzantium, only those fully assimilated into the

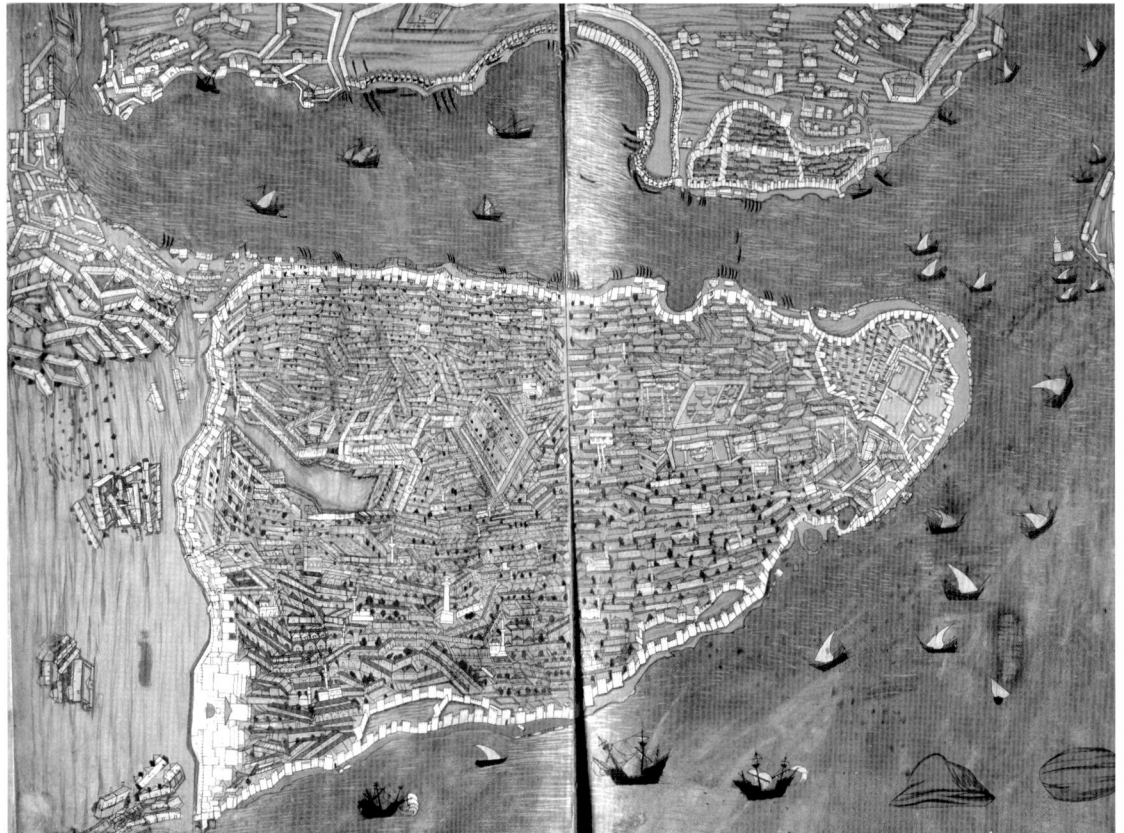

FIGURE 120
View of Istanbul, 1584–85, in Lokman bin Seyyid Hüseyin, *Hünernāme*, Topkapı Palace Museum, H 1523, fols. 158v–159r.

Ottoman order are represented. In other images, such as the *Hünernāme* view, or those in copies of Piri Reis's *Kitāb-ı Baḥriye,* which adapt the conventions of the perspective view to the miniature idiom and change the orientation once more to capture the city's monumental prospect to the north, the memory of Istanbul's former self is further silenced: Hagia Sophia, the Hippodrome (in the former view), and the city walls are the only visible remnants of Byzantium (figs. 120, 121). In these images, produced at a time when new definitions of Sunni Islam were articulated to become central constituents of Ottoman polity, the city's Islamic identity is given increasing emphasis.

If the cartographic image of Constantinople was transformed in the course of the sixteenth century to emphasize a newly defined Ottoman identity, the visual image of Byzantium was not completely forgotten. Removed from "realistic" depictions of the city, it was transposed to the realm of myth and memory. Thus appears an image of Hagia Sophia and Justinian in the *Tercüme-i Miftāḥ-ı Cifrü'l-Cāmi',* a kabbalistic text from the end of the sixteenth century (fig. 122).[67] Illustrating a description of Kostantiniyye that includes a remarkably detailed account of Justinian's statue, the painting shows Hagia Sophia and the statue, as well as the three columns of the Hippodrome, as isolated objects in an otherwise empty landscape. This is an icon of the symbolic center of Constantinople, the site where the two most potent symbols of the city once complemented each other in representing the political and religious power of Byzantium. It is reminiscent of those Buondelmonti views

FIGURE 121
Map of Istanbul in Piri Reis's *Kitāb-ı Baḥriye,* second half of the seventeenth century, Staatsbibliothek zu Berlin, Preußischer Kulturbesitz, Orientabteilung, Diez A. Foliant 57, fol. 28, quarters a, b.

FIGURE 122
Hagia Sophia, Justinian's
column, and columns of
the Hippodrome in ʿAbd
al-Rahman al-Bistami, *Tercüme-i
Miftaḥ-ı Cifrü'l-Cāmiʿ*. Istanbul
University Library, T.6624.

that featured only these two monuments within
an otherwise empty peninsula. But the context
in which the picture appears is not that of geography or history but that of *cifr*, which situates
these monuments not only in the past but also
against the backdrop of doom and destruction.

In the West, too, the equestrian statue of
Justinian reappeared in the context of doom
and destruction. A Nüremberg broadsheet
giving news of the earthquake that shook Constantinople in 1556 provides a glimpse of the
continued significance of this powerful symbol
one hundred years past its destruction.[68] The
article not only gives readers information on
the earthquake, it is equally keen on underlining the significance of the disaster: this was a
sign from God, a punishment of the infidels for
their misdeeds. In the illustration to this apocalyptic news article, in the midst of a destroyed
city where those who survive run helplessly
to escape, Justinian's statue stands on its lofty
column near a falling Hagia Sophia, untouched
by the fury of the heavens, perpetually pointing
toward the east (fig. 123).

THE LITERARY IMAGE OF THE CITY AND ANOTHER DEBATE

The letters dispatched from Istanbul to a number
of Muslim courts in the months following the
conquest of Constantinople are woven around
themes starkly contrasting with the images of
kingship and territorial domination the Ottoman court highlighted in its correspondence
with Western powers and in the imagery projected on such objects as portrait medals and
city views. In letters sent to the Mamluk and
Kara Koyunlu courts and to the sherif of Mecca,
the main theme is *gaza*, or *jihad*, the conquest of
an abode of the infidel remaining in the midst of
Muslim territory. In these letters, descriptions
of the siege, conquest, looting, and annihilation
or capture of the city's inhabitants evoke the
narratives of the same events by those who lived
through or witnessed the city's fall.[69] The letters
evoke traditions according to which the prophet
alluded to Constantinople as the object of Muslim warfare, and they speak of the minting of
coins and the reading of the Friday sermon in

Ein erschrocklich wunderzeichen/von zweyen Erdbidemen/ welche geschehen seind zu Rossanna vnnd Constantinopel—Im M. D. Lvj. Jar.

FIGURE 123
Istanbul during the earthquake of 1556, woodcut, whose caption reads: "Ein erschrocklich wunderzeichen von zweyen Erdbidemen welche geschehen seind zu Rossanna unnd Constantinopel—Im M. D. Lvi. Jar" (A frightening omen of two earthquakes that took place at Rossanna and Constantinople in the year 1556).

the city as powerful signs of the establishment of Muslim rule. The physical attributes of the city, its singular geographic layout and the strength of its walls, are noted only to highlight the mastery and final victory of the conquering army.

It may be significant that within these texts the only description in aesthetic (and not solely religious) terms and the only references to the city's beauty are found in a letter sent from the Kara Koyunlu court at Tabriz.[70] Following a eulogy to the conqueror, the letter describes Constantinople as a bride of matchless beauty whose skirts had not been touched until then by any ruler of Islam. Her beautiful and adorned face had been expecting the exalted deeds of a (Muslim) monarch. The city's heart-attracting plan was drawn in light in the dark of a black eye; neither thought nor imagination had seen its like. Kneaded with amber, musk, and rose water at the time of creation, Constantinople was brought down to earth by the keeper of paradise in order to adorn and beautify it. To be sure, this imaginary commentary (neither the Kara Koyunlu ruler, Jihan Shah Mirza, nor the composer of his letters were likely ever to have set eyes on the city) representing Constantinople as a beautiful bride and heavenly abode on earth was not completely devoid of images of religious war and conquest. The Muslim ruler, the letter notes, purified this heavenly creation of the stains of the infidel.

At the time such letters were proclaiming the Islamization of the city (the letters to the Mamluk court and to the sherif of Mecca are dated October and November 1453 respectively)—emphatically boasting of the issuing of coins, the reading of the Friday sermon, and the conversion of churches into mosques (masjids, minbars, and mihrabs replaced the churches of the infidel, repeated the letters and the answers written to them)— Hagia Sophia was the only converted church in the city. It will be remembered that few churches in fact were converted into mosques during the reign of Mehmed II, and that the two city views representing Ottoman Constantinople pictured it with a host of churches alongside mosques. The contrasts between these images of conquest and Islamization projected to the Islamic world and those images projected to and manufactured in the West underline not only the multiplicity of the audiences of the Ottoman court but the typical ease with which it used a range of discourses and representational strategies to address itself to the different worlds to which it was connected and in the midst of which it was located.

The letters sent from the Ottoman court, alongside gifts (and, in the case of Mecca, shares of the booty from Constantinople to be distributed to the descendants of the prophet, attendants of the holy sites, and the city's poor), at once shared the achievement of this millennial goal with the rest of the Muslim world and projected an image of the conquered city largely cast in religious terms. The topoi that shaped representations of the city in Ottoman historical and literary writing of the decades following 1453 were rooted in a different problematic. The increasingly articulate centralizing policy of the Ottoman state following the conquest, it has been noted earlier in this study, prompted tensions between those at the center of this new configuration and those who were marginalized by it. Contemporary literary representations of the city, its history, and its monuments, produced in a range of milieus and addressing a range of Ottoman audiences, reflect this tension and partake in the articulation of the attitudes and opinions of the different parties involved. As Stéphane Yerasimos's in-depth study of the traditions of Constantinople and Hagia Sophia demonstrates, history and myth were translated, manipulated, and invented to manifest the ideologies, positions, and attitudes of different segments of fifteenth- and early-sixteenth-century Ottoman society regarding the new orientation of the Ottoman state.[71] With regard to ideological disposition, Yerasimos discerns two types of narrative, which he terms pro- and anti-imperial. Neutralized and stripped of its anti-imperial aspects in the course of the sixteenth century, he notes, the latter type of narrative was in large part absorbed into "pro-imperial" texts.

At the time of their articulation by different segments of Ottoman society, however, these narratives were informed by ambiguities and incongruities, as were contemporary visual images of the city. The creation of an Ottoman literary discourse on the city began with Mehmed's order for the translation of the *Patria*, a Greek copy of which he already possessed, into Persian and Turkish.[72] Significantly, the Byzantine epic of the city and the construction of its church was only partially translated: only those sections narrating the construction of Hagia Sophia and the erection of the column of the Augustaion are found in the Persian and Turkish texts, while the city's foundation narratives and subsequent history are reduced to a summary sentence.[73] The image conveyed in the *History of the Building of the Great Hagia Sophia,* as Şemsüddin Karamani's translation of the *Patria* is titled, is that of a pious Justinian building the grand and spectacular church for the glory of Christendom.[74] The royal grandeur of the project is conveyed through detailed accounts of material brought from all parts of Justinian's realm, gifts sent upon its completion by sovereigns of other kingdoms, and precious objects with which the building was decorated. In underlining the piety of the emperor, Şemsüddin is not concerned with particularities of religious identity. Having complete faith in the continuity between one imperial order and the other (not unlike his patron), Şemsüddin presents Justinian and his project within the same conceptual framework as he would a Muslim monarch. Thus he has Justinian's architect place a mihrab in the church and a platform from which the mufti would preach; the emperor establishes a waqf for Ayasofya and, like Mehmed, orders his viziers to construct churches and other buildings in the city.[75] Şemsüddin's presentation of the equestrian statue of Justinian flanking the Great Church, too, is conveniently neutralized: The emperor holds a gilded orb in one hand "so that onlookers will know that [he] captured the whole world and, holding it like a ball, ruled over it." Justinian's other hand, which to most onlookers on either side of the Bosphorus seemed to gesture threateningly toward the east, is to Şemsüddin nothing more than an empty hand, a symbol of the transience of worldly power.[76]

The narrative of the construction (and destruction) of Constantinople that takes up considerable space in the anonymous chronicles of the House of Osman casts a radically different light on the city, as it does on its fifteenth-century onlookers.[77] Unlike Şemsüddin, the authors of this alternative narrative dwell at length on the foundation of the city. And significantly, they agree that an ill omen prophesied its doom and destruction at the very hour of its foundation.[78] Beginning with Yazıcıoğlı Ahmed, whose *Dürr-i Meknūn* is the earliest text in Turkish to tell this frightful tale, a number of Ottoman authors turned to a well-established apocalyptic tradition in Arabic literature that, from Abbasid times onward, saw in the destruction of Constantinople a sign of the approaching Day of Judgment.[79] The city, in this version of its history, was built three times and destroyed three times. Its rulers were always driven by greed; oppression, cruelty, and intrigue (*zulm, fitne fesād*) were the tools of their trade. The author of the 891/1486 text (the version of the traditions Yerasimos identified as the most outspoken in its opposition to Mehmed's policies) states in no subtle terms his opposition to notions of kingship. Hence Kostantiniyye, the indubitable locus of kingship, is doomed to destruction.

Only when he turns to Constantine's erection of Hagia Sophia does the anonymous author's representation become more favorable. To the author, Ayasofya is the benchmark against which to measure the cruelty and oppression practiced by Mehmed in his architectural endeavors. At the time Hagia Sophia was raised, cruelty was not the means by which rulers built; they paid their workers, and craftsmen were held in respect. Constantine is praised for building Constantinople in forty days, whereas Mehmed took three, four years just to repair it, and "so many parts of it are still in ruins."[80]

This change in tone is doubtlessly shaped not only by resentment toward Mehmed's unrelenting policies in building the city and the empire but also by the awe and admiration Hagia Sophia had inspired in the Islamic world from very early on. Thus the latter part of the narrative, following the construction of the church, is largely an account of Muslim raids on the city and includes the story of Ayyub and his praying in Ayasofya. As Gülru Necipoğlu has noted, this text emphasizes the sacred character of the building, whereas Şemsüddin emphasizes its regal associations. This marks another channel in the symbolic appropriation of the building and its history, making it an object of popular piety.[81]

Like the Constantinople of the city views, the Kostantiniyye of the anonymous histories presents a polysemous image, shaped in part by the other's (in this case the Ottoman center's) construction of the city and its history: it is the doomed city, its destruction worked into and prophesied at its foundation. But at the same time, it is home to Hagia Sophia, whose legends of construction had become part of Islamic lore long before the Ottomans appeared on stage, and which had, through the first Ottoman centuries, become the symbolic aim of their expansionist warfare. The city is doomed, but its church, idealized against Mehmed's imperfectly, cruelly, and unjustly built mosque, is present in all its splendor, boasting the stones and marbles of Solomon's Temple and the beams of Noah's Ark.

Admiration for Hagia Sophia and contempt for Constantinople is in fact a theme that runs through all histories and traditions rooted in the ghazi milieu in this period, from the *Dürr-i Meknūn* to the *Ṣalṭuḳnāme* and the anonymous histories. The *Ṣalṭuḳnāme,* a compilation of ghazi traditions presented in 1474 to Cem Sultan, Mehmed II's younger heir, at the time resident in Edirne, is the most explicit among these in the expression of this contempt and in its opposition to Constantinople's being made the Ottoman capital.[82] Hence it is also the text that most dramatically contrasts the city and its church, cursing one while sparing the other. References to Constantinople as the doomed city, and comparisons between it and Edirne, become increasingly more frequent in the final sections of the epic, as Saru Saltuk becomes more of a figure of the present time and place and less of one of a legendary past and legendary places. Toward the very end of the *Ṣalṭuḳnāme,* Mehmed's begs, knowing that he has his mind set on the conquest of Constantinople, advise him as follows:

It is a difficult fort, hard to control, and it is also inauspicious. The reason for its inauspiciousness is that when the devil—may the curse of God be on him—came down to earth, he stepped his ill-omened foot first on this site. Because of this it is destroyed; it is ruined in every age. They say that when it fell, because of adultery and sodomy and lewdness and debauchery, black waters emerged from its ground at night, and it remained ruinous. It is a sign that earthquakes destroyed it so many times. It is also a place of the plague, which resides underneath this city. A tradition of the prophet says that famine and drought never leave this city; it is not a place of serenity and joy. If you see [conquer] it, build a wall around Ayasofya and destroy the rest. If you rebuild this city, it will destroy the world, and you will be the cause of this destruction. It will never flourish. However many times you build it, it will fall back into ruin again.[83]

While Hagia Sophia and its builders were loci whose contrasting representations registered varying cultural and political Ottoman attitudes regarding the past and present of Constantinople, the city at large became the subject of the first eulogies in a literature of praises to the city that was to be refined, elaborated, and reshaped through the following centuries. Unlike the official dispatches of 1453, in which references to the city for the most part concern its passage to Islamic rule and the signs of that passage, these texts merge an understanding of the city's political significance with perspectives on its physical and social space. In his *History of Mehmed the Conqueror,* Tursun Beg, one of the authors to lay the groundwork for eulogies to the city, places emphasis on the strength of its fortifications, describes its geographic location as a gateway to Rumelia between the Black Sea and the Mediterranean, and praises its well-protected and vast port. Entering that well-protected enclosure of grand dimensions, Mehmed, according to Tursun, mounted on his Burak-like horse, viewed and contemplated it as if it were paradise, before announcing his desire to see Hagia Sophia, comparable to the highest sphere of heaven.

To the Ottoman audience within the courtly sphere, the Constantinopolitan landscape was conditioned by the metaphor of kingship: a metaphor articulated and elaborated by a set of authors and simultaneously inscribed into architectural spaces created for the Ottoman rule. Both the Topkapı Palace and the New Mosque complex were shaped by and represented through ideas of dominion over the geography of seas and lands locked together by the city.[84] The kingship metaphor inscribed in Constantinopolitan landscape was elaborated further by Bidlisi. The city was "a fort whose moat was the deep Roman sea; its walls were the lands and the seas of Rome and Greece, [situated as it was] between the two grand realms of Rūm, that is, Rumelia and Anatolia."[85] Earlier in the *Heşt behişt,* Bidlisi had expounded on the city as the seat of kingdom (*dārü'l-mülk*), which, between the fifth and the sixth climes, was the place of origin of ancient kings, the

throne of sovereign rulers.[86] He evoked Rome, the imperial city in whose image Constantinople was first created, noting the latter's seven hills rising within its impregnable triangular enclosure on the shores of the green waters of the Roman sea.

The kingship metaphor remained a central trope in the representation of Istanbul's geography, while images of resplendence and beauty were articulated in poetry and prose as attributes of the city and of its parts. As particular monuments, such as the Topkapı, the New Mosque, and the mosque of Mahmud Pasha, were represented (by authors writing for the patrons of these structures) in terms of the value of their materials, the artfulness of their construction and decoration, and the loftiness of their structures, the city too became the subject of poetic representation as images of resplendence were transposed from particular buildings to the larger urban entity. The poet 'Ayni highlights Constantinopolitan luster and shine with the refrain of his poem "The splendor of this universe is in the city of Constantine."[87] Each of the six quatrains ending with that line, in turn, represents a different aspect of the city and urban life.

> The greatest city, constructed of water and
>   of earth
> Heaven is at once above and beneath it
> The news that circulates is apparent and hid-
>   den at once
> The splendor of this universe is in the city of
>   Constantine

The beginning quatrain, which evokes the city as the heavenly abode built of water and earth, is followed by tropes that were to become central to poetry and prose on Ottoman Istanbul: the royal city as paradisal garden (Sultan

Mehmed conquered it and made it his abode; the lofty buildings he constructed turned it into a beautiful garden of paradise); the city as full of mosques (those bearers of the world had filled every corner of it; reciters were the ornaments of their lodges). The city not only as blessed site but also as social paragon is part of this portrait of splendor: as the shining moon of society casts its light on the ground, beautiful narcissi flourish, and every corner of the city turns green.

Duality and opposition, worked into the city's images to conflate and contrast its multiple selves, Ottoman and Byzantine, heavenly and unblessed, kingly and wretched, find further meaning in ʿAyni's poem, as he elaborates images of opposition between the cities of Constantinople and Galata. "If you desire to see two universes in one life," he writes, "go to the city of Galata, have the pleasure of crossing the sea. Ask for wine, and drink your life away with the wine of beauties." The representation of the two cities as other is not new in itself: Orthodox Constantinople had been contrasted to Catholic Galata in the writings of Christian pilgrims to the Byzantine city; city views juxtaposed the empty and desolate Byzantine capital with the densely built, thriving Genoese colony. Contrasts embodied and enhanced by the city's geography now highlighted differences between its Muslim and Christian selves, written in the sensual pleasures the largely Christian Galata offered a Muslim Constantinopolitan. While the city proper, where non-Muslims constituted more than 40 percent of the population, was far from being a monolithic Muslim entity socially, spatially, or institutionally, the presence of the largely Greek and Italian Galata at its edge rendered such opposition possible and meaningful. The following centuries were to see a growing Muslim presence in Galata, but the otherness of the former colony prevailed as

a long-term attribute, changing (and preserving) its meaning into the modern era.

As the space of the city was reconstructed through the decades that followed its conquest, the image of Constantinople too was remade to situate it at the core of an Ottoman geography. The construction of a new image of Constantinople, center and symbol of transformations that followed its fall/conquest, entailed the remaking of the city's cultural meaning in a range of political and cultural spheres: in the political arena between the Ottomans and the powers that lay to their east and west, as well as within an internal political field. Ongoing conflicts and contestations within those spheres were the backdrop against which the meaning of the city was contested and negotiated. That the emerging political power was the one eventually to determine the shape of the image is in itself unsurprising.[88] What lends fifteenth-century representations of Constantinople their fascination is that both in the space of Ottoman-European encounters and in the space of the internal conflict that opposed Edirne to Constantinople, the city's new image took shape through dialogues between the contrasting visions of its contenders. Never pure assertions of a particular and singular vision concerning this site of immense significance, the images embody, and at times embrace, residues of the other's construction of place. Their ambiguities capture the process through which a cultural meaning was transformed and remade.

In Mehmed's *Dīvān* is an ode to a beautiful youth of Galata:[89]

> I saw a sun-faced angel; he is the moon of
>   the universe
> Those black hyacinths of his are the sighs of
>   his lovers

Clad in black like the radiant moon that
  graceful cypress
Of the dominion of the Frank, he is the shah
  of beauty
The one who is not enamored with the knot
  of the beloved's girdle
Is not a believer, but a heretic among lovers
His lips give life when his glance has killed
If that giver of spirits has faith, it is the path
  of Christ
O 'Avni, do not doubt, that beauty will yield
  to you
You are the shah of Istanbul and he the shah
  of Galata

Clad in black and adorned with black hyacinths, the Galatan youth is decribed by Mehmed as the embodiment of Frankish beauty and a follower of the path of Christ. But as he circuitously gave voice to self-doubts in this erotic chase cast in tones of a rivalry among monarchs (or a rivalry between monarchs cast in erotic tones?), perhaps the conqueror, too, partook of the ambiguity and the rhetoric of oppositions that shaped the city's images created by his contemporaries.

Istanbul Inhabited

CHAPTER 4

The earliest extant census of Ottoman Istanbul, dating to the year 1477, yields a population of 16,324 households living in the walled city and in Galata.[1] The city's population at this date has been estimated as between sixty thousand and one hundred thousand; recent work on early modern demography suggests that the lower figure might be more plausible.[2] It must of course also be remembered that the census was taken at a tumultuous period in the history of the city. Offers of free property, which did lure a number of immigrants to the city, shortly proved unsustainable. Fluctuations in policy regarding the status of Byzantine property continued to affect population movements (as well as the political attitudes of inhabitants) and became one of the factors that marked the contentious nature of resettlement. Whether in bold manifestations or covert suggestions (often depending on their distance from or proximity to the center), contemporary authors noted conflicts regarding resettlements and imposition of rents on urban property and voiced reactions to the court's measures. As already noted in the context of the commercial infrastructure, wealthy merchants and craftsmen were primary targets of such ventures, which fact was another source of contention.[3] The larger part of the population consisted of communities forcefully deported to the city and its environs. Movements between Istanbul and the places of origin of deported subjects were not infrequent; families could be left behind when individuals were taken to the new capital.[4] Two plague epidemics, in 1466 and 1470, dealt harsh blows to the city's new inhabitants; in 1466, Kritovoulos wrote of six hundred deaths each day.[5]

		Households	%
Istanbul:			
	Muslims	8951	60
	Greek Orthodox	3151	21.5
	Jews	1647	11
	Caffans	267	2
	Armenians of Istanbul	372	2.6
	Armenians and Greeks of Karaman	384	2.7
	Gypsies	31	0.2
Galata:			
	Muslims	535	35
	Greek Orthodox	592	39
	Europeans	332	22
	Armenians	62	4

Constantinople in the fifteenth century was not a particularly desirable resettlement destination for Ottoman subjects residing elsewhere. Several accounts attest to the plight of the deported peoples: "He said to remove men with their families / To bring and settle them in this city / This brought great grief to the Turkish nation / Who are lamenting with bitter tears / For they separated fathers from sons / They separated daughters from mothers / They separated brothers from one another / They deprived many of their ancestral homes," wrote Abraham of Ankara in his lament on the fall of Constantinople.[6] Another lament closed the manuscript copied by an Armenian scribe in 1480: "I copied this in times of bitterness, for they brought us from Amasia to Kostandinupawlis by force and against our will; and I copied this tearfully and with much lamentation."[7] "I have come to be like the nipples of a virgin, and have been transferred from one community to another," wrote the Jewish doctor and preacher Ephraim ben Gershon, who called himself "the exile." "The exile does not permit me to sleep, I have come to look like a pitchfork," he wrote elsewhere.[8]

Mass resettlements were not a novelty to the Ottoman polity, nor were they to the medieval polities of the larger region. Movement of populations into or from newly conquered territory, for purposes of colonization, control, and stabilization, had been implemented by Ottomans from early on and had resulted in considerable shuffling between Anatolia and the Balkans. Such deportations had been implemental in the Byzantine world too, though city-building ventures in the Ilkhanid and the Timurid worlds were the conceptually closer model. Similar to Timur's population of his capital city, Samarqand, through deportations from other cities, Mehmed's population of Istanbul was accomplished largely by fiat.[9] Beginning with the campaigns into the Peloponnese in 1458, and up to the conquest of the Genoese colony of Caffa in 1475, massive deportations of communities from newly acquired territories to Constantinople accompanied Ottoman territorial expansion.[10] Deportations to the city were to continue into the reign of Selim I (1512–20), but the census document of 1477 captures the end result of Mehmed II's endeavor and substantiates information found in narrative sources regarding the demographic makeup of the urban population and the range of ethnic communities forcefully brought to the city. In the city proper, 60 percent of the inhabitants were Muslims, while the remaining 40 percent consisted of Orthodox Greeks, Jews, Catholic Caffans, Istanbulite Armenians, Armenians and Greeks from Karaman, and Gypsies. In Galata, the Muslim to non-Muslim ratio was reversed: 35 percent of the town's population consisted of Muslims, while Orthodox Greeks and Europeans constituted the majority of the former Genoese colony's population.[11] The establishment of the Greek Orthodox patriarchate and relationships with religious and civil authorities of other communities were integral to the consolidation of Ottoman power in the city, on the one hand, and to enticing movement into Constantinople, on the other. The institutional organization of the non-Muslim communities and their relations to the Ottoman court through these decades, it might be noted, were much more varied and ambiguous than has been generally assumed.[12]

What follows is an exploration of the immediate material environment of the city's inhabitants. Turning from the monumental structure and image of Ottoman Constantinople to the social, political, and spatial constituents of its residential fabric, I map out a residential topography of the newly declared capital and delineate its relationship to the city's monumental order. I focus on the organizing principles of the documents relevant to the topic to highlight their representational strategies, which will in turn expose ruptures between representations of the urban body and the practices that shaped it. This, I hope, will shed light at once on Ottoman concepts of the city and its construction and on modern interpretations of those concepts, informed at times by highly literal readings of the documents in question.

THE IDEA OF A NEIGHBORHOOD, THE IDEA OF A CITY

The documents registering urban property in Istanbul through the early decades of the 1500s evoke an image of Ottoman surveyors in the very act of creating an urban toponymy, projecting on a ruinous landscape a matrix of names that correspond to a network of authority. In this section I examine the shape and meaning of that matrix and its relation to the space of the city.

Endowment deeds and surveys of endowed property, the main sources of information on the city's layout, together present a particular urban vision through their manner of organizing and representing information relevant to the control and administration of endowed property.[13] The earliest documents of this type, the endowment deeds of the Mehmed II foundation, contain lists of new religious and charitable foundations recorded according to the quarters (maḥallāt) in which they were located and to which they gave their names: hence Mehmed II's New Complex is located in the Maḥalle-i Cāmiʿ-i Cedīd (quarter of the New Mosque), the mosque of Zeyrek (the Pantokrator) in the quarter of the Zeyrek mosque. The income-generating property that follows, too, is similarly presented: caravanserais and baths, alongside smaller-scale houses and shops, are

listed according to the neighborhoods in which they were located, and their boundaries are described. Neighborhoods also constitute the organizational matrix of the property surveys of the Ayasofya foundation, documents equally central to Istanbul's urban history.[14]

A later document relevant to the history of the city, the citywide survey of pious endowments drawn in 953/1546, represents an elaboration on this scheme of the city divided into a set of neighborhoods.[15] Since the earlier documents I have mentioned deal exclusively with the Mehmed II foundation and refer to the property of other individuals only in the context of neighborhood names and property boundaries, the 1546 survey remains an important source for the fifteenth-century city. The survey is the first extant document that arranges the city into thirteen districts, dividing each district (nāḥiye) into a number of neighborhoods.[16] Beginning with the foundation of the quarter mosque or masjid, it registers all the endowments of that neighborhood's residents. Here, a summary of each endowment deed is recorded, except for the few cases where it was not available, and the current state of the foundation (property endowed, incomes, expenses, beneficiaries, etc.) registered.[17] The only omissions in this citywide survey of 219 neighborhoods and 2,490 foundations are the royal ones.

Studied individually, these documents all draw a similar picture of the city. Each suggests an established urban structure, a conglomeration of smaller units that add up to the city itself. Each document represents the city as neatly divided into neighborhoods, which are the reference points for the dealings of and with the city (which in our period have to do with property). Property (alienated or otherwise) belonging to the ruler as well as to the subjects is registered within the city's neighborhoods. In each consecutive document, one finds a larger number of neighborhoods, an increase that has been interpreted as an indication of urban growth.

A telling disjunction between representation and practice reveals itself when this set of documents is studied as a group. Whereas individual documents represent a cellular structure that is a constant feature of the urban whole from the early years of Ottoman rule onward, together they suggest that that structure—at least in the early decades—existed only in the minds of the city's surveyors. The following comparisons may demonstrate this point: In the first waqfiyya of Mehmed's foundation, of ca. 1474, fifty-five neighborhoods are mentioned, while in the second deed, of ca. 1479–80, there are sixty-one. Only thirty names appear in both documents, suggesting not that six new neighborhoods were added between 1474 and 1480 to those already existing, but that what the officials considered to be *maḥallāt,* or the location they considered to be the reference point within each quarter, changed considerably in the course of the five to six years between the drawing of the two foundation deeds. The same pattern emerges in a comparison of the surveys of the sultanic waqf and the larger survey of 1546: while a number of quarters are mentioned in all the documents, a considerable portion are mentioned only once or twice in the whole set.[18]

The centrality of the town quarter in documents relevant to Istanbul's urban history finds a reflection in the centrality of the topic in the scholarship on the city. Understanding what constituted this basic unit of the urban whole might lead to an understanding of that unit's primacy in the city's historical documents and in modern studies alike. In a highly informative article on Ottoman Istanbul, Halil İnalcık provides a definition:

The *maḥalle* was an organic unity, a community with its own identity, settled around a mosque, a church or a synagogue. The individuals of this community were linked not only by a common origin (in many cases), a common religion and a common culture, but also by external factors making for social solidarity. The meeting-place of the community and the symbol of its unity was the place of worship, the repair of which and the maintenance of whose staff were the joint responsibility of the inhabitants, and after which the *maḥalle* was named.[19]

İnalcık's definition of an Ottoman town quarter has significant points in common with definitions offered by Muslim jurists from the medieval era onward, underlining the central place of the quarter and its mosque in urban practices across the core areas of the Islamic world. The corporate responsibility placed on the inhabitants of the quarter regarding the maintenance and the administration of the quarter mosque, and the role of the mosque in mediating a social and religious identity, have been noted.[20] What did the town quarters of fifteenth-century Istanbul share with these definitions that refer to Ottoman and Islamic urban practices at large? What do the incongruities between the definitions and the documents signify? If a religiously and/or ethnically unified community gathered around an administratively and symbolically central house of worship is the most salient aspect of the picture presented above, fifteenth-century neighborhoods of Istanbul seem to fail, at least by half, to correspond to it. The waqf documents of the Mehmed II foundation and the survey of 1546 feature a total of 126 neighborhoods extant in Mehmed II's Istanbul.[21] Of these, sixty-four carry the names of mosques and masjids; the rest fall into several categories. There are neighborhoods named after their commercial centers, such as Un Kapanı, Balık Bazarı, Balat Bazarı (or Suk-ı Balat); those named after city gates, such as Bab-ı Orya (Neorion Gate), Odun Kapusı, Bab-ı Silivri; and those designated by Byzantine landmarks in the city: Aslanlı Ev ("The House with Lions," in the vicinity of Taht al-kalʿa, most likely a Venetian palace), Tekvur ("Prince," near the Blachernae Palace), Kıztaşı (the Maiden's Column), Libs Manastırı (the monastery of Constantine Lips), Ayulanga (Langa). The two neighborhoods named Fil Damı (Elephant House), one near the Bab-ı Semek (the gate and the bazaar of the fishmongers) and the other near Balat, were possibly named after large Byzantine buildings used as menageries. Some neighborhoods were named after baths built during the reign of Mehmed, such as Sırt Hamamı, Alaca Hamam, Kazasker Hamamı, Gedik Pasha Hamamı. Others were named after the places of origin of deportee communities, such as Balat, Edirneli Yahudiler (Edirne Jews), Aksaray. And finally, there are those areas named after prominent individuals who resided in them. Among these are the neighborhoods of Mehmed Pasha (possibly Rum Mehmed Pasha), to the southwest of the first palace, and (Gedik) Ahmed Pasha and one named Topcu Urban Evleri, or Houses of Urban the Cannon Maker (the Hungarian cannon maker whose services to the Ottomans had been crucial to their military success in 1453, we learn, was among those who received a donation of buildings).

Two poll-tax registers, dating to 1540 and 1545, list non-Muslim quarters and communities in the city, most of which were populated by deportees during the reign of Mehmed II. They provide a similar picture. In these documents, where tax-paying non-Muslims of the city were registered on the basis of their residential quarters, communities, or profession, appear few *maḥallāt* carrying the name of a house of worship: of the forty-two Greek quarters within the walled city, seven carry the names of churches, while the rest are named after communities' places of origin or landmarks in the area.[22] Jewish residents, too, were registered by Ottoman officials as members of *cemāʿat* (communities) in relation to their places of origin, but not in relation to their houses of worship. A number of synagogues in present-day Istanbul, those of Ohrid, Yanbol, Veria, İştipol, and Çana in Balat, and Kastorya in Tekfur Saray, carry the names of deportee communities brought to the city during the reign of Mehmed II.[23]

How, then, did the picture in the 953/1546 survey, where the great majority of the city quarters were named after and presumably centered around a mosque or a masjid, come into being? Locating on a map all the neighborhoods and, wherever known, the particular buildings (mosques, baths, gates, etc.) these were named after demonstrates that in particular areas of the city numerous *maḥallāt* did not make it to the (waqf documents of the) mid–sixteenth century (map 3).[24] These are the Taht al-kalʿa area, the Un Kapanı area, and the environs of the aqueduct and Mehmed's New Mosque complex, in addition to several locations along the land and sea walls, mostly near city gates. In some instances it is possible to follow the change of neighborhood designation from a nonreligious landmark to a masjid. Such was the case with the many *maḥallāt* near Taht al-kalʿa and Un Kapanı. In Taht al-kalʿa, the quarters of Bozahaneler, Edirneli Yahudiler, Aslanlı Ev, Orya Kapu, Taht al-kalʿa, and Vasiliko (Fesleğen) Kapusı were replaced by the neighborhoods carrying the names of masjids: Hacı Halil and Bezzaz-ı Cedid. Instead of the neighborhoods of Debbagin, Azebler Hammamı, Sinan Halveti, and Tatarlar around

Un Kapanı, one finds the quarters of the Elvan Çelebi and Yavuzer Sinan masjids.[25]

The 1546 survey thus presents a Muslim map of the city: it "corrects" earlier nonreligious designations or omits non-Muslim neighborhoods altogether, probably registering any endowed property in these areas as parts of larger Muslim enclaves: the masjid of Elvan Çelebi, its endowment deed dating to 887/1482–83, was built next to the Azebler bath, which dates to before 1474. As late as the 926/1520 survey of the Ayasofya endowment, the area was referred to as the neighborhood of the bath, and only in the 953/1546 survey was it named after the masjid. Similarly, in 953/1546 one finds the quarter of the Ferhad Ağa masjid in the area where in the 1470s the quarters of Kırkçeşme, Topcu Urban Evleri (Houses of Urban the Cannon Maker), and Manastır (Monastery) had been registered.[26] In the same period, two Greek quarters near Kırkçeşme, those of Panaghia and Gedikçi, were recorded in the poll-tax document, while nothing of the quarter of Houses of Urban the Cannon Maker is to be found beyond the fifteenth century.

The *maḥalle* centered by its mosque provided the Ottomans with an operative concept through which urban space could be conceived and constructed, as a cellular structure that added up to the city itself. This was in line with conceptualizations of the city in Hanafi law, particularly as practiced by Mamluk and Ottoman jurists, as Baber Johansen has elucidated.[27] At the expense of socioeconomic and multidimensional definitions of the town, Johansen demonstrates, Hanafi jurists favored definitions that centered on the congregational mosque as the defining element of the town, along with those definitions that lay emphasis on the representation of the state in the town or on the size of population. The definition through the mosque, significantly, elaborated a hierarchy

of religious structures whereby the multiple Friday mosques of a town ranked highest, to be followed by the mosques of the quarter, the mosques of the marketplace or the throughway, and other places of worship such as convents.

A definition of the city through a multiplicity of places of worship and a concomitant hierarchy that orders them, the quarter mosque ranking highest after the congregational mosque, corresponds almost exactly to the listings in the surveys, particularly the citywide survey of 1546. The cellular structure implied in legal definitions and documents alike, however, was far from being a constant in the city's physical and social configuration. Particularly through the early decades of Ottoman rule, these cells tended to be amorphous and permeable, their social and physical boundaries prone to change. Although change and flexibility of a town quarter's social and physical boundaries characterized not only Istanbul through this period but most Ottoman cities through the early modern era,[28] the vicissitudes involved in creating an urban population through forced deportations, and the concomitant need to survey and thereby control urban space in the years following the conquest, magnified such flexibility.

The centrality of an image of the city composed of quarters, a representational constant in the face of rapid spatial and demographic changes, is significant not only for insights into Ottoman notions of urban order. That image has also had a considerable impact on the city's modern historiography, for it informed the narrative of a linear urban development in Ottoman Istanbul from the first years following the conquest onward. Most accounts of Istanbul's residential history can be traced back to the work of Ekrem Hakkı Ayverdi, who in a short but much used work published in 1958, based on the documents cited above, concluded that at the end of Mehmed II's reign the walled city comprised 181 neighborhoods.[29] Not unlike the city's surveyors several centuries earlier, Ayverdi projected on the city's empty and ruinuous space and its amorphous and indistinct residential areas his idea of an Istanbul neatly divided into a rather exaggerated number of neighborhoods, which had distinct boundaries and functioned as sixteenth-century and later town quarters did. Keen on attributing a Turkish and Muslim character to the newly inhabited capital, Ayverdi reached his conclusions through a process of addition (of later structures falsely attributed to this era)[30] and elimination (of quarters that were registered in the early surveys but were absent in later waqf documents, as they did not house mosques). Most of such non-Muslim city quarters included in the early surveys but excluded from Ayverdi's list are to be found intact in the poll-tax registers of the mid–sixteenth century. As I stated earlier, in these documents of 1540 and 1545 taxpaying individuals are registered as members of communities (*cemāʿat*), of neighborhoods (*maḥallāt*), or by profession.[31] That not all authors using Ayverdi's account have shared his agenda is, in one sense, of little import, since his figures have been continuously used, leading, in turn, to oversights regarding changes in urban policy, patronage patterns, and political orientations between the later fifteenth and mid sixteenth centuries.[32]

A REVISED PICTURE

The highest concentration of settlement through the first decades of Ottoman rule in Constantinople was in the northeastern part of the peninsula, while residential areas were found also along the city's main arteries and around city gates (map 3). The earliest Ottoman settlements were in the area to which late Byzantine Constantinople had shrunk,

within the stretch along and on the slopes of the Golden Horn, especially the shoreline between the Neorion (Orya) Gate and Un Kapanı and the slopes to the south of these. Not surprisingly, documents of the Mehmed II foundation, which often specify Byzantine structures as *kāfirī al-binā'* (infidels' buildings), locate the majority of these buildings in this area. The same documents indicate that members of deportee communities were living in such "infidels' buildings." These were the Byzantine structures given out first as freehold property and later rented out to the city's new inhabitants.[33]

Several reasons suggest themselves to explain the dense settlement in this area of the city. While concerns with security through the last centuries of Byzantium doubtless had a role in the shrinking of Constantinople's urban settlement to this area, equally important was the natural concentration of trade and crafts here, along the shore, as well as along main arteries, the Mese and the Makros Embolos. The first chapter of this study delineated the continuities in the uses of commercial space through the Byzantine and Ottoman periods, with the sizable additions of the bedestan and the markets in the vicinity of the New Mosque. Hence the quarters of Debbagin (tanners),[34] Balat Bazarı (the market of Balat), Balık Bazarı (fishmongers' market), Un Kapanı (the weighing station for flour), Odun Kapanı (the weighing station for wood), and Bozahaneler (*boza* houses) along the Golden Horn. The construction of the bedestan encouraged settlement along the Uzunçarşı, for new quarters are found on it or in its vicinity in the later fifteenth century: quarters of the Sırt Hamamı (later the Mercan Ağa mosque) and the Yavaşca Şahin, Merdivenli, and Samanviran masjids are among these. Significantly, the majority of the Jewish deportees, along with a number of Muslim communities, were settled in this area, which retained its centrality to trade and procurement throughout the city's history.

Also in the northern part of the peninsula, but farther away from the shore, along the course of the Mese where the majority of the large-scale Ottoman foundations were located, lay other newly founded masjids and settlements. The first palace and the commercial center, the restored aqueduct and its fountains, and finally Mehmed's New Complex provided loci for deportee communities. Hence the presence of the largely Greek neighborhoods of Kırkçeşme, Manastır (Monastery), and Topcu Urban Evleri (Houses of Urban the Cannon Maker) in the vicinity of Kırkçeşme, the Forty Fountains from which the waters of the newly restored aqueduct flowed (map 3 [D5]). The first neighborhoods around Mehmed's New Mosque were those of the Larger and the Smaller Karaman and Gürci (the Georgians), named after deportee communities settled here during the construction of the complex, and those of Sultan Bazarı and Demirciler (ironmongers), pointing to the presence of commerce and crafts in the area, supplying the janissary barracks nearby (map 3 [D5]). To the west and east of the New Mosque, two architects whose names are attached to its construction, Atik Sinan and Ayas, built masjids (map 3 [D4, D5]).

Like the major monuments, several small neighborhood mosques were built on or very close to the Mese, among them the masjids of Mevlana Gürani, Nurlu Dede, Emin Beg, and Hubyar (map 3, [C6, C7, E7]). The determining factors in the choice of site for these buildings may have been similar to those that informed the construction of sultanic and vizierial foundations: ease in transportation, proximity to waterways, visibility, and, especially for those farther away from the center, security.[35]

The length of the sea and land walls of the city was dotted with settlements. The commercial stretch on the Golden Horn bore the quarters of Balık Bazarı, Odun Kapanı, and Un Kapanı (names that were used interchangeably with those of the city gates they flanked, that is, Odun Kapusı and Un Kapusı), among others. Stéphane Yerasimos, on the ground of the 1540 and 1545 poll-tax surveys, has delineated a pattern of Greek settlements along the city walls, in a largely unbroken band beginning in the Petrion quarter to the west of Cibali on the Golden Horn and following the land walls to the Marmara, in a number of settlements that reached the Kumkapı/Kontoskalion area.[36] At the northern end of this stretch Greek and Jewish communities were merged, while at its southern end a number of Armenian settlements coexisted with the Greek quarters. Fifteenth-century surveys also feature both Muslim and Christian settlements, near the Edirne (Charisios), Top (Hagios Romanos), and Silivri (Pege) Gates along the land walls.

A number of these owed their existence to activities related to the city gates—trade in the case of those along the Golden Horn, control and payment of customs for goods brought to the city by land routes in the case of gates in the land and Marmara sea walls, such as Edirnekapı (Charisios Gate), Topkapı (Aya Romano), and Yenikapı.[37] Other non-Muslim communities were possibly settled around monastic establishments extant in these sections of the city. Such was the case with the Silivri (Pege) Gate and the environs of the Peribleptos abbey, where a Greek and an Armenian community lived.

By contrast, the area west of Mehmed II's and Has Murad Pasha's foundations was largely empty, save for few settlements on arteries that led to the city gates. In the southwestern section of the walled city, in what was to become the districts of Topkapı and Koca Mustafa Pasha, were four masjids whose expenses were covered by Mehmed's foundation, and another four paid for by the imperial treasury (*beglikden,* or *ḫāṣṣa ḫarcdan*).[38] None is included in Mehmed II's endowment deeds. It has been suggested that these might be masjids established during the reign of Mehmed by those individuals whose names they still carry, masjids that became, possibly due to their remote location, impoverished in the course of time.[39] It is also possible that these were later constructions incorporated into the foundation of Mehmed II. Except for the largely Greek quarter of Altımermer, in the vicinity of İsa Kapu (the last extant gate along the Constantinian land walls), all dated foundations in this area were from the last decades of the fifteenth century or from the sixteenth century (map 3, [B7]).[40] During Bayezid II's reign, numerous Sufi convents were to spring up in this area. The largest and best endowed among these was founded by Koca Mustafa Pasha for the Halveti sheikh Sünbül Sinan and was housed in the converted church of St. Andrea in Krisei and in the complex that was built around it.[41]

This survey renders visible the connections between the city's residential quarters and its administrative, commercial, and religious loci. Although clear-cut divisions are difficult to draw, it is possible to single out foundations by patrons related by background or profession in locations connected to their particular activities. In chapter 2, I have noted the location of vizierial establishments close to Mehmed II's palaces: Mahmud Pasha's foundation to the west of the Topkapı Palace and Hagia Sophia, that of İshak Pasha across from the palace walls to the south of Hagia Sophia, the palace of Rum Mehmed Pasha to the northwest of the first palace (map 1). These complexes spurred the formation of residential quarters around them. The strand of the Golden Horn between the Neorion Gate and the Un Kapanı, and the environs of the Uzunçarşı, were marked mostly by foundations of merchants, craftsmen, and those members of the military elite who were involved in the procurement of goods for the capital. The large numbers of *ḫāce*s (merchants) among the founders of mosques in this area, and the frequent notes in Ayvansarayi on the backgrounds of patrons as overseers of the trade, support this point.[42] The area to the west and northwest of the first palace, the Vefa district of the sixteenth century and later, became marked by foundations of the religious elite; in this area was the mosque and convent of Şeyh Vefazade, founded by Mehmed II, along with foundations of other members of the learned hierarchy: prominent figures such as Mevlana Husrev, who served as kadi of Istanbul, as mufti, and as professor at the Ayasofya madrasa; Mevlana Gürani, *ḳāḍī'asker* and also mufti; and Hızır Beg, the city's first kadi; but also lesser-known individuals—all of these endowed masjids that constituted the cores of new residential quarters in this area (map 3 [E5, E6]).[43]

Were these, as scholarship on Ottoman Istanbul has for the most part assumed, ethnically and religiously homogeneous units? While the assumption that Ottoman town quarters constituted such units has not gone unquestioned in writings on Ottoman cities at large, it has not lost its centrality in narratives of the construction of the Ottoman capital city.[44] To summarize this view briefly: Muslim and non-Muslim communities deported from elsewhere in the Ottoman realm were settled separately, in residential quarters centered by their places of worship. It would of course be wrong to attribute the making of this picture of cellular homogeneity to modern scholars alone. As early as the later fifteenth century, Giovan Maria Angiolello, Vicenzan captive in the court, described the deportee communities of Istanbul, each living in its own quarter. He drew a detailed portrait of the Caffan quarter, with its honorable houses and churches, beautiful streets, shops and markets, which, he wrote, because of the love of the inhabitants for their town of origin, was now called Caffa.[45] Some archival and narrative sources support this description. The settlement of the deportees from Karaman in the environs of Mehmed II's and Murad Pasha's foundations has already been noted.[46]

Perhaps it is the orderliness of this picture that has led contemporary witnesses and modern scholars alike to pay less attention to contrary evidence. In the poll-tax registers of 1540 and 1545 the non-Muslim communities of Istanbul and Galata, the majority of them deported to the city during the later fifteenth century, are registered according to their places of origin and the neighborhoods in which they lived. Thus one finds the Greeks of Karaca Foça, brought to the city in 1459, living in Kumkapı (Kontoskalion), Kadırga, Fener, and Galata; or the deportees from Mytilene, deported in 1461, dispersed to eleven neighborhoods within the walled city and in Galata.[47]

The range of names one encounters in the waqf documents of the later fifteenth century within particular quarters shows that ethnic (and religious, linguistic, and cultural) homogeneity marked only some areas of the city at the time. To give one example: in the quarter of Mevlana Husrev, near the Aya Kenisası and the bath of Mustafa Pasha,[48] lived Fāṭima bint-i Mürsel, Naṣūḥ bin Ḳarabula, Ḥamza the Carpenter, Mārodḳō Ṭōdoros the Christian, Balabān the Porter, Ḳaragöz bin ʿAbdullah, Mātyōs bin Dōḳa the Christian, Muṣṭafā bin Yānī the Orphan, Ḳōsta from Mytilene the Christian, Ḳocabāz the Christian, and Raḫūs of Trabzon the Christian. In the neighboring quarter of Aya Kenisası, later to be registered as part of the quarter of Mevlana Husrev, we find Ḥacī Sinān the Butcher, Ḥamza bin Rukneddīn of Ankara, Muṣṭafā Faḳīh, el-Ḥāc Ṭūrdı the Waterway Builder. Here lived not only a religiously heterogeneous population but also deportees from different places and a number of recent converts to Islam (map 3 [E3, E4]).[49] Such heterogeneity marked particularly the areas along the Golden Horn, while it could be observed in many other quarters as well. The mosque of Hacı Halil, already mentioned in the context of interventions in the city's commercial fabric, stood in the mostly Jewish quarter of Bozahaneler near the Vasiliko Gate. Here lived the imam and the müezzin of the mosque, and also one ʿAbdurrahman al-ʿArab and one Hacı Seydi.[50] The neighboring quarters of Acemoğlu, Halil Pasha Bergosu, and Edirneli Yahudiler housed Jewish inhabitants as well (and at least three synagogues), but also a number of Muslims and Christians (map 3 [F5]). One of them was a Frank (Efrenc), possibly a member of the Venetian establishment that remained in this area into the middle decades of the sixteenth century.[51]

Founded four years after the conquest in 861/1457, the masjid of Hacı Halil is one of the earliest in the city (see fig. 18). Exactly when a Jewish community from Edirne was settled here is not known, but they probably arrived within the first decade of Ottoman rule. Given that the construction of the mosque and the settlement of the inhabitants were nearly contemporaneous, one can safely assume that either the patron chose the Jewish quarter in which to found his masjid or the Jewish community was given an area where a masjid already stood. The quarter was referred to as that of the Jews of Edirne until the 1546 survey, when it was recorded as the quarter of the Hacı Halil masjid. The coexistence of Muslims and Jews in the area was not deemed undesirable until the conception of the Yeni Valide mosque complex in the later decades of the sixteenth century.[52]

WAQF AND NEIGHBORHOODS

In the 1470s an increasing number of Istanbul's residential quarters, nearly half of them at the time, housed a mosque, founded within the institutional framework of the waqf: commercial and/or residential property in the vicinity of the foundation and/or in the commercial district, newly built or donated by the sultan, would be endowed, its income in most cases to be shared between the founded institution and the founder's family. Hence the social and spatial implications of the foundation of a mosque largely exceeded the construction and functioning of a house of worship alone. An examination of the interrelationships between founders, endowments, and users that takes into consideration patterns of land use and city dwellers' uses of endowed institutions should throw light on the social and spatial processes through which a house of worship came to occupy the social and symbolic center of a residential quarter. Since evidence regarding the formation of individual quarters is in large part waqf related, the resulting picture of the making and workings of a residential quarter in fifteenth-century Istanbul will necessarily remain incomplete. Excluded from this picture are non-Muslim quarters and those which were not, in this period at least, marked by a pious foundation.

The leading founders were members of the military elite, followed by merchants and craftsmen, then members of the religious hierarchy.[53] Of the roughly seventy quarter mosques, thirty-one can be attributed to members of the military elite with some certainty. Four foundations were established by women, three of them by members of the royal family.[54] In Istanbul, as in other newly conquered cities, women assumed relative visibility and prominence as patrons of religious and charitable foundations only after the formation of a (largely male) network of patronage. Seventeen were founded by merchants and craftsmen, and eleven by members of the learned hierarchy.[55] Significantly, these numbers are in line with Halil İnalcık's count for mid-sixteenth-century Istanbul. İnalcık notes that the military elite was the leading group among the founders of mosques (for reasons of social and political prestige and also as a means of tying down funds); they were followed by merchants (the only group besides the ruling class to accumulate cash capital) and craftsmen, and lastly by members of the learned hierarchy. The intervening period, particularly the reign of Bayezid II, witnessed a significant rise in the power and status of the religious elite; concomitantly, the ulema became more prominent patrons of urban institutions than were merchants and craftsmen. The prominence of state officials (of the military or the religious track) as founders of religious institutions in the new capital is nevertheless significant.[56]

How did such a configuration emerge? Mehmed's claim to the stones and the land of the city was not merely an attempt to mitigate the damages of the sack that followed the conquest. ("The stones and the land of the city and its appurtenances belong to me; all other goods and property, prisoners and foodstuffs are booty for the troops," he said, observing the devastation of the city by the conquering army.)[57] The monarch's possession of the city's land and buildings was literal. This can be gleaned from many fifteenth-century freehold deeds preserved at the Topkapı Palace Archives and from endowment deeds, which often include notes on the sultan's granting ownership of a building or plot of land to an individual.[58] One needed a *mülknāme* (freehold deed) to carry a fountain lying in the moat outside a city gate to one's mosque and to use it there, just as one did to acquire the land on which to build that mosque.[59] It is perhaps not coincidental that sales documents of urban property dating to the reign of Mehmed are rare,[60] as are references in waqf documents to property bought from other individuals. Starting with Bayezid's reign these are plenty; in some instances one can trace an individual's expansion of his possessions in a certain area of the city, as with Kapu Ağası Hüseyin Ağa, who acquired land in the area between his mosque-and-lodge (the Küçük Ayasofya/SS. Sergius and Bacchus) and the Hippodrome, or Koca Mustafa Pasha in the Taht al-kal'a area.[61] By contrast, through Istanbul's first Ottoman decades, it was a rare event for urban property to be bought and sold between individuals. Most frequently, land and buildings (and stones, as in the case of the fountain) moved in one direction only, from the possession of the sultan to the possession of individuals of all ranks and backgrounds.

If one's access to urban property was largely, if not exclusively, dependent on the sultan's favor, it follows that allotments of land reflected and reproduced his (and the administration's) understanding of the role to be played by city dwellers in its settlement. Freehold and endowment deeds that document donations of land by the sultan delineate a hierarchy of social categories and of individuals within those categories. Thus the types, sizes, and locations of land and buildings endowed to the city's inhabitants ranged from the most modest single-room house in the vicinity of the Hippodrome given to Mariya the Çengi (musician or dancer) with the right to own, sell, or endow it and to use it in whatever way she wished,[62] to the church and the two large plots given to the architect Atik Sinan to build his house and a mosque on,[63] to land encompassing the larger part of the slopes

between the first and the second hills of the walled peninsula, given to Mahmud Pasha as site for his palace, socioreligious complex, and commercial and residential structures, which added up to several hundred units.

A hegemonic vision of the city and its builders underlay this manner of disposing of urban property through donations to individuals in accordance with their professional backgrounds and status. Prominent members of the military and religious hierarchy and those individuals who partook in the provisioning of the city were simultaneously the builders of urban institutions. Donations of urban property and foundations created through such donations charted out political and professional hierarchies on the space of the city, concomitant with their role in the making of an Ottoman social and spatial fabric in Constantinople and their role in enhancing the status of founders. Edward Mitchell has interpreted the creation of foundations not only as the realization of Mehmed II's command of 1459 but also as the self-realization of the ruling class.[64] As the creation of a new monumental order gave concrete form to a resignification of urban space, minor focal points, in less conspicuous ways, contributed to that process, which would at once manifest the political order within the city and be instrumental in its reproduction. This was in line with earlier Islamic and Ottoman practice, whereby pious endowments were used in the appropriation and institutionalization of newly acquired territory.

Mehmed, wrote Kritovoulos of the sultan's order of 1459, commanded his grandees to undertake constructions in places of their choice. In the context of Byzantine buildings given to individuals as freehold property in the first years after the conquest, İnalcık has noted that inhabitants chose particular buildings and then petitioned the court for ownership.[65]

The few extant fifteenth-century documents regarding permissions given for constructions in the capital city and elsewhere suggest that the court exercised more control over *what* was to be built than *where,* defining the area of construction rather than the exact location. Thus permission was given to Hacı Müslihüddin, overseer of the Koca Mustafa Pasha foundation, to build a double bath and a sheep's-head shop in the vicinity of İsa Kapu, "wherever he may choose" (*her ne yerde isterse*). Hacı Müslihüddin was also granted permission to build shops, as many as he wanted, on his property as well as on state-owned land.[66] By contrast, one Çatladı Kasım was not given permission by Mehmed II to operate the bath he had built in the vicinity of the Hippodrome; he petitioned the court once again when Bayezid II took over, and did, this second time, obtain the desired license.[67]

Extant documents regarding permissions granted (or withheld) for the construction and operation of buildings treat commercial property, baths, shops, and one caravanserai. The deeds related to construction of commercial property underline a concern with protecting the interests of other individuals who owned buildings with similar functions in the areas in question, while the availability of water was also an important point of consideration. Mevlana Gürani, professor of Mehmed II, *ḳāḍī'asker,* kadi of Istanbul, and finally mufti in 1480, petitioned the court to have one measure (*māṣūra*) of water for his *dārü'l-ḥadīṣ* (school for the study of hadith) from the palace waterways and was rejected, on account of the scarcity of water in the system.[68] Where religious buildings were concerned, no documents seem to have survived to attest to the process of appeal and approval between founders and the court. Collections of jurisprudential opinion (*fetvā*) from the early sixteenth century onward, however, contain references to permissions from the

court granted or withheld for the construction and use of masjids and congregational mosques (or the conversion of masjids into congregational mosques), suggesting that similar procedures were in place at an earlier date as well.[69] The very small number of congregational mosques in the city in this period, all endowed by the sultan and members of the imperial council, suggests that religious or customary law put restrictions on who could found one.[70]

Regarding the types of foundations established by individuals to whom land was donated, tacit acceptance of established forms and hierarchy of architectural patronage, if no explicit orders, seems to have been at work. The shift in the sultanic and vizierial foundations from convent-masjids to Friday mosques, signifying transformations in political hierarchy and shifts in power bases, paralleled changes in the composition of neighborhoods: while the foundation of a congregational mosque remained the prerogative of the sultan and his high-ranking viziers, small-scale religious foundations that were functional in the formation of new settlements were almost exclusively masjids with allotments only for a prayer leader and a reciter for the call to prayer (imam and a müezzin), rather than convents or multifunctional convent-mosques, spaces of accommodation and of Sufi practices instrumental in the formation of new communities in conquered territory in an earlier era.[71] This is not surprising, considering Mehmed's unfavorable disposition toward the Sufi sects, which had formerly been central constituents of the Ottoman political spectrum, and the dervishes' equally unfavorable disposition toward the restoration of the city to its former imperial splendor. A new type of patronage, exercised by a group of patrons largely different from that of the earlier era, is discernible: a new urban elite, consisting in large part of members of the new military establishment, built for an urban population in large part forcefully deported to the city.

Only a few convents in Istanbul are dated to the reign of Mehmed with some degree of certainty. Among these are three royal foundations; only one, the foundation of Sheikh Vefa (whose attribution as mosque or convent was vague, as was noted in the second chapter), figures as the center of a residential quarter. It will be remembered that the Eski İmaret (Old Hospice) was converted into a mosque upon the completion of the lavishly constructed and generously endowed guesthouse within the New Mosque complex, and that the Kalenderhane did not give its name to a neighborhood until the early sixteenth century, when it was converted into a mosque.[72] The vizierial mosques, I have noted in the second chapter, were variations on the well-established convent-masjid type, but there is no indication in their waqfiyya summaries or in narrative sources of ritualistic uses of these spaces. One convent did give its name to a residential neighborhood in this period: that built for the chronicler Aşıkpaşazade by the architect Sinan, flanked by a masjid, possibly endowed by the chronicler himself.[73] A few of the masjids in the western part of the city whose maintenance was covered by the imperial treasury (Kovacı Dede, Mirza Baba, Tarsus) functioned also as convents, significantly, from the late 1480s onward (map 3 [D4, B8, A6]). Private endowments of the quarters' inhabitants supported the expenses of the convents. A convent of Karaca Ahmed in the Langa area is mentioned in a document of 1479, perhaps an indication that the areas farther away from the center were deemed more favorable by the users of these spaces.[74]

This is in line with what Küçük Abdal writes in the Velāyetnāme of Otman Baba, the marginal Sufi leader mentioned earlier in the context of his displays of power in the commercial

area. Numerous convents, whose followers were possibly adherents of popular Sufi orders, are encountered in this narrative, most of them in the western and southwestern sections of the city. The dervish lived in a convent near the Silivri/Pege Gate (it is not certain whether this is the same place as the Kılıç Manastırı [the Monastery of the Sword], where he might have been kept in custody during his second stay in Istanbul);[75] he visited the Hindiler convent and the Edhemi convent, both located "within orchards" in the vicinity of the Murad Pasha mosque, and another convent "below the Old Palace."[76] None of these convents is mentioned as a quarter masjid in contemporary sources, implying a significant contrast with their prominence during the reign of Bayezid II, when the number of convents in Istanbul visibly increased. Many of these, especially convents of the prominent Halvetiyye order (who had supported Bayezid as heir to the throne during his strife with Cem) and the Nakshibendiyye, were well-endowed institutions. Some are registered as neighborhood centers in official documents.[77]

The involvement of the founder in the actual physical development of a quarter varied greatly. As in the case of the sultan or of Mahmud Pasha, one could "develop" a huge district of the city through the establishment of a host of religious, charitable, residential, and commercial structures. The minor foundations that are the subject of this section echo this pattern in differing degrees. The endowment deeds of the architect Ayas, or that of Çelebizade 'Alaüddin, suggest that some founders created tiny models of the Mahmud Pasha foundation: Ayas's foundation to the east of the New Mosque, dated to 879/1475, consisted of a mosque situated on the main artery, a primary school, his own residence, a compound referred to as oṭalar (rooms)—containing sixteen rooms, a latrine, a water well, and thirty-two shops—and another compound laid out around two courtyards, all newly built on the same plot of land. Similarly, the smaller foundation of Çelebizade 'Alaüddin, a merchant, consisted of a mosque he built near the Alaca bath in the commercial district, for which he endowed a total of thirteen rooms, all in the vicinity of the mosque and bath. The *maḥalle* of Çelebizade 'Alaüddin, according to surveys of the Mehmed II foundation, housed a Muslim and a Jewish community.

Such spatial unity characterizes only some of the smaller foundations of the period. Individuals of higher means (or standing vis-à-vis the sultan) could found a number of religious structures and be involved to differing degrees in the areas where they endowed property. Such is the case of Mevlana Husrev, the most prominent member of the religious elite of this period, who held the office of kadi of Istanbul between 1459 and 1473 and served as the mufti from 1473 until his death, in 1480. In 1465, when he held the office of kadi of the capital city, Mevlana Husrev drew an endowment deed for three mosques he founded in areas of the walled city quite distinct from one another. One of these was located to the west of the Old Palace, in an area that was to be marked by foundations of the religious elite, and in the vicinity of three largely Christian neighborhoods at the time, Kırkçeşme, Manastır, and Houses of Urban the Cannon Maker. Private property near Mevlana Husrev's mosque belonged mostly to Christians; judging from the presence of one Tengrivermiş (Gift of God, more often an Armenian name used in Anatolia), some of them at least were deportees, but one Tōdōrōs al-Istanbūlī, most likely a native of Constantinople, also lived here. Mevlana Husrev's second mosque, located near the Aya Kenisası and the bath of Mustafa Pasha, has already been noted in the previous section, in the context of the ethnic makeup of the city's residential areas. Among others, deportees from Trabzon and Mytilene, brought to the city in 1461 and 1462 respectively, lived here; the construction of the mosque, endowed in 1465, might have postdated the settlement of Christian deportee communities in the area. While the locations of these two masjids suggest that Islamizing largely non-Muslim districts might have been a factor in the choice of site, the third structure was built in an area with a markedly different character. North of the Forum Bovis, where Has Murad Pasha was to build his complex, this was the area where the deportees from Aksaray were to be settled following the Karaman campaigns. The lack of any reference to this location in the documents of the Mehmed II foundation suggests that no inhabitable Byzantine structure existed here.

For the three mosques Mevlana Husrev endowed a host of commercial structures in the commercial district, near the bedestan, in the Mahmud Pasha quarter, and within the flea and the fowl markets. He was not involved any further with the physical development of the areas where he undertook religious constructions. The waqfiyya summary does not specify where the kadi's own dwelling was; it might have been near the first foundation, west of the Old Palace, as this would become an area marked by foundations and residences of the religious elite.

Another large and disperse foundation, that of the architect Sinan, suggests a more entrenched relationship with different locales in the city. Judging from the extent of his foundation, the architect of the New Mosque enjoyed the sultan's highest favor before he met his tragic end. In the quarter of the Maiden's Column, to the west of the New Mosque, Sinan founded the mosque that was to acquire the name Kumrulu Mescid, "the Mosque of the Doves," due to the spoliated frieze of doves attached to its façade. An elementary school, possibly functioning within the mosque initially, was to be given its separate building by 1469, when Sinan drew his second foundation deed. Within the same quarter a church with two adjoining rooms (chapels?) and a large courtyard with a water well and cypress trees was endowed for the founder's family. How would a convert to Islam, most possibly an Orthodox Greek by birth, make use of a sultanic gift of an Orthodox church? What did the classification of this property as a private foundation, rather than a pious one, signify? The most likely answers to these questions would take into account the possibility that the architect's family did not convert to Islam but remained practicing Christians, in which case the church would have been used as a family chapel.[78] Unfortunately, contemporary and later documents provide no clear answers.

The endowment deed of Sinan, however, does offer a revealing connection to an unexpected locale and individual, given that person's occupation and background: in a quarter of the Fener district referred to interchangeably as that of Baba Saltuk and that of Aşık Pasha, after the legendary hero of Ottoman expansion and the fourteenth-century mystic and man of letters respectively, the architect endowed a convent and stipulated its sheikhdom to Aşık Pasha's great grandson, the chronicler Şemseddin Ahmed bin Yahya, better known as Aşıkpaşazade. Adjacent to the convent was the mosque of Aşık Pasha. The masjid might have been founded by the chronicler: Aşıkpaşazade owned commercial property in at least three different places in the Un Kapanı area, suggesting that he might have had the means to found a mosque. (Possibly the dervish was among those who suffered through policy changes regarding property initially given to settlers as freehold, for which they later had to pay rent: a topic that merited a lengthy and highly critical account

in his chronicle.)[79] The exact nature of the link between the buildings, the architect, and the chronicler remains in the dark. Nevertheless, the architect's and the chronicler's names are connected to the same quarter and buildings, suggesting a relationship between the dervish-chronicler and the convert, a connection reminiscent of an earlier era when prominent and charismatic mystics were instrumental in proselytizing Islam.[80]

The commercial properties Sinan endowed for his charities, too, were dispersed in different areas of the city: the two deeds list numerous shops in the vicinity of the newly built bedestan, near his mosque, and in the quarter of Ḥacaru'l-ʿAmūd (Stone Column). The identity of this column remains unknown, but the description of property boundaries and owners of neighboring plots suggests that it was located in a largely Jewish neighborhood.[81] Judging by the expansive residential compound built on a large plot of land donated by the sultan and endowed for his family and his heir in the quarter of the New Mosque, Sinan lived in the vicinity of the two mosques he built, for the sultan and for himself. His connections within the city, through a wide range of patronage relationships mediated through his pious foundation, extended far beyond the limits of his neighborhood.

An extensive body of work has delineated the role of the waqf institution in the formation and sustenance of social and political networks and in shaping the material environment within the Islamic world. Pious endowments provided an institutional framework for interactions that connected a range of social groups vertically and horizontally, creating spaces for charity, patronage, and accommodation.[82] The scope and quantity of extant documentation on fifteenth-century Istanbul, however, do not allow for a full picture of social and spatial networks framed by the waqf institution of that time and place. But the sources do provide a number of answers to more specific questions regarding the workings of pious endowments in the creation of residential patterns and the human network of the residential quarter.

Where the founder resided near the mosque he built, and where he perhaps built and/or endowed other commercial and residential structures, a tighter net of social relations revolving around the foundation emerged. By extension, the founder, most likely a state official, was a leading member of the community, landlord to a large number of the residents of the quarter, and perhaps the head of a large household that resided there. He might have been influential in the workings of the quarter or in mediating the demands of the residents. When, as in the case of the Mevlana Husrev foundation, the patron was not a resident of the quarter where he founded public institutions, waqf employees were the link between the patron and the community.[83]

This, however obvious, is to some extent speculative: archival or narrative sources on the city in this period provide little precise information on social interactions at the neighborhood level. It may indeed be significant that the neighborhood mosque, so central to the scholarship on the residential history of the city, is completely absent from narrative sources of this period. One may of course reason that such humble settings did not figure in the stories of the exalted. But one might still ask why Taşköprizade's highly anecdotal biographical dictionary of the learned does not refer to mosques as settings to any of its narratives. One may also easily guess why these new buildings never figure in narrative sources that originated in the dervish/ghazi milieu, such as the *Ṣaltūḳnāme* or the *Velāyetnāme* of Otman Baba, except for those instances when a figure of the

religious establishment had to be taught a lesson.[84] In rural areas as well as in cities, convents, not mosques, were the architectural settings of the dervishes, and these buildings do figure very centrally in both texts as sites of a host of narratives.

A close look at the survey of pious foundations completed in 1546 sheds some light on the absence of quarter mosques in the narrative sources of the postconquest era. Under headings for each district of the city proper, and each quarter within each district, the survey lists all endowments of the inhabitants from the beginning of the Ottoman rule onward, starting with the foundation of the neighborhood masjid. An overview of the deeds registered in any given quarter shows that the functioning of the quarter's masjid did not involve the founder only. In any quarter at least half, and usually more, of the foundations involved the masjid in some way.[85] In the majority of the cases, this involvement is in the form of an endowment to the prayer leader or to the reader of the call to prayer, in return for his reading a part of the Koran on a regular basis—one section daily or the entire book yearly (*ḥatim*) and so on. In some cases the endowment is more general, stipulating that the income from a certain property or the interest from a certain amount of money be spent for the masjid. More particularly, one could allot money for repairs and restorations necessary for the masjid. Many founders of family foundations stipulated that in case the family line became extinct, the income and the overseeing of the foundation go to the prayer leader of the neighborhood masjid.[86] Individuals made endowments for oil for the lamps in their quarter's mosque; they endowed objects to be used in the mosque or by the employees of the mosque, Korans and Koran stands mostly, but also candles and candlesticks, cauldrons, pans and ladles. In fewer cases, an inhabitant of a quarter would endow residences for the imam and the müezzin, even when the mosque's endowment already had an allowance for this.[87]

An overview of foundations in a given city quarter, then, presents a picture in which the mosque, as a building and an institution, stands at the center of the quarter, at least as far as the inhabitants' acts of charity and the patronage relations embedded in those acts are concerned. In this picture, charity flows not only in one direction, from the founder to the mosque to the inhabitants of the quarter, but also in the reverse direction, from the inhabitants to the mosque. While this is a partial portrait of the workings of the city quarter, presenting only what has gone through the filter of Muslim charity, it is nevertheless significant in that it displays patronage relations embodied in and engendered by the waqf institution.

The 1546 survey presents a still picture of a network of donors and beneficiaries of charities, as well as their material settings. At the same time, it reveals a process encapsulated in changes in the types of endowments and the stipulations of the founders over a period of almost a century, between the 1450s and the 1540s. A close reading of the survey as a set of documents regarding differently dated, sized, and constituted units, then, offers a glimpse into the social formation of the town quarter. A striking, if not surprising, aspect of the survey in this regard is the scarcity of endowments that date from the first Ottoman decades of the city, and the scarcity among these of donations by residents of a quarter that involve that quarter's public institutions. To give some numbers: the survey includes some seventy mosque foundations between the dates 857/1453 and 895/1489–90,[88] while during the same period sixty-nine other endowments by other individuals were founded. Of these, thirty-five, about half, had no ties to the mosque of the quarter in

which they were registered: either their income was allotted for the founders' descendants,[89] or their charities were directed elsewhere, to the paying of alms or to religious foundations other than the quarter mosque. To give some examples: in the quarter of the architect Sinan ten of the twenty-four deeds registered involve the quarter mosque (two of the ten direct funds to the supervision of the endowment). Among these, the earliest dates to 895/1490, the next one to 901/1495, the rest to the 1520s and later.[90] In the quarter of the mosque of Aşık Pasha, only five of the nineteen deeds registered involve the convent or the masjid. Among these, two have considerably early dates, 876/1471 and 883/1479.[91] Three foundations have endowments for the masjid of Hacı Ferhad, which must have been located in the area. In the quarter of the masjid of Saru Bayezid, nine of the ten deeds registered involve the masjid. Of these, two date to 899/1494 and one to 901/1495; the rest are from the 1510s and later. In the majority of the quarters, the earliest foundations that have donations for the quarter mosque date to the later 1480s. These figures seem to point in the same direction as the lack of references to neighborhood mosques in narrative sources. The neighborhood as a social entity in Ottoman Istanbul did not form contemporaneously with "quarter mosques" through the first decades of Ottoman rule. The flow of charities in their direction suggests that when neighborhood communities did develop, in the later decades, mosques in most cases became the religious centers of communities, and hence mediators of the social relationships within.

There were instances when this did not happen. The Mevlana Husrev masjid built to the north of the Murad Pasha mosque, already mentioned in the context of the kadi's patronage, represents such a case. Two convents of the Halveti order were founded in the vicinity of the mosque in the 1490s, one of them across the street from the kadi's mosque.[92] While the quarter continued to be named after the mosque of Mevlana Husrev in official documents, it was the two convents that received inhabitants' charities. Of the twenty-four waqfs registered in the neighborhood in 1546, twenty-one directed funds to the convents, while only one inhabitant made an endowment for the mosque. One of the deeds refers to the quarter as that of the Şeyh Süleyman Halife convent, rather than that of Mevlana Husrev.[93] This exposes a distinction between the official *maḥalle* and that of the inhabitants; one may safely assume that here convents were the sites around which the quarter's network of relationships revolved. Clearly the idea of a neighborhood underlay the foundation of mosques and in turn the making of the city's official documents, but the official version of events does not necessarily correspond to the practices and experiences of the city's inhabitants. In this city of resettled communities and individuals, the formation of quarters as social and physical entities followed later, and sometimes in ways not foreseen by the founders.

A further conclusion suggested by this reading of sources is that the *maḥalle* was both an administrative entity (the city composed of quarters as a matrix imposed by the state on urban space for control of the population and collection of revenues) and a social and political entity, one of the sites in the city where social and political interactions took place and where patronage mechanisms and loyalties were established and reproduced. The first definition has to do with the particulars of administration; the second with the perceptions of the urban population regarding their social and spatial environment and their self-definitions in relation to their immediate surroundings. The ever-present inconsistencies in documents concerning names and boundaries of the quarters, and the general instability of these over any period of time, suggest that the two meanings of the *maḥalle,* in the minds of the city's surveyors and in the minds of its inhabitants, never completely coincided.[94]

THE ARCHITECTURE OF THE NEIGHBORHOOD

If in fifteenth-century Istanbul the masjid lacked the nearly absolute centrality modern scholarship has attributed to it as the social center of the quarter, what was its role in the making of the visual and spatial fabric of the city's residential areas? A striking aspect of the neighborhood masjids of the period is their unspectacular architecture. The majority were built over short periods of time, not with durable building materials, and perhaps not with all the necessary skills either: a remarkably small number of masjids built in this period preserve something of their original form. Several were demolished to open space for mosques of a monumental order, as ambitious building projects of the later sixteenth century focused on locations formerly endowed with a masjid. Many were altered completely through radical rebuilding operations.[95] From this point of view, the nearly seventy neighborhood masjids of Mehmed's Istanbul stood in stark contrast with the few monumental mosques of the city. The contrast can also be extended to contemporary and earlier masjids of Bursa and Edirne, which exhibit a stylistic unity that characterizes the architecture of each city.[96] In this comparison, too, the smaller mosques of Istanbul emerge as the lesser ones in terms of their formal architectural features as well as in their use of building materials.

The comparison between smaller-scale religious buildings in major Ottoman cities through the fifteenth century highlights at once the dire conditions that accompanied Istanbul's reconstruction and the sheer will power that made construction possible. Lack of skilled craftsmen and difficulties in the procurement of labor and materials concurred with the task of rapidly building and inhabiting the city and providing it with a network of Muslim houses of worship. Hence the scarcity of fifteenth-century buildings that have survived in their original form. A vulnerability to the effects of nature marked in fact many buildings of this period; one may remember the fate of Mehmed's own religious building projects, particularly the New Mosque and the Ayyub mosque, which could not survive natural disasters. Very few of the masjids of this period have reached our day intact, which points not only to the meager means available to the founders but also to the priorities they held: they were concerned little with the formal features of their buildings or with the use of expensive materials and craftsmanship. The construction, nevertheless, of about seventy masjids within the course of twenty-five years suggests the centrality of these institutions to the Ottoman project.

The role assigned to quarter mosques by the Ottoman ruling body presents itself as a question if one remembers that several were located in areas with heavily non-Muslim populations. If at least some of these structures were not built to answer the immediate needs of particular communities, and if their architectural modesty suggests that private or shared manifestations of wealth or power were not central to their conception, one may ask what other reasons may have prompted their construction. The notion of a mosque as a sign simultaneously of Muslim and Ottoman presence in the city might have been the foremost factor that led Ottoman rulers to encourage and patrons to undertake these constructions over short stretches of time and with limited

FIGURE 124
Hace Hayrüddin mosque, exterior, from the north.

means. The required presence (and, often, residence) of an imam and a müezzin in the vicinity of the mosque, when construction in a largely or solely non-Muslim area was in question, might have been a related consideration, as the mosque employees would have constituted a connection between the founder, often an official or member of the learned hierarchy, and the inhabitants of the area. Proselytizing the Muslim faith might have been a related motive.

Excepting the few monumental structures such as the Hagia Sophia, the New Mosque, and several viziers' mosques that gave their names to city quarters, the quarter mosques of the period were in large part small buildings constructed of rubble stone or composite masonry. A small number were domed buildings, such as the Hace Hayrüddin, Yavuzer Sinan, and Yavaşca Şahin masjids, all built by merchants within or in the vicinity of the commercial district (figs. 124–126).[97] The majority, however, featured pitched wooden roofs, as

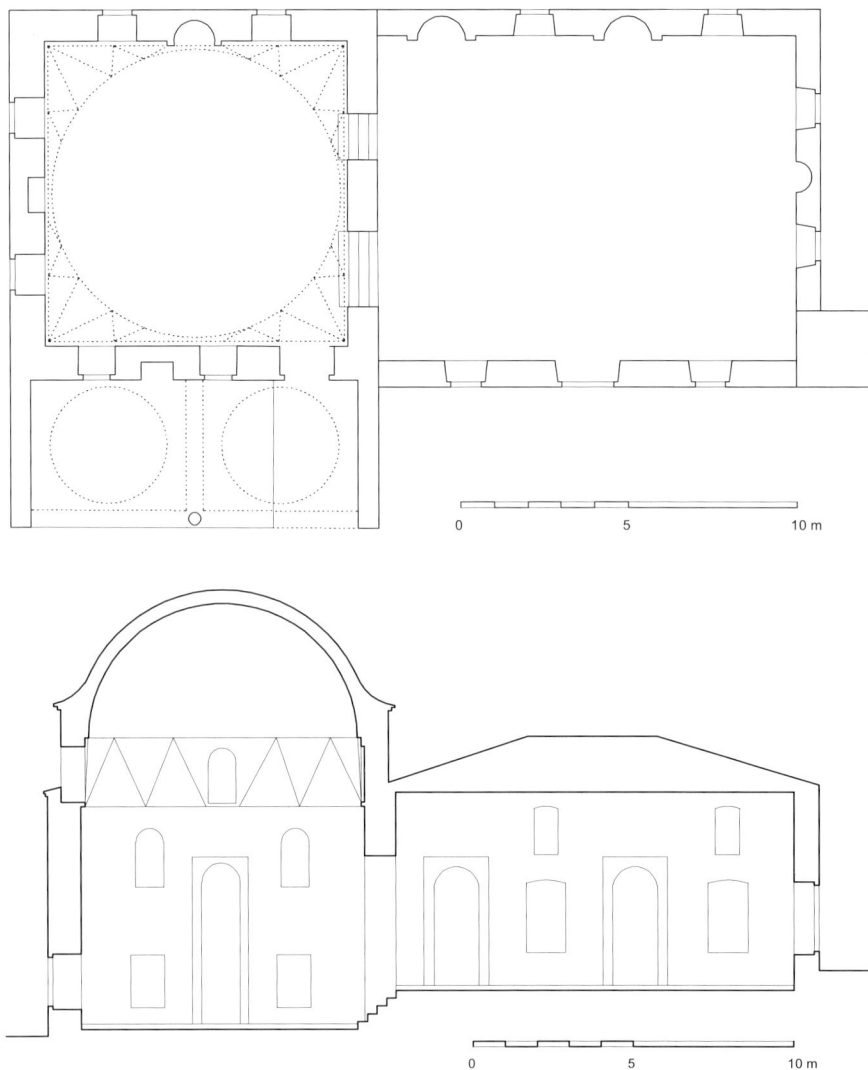

FIGURE 125
Hace Hayrüddin mosque, plan.

FIGURE 126
Hace Hayrüddin mosque,
section.

The surrounding fabric, or the lack of one, determined the layout of masjids. From early on, the dense settlement pattern of the commercial district led builders to make optimum use of available land here (see fig. 17). The masjid of Hacı Halil in Un Kapanı, with its trapezoidal plan, and that of Samanviran, with its minaret located at the curve of a street and its enclosure wall following that curve, bespeak an urban sensibility in their use of topography and the extant fabric to lend prominence and visibility to new structures (fig. 128).[98] A number of masjids in the commercial district were on the second stories of buildings whose ground floors were used for commercial purposes. Sarı Timur and Hacı Timurtaş were such *fevḳānī* masjids to the west of the Taht al-kalʿa that have lost relatively little of their original construction to later alterations (figs. 129, 130).[99] It will be remembered that the architect of the Mahmud Pasha mosque created a higher platform for that building while using the slope for commercial space. In the later sixteenth century, the architect Sinan was to monumentalize this type of building when he designed the Rüstem Pasha mosque in Taht al-kalʿa over a ground floor of commercial space. Elsewhere in the city, where land was readily available, one does not encounter *fevḳānī* masjids or any that abandon the orthogonal geometry of the prayer hall to fit in tight and irregular plots.

Mosques and masjids, it will be remembered, marked and defined about half of the city quarters through the first decades of Ottoman rule in the city. In several quarters baths were the more monumental structures compared to mosques, while a large number were defined in Ottoman documents by nonreligious focal points—gates, markets, prominent Byzantine buildings and monumental columns—suggesting that these structures were spatially, if not institutionally, central to their respective

did most dwellings and commercial structures that surrounded them (fig. 127). Often the most conspicuous sign of their presence was their minarets, in stark contrast to Istanbul's later mosques, distinguished from the surrounding fabric by their ashlar or composite masonry construction and their lead-covered domes. The demolition of bell towers and construction of minarets in their stead is a trope of Ottoman conquest narratives, highlighting the importance of signs of religious identity in this era of rapidly transforming social and physical landscapes.

areas of settlement. Little is known of non-Muslim places of worship from this period in the city's history. Waqf documents do not refer to churches and synagogues as neighborhood centers, while poll-tax registers documenting the non-Muslim communities refer to these by their places of provenance, rather than the names of their places of worship. One building that retains the memory of its former deportee community is the Kefeli church/mosque, possibly part of a Byzantine monastic complex, given to the Dominican Catholic community deported from the northern Black Sea port city of Caffa upon its takeover by the Ottoman navy in 1475 (fig. 131).[100] Istanbul today houses a single Greek Orthodox church that has retained its original architecture and function through the Ottoman and republican eras: the Panagia Mougliotissa in the Fener district, which is also associated with the Greek architect of Mehmed II's New Mosque (fig. 132). As has been noted earlier, several Jewish synagogues carry the names of the places of origin of their respective communities; the buildings themselves have all been rebuilt or radically altered.

Nothing remains of individual residential structures that surrounded these buildings. What we have are descriptions in waqf documents of a range of structures that constituted the city's residential fabric.[101] Although not encompassing the whole expanse of the city, documents of the Mehmed II foundation provide a wealth of information regarding the density of settlement and the types of buildings that shaped the urban fabric in different areas of the city. The majority of the residential structures were ḥöcerāt (rooms), buyūt (literally "houses," but at times denoting rooms in a house), and menāzil (compounds of a number of units). The surveys list mostly two-story structures in the northeastern section of the peninsula, the densest area of late Byzantine settlement. If not Byzantine

FIGURE 127
Istanbul between the Un Kapanı area along the Golden Horn and the Valens aqueduct, detail from the panorama by Melchior Lorichs, 1559, 1561–62.

FIGURE 128
Samanviran masjid, exterior (drawn by Süheyl Ünver).

FIGURE 129
Hacı Timurtaş masjid, from the west, second-story mosque in the commercial area, with shops in the ground floor.

FIGURE 130
Hacı Timurtaş masjid, ground-floor and second-floor plans.

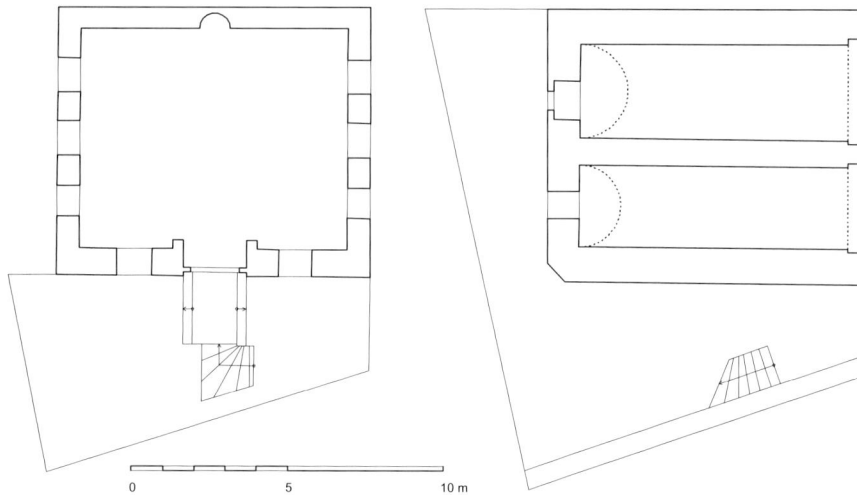

0   5   10 m

drawings, by Melchior Lorichs and Salomon Schweigger respectively, illustrate such structures, which continued to mark the residential fabric of the capital (fig. 133, 134).

Larger complexes laid out around multiple courtyards and featuring amenities of wealthier residences (such as a garden, stables, furnace, water well, numerous rooms) are found in the endowment deeds of a number of foundations. The two architects whose names are connected to the construction of the New Mosque, Sinan and Ayas, both built such compounds in the vicinity of the mosque, on land donated by the sultan. Large compounds were built not only in the sparsely populated western sections of the peninsula but also in the densely inhabited northeastern sections of the city. The description of Mercan Ağa's buildings in the vicinity of his mosque on the Uzunçarşı, a large *menzil* in two parts, suggests a layout with separate family and men's quarters. One part included two winter rooms (*beyteyn şatūbeyn*), an anteroom (*ṣuffa*), an upper room (*ġurfe*), and a toilet (*kenīf*), while the other consisted of one ground-floor and one second-floor room (*'ulvī ve suflī*), an anteroom, five cells (*ḥöcerāt*), a toilet, a courtyard, and a garden. Across from this compound and near a church-turned-depot, Mercan Ağa endowed another house with five rooms, two of which were also described as winter rooms, an anteroom, stables, "an old building known as the cellar" (*bōdrūm,* possibly part of the adjacent church), and a courtyard. This second compound, most likely because it incorporated parts of a Byzantine structure, is not specified as new in the endowment deed.[103]

Courtyard houses, a perennial feature of eastern Mediterranean residential architecture, seem to have been shared by Byzantine and Ottoman traditions alike. Some of the larger compounds including courtyards incorporated parts of former Byzantine (or Italian)

structures, these must have been newly built following extant patterns. One- or two-story houses of modest size and material characterized the residential areas of the city through the earlier part of the sixteenth century, as attested to by Ramberti in the 1530s, who wrote that the city was "full of houses, not many of which are good, being made of clay and wood and only a few of stone."[102] Mid- and late-sixteenth-century structures. The large *menzil* bought by Kapu Ağası Hüseyin Ağa in 883/1478 from a certain Jewish woman by the name of Uķūmiya daughter of Ilya might be such a structure.[104] This compound, in the Çelebioğlu quarter, possibly a Byzantine building given to Uķūmiya's family at the time of their deportation to the city, comprised two groups of rooms—one with four ground-floor rooms and an upper-story room, and the other, near these, with five upper-story rooms—in addition to two furnaces, a water well, a toilet, and a courtyard with trees.[105] In the nearby Hace Sinan bin Elvan quarter, where Jewish deportees were settled in the first years following the conquest, stood the large *menzil* of Sinan Ağa bin Abdullah, keeper of the treasury. With eight rooms built above the stables, four others on the ground floor, a courtyard with a well and trees, a toilet, and a garden with a furnace room, this too might have been, in whole or in part, a Byzantine structure.[106]

Of larger residential complexes belonging to the high-ranking members of the military and religious elite, the earliest extant documents date to the last decades of the fifteenth century. The palaces of Firuz Ağa near the Hippodrome, that of Çandarlı İbrahim Pasha in the proximity of the first palace and the commercial center, that of Kapudan Sinan Pasha in the quarter of Mahmud Pasha, all featuring arrangements reminiscent of Mehmed II's New Palace, might not have been radically different from the palaces of Mehmed's viziers. The double courtyard *dār* (residence) of Firuz Ağa near the Hippodrome and the masjid he built in 1490 featured adjacent ground and upper-story rooms and anterooms (*ṣufāf*), a bath, stables, a garden within the inner courtyard, and two gardens within the outer courtyard. Situated above the Philoxenos/Binbirdirek cistern, the inner courtyard used the Byzantine structure both as a foundation and as a means of

elevating the new building and lending it more prominence within the urban fabric.[107] If it followed the boundaries of the cistern beneath, it was a spacious enclosure sixty-four meters in length and fifty-six in width.[108] Another prominent figure of the reign of Bayezid II, Çandarlı İbrahim Pasha, endowed only the *selāmlıķ,* or men's quarters, and the stables of his palace, keeping private ownership of the other *menāzil,* rooms, and a garden across from this building,

FIGURE 131
Kefeli church/masjid, lithograph, 1877.

FIGURE 132
Theotokos Panagia Mougliotissa, lithograph, 1877.

FIGURE 133
Melchior Lorichs, view of
houses in Istanbul, with domed
building and minaret in the
background, ca. 1559.

most likely the family quarters. The men's section, situated near and to the south of İbrahim Pasha's mosque, "had the form of a *burġaz* [tower]," suggesting that a Byzantine tower was incorporated into the palace. Above five ground-floor rooms, another room was reached by a double staircase: possibly this was the vizier's audience hall.[109]

Such larger compounds and viziers' palaces must be those dwellings represented by Matrakcı Nasuh in his ca. 1537 view of the Ottoman capital, an image I will turn to in the Epilogue. Numerous dwellings are depicted here, and Matrakcı's precision in portraying public structures of the imperial capital suggests that the residences he chose to include in his view of Istanbul were not stylized images signifying generic houses but representations of particular buildings. These are mostly of stone, brick, or composite masonry and feature a number of adjacent sections, suggesting a sprawl of connected buildings. Loggias

sporting roofs over what seem to be elegantly proportioned columns provide views onto the street, unlike the more introverted residential style that was to gain prominence in Istanbul in the later centuries (fig. 135). Evidence from the middle Byzantine era for mansions organized around courtyards and occasionally featuring projecting sunrooms on their upper floors suggests continuities in Byzantine and Ottoman housing patterns.[110]

Across the Golden Horn, Galata housed a markedly different urban fabric. Buildings of stone and/or brick rose two or three stories above underground storage spaces (*maḥzen*).[111] References to vaulted streets with rooms above suggest dense construction, as do wooden additions to *kāfirī* buildings noted in the early sixteenth century.[112] Galata was often likened to an Italian city, and particularly to Genoa, its founder to the west (fig. 136; in fig. 114 and plate 6 the denser urban fabric of the colony is observed).[113] The residential buildings it

FIGURE 134
Salomon Schweigger, houses in
Constantinople, 1608.

housed, too, were possibly more like those of Genoa than those of the city opposite. The earliest non-Muslim waqfiyya in the Directorate of Pious Endowments, drawn for a certain Doka son of Bedros, provides a detailed description of his house in Galata's Lonca (Loggia) quarter. The house is endowed, along with other property whose income is stipulated to his poor relatives, the Orthodox Patriarchate, and a nursing home for the elderly and the poor of Galata.[114] Possibly because it featured a multicolor façade, Doka's house was referred to as Alaca Ev. A public street divided its basement level and ground floor in two, one side housing three cellars, three rooms above these, and a toilet; the other side a well and a cellar, with two rooms and two toilets above. The second floor had an anteroom "known as a *kamina* (?) in the founder's language," another room called a *kamina*, two

kitchens, four other rooms, and three toilets. The third floor also had an anteroom called a *kamina*, five other rooms, and two toilets.[115] While other endowment deeds that include property in Galata do not provide similarly detailed descriptions, they indicate nevertheless the presence of such multistory buildings.

Both in Galata and in the city proper, Byzantine buildings constituted a highly prominent and visible part of the urban fabric through the first decades of the sixteenth century. In both places the surveys include a large number of residential and commercial buildings specified as *kāfirī al-binā'* (infidels' buildings), those structures that were endowed for the Hagia Sophia foundation in the early years of Ottoman rule in Constantinople. Unfortunately, the deeds and surveys do not provide detailed descriptions of these; they often record no more than the number of rooms and floors. It seems unlikely, moreover, that all Byzantine buildings were specified in these documents, as not all property given out first as freehold and rented out later is registered in the surveys as *kāfirī*.[116]

It has already been noted that the number of churches converted into mosques or charitable institutions during the reign of Mehmed II was extremely limited, and the founder, in all cases, was the sultan himself. The wave of conversions, contrary to assertions made in narrative sources, would come during the reign of Bayezid II. Many churches, on the other hand,

FIGURE 135
The Old Palace, Bayezid II complex, and commercial structures at the left, and residential complexes at the right, detail from Nasuhü's-Silahi [Matrakcı], view of Istanbul in the *Beyān-ı menāzil-i sefer-i ʿIraḳeyn,* ca. 1537 (plate 7). Istanbul University Library, T.5964, fol. 8v.

were used for nonreligious purposes. Mehmed, according to Kritovoulos, gave his grandees beautiful churches as their residences.[117] Apart from the Hagia Sophia, converted into a mosque, the Monastery of Mangana, taken over by dervishes, and the Pantokrator, all churches in the city "were occupied by Turks with their wives and children," writes Doukas.[118] Endowment documents provide further evidence for such uses. In 868/1464, Hace Üveys endowed a church known as Eski Kenīse (the Old Church, in the vicinity of the masjid he built) as a residence for his freed slaves and their descendants. The building is described as consisting of a large ground-floor room, a small ground-floor room, and an adjacent garden twenty-one cubits in length and as wide as the length of the church.[119] Churches were incorporated into larger residential complexes, as was done by Defteri Muhyiddin Çelebi, who endowed a compound including two churches in the Mevlana Husrev quarter, near the mosque of Şeyh Vefa. One of these is described as a four-story structure, while the other had two stories and adjacent ground-floor rooms. The lengthy list of units endowed within the same compound and registered in the deed suggests a rather large enclosure, which might have been in part or in whole a former monastic establishment.[120] Endowed for his descendants, this was possibly Muhyiddin Çelebi's residence.

Several large Byzantine buildings were used for keeping animals. There was a Fil ṭāmı (elephant house) and an Öküz ṭāmı (ox stall) in the Jewish quarter to the east of Taht al-kalʿa. Two churches close to the Hippodrome and the Topkapı Palace were used as menageries.[121] In (or before) 1486 Hüseyin Ağa, the founder of the Küçük Ayasofya mosque (the SS. Sergius and Bacchus), converted another structure in the vicinity of the bedestan, in use until then as a horse market, into a congregational mosque.[122]

FIGURE 136
Pera, detail from the map of
Constantinople in Cristoforo
Buondelmonti's *Liber Insularum
Archipelagi*, ink drawing, ca. 1481
(fig. 111). Universitäts- und
Landesbibliothek, Düsseldorf,
MS G 13, fol. 54r.

Other churches were put to commercial use, as were those in the Mercan Ağa quarter and in the quarter of the New Mosque.[123] Such was also the fate of the Pantokrator monastery, until it was converted into a madrasa: "Fullers entered the monastery of the Pantokrator and took up quarters there, and shoemakers were busy at work in the center of the church," writes Doukas.[124] In the Hace Hayrüddin quarter a bell tower ("the building known as *çānlık*") belonging to the Hagia Sophia foundation was used as a shop.[125] Several of the towers along the city walls of Istanbul and Galata were also endowed and rented out as shops and depots.[126]

The center of the Venetian colony in the commercial area stayed intact through the fifteenth century, and most probably it continued to house the Venetian bailo, though it now lay in a largely Jewish quarter.[127] Close to the Fishmongers' Gate were two churches, one of them referred to as the Kenīse-i Venedīk, with a cellar (*bōdrūm*) beneath, a large house known as the Menzil-i Bālyōz (the bailo's house), and near it

stables with rooms above. All of this was in the possession of the sultan until 1502, when it was donated by Bayezid II to Sinan Pasha, keeper of the treasury, who endowed it.[128] The official decree of donation and the foundation deed drawn by the vizier provide information on the layout of the complex, while another copy of Sinan Pasha's waqfiyya registers the Venetian buildings within the Fil Damı quarter, close to the elephant and ox houses, suggesting that the latter, too, were part of the city's Venetian heritage.[129]

The ubiquity of references to these buildings in later-fifteenth-century sources does not only demonstrate the predominance of a Byzantine urban fabric through the first decades of Ottoman rule in the city. It simultaneously underlines an awareness of this predominance on the part of the city's new rulers and inhabitants. A comparison between fifteenth- and early-sixteenth-century sources and the survey of 1546 highlights the centrality of the city's former history to the urban perceptions of

Ottoman Istanbul's earlier residents. References to *kāfirī* buildings or to the original functions of Byzantine structures abound in the earlier documents and are sparse in the 1546 survey. To give two examples: the foundation deed of Mevlana Gürani dated to 1484 indicates that the mufti endowed "a church in Galata and a mosque within the church," and that of İbrahim Pasha, drawn in 1481, indicates that the vizier endowed the church near his palace as a school for children. In the 1546 survey, which in its details is otherwise similar to the original deeds, only a mosque and a school are recorded; no reference or allusion to the original functions of these buildings is to be found.[130] The Epilogue, an overview of the decades preceding the citywide survey, will reveal that the absence of references to the city's Byzantine past in the 1546 document was not due solely to an oversight on the part of the surveyors.

Epilogue

A PICTURE FROM CIRCA 1537

One of the most celebrated manuscripts held in Istanbul's libraries, Matrakcı Nasuh's *Beyān-ı menāzil-i sefer-i 'Irakeyn,* features a well-known image of the city (plate 7). This is the first of 107 topographic images of cities, landscapes, and detached monuments and shrines to illustrate this narration of Süleyman's Iraqi campaign of 1533–36, a double-page painting depicting the city proper on one page, and its suburbs, Galata, Üsküdar, and Eyüp, on the other, divided by the waters of the Bosphorus and the Golden Horn.[1] Buildings of importance in the walled city and three suburbs of greater Istanbul are depicted in meticulous detail, against the background of a green garden of cypresses, blossoming trees, and flowers.

This painting represents Ottoman Istanbul at the end of the 1530s, that is, on the eve of the wide-scale building campaign launched by Süleyman and his grandees and realized by the master architect Sinan and the imperial office of architects working under him. Comparable to, if grander than, Mehmed II's, the new phase of construction was to transform the city, now the capital of a world power, once more, consolidating a new imperial image, endowing Istanbul with a tighter network of public buildings of monumental order and with its famed silhouette. Understanding Matrakcı's painting is therefore important to this study, because it provides an epilogue to the process whose first steps I have traced in the preceding chapters. What is the image of the Ottoman capital projected in the *Beyān-ı menāzil*? In what ways is it related to images of Constantinople produced during the first decades of Ottoman rule? If there are differences between Matrakcı's and earlier views beyond immediately visible formal ones, what is their significance?

Matrakcı's painting represents Istanbul in bird's-eye view, or rather views: the city proper, Eyüp, and Üsküdar are depicted as seen from the west, while Galata, viewed from the south, faces the city proper. A familiarity with the representational conventions of the Buondelmonti views, discussed in an earlier chapter, reveals at first glance that the Matrakcı image owes its greatest debt to that tradition.[2] As is the case with European city views produced within this idiom, the walls of the city proper and Galata are laid out in plan and rendered in elevation. Monuments and landmarks are then placed within, rendered either in elevation or in bird's-eye view. A number of significant sites outside the walled enclosures, too, are depicted. The most striking departure from the conventions of the European bird's-eye view is in the multiple points of view employed. Alessandro Strozzi in his view of Rome, Pietro del Massaio and his workshop in the city views that illustrated Ptolemy's *Geography,* and the makers of the views in the *Isolario* manuscripts maintained a single point of view for representations of urban entities. The Matrakçı view, like other topographic images in the manuscript and a host of topographic representations illustrating Ottoman historical and geographic texts from the early decades of the sixteenth century onward, merges the representational idiom of the European bird's-eye view with that of the miniature painter.[3] Having recourse to a Persianate mode of spatial representation that juxtaposed different viewpoints in depictions of complex structures, the Ottoman painter configured a new mode of representing the urban environment. Limitations of space and the underlying logic and structure of the image led to the juxtaposition of multiple points of view; individual monuments or their parts are depicted as seen from different angles. Hence the layout of the Topkapı Palace, where the successive courtyards make a ninety-degree turn following the first courtyard; hence the aqueduct of Valens and the janissary barracks, depicted as in line with and diagonal to the main point of view; and hence the city of Galata, represented as facing Istanbul, underlining the subordination of the former colony to the Ottoman capital.

Like other topographic images and city views produced by the Ottomans in the sixteenth century, the Matrakçı view exhibits European inspiration, as well as transformation of that inspiration through the use of conventions of miniature painting and through the intent of the image. Models for the view of Istanbul (and, if one can imagine a transfer of a nautical itinerary to an earthbound one, also for the manuscript) would have been readily available to Matrakçı, as copies of the *Isolario,* with their views of Constantinople and depictions of the Aegean islands, did circulate in Ottoman hands.[4] Buondelmonti's book of islands, written and reproduced at the Byzantine-Italian interface, housed an image of the Byzantine capital meant for an Italian audience eager to sustain an unchanging portrait in the face of radical transformation. The *Beyān-ı menāzil,* which opens with a sumptuous image of the same city, too is an itinerary. But unlike the *Isolario,* it follows the route of one of the most ambitious of Ottoman military campaigns of the sixteenth century. A presentation of the imperial territories to the monarch as much as a record of a military campaign, it has a representational agenda and an intended audience that are much different from those of the *Isolario.*[5]

The obviousness of the formal source of inspiration for Matrakçı's and other city views produced by the Ottomans from the early decades of the sixteenth century onward should not obscure the larger significance of this imagery. Just as city images began to illustrate texts with no explicit urban subject matter in fifteenth-century Europe, such as the *Isolario* or Ptolemy's *Geography,* so city images illustrated Ottoman texts such as the *Menāzil* or the *Kitāb-ı Baḥriye.* Like their Western counterparts, the city portraits are indicative of an interest in the city as an entity, as a carrier of meaning in its own right. It was not only visual imagery that captured the emerging interest in the city and its representation. The same decades that witnessed the growing popularity of urban views witnessed also the creation of the first examples of the *Şehrengiz* genre in Ottoman literature, works in verse that dealt with the beauties of a city, beginning with its monuments and continuing with its men (and sometimes women). As the increasing vivacity of Ottoman urban life from the later fifteenth century onward rendered the city more imageable formally as well as socially, visual and literary images of cities, repositories of a wide range of meanings, reflected that vivacity and ultimately realized an "objectification of urban space."[6]

The first impression conveyed by the Matrakçı view is that of a densely built-up city, boasting myriad buildings and sites of importance. This impression is conveyed through a manipulation of the peninsula's shape and the location of particular buildings.[7] Keen on representing the urban enclosure as densely developed and on including every building of significance, Matrakçı has recourse to the same deceit the maker of the Vavassore image had resorted to earlier: he extends the built-up section of the city toward the west and the south, whereas the area beyond Mehmed II's New Mosque was never densely settled throughout Istanbul's Ottoman history. Here, the districts to which Ottoman patrons had paid less attention appear as densely built-up as the eastern and northern sections. In order to create space to fit in all the monuments of importance in the eastern end of the peninsula, on the other hand, Matrakçı alters the triangular shape of the city to a rough rectangle that is wider at the eastern end.

As in other bird's-eye views of this type, emphasis is not on the representation of urban space as a complex of developed and empty areas but on individual buildings as entities adding up to the city itself. In other words, this is a city conceived as a collection of significant sites, comparable to the city represented on pilgrimage maps of Rome. Producing an exact map with a uniform scale was not a concern for the painter; he approximated the places of monuments in relation to urban boundaries and in relation to other structures. As Walter Denny has observed, the relative importance of particular buildings is suggested by their sizes and by the degree of precision in their depiction.

This manner of locating buildings within the city's boundaries is far from arbitrary. There is an underlying structure that binds these myriad buildings to a higher order and, through it, to each other. The religio-political loci of the city, Hagia Sophia, Bayezid's Friday mosque, the Old Palace, and Mehmed's New Mosque, form a central axis that runs through the middle of the rectangular enclosure and points toward the East. The most significant sites of Ottoman Istanbul (excepting the Topkapı) together form a symbolic spine to the city and the rest of the buildings that flesh it out.[8] The city's urban layout, with its main arteries, developed and undeveloped areas, is subordinated to the painting's axial structure and the floral imagery that forms its background. İffet Orbay has observed that symbolic axes are extended to the suburbs of the city, imparting to the image an underlying structure that highlights the political order that governs it and the hierarchy of its parts: another imaginary axis runs between the Old Palace, at the center of the city proper, and the Genoese tower of Galata, symbolically connecting the largest suburb of the city to the mainland. The two other suburbs, Üsküdar and Eyüp, are placed in a symmetrical relation to the two sides of Galata.[9]

This city structured by the central axis of its religio-political loci presents a wealth of buildings. Hagia Sophia and Mehmed's New Mosque mark the two ends of the central spine. They are shown, though from different points of view, as comparable to each other in size and style. In the middle is the Old Palace, a walled enclosure with a complex of buildings within. Above it is the mosque of Bayezid II, flanked by its dependencies. Another conspicuous site is the Topkapı, represented, with its strongly fortified walls, almost as another city within the peninsula. The Hippodrome occupies a vast space at the eastern end of the peninsula; it is drawn with its sphendone and its monumental columns and is flanked by the palace of İbrahim Pasha, whose size is vastly exaggerated. The bedestan, surrounded by streets of shops, too occupies a central location. To the right of

Mehmed II's mosque complex is that built for Selim I. The citadel at the Golden Gate, Yedikule, is another prominent site within the walls.

These are the buildings visible at first glance. "Lesser" buildings do not exhibit the same concern for precision. As Walter Denny has observed, numerous religious, charitable, commercial, and residential structures are represented as types to be found in different parts of the city rather than as particular and recognizable structures. Because of the absence of legends, not all of these are readily identifiable. Whether they were meant to be identified is a question I will turn to shortly. Nevertheless, it is still useful to engage in a search for correspondences between particular sites in early-sixteenth-century Istanbul and individual buildings represented by Matrakcı, for such identification, even if speculative and incomplete, will provide one path to an interpretation of the image.[10]

Three representational models correspond roughly to major mosque types in Ottoman Istanbul. A domed structure preceded by a three-bay portico represents mosques built (and in one case converted) by grandees Mahmud Pasha, Atik Ali Pasha, and Davud Pasha. The SS. Sergius and Bacchus, converted by the chief white eunuch Hüseyin Ağa, is also represented in this manner. Most other converted structures are portrayed with lead-covered domes flanked by smaller or half domes, their high drums evocative of middle and late Byzantine churches of Constantinople. The St. Andrea in Krisei and the Toklu Dede Mescidi, both converted and founded as mosques by Koca Mustafa Pasha, and Bodrum Cami (the Myraleion) are represented in this manner, as is the newly built mosque of Has Murad Pasha. The mosque with a pitched roof, the most ubiquitous, if also the most modest, type of house of worship in Ottoman Istanbul,

is the one that is least visible in Matrakcı's image. The most easily recognizable among these is the Çandarlı İbrahim Pasha mosque, near the bedestan.[11] Not falling within these types but depicted with more precision are the Gül and the İmrahor (St. John Studius) mosques; the particularities of their architecture seem to have led the painter to create likenesses of these buildings rather than represent them as types.

Also in the image are dependencies of the larger complexes: the madrasas of Hagia Sophia, Atik Ali Pasha, Bayezid II, Selim I, and Mehmed II, represented as rows of rooms, and the public kitchens of Bayezid II and Selim I, discernible by their lanterned domes.[12] The many baths of early Ottoman Istanbul, too, are among the buildings that can largely be identified: there is one in the commercial area (Mahmud Pasha or Taht al-kal'a), besides those of Balat, Hüseyin Ağa, Gedik Ahmed Pasha, Nişancı Mehmed Pasha, and Davud Pasha. Commercial structures depicted as arcades are dispersed throughout the peninsula.

It is more difficult to associate residential structures in the image with their owners. As I have shown in the previous chapter, both contemporary waqf surveys and travelers' accounts suggest that the majority of Istanbul's residential structures were small, single-story dwellings at this date. Those depicted by Matrakcı are almost all two-story buildings with several sections, overhangs, and, interestingly, loggias (see fig. 135).[13] Most of these have a single gate, which suggests that they represent residential complexes rather than rows of individual houses. They may either be specific palatial buildings or representational types signifying the presence in the city of a large number of such sizable residential complexes. An exception is the palace of Süleyman's grand vizier İbrahim Pasha, a large, multi-courtyard structure overlooking the Hippodrome, built in the early sixteenth century and confiscated by the sultan following the vizier's execution in 1536.[14]

Across the Golden Horn, tripartite Galata is represented with its four land walls crowned with the Genoese tower. At the center of the town is the Dominican church converted into a Friday mosque by Mehmed II, marked with a gilded crescent atop its bell tower–turned–minaret. Galata is home to a number of basilical churches, three mosques in the western part of the city and on the shore, a bath, markets, and residential structures. The arsenal, the cannon foundry, mansions, and possibly dervish lodges are scattered in the environs of Galata. Eyüp features the complex built for the prophet's companion, and houses that were cut out when the image was trimmed to adapt it to the size of the manuscript. At the other end Üsküdar is shown as a larger settlement, housing the (trimmed) mosque of Rum Mehmed Pasha, a market, and residential buildings.

In view of the previous discussion of Istanbul's fifteenth-century images, one aspect of this representation will have become clear: the reduced presence of Byzantine structures in the city proper. Unlike the makers of Constantinople's fifteenth-century images, Matrakcı represents only those Byzantine buildings and sites that are completely appropriated by the Ottoman order: in particular those at the eastern end of the peninsula, Hagia Sophia, the Hippodrome, and the two churches in the environs of the Hippodrome used as the sultan's menagerie.[15] The monumental columns of the city are all there: those in the Hippodrome, the porphyry column of Constantine (painted red), and those of Arcadius and Marcian are placed in their approximate positions within the city. There is only one building that is readily identifiable as a church: a basilica without a minaret sandwiched between two mosques.

Its location, close to the southern shore of the peninsula, suggests that this might represent the Armenian patriarchate; it might also be a church put to nonreligious use. Another structure resembling the converted and newly built mosques, but without a minaret, may represent the Pammakaristos abbey, the seat of the Greek patriarchate. In all, the image does not deny the Byzantine past of Constantinople, or the presence of a religiously mixed population in it. But Byzantine buildings and those related to the non-Muslim communities are here completely subordinated to the civil and religious monuments of the Ottoman elite.

Along the wide scale of realism and recognizability that shaped the representation of buildings in the image, royal buildings (palaces, mosques, citadel, important commercial structures) rank highest: precise representation of their architectural features and their approximate locations was a priority of the artist. Via a familiarity with the city's topography we can guess at the identity of other buildings, but exact representations of the charities and residences of the Ottoman elite was not a concern for the artist. Rather, he lent the image a sense of unity and coherence through the repetition of generic types over the space of the city. Looking at any one segment of the painting, the viewer will see a number of religious and charitable buildings, baths, markets, and residences. The total impact of these structures, public and private buildings of the ruling elite dispersed evenly through the city and tied together with a central axis, is key to the message of the image. This totality speaks for the uniform identity of the city, the capital of the Ottoman dynasty and its extended household.

The background against which the buildings are placed contributes to this sense of unity and underscores the painting's royal character. The imagery of a garden of cypresses, blossoming trees, and flowers permeates Matrakcı's view within and without the walled peninsula, with one conspicuous exception: Galata. The representation of Istanbul, its (largely Muslim) suburbs, and its environs as a blossoming garden evokes the paradisal imagery that pervaded the conception and representation of monumental spaces in the Ottoman realm from the fifteenth century onward. It will be remembered that the city and its individual monuments were described and interpreted through paradisal allusions in contemporary chronicles and poetry, in an Ottoman appropriation of mostly Persianate poetic images of gardens with aesthetic, cosmic, and political associations.[16] The blossoming background of the Matrakcı painting extends the paradisal metaphor to the entire space of the city. While highlighting the beauty of the Ottoman capital, the paradisal metaphor simultaneously brings the city's royal character into sharp focus. Significantly, the garden imagery stops at the walls and gates of the largely non-Muslim Galata. The contrast between Galata and the rest of the city underlines the centrality of Istanbul's religious identity: if the background of cypresses, blossoming trees, and flowers was in fact meant to evoke paradise, then this was an "Islamic" paradise; the city's largely non-Muslim suburb was excluded from it.

It was argued earlier in this study that fifteenth-century representations of Istanbul were marked with a fluidity of meaning: whether images of the Byzantine or the Ottoman city, they presented side by side some of the most powerful symbols of the two worlds and underlined the ambiguous identity of the city during the decades following its fall/conquest. In the Matrakcı view, a new image emerges: this is an Ottoman city that has completely absorbed its Byzantine past. The monuments represented, as well as the representational mode itself,

express the city's royal character and Islamic identity. Unlike the Düsseldorf and the Vavassore views, in which Byzantine and Ottoman monuments are boldly juxtaposed in portrayals of the newly reconfigured city, the Matrakcı image represents Istanbul as a creation of the Ottoman ruling elite: a city boasting of myriad civic and religious buildings, all built or converted from Byzantine structures by sultans and their extended households. The central axis of royal buildings in the city proper, and its extensions into the suburbs, highlight the underlying order that holds this collection of monuments together and renders them meaningful. This beautifully portrayed garden-city is a confident proclaimer of the primacy of the capital among all the cities the reader will encounter turning the pages of the *Beyān-ı Menāzil.*

If the monumentalization of Istanbul during the reign of Mehmed II was a collective enterprise on the part of the ruling elite aiming to create the imperial capital, the Matrakcı view presents the results of that enterprise. But the salient point is that the picture from 1537 seems to be the product of a trajectory different from that laid out by Mehmed. The most significant difference between the cityscape at the end of Mehmed's rule and that illustrated in the 1530s is that the latter image projects the city's Islamic identity as a central aspect of its Ottoman character.

What made such a representation possible? In what ways were changes in the Ottoman polity in the roughly six decades between the end of Mehmed II's reign and the making of the Matrakcı painting reflected in the space and the image of the capital city? Although the trajectory Mehmed II plotted, beginning with the conquest of the Byzantine capital and continuing with the subsequent restructuring of the Ottoman administrative apparatus, was not challenged through the following centuries, significant political and cultural changes did mark Bayezid II's thirty-one-year rule. A departure from Mehmed's cosmopolitanism and a growing visibility of the religious establishment and of Sufi orders within the political sphere were the most salient aspects of this change, finding reflections in the image of the sultan as well as in particular policies of the Ottoman state.

Dynamics internal and external to the Ottoman polity underlay reorientations in the political and cultural realms. Immediately visible among these were reactions against Mehmed II's relentless and uncompromising measures in building the centralized state apparatus and his equally uncompromising cosmopolitanism. Alongside his harsh financial and demographic policies and his marginalization of centrifugal elements within the Ottoman polity, his cultural pluralism and patronage of non-Muslims, Iranians, and Europeans had gained him considerable resentment.[17] A verse presented to Mehmed by a certain Çatladı, one of his courtiers, captures this sentiment:

> If you wish to stand in high honor on the
>   sultan's threshold,
> You must be a Jew or a Persian or a Frank,
> You must choose the name Habil, Kabil,
>   Hamidi,
> And behave like Zorzi: show no knowledge.[18]

Bayezid II did not radically reorient Ottoman polity; neither did he envision a return to the era of the ghazi principality. Likewise, he did not completely turn his back on imperial cultural enterprises initiated by his father: he extended invitations to Leonardo da Vinci and Michelangelo for work in royal projects in Istanbul, and literati hailing from the Persian cultural sphere continued to have a visible presence in the Ottoman court. But at the same time,

Bayezid accommodated the complaints rooted in reactions to his father's policies captured in Çatladı's poem. Restitution, to individuals and cities alike, of rights and possessions appropriated by his father was a prominent feature of Bayezid's rule. Thus he returned to their original founders and owners endowed and private property confiscated by his father in support of the growing centralized army and costly state-building operations (of which architectural projects in Istanbul were part), and constructed prestigious building complexes in Amasya and Edirne, rescuing these cities from the obscurity into which they had fallen during Mehmed II's reign. He reestablished the prestige of the Çandarlı vizier family and restored the honor (and at least part of the large pious foundation) of Mehmed's executed grand vizier Mahmud Pasha. Bayezid's highly pious disposition, too, contributed to these reversals of Mehmed's policies. So devout and benevolent that he earned himself the title saint (*velī*) during his lifetime, as well as a place in the genealogies of the prominent Halveti order, Bayezid allegedly condemned his father for being an unbeliever.[19] Cultivating a self-image that was the opposite of his father's, Bayezid may have hoped to gain the favors and support his predecessor had lost.

Equally important to changes in cultural politics and the reinforced religious identity of the Ottoman state was the rise of the Safavid dynasty in Iran at the turn of the sixteenth century. The consolidation of a Shiite polity at its eastern border meant the presence of a continuous threat to the Ottoman Empire by a rival state with claims to Ottoman territory and with a spiritual and political alternative to offer Anatolian communities with Alid loyalties. Uprisings led by Safavid sympathizers that devastated central and western Anatolian towns bespeak the tangibility of the threat posed by the Ottomans' eastern neighbors. As the

Ottoman polity sought to articulate responses to the new political configuration, a focus on the Sunni identity of Ottoman state and society emerged as a way of reinforcing and safeguarding Ottoman political and cultural integrity (although the nature of Ottoman Sunni identity and conduct were then, and would remain through the following centuries, open to varying degrees of contestation).[20] Hence the growing visibility and influence of the religious establishment, and hence the support and patronage extended to particular Sufi sects from the early decades of the sixteenth century onward. The Halvetiyye, and to a lesser extent the Nakshibendiyye, enjoying considerable prestige and extensive favors under Bayezid II and his grandees, became increasingly central components of political and cultural life through the rule of his successor, Selim I.[21]

Bayezid founded his royal complex in Istanbul twenty years after his accession to the throne. This delay was not due to his lack of enthusiasm for architectural patronage: within the first years of his rule he built two large

FIGURE 137
Firuz Ağa mosque, view from the north.

socioreligious complexes in Amasya and Edirne in an attempt to counteract the imbalance created during his father's reign to the advantage of the new capital and to the detriment of other urban centers of symbolic significance. Neither did many members of the ruling elite launch large-scale architectural projects during the same years. Except for two, the major constructions in the capital during Bayezid's reign date from the 1490s and the first decade of the sixteenth century. The realization of so many Istanbulite projects during Mehmed II's reign, which endowed the capital with the necessary infrastructure and public services, allowed Bayezid to focus on other cities (of political importance) within the Ottoman realm.

When construction of public works in the capital resumed, the base of patronage had widened. During the reign of Mehmed, builders of the largest complexes were, alongside the sultan, grand viziers and one commander in chief. Under Bayezid II the ranks were opened up: alongside members of the imperial council and commanders in chief, patrons of architectural projects included figures such as Hüseyin Ağa, the chief white eunuch, and Firuz Ağa, keeper of the treasury. The former converted the SS. Sergius and Bacchus into a mosque and built convent rooms, a public kitchen, and a bath as its dependencies; the latter built his masjid at the highly prominent location where the Mese met the Hippodrome. Close by, above the Philoxenos/Binbirdirek cistern, Firuz Ağa built his palace.[22]

The sites chosen for architectural projects of Bayezid's ruling elite indicate strong continuity with the era of Mehmed II (map 2). During Bayezid's reign the Mese turned into the Divan Yolu of the Ottoman capital, the city's main ceremonial artery, marked by a sequence of monumental structures built by the ruling elite. At its very beginning stood the masjid of

Firuz Ağa, built in 896/1490 (figs. 137, 138). Less than five hundred meters further up the artery, on the Forum of Constantine, centered by its porphyry column, grand vizier Atik Ali Pasha founded his complex in 915/1509. The mosque, a massive structure completed in 1496, was situated to the north of the artery and occupied part of the forum area (fig. 139). The dependencies of the mosque, the Elçi (Ambassadors') Han and the madrasa were located across the street from it.[23] Past it one arrived at the Forum Tauri, its northern section now enclosed by the wall surrounding the Bayezid II complex. Further ahead on the northern branch of the Mese, between Mehmed's Friday mosque and the Edirne Gate, Atik Ali Pasha built another congregational mosque and a large bath facing the main street. Close to the southern branch of the Mese, to the west of the Arcadian Forum, Davud Pasha built his complex of a convent-mosque, public kitchen (now demolished), and

madrasa (fig. 140). The convent-mosque was completed in 1485.

The continuing monumentalization of the Mese is most clearly observed in the layout of Bayezid II's complex, occupying the southern end of the Old Palace grounds, which had in turn enclosed part of the Forum Tauri (figs. 141, 142).[24] The plan of the second Ottoman royal complex within the walled city showed little consideration for the uncompromising geometry and axiality of its predecessor's. But it has another, equally conspicuous logic: its buildings stretch along the main artery through the length of the Forum area. Situated at some distance from each other, the mosque, the madrasa, and the bath mark the course of the Mese with their monumental dimensions and ashlar masonry. The smaller Koran school at the eastern end marks the beginning of this sequence. The large public kitchen and caravanserai complex is located to the north of the mosque, at

FIGURE 138
Pieter Coecke van Aelst, Friday procession of Sultan Süleyman through the Hippodrome, woodcut, 1553, after drawings made in 1533. Firuz Ağa mosque at center, and the mosque of Mehmed II on the horizon at the left.

VII   La Ville de Constantinoble, avec tous leurs Mosquées ou temples, Obelisques, Eguilles, er Coulonnes avec le Serpent de cuyure, a tenir par le dedans. Item, contenant en vn quelle maniere le iy et Turcq ayant deuant lny allans douze halquebutiers ou archiers : er apres loy feyent deux de ses plusbe Sus Chamberlans . Et ainsi conuersant la ville fasst sa demonstration.

FIGURE 139
Mese/Divan Yolu and the
column of Constantine, with the
mosque and public kitchen of
Atik Ali Pasha, photograph by
Guillaume Berggren, ca. 1890.

the complex are oriented to the qibla line, this pattern is broken by the bath, aligned with the artery, thus reinforcing the centrality of the Mese in the conceptualization of the layout of the ensemble (figs. 143, 144).

The column of Theodosius, at the southwestern corner of the Old Palace enclosure and visible in the Vavassore and the Düsseldorf views as a prominent landmark at the edge of the palace grounds, was pulled down to open space for the bath (see fig. 8, map 4 [19], map 5 [15]).[25] This act of destruction highlights the contrast between the attitudes of Mehmed and Bayezid toward the Byzantine past: while Mehmed enclosed the column within the palace grounds and commissioned an Italian artist, possibly Gentile Bellini, to reproduce its narrative reliefs in detailed drawings, his successor removed it to build in its stead a charity.[26] It is also telling that the demolition of the Byzantine monument was not total: fragments of the column's base were used as spolia in the bath construction.[27] These fragments, with representations of military scenes, were conspicuously displayed on the walls of the building facing the Mese and the side street, marking another manner of appropriating the city's Byzantine past (fig. 145).

The location of Bayezid's mausoleum, too, underlines the centrality of the Mese as an integral element of architectural design and urban configuration in Ottoman Istanbul. Like his father, Bayezid was buried in a monumental mausoleum behind the qibla wall of his mosque, built by his successor, Selim. At the edge of the Mese/Divan Yolu and separated from it only by a window-pierced enclosure wall, the domed polygonal structure of ashlar masonry was prominently displayed on the city's ceremonial artery. In retrospect there is nothing exceptional in this arrangement: starting with Mehmed II and with few exceptions, every Ottoman ruler was buried in a domed

the edge of the road that ran northward along the palace grounds to reach the port area. All the buildings were thus situated along arteries that surrounded the plot; the distances between those lining the Mese suggests that marking and monumentalizing a long stretch of the main road was a primary design concern. While the religious and charitable buildings of

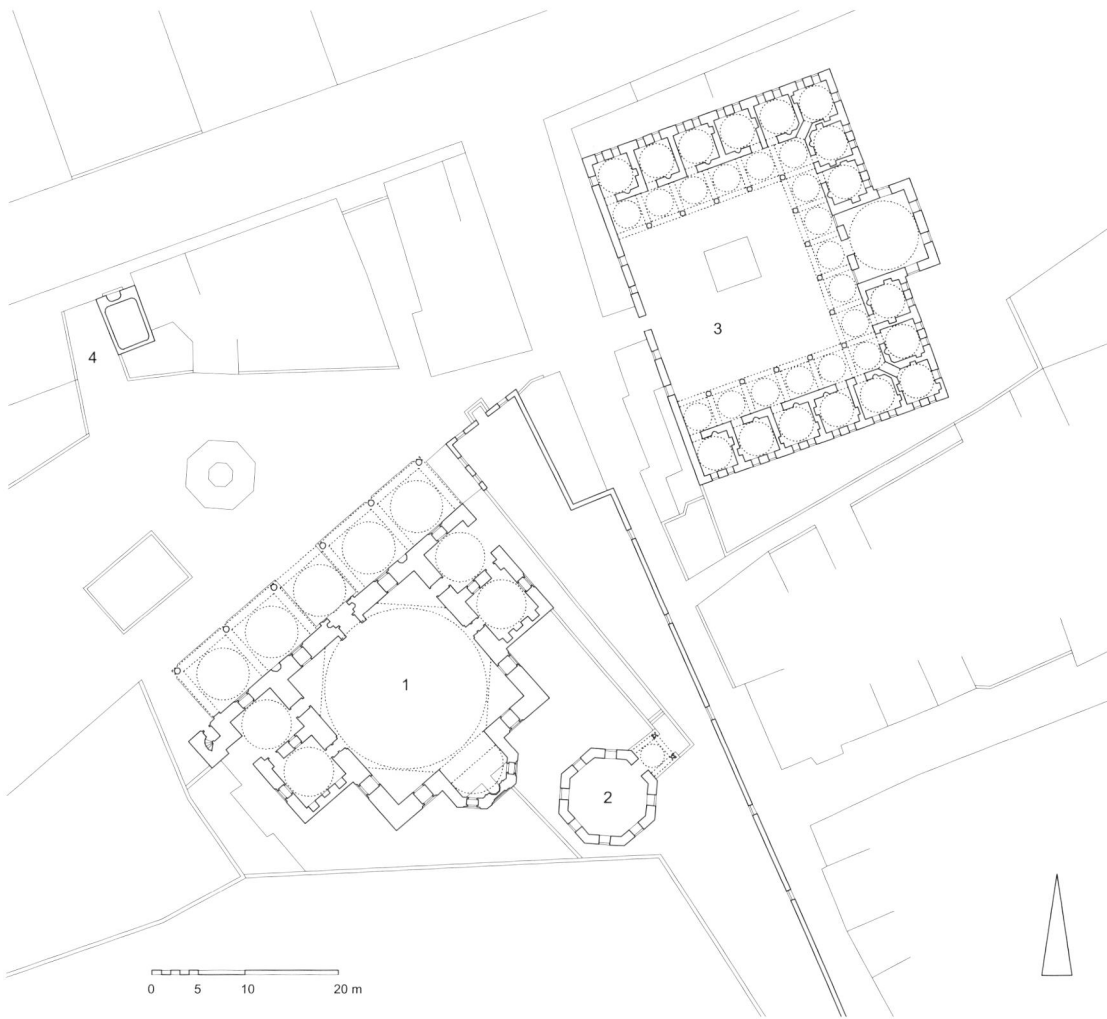

0 5 10 20 m

mausoleum near his congregational mosque, built by his successor upon his death.[28] Bayezid's mausoleum, however, so conspicuously displayed on the city's ceremonial artery, was built only through a violation of the deceased ruler's will: a (rather atypical) note in the endowment deed of the Bayezid II foundation indicates that the sultan willed to be buried near the mausoleum of Ayyub on the Golden Horn, in a grave that would be covered with earth only.[29] Obligations to empire and to the imperial city must have proved stronger than the sultan's will.

The constructions of the Ottoman ruling body on the Mese consolidated the character of the city's main artery as its ceremonial route, dotted with significant sites. With the exception of baths and inns, these buildings did not present façades to the main artery but for the most part were enclosed within window-pierced walls. Their large dimensions, ashlar masonry, and lead-covered domes, their display of precious building materials and high-quality craftsmanship, distinguished them from the surrounding fabric. As noted earlier in this study, the uniform appearance of the street, achieved through standardizing measures and practices or through the creation of straight arteries, was never a concern for Ottoman

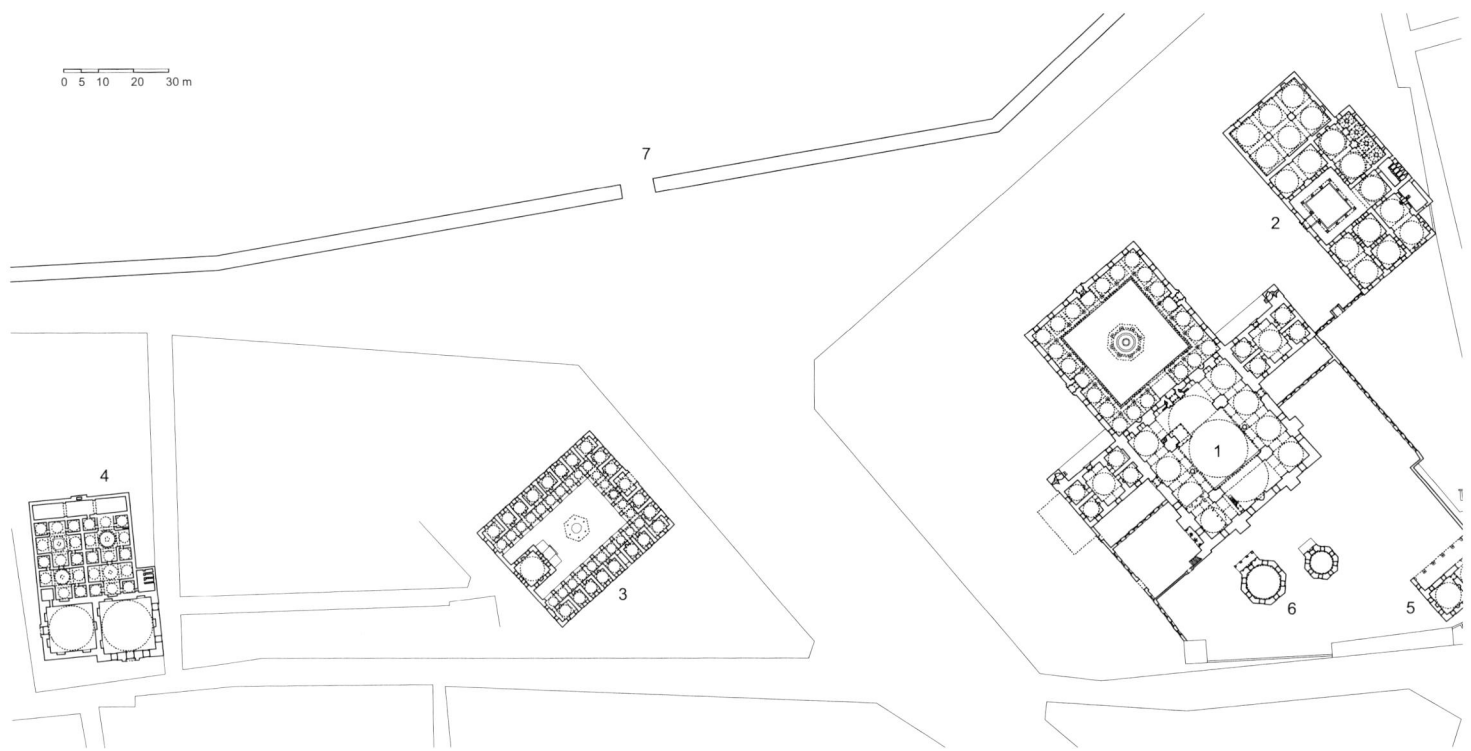

FIGURE 141
Bayezid II complex, plan:
(1) mosque, (2) hospice and
caravanserai, (3) madrasa,
(4) double bath, (5) elementary
school, (6) mausolea of
Bayezid II and his daughter
Selçuk Hatun, (7) Old Palace.

patrons and architects until the modern era. Matrakcı's painting, too, reflects this attitude. With all its focus on creating the image of a monumentalized Istanbul, one cannot readily recognize a single street. This was not, however, an indication of the "inward-oriented" nature of Ottoman urbanism, as has been suggested.[30] To the contrary, the Mese/Divan Yolu, along with a number of other arteries, mostly in the dense commercial area, were to become sites where Ottoman architects articulated various ways of relating monumental structures to the street and hence exhibiting them to users of the arteries. Initiated through the first decades of Ottoman reign in Constantinople, in structures such as the complexes of Mehmed II, Murad Pasha, and Mahmud Pasha, this trend was consolidated through the later fifteenth and early sixteenth centuries. The Divan Yolu gained the character of a processional route, marked with a sequence of significant sites that lent meaning to the setting and to rituals enacted on it and on

particular sites along it.[31] The Ottoman Divan Yolu is in this sense comparable to other arteries displaying, in Allan Ceen's words, characteristics of "processional-route architecture," such as the Via Papale in Rome, taking shape through the early decades of the sixteenth century, or the al-Moaz street in Cairo, where street-oriented Mamluk buildings created a uniquely continuous ensemble from the thirteenth century onward.[32] In all three cases, the city's main processional route was monumentalized through constructions of the urban ruling elite. The emphasis, in all three cases, was not on the straight axis but on situating significant buildings on the route and lending them visibility and prominence through choices in siting and architectural design. The varying political processes that prompted these constructions, and the diverse architectural idioms in the Mamluk, Italian, and Ottoman contexts, render these three processional routes comparable but distinct.

Constructions of this period contributed to Istanbul's skyline, defined by sultanic mosques, with their monumental hemispherical domes and multiple minarets, surrounded by a host of dependencies. With its elevated location, the Bayezid mosque added another focus to the city's skyline; the trend continued with the construction of Selim I's mosque complex, located on the fifth hill of the peninsula that juts toward the Golden Horn, completed some years before the Matrakçı painting. Unlike the major works of architecture dating from the first decades of Ottoman rule in the city, those of the later period were much more uniform in their building techniques, proportions, materials, and hence in their overall formal features. The formation, in the early decades of the sixteenth century, of a community of architects working for the court accounts for the making of this stylistic unity, consolidated during the period the office of chief architect was held by Sinan.[33]

With its architecture and imperial symbolism revived through the constructions of Mehmed and his viziers, Hagia Sophia continued to inform the architecture of sultanic and vizierial mosques. The major sultanic mosque of the period, that of Bayezid II, followed the trend established by that built by Mehmed II. With its prayer hall covered by a central dome flanked by two semidomes on the qibla axis, its superstructure had a closer affinity to the Byzantine monument than the former. The mosque of Atik Ali Pasha on the Constantinian Forum was comparable in design to the mosques of Mehmed II and of Rum Mehmed Pasha in Üsküdar, with its central dome flanked by a semidome on the qibla side (figs. 146–48). It differed from the latter building in its incorporation of the side spaces into the mosque's prayer space. The most telling manifestation of the centrality of the Hagia Sophia image to the

Ottoman architectural enterprise is the fate of the St. Andrea in Krisei, converted to a convent-mosque by Koca Mustafa Pasha. In the process of conversion, remodeling, and ninety-degree change of the building's orientation, its superstructure too was altered. The result was that a typical late Byzantine church was transformed into a mosque whose new superstructure, with two half domes flanking the central dome, now emulated that of the city's primary Justinianic monument (fig. 149).[34]

FIGURE 142
Divan Yolu and Bayezid II complex: mausoleum, elementary school, and mosque.

FIGURE 143
Divan Yolu and Bayezid II complex: mosque and madrasa.

Alongside continuities with practices established in Mehmed II's Istanbul, new trends, largely rooted in transformations in the state's religious politics, inscribed changes in urban space. Aiming to create a strictly hierarchical institutional framework to house the religious elite, Mehmed had kept popularly leaning Sufi orders at a safe distance from the state; that distance assumed spatial definition in the architecture of the New Mosque complex. The struggle for the throne between Bayezid and his brother Cem, and the former's assumption of power, by contrast, were played out against the growing prominence and visibility of the Halvetiyye order, which had had an important center in Amasya since the 1460s

FIGURE 144
Bayezid II bath, exterior.

FIGURE 145
Bayezid II bath, exterior, fragments from the Theodosius column base.

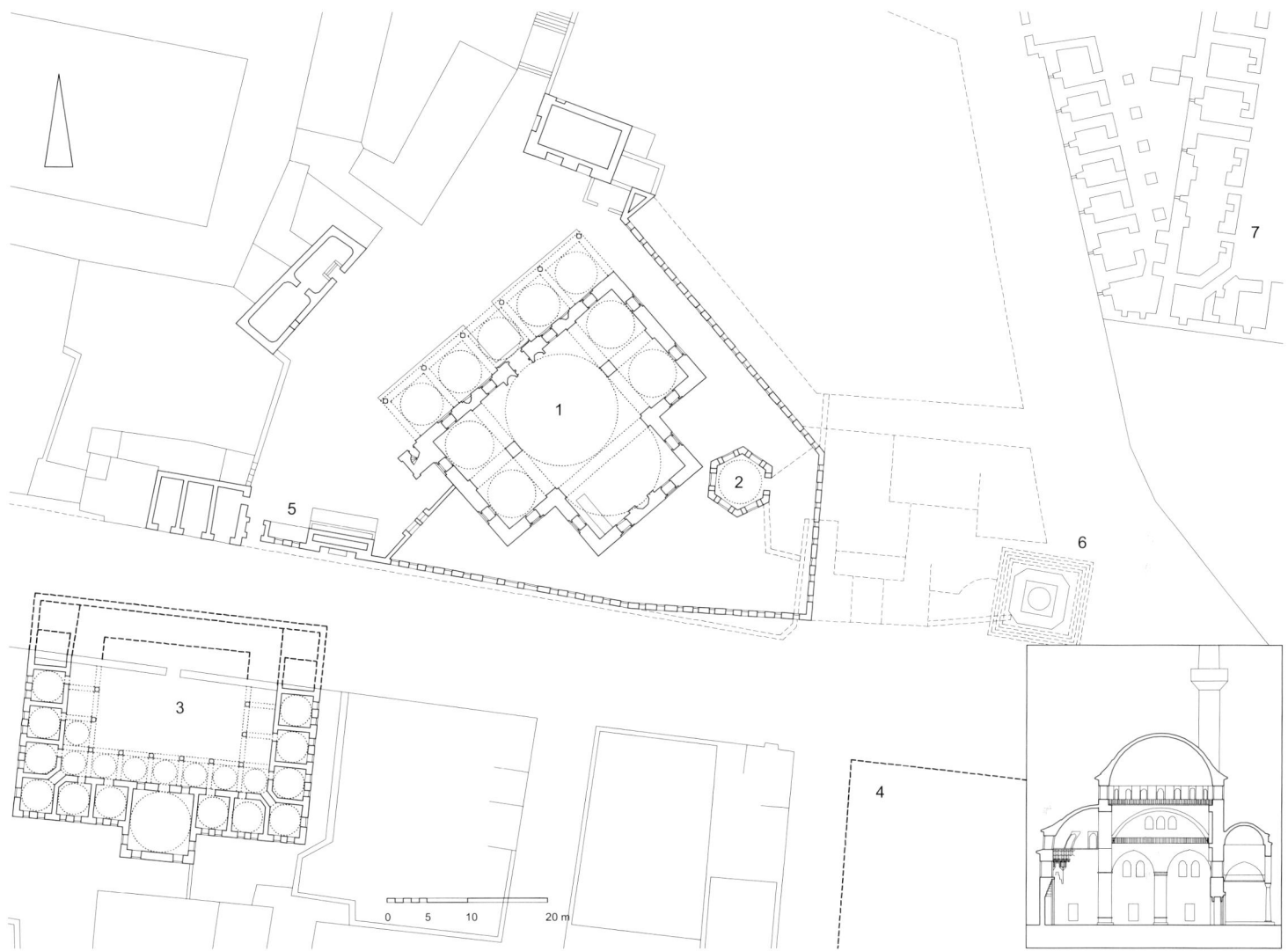

FIGURE 146
Atik Ali Pasha complex, plan,
and section of the mosque:
(1) mosque, (2) mausoleum,
(3) madrasa, (4) khan,
(5) fountain, (6) column of
Constantine, (7) Vezir han.

and whose leading members were prominent figures of Bayezid's princely court in that city. The Halvetiyye, led by Çelebi Halife, who was the spiritual (and perhaps political) guide to Bayezid, was instrumental in the latter's emergence as the victorious party in the struggle for the throne.[35] Bayezid's rule, in turn, saw the beginning of a close rapport between the state and the Sufi order, which made it the dervish order most actively supported by the Ottoman ruling body, particularly through the sixteenth century. The most decisive step in bringing the Halvetiyye to the center stage of Ottoman politics was the invitation extended by Bayezid II to Çelebi Halife to move, with his disciples, from Amasya to Istanbul. The sponsorship the spiritual leader and his followers enjoyed in the capital city marked a radical turn in Ottoman architectural patronage: beginning with the mosque-and-lodge complex founded in 1486 by Koca Mustafa Pasha for Çelebi Halife (fig. 150), a significant number of major religious establishments founded through Bayezid's reign were designed to accommodate the Halveti order.

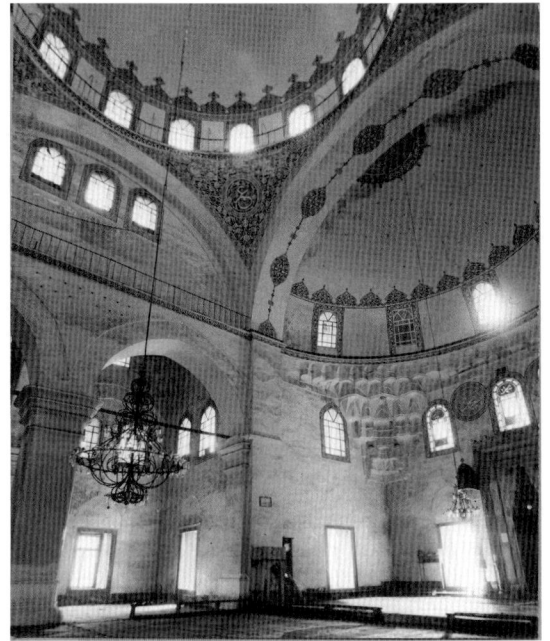

FIGURE 147
Atik Ali Pasha mosque, from
the east.

FIGURE 148
Atik Ali Pasha mosque, interior,
toward the east.

FIGURE 149
St. Andrea in Krisei/Koca
Mustafa Pasha mosque, section.

The new relationship between the state and Sufi orders found royal expression in the congregational mosque Bayezid built in Istanbul, which was, as already noted, a structure designed in the image of Hagia Sophia. What distinguished the building from former congregational mosques built by Ottoman rulers was the addition of convent sections to the two sides of the prayer hall. The bold statement embodied in the design of Mehmed's complex, with its madrasas lined up around the centrally placed mosque and its hospice removed from the religious space and enclosed within its own walls, was rejected by an equally bold and clear statement: the convent, symbolizing the state's accommodation of Sufis, assumed a new centrality as it was now housed within the royal mosque (figs. 141, 142). The next sultanic mosque to be built in the city, that of Selim I, completed by his son Süleyman, was also flanked by convent rooms.[36] It would be Süleyman, with his grand mosque complex a bold manifestation of Ottoman Sunni orthodoxy, who brought a final end to the sultanic

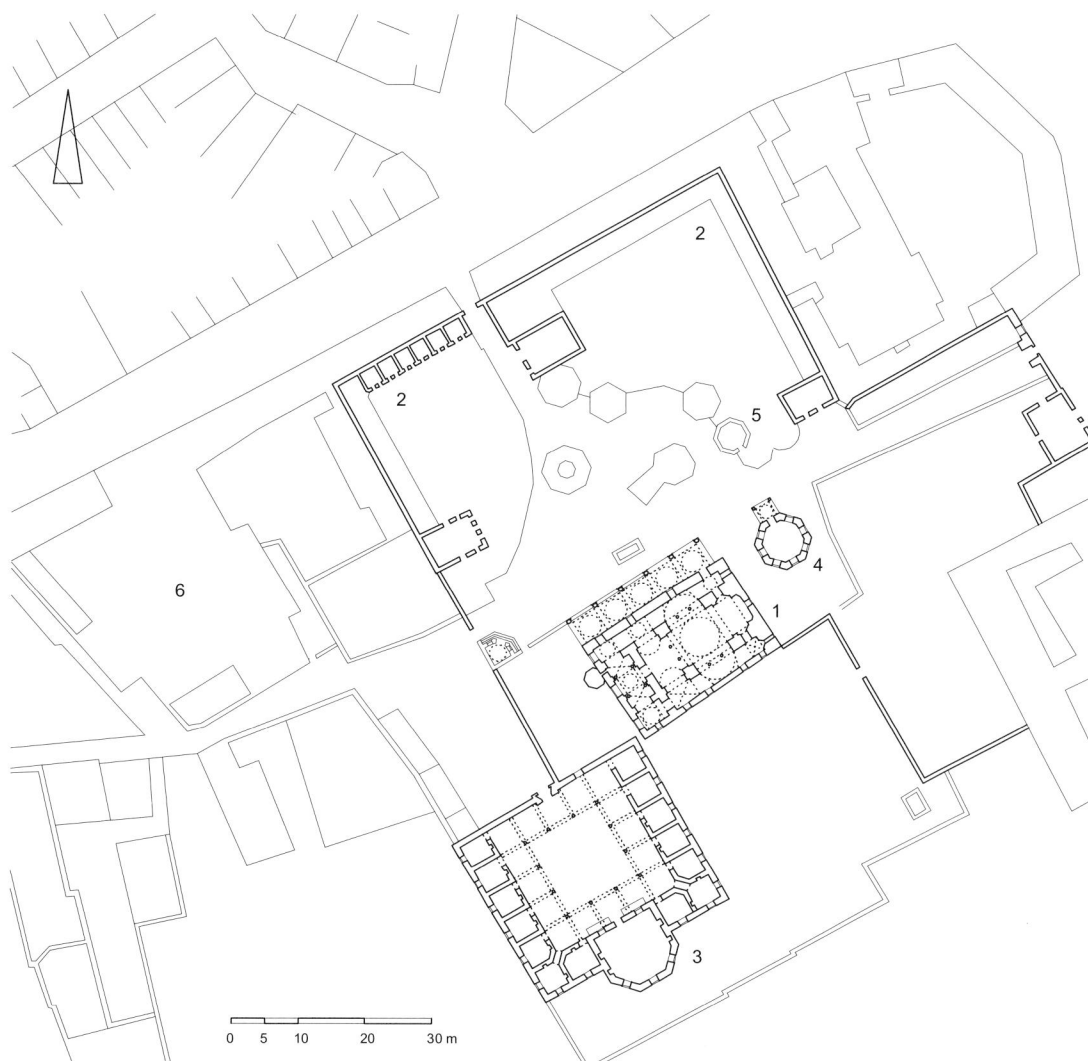

FIGURE 150
Koca Mustafa Pasha
complex, plan: (1) church/
mosque, (2) convent rooms,
(3) madrasa, (4) mausoleum
of Safiye Hatun, the founder's
daughter, (5) mausoleum of
Sünbül Sinanüddin Efendi,
(6) double bath.

convent-mosque.[37] (Before its final demise, this architectural legacy of early Ottoman culture, it will be remembered, had already undergone a significant transformation, as its function in the aftermath of the conquest changed from convent-masjid to convent-mosque and its denomination from *'imāret* to *cāmi'*.)

The Koca Mustafa Pasha foundation, established at the monastery of St. Andrea in Krisei, remained a major center of the Sünbüli branch of the Halveti order through the Ottoman history of the city.[38] The turn of the sixteenth century witnessed the foundation of other sizable

establishments housing Halveti convents. Atik Ali Pasha's complex on the Constantinian Forum housed convent functions, as did the church of SS. Sergius and Bacchus, endowed by Kapu Ağası Hüseyin Ağa. The Küçük (Little) Ayasofya, as the Justinianic church was to be named by its Ottoman users, was converted in 1505 into a mosque-and-lodge complex adjoined by a soup kitchen, a primary school, and a double bath (figs. 151, 152). Another early Byzantine church, the St. John Studius, was converted into a mosque and Halveti lodge in 1506–7 by Mirahor İlyas Beg.[39] As was the case

FIGURE 151
SS. Sergius and Bacchus/Küçük
Ayasofya convent-mosque
complex, plan: (1) church/
mosque, (2) convent rooms,
(3) mausoleum, (4) double bath,
(5) city walls.

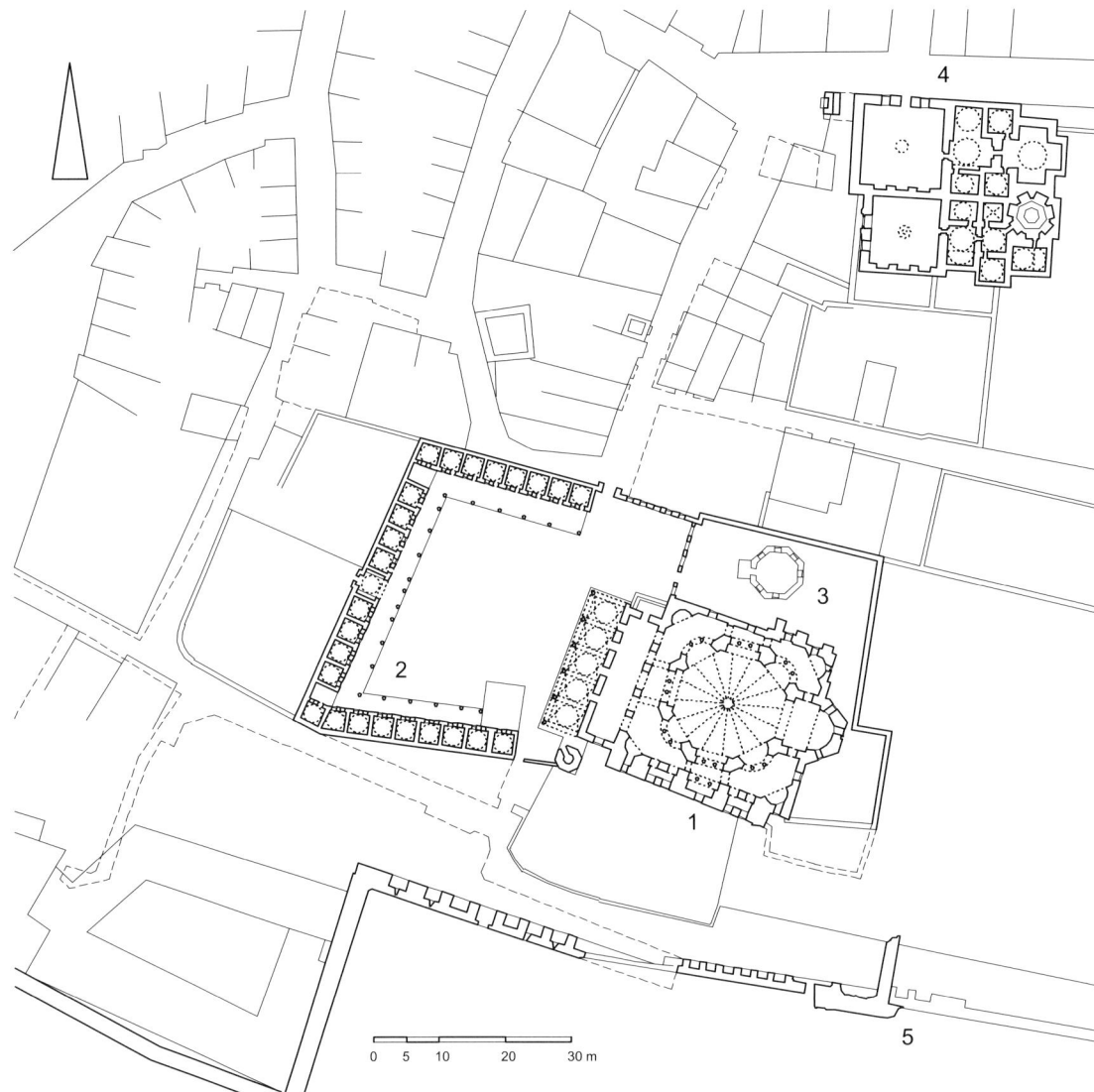

with the convent-mosque built by Mehmed II for the Zeyni sheikh Vefazade, also in newly built and converted structures, the main domed hall served simultaneously as mosque and ritual space.[40] While tracing the formation of residential quarters of the city, I noted that a number of lodges were established during the reign of Bayezid II and at times served as quarter mosques. A number of masjids founded during the reign of Mehmed II began to function also as Sufi lodges in the same period. The

Pantokrator, which had started its Ottoman life as the madrasa of Mevlana Zeyrek and had been turned into a quarter mosque upon the completion of the madrasas around the Mehmed II complex, now housed also a Nakshibendiyye lodge.[41] It will be remembered that concomitant with the increase in numbers of Sufi lodges and their growing centrality as urban institutions was the increasing visibility of the religious elite as founders of such institutions.

Apart from the Hagia Sophia, the monastic churches of the Pantokrator, Kyriotissa, and the Pantepoptes were among the few Christian structures converted for religious use by the Ottoman administration during the reign of Mehmed II. The Ayasofya mosque, the Zeyrek madrasa, the Kalenderhane, and the Eski İmaret all belonged to the Mehmed II foundation and were founded within the first years after the conquest. Following the sultan's order in 1459, the Ottoman ruling elite focused on new constructions. Bayezid's reign, by contrast, saw a wave of conversions, which may in part be understood as the Ottoman state's inscription of its strengthening religious identity into the space of the capital city. Three of the four Halveti lodges just mentioned were housed in converted Byzantine churches. The Myrelaion (Bodrum Cami, founded by Mesih Pasha), Gül Cami (whose Ottoman founder, like its Byzantine identity, remains unknown), the Chora (founded by Atik Ali Pasha, who built two other congregational mosques in Istanbul), the monastery of Constantine Lips (founded by Fenarizade Alaüddin Beg), and Toklu Dede Mescidi (founded by Koca Mustafa Pasha, who also converted the St. Andrea in Krisei) were turned into mosques during this period. At least two of these, the Gül Cami and the Constantine Lips, were in use as churches up to the time of their conversion. Another layer of the memory of Byzantium was thus absorbed into the Ottoman order as the capital city's Islamic identity became an increasingly central constituent of its image. (The figural mosaics of the Chora, like those of Hagia Sophia and possibly other converted churches, were, however, intact and visible.)[42] Hence Matrakcı's painting represents these converted churches with the same conventions it uses for newly built mosques, rendering them part of an Ottoman visual order. That visual order, I noted

FIGURE 152
SS. Sergius and Bacchus/Küçük Ayasofya convent-mosque, west façade with the Ottoman portico.

earlier in this chapter, represented in turn a tightly structured political order.

Matrakcı's painting, then, allows us entry into an Istanbul whose constitution was at once similar to and different from that conceived and shaped through the first decades of Ottoman rule. The contrast between Matrakcı's painting and the city's earlier images underlines the passage of an era when Byzantine and ghazi legacies, immediately accessible to Constantinople's new rulers, merged with an idiosyncratic vision of empire to construct the Ottoman capital city. And perhaps the cultural syncretism of the era was founded, in part, on the very tangibility of those diverse pasts.

The disparate urbanistic devices and signifying practices that shaped the spaces and images of Constantinople/Istanbul did not constitute a set of arbitrary solutions to the problems of building an Ottoman city on Byzantine foundations. The centralizing absolutist polity led by Mehmed II was heir to a frontier culture that had learned, through the preceding century and a half, to include, appropriate, and embody elements of the other and to use the resultant heterogeneity and ambiguity to its own ends.[43] The urban project that reshaped Constantinople as the Ottoman capital was a product of the most momentous of those encounters with the other, for the entity that was encountered was the millennial locus of empire. Through multiple ways of reconfiguring and imagining urban space, that project sought to represent and reproduce a new political and social order. At the same time, it sought to encompass, address, and be legible to the diverse actors in a varied, complex, and at times conflicted social and cultural spectrum.

Introduction

1. Possibly the Byzantine church later converted to a mosque as the Gül Cami.

2. Barthes, *S/Z*, 107. If this is too abrupt a recontextualization of Barthes's text, it may be justified for the interpretative light it sheds on the city and its images, particularly on the displacement, suspension, and interpenetration of its multiple identities through this particular period. "Constantinople" and "Istanbul," it will be noted, do not denote the Byzantine and Ottoman cities respectively. "Constantinople," in its arabicized form "Kostantiniyye," denoted the city (often but not exclusively in official and literary contexts) throughout its Ottoman history; it was used interchangeably with "Istanbul," which is encountered more frequently in unofficial/vernacular contexts.

3. On transformations of the Ottoman polity in the later fifteenth century, see Yerasimos, *La fondation de Constantinople et de Sainte-Sophie;* G. Necipoğlu, *Architecture, Ceremonial, and Power;* Kafadar, *Between Two Worlds.* Recent work suggests that Balkan frontier lords remained important political actors into the sixteenth century; Çıpa, "Centrality of the Periphery."

4. On Mehmed II, see İnalcık, *The Ottoman Empire,* 23–34, 59–103; Kafadar, "The Ottomans and Europe," 595ff.; Finkel, *Osman's Dream,* 48–80.

5. On Mehmed II's law code, see Özcan, "Fâtih'in Teşkilât Kanunnamesi," and G. Necipoğlu, *Architecture, Ceremonial, and Power.*

6. On the cultural patronage of Mehmed II, see Raby, "El Gran Turco," and G. Necipoğlu, *Architecture, Ceremonial, and Power.*

7. Contrary to the widespread assumption that the Greek and Armenian patriarchates and the chief rabbinate of the Jewish community were established shortly after the conquest, the Greek patriarchate was the only non-Muslim religious authority established and recognized by the court during the early decades of Ottoman rule in Istanbul. The date of Gennadios's assignment to the post is January 1454; Kritovoulos, *History of Mehmed the Conqueror,* 94–95. For discussions of the relationship of non-Muslim communities to the Ottoman court and its diverse institutional frameworks, see Braude, "Foundation Myths of the *Millet* System"; Bardakjian, "Rise of the Armenian Patriarchate of Constantinople"; Epstein, "Leadership of the Ottoman Jews in the Fifteenth and Sixteenth Centuries."

8. For a compilation of Byzantine, Ottoman, and European texts pertaining to the fall of the city, see *La caduta di Costantinopoli,* ed. and trans. Pertusi. For an overview and interpretation of the varying perceptions of the city and of the events of 1453 by Byzantine, European, and Ottoman witnesses, based largely on Pertusi's translations, see Balard, "Constantinople vue par les témoins du siège de 1453." In a number of narratives originating in the Byzantine milieu, an angel saves the emperor Constantine during battle with the Turks and hides him in a cave near the Golden Gate. From then on the Sleeping Emperor, Constantine, waits there for the moment when God will restore him to life and give him back the sword he used to defend the city during the siege; the emperor will then march into Constantinople to rid it of the Turks. For a discussion of Greek legends of Constantine, of the fall and awaited recovery of the city, see Nicol, *Immortal Emperor,* 95–108.

9. Neşri, *Kitâb-ı Cihan-nümâ,* 713.

10. Saʿdüddin, *Tacüʾt-tevarih,* 1:581.

11. *Evliya Çelebi Seyahatnamesi,* bk. 1, fol. 114r.

12. The process of inscription continued into the twentieth century: in 1953, a committee of historians and art historians taking part in the celebrations for the 500th anniversary of the conquest placed plaques bearing the date 1453 on the structures mentioned by Ayvansarayi. The plates, or their replacements, are still visible on many monuments in Istanbul. Needless to say, none of these structures was built in 1453.

13. *Die altosmanischen anonymen Chroniken,* 1:94, my translation, as are all others underless otherwise stated.

14. Ebuʾl-Hayr-i Rumi, *Ṣalṭuḳnāme,* fol. 616v. For a discussion of this passage, see chapter 3.

15. Namık Kemal, *Evrāḳ-ı perīşān,* particularly 8–38, "Devr-i istīlā" [Age of Conquest], and 129–286, "Fātiḥ" [The Conqueror]; idem, *Osmanlı tarihi.* The other two chapters of *Evrāḳ-ı perīşān* (Scattered Papers) are devoted to Salahaddin Ayyubi, the Ayyubid ruler who fought the Crusaders to return Jerusalem to Islamic rule, and Selim I, the Ottoman sultan who conquered Syria and Egypt in 1516. For an evaluation of Namık Kemal's historical writings within the context of his political thought, see Mardin, *Genesis of Young Ottoman Thought,* and Ersoy, "Namık Kemal." Mardin notes that Kemal's *Ottoman History* (which originally included sections on Roman and early Islamic history) came at the end of his writing career, when, in exile, he had given up on the idea of a multiethnic Ottoman "nation," turning his eyes instead to the "people of Islam."

16. Said, *Beginnings,* 29–43.

17. For discussions on the discourse and imagination of the conquest in Turkey at the turn of the twenty-first century, see Bora, "Fatih'in İstanbul'u," *İstanbul'un Fethinin 550. Yılında* and Çinar, "National History as a Contested Site."

18. In the introductory essay to the third volume of *Realms of Memory,* Pierre Nora distinguishes between

227

imposed and constructed sites of memory as central images of collective memory and identity. The latter, he notes, are places, individuals, and objects that are transformed into important and durable national symbols through complex historical processes; Nora, *Realms of Memory,* 3:ix–xii. In the introductory essay to the whole work, he articulates the notion of *lieu de mémoire* in its relations to changing historical consciousness and circumstances.

19. For an assessment of the "intertwined strands" of orientalist and nationalist paradigms as they have shaped Western as well as Middle Eastern scholarship on the visual culture of the Islamic world, see Bozdoğan and Necipoğlu, "Entangled Discourses."

20. E. H. Ayverdi's extensive surveys of early Ottoman architecture exemplify such debates; see, e.g., Ayverdi, *Osmanlı miʿmârîsinde Fâtih devri, 855–886 (1403–1451).* In an article published in 1956 and titled "Turkish and Byzantine Architectural Elements," the author expressly rejected any Byzantine "influence" in Ottoman architecture. Recent scholarship on Byzantine and Ottoman architectural practices and on Istanbul has been more interested in the interrelationships of the two traditions. See G. Necipoğlu, "The Life of an Imperial Monument"; idem, *Age of Sinan;* and Ousterhout, "Ethnic Identity and Cultural Appropriation in Early Ottoman Architecture."

21. Major reference works on the period are Kuran, *The Mosque in Early Ottoman Architecture;* Ayverdi, *Osmanlı miʿmârîsinde Fâtih devri, 855–886 (1403–1451);* Goodwin, *History of Ottoman Architecture;* Müller-Wiener, *Bildlexikon zur Topographie Istanbuls;* Necipoğlu, *Architecture, Ceremonial, and Power;* and Kuban, *Osmanlı mimarisi.* Julian Raby's "El Gran Turco" remains the most comprehensive study of the artistic patronage of Mehmed II.

22. For two historiographic assessments of the earlier formulations of the Islamic city model and its later uses, see Abu-Lughod, "Islamic City," and Raymond, "Islamic City, Arab City." For an overview of recent work on Middle Eastern cities and a discussion of the notion of the "Islamic city" as it bears

on the study of urban history, see Çelik, "New Approaches to the 'Non-Western' City." Çelik notes that while the debate on the Islamic city continues to problematize this concept, studies focusing on particular cities or periods bring its limitations into sharper focus. The persistence of the model, and the notion that religion is the primary determinant of urban practice, are perhaps best illustrated in general surveys and work on Western theory of architecture and urbanism. Spiro Kostof's wonderful book *The City Shaped* turns to religious law of the first centuries of Islam, and to tradition, ownership, and the Muslim's right to visual privacy, to explain "Islamic" city form. Kostof, *The City Shaped,* 62–64. Françoise Choay, in an important volume on Western urban theory, comments on the "oblique manner in which religion came to impose upon [Islamic cities] its order," and finds that in the last analysis urbanistic practices refer to a single book, the Koran. See Choay's comparative discussion of urbanism and urban theory in *The Rule and the Model,* 22–24.

23. A 1990 article by Halil İnalcık titled "Istanbul: An Islamic City" may be considered a somewhat belated attempt to locate Istanbul squarely within this conceptual framework. Doğan Kuban's urban history of Istanbul, *Istanbul, an Urban History,* also exemplifies this trend, as its interpretations of the city's spatial configurations are often tacitly based on the Islamic city model. For an overview of work on the Ottoman city, see the introductory essay, "Was There an Ottoman City?" in Eldem, Goffman, and Masters, *The Ottoman City Between East and West,* 1–16.

24. An in-depth discussion of "organic" urban patterns is found in Kostof, *The City Shaped,* 43–93, where the author critiques notions of spontaneity and lack of cohesion associated with lack of geometric order. Kostof surveys a series of urban environments to expose the ways in which "organic" configurations were in fact deliberately constructed and sustained.

25. Features of urban space that relate Ottoman Istanbul to a significant number of medieval and early modern cities of the Old World—the lack of a

geometric order and use of perspectival devices in its layout, its winding streets and dead ends (which it shared with cities both east and west of the Mediterranean basin)—have been read as indicators of its Islamicness and/or of the spontaneity of its urban processes. Comparative studies into the social, political, and institutional structures that shaped and sustained particular patterns of urban spatiality are needed for valid interpretations of connections and ruptures rendered obscure through nationalistic or civilizational divides in historiography. An important step in this direction has been taken in the exhibition Secular Medieval Architecture in the Balkans, 1300–1500, and Its Preservation, held in Thessaloniki in 1997, and in the volume that accompanied the exhibition, edited by Ćurčić and Hadjitryphonos. Articles in *The Ottoman City and Its Parts: Urban Structure and Social Order,* ed. Bierman, Abou-el-Haj, and Preziosi, and Watenpaugh's *Image of an Ottoman City* exemplify novel approaches to Ottoman urban configurations within larger cultural and political contexts. Another compilation of studies that approach questions of urban form from the point of view of architectural history is *Istanbul: An Urban Vision,* a special issue of *Environmental Design* 1–2 (1987).

26. I subscribe to Henri Lefebvre's definition of monumentality, which underlines the multiplicity of meanings a monument embodies, and proposes a reading of monumental space through its perception and use as well as its conceptualization; Lefebvre, *Production of Space,* 220–28.

27. After Barthes, *S/Z,* 5: "To interpret a text is not to give it a (more or less justified, more or less free) meaning, but on the contrary to appreciate what *plural* constitutes it."

28. Michel de Certeau's focus on users of urban space in his *Practice of Everyday Life,* an inquiry into relations between spatial and signifying practices as they bear on urban discourses and on the city as symbolic order, has provided insights for my interpretations of the urban fabric and its uses.

29. Henri Lefebvre outlines a triad of conceived, represented, and lived spaces in the introduction to his

Production of Space, 1–67. Conceived space, according to Lefebvre, is the space of scientists, planners, urbanists; among the constituents of conceived spaces are intellectually articulated signs, codes, "frontal" relations. These are "representations of space" that are tied to the larger order, itself connected to particular relations of production. Perceived space is what ensures the continuity and cohesion of social formation, as each social formation creates its particular locations and spatial sets enabling the production and reproduction of a particular order. Finally, lived space, or representational space, is the space of users and inhabitants, and of artists, "lived through its associated images and symbols," the space "the imagination seeks to change and appropriate." Lefebvre's definition of codes as partaking of a practical relationship between subjects and their surroundings, and his proposal to trace the coming-into-being and disappearance of codings and decodings, has been important to my interpretation of Ottoman monuments and their representations.

30. A number of works that emphasize the relational and dynamic aspects of processes of signification have provided important insights for this exploration. The notion of "reckoning" as elucidated by Donald Preziosi (*Rethinking Art History*), which brings into sharp focus the user as an "always active, complicit, constructing and construing subject," has shed light on Ottoman responses to the Constantinopolitan cityscape. Carlo Ginzburg's inquiries into the polysemy and dialogic of historical sources (in *Myths, Emblems, Clues*) have opened vistas for the interpretation of documents produced by a cultural environment of encounters and oppositions. My interpretations of urban spatiality and its representations owe debts to Spiro Kostof's focus on the dynamic and complex processes that give shape and meaning to the urban environment (in *The City Shaped*). Equally important to my formulations is the work on Ottoman architectural and cultural history of the past two decades, which has covered important ground in contextualizing the processes through which

cultural artifacts are produced and used, and in offering novel perspectives on traditionally accepted disciplinary or cultural boundaries. For a literature survey, see the doctoral dissertation on which this book is based, Kafescioğlu, "The Ottoman Capital in the Making," 13–18.

31. On Ottoman historical writing of the fifteenth century, see İnalcık, "Rise of Ottoman Historiography"; idem, "How to Read Ashik Pasha-zade's History"; Ménage, "Beginnings of Ottoman Historiography"; and Kafadar, *Between Two Worlds.*

32. Kafadar, *Between Two Worlds,* 90–105.

33. Yerasimos, *La fondation de Constantinople et de Sainte-Sophie;* Kafadar, *Between Two Worlds.*

Chapter 1

1. Tafur, *Travels and Adventures,* 145–46; Clavijo, *Embassy to Tamerlane,* 87–88; Buondelmonti, *Liber Insularum Archipelagi* (1897), 245; Magdalino, "Medieval Constantinople," 535–36; N. Necipoğlu, "Social and Economic Conditions in Constantinople During Mehmed II's Siege."

2. Doukas, *Decline and Fall of Byzantium to the Ottoman Turks,* 235.

3. Tursun Beg, *History of Mehmed the Conqueror,* fol. 54v.

4. Kritovoulos, *History of Mehmed the Conqueror,* 83.

5. Without indicating sources, Babinger, in *Mehmed the Conqueror and His Time,* 150, notes that Mehmed moved the palace to Istanbul permanently in 1457. One chronicler notes the winter of 1458 as the first lengthy stay of Mehmed II in Istanbul. That year probably marked a turning point, as the anonymous chronicle attributed to Ruhi reports of Mehmed's spending the winter of 1459 "established" in the city; the winter of 1460 too was spent in Istanbul, with Mehmed "favorably disposed" toward the city, where he was busy administering justice and equity; Cengiz and Yücel, "Rûhî Târîhi," 448–55.

6. See Aşıkpaşazade, *Tevârîh-i Âl-i Osman,* 198–99, and Kemalpaşazade, *Tevârîh-i Âl-i Osman,* 139–43.

7. Kritovoulos mentions fifty thousand captives held by the Ottoman

army, though the number was probably smaller. The population of Constantinople before its fall is estimated to have been around fifty thousand. Since many were killed and many fled before and during the siege, the number of those who were enslaved by the Ottomans must be smaller. For population estimates, see N. Necipoğlu, *Byzantium Between the Ottomans and the Latins,* and Yerasimos, "Osmanlı İstanbulʾunun Kuruluşu."

8. Halil İnalcık, in "The Policy of Mehmed II," discusses the initial measures intended to populate the city and alterations in the status of urban property. I discuss the repopulation and deportations in some depth in chapter 4.

9. For the Ottoman history and meaning of the monument, see G. Necipoğlu, "The Life of an Imperial Monument."

10. Ebuʾl-Hayr-i Rumi, *Şalṭuḳnāme,* fols. 614r–v; Tursun Beg, *History of Mehmed the Conqueror,* fols. 51r–53r. The translation of the couplet is from Babinger, *Mehmed the Conqueror and His Time,* 96.

11. For a discussion of Arab perceptions and representations of Constantinople in the twelfth and thirteenth centuries, see El-Cheikh, "Byzantium Through the Islamic Prism." It may be interesting to note that the Hagia Sophia in Thessaloniki and that in Trebizond, too, preserved their names, as they were named Ayasofya mosques. In most conversions, the building would be renamed after the founder of the mosque, and less frequently, after its location.

12. For an in-depth analysis of the Ottoman histories of Hagia Sophia produced through the later decades of the fifteenth century, see Yerasimos, *La fondation de Constantinople et de Sainte-Sophie.* See G. Necipoğlu, "The Life of an Imperial Monument," for another interpretation underlining the dynastic significance of the monument.

13. Not only Mehmed II's New Mosque but the convent-mosque built near the mausoleum of Ayyub al-Ansari, that built for Sheikh Vefa, and that of Rum Mehmed Pasha featured aspects of Hagia Sophia's superstructure. The trend would continue

into the mid–sixteenth century with Bayezid II's mosque in Istanbul and with vizierial mosques such as those of Atik Ali Pasha and Koca Mustafa Pasha (who restructured a late Byzantine church to support a central dome flanked by two half domes). On these buildings, see the final section of chapter 1, chapter 2, and the epilogue. On the classical formulation of the Süleymanic age, when the domical structure of Hagia Sophia became an exclusive feature of royal mosques, see G. Necipoğlu, *Age of Sinan*.

14. G. Necipoğlu, "The Life of an Imperial Monument," 204.

15. Cyril Mango notes that some of the mosaics must immediately have been plastered over, as Marino Sanuto reported that they were revealed when the plaster fell during the 1509 earthquake. Mango observes that the dome mosaics remained in place until around 1630. Gülru Necipoğlu notes that those mosaics that remained above and beyond the view of the Muslim congregation remained intact through the early seventeenth century; she also provides a repair document dated 1607–9 for the covering of the Pantokrator image. Mango, *Materials for the Study of the Mosaics of St. Sophia at Istanbul;* G. Necipoğlu, "The Life of an Imperial Monument," 203–4, 211–13.

16. Müstakimzade Süleyman Sadeddin, *Tuḥfet-i-ḫaṭṭāṭīn,* 78; İdris Bidlisi, *Heşt behişt,* fols. 79v–91r.

17. On the minarets, see Emerson and Van Nice, "Hagia Sophia and the First Minaret Erected After the Conquest of Constantinople," and G. Necipoğlu, "The Life of an Imperial Monument," 206–9. Emerson and Van Nice, referring to a 1573 royal edict published by Ahmet Refik in his *İstanbul hayati* series (ordering the replacement of the wooden minaret on a buttress on the qibla side with a brick one), note that the brick minaret that stands at the southeast corner is a replacement for the first wooden minaret of Hagia Sophia. They suggest that the second masonry minaret might have been built by Bayezid II or Selim I. Gülru Necipoğlu refers to Mehmed ʿAşık's late-sixteenth-century *Menāẓırü'l-ʿavālim,* where the first two minarets are dated to Mehmed II's reign. The

dating of these minarets to Mehmed's rule is supported by the fact that the mosque of Ayyub al-Ansari, too, was given a second minaret during this time, possibly following the construction of the New Mosque. The dissimilarity of the two minarets built by the same patron would otherwise be difficult to explain. For the Ayyub al-Ansari mosque, see further in chapter 1.

18. For the first survey of property, see İnalcık, "The Policy of Mehmed II."

19. No endowment deed for the Ayasofya foundation has surfaced. What we know is provided by a later document, the account book of the endowment dating to between 893/1487–88 and 895/1489–90; BBA MM 19 (*Ayaṣofya vakfı taḥrīr defteri,* A.H. 895). At least quantitatively, this most probably reflects the original state of the endowment, as the later religious and charitable foundations in the city were included in the foundation of the New Mosque complex. Changes in the uses of buildings followed the completion of Mehmed's religious complex: the Zeyrek Madrasa and the convent were converted into mosques; a madrasa of the Kalenderhane is registered in the document, suggesting that by that date the church given to the Kalenderi dervishes as a convent was converted into a madrasa. Another converted church, the Güngörmez masjid, is also registered, suggesting that only recently had it begun to be used as a gunpowder depot, which made it the scene of a catastrophic explosion in 895/1490. The masjids of Güngörmez, of the new caravanserai, and of the tanneries outside the Golden Gate were possibly later additions to the foundation.

20. The Pantokrator was occupied by fullers before its conversion to a madrasa; Doukas, *Decline and Fall of Byzantium to the Ottoman Turks,* 243.

21. For a discussion of the Kalenderhane, see chapter 2.

22. Nothing is known on the location and date of this building, though its name implies that, like the Akataliptos imareti (also noted in an early waqf document), the Aristo bīmārḫānesi, too, was a Byzantine structure.

23. Kritovoulos, *History of Mehmed the Conqueror,* 93.

24. G. Necipoğlu, *Architecture, Ceremonial, and Power,* 3–4.

25. Other fragments of the city's past were transported to the palace grounds, to form parts of the sultan's private collection of Byzantine relics. See chapter 2. For Bayezid's bathhouse, see the epilogue.

26. See the anonymous letter narrating Mehmed's funeral, *Testament de Amyra Sultan Nichemedy,* in *Fatih Sultan Mehmed'in ölümü ve hadiseleri üzerine bir vesika,* 24–25.

27. The Topkapı, too, was to feature such a gate complex, which communicated with the remains of the Chalke Gate complex of the Byzantine Great Palace across from the Augustaion, simultaneously constituting a node between the palace and the city; G. Necipoğlu, *Architecture, Ceremonial, and Power,* 37–40.

28. For the Taht al-kalʿa, see further in chapter 1. For the citadel as palace and military stronghold in the larger Islamic world from the eleventh and twelfth centuries onward, see Bacharach, "Administrative Complexes, Palaces, and Citadels," and G. Necipoğlu, "An Outline of Shifting Paradigms."

29. For a discussion of fortified palatial residences in the Balkans in relation to military and palatial architecture through the late medieval era, see Ćurčić, "Architecture in the Age of Insecurity," 37ff.; for examples of such structures, see Ćurčić and Hadjitryphonos, *Secular Medieval Architecture in the Balkans,* 241ff.

30. For negotiations between the papacy and the Austro-Hungarian Empire for the organization of a Crusade against the Ottomans (about which the Ottomans were probably informed), see Setton, *The Papacy and the Levant,* 2:138–60. The construction of two fortresses on the Dardanelles, possibly over the same years, bespeaks similar concerns. For Crusade literature of the period, see Hankins, "Renaissance Crusaders."

31. Kritovoulos, *History of Mehmed the Conqueror,* 93. For a discussion of the citadel in the context of Byzantine internal conflicts and Byzantine-Ottoman relations, see Reinert, "The Paleologoi, Yıldırım Bāyezīd,

and Constantinople," 312–33. For the Golden Gate and the citadel, see Janin, *Constantinople byzantine,* 272–73; Guberti Basset, "John V Palaiologos and the Golden Gate in Constantinople"; and Mango, "The Triumphal Way of Constantinople and the Golden Gate," 181ff.

32. Angiolello, *Viaggio di Negroponte,* 25, notes that the money of the Grand Turk was kept in the citadel. For the citadel as refuge and treasury, see G. Necipoğlu, *Architecture, Ceremonial, and Power,* 10, 53.

33. Menavino, *I costumi et la vita de Turchi,* 137.

34. The road to Edirne and, along with it, the northern branch of the Mese connecting to this road through the Charisios Gate were to gain in importance instead.

35. On the Golden Gate as triumphal monument, and a reconstruction of its structure and form, see Mango, "The Triumphal Way of Constantinople and the Golden Gate."

36. Meyer-Plath and Schneider, *Aufnahme, Beschreibung und Geschichte,* 39–63.

37. Mango, "The Triumphal Way of Constantinople and the Golden Gate," 182 n. 58, and Doukas, *Decline and Fall of Byzantium to the Ottoman Turks,* 75.

38. On the citadel within the context of Mehmed's patronage of Italian artists and interest in Renaissance Italy, see Restle, "Bauplanung und Baugesinnung unter Mehmed II Fatih," and Raby, "El Gran Turco," 282–86.

39. Raby, "El Gran Turco"; Restle, "Bauplanung und Baugesinnung unter Mehmed II Fatih."

40. The reference is to Emanuele Filiberto (1559–80) and the citadel of Turin completed in 1566. In her study of Turin, Martha Pollak notes that the citadel was a central component of the independence of the duchy and of the city's image. Pollak situates the construction of Turin's citadel within the sixteenth-century discussion of the ideal city and its military component, demonstrating the central role of the citadel in this discussion; Pollak, *Turin, 1564–1680,* 13–34.

41. The aim of this section is not to recount all commercial structures known to have been in use during the reign of Mehmed II but rather to elucidate the emerging urban pattern in the commercial area of this period. I focus on the main areas of reuse and new construction and highlight the principal motives behind the decisions concerning the commercial district.

42. Apart from the first bedestan and the commercial area around the New Mosque complex of Mehmed II, it is not possible to know exact or approximate dates for construction of commercial structures. There is no clear chronological reference in contemporary sources relating to the Taht al-kalʿa area and the numerous hans. The order for the construction of the bedestan and the baths, on the other hand, suggests that in this period particular attention was paid to the construction of the commercial area. The Taht al-kalʿa bath, possibly built upon this order, is one of the largest in the city. The commercial area continued to grow in later decades; I will, however, deal with this topic as a whole in this section, in order to better demonstrate the interrelationships between its different segments and to address questions pertaining to its development.

43. Kritovoulos, *History of Mehmed the Conqueror,* 104–5.

44. The almost complete dependence of the city on outside resources is stressed and different aspects of its provisioning studied in a number of articles in the volume edited by Mango and Dagron, *Constantinople and Its Hinterland.* See esp. the articles by Durliat, Magdalino, Mango, and N. Necipoğlu. For an assessment of the same situation in the Ottoman period, see Mantran, *Istanbul dans la seconde moitié du XVIIe siècle,* 22–23.

45. For the Makros Embolos, see Janin, *Constantinople byzantine,* and Mordtmann, *Esquisse topographique de Constantinople,* 22. The similarity between the layout of the commercial areas of Istanbul and Ankara is striking; each has a two-centered structure with the bedestan and the Taht al-kalʿa and with the Uzunçarşı connecting them. Their contemporaneous development, one largely by Mehmed and the other largely by Mahmud Pasha, suggests that this was a favored arrangement for commercial centers. For Ankara, see Ergenç, "Osmanlı şehrinde esnaf örgütlerinin fizik yapıya etkileri," and idem, "16. yüzyıl Ankaraʾsı." Cemal Kafadar draws attention to the fact that during the fifteenth century Ankara became a major center of camlet production and the city's bedestan a center for camlet distribution; Kafadar, "A Death in Venice (1575)," 205–6.

46. Anhegger and İnalcık, *Ḳānūnnāme-i sulṭanī ber mūceb-i ʿörf-i ʿoṣmānī,* 41–50, 57–60, 82–85.

47. Ankara, with an estimated population of 25,000 in 979/1571–72, had two bedestans, fifteen khans, and 836 endowed shops. Kayseri, with a population between 30,000 and 33,000 in 992/1584, had two bedestans, two khans, and 43 (known) endowed shops; the figures are from Faroqhi, *Towns and Townsmen of Ottoman Anotolia.* Istanbul, at the end of Mehmed's reign, had an estimated population of around 50,000 and commercial structures that were comparable to or greater than those of the main commercial centers of Anatolia: two bedestans, fifteen khans, and 2,300 shops in Mehmed's foundation only, about 1,650 of them in the commercial area, some 420 around the New Complex, and the rest dispersed in the city. Ayverdi, *Osmanlı miʿmârîsinde Fâtih devri, 855–886 (1451–1481),* 4:556, notes that the number of endowed and privately owned shops in Istanbul and Galata at the end of Mehmed's reign was 3,927, citing a document in the Topkapı archives. Suraiya Faroqhi's research has revealed that the majority of endowed commercial buildings in Anatolian cities were built before 1500. Thus a quantitative comparison between the commercial structures of the capital as known from fifteenth-century sources and the Anatolian cities as revealed by sixteenth-century documents is less anachronistic than it might seem at first sight; Faroqhi, *Towns and Townsmen of Ottoman Anotolia,* 23–48. Istanbul toward the end of the sixteenth century, as could be expected, far surpassed Anatolian cities in terms of the expanse of the commercial area.

48. Given the population estimates at hand, one can safely assume that, at least in the first decade of Ottoman rule, the commercial space

restored to its functions or newly created was setting to a commercial life less vigorous than that of other Ottoman urban centers. Suraiya Faroqhi has noted that the construction of commercial buildings did not necessarily indicate economic prosperity. The Ottoman ruling groups, who were the main builders of commercial structures, could be willing to undertake such constructions in seemingly unfavorable sites as long as they were able to bear the construction expenses; Faroqhi, *Towns and Townsmen of Ottoman Anatolia*, 23–24.

49. İnalcık cites BBA Maliye 7387, which indicates that in 1479 the Istanbul customs zone gained 13 million *akçe* in three years, while the Bursa silk customs zone gained 700,000 yearly and that of Antalya 150,000; İnalcık, "Mehmed II," in *İslâm ansiklopedisi*, 7:534. On customs zones in the Ottoman customs system, see İnalcık, *Sources and Studies on the Ottoman Black Sea*, 1:91–113.

50. On the issue of deportations to Constantinople during the reign of Mehmed, its implications and consequences, see İnalcık, "The Policy of Mehmed II." For a discussion of the deportations as a policy of the Ottoman state within its larger context, see Lowry, "From Lesser Wars to the Mightiest War." For an overview of resettlement of specific communities to specific sections in the city, see Yerasimos, "Osmanlı İstanbul'unun Kuruluşu," and idem, "La communauté grecque-orthodoxe de Constantinople." The deportations to Istanbul are discussed in some detail in chapter 4.

51. Hadidi, *Tevārīḫ-i ʾĀl-i ʿOşmān*, fols. 23b–24a; İnalcık, "The Policy of Mehmed II," 237.

52. The granting of privileges and real estate to, and the increasing prominence of, the Italian trading colonies settling along the Golden Horn had marked the definitive establishment of the city's ports in this area from the eleventh century onward. For a study of this area and of the fluctuations between the city's southern and northern harbors as the main points of disembarkment in previous centuries, see Magdalino, "Maritime Neighborhoods of Constantinople."

53. The correspondence between the Byzantine and Ottoman names of the city gates is not known with certainty, though it has generally been accepted that the Neorion Gate, referred to in early Ottoman documents as the Orya Kapı, is the later Bahçekapı, that the Drungarii Gate is the Odun Kapısı, and that the Platea Gate is the Ottoman Un Kapanı Kapısı. Until the Fourth Crusade and the establishment of Latin rule, commercial areas were also scattered at different points on the Mese and the city's fora. Janin, *Constantinople byzantine*, 87–105, 235–36; Mundell-Mango, "The Commercial Map of Constantinople." Mundell-Mango has suggested that some commercial property did exist along the Mese through the first half of the fifteenth century.

54. For the Venetian quarter in the Byzantine city, see Bertelè, *Il palazzo degli ambasciatori di Venezia a Costantinopoli*, 19–32; Magdalino, *Constantinople médiévale*; idem, "Maritime Neighborhoods of Constantinople"; Yerasimos and Bacqué-Grammont, "La résidence du Baile de Venise à Balıkpazarı"; and Ağır, "İstanbul'un Eski ʿVenedik Ticaret Kolonisi'nin."

55. For a discussion of the constituents of Italian trading quarters, see Magdalino, "Maritime Neighborhoods of Constantinople," 224–26.

56. For a survey of the principal commercial districts and buildings of early Ottoman Istanbul, see Eyice, "İstanbul," 1214/114–1214/118, and İnalcık, "Istanbul," 227–29.

57. "Old" buildings comprising a shop and a residential room on top or combining a shop, a cell (*ḥöcre*), and a residence on the second floor are frequently encountered in this area. See, for example, houses in the Timurtaş quarter, the former quarter of the "House with the Lion"; Istanbul Atatürk Library M.C. O.64 (*Ayaṣofya vakfı cibāyet defteri*, A.H. 926), fols. 129v, 131r.

58. Aspects of inhabitation and of religious and ethnic denomination within residential quarters are discussed in chapter 4.

59. The capitulations granted to Venetians residing in the city, in 1521 and 1540, note that the bailo resided in Constantinople. For the 1521 treaty,

see Şakiroğlu, "1521 tarihli Osmanlı-Venedik antlaşmasının asli metni"; the 1540 treaty has been published by Tayyib Gökbilgin; Gökbilgin, "Venedik devlet arşivindeki vesikalar külliyatında Kanuni Süleyman devri belgeleri," 121–27. Ağır discusses evidence that the Venetian bailo might have resided in the city as late as 1567, while Yerasimos takes 1540 as the latest date when the bailo's presence in the city proper is noted. Ağır, "İstanbul'un Eski ʿVenedik Ticaret Kolonisi'nin," 91–92; Yerasimos and Bacqué-Grammont, "La résidence du Baile de Venise à Balıkpazarı."

60. Since Jewish communities were largely settled in the port area, this may well be where he went. Harff, *Pilgrimage*, 244; Ibn Battuta, *Travels in Asia and Africa*, 160.

61. In these documents the word *zuḳāḳ* was also used to denote the paved streets of Galata; apart from the commercial area, such streets are recorded only in two locations within the walled city, one near Hagia Sophia and the other near the citadel at the Golden Gate. As the two ends of the city's main artery, both were likely locations for paved streets. *Fatih Sultan Mehmed'in vakfiyeleri*; BBA MM 19. For references to paved streets in travel accounts of the period, see Yerasimos, "Galata á travers les récits de voyage," 117.

62. Since this is a detached page and the only one in the volume that deals with this topic, it is not possible to know whether other streets were involved as well. See the account book of royal and vizierial endowments dating to between 891 and 898/1486 and 1493, the page entitled "The pavements to be built and to be restored at the present time" (Şimdiki ḥālde bināʿ olıcak ve meremmet olıcak ḳaldırımları beyān eder), between fols. 79 and 80 in the *Muḥāsebe icmāl defteri*, M.C. O.91. Gökbilgin and Barkan have published relevant parts of this volume in their studies of royal and vizierial endowments and property, in Edirne and in Istanbul respectively. Gökbilgin, *XV.–XVI. asırlarda Edirne ve Paşa livası*; Barkan, "Ayasofya Cami'i ve Eyüb Türbesinin 1489–1491" and "Fatih Cami ve Imareti Tesislerinin 1489–1490." There are several such detached pages in the book; the paper and the

handwriting of this one suggest that it is contemporaneous with the rest of the document. For the paving of streets in Ottoman cities, see Orhonlu, "Mesleki bir teşekkül olarak kaldırımcılık." Orhonlu notes that the earliest documents for the paving of streets are from the middle of the sixteenth century. For a reference to such a newly laid-out street, see the section on Mehmed's foundation in part 1 of chapter 2.

63. Paul Magdalino has suggested that the east-west *emboloi* mentioned in twelfth- and thirteenth-century descriptions of Pisan, Genoese, and Venetian quarters along the Golden Horn might have been parts of the same street mentioned in the *Patria*; Magdalino, "Maritime Neighborhoods of Constantinople," 224.

64. The same gate is referred to as Zindan Kapı in later documents.

65. André Raymond has argued in the context of Arab cities under Ottoman rule that the formation of "below-the-citadel" areas of trade had to do with the desire of the alien rulers to control commercial activity. Hence, he noted, the commercial center was located close to the governor's residence. However, since Anatolian towns featured a similar configuration, the proximity of the locus of rule to the locus of commerce was clearly deemed important for the efficient supervision of commercial activity, regardless of issues of ethnicity and alien rule. This is also reflected in Mehmed's order, as noted by Kritovoulos, for the construction of the bedestan near the (first) palace; Raymond, *Grandes villes arabes,* 170, 194–95. The *ḳalʿa* did not necessarily refer to the citadel in all cities where a *taḫt al-ḳalʿa* existed; in Bursa and Edirne, it simply meant the walled city.

66. BBA MM 19 (*Ayaṣofya vaḳfı taḥrīr defteri,* A.H. 895), fol 9a. The street running along the city walls, the masjid, the bath, and a number of smaller plots owned by, or belonging to individuals are noted as boundary markers of the *ṣaḥn.* There is no indication in any of the documents that the shops were Byzantine or Venetian structures.

67. "Taḫt al-ḳalʿa meydānı," BBA MD 67, p. 11.

68. No khan or weighing station was present here, and the edicts that specify locations where goods were to be initially brought into the city, compiled in Mehmed's *ḳānūnnāme,* make no reference to this area.

69. Suggested independently by Mundell-Mango, "The Commercial Map of Constantinople," 205–6, and Magdalino, "Maritime Neighborhoods of Constantinople," 221. Magdalino refers to Albrecht Berger's discussion of the Leomakellon, a meat market popularly associated with Leo I; Berger, "Zur Topographie der Ufergegend am Goldenen Horn in der byzantinischen Zeit." For the fourteenth-century account, see Majeska, *Russian Travelers,* 150.

70. Tommasso Bertelè has argued that the Balkapan Hanı was the palace of the Venetian bailo in the Byzantine period. The Yemiş Kapanı (weighing station for fruits and vegetables) of late-fifteenth- and early-sixteenth-century documents, it has also been argued, was this building. It is not possible to establish more than the pre-Ottoman origins of the structure; Bertelè, *Il palazzo degli ambasciatori di Venezia a Costantinopoli,* 23–28; Müller-Wiener, *Bildlexikon zur Topographie Istanbuls,* 343. For a recent survey and discussion of the building, see Ağır, "İstanbul'un Eski 'Venedik Ticaret Kolonisi'nin," 209–23. For the House with the Lion, see BBA MM 19, fol. 10a. For the use of the lion of Saint Mark on public and palatial buildings in other Venetian colonies, see Georgopoulou, *Venice's Mediterranean Colonies,* 79–103, passim.

71. Istanbul Atatürk Library M.C. O.64 (*Ayaṣofya vaḳfı cibāyet defteri,* A.H. 926), fol. 130v. The garden is within the quarter of the Timurtaş mosque, which replaced the quarter of the House with the Lion of the earliest documents, and belonged to Mahmud, the son of Piri Pasha.

72. BBA AE Mehmed II, 70. This must be the same structure noted by a Russian pilgrim in the earlier part of the sixteenth century; Majeska, *Russian Travelers,* 353.

73. August Mordtmann noted, without referring to a particular source, that this was the S. Akindini; Mordtmann, *Esquisse topographique de Constantinople,* 46. Aygül Ağır has suggested that this church lay to the east of the Drungarii/Odun Gate and therefore could not have been the masjid; Ağır, "İstanbul'un Eski 'Venedik Ticaret Kolonisi'nin," 74–75. Selma Özkoçak refers to a firman of 1562–63 that gives the measures 248 *zirāʿ* for the Hacı Halil mosque and 788 *zirāʿ* for the sixteenth-century building; Özkoçak, "Urban Development of Istanbul," 89.

74. For an evaluation of the baths built in this period, see chapter 3. Gülru Necipoğlu has established that the construction of the Rüstem Pasha started in 1562, that is, after the drawing of the Lorichs panorama; G. Necipoğlu, *Age of Sinan,* 321.

75. For the survey of the building that preceded its restoration, see Aktuğ and Erzen, "Bir 15. yüzyıl yapısı olan Tahtakale Hamamında uygulanan bazı yapım teknikleri."

76. Ağır, "İstanbul'un Eski 'Venedik Ticaret Kolonisi'nin," 61. Albrecht Berger has also drawn attention to ancient features of the street network of this area; Berger, "Streets and Public Spaces in Constantinople."

77. Barkan, "Fatih Cami ve İmareti Tesislerinin 1489–1490," 306–7.

78. For an economic and social history of the Istanbul bedestan, see İnalcık, "Hub of the City." For an architectural survey of the building, see Ayverdi, *Osmanlı miʿmârîsinde Fâtih devri, 855–886 (1451–1481),* 4:557–74. Ayverdi's reconstruction includes the colonnaded streets that surrounded the building, which are omitted in most studies of the bedestan (and excluded in the published plans) and therefore have not been discussed in terms of the design of the bedestan-markets complex. For studies on the Ottoman bedestans in general, see Eyice, "Les 'bedestens' dans l'architecture turque," and Kreiser, "Bedesten-Bauten im Osmanischen Reich." For a comparative architectural study of the Ottoman bedestans, see Cezar, *Typical Commercial Buildings,* 159–250. For Roman prototypes, see Macdonald, *The Architecture of the Roman Empire,* 1:86–88; for medieval Islamic prototypes, see Sims, "Trade and Travel," 106–9.

79. Gilles, *Antiquities of Constantinople,* 30–31; Chesneau, *Le voyage de Monsieur d'Aramon,* 34–35. See also Nicolay, *Dans l'empire de Soliman le Magnifique,* 140, in which the author notes the difference of scale between

the bedestan and the surrounding markets.

80. The building's arrangement, with interior storage spaces facing the courtyard and exterior shops facing outward on all four sides, is similar to that of several of the bedestans built earlier in Ottoman cities, notably the bedestan of Bursa built by Bayezid I and that of Edirne built by Mehmed I.

81. The shops that now occupy much of the interior and leave only narrow lanes between blocks were built only in the 1950s.

82. He also wrote that in parts of the building merchants had widened their benches, making it difficult for three persons to walk side by side; Dernschwam, *İstanbul ve Anadolu'ya seyahat günlüğü*, 130–31. Gilles also noted the temporary nature of the warehouses in the bedestan, describing the two-doored presses that were attached to the walls of the building and were removable at pleasure; Gilles, *Antiquities of Constantinople*, 31. Ayverdi wrote in the early 1970s that the shops in the building at that time had been built some fifteen years earlier; Ayverdi, *Osmanlı miʿmârîsinde Fâtih devri, 855–886 (1451–1481)*, 4:561.

83. The Galata bedestan was a later-sixteenth-century structure built on Byzantine foundations at the request of the city's residents, as attested to by a firman carrying the date 1585. Özkoçak, "Urban Development of Istanbul," 99 n. 234; Refik, *On altıncı asırda Istanbul hayatı (1553–1591)*, 133–34. For loggias in Venetian colonial settlements, see Georgopoulou, *Venice's Mediterranean Colonies*, 79ff.

84. Ergin, "Bedesten," in *İslâm ansiklopedisi*, 2:441; Özdeş, *Türk çarşıları*, 46–47; Ayverdi, *Osmanlı miʿmârîsinde Fâtih devri, 855–886 (1451–1481)*, 4:558–60; Cezar, *Typical Commercial Buildings*, 174–78.

85. One could add to Ayverdi's example other bird motifs on at least two fifteenth-century buildings, the Kazlıçeşme (Fountain with the Goose), outside the Golden Gate, and the masjid of the architect Sinan, whose relief of doves is also of Byzantine origin. But the point here is not to establish the number of spoliated Byzantine bird reliefs in Ottoman Istanbul. None

of these images carries the significance of the eagle motif, the imperial symbol of Byzantium.

86. The imperial symbol of the Palaeologan dynasty was the double-headed eagle. The eagle, as is well known, was also a royal symbol of the Seljuks of Rum, an image whose form and meaning the Seljuks possibly appropriated from the neighboring Byzantine Empire. Konya, soon to become Ottoman territory, and other royal Seljuk sites often featured images of eagles, inscribed "sultan," over city gates and walls and on palatial buildings. Unlike the Seljuks, the Ottomans did not use the royal image consistently or for long. For a discussion of this imagery and its royal associations for the Seljuk rule, see Redford, "Seljuks of Rum." For images of the Ottoman city that feature the double-headed eagle, see figure 114 and plate 6, discussed in chapter 3.

87. Needless to say, Ergin's familiarity was through an intellectual, rather than contextual, channel. That the image did lose its connotative power once the Byzantine past lost its immediacy is evident in Evliya Çelebi's description of the "formidable bird opening its wings" over the eastern gate of the bedestan, which he interpreted as an allegory of profit and trade; *Evliya Çelebi Seyahatnamesi*, bk. 1, fol. 200v. The eagle relief is visible in a seventeenth-century album painting that depicts the bedestan and commercial transactions around it; Taeschner, *Alt-Stambuler Hof- und Volksleben*, pl. 3.

88. Ayverdi's study suggests that originally the eastern side also had such a portico; Ayverdi, *Osmanlı miʿmârîsinde Fâtih devri, 855–886 (1451–1481)*, 4:563–68. Gilles relates having seen the "old basilica" thanks to the fire that burned down the whole bazaar except for the two basilicas, which could not be viewed earlier because of the "shops and public houses" surrounding them. He notes "two additional buildings like wings joining the main building, each of which was divided into sixty apartments, which were all arched overhead." He also says that the building was covered with brickwork and leaded at the top, which may indicate that the shops on the

exterior and the arcades were originally covered with roof tiles, while the domes of the main hall were covered with lead; Gilles, *Antiquities of Constantinople*, 30–31.

89. Çelik, *The Remaking of Istanbul*, 4.

90. On *emboloi* in the Byzantine city, see Mundell-Mango, "The Commercial Map of Constantinople," 194–97, 203–4. According to Chrysoloras, the porticoes and arcades in the city about a decade before its fall provided protection from rain and sun; Chrysoloras, "Comparison of Old and New Rome."

91. BBA MM 19 (*Ayaṣofya vaḳfı taḥrīr defteri*, A.H. 895), fols. 24a–25a.

92. For the Mahmud Pasha foundation, see chapter 2.

93. Bursa's commercial district also had a *Gelincik bāzārı*, the streets running from the two sides of the Geyve Khan, built by Haci Ivaz Pasha in the early fifteenth century; Dalsar, *Türk sanayi ve ticaret*, 256–57.

94. That the flea market should be in the immediate vicinity of the bedestan is not surprising. In his analysis of the Cairo Geniza documents, S. D. Goitein draws attention to the importance of the flea market in the medieval city, where exchange of used clothing was part of everyday life, a practice difficult to imagine in view of modern habits of consumption; Goitein, *Mediterranean Society*, 1:151.

95. Seventy-two shops were adjacent to it, and eighteen shops across from it; *Fatih Sultan Mehmedʾin vakfiyeleri*, 7.

96. *Zwei Stiftsurkunden des Sultan Mehmed II. Fatih*, 22.

97. These possibly constituted a later addition, as they are not mentioned in the first waqfiyya. The han is noted in the second waqfiyya as lying in the vicinity of the Old Palace, and in the 926/1520 survey as flanking the small (Sandal) bedestan; one of the surveyors seems to have confused two buildings; Istanbul Atatürk Library M.C. O.64 (*Ayaṣofya vaḳfı cibāyet defteri*, A.H. 926), fol. 22a.

98. Anhegger and İnalcık, *Ḳānūnnāme-i sulṭanī ber mūceb-i ʿörf-i ʿoṣmānī*, 41–44, nos. 31, 32; 46–47, no. 34. This also explains the khan built

alongside the bedestan of Ankara by Mahmud Pasha. On commercial and accommodation functions of urban khans in the Islamic world, see Raymond, *Grandes villes arabes*. Both works emphasize the role of these buildings in long-distance and wholesale trade.

99. Gilles, *Antiquities of Constantinople*, 30–31. For the restoration of shops, on the other hand, and for the repair of the Khan of Süleyman Pasha, expenses for stone and stone workers are also mentioned; Barkan, "Ayasofya Camiʾi ve Eyüb Türbesinin 1489–1491," 362–68.

100. La Broquière, *Le voyage d'outremer*, 83–84.

101. Dernschwam, *İstanbul ve Anadoluʾya seyahat günlüğü*, 130–31.

102. Taşköprizade relates that Mehmed heard about the *mevlana*'s drinking wine in the bedestan and spilling his impure drink on the Muslims; he was given an ʿulūfe of ten *akçe* a day upon quitting his habit; Mecdi Efendi, *Tercüme-i şaḳāyıḳ*, 232–33. (According to biographers of poets, rather than the biographer of scholars, the encounter with the ruler failed to persuade the poet to change his lifestyle, as he continued to spend his days in the taverns of Taht al-kalʿa; Kınalızade Hasan Çelebi, *Tezkiretüʾş-şuʿarā*, 923–24; Latifi, *Tezkiretüʾş-şuʿarā ve tabsıratüʾn-nuzamā*, 504–5.) Stories of this popular poet are many in sixteenth-century biographies of Ottoman poets, the most fantastic recounting his recourse to an enema in an attempt to get alcohol into his system. On Melihi and his poetry, see Tekin, "Fatih devri Türk edebiyatı," 192–93.

103. Angiolello and Lezze, *Historia turchesca (1300–1514)*, 119–20.

104. "ve Eski Sarāy altında bir caʿdde ulu yol var idi ki mecmūʿmā ḥalḳuʾllāh ol aradan gelür geçer idi"; Küçük Abdal, *Velāyetnāme-i Sulṭān Otman*, fol. 111a.

105. For an evaluation of Otman Baba's hagiography within the context of fifteenth-century religio-political currents in the Ottoman realm, see İnalcık, "Dervish and Sultan."

106. A dervish known as Şücāʿ Dervişi, also there with his *abdāllar*, becomes envious of the popularity of Otman Baba and rushes to the

New Mosque to inform the ulema of this act of heresy. After debates and negotiations involving the ulema, the sultan, and the dervish, Otman Baba ultimately exercises his powers over the elements to convince the people of Istanbul that this was in fact a holiday; Küçük Abdal, *Velāyetnāme-i Sulṭān Otman*, fols. 111a–112a.

107. The market was referred to as the Mahmud Pasha *dükkānları* (the shops of Mahmud Pasha). It comprised 265 shops laid out on a quadrangular plot of land. The survey of the Hagia Sophia endowment dating to A.H. 895 records the "suk with four sides, sections of it situated across from other parts, and, in addition to this, the shops built to the back of it and those built around it." The 220 shops that the surveys note were returned to the Mahmud Pasha endowment by an imperial edict during the reign of Bayezid II refer in all probability to the same market.

108. Since the layout of the Sandal Bedestanı suggests that it occupied a plot of land whose boundaries had already been determined by surrounding plots, it is possible that this bedestan replaced the grand vizier's market. The construction date of the second, small bedestan of Istanbul, called the Sandal after the type of silk traded there, is unclear. The earliest mention of a second bedestan is in the 926/1520 survey, where "the small bedestan in which the cotton merchants reside" is registered. Ayverdi dated it to the reign of Mehmed and argued that it was the quadrangular suk mentioned in the surveys. This seems far-fetched, for it is based only on the reference to a four-sided structure in the area. Kreiser notes that Ayverdi's argument is at the best plausible, taking the reference to the small bedestan in the 926/1520 survey of the Ayasofya foundation as a *terminus ante quem* for the building. İnalcık, noting that the 926/1520 document refers to the building as the home of the cotton merchants, as opposed to the silk merchants who gave the building its later name, and noting the small number of shops registered (sixty inside and twelve outside), asserts that the present structure replaced a former, smaller building; Ayverdi, *Osmanlı miʿmârîsinde Fâtih*

devri, 855–886 (1451–1481), 4:568–69; Kreiser, "Bedesten-Bauten im Osmanischen Reich," 384–85; İnalcık, "Hub of the City," 4–5. For a discussion of Mahmud Pasha's commercial establishment, see chapter 3.

109. Some of the commercial properties endowed by these and other individuals are listed as forming the boundaries of the Mehmed II endowment. Others are listed in the waqf survey of 953/1546, where all nonroyal foundations within the walled city are registered. The nature of the builders' (the sultan's and the grandees' in most cases) involvement in the commercial life of the particular locations at which they endowed buildings and the particular trades and crafts their buildings served is not known with certainty. For the foundations of Mahmud Pasha and Murad Pasha, see part 2 of chapter 2. Smaller foundations, mostly endowed in the later decades of the fifteenth century, are discussed in chapter 4.

110. Royal endowment deeds and surveys are the primary sources of information on the urban fabric and growth in Galata in the decades following the city's fall. The account that follows in the text is largely based on these documents, on İnalcık's discussion of Mehmed's policies regarding the Genoese colony and of the development of Galata under Ottoman rule, and on Kate Fleet's work on Ottoman-Genoese commercial relations through the reign of Mehmed II. An important source for İnalcık's study is the earliest land survey of the city, dating to 1455, which he is preparing for publication and which has not been available to this author. A question not addressed by İnalcık, and one whose answer would be useful in evaluating the material environment of commerce in both cities, is the character and dimensions of the commercial activity in Galata in relation to Constantinopolitan trade in the same period; İnalcık, "Ottoman Galata." Kate Fleet surveys the consequences of the fall of Constantinople with regard to Ottoman-Genoese commercial relations and concludes that, contrary to received opinion, the volume and nature of Genoese trade did not change radically during the reign of Mehmed and that, while the volume of trade before and after the conquest

remains largely unknown, there is no evidence for a change in Ottoman policy regarding Genoese trading establishment in Galata. Fleet also surveys increasing state control of commodity flow and imposition of state monopolies, actions that marked Mehmed II's commercial policy toward the Italian trading establishments within Ottoman territory; Fleet, *European and Islamic Trade in the Early Ottoman State,* 122–33.

111. İnalcık traces the development of Galata from 1455 (the date of the first property survey) through the early sixteenth century, demonstrating the restoration of the city to its former prosperity; İnalcık, "Ottoman Galata."

112. The Galata bedestan popularly attributed to Mehmed is a later-sixteenth-century structure, not mentioned in any fifteenth- or early-sixteenth-century document. See note 83 above. It was placed at the commercial heart of the city, in the Lonca neighborhood, near the khan built by Rüstem Pasha in the 1550s or 1560s.

113. The khan is mentioned in the first waqfiyya of Mehmed's foundation; *Fatih Sultan Mehmed'in vakfiyeleri,* 32. For the complex of Rum Mehmed Pasha, see "An Ottoman Monument on the Asian Shore," in part 2 of chapter 2.

114. As precedents, consider early Christian Rome, with its first shrines at the edges or outside of the urban core, the host of Muslim shrines established at the edges of medieval Anatolian cities, and the creation of a shrine over the discovered grave of the Sufi scholar İbn al-Arabi in suburban Salihiyya following the Ottoman conquest of Damascus.

115. Parts of the deed have been reproduced in *Fatih Mehmed II vakfiyeleri,* 336–39.

116. İnalcık, "Eyüp projesi." Yerasimos too stresses the legitimization rationale that informed the discovery and the construction, but he argues that the discovery of the grave was linked not to the conquest but to the decision to move the capital from Edirne to Constantinople, and dates the discovery to around 1458–59. He disregards, however, the presence of a convent near the grave already in 1457; Yerasimos, "Osmanlı İstanbul'unun Kuruluşu."

117. Through a careful study of the sources on the subject, Wittek

reconstructed the fifteenth-century debate on the location of the grave and argued that present-day Ayvansaray could have been the alternative site for the grave of the Arab warrior; Wittek, "Ayvansaray."

118. İdris Bidlisi, *Heşt behişt,* fols. 49b–51b.

119. Wittek, and more recently Yerasimos have driven attention to conflations in names and practices; Wittek, "Ayvansaray"; Yerasimos, *La fondation de Constantinople et de Sainte-Sophie,* 172. SS. Cosmas and Damian was most likely on the hill above Eyüp, where substantial Middle Byzantine substructures have been identified. The "small church" on the site of the Ayyub mausoleum remains unidentified. My thanks to Robert Ousterhout for driving my attention to the disparate locations of SS. Cosmas and Damian, and the Ayyub complex. For the identification of the site with that of the church and monastery of SS. Cosmas and Damian, see Janin, *Constantinople byzantine,* 456.

120. Yerasimos, in his study of the Hagia Sophia legends, studied the debate within the context of the ghazi reaction to the establishment of the imperial state with Constantinople as its locus; Yerasimos, *La fondation de Constantinople et de Sainte-Sophie,* 172–74.

121. *Menāḳıb-ı Aḳşemseddīn,* 132–36; Mecdi Efendi, *Tercüme-i şaḳāyıḳ,* 244–48; VGMA 625:141.

122. No clear construction date has been set for the mausoleum. Wittek's contention that it was there in 861/1457 is not completely convincing, since the term in the relevant document of that date, *ravzat,* might mean the mausoleum but more likely denotes the site only; Wittek, "Ayvansaray," 521 n. 1; *Fatih Mehmed II vakfiyeleri,* 336–38. Ayvansarayi cites an inscription with the date 863/1458–59 for the mosque, which I consider the date of completion of the building, and I assume that the other buildings of the complex were also built around this time; Ayvansarayi, *Garden of the Mosques,* 244. For a survey of the buildings and a reconstruction of the mosque, see Ayverdi, *Osmanlı miʿmârîsinde Fâtih devri, 855–886 (1451–1481),* 3:348–56. For

a recent reconstruction of the mosque that improves on that of Ayverdi, see Kuran, "Eyüp Külliyesi."

123. For a discussion of the establishment of the complex and Ottoman ceremonial centered around it, see G. Necipoğlu, "Dynastic Imprints on the Cityscape." For a discussion of the Ottoman shrine within the context of the making of a cult of saints, see Berktay, "Azizler, cismani kalıntılar, haclar, yatırlar."

124. Angiolello, *Viaggio di Negroponte,* 26–27.

125. Barkan, "Ayasofya Camiʾi ve Eyüb Türbesinin 1489–1491," 373–79.

126. Wittek, "Ayvansaray," 525.

127. Kuran's reconstruction improves on the earlier and widely accepted reconstruction by Ayverdi, who in typical inflation of fifteenth-century achievements had added two half domes to the lateral sides of the prayer hall. Evliya, however, mentions only a single small half dome over the mihrab niche, and "strong arches supporting the dome."

128. Kuran notes that the first scheme would make this resemble the Davud Pasha mosque, constructed in the 1480s. For the Rum Mehmed Pasha mosque, see chapter 2. The use of this second scheme in a number of fifteenth- and early-sixteenth-century mosques (those of Mehmed II, Rum Mehmed Pasha, Atik Ali Pasha) suggests that it could have been used in this earliest monumental Ottoman mosque in the city.

129. For Hagia Sophia in the Ottoman period and its impact on Ottoman religious architecture, see G. Necipoğlu, "The Life of an Imperial Monument," and Ahunbay and Ahunbay, "Structural Influence of Hagia Sophia."

130. The formalization of architectural hierarchies in the hands of Sinan and his dynastic patrons in the mid–sixteenth century would limit the use of these architectural elements to dynastic monuments only; G. Necipoğlu, *Age of Sinan.*

131. Since the building is depicted with two minarets in the Düsseldorf view drawn ca. 1481, and in Bidlisi's narrative, the addition was possibly made soon after the completion of the building (fig. 111).

132. Tanman, "Eyüp Sultan Külliyesi."

133. Kuran, "Eyüp Külliyesi"; Ayverdi, *Osmanlı miʿmârîsinde Fâtih devri, 855–886 (1451–1481)*, 3:348–56.

134. Having had access to an earlier (perhaps the original) waqfiyya, Bidlisi also indicates the wages and numbers of the employees of the foundation. The figures he gives and those in the account book of the foundation of 96/1491 are comparable, while those in the 990/1582 deed are considerably higher: 2-*akçe* stipends for 9 students and a 28-*akçe*/day wage for the *müderris* in the 896/1491 document; 2-*akçe* stipends for 10 students and a 36-*akçe*/day wage for the *müderris* in Bidlisi; 11 students and a 50-*akçe*/day wage for the *müderris* in the 990/1582 deed. Barkan, "Ayasofya Camiʾi ve Eyüb Türbesinin 1489–1491," 375–76; İdris Bidlisi, *Heşt behişt*, fol. 51b. Originally, the bath and the land around the tomb were the only income-generating properties in the vicinity of the foundation, the rest being villages in Thrace and western Anatolia, as seen in the account book of 896/1491; Barkan, "Ayasofya Camiʾi ve Eyüb Türbesinin 1489–1491," 373–79. In the waqfiyya of the Ayyub foundation dating to 990/1582, a large number of houses and shops in the township (*ḳasaba*) of Ayyub are endowed, which attest to the growth of the endowment as well as to the urban development in the area within a century; "Eyyup vakfiyesinin faksimilesi," 291–94. Thus, before or at the time the deed was drawn, the foundation was considerably enlarged, with a larger number of employees and higher wages. The growth in the endowment corresponded to additions to the complex and its income-generating property. This makes the deed a less relevant document for the earlier history of the foundation.

135. For discussions of the site in the context of later Ottoman ceremonial, see Kafadar, "Eyüpʾte kılıç kuşanma törenleri," and Vatin, "Aux origines du pèlerinage à Eyüp des sultans ottomans."

136. "Padişah gah gah Ebu Ayyuba ziyarete gider iken," Taşköprizade writes. The sultan would stop at the house of Mevlana Hüsamüddin, located on his way to the site, to drink the sherbet offered to him. Taşköprizade writes that the source of this story was a descendant of the *mevlana;* Mecdi Efendi, *Tercüme-i şaḳāyıḳ,* 210–12.

137. İnalcık, "The Policy of Mehmed II," 237.

138. Parts of the deed have been reproduced in *Fatih Mehmed II vakfiyeleri,* 336–39.

139. Angiolello, *Viaggio di Negroponte,* 26–27.

140. İdris Bidlisi, *Heşt behişt,* fol. 50b.

141. Taşköprizade writes that Mevlana Kestelli, Alaüddin Arabi, Alaüddin Ali, among others, were buried in the mosque graveyard; Mecdi Efendi, *Tercüme-i şaḳāyıḳ,* 166, 176, 184, 187, 196. Süheyl Ünver cites a narrative of the Abu Ayyub story dating from the mid–sixteenth century that includes a further list of scholars and high-ranking members of the religious elite buried in the graveyard, among them a professor of Mehmed II, Mevlana Kırimi, Babazade Efendi, Mevlana Hatibzade, Mevlana Samsunizade; Ünver, *İlim ve sanat bakımından Fatih devri notları,* 50–52. A prosopographic index based on Evliya Çelebi and Ayvansarayi is added to Bacqué-Grammont's study of the tombs in Eyüp; Taşköprizade and the anonymous manuscript add substantially to this list, particularly the names of those buried there in the late fifteenth and early sixteenth centuries; Bacqué-Grammont, "Eyüp mezarlıklarının incelenmesi üzerine düşünceler," 70–105.

142. The waqfiyya of Bayezid II, VGMA 2113:195–203.

143. Preziosi, *Rethinking Art History,* 123–55.

Chapter 2

1. In his translation of the Greek text, Charles Riggs has rendered the word *kosmein* as "to beautify" and "to adorn," and the word *agallein* as "to embellish." It is possible to expand this vocabulary somewhat, as *kosmein* connotes "ordering" as well as "beautifying," while *agallein* connotes "glorifying" and "paying honor to God" in addition to "embellishing." I am grateful to Christoph Lüthy for comparing the original Greek text with the English translation.

2. Kritovoulos, *History of Mehmed the Conqueror,* 140–41.

3. "Such was his enthusiasm that he could not wait to begin the work; he himself designed the general layout of the new town, indicating the position of the market square, the number of temples to be built, and what gods they should serve." Arrian, *Campaigns of Alexander,* 149.

4. Tursun Beg, *History of Mehmed the Conqueror,* fol. 59v; Muʿali, *Hünkārnāme,* fol. 8v.

5. *Zwei Stiftsurkunden des Sultan Mehmed II. Fatih,* 6, and most of the chronicles of the period.

6. Christine Smith discusses the impact of the ekphrasis tradition on architectural writing in the Renaissance in her *Architecture in the Culture of Early Humanism.* For examples of fifteenth-century ekphrastic texts, see Cardinal Bessarion's description of the Palace of Trebizond, translated by Cyril Mango, and Manuel Chrysoloras's "Comparison of Old and New Rome," a letter addressed to John Palaeologus comparing the cities of Rome and Constantinople, translated and discussed by Christine Smith. Mango, *Art of the Byzantine Empire,* 252–53; Smith, *Architecture in the Culture of Early Humanism,* 171–215.

7. Christine Smith has demonstrated that notions of urban order and architectural value in the early Renaissance were to a significant extent attributable to late Byzantine notions of architectural value, while John Onians has convincingly argued that the Constantinople-educated Francesco Filelfo had an important role in the making of Filarete's treatise. Smith, *Architecture in the Culture of Early Humanism;* Onians, "Alberti and Filarete."

8. By the middle of the sixteenth century, with the addition of several other large building complexes, the number of the city's districts was to reach thirteen; İnalcık, "Istanbul," 228–30; idem, "The Policy of Mehmed II," 237. İnalcık's highly influential studies have shaped the readings of many other historians who have worked on Istanbul's urban structure and institutions. There is no evidence, however, that these foundations were conceived of as centers of districts. The

first extant document that orders the city within the framework of *nevāḥi*, each with a number of neighborhoods, is the waqf survey of 953/1546. It was not the conditions of the still sparsely populated Istanbul but only those of a grown city that necessitated the ordering of neighborhoods within larger units of urban administration. The 953/1546 survey, based on an earlier one no longer extant, is discussed in detail in chapter 4 as a source for the fifteenth-century city.

9. For the law code of Mehmed II, see Özcan, "Fâtiḥ'in Teşkilât Kanunnamesi." For an evaluation of Mehmed's own buildings, his new palace and mosque complex, as accommodating the hierarchical structure devised in the *ḳānūnnāme*, see G. Necipoğlu, *Architecture, Ceremonial, and Power*, 15–16. For a study of the transformation of the vizierial post under Mehmed, see Stavrides, *Sultan of Vezirs*, esp. 37–70.

10. Edward Mitchell also discussed the order of the sultan, as recorded by Kritovoulos, as a central source on the construction of the capital. He did not, however, question the text for its implications concerning architecture and urban space; Mitchell, "Institution and Destitution," 248–52.

11. In her *Architecture, Ceremonial, and Power: The Topkapı Palace in the Fifteenth and Sixteenth Centuries*, based on a study of its architecture and contemporary primary sources, Gülru Necipoğlu locates the building within its fifteenth- and sixteenth-century aesthetic, cultural, and political context.

12. There is to date no satisfactory reconstruction of the fifteenth-century layout of the palace. I use here the plan proposed by Sedad Eldem and Feridun Akozan, although this too does not completely correspond to the textual information on the palace through the fifteenth century.

13. Referred to as a *loggia* in fifteenth- and early-sixteenth-century Italian sources, this is the building known today as the Chamber of Petitions. In addition to this name (*'arż otası*), the building was referred to in the sixteenth-century Ottoman sources as the "inner audience hall" (*dīvanḫāne-i enderūnī*) and the "royal council hall of the interior" (*dīvān-ı*

ḫāṣṣa-i enderūnī). Unlike other royal buildings within the inner court whose functions were altered, the audience hall rebuilt by Süleyman between 1526 and 1528 retained its original function. For the construction, contemporary descriptions, and Süleyman's new building, see G. Necipoğlu, *Architecture, Ceremonial, and Power*, 96–101.

14. For architectural evidence on the location and layout of the harem in the fifteenth century, see Ayverdi, *Osmanlı mi'mârîsinde Fâtih devri, 855–886 (1451–1481)*, 4:732–36; for contemporary sources and the organization of the harem in this era, see G. Necipoğlu, *Architecture, Ceremonial, and Power*, 159–62. What is known of the boundaries of the fifteenth-century palace suggests that the harem was possibly organized around another trapezoidal courtyard adjacent to the third courtyard. See Ayverdi, *Osmanlı mi'mârîsinde Fâtih devri, 855–886 (1451–1481)*, vol. 4, fig. 1039; Eldem and Akozan, *Topkapı Sarayı*, plan 3.

15. Two of the belvedere towers were replaced by the Baghdad and the circumcision kiosks built in the sixteenth and seventeenth centuries. One of the towers, today referred to as Hekimbaşı, or Lala tower, remains; G. Necipoğlu, *Architecture, Ceremonial, and Power*, 183–89; Eldem and Akozan, *Topkapı Sarayı*, pl. 91.

16. The first representational buildings around the Hippodrome were built, not during the reign of Mehmed, but during that of his successor. The narrative of Mehmed throwing his maze at the Serpent Column to the express discontent of the patriarch Gennadios, and the narrative of Otman Baba being brought there upon capture by authorities, on the other hand, suggest that the significance of the Hippodrome as an integral part of the city center was recognized from early on; Lokman bin Seyyid Hüseyin, *Hünernâme*, fols. 161v–162r; Küçük Abdal, *Velāyetnāme-i Sulṭān Otman* 94v–97r.

17. Several versions of the *Patria*, in Turkish and Persian translations as well as in the original Greek, circulated in fifteenth-century Constantinople. Two main texts, a partial translation from Greek and a rewriting loosely

based on it, offered different views on Byzas and the city's foundations, while both lay emphasis on monumental and complex underground structures that were attributed to the city's eponymous founder; Şemsüddin Karamani, *Tercüme-i Tārīḫ-i Cāmi'i Ayāṣofyā; Die altosmanischen anonymen Chroniken*. On the *Patria*, see Dagron, *Constantinople imaginaire*; on the Ottoman traditions on the foundation of Constantinople, see Yerasimos, *La fondation de Constantinople et de Sainte-Sophie*, and chapter 3. On versions of the Greek text held at Mehmed II's palace library, see Ebersolt, *Mission archéologique de Constantinople*, 55–65; Deissmann, *Forschungen und Funde im Serai*, 45–46, 58; Raby, "El Gran Turco," 386.

18. Gülru Necipoğlu has discussed other reasons for moving the palace from the center of the city to its edge: ideals of imperial seclusion, concerns for security, the prestige of the site, among others; G. Necipoğlu, *Architecture, Ceremonial, and Power*, 4–22.

19. While the accepted opinion on these pieces was that they had been transported to the palace to be used as spolia in later constructions, Julian Raby has convincingly argued that these imperial sarcophagi and fragments of ancient monuments, all discovered within the second courtyard, were deliberately collected and exhibited here; Raby, "El Gran Turco," 222–28. For sarcophagi discovered in the palace grounds, see Mango, "Three Imperial Byzantine Sarcophagi." For a catalogue of the sarcophagi and architectural and sculptural fragments, see Tezcan, *Topkapı Sarayı ve çevresinin Bizans devri arkeolojisi*.

20. Gilles, *Antiquities of Constantinople*, 97–98.

21. Cited in Tezcan, *Topkapı Sarayı ve çevresinin*, 165.

22. Kritovoulos, *History of Mehmed the Conqueror*, 207.

23. Discussed in chapter 3.

24. On the gates, see G. Necipoğlu, *Architecture, Ceremonial, and Power*, 32–40, 50–52, 88–90; Raby, "El Gran Turco," 301; Eldem and Akozan, *Topkapı Sarayı*, pls. 21, 22, 31, 32, 33; Ayverdi, *Osmanlı mi'mârîsinde Fâtih devri, 855–886 (1451–1481)*, 4:695–704, 714–15.

25. Italian sources refer to the Chamber of Petitions as a loggia. Probably surrounded by a colonnade, the original audience hall might also have imparted an Italianate visual idiom to this space; Angiolello, *Viaggio di Negroponte*, 23; G. Necipoğlu, *Architecture, Ceremonial, and Power*, 97–98. The incongruity of the Italianate arcade of the treasury with the rest of the courtyard buildings, particularly as they were transformed during later centuries, has led to suggestions that the arcade may be a later, eighteenth-century addition. Both historical and archaeological evidence, however, confirm that the arcade has preserved its original structure while losing its original decorative revetment of mosaics, noted by Jean-Baptiste Tavernier in the later sixteenth century; Tavernier, *Nouvelle relation de l'intérieur du serail du grand seigneur*, 129–30; Ayverdi, *Osmanlı miʿmârîsinde Fâtih devri, 855–886 (1451–1481)*, 4:715–17.

26. Onians, *Bearers of Meaning*, 42–48, 150, 154.

27. On the pavilions, see Raby, "El Gran Turco," 295–99, and G. Necipoğlu, *Architecture, Ceremonial, and Power*, 210–17. Two other fifteenth-century pavilions in the outer gardens are noted in contemporary sources: the pavilion whose foundations and ground floor are below the present Mecidiye kiosk, and the Ishakiye kiosk built by the grand vizier İshak Pasha.

28. Chrysoloras, "Comparison of Old and New Rome."

29. G. Necipoğlu, *Architecture, Ceremonial, and Power*, 210.

30. La Broquière, *Le voyage d'outremer*, 187–89.

31. Modern sources refer to the tower in the Edirne palace as the Cihannüma kiosk. Ayverdi, who has drawn attention to the otherwise inexplicably bulky basement floor walls of the privy chamber, has suggested that the building might initially have been designed as a multistoried tower; Ayverdi, *Osmanlı miʿmârîsinde Fâtih devri, 855–886 (1451–1481)*, 4:682, figs. 1054a, b, d. For a plan of the basement level of the New Palace's two inner courtyards, see also Eldem and Akozan, *Topkapı Sarayı*, pl. 19. More recently, Ayda Arel has explored

Ayverdi's suggestion more broadly, demonstrating the centrality of multifunctional towers serving as treasury, audience hall, and belvedere in early Ottoman palaces. Arel locates the emergence of such structures to the rule of Murad II and traces the continued use of tower-palaces in the Ottoman world into the sixteenth century; Arel, "Cihannüma Kasrı." The correspondence in functions can also be traced to the denominations of the Edirne tower. Rifat Osman has noted that the tower was referred to with several names, among them Kasr-ı Padişahi (Royal Palace), Taht-ı Hümayun Kasrı (Palace of the Royal Throne), Cihannüma Kasrı (Belvedere Palace), Hasoda (Privy Chamber), and Hasoda Köşkü (Privy Chamber Kiosk); Rifat Osman, *Edirne Sarayı*, 69.

32. The "tower of justice" of the later centuries. Changes in the uses of the tower and the configuration of the council hall–treasury–tower complex are discussed in G. Necipoğlu, *Architecture, Ceremonial, and Power*, 84–86.

33. For the Topkapı's relation to other palatine traditions, see G. Necipoğlu, *Architecture, Ceremonial, and Power*, 242–58; idem, "An Outline of Shifting Paradigms." For an evaluation of late antique palaces in terms of urban context, see Ćurčić, "Late-Antique Palaces." On Timurid palaces, see O'Kane, "From Tents to Pavilions."

34. G. Necipoğlu, "An Outline of Shifting Paradigms," 12–19. Slobodan Ćurčić has drawn attention to the origins of the fortified urban palaces of the medieval Western world in late antique palatial enclosures; Ćurčić, "Late-Antique Palaces," 90.

35. The tower-punctuated enclosure linked Mehmed's New Palace to medieval citadel-palaces and from there back to military architecture. On the tower as an integral element of medieval palatial architecture of the Balkans, see Ćurčić and Hadjitryphonos, *Secular Medieval Architecture in the Balkans*, 213ff. On Ottoman uses of tower structures in palatial contexts, see Arel, "Cihannüma Kasrı." On the urban citadel-palace in the medieval Islamic world, see Bacharach, "Administrative Complexes, Palaces, and Citadels"; G. Necipoğlu, "An Outline of

Shifting Paradigms"; and Rabbat, *Citadel of Cairo*.

36. This is less visible today, particularly on the Golden Horn façade of the palace, where the opening of the third courtyard through replacement of towers with domed pavilions, and the expansion of the harem from the sixteenth century onward, have endowed the complex with a residential character that it did not have at the time of its foundation.

37. G. Necipoğlu, *Architecture, Ceremonial, and Power*; idem, "Framing the Gaze in Ottoman, Safavid, and Mughal Palaces."

38. These foundations and their links to the palace are discussed in part 2 of this chapter.

39. "Yapıldı ʿadl-u bezl erkānı üzre / Anuñla oldı İstānbūl maʿmūr"; Tursun Beg, *History of Mehmed the Conqueror*, 60v.

40. Kostof, *The City Shaped*, 165.

41. Scholarship has generally accepted that Mehmed's mosque was built on the same site as the Holy Apostles, following the early studies of Philipp Forchheimer, Josef Strzygowski, and Karl Wulzinger; Forchheimer and Strzygowski, *Die byzantinischen Wasserbehälter von Konstantinopel*; Wulzinger, *Die Apostelkirche und die Mehmedije zu Konstantinopel*. Contemporary and later Ottoman sources too note that the New Mosque was built on the site of the Holy Apostles; the remains of the Byzantine complex standing close to the new buildings were visible to an anonymous Greek author and to Bidlisi, both writing in the early decades of the sixteenth century. Albrecht Berger has disputed this, noting that the dimensions of the two structures and the adjoining mausolea were not comparable; Berger, "Streets and Public Spaces in Constantinople." Remains of a former structure were detected under the mosque in a recent radar survey, also supporting the hypothesis that the mosque was built on the site of the church; Yılmaz and Eser, "Ground-Penetrating Radar Surveys." The New Complex might have been built slightly to the southwest of the Holy Apostles complex, but this does not subtract from the symbolic significance of the new project in terms of its relation to the Byzantine legacy.

That both complexes occupied the summit of the peninsula's highest hill is without doubt.

42. Gennadios's request has been noted in an anonymous fifteenth-century Greek chronicle; *Emperors, Patriarchs, and Sultans of Constantinople,* 57.

43. Since the column was visible to early-fifteenth-century visitors to the city, it might have been taken down following the conquest or during the construction of the mosque. Ottoman sources make no mention of the column or the group statue that adorned it, while they do note the disassembly of Justinian's statue in the Augustaion and the removal of the monumental cross atop the column of Constantine. For Michael VIII's monumental column, see Talbot, "Restoration of Constantinople," 258–60.

44. On the mosque complex, see also Ağaoğlu, "The Fatih Mosque at Constantinople"; Konyalı, *Fatihin mimarlarından Azadlı Sinan,* 89–110; Kuran, *The Mosque in Early Ottoman Architecture,* 191–93; Ayverdi, *Osmanlı miʿmârîsinde Fâtih devri, 855–886 (1451–1481),* 4:356–406; Raby, "El Gran Turco," 261–76; Restle, "Bauplanung und Baugesinnung unter Mehmed II Fatih"; Yerasimos, *La fondation de Constantinople et de Sainte-Sophie,* 150–53, G. Necipoğlu, "The Life of an Imperial Monument"; and idem, "Anatolia and the Ottoman Legacy."

45. İdris Bidlisi, *Heşt behişt,* fols. 81v–82r. *Emperors, Patriarchs, and Sultans of Constantinople,* 57; Gilles, *Antiquities of Constantinople,* 169–70. By the time Pierre Gilles was searching for antiquities in Constantinople, nothing remained of the church.

46. For the substructure, see Forchheimer and Strzygowski, *Die byzantinischen Wasserbehälter von Konstantinopel,* and Kunter and Ülgen, *Fatih Camii ve Bizans Sarnıcı,* 16. Ground-penetrating radar surveys at the Mehmed II or Fatih Mosque provide evidence for the substructures and possibly the remains of the Holy Apostles complex underneath the mosque; Yılmaz and Eser, "Ground-Penetrating Radar Surveys."

47. It should be noted that the path for this trend was opened by Murad II in Edirne, when he converted the reversed T-type convent-masjid he had built for Mevlevi dervishes into a congregational mosque. The building was the centerpiece of a multi-functional complex endowed in 1426–27 in the outskirts of the city. Founding the Üç Şerefeli not too far away from Mehmed I's Eski Cami, Murad II moreover became the first patron to endow an Ottoman city with multiple congregational mosques. The newly added mosque was flanked by a madrasa. For a survey of the buildings and their endowments, see Ayverdi, *Osmanlı miʿmârîsinde Çelebi ve II. Sultan Murad devri, 806–855 (1403–1451),* 405–15, 422–62.

48. For a discussion of the sultanic complexes as funerary monuments manifesting dynastic continuity in the Ottoman capital, see G. Necipoğlu, "Dynastic Imprints on the Cityscape."

49. Mehmed's mausoleum, following Ottoman practice, was built by his son after his death. The wills of Murad II and Bayezid II, Mehmed's father and son, regarding the location and form of their graves have been preserved. It is therefore likely that Mehmed too had specified the location of his mausoleum. For the construction of Mehmed's mausoleum by Bayezid II, see Caʿfer Çelebi, *Heveşnâme,* 28–29. For the will of Murad II, see Uzunçarşılı, "Sultan İkinci Murad'ın Vasiyetnamesi." Bayezid II's will is preserved in his waqfiyya: VGMA 2113:195–203.

50. Mesarites, "Description of the Church of the Holy Apostles at Constantinople," 861–67, 890–97.

51. It is not known with certainty when the educational institutions connected to the Holy Apostles ceased functioning; it seems unlikely that they were functioning through the earlier fifteenth century.

52. Spiro Kostof has noted the novelty of the scale, proportions, and axiality of the complex. "[A]ll this has the authority of ancient Rome," he writes. "Nothing so early in the Western Renaissance has this grandeur." Kostof, *History of Architecture,* 459.

53. For Bidlisi's comments, see further in chapter 2.

54. I thank Christine Smith for this suggestion.

55. Alberti, *On the Art of Building,* 126 (bk. 5, chap. 6). The same idea is elaborated in the next section: "The monastery is a form of religious military camp, where a number of men (such as those who dedicate their lives to religion, and who take the holy vow of chastity) may come together for a life of piety and virtue"; ibid., 127 (bk. 5, chap. 7).

56. Ackerman, "The Certosa of Pavia," 277. On Filarete, see also Lazzaroni and Muñoz, *Filarete; Filarete's Treatise on Architecture;* Onians, "Alberti and Filarete"; Giordano, "On Filarete's *Libro Architettonico.*" On the connections of Filarete's treatise to medieval Mirrors of Princes literature, and on microcosmic associations in Sforzinda, see Lang, "Sforzinda, Filarete, and Filelfo." On the political dimensions of Filarete's treatise and his ideal city as princely capital, see Pierotti, *Prima de Machiavelli.*

57. The similarities between the two projects and the possible involvement of Filarete have been discussed by Franz Babinger, Marcell Restle, and Julian Raby; Babinger, *Mehmed the Conqueror and His Time,* 246, 465; Restle, "Bauplanung und Baugesinnung unter Mehmed II Fatih"; and Raby, "El Gran Turco," 261–76.

58. Among other complexes with similar layouts are a school for boys and a merchants' piazza; *Filarete's Treatise on Architecture,* 230–42, 74–76.

59. Raby, "Pride and Prejudice," 189–90.

60. Restle, in "Bauplanung und Baugesinnung unter Mehmed II Fatih," has argued that the Ottoman *arşın,* the Byzantine foot, and the Florentine braccio were all used in the construction of the complex; according to his findings, while the dimensions of the plaza conformed to all three measurements, those of the courtyard of the mosque conformed to the Byzantine foot, and the madrasas could be easily measured with the Florentine braccio. As neither the Byzantines nor the Ottomans used a standardized system of measurement, Restle's findings may also be the result of a coincidental correspondence between similar premodern units of measurement. Restle's contention (based on Mesarites' description of the Holy Apostles and

the proportions of the aqueduct) that the boundaries of the plaza were those of the Holy Apostles and its dependencies, and that these followed Byzantine property divisions, is not plausible, as there is no clear evidence of an orthographic street layout and property division in Byzantine Constantinople. The description by Mesarites that mentions the patriarchal chancery situated close to the church does not provide precise information regarding the arrangement of the buildings; Mesarites, "Description of the Church of the Holy Apostles at Constantinople," 861–67, 890–96.

61. No such drawing or treatise that can be traced to Italy has surfaced in the Turkish collections. For a discussion of Mehmed's various Italian contacts and the dates of Filarete's intended visit, see Raby, "El Gran Turco," 1–56, 260–62, and passim. For a discussion of Mehmed's collection of Western manuscripts and prints in the context of the maps and views of the city produced during his reign, see chapter 3.

62. For the plans, see G. Necipoğlu, "Plans and Models."

63. Particular references to the treatises of Alberti and Filarete are to be found in the following discussion. For urban theory and notions of the ideal city in fifteenth-century Italy, I have benefited mostly from Eden, "Studies in Urban Theory"; Onians, "Alberti and Filarete"; Westfall, *In This Most Perfect Paradise*; Tafuri, "Cives esse non licere"; Burroughs, *From Signs to Design*; Kostof, *The City Shaped*, 159–209; Choay, *The Rule and the Model*; Giordano, "On Filarete's *Libro Architettonico*."

64. As Charles Burroughs has observed, despite Alberti's clear distinction between tyrant and king and between their respective urban orders, his suggestions to the tyrant often seem directed to the king as well. For an interpretation of this ambivalence in the context of papal politics through the pontificate of Nicholas V, see Burroughs, *From Signs to Design*, 173ff.

65. Raby has discussed the use of this ideal plan with clear Italian roots within the framework of artistic influence, while Yerasimos has seen in its use primarily the appeal of an orderly plan.

Restle did not discuss the political and cultural implications of the connection between the plan of the New Complex and Italian architectural practice. Raby, "El Gran Turco," 261–63; Yerasimos, *La fondation de Constantinople et de Sainte-Sophie*, 152; Restle, "Bauplanung und Baugesinnung unter Mehmed II Fatih."

66. Onians, "Alberti and Filarete."

67. On the layout of the complex as reflecting the growing power of the ulema and their subordination to the sultan within the framework of the hierarchical state apparatus, see G. Necipoğlu, "The Süleymaniye Complex in Istanbul," 96, 114 n. 13; Yerasimos, *La fondation de Constantinople et de Sainte-Sophie*, 153–54; and Crane, "Ottoman Sultans' Mosques," 179–80. For a discussion of the religious hierarchy during the rule of Mehmed within the framework of his *ḳānūnnāme*, see Repp, *Mufti of Istanbul*, esp. 27–72, 125–96.

68. Its prayer hall largely collapsed; the courtyard and the entrance and qibla walls are the only parts dating from the fifteenth century. Ayverdi's architectural survey of the complex is to date the most thorough. It includes a reconstruction of the mosque based on his archeological findings and documentary evidence; Ayverdi, *Osmanlı mi'mârîsinde Fâtih devri, 855–886 (1451–1481)*, 3:356–406. The main primary sources that describe the building's original form are Tursun Beg, *History of Mehmed the Conqueror*, fols. 56a–57b; Angiolello, *Viaggio di Negroponte*, 34–35, İdris Bidlisi, *Heşt behişt*, fols. 46b–49a; Mu'ali, *Hünkārnāme*, fols. 8a–b; Ca'fer Çelebi, *Heveṣnāme*, 22–29; Mehmed bin Ömer Bayezid el-'Aşık, *Menāẕirü'l-'avālim*, fols. 262b–265b; Evliya Çelebi *Seyahatnamesi*, bk. 1, fols. 39b–41a; Hezarfen Hüseyin Efendi, *Telhīsü'l-beyan fī kavānīn-i Āl-i Osmān*, 48–49.

69. See G. Necipoğlu, "Anatolia and the Ottoman Legacy," 152–53.

70. On the absorption of features of Hagia Sophia's architecture into the architecture of Ottoman sultanic mosques, see Kuban, "The Style of Sinan's Domed Structures"; G. Necipoğlu, "The Life of an Imperial Monument"; idem, "Anatolia and the Ottoman Legacy"; and idem, *Age of Sinan*.

71. Its dome was seriously damaged in the great earthquake of 1509. The building suffered additional damages in the earthquakes of 1556, and 1690; Ambraseys and Finkel, *The Seismicity of Turkey and Adjacent Areas*, 38, 48, 94.

72. The inscription on the tombstone of the architect gives the date 876/1471–72. According to the chronicle attributed to Ruhi of Edirne, he was executed when the construction of the mosque reached the level of the windows; but accepting the date on the tombstone and the previous year as that in which the building was completed, this does not seem to be possible. The anonymous chronicles note that the sultan executed the architect who built for him the mosque and the eight madrasas, suggesting that the execution took place after the completion of the mosque. Discussing the evidence, Raby suggests that Sinan's fault lay not in cutting the columns of the mosque short and therefore making the building lower than Hagia Sophia, as is narrated in the sources. It must have been evident long before its completion that the building would not be as high as Hagia Sophia. Raby, "El Gran Turco," 269–76, suggests that the weakness of the dome might have become evident shortly after its completion, and this might have caused the architect's unfortunate end. By the time the architect's story reached Evliya (or perhaps *at* the time it reached Evliya), it told of an architect who had lost not his life but his hands because he had shortened the columns, a just Mehmed who stood in front of a kadi side by side with the architect who had had him summoned to the court, and also a dragon kept under the kadi's carpet as a last resort in case the sultan refused to abide by the law; *Evliya Çelebi Seyahatnamesi*, bk. 1, fol. 41a. For Ruhi's comment, see Ménage, "Edirne'li Ruhi'ye Atfedilen Osmanlı Tarihinden İki Parça," 330–31. The architect's tombstone has been published in Ayverdi, *Osmanlı mi'mârîsinde Fâtih devri, 855–886 (1451–1481)*, 3:442. For the architect's charitable endowment, see chapter 4.

73. The four bands of green marble in the nave of the church symbolized the four rivers of paradise and were also noted as such in the *Patria*; Dagron,

Constantinople imaginaire, 207, 209, 254 n. 188.

74. Şemsüddin Karamani, *Tercüme-i Tārīḫ-i Cāmiʿi Ayāṣofyā*, fol. 20b. The cypresses are not mentioned in the Greek versions of the *Patria*, but according to Majeska, they are mentioned in the Persian translation (which also explains Şemsüddin Karamani's note). Four cypresses around the fountain were also noted in a late-fourteenth-century anonymous Russian description of Constantinople, and by Ibn Battuta who saw the building in the fourteenth century; Majeska, *Russian Travelers*, 138, 200; Ibn Battuta, *Travels in Asia and Africa*, 157. The cypresses in the New Mosque courtyard are described in fifteenth-century sources discussed below and are visible in the seventeenth-century Köprülü drawing (fig. 34); cypresses still surround the courtyard fountain today.

75. Georgius de Hungaria wrote of how Mehmed went to mosques and baths accompanied only by two pages. He was especially struck by the simplicity of the sultan's conduct when riding his horse in the city's streets and when praying in the mosque; Georgius de Hungaria, *Chronica*, 27–28.

76. For a discussion of the formulation of notions of imperial seclusion during Mehmed's reign, and its impact on court ceremonial and the architecture of the palace, see G. Necipoğlu, *Architecture, Ceremonial, and Power*, 15–22.

77. The destruction of the mosque's prayer hall during the 1766 earthquake has made it impossible to fully reconstruct the epigraphic program of the building. Only the hadith on the mihrab, and those inscriptions that were located in the courtyard, have partially survived. The Fatiha (1:1) is engraved in the marble lunettes of the windows of the courtyard façade, and the end of the Throne verse (11:256) has remained on the cuerda seca tiles of the portico window lunettes. Although these are verses common to the epigraphic programs of many Islamic monuments, the royal imagery evoked by the latter verse should still be noted, particularly as it was here used on an Ottoman monument for the first time. The interior housed other inscriptions:

Angiolello noted "a circle made of Arabic letters," possibly a calligraphic roundel marking the summit of the dome; Mehmed ʿAşık described wooden panels inscribed with Arabic verses. Angiolello, *Viaggio di Negroponte*, 33–34; Mehmed bin Ömer Bayezid el-ʿAşık, *Menāẓirüʾl-ʿavālim*, fol. 263r.

78. The mausolea of Mehmed II and Gülbahar Hatun were rebuilt after the earthquake of 1766 on the foundations of the original buildings.

79. These preparatory schools for lower-ranking students might have been built of less durable materials, as nothing of their structures has survived. Ayverdi notes that those situated to the southwest of the complex were standing in 1928, when they were pulled down to open space for the artery reaching the Edirne Gate; Ayverdi, *Osmanlı miʿmârisinde Fâtih devri, 855–886 (1451–1481)*, 3:363.

80. In the endowment deed, only the "house for guests" (i.e., the hospice) and the imaret (public kitchen) are indicated; the stables were probably considered part of the hospice. *Zwei Stiftsurkunden des Sultan Mehmed II. Fatih*, 15.

81. Evliya Çelebi writes that the hadith is placed to the right of the qibla gate, when leaving the mosque. He might have been mistaken, or the place of the inscription might have been changed during the rebuilding of the mosque. *Evliya Çelebi Seyahatnamesi*, bk. 1, fol. 40a.

82. The main theme in the foundation inscriptions of earlier sultanic mosques was piety, acts of ḫayr and ṣadaḳa (charity and almsgiving). Though the sultan's titles and immediate ancestors are cited in most, significantly only the convent-mosque of Mehmed I, a symbol of the consolidation of Ottoman power following the civil war between Bayezid I's sons, features the whole genealogy of the House of Osman up to Orhan in its foundation inscription. The foundation inscription of the Üç Şerefeli Mosque of Murad II, containing little more than the name and title of the founder and the building founded, and stressing his piety through Koranic quotations, contrasts strongly with that of his son. For the text of this inscription, see Dijkema,

Ottoman Historical Monumental Inscriptions in Edirne, 26–31. This shorter but tripartite foundation inscription placed above the three entrances foreshadowed the more elaborate inscription scheme of the New Mosque. The New Mosque's inscription plates in turn were to be the model for the foundation inscriptions of later sultanic mosques. For a comparison of the inscriptions of Mehmed's mosque and that of the Süleymaniye, see G. Necipoğlu, "The Süleymaniye Complex in Istanbul," 107–9.

83. For a discussion of Mehmed's "private" collection of Byzantine relics and antiquities, see Raby, "El Gran Turco," 226–28. In the 1530s one porphyry and marble sarcophagus, ten feet by five feet, stood, without a cover, near the Mese on the site of the Holy Apostles. It was believed by Greeks and Turks alike to be the grave of Constantine the Great; Gilles, *Antiquities of Constantinople*, 172. The sarcophagus was drawn by Melchior Lorichs in the later sixteenth century.

84. Muʿali, *Hünkārnāme*, fols. 8r–v.

85. Kritovoulos, *History of Mehmed the Conqueror*, 140.

86. Tursun Beg, *History of Mehmed the Conqueror*, fol. 56r.

87. Kemalpaşazade, *Tevârîh-i Âl-i Osman*, 102.

88. Caʿfer Çelebi, *Heveşnāme*, in Çelebi, *Divan şiirinde İstanbul*, 22. On Caʿfer Çelebi, who served as nişancı and kazasker during the reigns of Bayezid II and Selim I, see Gökbilgin, "Cafer Çelebi," 98–100.

89. İdris Bidlisi, *Heşt behişt*, fol. 47r. Bidlisi uses the term "iwan" to refer to the spaces below the sanctuary dome and half dome.

90. Ibid., fols. 46r–49v.

91. Ibid., fols. 47r–v.

92. Ibid.

93. Gülru Necipoğlu has suggested that the geometry in the layout of the complex creates a paradisal axis running through the courtyard, with its pond and cypresses, the gate and the mihrab, which stand for the gates of heaven, and culminating in the garden behind the qibla wall, which housed the mausolea of the sultan and his consort, another symbol of paradise; G. Necipoğlu, "Anatolia and the Ottoman Legacy," 154.

94. The *Patria* of Constantinople, a collection of texts devoted to the history and the monuments of the city, have been published by Théodor Preger, *Scriptores Originum Constantinopolitanarum,* 2 vols. (Leipzig, 1901–7). For a translation and analysis, see Dagron, *Constantinople imaginaire.* On the Persian translations, see Tauer, "Notice sur les versions persanes."

95. Sirozlu Sa'di, *Gazel,* in Çelebi, *Divan şiirinde İstanbul,* 35.

96. İdris Bidlisi, *Heşt behişt,* fol. 46v.

97. Mu'ali, *Hünkārnāme,* fol. 8v.

98. Ca'fer Çelebi, *Heveşnāme,* in Çelebi, *Divan şiirinde İstanbul,* 22–23.

99. The parallels between the descriptions of the Süleymaniye and Mehmed II's mosque—the emphases on paradisal analogies, precious materials, and the strength of the building—suggest that from the fifteenth century onward these became the main themes in understanding a sultanic religious monument in the Ottoman realm. Commentaries on Süleymaniye differ in their emphasis on the Sunni dimension of Islam and the reflections of this in the mosque's architecture and decoration. For a discussion of the meaning of the Süleymaniye and the contemporary descriptions of it, see G. Necipoğlu, "The Süleymaniye Complex in Istanbul."

100. Aşıkpaşazade, *Tevârîh-i Âl-i Osman,* 192. For a recent historiograhic analysis of Aşıkpaşazade, see Kafadar, *Between Two Worlds,* 96–114.

101. Aşıkpaşazade, *Tevârîh-i Âl-i Osman,* 202–3.

102. I cite the ca. 896/1490 version of the anonymous chronicles edited by Friedrich Giese; *Die altosmanischen anonymen Chroniken,* 1:98–100. For a historiograhical analysis of the chronicles, see Kafadar, *Between Two Worlds,* 102–16.

103. In his study of the traditional accounts of the construction of Constantinople and the Hagia Sophia, Yerasimos has drawn attention to passages on Mehmed II's mosque in the anonymous chronicles. He has discussed the authors' negative evaluation of the project and the building as indicative of their rejection of Mehmed's imperial project at large; Yerasimos, *La fondation de Constantinople et de*

Sainte-Sophie, 154–59. The negative assessment of Mehmed II's patronage by groups marginalized by his policies may be compared to the criticism of Mathias Corvinus of Hungary's artistic and architectural endeavors, a criticism again rooted in a broader political reaction against the ruler's policies; Feuer-Tóth, *Art and Humanism in Hungary.*

104. *Die altosmanischen anonymen Chroniken,* 1:99–100.

105. Ibid., 99.

106. Ibid.

107. Uruç bin 'Adil, *Die frühosmanischen Jahrbücher des Urudsch,* 216.

108. Sennet, *Flesh and Stone,* 96–97. Sennet, admittedly, is writing about a different time and place: about the emperor Hadrian, whose design for the Temple of Venus and Roma was criticized by the architect Apollodorus, who met the same tragic fate as did Sinan.

109. An employee of the waqf was paid two dirhams a day to protect the enclosure of the mosque from those who might write or engrave on it; *Zwei Stiftsurkunden des Sultan Mehmed II. Fatih,* 122. The lower-ranking *tetimme* have been demolished, but a description is found in the endowment deed; *Zwei Stiftsurkunden des Sultan Mehmed II. Fatih,* 14–15.

110. In large part these served the janissary barracks situated close by. The same waqfiyya lists 843 shops in the commercial area around the bedestan, about twice the number around the New Complex. *Zwei Stiftsurkunden des Sultan Mehmed II. Fatih,* 20–21.

111. Angiolello, *Viaggio di Negroponte,* 33–36. What is referred to as the Sultān Bāzārı in the waqfiyya may be the market referred to as the Karaman Pazarı in this and other sources.

112. For a discussion of the relation of the Holy Apostles complex to the Mese, and proposals regarding the layout of streets surrounding the complex, see Berger, "Streets and Public Spaces in Constantinople."

113. Gilles, *Antiquities of Constantinople,* 172. Travelers' and pilgrims' accounts from the fourteenth and the fifteenth centuries, on the other hand, do not mention the section of the artery between the Forum Tauri and the Charisios Gate. The only street to which travelers of this period refer is

the main part of the Mese between the Hippodrome and the Forum Tauri. For these accounts, see Majeska, *Russian Travelers;* Tafur, *Travels and Adventures;* and Clavijo, *Embassy to Tamerlane.* For reconstructions, see Müller-Wiener, *Bildlexikon zur Topographie Istanbuls,* 21, 25.

114. The masjids of the architect Sinan, Efdalzade, and Üçbaş and the mosque of Atik Ali Pasha are the earlier structures on this course.

115. That several Jewish physicians were employed in the hospital of the New Mosque complex points in the same direction.

116. Barkan, "Ayasofya Cami'i ve Eyüb Türbesinin 1489–1491"; idem, "Fatih Cami ve Imareti Tesislerinin 1489–1490"; Gökbilgin, *XV.–XVI. asırlarda Edirne ve Paşa livası,* 301–15. In 1477 Istanbul counted 16,324 households; the population is estimated between 60,000 and 100,000 people; İnalcık, "Istanbul," 238–39.

117. Along with Lefebvre's notion of the social production of space, Richard van Leeuwen's application of Pierre Bourdieu's concept of field to his study of Damascene waqfs may prove beneficial here: Bourdieu defined fields as sets of coherently articulated relationships, constituting the framework for power struggles and for the competition for and exchange of symbolic commodities. Waqfs were such fields, Leeuwen argued; as such they were instrumental in the regulation of power struggles and in the stabilization, reproduction, and transformation of power configurations; van Leeuwen, *Waqfs and Urban Structures;* Bourdieu, *Distinction;* Lefebvre, *Production of Space.*

118. The endowment deeds of Mehmed's foundations, preserved in a number of copies dating from ca. 1472 onward, constitute the main source for the wider network of buildings and activities encompassed by the sultanic waqf. Unlike another deed, comprising only the New Complex and its income-generating property, the 1496 copy in the Topkapı Palace Archives (E 7744-4, published in *Zwei Stiftsurkunden des Sultan Mehmed II. Fatih*) does not mention a keeper for Mehmed's mausoleum. This suggests that the original of this version of the endowment deed was

drawn during the rule of Mehmed. In her recent study of the various endowment deeds of the Mehmed II foundation, Kayoko Hayashi has argued that this copy must date from Bayezid II's reign, on the evidence that a merchant by the name of Elvanoğlu Sinan, known to have drawn his own waqf in 1482, is referred to here as "the deceased." This in itself does not, in my view, constitute evidence for the dating of the deed, as the adjective *merḥūm* (deceased) could easily have been added by the scribe of the 1496 copy. Other prominent personages of the period, such as Mevlana Husrev (d. 1481) and Mevlana Gürani, as Hayashi also notes, are referred to without the title "deceased." Hayashi, on the other hand, is also of the opinion that the Topkapı deed E 7744-4 is significant in bringing together all foundations and endowed property of Mehmed; Hayashi, "Fatih Vakfiyelerinin Tanzim Süreci Üzerine."

119. That the New Complex was perceived as the center of the endowment and not as *one* among the numerous foundations of Mehmed II is suggested by John Sanderson, who was in Istanbul in the last decade of the sixteenth century and described the complex: "The said Sultan Mahemett left for the maintenance hearof sixty thowsand ducketts yearelie rent in that time, which now doth import above 200,000; for they have of the rents of Sofia, to which also, besides other revenewe, belongeth the besistans and in a mannerr all the principall shopps in the citie, even untill you come to the Seralio of the Great Turke, which paieth rent therto 1001 aspers per day." *The Travels of John Sanderson in the Levant,* 70. Though Sanderson's note postdates the 1496 document by nearly a century, it is telling in that it reveals the primacy of the new foundation for those who informed the author.

120. The numerous surveys of the Ayasofya endowment's holdings and registers of its accounts attest to its continuation. The accounts of 894–95/1489–90 for this endowment and the New Mosque's waqf show that new commercial and residential buildings were added to the former foundation, while baths, endowed villages, and the jizya of non-Muslims in Istanbul and Galata formed the income of the latter; Barkan, "Ayasofya Camiʾi ve Eyüb Türbesinin 1489–1491"; idem, "Fatih Cami ve Imareti Tesislerinin 1489–1490."

121. Literally, "from the smaller to the greater *jihad*"; *Zwei Stiftsurkunden des Sultan Mehmed II. Fatih,* 4–10. Ayverdi and, later, Lowry have drawn attention to the significance of this phrase with regard to the rebuilding of the city, translating *jihad* solely as war. The notion of the "greater *jihad*," on the other hand, was used in Islamic scholarly literature in opposition to the "smaller *jihad*," that is, the *jihad* of the sword, to denote a peaceful endeavor for spiritual perfection; Tyan, "Djihad"; Peters, *Jihad in Classical and Modern Islam.*

122. Only the minaret remains of the mosque today.

123. Zakir Şükri Efendi, *İstanbul Hankahları meşayihi,* 21. This list of convents and the succession of their sheikhs does not provide information on the layout of any of the structures. The dervishes of the Nakshibendi order residing in the Zeyrek convent are also mentioned in a collection of jurisprudential opinion by the early-sixteenth-century mufti ʿAli Cemali Efendi; Zenbilli ʿAli Cemali Efendi, *Mecmuʿa-i Fetāvā,* fol. 67r.

124. For the Zeyniye, see Margoliouth, "Zayn al-Din," and Kara, *Bursaʾda tarikatlar ve tekkeler,* 83–114. For Şeyh Vefazade, see Mecdi Efendi, *Tercüme-i şakāyık,* 251–54 and passim. According to Taşköprizade, the sheikh never agreed to see or converse with either of the sultans who extended their favors to him. It is interesting that this author refers to the mosque and the convent that "Vefazade had built," with no reference to Mehmed's patronage.

125. A summary copy of this endowment is found in the 953/1546 survey; Barkan and Ayverdi, *İstanbul vakıfları tahrir defteri 953 (1546) tarihli,* 159. The waqf was impoverished during the reign of Bayezid, and the dervishes of the convent petitioned the court to ensure its continuance; TKSA E 6131. Possibly the impoverishment of the foundation had to do with the sheikh's fall from favor, since during the struggle for the throne that followed the death of Mehmed II (and ended in Bayezid's accession) Şeyh Vefazade had supported Cem rather than Bayezid.

126. This is the date given by Ayvansarayi with the chronogram *cāmiʿ ḥāḳāniyye* (sultanic mosque); he also says that it was built by Bayezid. Ayvansarayi, *Garden of the Mosques,* 130–31. This date would be consistent with the information in the endowment deeds, as the mosque does not appear in the first deed but in the second; *Zwei Stiftsurkunden des Sultan Mehmed II. Fatih,* 134–35.

127. The mosque was demolished early in this century; it is known through the plan, elevation, and view of the interior published by Cornelius Gurlitt in 1907; Gurlitt, *Die Baukunst Konstantinopels,* 1:43.

128. Saʿdüddin, *Tācüʾt-tevārīḫ,* 1:580; *Evliya Çelebi Seyahatnamesi,* bk. 1, fol. 106v. Ayvansarayi notes "the great square in the direction of the tomb . . . the well-known Vefa Meydanı"; Ayvansarayi, *Garden of the Mosques,* 146.

129. Berger, "Roman, Byzantine, and Latin Periods."

130. Ocak, *Osmanlı İmparatorluğuʾnda marjinal Sûfîlik,* 122–24; *Zwei Stiftsurkunden des Sultan Mehmed II. Fatih,* 13.

131. It has been noted that the period immediately following the conquest was the only time when this sect was given convents in Istanbul or the provinces by the central authority, and that a concern with controlling its often heretical members and simultaneously their high prestige as frontier warriors must have played a role in this patronage. Taking into consideration the central location of the convent, which, apart from accommodation, also provided the setting for the range of activities foreseen for them in the waqfiyya, it is possible to read both motives in the foundation of a *ḳalenderḫāne* near the first palace, on the Forum of Taurus. Two other Kalenderi convents, at least one of them far removed from the center in Davud Pasha, were noted in the account books of the Ayasofya waqf of 894–95/1489–90; Barkan, "Ayasofya Camiʾi ve Eyüb Türbesinin 1489–1491," 355, 359. For a discussion of the later history of the Kalenderhane, see Göyünç, "Ottoman Period."

132. Such was the case with the Kalenderhane in Eyüp, also known as the convent of La'lizade Abdülbaki Efendi, which housed dervishes of the Melamiyye and the Nakshibandiyya as well as Kalenderis; Zarcone and Tanman, "Kalenderhane Tekkesi." The Kalenderhane is not among convents mentioned in the *Velāyetnāme* of Otman Baba, which mentions several such buildings in the city that the dissident sheikh frequented.

133. My thanks to Baha Tanman for sharing his views on the Kalenderhane regarding the stipulations in the waqfiyya and the subsequent change of the building's function. For the Kalenderhane in the middle of the sixteenth century, see Barkan and Ayverdi, *İstanbul vakıfları tahrir defteri 953 (1546) tarihli*, 437. Excavation and a survey carried on in the building and its immediate surroundings have revealed that a room at its northeast corner, a remainder from the earlier church standing here, was in use through the Palaeologan and Ottoman periods. In the eighteenth century this space was replaced by a newly built, approximately square room with a hearth, a cistern within the adjoining aqueduct arch, and three windows. The survey team has suggested that this room might have been used as a kitchen for the foundation. Striker and Kuban, *Kalenderhane in Istanbul*, 75.

134. For Taşköprizade's narration of the debate between Zeyrek and Hocazade, see Mecdi Efendi, *Tercüme-i şaḳāyıḳ*, 142–45.

135. None of the monumental baths of early Byzantine Constantinople were still functioning by the mid–fifteenth century. Ćurčić and Hadjitryphonos have drawn attention to possible connections between late Byzantine and Ottoman baths, noting that Ottoman uses of the Byzantine labor force and technical know-how had a role in the design and structuring of these buildings; Ćurčić and Hadjitryphonos, *Secular Medieval Architecture in the Balkans*, 309. For examples of three Byzantine baths (one of which was in use through the 1930s), see ibid., 310–15. Ćurčić notes that the Ottoman baths are more like late antique private bathing establishments than the giant structures built by imperial funds in the Roman

era; Ćurčić, "Architecture in the Age of Insecurity," 47.

136. Machiel Kiel, in an article on Ottoman baths in the Balkans, discusses their Seljuk precedents, particularly in their use of cross-axial arrangements. Kiel attributes their construction only to the need for ritual ablutions, which does not explain the large scales of these buildings, especially in comparison to baths elsewhere in the Muslim world. Kiel, "The Ottoman Hamam and the Balkans."

137. The building has attracted the attention of numerous scholars, from Charles Texier onward, who have discussed the possibility that this was originally a Byzantine structure. While Charles Texier and Albert Gabriel have noted the building might have Byzantine foundations, Ekrem Ayverdi and Sedat Çetintaş have argued the opposite. Çetintaş does make note of the popular Bursan lore concerning figural imagery (a mosaic?) decorating the floor of the caldarium pool. Texier, *Asie mineure*, 116–17; Gabriel, *Une capitale turque*; Ayverdi, *Osmanlı mi'marisinin ilk devri*, 276–83; Çetintaş, *Türk mimari anıtları*, 12–20.

138. Hıbri, *Enîsü'l-Müsâmirîn*, 45; Eyice, "Çardaklı Hamam." The presence of Byzantine foundations or architectural elements in the Çardaklı and Taht al-kal'a baths suggests that some of the other baths of the period, too, might have incorporated parts of Byzantine bathing structures.

139. For a survey of these buildings, see Ayverdi, *Osmanlı mi'mârîsinde Çelebi ve II. Sultan Murad devri, 806–855 (1403–1451)*, 2:471–77.

140. For assessments of Umayyad baths in their relationship to the late antique heritage, see Grabar, *Formation of Islamic Art*, 145–50; idem, "Umayyad Palaces Reconsidered"; and Fowden, *Qusayr Amra*.

141. For the bath in Roman architecture and culture, see Yegül, *Baths and Bathing in Classical Antiquity*. Yegül briefly discusses the question of Roman origins of the Ottoman bath. The Roman resonances in the Ottoman bath have received frequent comment. Gaspard Fossati, for example, commissioned for a major restoration of Hagia Sophia in 1847 along with other

building projects in the Ottoman capital, noted the Roman character of Ottoman bathhouses (and produced designs for one such structure). I thank Paolo Girardelli for this reference. For further information and a copy of the proposed design for a bath, see Girardelli's forthcoming article on the work of the Fossati brothers in Istanbul.

142. While few of the public baths belonging to the sultanic foundation have reached our day in their original form, several survive, and information on others is preserved in earlier drawings and depictions.

143. Kritovoulos, *History of Mehmed the Conqueror*, 105. For the Kırkçeşme waterways, see Nirven, *İstanbul'da Fatih II. Sultan Mehmed devri Türk su medeniyeti*, and Çeçen, *Mimar Sinan ve Kırkçeşme tesisleri*. Kemalpaşazade notes that the "forty fountains" were built by the "Roman sultans," had later fallen into disrepair, and had been restored by Mehmed; Kemalpaşazade, *Tevârîh-i Âl-i Osman*, 102. Evliya Çelebi, too, notes that "in the time of the infidels, there was no running water [fountain] in the city other than the Kırkçeşme": *Evliya Çelebi Seyahatnamesi*, bk. 1, 95r.

144. Kemalpaşazade, *Tevârîh-i Âl-i Osman*, 103. "Fire during the day and smoke during the night filled its furnace," wrote İbn Kemal.

145. Kritovoulos, *History of Mehmed the Conqueror*, 105.

146. *Külliyyāt-ı dīvān-ı Mevlānā Ḥamīdī*, 309, 323. Descriptions of and eulogies to newly constructed bathhouses, both private and public, are quite common in contemporary poetry, reflecting a trend that largely disappears with the diminishing importance of the public bath within the cityscape through the later sixteenth century.

147. Mango, "The Water Supply of Constantinople," 9.

148. It has been argued that these two types of structures often constituted the center of a neighborhood, though the construction of a bath usually depended on the density of population in the area; Özkoçak, "Urban Development of Istanbul," 31–36. The relation between public baths and population density in residential quarters has been explored by André Raymond

in the context of eighteenth-century Cairo; Raymond, "La localisation des bains publics au Caire." While the bath and the mosque may often have constituted the foci of a residential quarter, in the case of Istanbul, at least, the number of neighborhood mosques was far greater than that of baths.

149. Michell, *Architecture of the Islamic World*, 109–10.

150. In the New Mosque foundation account books dating to 1489–90, income from the fourteen public baths adds up to 243,893 *akçe;* during the same period, the poll tax of non-Muslims resident in Istanbul and Galata added up to 421,224 *akçe,* and revenues from the fifty-plus endowed villages in Thrace, 708,437 *akçe.* Barkan, "Fatih Cami ve Imareti Tesislerinin 1489–1490."

151. More than two centuries later, another major restoration and expansion in Istanbul's water-distribution system would bring the city its host of monumental public fountains. As Shirine Hamadeh notes, while this made the proliferation of public fountains in the city and its suburbs possible, work on the city's water-distribution system was only one of many factors that led to the construction and subsequent popularity of these structures; Hamadeh, "Splash and Spectacle."

152. It is important to remember that the residential areas of the walled city at the time were in large part of mixed population rather than religiously and ethnically segregated. See chapter 4.

153. The state controlled the distribution of water in the city and the construction of baths, at least through the early decades of the sixteenth century. Permission from the palace was required to build a bath. For further discussion of petitions and relevant documents, see chapter 4.

154. Scholarship on Islamic architecture has largely accepted that the social and sporting purposes of the Roman bath were replaced in the Muslim world by the concern with ritual and actual cleanliness. See, for example, Michell, *Architecture of the Islamic World*, 109–10. Students of Ottoman social and literary history, on the other hand, will note that the bath was a prime location of social interaction.

Significantly, a number of neighborhoods were named after baths in the early surveys of endowed property, which implies that, at least as far as the administration was concerned, the bath was the center of the neighborhood.

155. Kritovoulos, *History of Mehmed the Conqueror*, 105. Kritovoulos wrote in 1467, when, as Yerasimos has pointed out, deportations to Istanbul involved in large part non-Muslim communities; Yerasimos, "Osmanlı İstanbul'unun Kuruluşu." In 1477, a citywide census revealed that slightly less than 60 percent of all households in Istanbul and Galata were Muslim; Orthodox Greeks constituted the largest non-Muslim community.

156. Özcan, "Fâtih'in Teşkilât Kanunnamesi," 30; Stavrides, *Sultan of Vezirs,* 56–59.

157. Kritovoulos, *History of Mehmed the Conqueror,* 141.

158. On the political and military career of Mahmud Pasha, and the structuring of the post of grand vizier during this period, see Stavrides, *Sultan of Vezirs.*

159. The prominence of Mahmud Pasha in the urban undertakings of this period is attested also by his constructions in other cities: among his works are the bedestan of Ankara (which was built in the same years as the bedestan of Istanbul), the Friday mosque of Sofia (a monumental structure in the style of the Friday mosques of Bursa and Edirne), and his large khan in Bursa; Ayverdi, *Osmanlı miʿmârîsinde Fâtih devri, 855–886 (1451–1481),* 3:33–47, 4:854–57. For a survey of his foundation, including endowments in the other cities of the empire, and a discussion of the grand vizier's architectural patronage, see Stavrides, *Sultan of Vezirs,* 267–93.

160. None of the original endowment deeds of the main vizierial undertakings of the period have surfaced. A summary copy of Mahmud Pasha's waqfiyya is found in Barkan and Ayverdi, *İstanbul vakıfları tahrir defteri 953 (1546) tarihli,* 42–45. An architectural survey of his buildings is in Ayverdi, *Osmanlı miʿmârîsinde Fâtih devri, 855–886 (1451–1481),* 3:443–51.

161. *Menāķıb-ı Maḥmūd Pāşā-yı Velī,* fol. 11v. For the dating of the *Menāķıb,* see Stavrides, *Sultan of Vezirs,*

380–84. The other sources mentioning the church that stood on the site are Ayvansarayi, *Garden of the Mosques,* 191, and Konstantios I, *Constantiniade,* 109.

162. Muʿali, *Ḫünkārnāme,* fol. 9b. I thank Wheeler Thackston for his help with these passages.

163. Another example is the Yayla masjid, near the Mevlevihane Gate, where a Byzantine cistern was used as a platform for the construction; see Eyice, "İstanbul'da Yayla camileri."

164. Gilles noted in the 1540s that it was built on the highest eminence of the second valley; Gilles, *Antiquities of Constantinople,* 145–46. It should be remembered that when it was built, the mosque was not surrounded, as it is today, by the dense fabric of the commercial area, with its multiple-story structures and numerous khans.

165. İdris Bidlisi, *Heşt behişt,* 60a.

166. The main studies on these buildings are Eyice, "Ilk Osmanlı Devrinin dini-içtimai bir müessesesi"; Kuran, *The Mosque in Early Ottoman Architecture;* and Emir, "Erken Osmanlı mimarlığında çok işlevli yapılar." Kuran assesses its formal characteristics and its spatial features; Eyice's study establishes the multiple functions of the T-shaped buildings as convent-mosques; Emir stresses this multiplicity of functions and offers a critique of the buildings' characterization predominantly as places of worship. In his survey of Ottoman architecture, Doğan Kuban has highlighted the primarily accommodative and ritual functions of these buildings; Kuban, *Osmanlı mimarisi,* 75–122. In this book I distinguish the T-type multifunctional buildings of the pre-conquest era, which incorporate a prayer space but do not have allocations for congregational prayer, and which have been described as ʿimāret or zāviye (hospice or convent) in their foundation deeds and inscriptions, from those of the post-conquest era, buildings with a similar layout founded and used as congregational mosques while incorporating convent rooms as well. The first are designated here as convent-masjids (after Necipoğlu, *The Age of Sinan,* 49–50) and the latter as convent-mosques.

167. Historians of Ottoman architecture who have written on the building have often noted the "alien"

character of these features and have in general found this an unsuccessful example of this type of mosque. Ayverdi, *Osmanlı miʿmârîsinde Fâtih devri, 855–886 (1451–1481),* 3:446. Both Kuran and Eyice find in this arrangement a new turn in mosque architecture. Kuran notes that the corridor eliminates the need for the central hall that provided access to the prayer iwan and the convent rooms; Kuran, *The Mosque in Early Ottoman Architecture,* 143, 208; Eyice, "Ilk Osmanlı Devrinin dini-içtimai bir müessesesi," 42.

168. For the use of the ambulatory as a funerary space in the Pammakaristos and Constantine Lips monastery churches, see Ousterhout, *Master Builders of Byzantium,* 125–27.

169. A large number of people, among them artisans and craftsmen, had been forcibly deported to the city following the campaign, and settled near Mehmed's mosque. For a discussion of the origins of the artisans who built the Tiled Pavilion, see G. Necipoğlu, *Architecture, Ceremonial, and Power,* 213–17.

170. Mahmud Pasha was dismissed from the grand vizierate for the second time in 878/1473 and executed in 879/1474; the mausoleum must have been built before 878/1474. The inscription on its portal, possibly placed there after the execution, gives the date 878/1474 and refers to the "martyrdom" of the grand vizier. For a discussion of the chronology of the period, including dates of the appointments of grand viziers, see İnalcık, "Mehmed the Conqueror," and Stavrides, *Sultan of Vezirs.*

171. A piece of oral history attributed to Mükrimin Halil Yinanç by Süheyl Ünver, cited in Banoğlu, *Mahmud Paşa,* 76.

172. The ʿimāret (designating here the public kitchen) and the muʿallimḫāne are not extant, and their location is not known, though one may assume that they were in the proximity of the other buildings. Only the classroom of the madrasa is still standing, to the east of the mosque.

173. Bidlisi, who must have studied the endowment deed, notes that the instructor (müderris) was paid fifty akçe daily, and this is also the amount indicated in the 953/1546 register.

174. The fountain provides admittedly confusing evidence regarding its date of construction and its later history. The earliest inscription on it, still extant, has also been recorded by Evliya Çelebi, who wrote of the fountain: "Bülbülī gördi çu itmāmını didi tārīḫ / Yapdı Ḫāḳ yolına bu çeşmeyi Mahmud Paşa," yielding the date 1014/1605–6; *Evliya Çelebi Seyahatnamesi,* bk. 1, fol. 95v. The fountain also carries the date of a second restoration, in 1172/1758, while another inscription on the northern façade mentions an Osman Ağa of Egypt who restored the building in 1031/1621–22. On Mahmud Pasha's waterways, see Nirven, *İstanbulʾda Fatih II. Sultan Mehmed devri Türk su medeniyeti,* 45, and Çeçen, *Halkalı suları,* 70–72. Davud Pasha also built a fountain near his mosque.

175. Matrakcı's view is discussed in detail in the epilogue.

176. Of the two, the Servi masjid is noted by Ayvansarayi as a neighborhood masjid built by Mahmud Pasha close to his great mosque; Ayvansarayi, *Garden of the Mosques,* 127.

177. Saʿdüddin, *Tacüʾt-tevarih,* 1:221; *Evliya Çelebi Seyahatnamesi,* bk. 1, fol. 88b.

178. Kritovoulos, *History of Mehmed the Conqueror,* 141. They were part of the family endowment of the founder and recorded in the 953/1546 register summarily as ḫānehā-i vāḳıf-ı mezbūr (the houses of the said founder) in the quarter of Kasım Paşa el-Cezeri, with a high yearly income of 5,040 akçe; Barkan and Ayverdi, *İstanbul vakıfları tahrir defteri 953 (1546) tarihli,* 42. The only remaining part of the palace and the gardens of Mahmud Pasha that was not confiscated and allotted to subsequent grand viziers is a bath that had become part of the family waqf in 953/1546 and was called Şengül Hammamı.

179. Evidence concerning late-fifteenth- and early-sixteenth-century vizierial palaces is discussed in chapter 4 and the epilogue.

180. On the location and history of the Bab-ı Ali, or the palace of the grand vizier that was reshaped as the prime ministry in the nineteenth century, see Toprak and Tanyeli, "Babıali."

181. This is Kritovoulos's definition of the grand vizier's office, which mirrors the definition of the post in Mehmed II's law code; Kritovoulos, *History of Mehmed the Conqueror,* 141. For the Kiosk of Processions, see G. Necipoğlu, *Architecture, Ceremonial, and Power,* 32–34. I thank Gülru Necipoğlu for calling my attention to the relationship between the viziers' buildings and the polygonal towers of the imperial fortress. She suggests that the palace might have been given to another grandee, possibly Süleyman's grand vizier Rüstem Pasha in the sixteenth century.

182. For architectural surveys of these buildings, see Ayverdi, *Osmanlı miʿmârîsinde Fâtih devri, 855–886 (1451–1481),* 4:580–89, 602–6.

183. Albrecht Berger has suggested that this might be an early Byzantine street laid out as part of an orthogonal plan; Berger, "Streets and Public Spaces in Constantinople," 167.

184. The irregular courtyard of the khan has been completely demolished. In the photograph published by Gurlitt (fig. 85), a large gate with a window above is visible at the narrow end of the second courtyard, opening to the area at the intersection of the two streets; Gurlitt, *Die Baukunst Konstantinopels,* vol. 1, pl. 13a. It may be assumed that this portal resembled that the first courtyard, with its brick iwan jutting out toward the artery.

185. Belonging to the endowment were 265 shops called "the shops of Mahmud Pasha" in the 883/1478 waqf and 220 others in the 895/1490 survey. The 895/1490 document features a note indicating that by imperial edict the 220 shops are endowed to the waqf of Mahmud Pasha. This may be indicating the return of property to the original waqf. But the story does not end here, for about thirty years later, in the 926 survey of the Ayasofya endowment, the han of Mahmud Pasha figures as one of the six sultanic hans in the city; Istanbul Atatürk Library M.C. O.64 (*Ayaṣofya vakfı cibāyet defteri,* A.H. 926), fol. 98v. In the eighteenth century, Ayvansarayi noted that the khan and its masjid, built by Mahmud Pasha and Hacı Kuçek, respectively, both belonged to the Ayasofya endowment; Ayvansarayi, *Garden of the Mosques,* 184. On the other hand, the survey of

953/1546, too, features the khan among the endowed property of Mahmud Pasha. It had a meager income compared to the figures in earlier surveys, which suggests that only part of it belonged to the original waqf at that date.

186. By 1478, the foundation of the executed grand vizier was, in part or in whole, incorporated into the sultanic endowment comprising the New Mosque and Ayasofya foundations. Parts of its endowed property feature in surveys of the Ayasofya foundation dating to 1490 and 1520. As has been noted earlier, the original endowment deed has not surfaced; only a summary is available in the 953/1546 document. The account given there of the property and the expenses does not necessarily reflect those of the original deed, as the 1546 survey presents the current holdings and income of each foundation rather than the figures in the original deeds. The private waqf of the vizier seems to have remained intact and was mentioned in an undated petition from the daughters of Mahmud Pasha to Bayezid II concerning a property conflict between the vizier's daughters and his widow; Uzunçarşılı, "Fatih Sultan Mehmed'in Vezir-i Âzamlarından Mahmud Paşa İle Şehzade Mustafa'nın Araları Neden Açılmıştı?" 726–28.

187. The history of the Çandarlı family, through and after Mehmed's rule, presents a similar case. See Uzunçarşılı, Çandarlı vezir ailesi.

188. Mentioned in the earliest surviving copy of the endowment deed of Mehmed's foundation and in the 895/1489 survey of the property endowed to Hagia Sophia; Fatih Sultan Mehmed'in vakfiyeleri; BBA MM 19 (Ayaṣofya vaḳfı taḥrīr defteri, A.H. 895), fol. 39v.

189. The endowment deed of Rum Mehmed Pasha, in summary form, is in VGMA 617:83–84. This copy, which carries the dates 1315/1897–98 and 1317/1899–1900, also includes a reference to Rüstem Pasha as the holder of a zemīn, which makes it possible that the original of this particular copy dated to the latter half of the sixteenth century. This might be part of the garden palace of Süleyman's grand vizier Rüstem Pasha, which was adjacent to the mosque of Rum Mehmed Pasha. On this, see G. Necipoğlu, "Suburban Landscape of Sixteenth-Century Istanbul." The waqfiyya summary also includes notes on the contemporary state of the endowed property. Of the religious and charitable undertakings of the vizier, the expenses only for the mosque and the imaret in Üsküdar and the mosque in Tire are noted. The madrasa, a later addition to the complex, was in a ruinous state when Ayvansarayi wrote; this might be the reason why it does not appear in this copy. The Istanbul property of the vizier is noted also in the 953/1546 register; Barkan and Ayverdi, İstanbul vakıfları tahrir defteri 953 (1546) tarihli, 181. Interestingly, there is very little correspondence between the reports of property and income in the two documents, the 953/1546 register presenting considerably lower figures. Though it is not possible to know which one is closer in date to the original endowment, the references to a palace and an adjacent bath in the neighborhood of Hace Hayrüddin in both documents establish at least that the private residence of the vizier, either at the time of its foundation or some time before 953/1546, was endowed for the religious-charitable complex in Üsküdar.

190. As argued by İnalcık, who notes that Rum Mehmed was a member of the divan in 1470 and grand vizier between 1471 and 1472 (during which time his mosque in Üsküdar was completed). He was atabek (tutor and regent) to Cem Sultan in Karaman until 1474, when he was dismissed for the last time and executed. İnalcık, "Mehmed the Conqueror," 414–15.

191. Kemalpaşazade notes that Rum Mehmed was one of those captured in Istanbul during the conquest. Aşıkpaşazade wrote about Rum Mehmed's Constantinopolitan origins; Neşri too notes, also in the context of the rent issue, that Rum Mehmed was a native of Istanbul. Aşıkpaşazade, Tevârîh-i Âl-i Osman, 215–16; Kemalpaşazade, Tevârîh-i Âl-i Osman, 276–79; Neşri, Kitab-ı cihannuma, 71–11. See also Tekindağ, "Mehmed Paşa (Rum)"; de Groot, "Mehmed Pasha (Rum)"; İnalcık, "The Policy of Mehmed II," 241–45; idem, "Mehmed

the Conqueror," 414–15; and Stavrides, Sultan of Vezirs, 65, 329–32.

192. Twenty-seven shops and twenty-four houses are listed. The copier of the document left a blank slot for another set of shops, though the monthly rent is recorded; judging from the rents indicated for this and for the other set of shops, the number omitted was probably seven or eight. VGMA 617:83–84.

193. Ayverdi, Osmanlı miʿmârisinde Fâtih devri, 855–886 (1451–1481), 3:482–89. Ayverdi attributes the Byzantine look of the building to the Greek origin of its builder, to which he attributes the builder's disloyalty to the Ottoman state. The architecture of this era, of course, provides ample evidence that the ethnic identity of the patron and the architectural style of the building did not necessarily correspond. Immediate examples include the mosque of Vefazade, which Cornelius Gurlitt mistook for a converted Byzantine church, and Murad Pasha's most conventional of the reversed-T type mosques in the city, built by a nephew of the last Byzantine emperor, according to Angiolello.

194. Kuran, The Mosque in Early Ottoman Architecture, 96–97; Ousterhout, "Ethnic Identity and Cultural Appropriation in Early Ottoman Architecture," 50.

195. The figure is comparable to the incomes of the Alaca, Sırt, and Azeban baths in the commercial area, and higher than most baths in Mehmed's foundation. Incomes of these baths are noted in an account book of the Mehmed II foundation dating to 1489–90. Barkan, "Fatih Cami ve Imareti Tesislerinin 1489–1490," 306.

196. Part of the ḥarem constitutes a separate entity; this section is missing from the document.

197. VGMA 617:83–84; Barkan and Ayverdi, İstanbul vakıfları tahrir defteri 953 (1546) tarihli, 180.

198. Angiolello and Lezze, Historia turchescha (1300–1514), 105; Kemalpaşazade, Tevârîh-i Âl-i Osman, 341–45; Neşri, Kitab-ı cihannuma, 808–10; Babinger, "Eine Verfügung des Paläologen Châss Murâd-Paša"; Beldiceanu and Beldiceanu-Steinherr, "Un paléologue inconnu de la région de Serres."

199. Stavrides, *Sultan of Vezirs*.

200. I accept here Neşri's and Sa'düddin's chronology of the Karaman campaigns; Neşri, *Kitab-ı cihannuma*, 778–85. Kemalpaşazade, along with other chroniclers, notes the deportations; Kemalpaşazade, *Tevârîh-i Âl-i Osman*, 298–305. For an architectural survey of the complex and transliterations of the inscriptions, with chronograms, see Ayverdi, *Osmanlı mi'mârîsinde Fâtih devri, 855–886 (1451–1481)*, 3:466–74. For a summary of the endowment deed dating to 953/1546, see Barkan and Ayverdi, *İstanbul vakıfları tahrir defteri 953 (1546) tarihli*, 307–8.

201. Hadidi, *Tevārīḫ-i 'Āl-i 'Oṣmān*, fols. 123b–124a.

202. The Hindiler convent and the Edhemi convent were both close to the complex of Murad Pasha. For these, see chapter 4.

203. A khan and some shops were located near and within the coppersmiths' market; *Zwei Stiftsurkunden des Sultan Mehmed II. Fatih*, 40–41, 73. In 953, forty-five shops and thirteen rooms belonging to the waqf were situated close to the complex; Barkan and Ayverdi, *İstanbul vakıfları tahrir defteri 953 (1546) tarihli*, 307.

204. For the excavation results, see Dirimtekin, "Ayasofya ve ona bağlı binalarda araştırmalar," 3–5, and Janin, "Constantinople byzantine," 256.

205. Chrysoloras, "Comparison of Old and New Rome," 211. For the river god, see Fıratlı, *La sculpture byzantine*, no. 507. Cyril Mango notes that the statue must have been in place when Chrysoloras described it in the early fifteenth century; Mango, *Le développement urbain de Constantinople*, 70.

206. The identity of this spot has been a point of debate among scholars of Byzantine Constantinople. Wolfgang Müller-Wiener located the Forum Bovis in this spot, while Cyril Mango has noted that this might be the Forum Amastrianum and that the Forum Bovis must have lain further to the west. Whether this was the area of the Forum Bovis or not, it was the point of intersection of the river Lycus with the Mese (hence the presence of the river god) and, as suggested by the excavation results and textual evidence,

a monumentally defined spot. Müller-Wiener, *Bildlexikon zur Topographie Istanbuls*, 253–54; Mango, *Le développement urbain de Constantinople*, 70.

207. Kuban, *Türk ve İslam sanatı üzerine denemeler*, 184–90, and Çelik, *The Remaking of Istanbul*, 23, provide such interpretations.

208. In the first half of the fifteenth century, Pero Tafur and Clavijo described the city as full of gardens and orchards, marked with small settlements in between; Tafur, *Travels and Adventures*, 145–46; Clavijo, *Embassy to Tamerlane*, 87–88.

209. Gilles, *Antiquities of Constantinople*, 151.

210. It has been suggested that the height of the domes required the connecting arch between the two sections to be placed also at an unusual height, creating a more unified interior space; Kuran, *The Mosque in Early Ottoman Architecture*, 94–95.

211. A highly damaged freehold deed dated 886/1481 documents Mehmed's allotment of an Istanbul plot bearing a structure with a large dome on four supports and a half dome ("dört ayak üzerine bir büyük ḳubbe ve yarım ḳubbe āḫir"); BBA AE Mehmed II 33a. The waqfiyya carries the date 891/1486–87; it is not certain when exactly the construction was completed. For the waqfiyya of İshak Pasha, see Tamer, "Fatih Devri Ricalinden İshak Paşa'nın vakfiyeleri ve vakıfları." An architectural survey of the buildings is in Ayverdi, *Osmanlı mi'mârîsinde Fâtih devri, 855–886 (1451–1481)*, 3:425–27. The Istanbul part of the foundation is registered in the 953/1546 survey, which notes that the income from the bath is endowed for the imaret in İnegöl after the cessation of the founder's family; Barkan and Ayverdi, *İstanbul vakıfları tahrir defteri 953 (1546) tarihli*, 5.

212. The Greek and Armenian communities, as well as their churches and taverns of this area, were described by Eremya Çelebi Kömürcüyan in the seventeenth century; Kömürcüyan, *İstanbul tarihi*, 3–4. Hrand D. Andreasyan, in his notes to Kömürcüyan's description, refers to the colophon of an Armenian manuscript written in this church in 1480, which notes that the Karamanid community

was deported in 1479; Kömürcüyan, *İstanbul tarihi*, 80–81. According to Andreasyan, the building was doubtlessly built on the site of a former Byzantine church, as it housed a holy spring (*ayazma*), a feature exclusive to Byzantine and Greek churches. Kevork Pamukciyan provides the text of a 1719 sultanic edict noting that the church was given to the Armenian community following the conquest; Pamukciyan, "Kumkapı Patrikhane Kilisesi Ne Zamandan Beri Ermenilerin Elindedir?" 151–53.

213. The women's section of the bath is not extant, and the apodyterium dome of the men's section has collapsed. Ayvansarayi cites the foundation inscription whose chronogram yields the date 880/1475–76; Ayvansarayi, *Garden of the Mosques*, 209. The present mosque dates from the nineteenth century. For a survey of what remains of the foundation, see Ayverdi, *Osmanlı mi'mârîsinde Fâtih devri, 855–886 (1451–1481)*, 3:476–77. Siding with Cem in the struggle for the sultanate between Mehmed's two sons, Nişancı Mehmed Pasha was killed in the janissary revolt following the sultan's death; Karamanlı Nişancı Mehmed Paşa, *Osmanlı sultanları tarihi*, 330–34.

214. The patron, of Serbian descent, was governor-general of Anatolia, vizier and grand vizier in the imperial council, and commander of the navy that laid siege to Otranto in 1481; Stavrides, *Sultan of Vezirs*, 65. The waqfiyya of the foundation has not survived. The bath was in all probability part of the foundation Gedik Ahmed established in Afyon, including a convent-mosque, madrasa, and bath. The chronogram written for the Istanbul bath by Tacizade Ca'fer Çelebi yields the date 1474–75, which corresponds to the first year of the founder's grand vizierate; Ca'fer Çelebi, *Heveşnâme*, 59.

215. Waqf documents of the Mehmed II foundation mention a "garden of İshak Pasha" in this area, neighboring property belonging to the sultanic waqf; BBA MM 19 (*Ayaṣofya vakfı taḥrîr defteri*, A.H. 895), fol. 36a.

216. Nişancı Mehmed Pasha willed that the palace courtyard (possibly the outer courtyard) with its buildings and the stables near the masjid be used as a

dervish convent after the cessation of his line. This and another willed stipulation of the pasha, that no member of the imperial council and no merchant be allowed to reside there ("ehl-i dīvāndan ve tācirlerden kimesne sākin olmaya"), were not granted. In 953/1546, the resident of the palace was the commander of the janissary corps. Barkan and Ayverdi, *İstanbul vakıfları tahrir defteri 953 (1546) tarihli,* 137.

217. As Bayezid Pasha's madrasa and imaret in his hometown, Amasya, and Çandarlı İbrahim Pasha's imaret in his hometown, Iznik, suggest. Bayezid Pasha, vizier of Mehmed I, built a masjid and madrasa in the Ottoman capital, Bursa, while Çandarlı built a mosque and bath in the same city.

218. For a more detailed comparison of viziers' and commanders' patronage through the first half of the fifteenth century, see Kafescioğlu, "The Ottoman Capital in the Making," 74–76.

219. This definition owes much to Lefebvre, *Production of Space,* particularly to his discussion of monumentality in terms of use as well as signification. I have benefited also from the essays by Françoise Choay, Kurt Forster, and Val K. Warke in the *Harvard Architecture Review* 4 (1984), an issue dedicated to "Monumentality and the City," as well as from Françoise Choay's discussion of notions of the architectural monument; Choay, *Invention of the Historic Monument.*

220. Tafuri, "Cives esse non licere."

221. Braudel, *The Mediterranean and the Mediterranean World,* 1:344–52.

222. While prototypes of the building complex comprising a host of functions and conceived as an urban or suburban core are to be found elsewhere in the medieval Islamic world, the particular set of institutions that form these complexes varies largely according to historical context and with the politics of patronage that underlie their foundation.

223. The centrality of the hospice and public kitchen to Ottoman political culture is demonstrated well in contemporary sources, which dwell at length on such charities of the ruling elite. See especially Aşıkpaşazade's notes on the works (*āṣār*) of sultans and grandees, and references to feasts offered by

Mahmud Pasha; Aşıkpaşazade, *Tevârîh-i Âl-i Osman,* 230–49; *Düsturnâme-i Enverī,* 7.

224. Madrasas were not part of the original foundations of Has Murad and Rum Mehmed, while that of Mahmud Pasha was similar in rank to those founded by the sultan. The complex of Davud Pasha, completed in 1483 or 1485, some years after Mehmed's death, does include a madrasa, as do a number of vizierial complexes built during Bayezid II's reign.

225. Gedik Ahmed Pasha's complex in Afyon did feature a madrasa, suggesting that, whether implicitly or explicitly, different policies regarding the patronage of educational institutions applied in the capital and the provinces. The difference was possibly informed by the recent establishment of Mehmed II's eight madrasas within his complex and the subsequent hierachization of religious education.

226. Alberti, *On the Art of Building,* 121–24.

227. On Matthias Corvinus and the reception of Renaissance humanism and artistic ideals in fifteenth-century Hungary, see Feuer-Tóth, *Renaissance Architecture in Hungary,* and idem, *Art and Humanism in Hungary.*

228. This is in line with the recent work of Peter Burke, who, in *European Renaissance,* discusses the Renaissance as a movement rather than a period, in an attempt to historicize and take into account dynamic aspects of Renaissance culture. Burke suggests that a number of peripheries were receptive to aspects of Renaissance culture, Mehmed's Istanbul among these. For a recent discussion of cross-cultural influences between the Ottoman and the Italian worlds that directs attention to the cultural patronage of Mehmed II, see Jardine and Brotton, *Global Interests.*

229. On late medieval urban planning in Italy, see Friedman, *Florentine New Towns,* and idem, "Palaces and the Street in Late Medieval and Renaissance Italy."

230. Alberti, *On the Art of Building,* 189–92 (bk. 7, chap. 1), 261–68 (bk. 8, chap. 6).

231. *Filarete's Treatise on Architecture,* 26, 76, and passim. For a discussion of the roots of this arrangement

in urban centers of the Po region, see Giordano, "On Filarete's *Libro Architettonico,"* 64–65.

232. Parallels in early modern Europe, such as the Paris of Henry IV, where numerous large-scale building projects were part of an urban program that meant to revitalize the Bourbon capital with no explicit plan for restructuring the street system and creating axial arteries, have not been explored. See Ballon, *The Paris of Henry IV,* esp. 251–53.

233. Chrysoloras, "Comparison of Old and New Rome," 211, 214.

234. BBA MM 19 (*Ayaṣofya vakfı taḥrīr defteri,* A.H. 895), fols 24a–25a. On *emboloi* in the Byzantine city, see Mundell-Mango, "The Commercial Map of Constantinople," 194–97, 203–4. Information on the Mese in the Palaeologan era suggests that commercial activity was focused on particular locations rather than stretching alongside it.

235. Berger, "Imperial and Ecclesiastical Processions in Constantinople," 83–85; 86–87, for a map of processions in the Byzantine city.

236. Küçük Abdal, *Velāyetnāme-i Sulṭān Otman,* 94v–97r, 117v–118v.

237. Kritovoulos, *History of Mehmed the Conqueror,* 83, 105, 141.

238. George of Trebizond, *Collectanea Trapezuntiana,* 493.

239. See chapter 3 for a discussion of this text.

240. Françoise Choay underlines the coexistence of a largely medieval sense of familiarity and an emerging sense of historic distance, alongside utilitarian, political, and moral concerns, in the evolution of a new aesthetic sensibility regarding the antique in fifteenth-century Italy; Choay, *Invention of the Historic Monument,* 17–39. For an interpretation of fifteenth- and sixteenth-century Ottoman architecture that takes into account its connections and parallels with Renaissance architectural culture, see Necipoğlu, *Age of Sinan,* esp. 77–103. For revisionist conceptualizations of the Renaissance that explore its parallels and interactions beyond the European cultural sphere, see, among other works, Darling, "The Renaissance and the Middle East"; Jardine and Brotton, *Global Interests;* MacLean, *Re-orienting the Renaissance.*

241. A comparable articulation of a visual, rather than geometric, order in trecento Florentine urbanism has been explored by Marvin Trachtenberg in his *Dominion of the Eye.*

242. Dwarfed by the nearby Nuruosmaniye mosque and by larger projects realized during the following centuries, Mahmud Pasha's mosque today is not a focus in the urban silhoutte of Istanbul. That it once did mark the cityscape is evident in the Lorichs and the anonymous Paris panoramas (Bibliothèque nationale de France, Cabinet des Estampes, Res. B.10), as well as the Düsseldorf view.

243. G. Necipoğlu, *Architecture, Ceremonial, and Power,* 4–13, 123–200; idem, "Framing the Gaze in Ottoman, Safavid, and Mughal Palaces."

244. Mantran, *Istanbul dans la seconde moitié du XVIIe siècle,* 43; Guidoni, "Sinan's Construction of the Urban Panorama."

245. Gautier, "Un récit inédit du siège de Constantinople," 109, cited in Necipoğlu, "The Life of an Imperial Monument."

246. Küçük Abdal, *Velāyetnāme-i Sulṭān Otman,* fol. 11r.

247. *Ṣalṭuḳnāme,* fols. 393r–v.

248. Tursun Beg, *History of Mehmed the Conqueror,* fols. 33v, 52r.

249. Muꜥali, *Ḥünkārnāme,* fol. 8v.

250. One example is the *Book of Travels* of Evliya Çelebi, who, more than two centuries later, described in detail the spectacular view of the sultan's palace, the Golden Horn, the Bosphorus, and the suburbs of the city the congregation enjoyed from the courtyard of the Süleymaniye. Part of the same passage describes the view of the complex from Galata. *Evliya Çelebi Seyahatnamesi,* bk. 1, fol. 45r.

251. Explorations of the gaze in relation to pictorial representation, which underline its relational aspect, prove useful when considering the gaze and visuality within urban space. Margaret Olin, in her essay "Gaze," directs attention to the subjugating/destroying gaze, exemplified in traditional images of the evil eye and theorized by Sartre and Lacan. "The gaze, then, corresponds to desire, the desire for self-completion through another. There is struggle over the gaze: one gets to look, to be

master of the gaze; the other (or Other) is looked at. Therefore the power of the gaze extends beyond the struggle between the sexes." Significantly, Olin also examines alternatives to the subjugating/possessing/destroying gaze: the act of looking back, the shared gaze, she explains, evoking Bakhtinian dialogic interpretations, urges the viewers into a relation. Transposing Norman Bryson's search for an expanded subject-object relationship assumed in the concept of the gaze to an urban/spatial framework may also prove useful for an inquiry into the complex workings of the gaze within the city; Bryson, "The Gaze in the Expanded Field."

Chapter 3

1. I borrow the term from Denis Cosgrove, who articulates the notion of symbolic landscape in his discussion of the relation of the Venetian myth to the city's urban landscape; Cosgrove, "The Myth and the Stones of Venice."

2. Francesco II Gonzaga's *Camera delle citta* in his villa in Gonzaga, whose designs were to be provided by Gentile Bellini, is an example that has not survived but is mentioned in several sources. For the correspondence between Bellini and the representatives of Francesco Gonzaga, see Luzio, "Disegni topografici e pitture dei Bellini." For the de' Barbari view and a contextual study of city views before the publication of de' Barbari's Venice ca. 1500, see Schulz, "Jacopo de' Barbari's View of Venice." The decoration of the Qaꜥa al Ashrafiyya in the Mamluk citadel of Cairo with architectural imagery can be evaluated in the same context. Although their formal roots were in the Umayyad tradition, the meanings these images conveyed were comparable to the meanings of their counterparts produced in the Italian realm. For a discussion of these images, see Rabbat, *Citadel of Cairo,* 161–69.

3. In one of the earliest studies on visual images of cities, Pierre Lavedan coined the term "l'idéogramme urbain," referring to the highly stylized depictions of cities in regional or world maps, which usually render the boundaries of the city in geometricized form and place a number of buildings within; Lavedan, *Représentations des villes*

dans l'art de Moyen Âge, 33–35. Chiara Frugoni, in her study of urban imagery in medieval art and literature, explored transformations in the iconography of these representations within the context of the rising political prominence of communes in the late medieval era; Frugoni, *A Distant City.* Juergen Schulz, in his groundbreaking article on the de' Barbari view, has discussed in detail the "ideal content" of cartographic images, arguing that the representation of political and religious ideas, which had largely shaped medieval cartography, was grafted onto the more precise maps of the early modern period; Schulz, "Jacopo de' Barbari's View of Venice," 442–67. For a discussion of the interrelated problems of precision and meaning in architectural and urban imagery, see Grabar, *Mediation of Ornament,* 156–93.

4. J. B. Harley pioneered this interpretative trend in a series of works that transformed the study of cartography. For an assessment of his strategy, see Harley, "Maps, Knowledge, and Power." I have benefited from a number of studies concerned with issues of meaning in cartographic images, particularly Schulz, "Jacopo de' Barbari's View of Venice"; idem, "Maps as Metaphors"; Woodward, *Art and Cartography*; Harvey, "Local and Regional Cartography in Medieval Europe"; Nuti, "The Perspective Plan in the Sixteenth Century"; idem, "Mapping Places"; Marchitello, "Political Maps"; Buisseret, *Envisioning the City*; and Cosgrove, *Mappings.* Matthew Edney has noted that Foucauldian readings of topographic images pioneered by J. B. Harley offered too absolutist an interpretative strategy, and that resistances and negotiations, too, work their way into cartographic representation; Edney, "Theory in the History of Cartography," 189.

5. As I hope to demonstrate, the images themselves prompt such an exploration. At the same time, the ground here has been prepared by Carlo Ginzburg's search for polyphony in inquisitorial records dealing with witchcraft and his attempt to highlight, in Bakhtinian terms, the dialogic structure of these records, by Cemal Kafadar's emphasis on the fluidity and

plasticity of identities in late medieval Anatolia and Balkans and his search for reflections of this phenomenon in Ottoman histories and traditions, and by Stéphane Yerasimos's analysis of Ottoman myths of Constantinople. Ginzburg, *Myths, Emblems, Clues;* Kafadar, *Between Two Worlds;* Yerasimos, *La fondation de Constantinople et de Sainte-Sophie.*

6. Buondelmonti, *Liber Insularum Archipelagi* (1897), 241.

7. Turner, "Christopher Buondelmonti and the Isolario"; Manners, "Constructing the Image of a City." For an earlier discussion of the dating of the manuscripts, see Garand, "La tradition manuscrite du *Liber Archipelagi insularum.*" For a survey of the images of Constantinople in the Buondelmonti manuscripts and a classification, see Gerola, "Le vedute di Costantinopoli di Cristoforo Buondelmonti."

8. Ian Manners's assertion that the sixteenth-century views, with their focus on truthful representation of the city, are rooted in the tradition of Buondelmonti views (and his criticism of Lucia Nuti for distinguishing the sixteenth-century images from the earlier ones) should be questioned in this context. Their *concern* for truthfulness notwithstanding, these fifteenth-century images, in terms of their conceptualization of the city and their representational conventions, are radically different from those produced according to the conventions of the "perspective plan," which became widespread particularly in the print medium during the following century. Manners, "Constructing the Image of a City," 94–95; Nuti, "The Perspective Plan in the Sixteenth Century," 105, 122–23.

9. David Harvey has noted that behind the late medieval maps and bird's-eye views were the traditions of the diagrammatic "city ideograms" designating particular or generic cities in manuscript illuminations (which he thinks were a survival of an ancient tradition of picture-maps). Among these, he notes particularly images of towns in the Holy Land, especially of Jerusalem, which began to appear after the Crusades. Harvey, *History of Topographical Maps,* 68–72. For diagrammatic plans of Jerusalem from the twelfth and

fourteenth centuries, see Harvey, *History of Topographical Maps,* 71; Harvey, "Local and Regional Cartography in Medieval Europe," 475. A telling example of the fifteenth-century "bird's-eye view" in this fashion is a mid-century copy of an original plan of Vienna and Bratislava dating to 1421–22. This is the earliest city map with a scale; inside the walls few monuments of importance are visible. Reproduced in Harvey, "Local and Regional Cartography in Medieval Europe," 472.

10. Manners, "Constructing the Image of a City."

11. For a discussion of late-fifteenth-century French literary representations of the city, see Santucci, "Jérusalem, Rome, Constantinople dans l'œuvre de Molinet." This is not to overlook the vast body of European writings that dealt with the fall, but to direct attention to a literary parallel to the Buondelmonti views.

12. Turner, "Christopher Buondelmonti and the Isolario," 13.

13. For a discussion of the *Isolario* in the context of Venetian historical consciousness in the fifteenth century and the interest in Venetian territories in the Aegean, see Brown, *Venice and Antiquity,* 77–81.

14. A connection between the later manuscripts of the *Isolario* and the writings of Aeneas Silvius Piccolomini has been suggested. Piccolomini, as Pope Pius II, was to call for a crusade to rescue Constantinople from the Ottomans. Manners, "Constructing the Image of a City," 96.

15. For a facsimile of the manuscript, see Buondelmonti, *Liber Insularum Archipelagi* (2005). This publication was available to me only after the completion of my study. The image of Constantinople in the manuscript was first published by Ian Manners in "Constructing the Image of a City." My interpretation of this image differs from that offered by Manners in some respects.

16. Only the earliest known map, which is also one of the crudest, depicts the whole of the straits and the Black Sea. This is the image in the Venice Marciana manuscript, dating to ca. 1422, reproduced in Turner, "Christopher Buondelmonti," 211. Most other copies of the map stop at the double

columns of Diplokionion in present-day Beşiktaş.

17. This feature of the map may also be a sign of its relationship to the Vavassore view, as the boundaries of the city in the two images are remarkably similar. Since topographic accuracy has shaped the latter image much more than the former, it may be plausible to assume that the maker of the Düsseldorf image was aware of the latter drawing.

18. The inclusion of this building may in fact be a sign that the image, or this particular copy of it, was drawn after Mehmed II's death, as it was Bayezid II who built his father's mausoleum. Information on the construction of the mausoleum is found in *Heveşnâme,* p. 29, in Çelebi, *Divan şiirinde İstanbul.*

19. The cross that had replaced the monumental statue of Constantine was removed together with Justinian's statue in the Augustaion; both Aşıkpaşazade and Neşri note that the "copper horse" was melted along with "the cross" (in Aşıkpaşazade, *vidalu hac,* "the cross with screws") and bells taken from churches. Aşıkpaşazade, *Tevârîh-i Âl-i Osman,* 196–97; Neşri, *Kitab-ı cihannuma,* 720. Visiting the city in 1544, Pierre Gilles gave a very detailed description of the column with no reference to the cross it once supported; Gilles, *Antiquities of Constantinople,* 132–37.

20. For Justinian's column and statue, see Mango, "The Columns of Justinian and His Successors." For a review of the sources on the column and the statue, and for their history in Ottoman times, see Raby, "Mehmed the Conqueror."

21. Prokopius, translated in Mango, *Art of the Byzantine Empire,* 110–13.

22. Frederick Hasluck has convincingly argued that the Turkish legend of the "red apple" was prompted by the gilded orb held by the emperor; Hasluck, *Christianity and Islam Under the Sultans,* 2:736–40. On the transformations of the red-apple lore in the Ottoman context, see Yerasimos, "De l'arbre à la pomme."

23. Şemsüddin Karamani, *Tercüme-i Tārīḫ-i Cāmiʿi Ayāṣofyā,* fol. 50r; Angiolello, *Viaggio di Negroponte,* 27.

24. Drawing attention to the inconsistency in the sources—that is, to the fact that Gilles studied fragments of the statue in the Topkapı Palace in the 1540s, whereas Ottoman histories assert that Mehmed had it melted into cannons—Julian Raby has suggested that fragments of the statue might have been included in the sultan's private collection of Byzantine relics kept in the palace gardens, and that he might have tried to save it at least in part; Raby, "Mehmed the Conqueror," 148–49.

25. These conventions make it highly unlikely that Gentile Bellini was the maker of the view. Although none of the city views Gentile painted for the duke of Gonzaga or might have painted for Mehmed II survive, his narrative paintings set in Venice demonstrate without doubt that he was a keen observer and meticulous renderer of architecture and architectural space. His carefully constructed urban spaces and competent use of perspectival devices are far removed from the conventions used in the Düsseldorf image. For a discussion of architectural imagery and urban spaces in Bellini's paintings, see Brown, *Venetian Narrative Painting in the Age of Carpaccio,* 144–50.

26. TKS GI 24. For this, see Raby, "El Gran Turco," 394.

27. The four directions of the compass are indicated in the same cursive hand. All other images in the manuscript, too, are captioned in Ottoman Turkish.

28. Manners has suggested Mahmud Pasha as a possible patron, but this does not seem plausible, since the view features Mehmed II's mausoleum and therefore must postdate 1481, whereas the grand vizier was executed in 1474.

29. Converted to Islam, the Amirutzes sons apparently kept their contacts with the Christian establishment in the city: one of them was commissioned by Mehmed to translate the Bible into Arabic; he also appealed to Maximos II, the Greek Orthodox patriarch between 1476 and 1482, to prepare an exposition on Christianity for the sultan. Babinger, *Mehmed the Conqueror and His Time,* 247.

30. The view has been dated to ca. 1520 by Leo Bagrow, and Ian

Manners has suggested, in light of other work by the cartographer, that it should be dated to the 1530s. Vavassore's view of Venice also was dated by Juergen Schulz to the mid-1530s, which makes it plausible that this similar view of Constantinople too should have been published around the same time. Schulz, "Printed Plans and Panoramic Views of Venice," 23–24; Manners, "Constructing the Image of a City." For an introduction to the cartographic work of Vavassore, see Bagrow, *Giovanni Andreas di Vavassore.* For earlier references to this view of Istanbul, see Mordtmann, *Esquisse topographique de Constantinople;* Schneider, *Die Bevölkerung Konstantinopels;* and Babinger, *Drei Stadtansichten.*

31. Manners, "Constructing the Image of a City."

32. For this print, see Schulz, "Printed Plans and Panoramic Views," 42, 124–25.

33. It is not my aim to replace the de' Barbari view with the Vavassore as the "first" perspective plan, as I am not concerned with establishing primacy. Both images, I contend, partook in this newly emerging representational idiom, and the maker of the Istanbul view, possibly a Venetian like de' Barbari, was an artist who was aware of the latest developments in this medium. For the "perspective plan," see Nuti, "The Perspective Plan in the Sixteenth Century." Another insightful discussion of such images is found in Louis Marin's essay on Utopia, "The City's Portrait in Its Utopics"; Marin, *Utopics,* 201–37.

34. These are the early-sixteenth-century view of Florence attributed to Lucantonio degli Uberti and the anonymous 1538 view of Rome, both copies of Rosselli prints produced in the 1480s and 1490s.

35. As in the cities of Pisa and El Cuzco in the *Civitates;* Nuti, "The Perspective Plan in the Sixteenth Century," 121–22.

36. For discussions on the making of the Rosselli views, see Schulz, "Jacopo de' Barbari's View of Venice," 429–31; Fanelli, *Firenze,* 77–86; Nuti, "The Perspective Plan in the Sixteenth Century," 113–16; and Friedman, "Fiorenza." The view of Ferrara dating to ca. 1490 is also of interest: it exhibits a

rare attempt to employ single-point perspective in a city view, a mode that was not adequate—hence its rare use for this purpose—for the representation of an area of the size and formal complexity of a city; Nuti, "The Perspective Plan in the Sixteenth Century," 108.

37. The inventory, made after the death of Rosselli's son, included copper plates of the perspective views of Rome and Florence mentioned above, along with two lost views, of Pisa and Constantinople. As the originals of the Rome and Florence views are dated to the 1480s and 1490s through their contents, the same years as Vavassore's original is dated to, it is tempting to ask whether Vavassore copied Rosselli's Constantinople. The inventory is found in Hind, *Early Italian Engraving,* 1:304–9. Arthur Hind, and more recently David Landau and Peter Parshall, have suggested that Rosselli, who traveled to Hungary in the early 1480s, might have visited Constantinople and made the drawing himself; Landau and Parshall, *The Renaissance Print,* 94.

38. Francesco Rosselli, in addition to being one of the first printers to produce city views in the new idiom, was also to produce, with Matteo Contarini, the first printed world map to incorporate the findings of Christopher Columbus. Landau and Parshall, in their study of the Renaissance print, and Jerry Brotton, in his work on early modern cartography, have underlined the importance of printing in developments relating to surveying and mapmaking, on the one hand, and in the formation of European conceptions of the world, on the other; Landau and Parshall, *The Renaissance Print,* 240–44; Brotton, *Trading Territories,* 116–17.

39. Schulz, "Jacopo de' Barbari's View of Venice," 439–41; Nuti, "The Perspective Plan in the Sixteenth Century," 107–9, 121–22.

40. Marin, *Utopics,* 208–9.

41. Babinger, *Drei Stadtansichten.* Amirutzes died in 1475, before the creation of the view.

42. The commission to Bellini is noted in Angiolello and Lezze, *Historia turchescha (1300–1514),* 120. On Francesco II Gonzaga and Bellini, see Schulz, "Maps as Metaphors." On urban settings in Gentile Bellini's narrative paintings, see Brown,

Venetian Narrative Painting in the Age of Carpaccio.

43. On translations of and commentaries on works of Ptolemy George of Trebizond presented to Mehmed II (or attempted to do so unsuccessfully), see George of Trebizond, *Collectanea Trapezuntiana*, 281–84, 748–50. For discussions of the material pertaining to Mehmed II's geographic interest, see Raby, "El Gran Turco," 10 ff, Pinto, "Ways of Seeing," 42–146. Malatesta was accused by Pius II of treachery, and the Venetian merchants carrying the parcel were forced to hand over the gift. There is, however, a copy of the manuscript in the Topkapı Library collection.

44. Brotton, *Trading Territories*.

45. Zorzi Dolfin notes that Mehmed owned a map of Europe. Noted in Raby, "El Gran Turco," 13–14.

46. Raby, "El Gran Turco," 20–21. This map is presently held at the Istanbul Archeological Museum.

47. For a discussion of the album and the collection of prints it contains, see Raby, "Mehmed II Fatih and the Fatih Album." For a discussion of the prints in the context of fifteenth-century print production and collection, see Landau and Parshall, *The Renaissance Print*, 91–95.

48. Hind, *Early Italian Engraving*, 1:195, reproduced in vol. 3, pl. 268. For the interpretation of the headgear, see Campbell and Chong, *Bellini and the East*, 66.

49. For the portrait medals of Mehmed produced in Istanbul and in Italy by Italian artists, see Raby, "Pride and Prejudice."

50. Berger, "Zur sogenannten Stadtansicht des Vavassore," 335–38.

51. Such as the Myrelaion. This was possibly a residue of the conventions of the earlier type of city views, which showed the monuments from the most favorable standpoint instead of representing the city from a single, unified point of view. Rosselli's Florence and its later copy, otherwise "accurate" and possibly the product of measured drawings, also feature buildings depicted from various points of view; Harvey, *History of Topographical Maps*, 75; Friedman, "Fiorenza." For a survey of the monuments depicted in the Vavassore view, see Berger, "Zur

sogenannten Stadtansicht des Vavassore," 338–55.

52. The column was removed when the bath of the Bayezid II complex was built on its site in the first decade of the sixteenth century. Its base reliefs were used as spolia in the façade of the bath. See the epilogue. The mid-sixteenth-century drawings by Battista Franco must be copies of earlier drawings, possibly by an Italian artist resident at Mehmed II's court.

53. The artist spreads out the more densely built-up area of the city westward; his possible motive is to avoid depicting the area close to the land walls, which was never completely built up throughout the Ottoman history of the city, as undeveloped space. Matrakcı did the same in his map of Istanbul, in all probability with the same motive.

54. Braun and Hogenberg, in the introduction to their ambitiously conceived album of city views, noted that they had included the figural representations in the foregrounds of the images in order to prevent Turks from using the book. While the detailed version of Cristoforo Sorte's map of Venetian territory drawn in the 1560s was kept in the state archive, only a simplified version of it was allowed to circulate; the former was considered to contain strategic information; Cosgrove, "The Geometry of Landscape," 257. That papal authorities tried to prohibit Mehmed II from acquiring the map of Italy sent to him by Maletesta, already noted above, is another indication of such caution (see note 43 above).

55. He told, for example, of having had to measure the column of Arcadius secretly from inside the shaft; Gilles, *Antiquities of Constantinople*, 198, 221–23.

56. Brown, *Venice and Antiquity*, 89–90.

57. With very few exceptions, Berger limits his analysis to the sites that are marked with legends in the first or later reproductions of the print, without commenting on others. He concludes that since the view includes (that is, marks with legends) only the Christian sites in the city apart from Mehmed's buildings, it cannot have been a work of Ottoman patronage. Nevertheless, he notes, too, that new

legends were added and some older ones omitted in the later reproductions of the print. This suggests that the original print or drawing might have carried more detailed legends, and those that were obscure to Vavassore, such as legends marking vizierial buildings, might have been omitted when he produced his print.

58. St. Lucca (which Mango identified as the church of the Nea, possibly the Güngörmez Kilisesi), St. Sebastiano, St. Pietro, St. Todaldo, the Patriarchate, St. Andrea (later Koca Mustafa Pasha Camiʿ), St. Lazaro (possibly the Peribleptos abbey, which became the Armenian patriarchate during Ottoman rule), St. Helena, St. Katerina, St. Galatani, St. Veneranda. For suggestions regarding identifications of these buildings, see Berger, "Zur sogenannten Stadtansicht des Vavassore," 339–55.

59. The exterior of the rotunda is 41.80 meters in diameter, second only to the Pantheon—it may well be the "colisseo" in the image. For the complex of the Myraleion (Bodrum Camiʿ), its monastery, and the palace of Romanus I Lecapenus, see Striker, *The Myraleion*.

60. Schneider, *Byzanz*, 93.

61. On the *Liber Chronicarum*, see Wilson, *The Making of the Nuremberg Chronicle*.

62. Schedel, *Liber Chronicarum*, 129v–130r, 257r.

63. Ian Manners has argued that the double-page view of Constantinople in the book is a conventional and stylized representation of the city, one that reveals little of the emerging interest in the "actual appearance of places that had already begun to affect the construction of topographic maps and views in Italy by this time." Ian Manners, paper presented at the conference "Istanbul: The Making of a City" (State University of Texas at Austin, March 1995). Albrecht Berger and Jonathan Bardill argue that the image derives from the original of the Vavassore view and a Buondelmonti view. Though they support this argument by pointing to similarities in the content of these images, they do not explore the representational conventions of this particular image and their implications. Similarly, they do not question why

the artist should create this particular image based on the assumed prototypes. Berger and Bardill, "Representations of Constantinople."

64. The inaccuracy of the majority of the views in the book should not undermine the value of this particular image, as it was without doubt created by a draftsperson familiar with the city. Moreover, as Juergen Schulz has observed, the significant thing about the use of the city views in the *Liber Chronicarum* is not their inaccuracy or imaginary quality or the publisher's apparent disinterest in matching text and image but rather the pronounced interest in the city image itself, as suggested by the profusion of real, imagined, and mismatched images of cities in the book; Schulz, "Jacopo de' Barbari's View of Venice," 463–64.

65. Note also Adrian Wilson's remark that in its scope and style the *Liber Chronicarum* is an Italian history rather than a northern European one. Schedel was educated in Padua and took the writings of Aeneas Silvius Piccolomini as his model. Wilson, *The Making of the Nuremberg Chronicle*, 19–25. Piccolomini had, as the secretary of the Council of Basel, written one of the most beautiful descriptions of that city.

66. Bibliothèque nationale de France, Cabinet des Estampes, Res. B.10; Österreichische Nationalbibliothek, Cod. 8626.

67. ʿAbd al-Rahman al-Bistami, *Tercüme-i Miftaḥ-ı Cifrüʾl-Cāmiʿ*, fol. 224v. Another version excludes the three columns of the Hippodrome, presenting only the Hagia Sophia and the statue of Justinian; TKS B373, fol. 255a.

68. Reproduced in Ambraseys and Finkel, *The Seismicity of Turkey and Adjacent Areas*, 49.

69. Ateş, "İstanbul'un fethine dair Fatih Sultan Mehmed," 14–21, 24–26, 35–43.

70. Ibid., 44–50. The emphasis of the Persian text on worldly and heavenly beauty may be foreshadowing later Ottoman discourse on the city and its monuments. As has been noted in chapter 2, authors who hailed from the Iranian world had a share in fashioning an aesthetic discourse on Ottoman monuments.

71. Yerasimos, *La fondation de Constantinople et de Sainte-Sophie*.

72. For the *Patria*, see Dagron, *Constantinople imaginaire*. For Mehmed II's copy, dating to 1474, see Raby, "El Gran Turco," 386, and Yerasimos, *La fondation de Constantinople et de Sainte-Sophie*, 210.

73. On the Turkish versions, see Yerasimos, *La fondation de Constantinople et de Sainte-Sophie*, 210–14. I have used the translation by Şemsüddin Karamani.

74. Şemsüddin Karamani, *Tercüme-i Tārīḫ-i Cāmiʿi Ayāṣofyā*, fols. 4v–5r.

75. Ibid., fols. 5v, 17r–v, 23r–v.

76. "so that they will know that in the end nothing was left in my hands when I left the world," says Justinian to his son; Şemsüddin Karamani, *Tercüme-i Tārīḫ-i Cāmiʿi Ayāṣofyā*, fol. 25v.

77. The version of the text to which I refer is the one used by Yerasimos, dating to 891/1486; transliteration in Yerasimos, *La fondation de Constantinople et de Sainte-Sophie*, 5–48.

78. Yazıcıoğlu Ahmed Bīcan, *Dürr-i Meknūn*, fols. 61vff. Yerasimos regards *Dürr-i Meknūn* as the first of the "anti-imperial" texts on Constantinople; Yerasimos, *La fondation de Constantinople et de Sainte-Sophie*, 202–3.

79. For Arab traditions on Constantinople, see Massignon, "Textes prémonitoires et commentaires mystiques."

80. Yerasimos, *La fondation de Constantinople et de Sainte-Sophie*, 26–33.

81. Necipoğlu, "The Life of an Imperial Monument," 202.

82. See esp. fols. 482v–486v, 616v–618v. Cemal Kafadar has discussed the *Salṭuḳnāme* in relation to the ghazi reaction to the centralizing policies of the state and to Constantinople's being made the capital as a symbol of this process; Kafadar, *Between Two Worlds*, 146ff.

83. *Salṭuḳnāme*, fol. 616v.

84. G. Necipoğlu, *Architecture, Ceremonial, and Power*. The eight madrasas situated in rows of four to either side of the New Mosque were named the Mediterranean and the Black Sea madrasas, echoing the theme of territorial dominance reflected in the inscriptions of the New Palace.

85. İdris Bidlisi, *Heşt behişt*, fol. 65v.

86. Ibid., fol. 36v.

87. Çelebi, *Divan şiirinde İstanbul*, 7. The identity of the poet is obscure; he may or may not be ʿAyni of Karaman. The poem is not included in the collection of poems by the latter; Aynur, "Istanbul in Divan Poetry," 44–45.

88. It always does, observed Carlo Ginzburg, in relation to the trials of the *benandanti* as witches in sixteenth- and seventeenth-century Friuli; Ginzburg, *Myths, Emblems, Clues*, 160.

89. "Bir güneş yüzlü melek gördüm ki ʿālem māhıdur / Ol ḳarā sümbülleri ʿāşıḳlarınuñ āhıdur / Ḳāralar giymiş meh-i tābān gibi ol serv-i nāz / Mülk-i efrengüñ ki ḥüsn içinde şāhıdur / ʿUkde-i zünnārına her kimse ki dil bağlamaz / Ehl-i īmān olmaz ol ʿāşıḳlarıñ gümrāhıdur / Ġamzesi öldürdügine lebleri cānlar virir / Vār ise ol rūḥ-baḫşuñ dīn-i ʿĪsā rāhıdur / ʿAvniyā ḳılma gümān ki sāña rām ola nigār / Sen Sıtānbūl şāhısuñ ol Ḳalātā şāhıdur." *Fātiḥʾin şiirleri*, 41, facsimile p. 10. ʿAvni is the pen name of Mehmed II. Nongendered, Turkish leaves the gender of the poem's object ambiguous. The Persianate literary tradition, which supplied Ottoman poetry with some of its basic conventions, rendered the beloved a young male figure, and I have translated it as such here.

Chapter 4

1. The chart is from İnalcık, "Istanbul," 238–39. The census document of 1477 records 14,803 households in Istanbul and 1,521 in Galata. This number does not include soldiers, madrasa students, and slaves. On the 882/1477 census (TKSA D 9524), see Schneider, *Die Bevölkerung Konstantinopels*; Meriç, "Birkaç mühim arşiv vesikası"; Barkan and Ayverdi, *İstanbul vakıfları tahrir defteri 953 (1546) tarihli*, xiv–xv; İnalcık "Istanbul," 238–39.

2. Alfons Schneider's estimate of sixty to seventy thousand seems more plausible to me. Ömer Barkan's calculation assumes five people per household, while recent work on early modern demography has generally assumed between three and five per household, the figures varying considerably according to particular circumstances. In the decades following the conquest, the city's population consisted mainly

of deportees, some of whom had left their families behind. It seems reasonable to accept a smaller number of people per household. For a discussion of population estimates on the basis of households, see Jennings, "Population, Society, and Economy."

3. See chapter 1 for resettlement of merchants and craftsmen. Tursun Beg, in a lengthy and rather convoluted passage, suggests that the sultan was criticized for the imposition of rent on property given as freehold to newcomers, and was accused of a break of treaty (nakż-i ʿahd), while Aşıkpaşazade details popular objections to such measures; Tursun Beg, History of Mehmed the Conqueror, 56a–57b; Aşıkpaşazade, Tevârîh-i Âl-i Osman, 193. Halil İnalcık provides a detailed account of the rent issue in "The Policy of Mehmed II."

4. Movements within the city are attested in İnalcık, "Istanbul." The Archives of the Prime Ministry hold a number of documents concerning deportees who had left their families in their places of origin or who were persecuted for escaping to their hometowns or for marrying in both places; BBA A.DVN 790:10, 35.

5. Kritovoulos, History of Mehmed the Conqueror, 221–22.

6. Sanjian, "Two Contemporary Armenian Elegies," 259.

7. Sanjian, Colophons of Armenian Manuscripts, 326.

8. Cited in Hacker, "The Sürgün System and Jewish Society," 12.

9. On mass resettlements as central to Ottoman territorial expansion, see İnalcık, "Ottoman Methods of Conquest," and Barkan, "Osmanlı İmparatoluğunda bir iskan ve kolonizasyon metodu olarak sürgünler." On resettlement for military, economic, and demographic reasons in the Byzantine realm, see Charanis, "The Transfer of Population as a Policy in the Byzantine Empire." On the Ilkhanid world, see Allsen, Culture and Conquest, 198 ff. Timur's policy of developing the city of Samarqand through deportations from elsewhere in the empire forms a precedent for Mehmed II's measures; G. Necipoğlu, Architecture, Ceremonial, and Power, 250.

10. For comprehensive overviews of deportations to the city during the reign of Mehmed, see İnalcık, "Istanbul," 222–23; Yerasimos, "Osmanlı İstanbulʾunun Kuruluşu"; and idem, "La communauté grecque-orthodoxe de Constantinople."

11. İnalcık, "Istanbul," 238–39.

12. Braude, "Foundation Myths of the Millet System"; Bardakjian, "Rise of the Armenian Patriarchate of Constantinople"; Epstein, "Leadership of the Ottoman Jews."

13. The main waqf documents that provide information on the social and physical makeup of the city's residential areas in this period are the endowment deeds of the Mehmed II foundation and surveys of property endowed to Hagia Sophia and Mehmed II's complex; Fatih Sultan Mehmedʾin vakfiyeleri; Zwei Stiftsurkunden des Sultan Mehmed II. Fatih; BBA MM 19 (Ayaşofya vakfı taḥrīr defteri, A.H. 895); Istanbul Atatürk Library M.C. O.64 (Ayaşofya vakfı cibāyet defteri, A.H. 926). These documents have been studied by Ekrem Hakkı Ayverdi, Ali Saim Ülgen, and Halil İnalcık, among others. The 953/1546 survey of pious foundations in the city proper, edited by Barkan and Ayverdi, is another indispensable source on the topic. Excepting passing references in narrative accounts, these are the only sources at hand, for unlike later periods of Ottoman history, this is not an era rich in court documents and imperial edicts pertaining to urban life and its workings.

14. The surveys of the Ayasofya endowment are organized along similar lines, except that different types of commercial property (caravanserais, baths, suks, and shops) and residential property are registered separately, and the description and income of each are presented as surveyed by the property's own cābī, or collector of revenues; BBA MM 19 (Ayaşofya vakfı taḥrīr defteri, A.H. 895); Istanbul Atatürk Library M.C. O.64 (Ayaşofya vakfı cibāyet defteri, A.H. 926).

15. Barkan and Ayverdi, İstanbul vakıfları tahrir defteri 953 (1546) tarihli.

16. There are references in the survey to a defter-i ʿatiḳ (the old survey), which has not surfaced and whose manner of organization remains unknown.

17. The survey's singular value for the early history of the city notwithstanding, one must take into consideration the time differences between the dates of the foundations and the date of the survey, and the changes both in the endowment and its surroundings that might have taken place within that span of time. In those cases where the original deed is extant, the listed property is often defined differently in the original foundation deed and in the summary registered in 1546. More frequently, additions have been made to the original endowment, but in some cases property listed in the original deed is missing in the summary.

18. On the changes of names of quarters in other Ottoman cities, see note 28 below.

19. İnalcık "Istanbul," 234. İnalcık's study on fifteenth- and sixteenth-century Galata ("Ottoman Galata") shows that in the earlier decades of Ottoman rule in the city, ethnic and religious identity did not necessarily define the town quarter. The notions of the homogeneity of the quarter's social makeup, the absoluteness of the ethno-religious divisions, and the lack of political autonomy originating in the city's cellular structure have been challenged by recent studies on a number of Ottoman cities. Abraham Marcus working on eighteenth-century Aleppo, Özer Ergenç working on sixteenth- and seventeenth-century Ankara and Konya, and Suraiya Faroqhi working on seventeenth-century Ankara and Kayseri have challenged the notion of the exclusive town quarter defined by religious, class, or occupational affiliations; Marcus, The Middle East on the Eve of Modernity, 314–28; Ergenç, "Osmanlı şehrindeki ʿmahalleʾnin işlev ve nitelikleri üzerine"; idem, "16. yüzyıl Ankaraʾsı"; idem, XVI. yüzyılda Ankara ve Konya, 145ff.; Faroqhi, Men of Modest Substance, 23–64. Ethnic and religious heterogeneity of residential quarters has also been noted in recent work on Ottoman Istanbul; Yerasimos, "La communauté juive d'Istanbul"; idem, "Osmanlı İstanbulʾunun Kuruluşu"; Özkoçak, "Urban Development of Istanbul"; Rozen, A History of the Jewish Community in Istanbul, esp. 62–65, 214–15; Dursteller, Venetians in Constantinople, 152–58.

20. Johansen, "The All-Embracing Town and Its Mosques," 151. Johansen notes that the Ottoman period in particular witnessed a growing autonomy of the local mosque community, which led jurists to come close to recognizing a system of parochial religious organizations within the town. The jurists to whom he refers for their definitions of the quarter and its mosque are Saraḥsī (d. 1090, Syria), İbn Nugaim (1520–63, Cairo), İbn ʿĀbidin (d. 1842, Damascus), and Ḥaṣkafī (d. 1677, Syria).

21. These are the quarters listed in the waqf documents and those named after mosques founded during Mehmed's reign. As already noted, one has to keep in mind that at least in the cases of some of these mosques, quarters developed around them later, or their names were associated with their respective quarters later on. The question of non-Muslim quarters, only partly recorded in waqf documents, further complicates the issue. Thus 126 is not the absolute number of quarters in Mehmed's Istanbul, but the number of all *places* that, during that period or by the middle of the sixteenth century, were regarded as *maḥallāt*.

22. BBA TT 210, TT 240. Halil İnalcık has noted these documents in his *Encyclopedia of Islam* article on Istanbul; İnalcık, "Istanbul," 238. I am thankful to the late Stéphane Yerasimos for directing my attention to the relevance of these documents for the fifteenth-century city. As Yerasimos has noted, these documents represent a sixteenth-century configuration, where the non-Muslim communities were largely found along the sea and land walls of the city, whereas through the fifteenth century numerous Christian communities inhabited the inner sections of the walled city as well; Yerasimos, "Osmanlı İstanbul'unun Kuruluşu." The document nevertheless provides significant information on communities that remained intact between their resettlement in Istanbul and the date of the survey.

23. Güleryüz, *İstanbul sinagogları*, 25; Yerasimos, "La communauté juive d'Istanbul," 114.

24. Map 3 demonstrates patterns of settlement and trends of change through Istanbul's first Ottoman

century and, to the extent that available sources allow it, the locations of neighborhood centers through the 1540s. It does not present a finalized chart where sites of all quarters are indicated with precision; the available data come from disparate documents with distinct functions. The map incorporates information from the fifteenth- and early-sixteenth-century endowment deeds and surveys of the Mehmed II foundation, the citywide survey of 1546, and the poll-tax registers of 1540 and 1545, which present a survey of Istanbul's non-Muslim population, categorized under residential quarter (*maḥalle*) and community (*cemāʿat*). *Fatih Sultan Mehmed'in vakfiyeleri; Zwei Stiftsurkunden des Sultan Mehmed II. Fatih*; BBA MM 19 (*Ayaṣofya vakfı taḥrīr defteri*, A.H. 895); BBA TT 210 (*Cizye defteri*, A.H. 947), BBA TT 240 (*Cizye defteri*, A.H. 951); Istanbul Atatürk Library M.C. O.64 (*Ayaṣofya vakfı cibāyet defteri*, A.H. 926); Barkan and Ayverdi, *İstanbul vakıfları tahrir defteri 953 (1546) tarihli*. Quarters mentioned in the poll-tax registers for which no topographic information was available to me (Yeñice Foça, Apōstōl nām-ı, diger Gedikci tabiʿ Midilluyān, Limnōs tabiʿ Midilluyān, Yōrgi Kalfatcı, Tuzcıyān-ı Balıkcıyān, Ḳalliḳrata, Ḳalafatcıyān-ı Nigbōli, Lāzāri) have not been placed on the map. Quarter mosques mentioned by the eighteenth-century author Ayvansarayi in his *Garden of Mosques* as dating from the fifteenth and early sixteenth centuries and those registered in the 1546 survey without dates are indicated separately. Map 3 does not include the suburbs of Istanbul. Information on the development of neighborhoods in Eyüp and Üsküdar during the reign of Mehmed II is scarce, limited mostly to the foundations of the ruling elite. These have been discussed in chapter 2. Galata presents a different problem: here, the majority of the residential neighborhoods were named after inhabitants and are in many cases impossible to locate with any degree of certainty. İnalcık discusses the urban development and the neighborhoods of the township from the capture of the city onward in the light of waqf documents; İnalcık, "Ottoman Galata."

25. The masjid of Bezzaz-ı Cedid was constructed before 878/1473. The property endowed for its upkeep, contrary to accepted practice, was sold by the founder's son; the inhabitants of the quarter later made endowments for it. The waqf of the Yavuzer Sinan mosque was drawn in 889/1484 and that of Hacı Halil in 861/1547; Barkan and Ayverdi, *İstanbul vakıfları tahrir defteri 953 (1546) tarihli*, 87, 102, 184–85, nos. 472, 502, 1052.

26. Barkan and Ayverdi, *İstanbul vakıfları tahrir defteri 953 (1546) tarihli*, 240, no. 1402.

27. Johansen, "The All-Embracing Town and Its Mosques."

28. On the relation of demographic changes to neighborhoods, see the studies of Ronald Jennings on Kayseri, Karaman, Amasya, Trabzon, and Erzurum in the sixteenth century; Heath Lowry on fifteenth-century Trabzon and Salonika; Özer Ergenç on Ankara and Konya; and Suraiya Faroqhi on Ankara and Kayseri. Jennings, "Urban Population in Anatolia"; idem, "Population, Society, and Economy"; Lowry, "Ottoman Tahrir Defters"; idem, "Portrait of a City"; Ergenç, *XVI. yüzyılda Ankara ve Konya*; Faroqhi, *Men of Modest Substance*. Although the types of documents used in these studies, namely detailed population surveys and court records, are different from the ones available for fifteenth-century Istanbul, the town quarter's socially and physically flexible nature can be observed in all cases. Noteworthy in the case of Istanbul are the rapidity and the wide range of these changes, which are comparable only to Trabzon in the fifteenth century, a city where similar conditions prevailed.

29. These he presented on a map of the peninsula, charting out the presumed boundaries of each neighborhood. When editing the 1546 survey, Ayverdi and Barkan noted that Ayverdi's earlier mapping of neighborhood boundaries was problematic, as these were not likely to be known with any certainty; Barkan and Ayverdi, *İstanbul vakıfları tahrir defteri 953 (1546) tarihli*, IX.

30. Seventy-two of his 181 *maḥallāt* were dated to the reign of Mehmed only on the grounds that they had been listed as such in *Ḥadīḳatüʾl-Cevāmiʿ*, Hafız Hüseyin al-Ayvansarayi's

encyclopedic survey of Istanbul's mosques, completed as late as 1780–81. Many of Ayvansarayi's attributions to the era of Mehmed were made on the basis of traditions concerning the founders; in few instances the author provided specific dates. Of these, fifty-five were registered as *maḥallāt* in the survey of 1546 and thus had begun to be regarded as neighborhoods between the 1480s and 1546; the rest were masjids that came to be regarded as neighborhood centers only in the course of the two and a half centuries between the survey and the writing of the "Garden of Mosques." Following Ayvansarayi's dubitable attributions, Ayverdi identified as quarter centers in Mehmed II's Istanbul a large number of mosques that were possibly built during the reign of Bayezid II. Even ignoring the suspiciously apocryphal component in attributions such as "the baker of the conqueror" or "the conqueror's supervisor of rice," the actual construction dates of these buildings is not clear. Of the seventy-two mosques that are dated to Mehmed's reign only by Ayvansarayi, twenty-one have waqfiyyas that postdate 895/1489–90. The endowment deeds were often written some years after the completion of construction; but even allowing a ten-year margin for the drawing of the document, one would still have to date these constructions to the reign of Bayezid II.

31. BBA TT 210, TT 240.

32. Halil İnalcık, too, uses Ayverdi's account in his much cited "Istanbul" article in the *Encyclopedia of Islam*. He does note whether non-Muslim neighborhoods were included in the figures from the sixteenth century and later, but does not question the validity of the figure offered by Ayverdi for fifteenth-century Istanbul. Edward Mitchell's acceptance of Ayverdi's figures as representing "a long reign of Mehmed" has led to an oversight regarding the changes in patronage patterns between the reigns of Mehmed II and Bayezid II; Mitchell, "Institution and Destitution," 230–89.

33. For a discussion of the fluctuations in the policy regarding the donations of freehold property to the inhabitants, see İnalcık, "The Policy of Mehmed II."

34. The tannery within the city walls on the Golden Horn designated its *maḥalle* in the first waqfiyya of the Mehmed II foundation, of ca. 1473. Here one el-Hac Ivaz endowed shops in 880/1476. The tannery was removed by royal edict sometime before 953/1546; Barkan and Ayverdi, *İstanbul vakıfları tahrir defteri 953 (1546) tarihli*, 259, no. 1536.

35. The areas farther away from the center and from the Golden Horn were largely empty and hence could be unsafe. See chapter 2 for a discussion of the evidence.

36. Yerasimos, "La communauté grecque-orthodoxe de Constantinople."

37. For the text of the *yasaḳnāme*, which specifies Edirnekapı, Topkapı, and Yenikapı as the gates through which grain should be brought into the city, see Anhegger and İnalcık, *Ḳānūnnāme-i sulṭānī ber mūceb-i ʿörf-i ʿoṣmānī*, 46–47.

38. The masjids of Kavak, Koruk Mahmud, Sufiler, and Ereğli were funded from Mehmed's foundation, and those of Mirza Baba, Arabacı Bayezid, Tersisli, and Çavuş Muslihüddin from the treasury; Barkan and Ayverdi, *İstanbul vakıfları tahrir defteri 953 (1546) tarihli*, 373, 377, 379, 380, 385, 389, 394, 396, nos. 165, 169, 170, 173, 179, 186, 193, 194, 196.

39. Ayverdi, *Fatih devri sonlarında İstanbul mahalleleri*, 37–38.

40. That only three of the eight masjids, those of Mirza Baba, Tersisli, and Ereğli, are mentioned in the *Ḥadīḳatüʾl-Cevāmiʿ* as having been founded during the reign of Mehmed II seems to support this argument. For the masjid of Mirza Baba, Ayvansarayi mentions a waqfiyya dating to 886/1481–82. Judging from the founder's titles, Şeyh Derviş Mirza Baba ibn-i ʿÖmerüʾl-Buhari, and from the later name of the masjid, Etyemez Tekkesi, this might have been one of the few Sufi convents in Mehmed's Istanbul; Ayvansarayi, *Garden of the Mosques*, 32–33.

41. For an overview of projects realized during the reign of Bayezid II, see the epilogue.

42. Neighborhoods of this type include Hace Sinan bin Elvan, Hace Sinan bin Hace Kasım, Hace Keşkek, Hace Rüstem; Barkan and Ayverdi,

İstanbul vakıfları tahrir defteri 953 (1546) tarihli, 22, 26, 35, 58.

43. It is difficult to establish how this trend was initiated, as the dates of the waqfiyyas in most cases do not correspond to the mosque's construction dates.

44. Exceptions to this trend are Yerasimos, "La communauté juive d'Istanbul"; Özkoçak, "Urban Development of Istanbul"; and Rozen, *A History of the Jewish Community in Istanbul*.

45. Angiolello, *Viaggio di Negroponte*, 24; Angiolello and Lezze, *Historia turchescha (1300–1514)*, 80. The church of the quarter, which Andreasyan identified as St. Nicholas, served Armenian as well as Catholic Genoese deportees from Caffa. In 1629 it was converted into a mosque called Kefeli Mescidi. Müller-Wiener notes that there is no agreement on the pre-Ottoman history of the building. Kömürcüyan, *İstanbul tarihi*, 92–93 n. 28, 175 n. 22; Müller-Wiener, *Bildlexikon zur Topographie Istanbuls*, 166–68.

46. See chapter 2. Otman Baba's *Velāyetnāme* tells of another quarter of Karamanlı near Yenikapı—"bir maḥalle miḳdārı Ḳārāmānlı"; Küçük Abdal, *Velāyetnāme-i Sulṭān Otman*, fol. 112b.

47. BBA TT 240.

48. The quarter of Aya Kenisası was later to be registered as part of the quarter of Mevlana Husrev; BBA MM 19 (*Ayaṣofya vaḳfı taḥrīr defteri*, A.H. 895), fol. 37b.

49. *Zwei Stiftsurkunden des Sultan Mehmed II. Fatih*, 54–56. These are not all the inhabitants of quarters ca. 1480, but only those whose properties flanked the property endowed by the sultan.

50. *Zwei Stiftsurkunden des Sultan Mehmed II. Fatih*, 33–34.

51. On Venetian presence in the Ottoman city, see Yerasimos and Bacqué-Grammont, "La résidence du Baile de Venise à Balıkpazarı," and Ağır, "İstanbulʾun Eski ʿVenedik Ticaret Kolonisiʾnin," 88–93. İnalcık notes that only later in the history of the city did segregation of different religious communities became pronounced, which resulted in the concentration of different religious groups in particular parts of the city; İnalcık, "Istanbul," 240–42.

Court edicts concerning non-Muslims in Muslim quarters from the latter half of the sixteenth century suggest that the process of segregation had become an issue then. To give an example, in 967/1560, the Muslim merchants who rented shops in the Mahmud Pasha han petitioned the court to have the non-Muslims in the building expelled and their shops pulled down. Their request was accepted; *3 numaralı mühimme defteri (966–968/1558–1560),* 523. Official citywide surveys, as well as accounts of Ottoman and European observers, provide ample evidence for ethno-religious concentrations, on the one hand, and a lack of absolute segregation in most residential areas, on the other; Barkan and Ayverdi, *İstanbul vakıfları tahrir defteri 953 (1546) tarihli;* Canatar, *İstanbul vakıfları tahrir defteri 1009 (1600) tarihli.* Evidence from Jewish and Venetian archival documentation also corroborates this view; Rozen, *A History of the Jewish Community of Istanbul,* 62ff.; Dursteller, *Venetians in Constantinople,* 152ff.

52. For the Hacı Halil foundation, see Barkan and Ayverdi, *İstanbul vakıfları tahrir defteri 953 (1546) tarihli,* 102. For the Yeni Valide mosque complex, see Thys-Şenocak, *Ottoman Women Builders.* Yerasimos draws attention to other neighborhoods in the area with Muslim-Jewish populations; Yerasimos, "Osmanlı İstanbul'unun Kuruluşu," 206.

53. Considering only those mosques which were considered centers of quarters, and excluding some of Ayverdi's more dubitable attributions, my conclusion is in line with İnalcık's count for 1546. İnalcık notes in his "Istanbul" article that, in 953/1546, 65 percent of the founders of mosques were members of the military establishment. The second largest category of founders was that of merchants and craftsmen, who built sixty of the capital's 219 mosques by 1546, while ulema and sheikhs founded forty-six; İnalcık, "Istanbul," 231. Edward Mitchell, using Ayverdi's count of mosques built during the reign of Mehmed, reaches a comparable conclusion regarding the backgrounds of founders. He notes that the great majority of the mosques founded in Istanbul in this period were

sponsored by members of the state. Of these, the majority were members of the military elite. They were followed by members of the religious elite, then merchants and craftsmen. Mitchell, based on Ayverdi's catalogue of 192 mosques in Istanbul dating to the reign of Mehmed, provides a breakdown of patrons: 26 (14 percent) of mosques were founded by Mehmed, 86 (44 percent) by the military elite, 26 (13 percent) by the religious elite, 21 (11 percent) by merchants and craftsmen, 17 (9 percent) *for* dervishes (the majority by the sultan), 4 (2 percent) by women; Mitchell, "Institution and Destitution," 257–63. As I have noted in the preceding section of this chapter, Ayverdi's attributions are unreliable in parts (as Mitchell, too, notes). These numbers do, however, give a general impression of the involvement of the military and the religious elite in the religious undertakings in the city.

54. Daye Hatun, Mehmed II's wet nurse, founded two masjids; Selçuk Hatun, daughter of Mehmed I, and a certain Keyci Hatun were also founders of masjids. Unlike the other three, the mosque of Selçuk Hatun was not registered as the center of a residential quarter.

55. The numbers, as I have already noted, are not precise, and about ten of the mosques are not attributable to any one group. Any dogmatic insistence on specific numbers or percentages is bound to be problematic, since attributions for the most part are based merely on the title of the founder.

56. Once foundations dating to the reign of Bayezid were included in the overall picture (as has been done by Edward Mitchell, who followed patronage trends through the turn of the sixteenth century), the ulama, in accordance with their rising status through this period, emerged as the second group of founders following the military elite; Mitchell, "Institution and Destitution," 253ff.

57. Tacizade Ca'fer Çelebi, quoted by İnalcık, "The Policy of Mehmed II," 233. İnalcık discusses the legal background of this statement.

58. For a discussion of the *mülknâme,* see İnalcık, "The Policy of Mehmed II," 241–42.

59. For the freehold deed for the fountain found by Hacı Müslihüddin outside the Edirnekapı/Charisios Gate, see VGMA 654:25.

60. I have come across one sales document in the Topkapı Palace Archives, concerning one Hacı Hasan's purchase of a house from one Derviş Hacı Ahmed; TKSA E 3204. For a reference to the purchase of property by a founder, see the discussion on the foundation of the Architect Sinan, which follows in the text.

61. See the waqfiyyas of Hüseyin Ağa, TKSA D 6996, D 6936, D 6990, D 6977; Mustafa Paşa mevķūfāt defteri, VGMA 654.

62. TKSA E 7232.

63. Sinan's foundation is one of the larger to be endowed by an individual below the high-ranking administrative elite of the period: a masjid and convent endowed for the chronicler Aşıkpaşazade was supported by twenty-two shops and seventeen rooms, while thirteen shops and several plots of land supported his masjid near the New Mosque; VGMA 633:42–45; 1767:246–53. These have been published by Konyalı in his monograph on the architect; Konyalı, *Fatihin mimarlarından Azadlı Sinan,* 15–21, 29–40.

64. Mitchell, "Institution and Destitution," 247–55.

65. İnalcık, "The Policy of Mehmed II," 241.

66. The expression is *kendünin tapuya alınmış yerinde ve diger yerde,* that is, "on his and on other property." VGMA 654:118–21; BBA A.DVN 790:74.

67. TKSA E 5479.

68. See BBA A.DVN 790:14, 78. Upon the succession of Bayezid II to the throne, Mevlana Gürani petitioned the court again, reminding the sultan of his services to the state and the dynasty; TKSA E 6089.

69. Zenbilli ʿAli Cemali Efendi, *Mecmūʿa-i Fetāvā,* fol. 8r. The published fatwas of Süleyman's Sheikh al-Islam Ebusuud Efendi, too, contain references to sultanic permissions for the building and use of masjids and Friday mosques; Düzdağ, *Şeyhülislam Ebussuud Efendi fetvalari,* 73–77.

70. As noted above in the context of late-sixteenth-century fatwa collections, sultanic permission was required

for the construction of a Friday mosque or for converting a masjid into a Friday mosque. One must remember in this context that it was only Murad II, when building two congregational mosques in Edirne, the Üç Şerefeli and a convent-mosque used as a Friday mosque, who altered the tradition of the single congregational mosque in a city. The period of Bayezid II, on the other hand, was to witness a considerable increase in the number of such mosques in Istanbul, as well as a widening of the range of patrons who could build one. For this, see the Epilogue. For a discussion of the multiplicity of congregational mosques in the city, as reflected in Islamic juridical texts, see Johansen, "The All-Embracing Town and Its Mosques." On the use of donations of land and the foundation of pious endowments as a method in Ottoman colonization and expansion, see Barkan, "Osmanlı İmparatorluğunda bir iskan ve kolonizasyon metodu olarak vakıflar ve temlikler"; İnalcık, "Ottoman Methods of Conquest"; G. Necipoğlu, *Age of Sinan*, 71–76.

71. A large number of masjids were founded in Bursa and Edirne during the early fifteenth century (twenty-eight in Bursa and fourty-five in Edirne during the reigns of Mehmed I and Murad II). There existed, by the time of Murad II, also eight convents or convent-mosques in Bursa and seven in Edirne. Possibly these numbers were greater, but the chances of survival for minor convents were smaller, as they were usually modestly constructed buildings. The numbers are reached through a classification of the buildings Ayverdi has included in his study of early Ottoman Bursa and Edirne; Ayverdi, *Osmanlı mimârisinde Çelebi ve II. Sultan Murad devri, 806–855 (1403–1451).* Ayverdi himself proposes a different count, for he disregards a building's original function as a convent whenever it has later been turned into a mosque or a Friday mosque.

72. For a 993/1585 order regarding a convent of the Haydari order established by Mehmed II, see Ahmet Refik, *Onuncu asr-ı hicrîde İstanbul hayatı,* 217–18. This convent, too, does not seem to have had a direct link to any residential quarter of the city.

73. More on the foundation of the architect Sinan follows.

74. Waqfiyya of Çakır Ağa, VGMA 610/25:291. Baha Tanman, discussing the location of the Kazlıçeşme convent outside the Golden Gate/Yedikule, makes a similar point; Tanman, "La tekke bektachi de Kazlıçeşme, 11."

75. Küçük Abdal, *Velāyetnāme-i Sulṭān Otman,* fols. 95bff. I have not been able to identify the Kılıç Manastırı. For a discussion of Otman Baba and his dervishes' stay in Istanbul, based on the *Velāyetnāme,* see İnalcık, "Dervish and Sultan," 30–31.

76. Küçük Abdal, *Velāyetnāme-i Sulṭān Otman,* fols. 21a, 96a, 114a. The Edhemi convent was located to the west of the Murad Pasha mosque, within the quarter of Hacı Bayram. One Aişe Hatun bint-i Mehmed endowed a number of rooms for it in 941/1534; Barkan and Ayverdi, *İstanbul vakıfları tahrir defteri 953 (1546) tarihli,* 319, no. 1869. Two Bektashi convents are mentioned in the 953/1546 survey, one of them in the quarter of Mahmud Pasha and dated 891/1486, the other in the quarter of Balaban Ağa, to the west of the Old Palace, without a date; Barkan and Ayverdi, *İstanbul vakıfları tahrir defteri 953 (1546) tarihli,* 45, no. 272, and 153, no. 870.

77. Barkan and Ayverdi discuss the large number of convents encountered in the survey as receivers of charities. Again, all the examples they give, with the exception of the convent endowed for Aşıkpaşazade, are from the last decades of the fifteenth century or from the sixteenth century; Barkan and Ayverdi, *İstanbul vakıfları tahrir defteri 953 (1546) tarihli,* xxvii–xxx.

78. The identity of Atik Sinan and the possibility that his family remained Orthodox Christians have been discussed by Konyalı, *Fatihin mimarlarından Azadlı Sinan,* 73–85, and more recently by Yerasimos, who suggests that Christodoulos and Sinan, mentioned as architects of the New Mosque in different sources, were one and the same person; Yerasimos, *La fondation de Constantinople et de Sainte-Sophie,* 145–50.

79. El-Hac Ahmed bin Aşık Pasha owned property in the suk in Un Kapusı and in the neighboring

quarter of Üskübi. As these properties were recorded in the waqfiyya of the Mehmed II foundation only as borders of property endowed by the sultan, it is not possible to know more precisely what they were or whether Aşıkpaşazade owned other property that was not adjacent to the sultanic waqf; *Zwei Stiftsurkunden des Sultan Mehmed II. Fatih,* 46, 48, 54. The 895/1489 survey of the Hagia Sophia foundation registered a mill and another piece of property in the quarter of Hacı Abdî, and a shop in the suk in Un Kapanı, for which the chronicler paid rent (*muḳāṭaʿa*); BBA MM 19 (*Ayaṣofya vaḳfı taḥrīr defteri,* A.H. 895), fols. 34b, 36a.

80. It is significant that such connections continued to be operative in imperializing Istanbul. For a discussion of heterodox Sufi leaders' roles in conversion of non-Muslim communities of Anatolia between the thirteenth and the fifteenth centuries, see Ocak, "Bazı menâḳıbnâmelere göre xiii.–xv. yüzyıllardaki ihtidâlarda heterodoks şeyh ve dervişlerin rolü." Kafadar suggests that some of the followers of such figures might have been non-Muslims; Kafadar, *Between Two Worlds,* 74.

81. The quarter of the Stone Column might be the same as the quarter of the Maiden's Column, where Sinan built his mosque. But since no Jewish inhabitants are recorded near this Sinan property, it is likely that a different monument and quarter are intended. Ḥacaruʾl-ʿAmūd may refer to any of the monumental columns of the city. The earliest endowment deed of the Mehmed II foundation contains a reference to a quarter of Ḥacaruʾl-Manṣūb, also after a monumental column; *Fatih Sultan Mehmedʾin vakfiyeleri,* 42.

82. See, for example, Humphreys, "The Expressive Intent of the Mamluk Architecture in Cairo"; idem, *Islamic History,* 238–54; Lapidus, *Muslim Cities in the Later Middle Ages;* Behrens-Abouseif, *Egypt's Adjustment to Ottoman Rule;* and van Leeuwen, *Waqfs and Urban Structures.* Recent work on the waqf institution has explored such interactions as instrumental in the formation of a public sphere in Islamic societies; Hoexter, "The *Waqf* and the Public Sphere."

83. Mitchell, "Institution and Destitution," 262.

84. Küçük Abdal, *Velāyetnāme-i Sulṭān Otman*, fols. 71b–76a.

85. Barkan and Ayverdi, and İnalcık as well, have also noted that the neighborhood mosques were supported by the inhabitants of the quarter as much as by the original waqf; Barkan and Ayverdi, *İstanbul vakıfları tahrir defteri 953 (1546) tarihli*, XXVII; İnalcık "Istanbul," 234.

86. It was more common for the higher-ranking founders to leave the supervision of the waqf to another high-ranking official, usually the kadi, rather than the imam. In such cases, the endowment is more likely to be for a congregational mosque than a masjid; Barkan and Ayverdi, *İstanbul vakıfları tahrir defteri 953 (1546) tarihli*, 44, 308, 346.

87. A certain Bozacı Abdürezzak endowed two *kāfirī* (Byzantine) houses for the imam and the müezzin of the mosque of Yeni Bezzaz; Barkan and Ayverdi, *İstanbul vakıfları tahrir defteri 953 (1546) tarihli*, 89, no. 482.

88. As founders of charities often took some years after completion of construction to have their endowment deeds written, I give a margin of ten years after Mehmed II's death and consider structures endowed until 1490 likely to have been built during his reign.

89. What Barkan and Ayverdi have called *evladlık* foundations, that is, foundations whose incomes were allotted only to the founder's heir; Barkan and Ayverdi, *İstanbul vakıfları tahrir defteri 953 (1546) tarihli*, XXI–XXV.

90. Barkan and Ayverdi, *İstanbul vakıfları tahrir defteri 953 (1546) tarihli*, 290–93, nos. 1708, 1719.

91. Ibid., 273–78, nos. 1627, 1629.

92. The date of the endowment deeds of both convents is 916/1510. But the convent of Şeyh Alaüddin Halife must have been there at least as early as 894/1489, when one Hacı Sinan, a royal archer, endowed the income of several shops and one house to the imam, the müezzin, and the inhabitants of that convent. The convent of Şeyh Süleyman Halife must also have been there much earlier than the waqfiyya date, since in 897/1492 a certain Şüca bin Abdullah endowed his residence to its residents upon the cessation of his

family; Barkan and Ayverdi, *İstanbul vakıfları tahrir defteri 953 (1546) tarihli*, 310–14, nos. 1811, 1821.

93. Barkan and Ayverdi, *İstanbul vakıfları tahrir defteri 953 (1546) tarihli*, 312, no. 1815.

94. This discrepancy explains the many footnotes Barkan and Ayverdi had to append to their edition of the 953/1546 survey, offering corrections to *mahalle* names that were encountered in individual waqfiyyas but were otherwise unknown, or locations referred to as quarters only in individual waqf documents, such as "the quarter of Kapan Musasıoğlu," "the quarter of Hacı Hızır," "the quarter named İbn-i Marul," or "the quarter of Aksaray"; Barkan and Ayverdi, *İstanbul vakıfları tahrir defteri 953 (1546) tarihli*, 19, nos. 4 and 5; 377, no. 2; 312, no. 3. Another example of a similar nature is the inconsistency in the name of a certain area across different documents, or at times within the same document, such as Sırt Hamamı and the masjid of Mercan Ağa being used interchangeably for the same quarter in the same waqfiyya, as well as in the summaries of other foundations registered in that quarter; VGMA 741:93–96; Barkan and Ayverdi, *İstanbul vakıfları tahrir defteri 953 (1546) tarihli*, 84–87, nos. 452–71.

95. Ayverdi has noted that the difficulty of constructing domed buildings over a short period of time led to the construction of a large number of mosques with pitched roofs, which were much more vulnerable to the frequent fires that ravaged the city than masonry structures; Ayverdi, *Osmanlı mi'mârîsinde Fâtih devri, 855–886 (1451–1481)*, 3:308.

96. For the religious architecture of Bursa and Edirne in the fifteenth century, see Kuran, *The Mosque in Early Ottoman Architecture*; Ayverdi, *Osmanlı mi'mârîsinde Çelebi ve II. Sultan Murad devri, 806–855 (1403–1451)*; and idem, *Osmanlı mi'mârîsinde Fâtih devri, 855–886 (1451–1481)*.

97. On the single-domed mosque, see Kuran, *The Mosque in Early Ottoman Architecture*, 61–70. The mosque of Hace Hayrüddin was later called the Üç Mihrablı (the mosque with three mihrabs). Nusret Çam has suggested that the mihrabs were used by followers

of different schools of law. This would have been unusual in Istanbul, as Çam's own study shows that the use of multiple mihrabs to serve different sects was a practice followed particularly in southeastern Anatolia and Syria only. The building might nevertheless have served merchants of different schools of law, or the mihrabs might simply have accrued during later additions—the building was converted to a congregational mosque by Mehmed II after the founder's death and was enlarged once more by Bayezid; Çam, "İslam'da Bazı Fikhî Meselelerin ve Mezheplerin Türk Cami Mimarisine Tesiri," 382 n. 54; Ayverdi, *Osmanlı mi'mârîsinde Fâtih devri, 855–886 (1451–1481)*, 3:510–12.

98. Ayverdi, *Osmanlı mi'mârîsinde Fâtih devri, 855–886 (1451–1481)*, 3:412–13, 490–91. Using the 953/1546 survey, Ayverdi notes that the traditional attribution of the building to the "supervisor of hay" (*saman emini*) during the reign of Mehmed II is wrong; the builder must have been from a place named Samanviran, or Samanviranlu.

99. The Mevlana Husrev masjid near the Gül Cami, the Voynuk Şüca' masjid in Un Kapanı, the Çelebioğlu 'Alaüddin masjid near the Alaca Hammam, and the Çakır Ağa masjid on the Uzunçarşı are noted in the *Ḥadīḳatü'l-Cevāmi'* of Ayvansarayi as *fevḳānī* masjids; Ayvansarayi, *Garden of the Mosques*, 72, 148–49, 201, 218.

100. The church was converted into a mosque in 1626; Müller-Wiener, *Bildlexikon zur Topographie Istanbuls*, 166–68; Eyice, "Kefeli Mescidi."

101. In his *Encyclopedia of Islam* article on Istanbul, Halil İnalcık gives a brief account of the domestic architecture of the city as gleaned from the waqf documents and travelers' accounts. He classifies these residences as follows: rooms, *oda* or *hücre*, *mahalle* houses, one- or two-storied houses of wood and mudbrick, houses with gardens, palaces and villas, suburban villas and *yalılar* (seaside mansions). Although no narrative accounts on the residential architecture in the city during the first Ottoman decades exists, the documentary evidence suggests that, excepting the seaside mansions, these were the main types of residences from early on; İnalcık "Istanbul," 236–37.

102. Ramberti, "The Second Book of the Affairs of the Turks," 239.

103. VGMA 741:93–95.

104. The waqfiyyas of Hace Üveys, Mevlana Gürani, and Muhyiddin Çelebi contain further descriptions of this kind; TKSA D 7079, VGMA 570:221, VGMA 740:74.

105. TKSA E 3060.

106. Sinan Ağa endowed his large house to the Ayasofya foundation and stipulated his right to use it as long as he lived; TKSA D 10729.

107. TKSA D 6931, the waqfiyya of Firuz Ağa, dated 897/1491–92. On the cistern, see Müller-Wiener, *Bildlexikon zur Topographie Istanbuls,* 280. For a similar use of a Byzantine cistern as a base for an early Ottoman mosque, the Yayla Cami near Topkapı, see Eyice, "İstanbul'da Yayla camileri ve şehrin tarihi topografyasının yanlış izah edilen bir meselesi."

108. In 907/1502, Sinan Pasha endowed a complex in the quarter of Mahmud Pasha, which he had bought from Süleyman Beg bin Abdullah, the commander of Ohri. This seems to have had a layout similar to the palace of Firuz Ağa and, although not indicated in his waqfiyya, in all probability was his residence. It had (three?) courtyards (in the Arabic waqfiyya, *muḥavvaṭāt,* which suggests that there were more than two), ground-floor and upper-floor rooms, a kitchen, stables, toilets, a bath; Sinan Paşa Vakfiyesi, BBA KK Haremeyn Mukataası 3359, fols. 24b–25a.

109. VGMA 575:22ff.

110. Ousterhout, "Secular Architecture," 198–99.

111. *Zwei Stiftsurkunden des Sultan Mehmed II. Fatih,* 78–111; BBA MM 19 (*Ayaṣofya vakfı tahrīr defteri,* A.H. 895), fols. 27a–39b; Istanbul Atatürk Library M.C. O.64 (*Ayaṣofya vakfı cibāyet defteri,* A.H. 926), fols. 179b–242a.

112. Istanbul Atatürk Library M.C. O.64 (*Ayaṣofya vakfı cibāyet defteri,* A.H. 926), fols. 179b–242a.

113. Yerasimos, "Galata á travers les récits de voyage," 117.

114. This is the earliest non-Muslim endowment deed extant in the VGM archives, dating to 923/1517 and signed by Şeref Efendi bin Ivaz, the kadi of Galata; VGMA 624:286ff.

115. *Ḳamina* is spelled *ḳ-m-n-h* in the Ottoman text. Paolo Girardelli suggests that this might be a misspelling, or misunderstanding, of the Italian *camera* (room); private correspondence, June 2005.

116. The 895/1489 survey of the Hagia Sophia foundation indicates whether the holders of endowed property were paying rents or not—suggesting that these were the Byzantine buildings given out as freehold initially and rented out later. Not in all cases, however, are these structures recorded as *kāfirī.* A lesser number of *nev* (new) houses and shops are also registered in the 895/1489 survey. For an evaluation of archival and narrative sources regarding the uses of Byzantine structures in relation to Ottoman efforts to repopulate the city, see İnalcık, "The Policy of Mehmed II."

117. Kritovoulos, *History of Mehmed the Conqueror,* 83.

118. Doukas, *Decline and Fall of Byzantium to the Ottoman Turks,* 243–44.

119. TKSA D 7079.

120. A kitchen with two rooms above, a bath, three gardens, a ground-floor room with a large room above, a water well, a toilet, another room, a courtyard, two ground-floor rooms with an anteroom, six fountains, two ponds, and stables with five rooms and an anteroom above are recorded. Nothing is known about the founder except for what is suggested by his name and titles. The waqfiyya refers to him as Muḥyiddīn Çelebi ibn-i merḥūmu'l-maġfūr al-Ḥāce Şems bin al-merḥūm Şuʿayb al-Defterī; he was also known as Cenderecizāde. He must have been a keeper of land registers in the palace. The waqfiyya dates to 898/1492–93; there is a reference to another waqfiyya dating to 870/1465–66 in a related document; VGMA 740:73ff., VGMA 608:298.

121. Angiolello, *Viaggio di Negroponte,* 27; *The Pilgrimage of Arnold von Harff,* 238–39; Kömürcüyan, *İstanbul tarihi,* 5. See also Mango, *The Brazen House,* 149–69.

122. According to his endowment deed drawn in 913/1507–8, Hüseyin Ağa converted the *menzil* known as the Eski At Bāzārı (the former horse market) into a Friday mosque; TKSA D 6996.

123. In the Mercan Ağa quarter a church was used as a depot (*anbār*), while one of the two churches in the vicinity of the New Mosque was put to the same use; VGMA 741:94; BBA MM 19 (*Ayaṣofya vakfı tahrīr defteri,* A.H. 895), fol. 42a.

124. Doukas, *Decline and Fall of Byzantium to the Ottoman Turks,* 244.

125. BBA MM 19 (*Ayaṣofya vakfı tahrīr defteri,* A.H. 895), fol. 35a.

126. *Fatih Sultan Mehmed'in vakfiyeleri,* 12; BBA MM 19 (*Ayaṣofya vakfı tahrīr defteri,* A.H. 895), fol. 38b.

127. On the residence of the Venetian bailo during the first century of Ottoman rule in Constantinople, see Yerasimos and Bacqué-Grammont, "La résidence du Baile de Venise à Balıkpazarı."

128. Sinan Paşa Vakfiyesi, BBA KK Haremeyn Mukataası 3359, fols. 24a–b. Dated 907/1502.

129. TKSA D 10729.

130. VGMA 575:27; VGMA 570:221; Barkan and Ayverdi, *İstanbul vakıfları tahrir defteri 953 (1546) tarihli,* 83, 161.

Epilogue

1. The manuscript has been published in facsimile with an introduction and a transcription of the text by Hüseyin Yurdaydın; Nasuhü's-Silahi [Matrakcı], *Beyān-ı menāzil-i sefer-i ʿIraḳeyn-i Sulṭān Süleymān Ḫān.* The image of Istanbul has been studied by Albert Gabriel, Walter Denny, and Iffet Orbay. The first two authors deal with the identification of the buildings represented in the painting, while Denny also discusses its representational conventions. He discerns a hierarchy of buildings that is reflected in their relative sizes and the precision of their depiction. He argues that a concern for enumerating the monuments of the city shaped the image, rather than a concern for realistic depiction of all buildings and their spatial relationship to each other. Denny does not, on the other hand, question these conventions in relation to conventions used in contemporary European city views, or in terms of the image's meaning. Michael Rogers has drawn attention to the

image's affinity to European city views such as Strozzi's Rome, though he has asserted that this is a conscious Ottoman adaptation showing the principal Ottoman monuments of the capital. More recently, Iffet Orbay has explored the image within its manuscript context and has discussed issues of composition, viewpoint, and content in terms of their bearing on the intent and meaning of the image. Gabriel, "Les étapes d'une campagne dans les deux Iraq"; Denny, "A Sixteenth-Century Architectural Plan of Istanbul"; Rogers, "Itineraries and Town Views in Ottoman Histories," 238–39; Orbay, "Istanbul Viewed," 29–72. For a general assessment of the Matrakçı manuscript within the context of Ottoman topographic representation in the sixteenth century, see Ebel, "City Views, Imperial Visions."

2. European city images that use the conventions of the bird's-eye view have been discussed in chapter 3.

3. In his introduction to Ottoman cartography in the *History of Cartography,* Ahmet Karamustafa draws attention to the special standing of Ottoman works within the larger Islamic tradition, in its merging of the conventions of premodern European and Islamic traditions of mapmaking. Discussing Ottoman portolan charts and the work of Piri Reis, Svat Soucek directs attention to the impact of the *Isolario* tradition on the *Kitāb-ı Baḥriye.* Karamustafa, "Introduction to Ottoman Cartography"; Soucek, "Islamic Charting in the Mediterranean," 272–79.

4. Printed copies of the same book have been suggested as a source of Piri Reis's *Kitāb-ı Baḥriye;* Soucek, "Islamic Charting in the Mediterranean," 277–78.

5. Ebel, "City Views, Imperial Visions," 170–210.

6. Françoise Choay has discussed the objectification of urban space in the context of fifteenth-century representations of the city, particularly in the Italian realm; Choay, *The Rule and the Model,* 49ff. For the *Şehrengiz* as a literary genre, see Levend, *Türk edebiyatında şehrengizler ve şehrengizlerde İstanbul,* and Stewart-Robinson, "A Neglected Ottoman Poem." Cemal Kafadar suggests that the increasing popularity of the genre

was one of the indications of the emergence of a "modern" mentality and of the participation of the Ottoman realm in the cultural rhythms of the early modern world; Kafadar, "The Ottomans and Europe," 621–22.

7. Denny, "A Sixteenth-Century Architectural Plan of Istanbul," 50; Orbay, "Istanbul Viewed," 48–52.

8. Religious doctrine was one of the factors that affected the orientation in medieval maps. Another was the concern with making the best use of the picture plane. In the orientation of the Matrakçı view, both may have been influential. For an interpretation foregrounding Istanbul as "imperial look-out," see Orbay, "Istanbul Viewed," 60 ff. For a discussion of orientation in maps in terms of their geometric structure, see Harley and Woodward, *History of Cartography,* 1:505–6.

9. Orbay, "Istanbul Viewed," 56–59. She observes that because the painting has been trimmed to reduce it to the size of the manuscript, the symmetrical placement of the city's suburbs, achieved through a manipulation of its topography, has become less apparent.

10. I largely follow Walter Denny's legend to the map, with some additions and some suggestions for different identifications. See Kafescioğlu,"The Ottoman Capital," 381–89.

11. There is another such mosque at the eastern end of the city, one to the north of the first palace, and two near the Edirne Gate. The locations of the first two suggest they might be representing the İshak Pasha and the Vefazade mosques respectively, but if such is the case, then domed structures are depicted with pitched roofs.

12. Walter Denny identified the building to the right of the Atik Ali Pasha mosque as the second mosque built by the same patron close to the Edirne Gate, suggesting a mistake on the part of the painter. But however imprecise the details and the locations of the monuments may be, Matrakçı seems to have laid importance on representing mosques with their minarets, which this one does not have. This might be the madrasa of the founder. An unidentifiable building with a lanterned dome is located near the Edirne Gate.

13. This may be a legacy of Byzantine residential architecture that did not survive the later centuries. The building Denny identifies as the baths of Zeuxippus and I believe is a Byzantine church put to a nonreligious use is depicted as surrounded by such structures. This building and others with loggias overlooking the street are also seen in the drawing of Hagia Sophia and the Hippodrome in the Freshfield Album (Oxford, Bodleian OR 430). Another church depicted with an adjoining structure that features a loggia has been identified by Cyril Mango as the church of the Chalke (later Aslanhane/the royal menagerie). Mango notes references to Byzantine sources that describe the church with a terrace overlooking the Mese; Mango, *The Brazen House,* 152. On Byzantine residential structures and evidence for projecting sunrooms on the upper floors, see Ousterhout, "Secular Architecture," 198–99.

14. Tülay Artan notes the seventeenth-century chronicle of Solakzade, according to whom the palace was built during the reign of Bayezid II. She also makes note of a document recording a restoration of this building in 1520; Artan, "İbrahim Paşa Sarayı."

15. Gabriel identified the building to the right of Hagia Sophia (also featured in the Freshfield Album drawing, see note 13 above) as the church of St. Stephan, while Denny wrote that it represented the baths of Zeuxippus. The latter identification does not seem plausible to me, as there is no evidence that the baths were standing at this date. Mango asserts that this is the church of St. John of the Diippion. Mango also argues convincingly that the domed building above Hagia Sophia is the Chalke church, used as the menagerie and the artist workshops; Mango, *The Brazen House,* 149–69.

16. For a discussion of floral imagery as evocative of paradisal symbolism, see Grabar, *Mediation of Ornament,* 204ff. For interpretations of garden imagery and its paradisal associations in Persian literature, see Meisami, "Allegorical Gardens in the Persian Poetic Tradition," and idem, "Palaces and Paradises." Paradisal allusions to the city and its monuments by fifteenth-

century and later Ottoman authors have been noted in chapter 3.

17. İnalcık, "Mehmed II," 7:531–33.

18. In Ünver, *İstanbul'un mutlu askerleri ve şehit olanlar,* 24, and translated in Babinger, *Mehmed the Conqueror and His Time,* 508. Neither author indicates a specific source. Edward Mitchell suggests that this might be Çatladı Kasım bin Mehmed, who was denied permission to operate a bath he had built close to the Hippodrome; Mitchell, "Institution and Destitution," 264–65. For his petitions for permission, see chapter 4.

19. For references to Bayezid II as *velī* during his lifetime, see Raby and Tanındı, *Turkish Bookbinding in the Fifteenth Century,* 81. Nathalie Clayer notes that Bayezid appears as a *ḥalīfe* (successor) of Çelebi Halife in a Sünbüli genealogy that was in the possession of descendants of the İmrahor convent's last sheikh; Clayer, *Mystiques, état et société,* 66.

20. On the reign of Bayezid II, see Uzunçarşılı, "Bayezid II"; on changes in political and religious orientation in the Ottoman world following Mehmed II's reign, see Beldiceanu-Steinherr, "Le règne de Selīm 1er"; Melikoff, "Le problème Kızılbaş"; and Clayer, *Mystiques, état et société.* On shifts in Ottoman notions of the Sunna between the early sixteenth and the later seventeenth centuries in the context of broader political dynamics, and the contested nature of its meaning on the part of various groups within the Ottoman society, see Terzioğlu, "Sufi and Dissident," 190–276.

21. For state patronage of Sufi sects during this period, see Yazıcı, "Fetihten Sonra İstanbul'da İlk Halveti Şeyhleri"; and Clayer, *Mystiques, état et société.*

22. For these buildings, see Müller-Wiener, *Bildlexikon zur Topographie Istanbuls,* 177–83, 414, and Yüksel, *II. Bayezid Yavuz Selim devri,* 250–52. On the palace of Firuz Ağa, see chapter 4.

23. Semavi Eyice has demonstrated that the Elçi Han, or the Ambassadors' Inn, serving as the residence for high-ranking foreign visitors to the city through the eighteenth century,

was part of the Atik Ali Pasha complex; Eyice, "Elçi Hanı."

24. For the complex, see Müller-Wiener, *Bildlexikon zur Topographie Istanbuls,* 384–90, and Yüksel, *II. Bayezid Yavuz Selim devri,* 184–217.

25. Pierre Gilles notes that the column was taken down to open space for the bath; Gilles, *Antiquities of Constantinople,* 150.

26. On the drawings, see chapter 3.

27. For the column of Theodosius, see Müller-Wiener, *Bildlexikon zur Topographie Istanbuls,* 264–65.

28. Before the conquest of Constantinople, Ottoman rulers as well as other members of the dynasty were buried in Bursa, near royal convent-masjids rather than the city's congregational mosque.

29. VGMA 2113:202.

30. As argued in Kuban, *Türk ve İslam sanatı üzerine denemeler,* 180–84.

31. For a study of imperial complexes situated along the Divan Yolu in the context of funeral ceremonies that involved visits to the sultans' tombs, see G. Necipoğlu, "Dynastic Imprints on the Cityscape." On the Divan Yolu as it took shape through the later centuries, see Cerasi, *The Istanbul Divanyolu.*

32. In his study of the Via Papale (running between the Vatican and the Lateran) during the Renaissance, Allan Ceen defines the characteristics of processional-route architecture, stressing the sequential character of the route and its development. In his study of the al-Moaz (Bayn al-Qasrayn) street in Cairo, Nezar Alsayyad, too, stresses the sequential structure of the architecture along the route; Ceen, *The Quartiere di'Banchi,* 104–71; Alsayyad, "Bayn al-Qasrayn."

33. Early in the sixteenth century, the architects working for the court began to be recognized as a *cemā'at* (community or regiment) with a hierarchical organization. For the earliest documents referring to a centralized organization of court architects under Bayezid II, see Meriç, "Birkaç mühim arşiv vesikası," and G. Necipoğlu, *Age of Sinan,* 153.

34. In an analysis of the building made possible by a restoration that exposed its construction history,

Semavi Eyice has demonstrated that the conversion of the building involved a change in its orientation roughly from the east to the south, which turned the interior into a laterally placed rectangle more in tune with the needs of the Muslim congregation. The interior arrangement of the building was changed from that of a nave with vaulted corridors on three sides to one in which the ambulatories were incorporated into the main prayer area. No doubt the motive for these changes was to accommodate the preference for a less interrupted prayer area in a mosque. Eyice attributes the change in the superstructure to structural necessities brought about by the change of orientation; Eyice, "İstanbul'da Koca Mustafa Paşa Cami'i ve onun Osmanlı-Türk mimarisindeki yeri." The symbolic significance of the Hagia Sophia scheme, too, must have been an essential factor in this radical structural alteration.

35. On the rise to prominence of the Halvetiyye in connection with Bayezid's accession to the throne, see Kissling, "Aus der Geschichte des Chalvetijje-Ordens," 244–52, and Clayer, *Mystiques, état et société,* 65–66. The sultan himself, as already noted, was to find a place in Halveti genealogies as a disciple of Çelebi Halife.

36. Matrakcı's representation of the convent sections of the sultanic mosques with lanterned domes (the same convention he used for public kitchens) suggests that these were understood to be imarets. Their accommodative functions, in other words, were regarded as central.

37. For an interpretation of Süleyman's mosque complex, completed in 1566, within the context of the consolidation of Ottoman Sunni orthodoxy, see G. Necipoğlu, "The Süleymaniye Complex in Istanbul."

38. For an assessment of the central location of the convent within the emerging religio-political configuration in the capital, see Yürekli, "A Building Between the Public and Private Realms of the Ottoman Elite," 170–73.

39. On these convents, see Zakir Şükri Efendi, *İstanbul Hankahları meşayihi,* 7–8, 11–12, and Yazıcı, "Fetihten Sonra İstanbul'da İlk Halveti

Şeyhleri," 93ff. For assessments of former Byzantine churches as convents of the Halveti order, see Tanman, "Sünbül Efendi Tekkesi," and idem, "Küçük Ayasofya Tekkesi."

40. On the mosque-and-lodge foundations and the use of the prayer hall as ritual space in early Istanbul foundations, see Tanman, "Settings for the Veneration of Saints."

41. İstanbul Hânkâhları meşâyihi, 21.

42. Robert Ousterhout notes that Stephan Gerlach saw the Chora mosaics in 1578; Ousterhout, *The Architecture of the Kariye Camii in Istanbul,* 6.

43. As Cemal Kafadar's analysis and interpretation of the cultural and political makeup of late medieval Anatolia shows; Kafadar, *Between Two Worlds.*

BIBLIOGRAPHY

Abbreviations for Archival Documentation

BBA   Başbakanlık Arşivi (Archives of the Prime Ministry)
TKS   Topkapı Sarayı (Topkapı Palace Library)
TKSA   Topkapı Sarayı Arşivi (Topkapı Palace Archives)
VGMA   Vakıflar Genel Müdürlüğü Arşivi (Archives of the Directorate of Pious Endowments)

Archival Documents

Topkapı Palace Archives:
D 6541, D 6931, D 6936, D 6977, D 6990, D 6996, D 7079, D 9524, D 9637, D 10029, D 10729, E 298, E 299, E 3060, E 3204, E 3365, E 4223, E 4503, E 5479, E 6089, E 6131, E 6184, E 7222/1, E 7225, E 7232, E 8936, E 9300/4, E 9433, E 10053, E 11414, E 11570, E 11975, YY 360

Archives of the Directorate of Pious Endowments:
Akbaş Cundi. A.H. 903 Galata. [608:340; 2132:328]
Ayas bin ʿAbdullah. A.H. 879h. [610:17–18; 1760:382–84]
Başcı Hacı Mahmud bin Hacı Sinan. N.d., additions in A.H. 997 [633:304–5; 1384–87]
Bayezid II. A.H. 911. İstanbul. [2113:195–203; 2148:1–40]
Çakır bin ʿAbdullah. A.H. 885, 887, 889. [610/25:290–92; 1768:221–29]
Çelebizade Hace ʿAlaüddin. A.H. 866. [571:161; 1766:316–17]
Defteri Cendereli Muhyiddin Çelebi bin Hace Şems bin Şuʿayb. A.H. 898, 894. [740:73–75; 608:298]
Duka bin Bedros. A.H. 923. Galata. [624:286–89; 2132:1527–36]
El-Hac ʿAli bin Hasan al-şehir bi ibn-i Bereket. A.H. 906. Galata. [570:29–30; 1766:82–85]
El-Hac Şemsüddin bin Hüseyn bin Binaburi. A.H. 882. [633:176–77; 1768:252–57]
Emir Ahmed bin Mehmed el-Buhari. A.H. 918. [633:58–60; 2165:521–25]
Additions to the Emir Buhari foundation:
  Hasan bin ʿAli. A.H. 929, 933. [633:61; 2105:530]
  Muslihuddin Mustafa bin Cüneyd el-maʿruf biʾl-Hac Kıssa Han. A.H. 918. [579:229–31]
Firuz bin ʿAbdullah. A.H. 897. [570:105–7; 1767:422–26]
Hace Şemsüddin bin Hüseyn el-Nişaburi. A.H. 882. [633:172; 1768:292–93]
Hayrüddin bin ʿAbdullatif (Lala Hayrüddin Beg). A.H. 891. [571:263–64; 1768:1–5]
Hayrüddin bin Mustafa. A.H. 907. Galata. [583:101–2; 1767:275–79]
İbrahim Paşa bin Halil Paşa. [A.H. 886], A.H. 899, 903. [575:22–29; 588:109; 1862:28–51]
İshak Paşa bin İbrahim. A.H. 891. [211; 2148:203–10]

Koca Muhyiddin Mehmed bin Hüseyin Paşa. A.H. 907. [632:478–80]
[Koca] Mustafa Paşa mevḳūfāt defteri. A.H. 894–910. [654]
Mercan bin ʿAbdullah. A.H. 868, 884. [741:93–96; 1961:316–19]
Mevlana ʿAli Çelebi (Fenarizade Ahmed Pasha biraderi). A.H. 901. [592:112–14; 1767:146–50]
Mevlana Bayezid bin ʿAbdullah (Saru Bayezid). A.H. 875. [576:1–2; 1766:367–69]
Mevlana Şemsüddin Gürani. A.H. 889. [570:220–22; 1767:25–29]
Mevlana Şemsüddin Seyyid ahmed bin Seyyid Mehmed Buhari. A.H. 916. [618:1–5; 1766:44–56]
Mevlana Şeyh Muhyiddin Mehmed bin Musa Fakih. A.H. 903. [570:18; 1766:39–41]
Mustafa Paşa bin Mehmed Beg bin Hamza Beg. A.H. 882.
Okcı Sinan. A.H. 894. Galata [608:203–4; 2105:134–36]
Pir Mehmed Paşa bin Mehmed bin Cemalüddin-i Aksarayi. A.H. 923, 927. [747:466–70; 1991:181–215]
[Rum] Mehmed Paşa. Üsküdar n.d. [617:83]
Şahi Hatun bin Bayezid Beg, Musa Beg validesi. A.H. 930. Eyüb. [570:22–23]
Şeyh Mehmed bin Şeyh Geylani. A.H. 858. [625:141–42; 1767:441–44]
Sinan Çelebi (el-Hac). A.H. 901. [609:302–5]
Sinanüddin Yusuf, miʿmār-ı sulṭānī der İstānbūl. A.H. 869, 873. [633:42–45; 1767:246–53]

Archives of the Prime Mininstry:
A.DFE 1/5–10; A.DVN 1/8; A.DVN 790; AE Bayezid II, 36; AE Bayezid II, 37; AE Bayezid II, 48; AE Bayezid II, 49; AE Mehmed II, 33a; AE Mehmed II, 63; AE Mehmed II, 70; Başmuhasebe zimmet 2411; D.HMH 1/18; D.HMH 1/20; D.HMH 1/36; D.HMH.VKF 39/4; D.HMH.VKF 39/5; Evḳāf-ı icāre zemin defteri, 959h.; KK Haremeyn Mukataası 3359, VKF 6/17; MD 67; MM 19; KK 4988; TT 890; TT 210; TT 240; VKF 20/6

Istanbul Atatürk Library:
M.C. O.64: *Ayaşofya vaḳfı cibāyet defteri.* A.H. 926.
M.C. O.71: *Defter-i müsveddāt-ı inʿāmāt ve taṣadduḳāt ve teşrīfāt ve ġayrihi.* A.H. 909–17.
M.C. O.91: *Muḥāsebe icmāl defteri.* A.H. 891–98.

Published and Unpublished Primary Sources
ʿAbd al-Rahman al-Bistami. *Tercüme-i Miftāḥ-ı Cifrüʾl-Cāmiʿ.* Translated by Şerifı bin Seyyid Mehmed ibn-i Seyyid Burhan. Istanbul University Library, T.6624.

Alberti, Leon Battista. *On the Art of Building in Ten Books.* Translated by Joseph Rykwert, Neil Leach, and Robert Tavernor. Cambridge, Mass.: MIT Press, 1991.

ʿAli, Mustafa bin Ahmet. *Künhüʾl-Aḥbār.* Vol. 2. Edited by M. Hüdai Şentürk. Ankara: Türk Tarih Kurumu, 2003.

al-Tamgrouti, Abouʾl-Hasan Ali ben Mohammed. *En-nafhat el-miskiya fi-s-sifarat et-Tourkiye/Relation d'une ambassade marocaine en Turquie (1589–1591).* Edited and translated by Henry de Castries. Paris: Geuthner, 1929.

Die altosmanischen anonymen Chroniken: Tevârîh-i Âl-i ʿOsmân. Edited and translated by Friedrich Giese. 2 vols. Breslau, 1922–25.

Angiolello, Giovan Maria. *Viaggio di Negroponte.* Edited by Cristina Bazzolo. Vicenza: N. Pozza, 1982.

Angiolello, Giovan Maria, and Donado da Lezze. *Historia turchesca (1300–1514).* Edited by Ioan Ursu. Bucharest: Editiunea Academiai Romăne, 1909.

Anhegger, Robert, and Halil İnalcık, eds. *Ḳānūnnāme-i sulṭanī ber mūceb-i ʿörf-i ʿoṣmānī.* Ankara: Türk Tarih Kurumu, 1956.

Arrian. *The Campaigns of Alexander.* London: Penguin Books, 1971.

Aşıkpaşazade, Derviş Ahmet. *ʿAşıkpaşaoğlu Ahmed ʿAşıkī. Tevârîh-i Âl-i Osman.* Edited by Nihal Atsız. Istanbul: Türkiye Yayınevi, 1947.

Ateş, Ahmet. "İstanbulʾun fethine dair Fatih Sultan Mehmed tarafından gönderilen mektuplar ve bunlara gelen cevaplar." *Tarih dergisi* 4, no. 7 (1952): 11–50.

Ayvansarayi, Hafız Hüseyin al-. *The Garden of the Mosques: Hafız Hüseyin al-Ayvansarayi's Guide to the Muslim Monuments of Ottoman Istanbul.* Translated and edited by Howard Crane. Leiden: Brill, 1999.

Barkan, Ömer Lutfi. "Ayasofya Camiʾi ve Eyüb Türbesinin 1489–1491 yıllarına ait muhasebe bilançoları." *Tarih dergisi* 23 (1963): 343–81.

———. "Fatih Cami ve Imareti Tesislerinin 1489–1490 yıllarına ait muhasebe bilançoları." *Tarih dergisi* 23 (1963): 297–341.

Barkan, Ömer Lufti, and Ekrem Hakkı Ayverdi, eds. *İstanbul vakıfları tahrir defteri 953 (1546) tarihli.* Istanbul: Baha Matbaası, 1970.

Braun, Georg, and Franz Hogenberg. *Civitates Orbis Terrarum, 1572–1618.* With an introduction by R. A. Skelton. Cleveland: World Publishing Company, 1966.

Breydenbach, Bernhard von. *Peregrinatio in Terram Sanctam.* Translated by Nicolas Le Huen. Lyon: Michel Topie and Jacques Heremberck, 1488.

Buondelmonti, Cristoforo. *Liber Insularum Archipelagi: Description des Îles de l'Archipel grec.* Translated and edited by Emile Legrand. Paris: E. Leroux, 1897.

———. *Liber Insularum Archipelagi: Universitäts- und Landesbibliothek Düsseldorf MS. G 13: Faksimile.* Edited by Irmgard Siebert and Max Plassmann, with contributions by Arne Effenberger, Max Plassmann, and Fabian Rijkers. Wiesbaden: Reichert, 2005.

Byzantium, Europe, and the Early Ottoman Sultans, 1373–1513: An Anonymous Greek Chronicle of the Seventeenth Century (Codex Barberinus Graecus 111). Edited and translated by Marios Philippides. New Rochelle, N.Y.: A. D. Caratzas, 1990.

La caduta di Costantinopoli. Edited and translated by Agostino Pertusi. 2 vols. Rome: Fondazione L. Valla, 1976.

Caʿfer Çelebi, Taci-zade. *Heveşnâme.* Nuruosmaniye Library, 4373.

Canatar, Mehmet, ed. *İstanbul vakıfları tahrir defteri 1009 (1600) tarihli.* Istanbul: İstanbul Fetih Cemiyeti, 2004.

Çelebi, Asaf Halet. *Divan şiirinde İstanbul.* Istanbul: Halk Basımevi, 1953.

Cengiz, Halil Erdoğan, and Yaşar Yücel, eds. "Rûhî Târihi." *Belgeler* 14–18 (1989–92): 359–472, and facsimile.

Chesneau, Jean. *Le voyage de Monsieur d'Aramon.* Paris: E. Leroux, 1887.

Chrysoloras, Manuel. "Comparison of Old and New Rome." Translated and edited by Christine Smith. In *Architecture in the Culture of Early Humanism: Ethics, Aesthetics, and Eloquence, 1400–1470,* 171–215. New York: Oxford University Press, 1992.

Clavijo, Ruy González de. *Embassy to Tamerlane.* Translated by Guy le Strange. New York: Harper, 1928.

Dei, Benedetto. *La cronica dall'anno 1400 all'anno 1500.* Edited by Roberto Barducci. Florence: F. Papafava, 1984.

Dernschwam, Hans. *İstanbul ve Anadoluʾya seyahat günlüğü.* Translated by Yaşar Önen. Ankara: Kültür Bakanlığı Yayınları, 1992.

Doukas [Ducas]. *Decline and Fall of Byzantium to the Ottoman Turks.* Edited and translated by Harry J. Margoulias. Detroit: Wayne State University Press, 1975.

Enveri. *Düstūrnāme-i Enverī.* Edited by Mükrimin Halil Yinanç. Istanbul: Evkaf Matbaası, 1929.

Ebuʾl-Hayr-i Rumi. *Şalṭuḳnāme.* Edited by Fahir İz and Şinasi Tekin. 7 pts. in 3 vols. Sources of Oriental Languages and Literatures 4. Cambridge, Mass: Harvard University Printing Office, 1974–84.

Emperors, Patriarchs, and Sultans of Constantinople, 1373–1513: An Anonymous Greek Chronicle of the Sixteenth Century. Edited and translated by Marios Philippides. Brookline, Mass.: Hellenic College Press, 1990.

Evliya Çelebi. *Evliya Çelebi Seyahatnamesi, 1. kitap: İstanbul.* 3 vols. Edited by Şinasi Tekin and Gönül Alpay-Tekin. Cambridge, Mass.: Harvard University Press, 1989.

"Eyyup vakfiyesinin faksimilesi" [Facsimile of the Eyyup Waqfiyya]. In *Fatih Mehmed II vakfiyeleri,* 285–327. Ankara: Vakıflar Umum Müdürlüğü Neşriyati, 1938.

Fâtihʾin şiirleri. Edited by Kemal Edip Ünsel. Ankara: Türk Tarih Kurumu, 1946.

Fatih Mehmed II vakfiyeleri. Ankara: Vakıflar Umum Müdürlüğü Neşriyati, 1938. [Later sixteenth-century Turkish copy.]

Fatih Sultan Mehmedʾin ölümü ve hadiseleri üzerine bir vesika: Testament de Amyra Sultan Nichemedy. Edited and translated by Süheyl Ünver. Istanbul: İstanbul Fetih Cemiyeti, 1952. [Contains a transcription and facsimile of MS no. 168 in the Garret Collection of Medieval and Renaissance Manuscripts of the Princeton University Library.]

Fatih Sultan Mehmed'in vakfiyeleri. Edited by Osman Ergin. Istanbul: Belediye Matbaası, 1945. [Ca. 1472, Türk ve İslam Eserleri Müzesi copy.]

Filarete [Antonio Averlino]. *Filarete's Treatise on Architecture.* Edited and translated by John R. Spencer. 2 vols. New Haven: Yale University Press, 1965.

Fossati, Gaspard. *Aya Sofia, Constantinople: As Recently Restored by the Order of H. M. the Sultan Abdul Medjid.* London: R. & C. Colnagni, 1852.

George of Trebizond. *Collectanea Trapezuntiana: Texts, Documents, and Bibliographies of George of Trebizond.* Edited by John Monfasani. Binghamton, N.Y.: Renaissance Society of America, 1984.

Georgius de Hungaria. *Chronica unnd beschreibung der Türckey: Unveränderter Nachdruck der Ausgabe Nürnberg 1530, sowie fünf weiterer "Türkendrucke" des 15. und 16. Jahrhunderts.* Edited by Carl Göllner. Cologne: Böhlau, 1983.

Gilles, Pierre. *The Antiquities of Constantinople.* Translated by John Ball. New York: Italica Press, 1988.

Gökbilgin, M. Tayyib. *XV.–XVI. asırlarda Edirne ve Paşa livası.* Istanbul: Üçler Basımevi, 1952.

———. "Venedik Devlet Arşivindeki vesikalar külliyatında Kanuni Sultan Süleyman Devri Belgeleri." *Belgeler* 2 (1953): 121–220.

Hadidi. *Tevārīḫ-i ʾĀl-i ʿOṣmān.* Edited by Necdet Öztürk. Istanbul: Edebiyat Fakültesi Basımevi, 1991.

Hamidi. *Külliyyāt-ı divān-ı Mevlānā Ḥamīdī.* Edited by İsmail Hikmet Ertaylan. Istanbul: Milli Eğitim Basımevi, 1949.

Harff, Arnold von. *The Pilgrimage of Arnold von Harff.* Translated by Malcolm Letts. Hakluyt Society, 2nd ser., no. 94. Cambridge: Cambridge University Press, 1946.

Hezarfen Hüseyin Efendi. *Telhīṣüʾl-beyan fī kavānīn-i Āl-i ʿOṣmān.* Edited by Sevim İlgürel. Ankara: Türk Tarih Kurumu, 1998.

Hıbri. *Enîsüʾl-Müsâmirîn: Edirne Tarihi, 1360–1650,* translated by Ratip Kazancıgil. Edirne: Türk Kütüphaneciler Derneği Edirne Şubesi, 1996.

Ibn Battuta. *Travels in Asia and Africa.* Edited by H. A. R. Gibb. London: Routledge, 1929.

İdris Bidlisi. *Heşt behişt.* Süleymaniye Library, Esad Ef. 2198.

———. *Tercüme-i Heşt behişt.* TKS B 196.

İstanbul Hânkâhları Meşayihi, ed. Turgut Kut. Journal of Turkish Studies 19 (1933): 1–156.

Karamanlı Nişancı Mehmed Paşa. *Osmanlı sultanları tarihi.* Translated by İbrahim Hakkı Konyalı. Istanbul: Türkiye Yayınevi, 1949.

Kemal. *Selātīn-nāme (1299–1490).* Edited by Necdet Öztürk. Ankara: Türk Tarih Kurumu, 2001.

Kemalpaşazade [İbn Kemal]. *Tevârîh-i Âl-i Osman: VII. Defter.* Edited by Şerafettin Turan. Ankara: Türk Tarih Kurumu, 1954–83.

———. *Mecmūʿa-i Fetāvā.* Nur-u Osmaniye Library, 1967.

Kınalızade Hasan Çelebi. *Tezkiretüʾş-şuʿarā.* Edited by İbrahim Kutluk. 2 vols. Ankara: Türk Tarih Kurumu, 1989.

Kıvami. *Fetiḥnāme-i Sulṭān Meḥmed.* Edited by Franz Babinger. Istanbul: Maarif Matbaası, 1955.

Kömürcüyan, Eremya Çelebi. *İstanbul tarihi: XVII. asırda İstanbul.* Edited by Hrand D. Andreasyan and Kevork Pamukciyan. Istanbul: Eren, 1988.

Konstantios I. *Constantiniade, ou Description de Constantinople ancienne et moderne, compose par un philologue et archéologue.* Translated by M. R. Constantinople: A. Coromilla et P. Paspalli, 1846.

Kritovoulos. *History of Mehmed the Conqueror.* Translated by Charles T. Riggs. Princeton, N.J.: Princceton University Press, 1954.

Küçük Abdal. *Velāyetnāme-i Sulṭān Otman Baba.* Ankara Milli Kütüphanesi, microfilm no. A22.

la Broquière, Bertrandon de. *Le voyage d'outremer de Bertrandon de la Broquière.* Edited by Charles Schefer. Paris: E. Leroux, 1892.

Latifi. *Evsâf-ı İstanbul.* Edited by Nermin Suner. Istanbul: Baha Matbaası, 1977.

———. *Tezkiretüʾş-şuʿarā ve tabsıratüʾn-nuzamā (inceleme-metin).* Edited by Rıdvan Canım. Ankara: Atatürk Kültür Merkezi, 2000.

Lokman bin Seyyid Hüseyin. *Hünernāme.* 2 vols. TKS H 1523, H 1524.

Majeska, George P. *Russian Travelers to Costantinople in the Fourteenth and Fifteenth Centuries.* Washington, D.C.: Dumbarton Oaks Research Library and Collection, 1984.

Mecdi Efendi. *Tercüme-i şaḳāyıḳ.* [Istanbul]: Tabhane-i ʿAmire, [A.H.] 1269.

Mehmed bin Hüsam. *Fatih Aşhanesi Tevziʿnamesi.* Edited by Süheyl Ünver. Istanbul: Istanbul Fetih Derneği, 1953.

Mehmed bin Ömer Bayezid el-ʿAşık. *Menāẕirüʾl-ʿavālim.* Süleymaniye Library, Halet Efendi 616.

Menāḳıb-ı Aḳşemseddīn. Edited by Ali İhsan Yurt and Mustafa Kaçalın. In *Akşemseddin, 1390–1459: Hayatı ve eserleri,* 127–89. Istanbul: Marmara Üniversitesi İlâhiyat Fakültesi Vakfı yayınları, 1994.

Menāḳıb-ı Maḥmūd Pāşā-yı Velī. Süleymaniye Library, Aya-sofya 1940/2.

Menavino, Giovanni Antonio. *I costumi et la vita de Turchi.* Florence: Appresso Lorenzo Torrentino, 1551.

Meriç, Rıfkı Melûl. "Birkaç mühim arşiv vesikası." *İstanbul Enstitüsü dergisi* 3 (1957): 33–42.

Mesarites, Nikolaos. "Description of the Church of the Holy Apostles at Constantinople." Edited and translated by Glanville Downey. *Transactions of the American Philosophical Society* 47 (1957): 855–923.

Mihailović, Konstantin. *Memoirs of a Janissary.* Translated by Benjamin Stolz; historical commentary by Svat Soucek. Ann Arbor: University of Michigan, 1975.

Muʿali. *Ḫünkārnāme.* TKS H 1417.

Müstakimzade Süleyman Sadeddin. *Tuḥfe-i Ḫaṭṭātīn.* Istanbul: Devlet Matbaası, 1928.

Nasuhü's-Silahi [Matrakcı]. *Beyān-ı menāzil-i sefer-i ʿIraḳeyn-i Ṣulṭān Süleymān Ḫān.* Edited by Hüseyin G. Yurdaydın. Ankara: Türk Tarih Kurumu, 1976.

Neşri. *Kitâb-ı Cihan-nümâ.* Edited by Mehmed A. Köymen. Ankara: Kültür ve Turizm Bakanligi, 1983.

Nicolay, Nicolas de. *Dans l'empire de Soliman le Magnifique.* [1576.] Edited by Marie-Christine Gomez-Geraud and Stéphane Yérasimos. Paris: CNRS, 1989.

Promontorio, Iacopo di Campis. *Governo et entrate del Gran Turco 1475.* In *Die Aufzeichnungen des Genuesen Iacopo de Promontorio de Campis über den Osmanenstaat um 1475,* edited by Franz Babinger, Bayerische Akademie der Wissenschaften, philosophisch-historische Klasse, Sitzungsberichte, Jahrgang 1956, Heft 8. Munich: Bayerische Akademie der Wissenschaften, 1957.

Ramberti, Benedetto. "The Second Book of the Affairs of the Turks." In *The Government of the Ottoman Empire in the Time of Suleiman the Magnificent,* by Albert Howe Lybyer, 239–61. Cambridge: Harvard University Press, 1913.

Refik, Ahmet. *On altıncı asırda Istanbul hayatı (1553–1591): Istanbul'un fikrî, içtimaî, iktisadî ve ticarî ahvalile evakf, belediye, iaşe ve gümrük işlerine dair hazinei evrak'ın gayrı matbuʾ vesikalarını havidir.* Istanbul: Enderun Kitabevi, 1988.

Saʿdi Efendi [Saʿdullah bin İsa bin Amir Han]. *Fetāvā.* Süleymaniye Library, Şehid Ali Paşa, 1073.

Saʿdüddin. *Tācüʾt-tevārīḫ.* 2 vols. [Istanbul]: Tabhane-i ʿAmire, [A.H.] 1279.

Şakiroğlu, M. "1521 tarihli Osmanlı-Venedik antlaşmasının asli metni." *Tarih Enstitüsü dergisi* 12 (1982): 388–403.

Sanderson, John. *The Travels of John Sanderson in the Levant, 1584–1602.* Edited by William Foster. London: Hakluyt Society, 1931.

Schedel, Hartmann. *Liber Chronicarum cum Figuris et Ymaginibus ab Inicio Mundi.* Nuremberg: Anton Koberger, 1493.

Schweigger, Salomon. *Ein newe Reyssbeschreibung auss Teutschland nach Constantinopel und Jerusalem.* Edited by Rudolf Neck. Graz: Akademische Druck, 1964.

Şemsüddin Karamani. *Tercüme-i Tārīḫ-i Cāmiʿi Ayāṣofyā.* Istanbul University Library, T.259.

Spandounes, Theodore. *On the Origin of the Ottoman Emperors.* Edited and translated by Donald M. Nicol. Cambridge: Cambridge University Press, 1997.

Sphrantzes, George. *The Fall of the Byzantine Empire: A Chronicle by George Sphrantzes (1401–1477).* Translated by Marios Philippides. Amherst: University of Massachusetts Press, 1980.

Taeschner, Franz Gustav, ed. *Alt-Stambuler Hof- und Volksleben; ein türkisches Miniaturenalbum aus dem 17. Jahrhundert.* Hannover: Orient-Buchhandlung H. Lafaire, 1925.

Tafur, Pero. *Travels and Adventures.* Edited and translated by Malcolm Letts. London: G. Routledge, 1926.

Tavernier, Jean-Baptiste. *Nouvelle relation de l'intérieur du serail du grand seigneur.* Paris, 1675.

Tursun Beg. *The History of Mehmed the Conqueror.* Edited and translated by Halil İnalcık and Rhoads Murphey. Minneapolis: Bibliotheca Islamica, 1978.

3 numaralı mühimme defteri (966–968/1558–1560). Edited by Nezihi Aykut et al. Ankara: Devlet Arşivleri Genel Müdürlüğü, 1993.

Uruç bin ʿAdil. *Die frühosmanischen Jahrbücher des Urudsch.* Edited by Franz Babinger. Hanover, 1929.

van der Vin, J. P. A. *Travellers to Greece and Constantinople.* 2 vols. Istanbul: Nederlands Historisch-Archaeologisch Instituut te Istanbul, 1980.

Yazıcıoğlı Ahmed Bican. *Dürr-i Meknūn.* TKS Revan 1136.

Zakir Şükri Efendi. *İstanbul Hankahları meşayihi.* Edited by Turgut Kut. *Journal of Turkish Studies* 19 (1995): 1–156.

Zenbilli ʿAli Cemali Efendi [Mevlana ʿAlaüddin ʿAli bin Ahmed bin Mehmed Cemali]. *Mecmuʿa-i Fetāvā.* Süleymaniye Library, Fatih 2388.

Zwei Stiftsurkunden des Sultan Mehmed II. Fatih. Edited by Tahsin Öz. Istanbuler Mitteilungen 4. Istanbul: Istanbuler Mitteilungen, herausgegeben von der Abteilung Istanbul der Archäologischen Institutes des Deutschen Reiches, 1935. [Ca. 1480, TKS copy.]

Secondary Resources

Abu-Lughod, Janet. "The Islamic City—Historic Myth, Islamic Essence, and Contemporary Relevance." *International Journal of Middle East Studies* 19 (1987): 155–76.

Ackerman, James S. "The Certosa of Pavia and the Renaissance in Milan." *Marsyas* 5 (1947–49): 23–27.

———. "The Planning of Renaissance Rome, 1450–1580." In *Rome in the Renaissance: The City and the Myth,* edited by P. A. Ramsey, 3–17. New York: State University of New York Press, 1982.

Ağaoğlu, Mehmed. "The Fatih Mosque at Constantinople." *Art Bulletin* 12 (1930): 179–95.

Ağır, Aygül. "İstanbul'un Eski 'Venedik Ticaret Kolonisi'nin 'Osmanlı Ticaret Bölgesi'ne Dönüşümü." Ph.D. diss., Istanbul Technical University, 2001.

Ahunbay, Zeynep, and Metin Ahunbay. "Structural Influence of Hagia Sophia on Ottoman Mosque Architecture." In *Hagia Sophia from the Age of Justinian to the Present,* edited by Robert Mark and Ahmet Çakmak, 179–94. Cambridge: Cambridge University Press, 1992.

Aktuğ, İlknur, and Ahmet Erzen. "Bir 15. yüzyıl yapısı olan Tahtakale Hamamında uygulanan bazı yapım teknikleri." *TAÇ Vakfı Yıllığı* 1 (1991): 25–55.

Allsen, Thomas T. *Culture and Conquest in Mongol Eurasia.* Cambridge and New York: Cambridge University Press, 2002.

Almagià, Roberto. "On the Cartographic Work of Francesco Rosselli." *Imago Mundi* 8 (1951): 27–34.

Alsayyad, Nezar. "Bayn al-Qasrayn: The Street Between the Two Palaces." In *Streets: Critical Perspectives on Public Space,* edited by Zeynep Çelik, Diane Favro, and

Richard Ingersoll, 71–82. Berkeley and Los Angeles: University of California Press, 1994.

Ambraseys, N. N., and C. F. Finkel. *The Seismicity of Turkey and Adjacent Areas.* Istanbul: Eren, 1995.

Anhegger, Robert. "Muʿâlîʾnin Hünkarnameʾsi." *Tarih dergisi* 1, nos. 1–2 (1949–50): 145–66.

Arel, Ayda. "Cihannüma Kasrı ve erken Osmanlı saraylarında kule yapıları hakkında." in *Prof. Doğan Kubanʾa Armağan,* edited by Zeynep Ahunbay, Deniz Mazlum, and Kutgün Eyüpgiller, 99–116. Istanbul: Eren, 1996.

Artan, Tülay. "İbrahim Paşa Sarayı." In *Dünden bugüne İstanbul ansiklopedisi,* 4:128–30.

Aslanapa, Oktay. *Edirneʾde Osmanlı devri abideleri.* Istanbul: Üçler Basımevi, 1949.

Aynur, Hatice. "Istanbul in Divan Poetry: 1453–1600." in *Acta Viennensia Ottomanica: Akten des 13. CIEPO-Symposiums vom 21. bis 25. September 1998,* 43–50. Vienna: Im Selbstverlag des Instituts für Orientalistik, 1999.

Ayverdi, Ekrem Hakkı. *Fatih devri mimarisi.* Istanbul: İstanbul Fetih Derneği, 1953.

———. *Fatih devri sonlarında İstanbul mahalleleri, şehrin iskanı ve nüfusu.* Ankara: Vakıflar Umum Müdürlüğü, 1958.

———. *19. asırda İstanbul haritası.* Istanbul: İstanbul Fetih Cemiyeti, 1958.

———. *Osmanlı miʿmârîsinde Çelebi ve II. Sultan Murad devri, 806–855 (1403–1451).* Vol. 2 of a work lacking a collective title. Istanbul: İstanbul Fetih Cemiyeti, 1972.

———. *Osmanlı miʿmârîsinde Fâtih devri, 855–886 (1451–1481).* 2 vols. Vols. 3 and 4 of a work lacking a collective title. Istanbul: İstanbul Fetih Cemiyeti/İstanbul Enstitüsü, 1973.

———. *Osmanlı miʿmarisinin ilk devri.* Istanbul: İstanbul Fetih Cemiyeti, 1966.

Babinger, Franz. *Aufsätze und Abhandlungen zur Geschichte Südosteuropas und der Levante.* 3 vols. Munich: Südosteuropa Verlagsgesellschaft, 1962–76.

———. *Drei Stadtansichten von Konstantinopel, Galata ("Pera") und Skutari aus dem Ende des 16. Jahrhunderts.* Österreichische Akademie der Wissenschaften in Wien, philosophisch-historische Klasse, Denkschriften, 77/3. Vienna: Rudolf M. Rohrer, 1959.

———. "Francesco Scarella e i suoi designi di Costantinopoli (circa 1685)." In *Aufsätze und Abhandlungen zur Geschichte Südosteuropas und der Levante,* 3:97–111. Munich: Südosteuropa Verlagsgesellschaft, 1976.

———. *Mehmed the Conqueror and His Time.* Translated by Ralph Manheim. Bollingen Series 96. Princeton, N.J.: Princeton University Press, 1992 [original German ed., 1953].

———. "Eine Verfügung des Paläologen Châss Murâd-Pâşa." In *Aufsätze und Abhandlungen zur Geschichte Südosteuropas und der Levante,* 1:345–54. Munich: Südosteuropa Verlagsgesellschaft, 1962.

Bacharach, Jere. "Administrative Complexes, Palaces, and Citadels: Changes in the Loci of Medieval Muslim Rule." In *The Ottoman City and Its Parts: Urban Structure and Social Order,* edited by Irene A. Bierman, Rafaʿat A. Abou-el-Haj, and Donald Preziosi, 111–28. New Rochelle, N.Y.: A. D. Caratzas, 1991.

Bacqué-Grammont, Jean-Louis. "Eyüp mezarlıklarının incelenmesi üzerine düşünceler." In *Eyüp: Dün-Bugün,* edited by Tülay Artan, 62–105. Istanbul: Tarih Vakfı Yurt Yayınları, 1994.

Bagrow, Leo. *Giovanni Andreas di Vavassore: A Venetian Cartographer of the Sixteenth Century.* Jenkintown, Pa.: George H. Beans Library, 1939.

Balard, Michel. "Constantinople vue par les témoins du siège de 1453." In *Constantinople and Its Hinterland,* edited by Cyril Mango and Gilbert Dagron, 169–77. Aldershot, Hampshire: Variorum, 1995.

———. "L'organisation des colonies étrangères dans l'Empire byzantin (XIIe–XVe siècles)." In *Hommes et richesses dans l'Empire byzantin,* 261–76. Paris: Editions P. Lethielleux, 1991.

Ballon, Hilary. *The Paris of Henry IV: Architecture and Urbanism.* Cambridge, Mass.: MIT Press, 1991.

Banoğlu, N. Ahmed. *Mahmud Paşa: Hayatı ve şehadeti.* Istanbul: Gür Kitabevi, 1970.

Bardakjian, Kevork B. "The Rise of the Armenian Patriarchate of Constantinople." In *Christians and Jews in the Ottoman Empire,* edited by Benjamin Braude and Bernard Lewis, 1:89–100. New York: Holmes & Meier, 1982.

Barkan, Ömer Lufti. "Osmanlı İmparatorluğunda bir iskan ve kolonizasyon metodu olarak vakıflar ve temlikler." *Vakıflar dergisi* 2 (1942): 279–386.

———. "Osmanlı İmparatoluğunda bir iskan ve kolonizasyon metodu olarak sürgünler." *Iktisat Fakültesi mecmuası* 11 (1949–50): 524–61; 13 (1951–52): 56–78; 15 (1953–54): 209–37.

Barthes, Roland. *S/Z.* Translated by Richard Miller. New York: Hill & Wang, 1974.

Basset, Sarah. *The Urban Image of Late Antique Constantinople.* Cambridge: Cambridge University Press, 2004.

Behrens-Abouseif, Doris. *Egypt's Adjustment to Ottoman Rule: Institutions, Waqf, and Architecture in Cairo (16th and 17th Centuries).* Leiden: E. J. Brill, 1994.

Beldiceanu, Nicoara. *Recherche sur la ville ottomane au XVe siècle: Étude et actes.* Paris: Librairie d'Amérique et d'Orient J. Maisonneuve, 1973.

Beldiceanu, Nicoara, and Irène Beldiceanu-Steinherr. "Un paléologue inconnu de la région de Serres." *Byzantion* 41 (1971): 5–17.

Beldiceanu-Steinherr, Irène. "Le règne de Selīm 1er: Tournant dans la vie politique et religieuse de l'Empire ottoman." *Turcica* 6 (1975): 34–48.

Berger, Albrecht. "Imperial and Ecclesiastical Processions in Constantinople." In *Byzantine Constantinople: Monuments, Topography, and Everyday Life,* edited by Nevra Necipoğlu, 73–88. Leiden: E. J. Brill, 2001.

———. "Roman, Byzantine, and Latin Periods." In *Kalenderhane in Istanbul: The Buildings, Their History, Architecture, and Decoration,* edited by Cecil Striker and Doğan Kuban, 7–16. Mainz: Verlag Philipp von Zabern, 1997.

———. "Streets and Public Spaces in Constantinople." *Dumbarton Oaks Papers* 54 (2000): 161–72.

———. "Zur sogenannten Stadtansicht des Vavassore." *Istanbuler Mitteilungen* 44 (1994): 329–55.

———. "Zur Topographie der Ufergegend am Goldenen Horn in der byzantinischen Zeit." *Istanbuler Mitteilungen* 45 (1995): 152–55.

Berger, Albrecht, and Jonathan Bardill. "The Representations of Constantinople in Hartmann Schedel's *World Chronicle* and Related Pictures." *Byzantine and Modern Greek Studies* 22 (1998): 2–37.

Berktay, Halil. "Azizler, cismani kalıntılar, haclar, yatırlar: Tektanrıcılık içinde özümlenmiş paganizm." In *Eyüp: Dün-Bugün,* edited by Tülay Artan, 24–49. Istanbul: Tarih Vakfı Yurt Yayınları, 1994.

Bertelè, Tommasso. *Il palazzo degli ambasciatori di Venezia a Costantinopoli e sue antiche memorie.* Bologna: Casa Editrice Apollo, 1931.

Bierman, Irene A., Rafaʿat A. Abou-El-Haj, and Donald Preziosi, eds. *The Ottoman City and Its Parts: Urban Structure and Social Order.* New Rochelle, N.Y.: A. D. Caratzas, 1991.

Blunt, Anthony. *Artistic Theory in Italy.* Oxford: Clarendon Press, 1940.

Bora, Tanıl. "Fatih'in İstanbul'u." *Birikim* 76 (1995): 44–53.

Bourdieu, Pierre. *Distinction: A Social Critique of the Judgement of Taste.* Translated by Richard Nice. London: Routledge & Kegan Paul, 1986.

Bozdoğan, Sibel, and Gülru Necipoğlu. "Entangled Discourses: Scrutinizing Orientalist and Nationalist Legacies in the Architectural Historiography of the 'Lands of Rum.'" *Muqarnas* 24 (2007): 1–6.

Braude, Benjamin. "Foundation Myths of the *Millet* System." In *Christians and Jews in the Ottoman Empire,* edited by Benjamin Braude and Bernard Lewis, 1:69–88. New York: Holmes & Meier, 1982.

Braude, Benjamin, and Bernard Lewis, eds. *Christians and Jews in the Ottoman Empire.* 2 vols. New York: Holmes & Meier, 1982.

Braudel, Fernand. *The Mediterranean and the Mediterranean World in the Age of Philip II.* Translated by Sian Reynolds. 2 vols. Berkeley and Los Angeles: University of California Press, 1995. [Original French ed., 1966.]

Braunfels, Wolfgang. *Urban Design in Western Europe.* Translated by Kenneth J. Northcott. Chicago: University of Chicago Press, 1988.

Brotton, Jerry. *Trading Territories: Mapping the Early Modern World.* London: Reaktion Books, 1997.

Brown, Patricia Fortini. *Venetian Narrative Painting in the Age of Carpaccio.* New Haven: Yale University Press, 1988.

———. *Venice and Antiquity: The Venetian Sense of the Past.* New Haven: Yale University Press, 1996.

Brown, Peter. *The Cult of the Saints: Its Rise and Function in Latin Christianity.* Chicago: University of Chicago Press, 1981.

Bryer, Anthony, and Heath W. Lowry, eds. *Continuity and Change in Late Byzantine and Early Ottoman Society.* Birmingham: University of Birmingham; Washington, D.C.: Dumbarton Oaks Research Library and Collection, 1986.

Bryson, Norman. "The Gaze in the Expanded Field." In *Vision and Visuality,* edited by Hal Foster, 87–108. Seattle: Bay Press, 1988.

———. *Vision and Painting: The Logic of the Gaze.* New Haven: Yale University Press, 1983.

Buisseret, David, ed. *Envisioning the City: Six Studies in Urban Cartography.* Chicago: University of Chicago Press, 1998.

Burke, Peter. *The European Renaissance: Centers and Peripheries.* Oxford: Blackwell, 1998.

Burroughs, Charles. *From Signs to Design: Environmental Process and Design in Early Renaisance Rome.* Cambridge, Mass.: MIT Press, 1990.

Çam, Nusret. "İslam'da Bazı Fikhî Meselelerin ve Mezheplerin Türk Cami Mimarisine Tesiri." *Vakıflar dergisi* 21 (1990): 376–94.

Campbell, Caroline, and Alan Chong. *Bellini and the East.* London: National Gallery Company, 2005.

Carpo, Mario. *Architecture in the Age of Printing: Orality, Writing, Typography, and Printed Images in the History of Architectural Theory.* Cambridge, Mass.: MIT Press, 2001.

Çeçen, Kâzım. *Halkalı suları.* Istanbul: İstanbul Su ve Kanalizasyon İdaresi, 1991.

———. *Mimar Sinan ve Kırkçeşme tesisleri.* Istanbul: İstanbul Su ve Kanalizasyon İdaresi, 1988.

Ceen, Allen. *The Quartiere di'Banchi: Urban Planning in Rome in the First Half of the Cinquecento.* New York: Garland, 1977.

Çelik, Zeynep. "New Approaches to the 'Non-Western' City." *Journal of the Society of Architectural Historians* 58 (1999–2000): 374–81.

———. *The Remaking of Istanbul: Portrait of an Ottoman City in the Nineteenth Century.* Berkeley and Los Angeles: University of California Press, 1986.

Cerasi, Maurice. *The Istanbul Divanyolu: A Case Study in Ottoman Urbanity and Architecture.* Würzburg: Ergon Verlag, 2004.

———. "Place and Perspective in Sinan's Townscape." *Environmental Design* 1–2 (1987): 52–61.

Certeau, Michel de. *The Practice of Everyday Life.* Translated by Steven Rendall. Berkeley and Los Angeles: University of California Press, 1984.

Çetintaş, Sedat. *Türk mimari anıtları: Osmanlı devri: Bursa'da Murad I ve Bayezid I Binaları.* Istanbul: Milli Eğitim Basımevi, 1952.

Cezar, Mustafa. *Typical Commercial Buildings of the Ottoman Classical Period and the Ottoman Construction System.* Istanbul: Türkiye İş Bankası, 1983.

Charanis, Peter. "The Transfer of Population as a Policy in the Byzantine Empire." *Comparative Studies in Society and History* 3 (1961): 140–54.

Chiabò, Maria, et al. *Alle origini della nuova Roma, Martino V (1417–1431).* Rome: Nella sede dell'Istituto Palazzo Borromini, 1992.

Choay, Françoise. *The Invention of the Historic Monument.* Translated by Lauren M. O'Connell. Cambridge: Cambridge University Press, 2001.

———. *The Rule and the Model: On the Theory and Practice of Urbanism.* Cambridge, Mass.: MIT Press, 1997.

Çınar, Alev. "National History as a Contested Site: The Conquest of Istanbul and Islamist Negotiations of the Nation." *Comparative Studies in Society and History* 43 (2001): 364–91.

Çıpa, Hakki Erdem. "Centrality of the Periphery: The Rise to Power of Selim I, 1487–1512." Ph.D. diss., Harvard University, 2007.

Clayer, Nathalie. *Mystiques, état et société: Les Halvetis dans l'aire balkanique de la fin du xve siècle à nos jours.* Leiden: E. J. Brill, 1994.

Cosgrove, Denis. "The Geometry of Landscape: Practical and Speculative Arts in Sixteenth-Century Venetian Land Territories." In *The Iconography of Landscape: Essays on the Symbolic Representation, Design, and Use of Past Environments,* edited by Denis Cosgrove and Stephen Daniels, 254–76. Cambridge: Cambridge University Press, 1988.

———, ed. *Mappings.* London: Reaktion Books, 1999.

———. "The Myth and the Stones of Venice: An Historical Geography of a Symbolic Landscape." *Journal of Historical Geography* 8 (1982): 145–69.

Cosgrove, Denis, and Stephen Daniels, eds. *The Iconography of Landscape: Essays on the Symbolic Representation, Design, and Use of Past Environments.* Cambridge: Cambridge University Press, 1988.

Crane, Howard. "Ottoman Sultans' Mosques: Icons of Sultanic Legitimacy." In *The Ottoman City and Its Parts: Urban Structure and Social Order,* edited by Irene Bierman, Rafaʿat Abou-el-Haj, and Donald Preziosi, 173–243. New Rochelle, N.Y.: A. D. Caratzas, 1991.

Ćurčić, Slobodan. "Architecture in the Age of Insecurity: An Introduction to Secular Architecture in the Balkans, 1300–1500." In *Secular Medieval Architecture in the Balkans 1300–1500 and Its Preservation,* edited by Slobodan Ćurčić and Evangelia Hadjitryphonos, 19–51. Thessaloniki: Aimos, 1997.

———. "Late-Antique Palaces: The Meaning of Urban Context." *Ars Orientalis* 23 (1993): 67–90.

Ćurčić, Slobodan, and Evangelia Hadjitryphonos, eds. *Secular Medieval Architecture in the Balkans, 1300–1500, and Its Preservation.* Thessaloniki: Aimos, 1997.

Curcio, Giovanna. "'Nisi celeriter repararetur totaliter est ruitura': Notazioni su struttura urbana e rinnovamento edilizio in Roma al tempo di Martino V." In *Alle origini della nuova Roma, Martino V (1417–1431),* edited by Maria Chiabò et al., 538–54. Rome: Nella sede dell'Istituto Palazzo Borromini, 1992.

Dagron, Gilbert. *Constantinople imaginaire: Études sur le recueil des Patria.* Paris: Presses Universitaires de France, 1984.

Dalsar, Fahri. *Türk sanayi ve ticaret tarihinde Bursaʾda ipekçilik.* Istanbul: İstanbul Üniversitesi İktisat Fakültesi, 1960.

Darling, Linda. "The Renaissance and the Middle East." In *A Companion to the Worlds of the Renaissance,* edited by Guido Ruggiero, 39–54. Oxford: Blackwell, 2002.

Decei, Aurel. "Patrik II. Gennadios Skolariosʾun Fatih Sultan Mehmed için yazdığı Ortodoks itikadnamesinin Türkçe metni." *Fatih ve İstanbul* 1 (1953): 101–16.

de Groot, Alexander H. "Mehmed Pasha (Rum)." In *Encyclopedia of Islam,* 2nd ed., 6:1000.

Deissmann, D. Adolf. *Forschungen und Funde im Serai: Mit einem Verzeichnis der nichtislamischen Handschriften im Topkapu Serai zu Istanbul.* Berlin: Walter de Gruyter, 1933.

Denny, Walter. "A Sixteenth-Century Architectural Plan of Istanbul." *Ars Orientalis* 8 (1970): 49–63.

Dijkema, Fokke Theodoor. *The Ottoman Historical Monumental Inscriptions in Edirne.* Leiden: E. J. Brill, 1977.

Dilger, Konrad. *Untersuchungen zur Geschichte des osmanischen Hofzeremoniells im 15. und 16. Jahrhundert.* Beitrage zur Kenntnis Südosteuropas und des Nahen Orients, vol. 4. Munich: Trofenik, 1967.

Dilke, Oswald Ashton Wentworth. "Cartography in the Byzantine Empire." In *The History of Cartography,* vol. 1, *Cartography in Prehistoric, Ancient, and Medieval Europe and the Mediterranean,* edited by J. B. Harley and David Woodward, 258–75. Chicago: University of Chicago Press, 1987.

Dirimtekin, Feridun. "Ayasofya ve ona bağlı binalarda araştırmalar." *Ayasofya Müzesi Yıllığı* 1 (1959): 3–19.

Dodd, Erica Cruikshank, and Shereen Khairallah. *The Image of the Word: A Study of Quranic Verses in Islamic Architecture.* Beirut: American University of Beirut, 1981.

Durliat, Jean. "L'approvisionnement de Constantinople." In *Constantinople and Its Hinterland,* edited by Cyril Mango and Gilbert Dagron, 9–34. Aldershot, Hampshire: Variorum, 1995.

Dursteller, Eric, R. *Venetians in Constantinople: Nation, Identity, and Coexistence in the Early Modern Mediterranean.* Baltimore: Johns Hopkins University Press, 2006.

Düzdağ, M. Ertuğrul. *Şeyhülislam Ebussuud Efendi fetvaları ışığında 16. asır Türk hayatı.* Istanbul: Enderun Kitabevi, 1983.

Ebel, Kathryn A. "City Views, Imperial Visions: Cartography and the Visual Culture of Urban Space in the Ottoman Empire, 1453–1603." Ph.D. diss., University of Texas at Austin, 2002.

Ebersolt, Jean. *Constantinople byzantin et le voyageurs du Levant.* London: Pindar, 1966.

———. *Mission archéologique de Constantinople.* Paris: E. Leroux, 1921.

Ebersolt, Jean, and Adolphe Thiers. *Les églises de Constantinople.* Paris: E. Leroux, 1913.

Eden, W. A. "Studies in Urban Theory: The De re Aedificatoria of Leon Battista Alberti." *Town Planning Review* 19, no. 1 (1943): 10–28.

Edney, Matthew. "Theory in the History of Cartography." *Imago Mundi* 48 (1996): 185–91.

El-Cheikh, Nadia Maria. "Byzantium Through the Islamic Prism from the Twelfth to the Thirteenth Century." In *The Crusades from the Perspective of Byzantium and the Muslim World,* edited by Angeliki Laiu and Roy P. Mottahedeh, 53–69. Washington, D.C.: Dumbarton Oaks Research Library and Collection, 2000.

———. *Byzantium Viewed by the Arabs.* Cambridge, Mass: Harvard University Press, 2004.

Eldem, Edhem, Daniel Goffman, and Bruce Masters. *The Ottoman City Between East and West: Aleppo, Izmir, and Istanbul.* Cambridge: Cambridge University Press, 1999.

Eldem, Sedad H., and Feridun Akozan. *Topkapı Sarayı: Bir mimari araştırma.* Istanbul: Milli Eğitim Basımevi, 1982.

Emerson, William, and Robert Van Nice. "Hagia Sophia and the First Minaret Erected After the Conquest of Constantinople." *American Journal of Archaeology* 54 (1950): 28–40.

Emir, Sedat. "Erken Osmanlı mimarlığında çok işlevli yapılar: Yapısal ve işlevsel bir analiz." Ph.D. diss., Istanbul Technical University, 1992.

Epstein, Mark. "The Leadership of the Ottoman Jews in the Fifteenth and Sixteenth Centuries." In *Christians and Jews in the Ottoman Empire,* edited by Benjamin Braude and Bernard Lewis, 1:101–15. New York: Holmes & Meier, 1982.

Ergenç, Özer. "16. yüzyıl Ankara'sı: Ekonomik, sosyal yapı ve kentsel özellikleri." In *Tarih içinde Ankara,* edited by Erdal Yavuz and Ümit Nevzat Uğurel, 49–60. Ankara: Orta Doğu Teknik Üniveritesi, 1984.

———. *XVI. yüzyılda Ankara ve Konya.* Ankara: Ankara Enstitüsü Vakfı, 1995.

———. "Osmanlı şehrinde esnaf örgütlerinin fizik yapıya etkileri." In *Türkiye'nin sosyal ve ekonomik tarihi/ Social and Economic History of Turkey (1071–1920),* edited by Osman Okyar and Halil İnalcık, 103–9. Ankara: Meteksan, 1980.

———. "Osmanlı şehrindeki 'mahalle'nin işlev ve nitelikleri üzerine." *Osmanlı araştırmaları* 4 (1989): 69–78.

Ergin, Osman. "Çarşı." In *İslâm ansiklopedisi,* 3:360–62.

Ersoy, Ahmet. "Namık Kemal." In *Discourses of Collective Identity in Central and Southeast Europe (1770–1945),* vol. 2, 94–97. *National Romanticism: The Formation of National Movements,* edited by Balázs Trencsényi and Michal Kopeček. Budapest: Central European University Press, 2007.

Eyice, Semavi. "Atik Ali Paşa Cami'inin Türk mimari tarihindeki yeri." *Tarih dergisi* 19 (1964): 99–114.

———. "Les 'bedestens' dans l'architecture turque." In *Atti del secondo Congresso internazionale di arte turca,* 112–17. Naples: Istituto Universitario Orientale, Seminario di Turcologia, 1963.

———. "Çardaklı Hamam." In *Dünden bugüne İstanbul ansiklopedisi,* 3:471–72.

———. "Elçi Hanı." *Tarih dergisi* 24 (1970): 93–129.

———. "Ilk Osmanlı Devrinin dini-içtimai bir müessesesi: Zâviyeler ve zâviyeli camiler." *İktisat Fakültesi mecmuası* 23 (1964): 3–63.

———. "İstanbul (tarihi eserler)." In *İslâm ansiklopedisi,* 5:1214/44–1214/144.

———. "İstanbul'da Koca Mustafa Paşa Cami'i ve onun Osmanlı-Türk mimarisindeki yeri." *Tarih dergisi* 5 (1953): 153–82.

———. "İstanbul'da Yayla camileri ve şehrin tarihi topografyasının yanlış izah edilen bir meselesi." *Tarih dergisi* 7, no. 10 (1954): 31–42.

———. "Kefeli Mescidi." In *Dünden bugüne İstanbul ansiklopedisi,* 4:517–18.

———. "Sekbanbaşı İbrahim Ağa Mescidi ve İstanbul'un tarihi topoğrafyası hakkında bir not (Kyra Martha Manastırı)." *Fatih ve İstanbul* 2, nos. 7–12 (1954): 139–65.

———. *Son devir Bizans mimarisi: İstanbul'da Palaiologos'lar devri anıtları.* 2nd, exp. ed. Istanbul: Türkiye Turing ve Otomobil Kurumu, 1980. [First ed., 1963.]

Fanelli, Giovanni. *Firenze.* Rome: Editori Laterza, 1980.

Faroqhi, Suraiya. *Men of Modest Substance: House Owners and House Property in Seventeenth-Century Ankara and Kayseri.* Cambridge: Cambridge University Press, 1987.

———. *Towns and Townsmen of Ottoman Anotolia: Trade, Crafts, and Food Production in an Urban Setting, 1520–1650.* Cambridge: Cambridge University Press, 1984.

Feuer-Tóth, Rózsa. *Art and Humanism in Hungary in the Age of Matthius Corvinus.* Budapest: Akadémiai Kiadó, 1990.

———. *Renaissance Architecture in Hungary.* Translated by Ivan Feherdy. Budapest: Corvina Kiadó/Magyar Helikon, 1981.

Finkel, Caroline. *Osman's Dream: The Story of the Ottoman Empire, 1300–1923.* London: John Murray, 2005.

Fıratlı, Nezih. *La sculpture byzantine figurée au Musée archéologique d'Istanbul.* Paris: Librairie d'Amérique et d'Orient d'Adrien Maisonneuve, 1990.

Fleet, Kate. *European and Islamic Trade in the Early Ottoman State: The Merchants of Genoa and Turkey.* Cambridge: Cambridge University Press, 1999.

Forchheimer, Philipp, and Josef Strzygowski. *Die byzantinischen Wasserbehälter von Konstantinopel.* Vienna: Verlag der Mechitharisten-Congregation, 1893.

Fowden, Garth. *Qusayr Amra: Art and the Umayyad Elite in Late Antique Syria.* Berkeley and Los Angeles: University of California Press, 2004.

Friedman, David. "'Fiorenza': Geography and Representation in a Fifteenth-Century View." *Zeitschrift für Kunstgeschichte* 64 (2001): 56–77.

———. *Florentine New Towns: Urban Design in the Late Middle Ages.* Cambridge, Mass.: MIT Press, 1988.

———. "Palaces and the Street in Late Medieval and Renaissance Italy." In *Urban Landscapes: International Perspectives,* edited by J. W. R. Whitehand and P. J. Larkham, 69–113. London: Routledge, 1992.

Friedrichs, Christopher R. *The Early Modern City, 1450–1750.* London: Longman Group, 1995.

Frugoni, Chiara. *A Distant City: Images of Urban Experience in the Medieval World.* Princeton, N.J.: Princeton University Press, 1991.

Gabriel, Albert. *Une capitale turque: Brousse, Bursa.* 2 vols. Paris: E. de Boccard, 1958.

———. *Châteaux turcs du Bosphore.* Paris: E. de Boccard, 1943.

———. "Les étapes d'une campagne dans les deux Iraq d'après un manuscrit turc du xvie siècle." *Syria* 9 (1928): 328–49.

Garand, Monique-Cécile. "La tradition manuscrite du *Liber Archipelagi insularum* à la Bibliothèque nationale de Paris." *Scriptorum* 29 (1975): 69–76.

Gautier, P. "Un récit inédit du siège de Constantinople par les Turcs (1394–1402)." *Revue des études byzantines* 23 (1965): 100–117.

Georgopoulou, Maria. *Venice's Mediterranean Colonies: Architecture and Urbanism.* Cambridge: Cambridge University Press, 2001.

Gerola, G. "Le vedute di Costantinopoli di Cristoforo Buondelmonti." *Studi bizantini e neoellenici* 3 (1931): 249–79.

Ginzburg, Carlo. *Myths, Emblems, Clues.* Translated by John Tedeschi and Anne C. Tedeschi. London: Hutchinson Radius, 1986.

Giordano, Louisa. "On Filarete's *Libro Architettonico.*" In *Paper Palaces,* edited by Vaughan Hart, with Peter Hicks, 51–65. New Haven: Yale University Press, 1998.

Glück, Heinz. *Die Baeder des Konstantinopolis.* Vienna, 1921.

Goitein, S. D. *A Mediterranean Society: The Jewish Communities of the Arab World as Portrayed in the Documents of the Cairo Geniza,* vol. 1, *Economic Foundations.* Berkeley and Los Angeles: University of California Press, 1967.

Gökbilgin, M. Tayyib. "Cafer Çelebi." In *İslâm ansiklopedisi,* 3:98–100.

———. "Venedik devlet arşivindeki vesikalar külliyatında Kanuni Süleyman devri belgeleri." *Belgeler* 1 (1964): 119–220.

Goodwin, Godfrey. *A History of Ottoman Architecture.* New York: Thames & Hudson, 1971.

Göyünç, Nejat. "Ottoman Period." In *Kalenderhane in Istanbul: The Buildings, Their History, Architecture, and Decoration,* edited by Cecil Striker and Doğan Kuban, 17–21. Mainz: Verlag Philipp von Zabern, 1997.

Grabar, Oleg. "The Architecture of the Middle Eastern City from Past to the Present: The Case of the Mosque." In *Middle Eastern Cities,* edited by Ira Lapidus, 26–46. Berkeley and Los Angeles: University of California Press, 1969.

———. *The Formation of Islamic Art.* New Haven: Yale University Press, 1987.

———. "The Meaning of History in Cairo." In *The Expanding Metropolis: Coping with the Urban Growth of Cairo,* 1–24. Singapore: Concept Media for the Aga Khan Award for Architecture, 1984.

———. *The Mediation of Ornament.* Princeton, N.J.: Princeton University Press, 1992.

———. *The Shape of the Holy: Early Islamic Jerusalem.* Princeton, N.J.: Princeton University Press, 1996.

———. "Umayyad Palaces Reconsidered." *Ars Orientalis* 23 (1993): 93–108.

Guberti Basset, Sarah. "John V Palaiologos and the Golden Gate in Constantinople." In *To Hellenikon: Studies in Honor of Speros Vryonis, Jr.,* edited by Jelisaveta S. Allen, Christos P. Ioannides, John S. Langdon, and Stephen W. Reinert, vol. 1, *Hellenic Antiquity and Byzantium,* 117–33. New Rochelle, N.Y.: A. D. Caratzas, 1993.

Guidoni, Enrico. "Sinan's Construction of the Urban Panorama." *Environmental Design* 1–2 (1987): 20–32.

Güleryüz, Naim. *İstanbul sinagogları.* Istanbul: Naim Güleryüz, 1992.

Gurlitt, Cornelius. *Die Baukunst Konstantinopels.* 2 vols. Berlin: E. Wasmuth, 1907.

Hacker, Joseph. "The *Sürgün* System and Jewish Society in the Ottoman Empire During the Fifteenth to the Seventeenth Centuries." In *Ottoman and Turkish Jewry: Community and Leadership,* edited by Aron Rodrigue, 1–66. Bloomington: Indiana University Press, 1992.

Hamadeh, Shirine. "Splash and Spectacle: The Obsession with Fountains in Eighteenth-Century Istanbul." *Muqarnas* 19 (2002): 123–48.

Hankins, James. "Renaissance Crusaders: Humanist Crusade Literature in the Age of Mehmed II." *Dumbarton Oaks Papers* 49 (1995): 111–207.

Harley, J. B. "The Map and the Development of the History of Cartography." In *The History of Cartography,* vol. 1, *Cartography in Prehistoric, Ancient, and Medieval Europe and the Mediterranean,* edited by J. B. Harley and David Woodward, 1–42. Chicago: University of Chicago Press, 1987.

———. "Maps, Knowledge, and Power." In *The Iconography of Landscape: Essays on the Symbolic Representation, Design, and Use of Past Environments,* edited by Denis Cosgrove and Stephen Daniels, 277–312. Cambridge: Cambridge University Press, 1988.

———. *The New Nature of Maps: Essays in the History of Cartography.* Edited by Paul Laxton. Baltimore: Johns Hopkins University Press, 2001.

Harley, J. B., and David Woodward, eds. *The History of Cartography.* Vol. 1, *Cartography in Prehistoric, Ancient, and Medieval Europe and the Mediterranean.* Chicago: University of Chicago Press, 1987.

Harvey, P. D. A. *The History of Topographical Maps: Symbols, Pictures, and Surveys.* London: Thames & Hudson, 1980.

———. "Local and Regional Cartography in Medieval Europe." In *The History of Cartography,* vol. 1, *Cartography in Prehistoric, Ancient, and Medieval Europe and the Mediterranean,* edited by J. B. Harley and David Woodward, 404–501. Chicago: University of Chicago Press, 1987.

Hasluck, Frederick W. *Christianity and Islam Under the Sultans.* 2 vols. Oxford: Clarendon Press, 1929.

Hayashi, Kayoko. "Fatih Vakfiyelerinin Tanzim Süreci Üzerine." In *Essays in Honour of Halil İnalcık,* forthcoming.

———. "The *Vakıf* Institution in 16th-Century Istanbul: An Analysis of the *Vakıf* Survey Register of 1546." *Memoirs of the Research Department of the Tago Bunko* 50 (1993): 93–113.

Hind, Arthur M. *Early Italian Engraving: A Critical Catalogue with Complete Reproduction of All the Prints Described.* 2 vols. London: Bernard Quaritch, 1938–48.

Hoexter, Miriam. "The *Waqf* and the Public Sphere." In *The Public Sphere in Muslim Societies,* edited by Miriam Hoexter, Shmuel N. Eisenstadt, and Nehemia Levtzion, 119–37. Albany: State University of New York Press, 2002.

———. "Waqf Studies in the Twentieth Century: The State of the Art." *Journal of the Economic and Social History of the Orient* 40 (1998): 1–22.

Humphreys, R. Stephen. "The Expressive Intent of the Mamluk Architecture in Cairo: A Preliminary Essay." *Studia Islamica* 35 (1972): 69–119.

———. *Islamic History: A Framework for Inquiry.* Rev. ed. Princeton, N.J.: Princeton University Press, 1991.

Imber, Colin. *The Ottoman Empire, 1300–1650: The Structure of Power.* New York: Palgrave Macmillan, 2002.

İnalcık, Halil. "Dervish and Sultan: An Analysis of the Otman Baba Vilayetnamesi." In *The Middle East and the Balkans Under the Ottoman Empire: Essays on Economy and Society,* 19–36. Bloomington: Indiana University Turkish Studies, 1993.

———. "Eyüp projesi." In *Eyüp: Dün-Bugün,* edited by Tülay Artan, 1–23. Istanbul: Tarih Vakfı Yurt Yayınları, 1994.

———. "Ghulam: Ottoman Empire." In *Encyclopedia of Islam,* 2nd ed., 2:1085–91.

———. "Greeks in the Ottoman Economy and Finances, 1453–1500." In *To Hellenikon: Studies in Honor of Speros Vryonis, Jr.,* edited by Jelisaveta S. Allen, Christos P. Ioannides, John S. Langdon, and Stephen W. Reinert, vol. 2, *Byzantinoslavica, Armeniaca, Islamica, the Balkans, and Modern Greece,* 307–19. New Rochelle, N.Y.: A. D. Caratzas, 1993.

———. "How to Read Ashik Pasha-zade's History." In *Studies in Ottoman History in Honour of Prof. V. L. Ménage,* edited by Colin Heywood and Colin Imber. Istanbul: Isis, 1994.

———. "The Hub of the City: The Bedestan of Istanbul." *International Journal of Turkish Studies* 1 (1980): 1–17.

———. "Istanbul." *Encyclopedia of Islam,* 2nd ed., 5:224–48.

———. "Istanbul: An Islamic City." *Journal of Islamic Studies* 1 (1990):1–23.

———. "Mehmed the Conqueror (1432–1481) and His Time." *Speculum* 35 (1960): 408–27.

———. "Mehmed II." In *İslâm ansiklopedisi,* 7:506–35.

———. *The Ottoman Empire: The Classical Age, 1300–1600.* New Rochelle, N.Y.: A. D. Caratzas, 1973.

———. "Ottoman Galata." In *Première Rencontre internationale sur l'Empire ottoman et la Turquie moderne: Institut*

national des langues et civilisations orientales, Maison de sciences de l'homme, 18–22 janvier 1985, edited by Edhem Eldem, 17–116. Istanbul: Isis, 1991.

———. "Ottoman Methods of Conquest." *Studia Islamica* 2 (1954): 103–29.

———. "The Policy of Mehmed II Toward the Greek Population of Constantinople and the Byzantine Buildings of the City." *Dumbarton Oaks Papers* 23–24 (1969–70): 229–49.

———. "The Rise of Ottoman Historiography." In *Historians of the Middle East,* edited by Bernard Lewis and P. M. Holt, 152–67. London: Oxford University Press, 1962.

———. *Sources and Studies on the Ottoman Black Sea.* Vol. 1, *The Customs Register of Caffa, 1487–1490.* Sources of Oriental Languages and Literatures, Turkish Sources 22. Cambridge, Mass.: Deptartment of Near Eastern Languages and Civilizations, Harvard University, 1995.

———. "Yeni bulunmuş bir 'Gazavât-ı Sultan Murad.'" *Ankara Üniversitesi Dil ve Tarih-Coğrafya Fakültesi dergisi* 7 (1949): 482–95.

İstanbul Topkapı Sarayı Müzesi ve Venedik Correr Müzesi koleksiyonlarından XIV–XVIII yüzyıl portolan ve deniz haritaları/Portolani e carte nautiche XIV–XVIII secolo dalle collezioni del Museo Correr–Venezia, Museo del Topkapı–Istanbul. Exhibition catalogue. Istanbul: Güzel Sanatlar Matbaası, 1994.

İstanbul'un Fethinin 550. Yılında Fetihçilik ve Uygarlık Bilinci/ Panel-Forum, edited by Yıldız Uysal. Istanbul: TMMOB Mimarlar Odası İstanbul Büyükkent Şubesi, 2003.

Janin, Raymond. "Constantinople byzantine: Découvertes et notes de topographie." *Revue des études byzantines* 21 (1963): 254–57.

———. *Constantinople byzantine: Développement urbain et répertoire topographique.* 2nd ed. Paris: Institut Français d'Études Byzantines, 1964.

———. *La géographie ecclésiastique de l'Empire byzantine, première partie: Le siège de Constantinople et le patriarcat oecuménique.* Paris: Institut Français d'Études Byzantines, 1953.

Jardine, Lisa. *Worldly Goods: A New History of the Renaissance.* New York: Nan A. Talese, 1996.

Jardine, Lisa, and Jerry Brotton. *Global Interests: Art Between East and West.* London: Reaktion Books, 2000.

Jennings, Ronald C. "The Population, Society, and Economy of the Region of Erciyes Dağı in the 16th Century." In *Contributions à l'histoire économique et sociale de l'Empire ottoman,* edited by Jean-Louis Bacqué-Grammont and Paul Dumont, 149–250. Collection Turcica 3. Leuven: Éditions Peeters, 1983.

———. "Urban Population in Anatolia in the Sixteenth Century: A Study of Kayseri, Karaman, Amasya, Trabzon, and Erzurum." *International Journal of Middle Eastern Studies* 7 (1976): 21–57.

Johansen, Baber. "The All-Embracing Town and Its Mosques: Al-Miṣr al-Cāmiʿ." *Revue de l'Occident musulman et de la Méditerranée* 32 (1981–82): 139–61.

Kafadar, Cemal. *Between Two Worlds: The Construction of the Ottoman State.* Berkeley and Los Angeles: University of California Press, 1995.

———. "A Death in Venice (1575): Anatolian Muslim Merchants in the Serenissima." *Journal of Turkish Studies* 10 (1986): 198–218.

———. "Eyüp'te kılıç kuşanma törenleri." In *Eyüp: Dün-Bugün,* edited by Tülay Artan, 50–61. Istanbul: Tarih Vakfı Yurt Yayınları, 1994.

———. "The Ottomans and Europe." In *Handbook of European History, 1400–1600: Late Middle Ages, Renaissance, and Reformation,* edited by Thomas A. Brady, Heiko A. Oberman, and James D. Tracy, 589–635. Leiden: E. J. Brill, 1994.

Kafescioğlu, Çiğdem. "Heavenly and Unblessed, Splendid and Artless: The Mosque Complex of Mehmed II in Istanbul in the Eyes of Its Contemporaries." In *Essays in Honor of Aptullah Kuran,* edited by Çiğdem Kafescioğlu and Lucienne Thys-Şenocak, 211–22. Istanbul: Yapı Kredi Yayınları, 1999.

———. "The Ottoman Capital in the Making: The Reconstruction of Constantinople in the Fifteenth Century." Ph.D. diss., Harvard University, 1996.

———. "Reckoning with an Imperial Legacy: The Ottomans and Byzantine Constantinople." In *1453: The Fall of Constantinople and the Transition from the Medieval to the Early Modern Period,* edited by Antónia Kiousopoulou, 23–46. Rethymnon: University of Crete Press, 2005.

Kara, Mustafa. *Bursa'da tarikatlar ve tekkeler.* Bursa: Uludağ Yayınları, 1990.

———. *Tasavvuf ve tarikatlar tarihi.* Istanbul: Dergah Yayınları, 1985.

Karamustafa, Ahmet T. "Introduction to Ottoman Cartography." In *History of Cartography,* vol. 2, bk. 1, *Cartography in the Traditional Islamic and South Asian Societies,* edited by J. B. Harley and David Woodward, 206–8. Chicago: University of Chicago Press, 1992.

———. "Military, Administrative, and Scholarly Maps and Plans." In *History of Cartography,* vol. 2, bk. 1, *Cartography in the Traditional Islamic and South Asian Societies,* edited by J. B. Harley and David Woodward, 209–27. Chicago: University of Chicago Press, 1992.

Kazhdan, Alexander. "The Italian and the Late Byzantine City." *Dumbarton Oaks Papers* 49 (1995): 1–22.

Kidonopoulos, Vassilios. *Bauten in Konstantinople 1204–1328.* Wiesbaden: Harrassowitz Verlag, 1994.

Kiel, Machiel. "The Ottoman Hamam and the Balkans." *Art and Archeology Research Papers* 9 (1976): 87–96.

Kissling, Hans Joachim. "Aus der Geschichte des Chalvetijje-Ordens." *Zeitschrift der Deutschen Morgenländischen Gesellschaft* 53 (1953): 233–89.

———. "Einiges über den Zejnije-Orden im Osmanischen Reiche." *Der Islam* 39 (1964): 143–79.

Konyalı, İbrahim Hakkı. *Abideleri ve kitabeleriyle Üsküdar tarihi.* 2 vols. Istanbul: Ahmet Sait Matbaası, 1976.

———. *Fatihin mimarlarından Azadlı Sinan (Sinan-ı Atik) vakfiyeleri, eserleri, hayatı, mezarı.* Istanbul: İstanbul Fetih Derneği Neşriyatı, 1953.

Kostof, Spiro. *The City Assembled: The Elements of Urban Form Through History.* London: Thames & Hudson, 1992.

———. *The City Shaped: Urban Patterns and Meanings Through History.* London: Thames & Hudson, 1991.

———. *A History of Architecture: Settings and Rituals.* New York: Oxford University Press, 1985.

Kreiser, Klaus. "Bedesten-Bauten im Osmanischen Reich." *Istanbuler Mitteilungen* 29 (1979): 369–400.

Kuban, Doğan. *Istanbul, an Urban History: Byzantion, Constantinopolis, Istanbul.* Istanbul: Economic and Social History Foundation of Turkey, 1996.

———. *Osmanlı mimarisi.* Istanbul: Yapı-Endüstri Merkezi, 2007.

———. "The Style of Sinan's Domed Structures." *Muqarnas* 4 (1987): 72–97.

———. *Türk ve İslam sanatı üzerine denemeler.* Istanbul: Arkeoloji ve Sanat Yayınları, 1982.

Kunter, H. Baki, and Ali Saim Ülgen. *Fatih Camii ve Bizans Sarnıcı.* Istanbul: Cumhuriyet Matbaası, 1939.

Kuran, Aptullah. "Eyüp Külliyesi." In *Eyüp: Dün-Bugün,* edited by Tülay Artan, 129–35. Istanbul: Tarih Vakfı Yurt Yayınları, 1994.

———. *The Mosque in Early Ottoman Architecture.* Chicago: University of Chicago Press, 1968.

———. "A Spatial Study of Three Ottoman Capitals: Bursa, Edirne, and Istanbul." *Muqarnas* 13 (1996): 114–31.

Kut, Günay, and Turgut Kut. "Ayvansarayî Hafız Hüseyin b. İsmail ve eserleri." *I.Ü.E.F. Tarih dergisi* 33 (1980–81): 401–39.

Landau, David, and Peter Parshall. *The Renaissance Print.* New Haven: Yale University Press, 1994.

Lang, Susanne. "Sforzinda, Filarete, and Filelfo." *Journal of the Warburg and Courtauld Institutes* 35 (1971): 391–97.

Lapidus, Ira. *Muslim Cities in the Later Middle Ages.* New York: Cambridge University Press, 1984.

Lavedan, Pierre. *Représentations des villes dans l'art de Moyen Âge.* Paris: Vanoest, 1954.

Lazzaroni, Michele, and Antonio Muñoz. *Filarete: Scultore e architetto del secolo XV.* Rome: W. Modes, 1908.

Lefebvre, Henri. *The Production of Space.* Translated by Donald Nicholson-Smith. Oxford: Blackwell, 1991.

Levend, Agah Sırrı. *Türk edebiyatında şehrengizler ve şehrengizlerde İstanbul.* Istanbul: Baha Matbaası, 1957.

Loga, Valerian von. "Die Städteansichten in Hartmann Schedels Weltchronik." *Jahrbuch der königlich preußischen Kunstsammlungen* 9 (1888): 93–107, 184–96.

Lombardi, Giuseppe. "La città, libro di pietra: Immagini umanistiche di Roma prima e dopo Costanza." In *Alle origini della nuova Roma, Martino V (1417–1431),* edited by Maria Chiabò et al., 17–46. Rome: Nella sede dell'Istituto Palazzo Borromini, 1992.

Lowry, Heath W. "From Lesser Wars to the Mightiest War: The Ottoman Conquest and Transformation of Byzantine Urban Centers in the Fifteenth Century." In *Continuity and Change in Late Byzantine and Early Ottoman Society,* edited by Anthony Bryer and Heath W. Lowry, 261–74. Birmingham: University of

Birmingham; Washington, D.C.: Dumbarton Oaks Research Library and Collection, 1986.

———. "The Ottoman Tahrir Defters as a Source for Urban Demographic History: The Case Study of Trabzon (ca. 1486–1583)." Ph.D. diss., University of California, Los Angeles, 1977.

———. "Portrait of a City: The Population and Topography of Ottoman Selanik in the Year 1478." *Diptika* 6 (1980–81): 254–92.

Luzio, Alessandro. "Disegni topografici e pitture dei Bellini." *Archivio storico dell'arte* 1 (1888): 276–78.

Macdonald, William L. *The Architecture of the Roman Empire.* 2 vols. New Haven: Yale University Press, 1982, 1986.

MacLean, Gerald, ed. *Re-orienting the Renaissance: Cultural Exchanges with the East.* New York: Palgrave Macmillan, 2005.

Magdalino, Paul. "Aristocratic *Oikoi* in the Tenth and Eleventh Regions of Constantinople." In *Byzantine Constantinople: Monuments, Topography, and Everyday Life,* edited by Nevra Necipoğlu, 53–69. Leiden: E. J. Brill, 2001.

———. *Constantinople médiévale: Études sur l'évolution des structures urbaines.* Paris: De Boccard, 1996.

———. *The Empire of Manuel I Komnenos, 1143–1180.* Cambridge: Cambridge University Press, 1993.

———. "The Grain Supply of Constantinople, Ninth–Twelfth Centuries." In *Constantinople and Its Hinterland,* edited by Cyril Mango and Gilbert Dagron, 35–49. Aldershot, Hampshire: Variorum, 1995.

———. "The Maritime Neighborhoods of Constantinople: Commercial and Residential Functions, Sixth to Twelfth Centuries." *Dumbarton Oaks Papers* 54 (2000): 209–26.

———. "Medieval Constantinople: Built Environment and Urban Development." In *The Economic History of Byzantium: From the Seventh Through the Fifteenth Century,* edited by Angeliki E. Laiou, 2:529–37. Washington, D.C.: Dumbarton Oaks Research Library and Collection, 2002.

Maltezou Chrysa A. "Il quartiere veneziano di Costantinopoli (scali marittimi)." *Actes du xve Congrès international d'études byzantines* 4 (1980): 208–39.

Mango, Cyril. *The Art of the Byzantine Empire, 312–1453.* Englewood Cliffs, N.J.: Prentice-Hall, 1972.

———. *The Brazen House: A Study of the Vestibule of the Imperial Palace of Constantinople.* Copenhagen: Ejnar Munskgaard, 1959.

———. "The Columns of Justinian and His Successors." In *Studies on Constantinople,* chap. x, 1–20. Aldershot, Hampshire: Variorum, 1993.

———. "The Development of Constantinople as an Urban Center." In *Studies on Constantinople,* I/117–35. Aldershot, Hampshire: Variorum, 1993.

———. *Le développement urbain de Constantinople (IVe–VII siècles).* Paris: De Boccard, 1985.

———. *Materials for the Study of the Mosaics of St. Sophia at Istanbul.* Washington, D.C.: Dumbarton Oaks Research Library and Collection, 1962.

———. "Three Imperial Byzantine Sarcophagi Discovered in 1750." *Dumbarton Oaks Papers* 16 (1962): 397–402.

———. "The Triumphal Way of Constantinople and the Golden Gate." *Dumbarton Oaks Papers* 54 (2000): 174–88.

———. "The Water Supply of Constantinople." In *Constantinople and Its Hinterland,* edited by Cyril Mango and Gilbert Dagron, 9–18. Aldershot, Hampshire: Variorum, 1995.

Manners, Ian. "Constructing the Image of a City: The Representation of Constantinople in Christopher Buondelmonti's *Liber Insularum Archipelagi.*" *Annals of the American Association of Geography* 87 (1997): 72–102.

Mantran, Robert. *Istanbul dans la seconde moitié du XVIIe siècle.* Paris: A. Maisonneuve, 1962.

Marchitello, Howard. "Political Maps: The Production of Cartography and Chorography in Early Modern England." In *Cultural Artifacts and the Production of Meaning,* edited by Margaret J. M. Ezell and Katherine O'Brien O'Keefe, 13–40. Ann Arbor: University of Michigan Press, 1994.

Marcus, Abraham. *The Middle East on the Eve of Modernity: Aleppo in the Eighteenth Century.* New York: Columbia University Press, 1989.

Mardin, Şerif. *The Genesis of Young Ottoman Thought: A Study in the Modernization of Turkish Political Ideas.* Princeton, N.J.: Princeton University Press, 1962.

Margoliouth, D. S. "Zayn al-Din." In *İslam ansiklopedisi,* 13:556.

Marin, Louis. *Utopics: Spatial Play.* Translated by Robert A. Vollrath. Atlantic Highlands, N.J.: Humanities Press, 1984.

Mark, Robert, and Ahmet Çakmak, eds. *Hagia Sophia from the Age of Justinian to the Present.* Cambridge: Cambridge University Press, 1992.

Massignon, Louis. "Textes prémonitoires et commentaires mystiques relatifs à la prise de Constantinople par les Turcs." *Oriens* 6 (1953): 11–17.

Meisami, Julie Scott. "Allegorical Gardens in the Persian Poetic Tradition: Nezami, Rumi, Hafez." *International Journal of Middle East Studies* 17 (1985): 229–60.

———. "Palaces and Paradises: Palace Description in Medieval Persian Poetry." In *Islamic Art and Literature,* edited by Oleg Grabar and Cynthia Robinson, 21–54. Princeton, N.J.: Marcus Wiener Publishers, 2001.

Melikoff, Irène. "Le problème Kızılbaş." *Turcica* 6 (1975): 49–67.

Ménage, Victor Louis. "The Beginnings of Ottoman Historiography." In *Historians of the Middle East,* edited by Bernard Lewis and P. M. Holt, 168–79. London: Oxford University Press, 1962.

———. "Edirne'li Ruhi'ye Atfedilen Osmanlı Tarihinden İki Parça." In *Ord. Prof. İsmail Hakkı Uzunçarşılı'ya armağan,* 311–33. Ankara: Türk Tarih Kurumu, 1976.

Meriç, Rıfkı Melul. *Beyazıd câmii mimarı; 2. Sultan Bâyezid devri mimarları ile bazı binaları; Beyazıd câmii ile alâkalı hususlar, sanatkârlar ve eserleri.* Ankara: Ajans-Türk Matbaası, 1958.

Meyer-Plath, Bruno, and Alfons Maria Schneider. *Aufnahme, Beschreibung und Geschichte*. Pt. 2 of *Die Landmauer von Konstantinopel*. Berlin: Walter de Gruyter, 1943.

Michell, George, ed. *Architecture of the Islamic World: Its History and Social Meaning*. New York: Morrow, 1978.

Mitchell, Edward. "Âşık Paşa Çeşmesinin gizli tarihi." *Tarih ve toplum* 90 (1991): 366–71.

———. "Institution and Destitution: Patronage Tales of Old Stamboul." Ph.D. diss., University of California, Los Angeles, 1993.

Mordtmann, August J. *Esquisse topographique de Constantinople*. Lille: Desclée, 1892.

Müller-Wiener, Wolfgang. *Bildlexikon zur Topographie Istanbuls: Byzantion, Konstantinupolis, Istanbul bis zum Beginn des 17. Jahrhundert*. Tübingen: Wasmuth, 1977.

———. *Die Hafen von Byzantion, Konstantinupolis, Istanbul*. Tübingen: Wasmuth, 1994.

Mundell-Mango, Marlia. "The Commercial Map of Constantinople." *Dumbarton Oaks Papers* 54 (2000): 189–207.

Namık Kemal. *Evrāḳ-ı perīşān*. Istanbul, 1301 [1883–84].

———. ʿ*Oṣmānlı Tārīḫi*. Istanbul: Mahmud Bey Matbaası, 1326 [1910–11].

Necipoğlu, Gülru. *The Age of Sinan: Architectural Culture in the Ottoman Empire*. London: Reaktion Books, 2005.

———. "Anatolia and the Ottoman Legacy." In *The Mosque: History, Architectural Development, and Regional Diversity*, edited by Martin Frishman and Hasan-Uddin Khan, 141–57. New York: Thames & Hudson, 1994.

———. *Architecture, Ceremonial, and Power: The Topkapı Palace in the Fifteenth and Sixteenth Centuries*. Cambridge, Mass.: MIT Press, 1991.

———. "Dynastic Imprints on the Cityscape: The Collective Message of Imperial Funerary Complexes in Istanbul." In *Cimetières et traditions funéraires dans la monde islamique*. Ankara: Türk Tarih Kurumu, 1996.

———. "Framing the Gaze in Ottoman, Safavid, and Mughal Palaces." *Ars Orientalis* 23 (1993): 303–42.

———. "A Kânûn for the State, a Canon for the Arts." In *Soliman le magnifique et son temps*, edited by Gilles Veinstein, 195–216. Paris: La Documentation Française, 1992.

———. "The Life of an Imperial Monument: Hagia Sophia After Byzantium." In *Hagia Sophia from the Age of Justinian to the Present*, edited by Robert Mark and Ahmet S. Çakmak, 195–225. Cambridge: Cambridge University Press, 1992.

———. "An Outline of Shifting Paradigms in the Palatial Architecture of the Pre-Modern Islamic World." *Ars Orientalis* 23 (1993): 3–24.

———. "Plans and Models in 15th- and 16th-Century Ottoman Architectural Practice." *Journal of the Society of Architectural Historians* 45 (1985): 224–43.

———. "Suburban Landscape of Sixteenth-Century Istanbul as a Mirror of Classical Ottoman Garden Culture." In *Gardens in the Time of the Great Muslim Empires: Theory and Design*, edited by Attilio Petruccioli, 32–71. Leiden: E. J. Brill, 1997.

———. "The Süleymaniye Complex in Istanbul." *Muqarnas* 3 (1985): 92–117.

Necipoğlu, Nevra. *Byzantium Between the Ottomans and the Latins: Politics and Society in the Late Empire*. Cambridge: Cambridge University Press, 2009.

———, ed. *Byzantine Constantinople: Monuments, Topography, and Everyday Life*. Leiden: E. J. Brill, 2001.

———. "Economic Conditions in Constantinople During the Siege of Bayezid I (1394–1402)." In *Constantinople and Its Hinterland*, edited by Cyril Mango and Gilbert Dagron, 157–67. Aldershot, Hampshire: Variorum, 1995.

———. "Social and Economic Conditions in Constantinople During Mehmed II's Siege." In *1453: The Fall of Constantinople and the Transition from the Medieval to the Early Modern Period*, edited by Antōnia Kiousopoulou, 75–86. Rethymnon: University of Crete Press, 2005.

Nicol, Donald M. *The Byzantine Family of Kantakouzenos (Cantacuzenus), ca. 1100–1460*. Washington, D.C.: Dumbarton Oaks Center for Byzantine Studies, 1968.

———. *The Immortal Emperor: The Life and Legend of Constantine Palaiologos, the Last Emperor of the Romans*. Cambridge: Cambridge University Press, 1992.

Nirven, Saadi Nazım. *İstanbul'da Fatih II. Sultan Mehmed devri Türk su medeniyeti*. Istanbul, 1953.

———. *İstanbul suları*. Istanbul: Halk Basımevi, 1946.

Niutta, Francesca. "Prospettiva orientali: Momenti dell'incontro con la cultura greca." In *Alle origini della nuova Roma, Martino V (1417–1431)*, edited by Maria Chiabò et al., 205–24. Rome: Nella sede dell'Istituto Palazzo Borromini, 1992.

Nora, Pierre. "Between Memory and History: *Les lieux de mémoire*." *Representations* 26 (1989): 7–25.

———, ed. *Realms of Memory: The Construction of the French Past*. Translated by Arthur Goldhammer. 3 vols. New York: Columbia University Press, 1998.

Nuti, Lucia. "Mapping Places: Chorography and Vision in the Renaissance." In *Mappings*, edited by Denis Cosgrove, 90–108. London: Reaktion Books, 1999.

———. "The Perspective Plan in the Sixteenth Century: The Invention of a Representational Language." *Art Bulletin* 76 (1994): 105–28.

Oberhummer, Eugen. *Konstantinopel unter Sultan Suleiman dem Grossen*. Munich: R. Oldenbourg, 1902.

Ocak, Ahmet Yaşar. "Bazı menâkıbnâmelere göre XIII.–XV. yüzyıllardaki ihtidâlarda heterodoks şeyh ve dervişlerin rolü." *Journal of Ottoman Studies* 2 (1981): 31–42.

———. *Osmanlı İmparatorluğu'nda marjinal Sûfîlik: Kalenderiler*. Ankara: Türk Tarih Kurumu, 1992.

———. "Zaviyeler." *Vakıflar dergisi* 12 (1978): 247–69.

O'Kane, Bernard. "From Tents to Pavilions: Royal Mobility and Persian Palace Design." *Ars Orientalis* 23 (1993): 249–68.

Olin, Margaret. "Gaze." In *Critical Terms for Art History*, edited by Robert S. Nelson and Richard Shiff, 2nd ed., 318–29. Chicago: University of Chicago Press, 2003.

Öndeş, Osman, and Erol Makzume. *Fausto Zonaro: Ottoman Court Painter*. Istanbul: Yapı Kredi, 2002.

Onians, John. "Alberti and Filarete: A Study in Their Sources." *Journal of the Warburg and Courtauld Institutes* 34 (1971): 96–114.

———. *Bearers of Meaning: The Classical Orders in Antiquity, the Middle Ages, and the Renaissance.* Princeton, N.J.: Princeton University Press, 1988.

Orbay, Iffet. "Istanbul Viewed: The Representation of the City in Ottoman Maps of the Sixteenth and Seventeenth Centuries." Ph.D. diss., Massachusetts Institute of Technology, 2001.

Orhonlu, Cengiz. "Mesleki bir teşekkül olarak kaldırımcılık ve Osmanlı şehir yolları hakkında bazı düşünceler." *Güney-doğu Avrupa araştırmaları dergisi* 1 (1972): 93–138.

Ousterhout, Robert. *The Architecture of the Kariye Camii in Istanbul.* Washington, D.C.: Dumbarton Oaks Research Library and Collection, 1987.

———. "Constantinople, Bithynia, and Regional Developments in Later Palaeologan Architecture." In *The Twilight of Byzantium: Aspects of Religious and Cultural History in the Late Byzantine Empire,* edited by Slobodan Ćurčić and Doula Mouriki, 75–110. Princeton, N.J.: Department of Art and Archaeology, Program in Hellenic Studies, Princeton University, 1991.

———. "The East, the West, and the Appropriation of the Past in Early Ottoman Architecture." *Gesta* 43, no. 2 (2004): 167–78.

———. "Ethnic Identity and Cultural Appropriation in Early Ottoman Architecture." *Muqarnas* 12 (1995): 48–62.

———. *Master Builders of Byzantium.* Princeton, N.J.: Princeton University Press, 1999.

———. "Secular Architecture." In *The Glory of Byzantium: Art and Culture of the Middle Byzantine Era, A.D. 843–1261,* edited by Helen C. Evans and William D. Wixom, 193–99. New York: Metropolitan Museum of Art, 1997.

Özcan, Abdülkadir. "Fâtih'in Teşkilât Kanunnamesi ve Nizam-ı âlem için Kardeş Katli Meselesi." *Tarih dergisi* 33 (1980–81): 7–56.

Özdeş, Gündüz. *Türk çarşıları.* Istanbul: Pulhan Matbaası, 1953.

Özkoçak, Selma Akyazıcı. "Two Urban Districts in Early Modern Istanbul: Edirnekapı and Yedikule." *Urban History* 30, no. 1 (2003): 26–43.

———. "The Urban Development of Istanbul in the Sixteenth Century." Ph.D. diss., University of London, 1997.

Pamukciyan, Kevork. "Engürülü Rahip Apraham'ın Fetihnamesi." In *Ermeni kaynaklarından tarihe katkılar,* vol. 1, *İstanbul yazıları,* 50–60. Istanbul: Aras, 2002.

———. "Kumkapı Patrikhane Kilisesi Ne Zamandan Beri Ermenilerin Elindedir?" In *Ermeni kaynaklarından tarihe katkılar,* vol. 1, *İstanbul yazıları,* 148–53. Istanbul: Aras, 2002.

———. "Sulumanastır Surp Kevork Kilisesi Ne Zamandan Beri Ermenilerin Elindedir?" In *Ermeni kaynaklarından tarihe katkılar,* vol. 1, *İstanbul yazıları,* 143–47. Istanbul: Aras, 2002.

Panofsky, Erwin. *Renaissance and Renascences in Western Art.* Stockholm: Almqvist & Wiksell, 1960.

Paspatēs, A. G. *Vyzantinai meletai topographikai kai historikai.* Constantinople: A. Koromēla, 1877.

Peters, Rudolf. *Jihad in Classical and Modern Islam.* Princeton: Markus Wiener, 1996.

Pierotti, Piero. *Prima de Machiavelli: Filarete e Francesco di Giorgio consiglieri del principe.* Pisa: Pacini Editore, 1995.

Pinto, John. "Origins and Development of the Ichnographic City Plan." *Journal of the Society of Architectural Historians* 35 (1976): 35–50.

Pinto, Karen. "Ways of Seeing.3: Scenarios of the World in the Medieval Islamic Cartographic Imagination." Ph. D. Diss. Columbia University, 2002.

Pitcher, Donald Edgar. *An Historical Geography of the Ottoman Empire: From Earliest Times to the End of the Sixteenth Century.* Leiden: Brill, 1972.

Pollak, Martha. *Turin, 1564–1680: Urban Design, Military Culture, and the Creation of the Absolutist Capital.* Chicago: University of Chicigo Press, 1991.

Preziosi, Donald. *Rethinking Art History: Meditations on a Coy Science.* New Haven: Yale University Press, 1989.

Rabbat, Nasser. *The Citadel of Cairo: A New Interpretation of Royal Mamluk Architecture.* Leiden: E. J. Brill, 1995.

Raby, Julian. "Cyriacus of Ancona and the Ottoman Sultan Mehmed II." *Journal of the Warburg and Courtauld Institutes* 43 (1980): 242–46.

———. "El Gran Turco: Mehmed the Conqueror as a Patron of the Arts of Christendom." Ph.D. diss., Oxford University, 1980.

———. "Mehmed the Conqueror and the Byzantine Rider of the Augustaion." *Topkapı Sarayı Müzesi yıllık* 2 (1987): 141–53.

———. "Mehmed II Fatih and the Fatih Album." *Islamic Art* 1 (1981): 42–49.

———. "Pride and Prejudice: Mehmed the Conqueror and the Italian Portrait Medal." In *Studies in the History of Art,* vol. 21, *Italian Medals,* edited by J. Graham Pollard, 171–94. Washington, D.C.: National Gallery of Art, 1987.

———. "A Sultan of Paradox: Mehmed the Conqueror as a Patron of the Arts." *Oxford Art Journal* 5, no. 1 (1982): 3–8.

Raby, Julian, and Zeren Tanındı. *Turkish Bookbinding in the Fifteenth Century: The Foundation of an Ottoman Court Style.* London: Azimuth Editions, 1993.

Raymond, André. *Grandes villes arabes à l'époque ottomane.* Paris: Editions Sindbad, 1985.

———. "Islamic City, Arab City: Orientalist Myths and Recent Views." *British Journal of Middle East Studies* 21 (1994): 1–18.

———. "La localisation des bains publics au Caire au quinzième siècle d'après les *Hitat* de Maqrizi." *Bulletin d'études orientales* 30 (1978): 347–60.

———. "The Residential Districts of Cairo's Elite in the Mamluk and Ottoman Periods (Fourteenth to Eighteenth Centuries)." In *The Mamluks in Egyptian Politics and Society,* edited by Thomas Philipp and Ulrich Haarmann, 207–23. Cambridge: Cambridge University Press, 1998.

Redford, Scott. "The Seljuks of Rum and the Antique." *Muqarnas* 10 (1993): 148–56.

Reindl, Hedda. *Männer um Bayezid: Eine prosopographische Studie über die Epoche Sultan Bayezids II (1481–1512)*. Berlin: Klaus Schwarz Verlag, 1983.

Reinert, Stephen. "The Paleologoi, Yıldırım Bāyezīd, and Constantinople: June 1389–March 1391." In *To Hellenikon: Studies in Honor of Speros Vryonis, Jr.*, edited by Jelisaveta S. Allen, Christos P. Ioannides, John S. Langdon, Stephen W. Reinert, vol. 1, *Hellenic Antiquity and Byzantium*, 289–365. New Rochelle, N.Y.: A. D. Caratzas, 1993.

Repp, Richard Cooper. *The Mufti of Istanbul: A Study in the Development of the Ottoman Learned Hierarchy*. London: Ithaca Press, 1986.

Restle, Marcell. "Bauplanung und Baugesinnung unter Mehmed II Fatih." *Pantheon* 39 (1981): 361–67.

Rifat Osman. *Edirne Sarayı*. Edited by Süheyl Ünver. Ankara: Türk Tarih Kurumu, 1957.

Rogers, J. M. "Innovation and Continuity in Islamic Urbanism." In *The Arab City, Its Character and Islamic Cultural Heritage*, edited by Ismail Serageldin and Samir el-Sadik, 53–61. Medina: Arab Urban Development Institute, 1982.

———. "Itineraries and Town Views in Ottoman Histories." In *History of Cartography*, vol. 2, bk. 1, *Cartography in the Traditional Islamic and South Asian Societies*, edited by J. B. Harley and David Woodward, 228–55. Chicago: University of Chicago Press, 1992.

Rozen, Minna. *A History of the Jewish Community in Istanbul: The Formative Years, 1453–1566*. Leiden: Brill, 2002.

Runciman, Steven. *The Fall of Constantinople, 1453*. Cambridge: Cambridge University Press, 1965.

Said, Edward. *Beginnings: Intention and Method*. New York: Columbia University Press, 1975.

Sanjian, Avedis K. *Colophons of Armenian Manuscripts, 1301–1480*. Cambridge, Mass.: Harvard Univesity Press, 1969.

———. "Two Contemporary Armenian Elegies on the Fall of Constantinople." *Viator* 1 (1970): 223–61.

Santucci, Monique. "Jérusalem, Rome, Constantinople dans l'œuvre de Molinet." In *Jérusalem, Rome, Constantinople: L'image et le mythe de la ville au Moyen Âge*, edited by Daniel Poirion, 137–48. Paris: Presses de l'Université de Paris, 1986.

Scaglia, Gustina. "The Origin of an Archaeological Plan of Rome by Alessandro Strozzi." *Journal of the Warburg and Courtauld Institutes* 27 (1964): 137–63.

Scharabi, Mohamed. *Der Bazar: Das traditionelle Stadtzentrum im Nahen Osten und seine Handelseinrichtungen*. Tübingen: E. Wasmuth, 1985.

Schneider, Alfons Maria. *Die Bevölkerung Konstantinopels im XV. Jahrhundert*. Nachrichten der Akademie der Wissenschaften in Göttingen, philologisch-historische Klasse 9. Göttingen: Vandenheock & Ruprecht, 1949.

———. *Byzanz: Vorarbeiten zur Topographie und Archäologie der Stadt*. Istanbuler Forschungen 8. Berlin, 1936.

———. "Regionen und Quartiere in Konstantinopel." In *Kleinasien und Byzanz: Gesammelte Aufsätze zur Altertumskunde und Kunstgeschichte*, Istanbuler Forschungen 17:149–58. Berlin: Walter de Gruyter, 1950.

Schulz, Juergen. "Jacopo de' Barbari's View of Venice: Map Making, City Views, and Moralized Geography Before the Year 1500." *Art Bulletin* 60 (1978): 425–74.

———. "Maps as Metaphors: Mural Map Cycles of the Italian Renaissance." In *Art and Cartography*, edited by David Woodward, 97–122. Chicago: University of Chicago Press, 1987

———. "The Printed Plans and Panoramic Views of Venice (1486–1797)." *Saggi e memorie di storia dell'arte* 7 (1970): 11–182.

Sennet, Richard. *Flesh and Stone: The Body and the City in Western Civilization*. New York: W. W. Norton, 1994.

Setton, Kenneth M. *The Papacy and the Levant (1204–1571)*. Vol. 2, *The Fifteenth Century*. Philadelphia: American Philosophical Society, 1978.

Sims, Eleanor. "Trade and Travel: Markets and Caravanserais." In *Architecture of the Islamic World: Its History and Social Meaning*, edited by George Michell, 80–111. New York: Morrow, 1978.

Smith, Christine. *Architecture in the Culture of Early Humanism: Ethics, Aesthetics, and Eloquence, 1400–1470*. New York: Oxford University Press, 1992.

Soucek, Svat. "Islamic Charting in the Mediterranean." In *History of Cartography*, vol. 2, bk. 1, *Cartography in the Traditional Islamic and South Asian Societies*, edited by J. B. Harley and David Woodward, 263–92. Chicago: University of Chicago Press, 1992.

Stavrides, Theoharis. *The Sultan of Vezirs: The Life and Times of the Ottoman Grand Vizier Mahmud Pasha Angelovic (1453–1474)*. Leiden: E. J. Brill, 2001.

Stewart-Robinson, James. "A Neglected Ottoman Poem: The Şehrengiz." In *Studies in Near Eastern Culture and History: In Memory of Ernest T. Abdel-Massih*, edited by James A. Bellamy, 201–11. Ann Arbor: University of Michigan, Center for Near Eastern and North African Studies, 1990.

Striker, Cecil. *The Myraleion (Bodrum Camii) in Istanbul*. Princeton, N.J.: Princeton University Press, 1981.

Striker, Cecil, and Doğan Kuban, eds. *Kalenderhane in Istanbul: The Buildings, Their History, Architecture, and Decoration*. Mainz: Verlag Philipp von Zabern, 1997.

Taeschner, Franz. "Ein altosmanischer Bericht über das vorosmanische Konstantinopel." *Annali dell'Istituto Universitario di Napoli*, n.s., 1 (1940): 181–89.

Tafuri, Manfredo. "'Cives esse non licere'—The Rome of Nicholas V and Leon Battista Alberti: Elements Toward a Historical Revision." *Harvard Architecture Review* 6 (1987): 60–75.

———. "La 'nuova Costantinopoli': La rappresentazione della 'renovatio' nella Venezia dell'Umanesimo (1450–1509)." *Rassegna* 9 (1982): 25–38.

Talbot, Alice-Mary. "The Restoration of Constantinople Under Michael VIII." *Dumbarton Oaks Papers* 47 (1993): 243–61.

Tamer, Vehbi. "Fatih Devri Ricalinden İshak Paşa'nın vakfiyeleri ve vakıfları." *Vakıflar dergisi* 4 (1958): 107–24.

Tanman, M. Baha. "Eyüb Sultan Külliyesi." In *Dünden bugüne İstanbul ansiklopedisi,* 3:237–43.

———. "Küçük Ayasofya Tekkesi." In *Dünden bugüne İstanbul ansiklopedisi,* 5:149–50.

———. "Settings for the Veneration of Saints." In *The Dervish Lodge: Architecture, Art, and Sufism in Ottoman Turkey,* edited by Raymond Lifchez, 130–71. Berkeley and Los Angeles: University of California Press, 1992.

———. "Şeyh Vefa Külliyesi." In *Dünden bugüne İstanbul ansiklopedisi,* 7:173–76.

———. "Sünbül Efendi Tekkesi." In *Dünden bugüne İstanbul ansiklopedisi,* 7:105–7.

———. "Tariqah Buildings/Tekkes in Ottoman Architecture." In *Ottoman Civilization,* edited by Halil İnalcık and Günsel Renda, 288–307. Ankara: Ministry of Culture, 2002.

———. "La tekke bektachi de Kazlıçeşme, II: Emplacement, plan de situation, architecture et décoration." *Anatolia Moderna* 7 (1997): 111–24.

Tauer, Felix. "Notice sur les versions persanes de la légende de l'édification d'Aya Sofya." In *Fuad Köprülü armağanı: Mélanges Fuad Köprülü.* Istanbul: Ankara Üniversitesi Dil Tarih Coğrafya Fakültesi Yayini; Osman Talem Matbaası, 1953.

Tekin, Gönül. "Fatih devri Türk edebiyatı." In *İstanbul armağanı,* vol 1, *Fetih ve fatih,* edited by Mustafa Armağan, 161–236. Istanbul: İstanbul Büyükşehir Belediyesi Kültür İşleri Daire Başkanlığı, 1995.

Tekindağ, Şehabeddin. "Mehmed Paşa (Rum)." In *İslâm ansiklopedisi,* 7:594–95.

Terzioğlu, Derin. "Sufi and Dissident in the Ottoman Empire: Niyāzī-i Mıṣrī (1618–1694). Ph.D. diss., Harvard University, 1999.

Texier, Charles. *Asie mineure: Description géographique, historique et archéologique des provinces et des villes de la Chersonnèse d'Asie.* Paris: F. Didot, 1862.

Texier, Charles, and Richard Popplewell Pullan. *L'architecture byzantine.* London: Day et fils, 1864.

Tezcan, Hülya. *Topkapı Sarayı ve çevresinin Bizans devri arkeolojisi.* Istanbul: Arkeoloji ve Sanat Yayınları, 1989.

Thys-Şenocak, Lucienne. *Ottoman Women Builders: The Architectural Patronage of Hadice Turhan Sultan.* Burlington, Vt.: Ashgate, 2006.

Toprak, Zafer, and Uğur Tanyeli. "Babıali." In *Dünden bugüne İstanbul ansiklopedisi,* 1:519–23.

Trachtenberg, Marvin. *The Dominion of the Eye: Urbanism, Art, and Power in Early Modern Florence.* Cambridge: Cambridge University Press, 1997.

Turner, Hilary Louise. "Christopher Buondelmonti: Adventurer, Explorer, and Cartographer." In *Géographie du monde au Moyen Âge et à la Renaissance,* edited by Monique Pelletier, 207–16. Paris: Éditions du C.T.H.S., 1989.

———. "Christopher Buondelmonti and the Isolario." *Terrae Incognitae* 19 (1987): 11–28.

Tyan, E. "Djihad." *Encyclopedia of Islam,* 2nd ed., 2:538–40.

Ülgen, Ali Saim. *Fatih devrinde İstanbul 1453–1481.* Ankara: Vakıflar Umum Müdürlüğü, 1939.

Uluçay, M. Çağatay. "İstanbul saraçhanesi ve saraçlarına dair bir araştırma." *Tarih dergisi* 5–6 (1951–52): 147–64.

Unan, Fahri. *Kuruluşundan Günümüze Fâtih Külliyesi.* Ankara: Türk Tarih Kurumu, 2003.

Ünver, Süheyl. *İlim ve sanat bakımından Fatih devri notları.* İstanbul: Belediye Matbaası, 1947.

———. *İstanbul'un mutlu askerleri ve şehit olanlar.* Ankara: Türk Tarih Kurumu, 1976.

Uzunçarşılı, İsmail Hakkı. "Bayezid II." *İslâm ansiklopedisi,* 2:394–95.

———. *Çandarlı vezir ailesi.* Ankara: Türk Tarih Kurumu, 1974.

———. "Fatih Sultan Mehmed'in Vezir-i Âzamlarından Mahmud Paşa İle Şehzade Mustafa'nın Araları Neden Açılmıştı?" *Belleten* 28 (1964): 719–28.

———. "Sultan İkinci Murad'ın Vasiyetnamesi." *Vakıflar dergisi* 4 (1958): 1–17.

van Leeuwen, Richard. *Waqfs and Urban Structures: The Case of Ottoman Damascus.* Leiden: E. J. Brill, 1999.

Vatin, Nicolas. "Aux origines du pèlerinage à Eyüp des sultans ottomans." *Turcica* 27 (1995): 91–99.

Vryonis, Speros, Jr. "Byzantine Constantinople and Ottoman Istanbul: Evolution in a Millennial Imperial Iconography." 13–52 In *The Ottoman City and Its Parts: Urban Structure and Social Order,* edited by Irene A. Bierman, Rafaʿat A. Abou-El-Haj, and Donald Preziosi. New Rochelle, N.Y.: A. D. Caratzas, 1991.

———. *The Decline of Hellenism in Asia Minor and the Process of Islamization from the Eleventh Through the Fifteenth Century.* Berkeley and Los Angeles: University of California Press, 1986.

———. "The Ottoman Conquest of Thessaloniki in 1430." In *Continuity and Change in Late Byzantine and Early Ottoman Society,* edited by Anthony Bryer and Heath W. Lowry, 281–321. Birmingham: University of Birmingham; Washington, D.C.: Dumbarton Oaks Research Library and Collection, 1986.

Watenpaugh, Hegnar Zeitlian. *The Image of an Ottoman City: Imperial Architecture and Urban Experience in Aleppo in the 16th and 17th Centuries.* Leiden: E. J. Brill, 2004.

Westfall, Carroll William. *In This Most Perfect Paradise: Alberti, Nicolas V, and the Invention of Conscious Urban Planning in Rome, 1447–55.* University Park: Pennsylvania State University Press, 1974.

Wilson, Adrian. *The Making of the Nuremberg Chronicle.* Amsterdam: Nico Israel, 1976.

Wittek, Paul. "Ayvansaray: Un sanctuaire privé de son héros." *Annuaire de l'Institut de philologie et d'histoire orientales et slaves* 11 (1951): 505–26.

Woodward, David, ed. *Art and Cartography.* Chicago: University of Chicago Press, 1987.

Wulzinger, Karl. *Die Apostelkirche und die Mehmedije zu Konstantinopel.* Brussels, 1932.

Yazıcı, Tahsin. "Fetihten Sonra İstanbul'da İlk Halveti Şeyhleri: Çelebi Muhammed Cemaleddin, Sünbül Sinan ve Merkez Efendi." *İstanbul Enstitüsü dergisi* 2 (1956): 87–113.

———. "Gülşeni, Eserleri, ve Fatih ve II. Bayezid Hakkındaki Kasideleri." *Fatih ve İstanbul,* 2, nos. 7–12 (1954): 82–95.

Yegül, Fikret. *Baths and Bathing in Classical Antiquity*. New York: Architectural History Foundation; Cambridge, Mass.: MIT Press, 1992.

Yenişehirlioğlu, Filiz. "14–15 yy. Mimari Örneklerine göre Bursa Kentinin Gelişimi." In *IX. Türk Tarih Kongresi*, 2: 1345–53. Ankara: Türk Tarih Kurumu, 1989.

Yerasimos, Stéphane. "La communauté grecque-orthodoxe de Constantinople aux lendemains de la conquête ottomane." *Revue des mondes musulmans et de la Méditerranée* [online], nos. 107–10 (2005): 375–99.

———. "La communauté juive d'Istanbul à la fin du XVI siècle." *Turcica* 27 (1995): 101–30.

———. "De l'arbre à la pomme: La généalogie d'un thème apocalyptique." In *Les traditions apocalyptiques au tournant de la chute de Constantinople: Actes de la Table ronde d'Istanbul (13–14 avril 1996)*, edited by Benjamin Lellouch and Stéphane Yerasimos, 153–92. Paris: Harmattan, 1999.

———. *La fondation de Constantinople et de Sainte-Sophie dans les traditions turques: Légendes d'empire*. Istanbul: Institut français d'études anatoliennes; Paris: Librairie d'Amérique et d'Orient J. Maisonneuve, 1990.

———. "Galata á travers les récits de voyage." In *Première Rencontre internationale sur l'Empire ottoman et la Turquie moderne: Institut national des langues et civilisations orientales, Maison de sciences de l'homme, 18–22 janvier 1985*, edited by Edhem Eldem, 117–29. Istanbul: Editions Isis, 1991.

———. "Osmanlı İstanbul'unun Kuruluşu." In *Osmanlı Mimarlığının Yedi Yüzyılı: Uluslararası bir miras*, edited by Nur Akın, Afife Batur, and Selçuk Batur. Istanbul: Yapı Endüstri Merkezi, 1999.

———. "Sinan and His Patrons: Programme and Location." *Environmental Design* 1–2 (1987): 124–31.

Yerasimos, Stéphane, and Jean-Louis Bacqué-Grammont. "La résidence du Baile de Venise à Balıkpazarı: Essai de localisation." *Anatolia Moderna* 6 (1996): 1–11.

Yılmaz, Öz, and Murat Eser. "Ground-Penetrating Radar Surveys at the Fatih Mosque and the Church of St. Sophia, Istanbul." *SEG Technical Program Expanded Abstracts* (2005): 1125–28. http://scitation.aip.org.

Yüksel, İ. Aydın. *Osmanlı miʿmârîsinde II. Bayezid Yavuz Selim devri, 886–926/1481–1520*. Istanbul: Fetih Cemiyeti, 1983.

Yürekli, Zeynep. "A Building Between the Public and Private Realms of the Ottoman Elite: The Sufi Convent of Sokollu Mehmed Pasha in Istanbul." *Muqarnas* 20 (2003): 159–85.

Zarcone, Thierry, and M. Baha Tanman. "Kalenderhane Tekkesi." In *Dünden bugüne İstanbul ansiklopedisi*, 4:398–400.

construction (cont'd)
    empire and, 1–3, 4–5, 51, 54–55,
      130–42, 207, 225–26
    of Hagia Sophia, 4
    historiography of, 5–10, 54–55
    of masjids, 196–97
    by Mehmed II, generally, *xix*, 17–18,
      22, 51–52, 53–56, 138, 212–13, 225
    of mosques, 196–98
    in neighborhoods, 189–93
    of New Mosque, 53, 54, 56–57, 88–89,
      90–92
    of New Palace, 53, 54, 56–59, 110
    non-Muslims and, 17–18
    patronage and, generally, 109
    of streets, 42
    by Süleyman I, 207
    of waterways, 28
Contarini, Matteo, 253n. 38
convent-masjids, 79, 110–14, 190–91,
    246n. 166. *See also* convent-
    mosques; hospices; masjids
convent-mosques, 108–9, 120–21, 124–25,
    131, 222–23, 246n. 166. *See also*
    congregational mosques; con-
    vent-masjids; hospices; mosques
convents, 194–95. *See also* convent-
    masjids; convent-mosques;
    hospices
crosses, 21, 151, 152, 166, 240n. 43,
    252n. 19
Crusades, 24
Çukur Hamam, 82, 104, 108
Cyriacus of Ancona, 162

Davud Pasha, 116, 210, 215, 217, 236n. 128,
    250n. 224
deeds. *See* endowments; freehold deeds
Defteri Muhyiddin Çelebi, 204
Denny, Walter, 209, 210, 262n. 1
deportation
    Byzantine practices of, 179
    commerce and, 30, 43–44
    construction and, 91
    Has Murad Pasha and, 123
    Ilkhanid and Timurid practices of,
      179
    inhabitation by, generally, 178–79,
      182, 186–87, 192
    Mehmed II and, generally, 178–79,
      182
    New Complex and, 93
    non-Muslims and, 182
    Rum Mehmed Pasha and, 119
    Selim I and, 179
De re militari (Valturio), 159
Dernschwam, Hans, 37, 42
devşirme, 3, 109

Die Bader Konstantinopolis (Glück), 125
districts. *See nāḥiye*, neighborhoods
Divan Yolu. *See* Mese
Doka son of Bedros, 203
Dome of the Rock, 72
Doukas, 12, 16, 25, 204, 205
Dürr-i Meknūn (Yazıcıoğlı Ahmed),
    12, 173
Düsseldorf manuscript. *See*
    Buondelmonti

eagle, Byzantine, 2, 37, 39, 142
earthquakes, 48, 77, 170, *171*, 174
Edirne
    baths of, 104
    building complexes of, 139
    as capital, 16–17, 54
    construction at, 213, 214
    convent-mosques in, 260n. 71
    maps of, *134*
    masjids of, 196, 260n. 71
    mosques of, 77–78, *78*, 79, 104
    palace at, 64
    urban order of, 131
education, 3, 21, 22, 56, 57, 70, 84, 115
Eight Colleges. *See* New mosque
    complex
"El Gran Turco," 2, 159, 165, *plate 5*
El-Hac Ahmed bin Aşık Pasha. *See*
    Aşıkpaşazade
    Ayyub al-Ansari shrine and, 51, 52
    Bayezid II and, 92
    Constantinople and, generally, 16,
      54–55, 130–42, 143, 207, 225–26
    construction and, 1–3, 4–5, 51, 54–55,
      130–42, 207, 225–26
    Hagia Sophia and, 18–20
    kingship and, 170–77
    Mehmed II and, 2–5, 16, 51–52, 62,
      66–67, 84–85, 90–92, 159
    monumentalization and, 54–55,
      130–42, 207
    nationalism and, 7–8
    New Complex and, 52, 82–85
    New Mosque and, 66–67, 82–85,
      90–92
    New Palace and, 52, 62, 65
    Ottomans and, generally, 1–3
    representation and, 143, 161, 170–77,
      211–12
    urban notions and, 1–2, 2–3, 4–5,
      130–42, 225–26
employment, 96–98, 115, 243n. 109,
    243n. 115. *See also* commerce,
    endowments
endowments. *See also individual found-
    ers*; patronage
    of Ayas (architect), 191

    at Ayyub al-Ansari shrine, 46, 50
    of Atik Sinan, 192–93, 195, 200
    Bayezid II and, 205, 213, 217
    bedestan and, 43
    churches and, generally, 204
    commerce and, 96–98, 190, 192, 193
    at Constantinople, generally, 21,
      96–103
    convents and, 194–95
    deeds for, 13, 98, 180, 188, 194–96, 200
    of Elvan Çelebi masjid, 183
    employment and, 96–98, 115, 118,
      128, 194, 197, 237n. 134, 243n. 109,
      243n. 115
    on Golden Horn, 31, 40
    government and, 189
    Hagia Sophia and, 40, 97, 98, 180, 183,
      230n. 19, 262n. 116
    income from, generally, 180, 188, 194,
      195
    income from baths, 35, 99, 107, 121
    income from rents, 97, 98, 178, 203
    Islam and, 189, 193–94
    masjids and, 190–91, 194–95
    Mehmed II and, 32, 96–109, 180,
      181–82, 185–86, 188–90, 213, 225
    of Mevlana Husrev, 43, 186, 192, 193,
      194
    mosques and, 190–91, 192–93, 194–95
    neighborhoods and, 180–84, 186, 187,
      188–96, 205–6
    New Complex and, 97, 98
    New Mosque and, 96, 98
    of Sinan Pasha, 205
    of Sinanü'd-din Yusuf Pasha, 46, 50
    surveys of, 180–83, 194–96, 205–6
    urban order and, 96–103, 189–93
    waterways and, 190
    women and, 188, 259n. 53
Enveri, 113
Ephraim ben Gershon, 179
Ergin, Osman, 37
Eski Cami, 240n. 47
Eski İmaret, 22, 191
Eski Kaplıca bath, 104, *105*, *106*
Eski Kenise, 204
Evliya Çelebi
    on Atik Sinan, 241n. 72
    on Ayyub al-Ansari shrine, 48–49
    on bedestan eagle relief, 234n. 87
    on Constantinople, 6
    on Mahmud Pasha complex, 116, 130
    on New Mosque, 95, 242n. 81
    on waterways, 245n. 143
Eyice, Semavi, 246n. 166, 264n. 34
Eyüp suburb
    Ayyub al-Ansari shrine at, 18, 45–51,
      137

Urban the Cannonmaker, 182. *See also* neighborhoods: Topcu Urban Evleri

urban practices and notions. *See also* construction; neighborhoods
architecture and, 133–35, 141–42
baths and, 103–9
bedestan and, 37–42
of Bursa, 131
Byzantine Constantinople and, 1–2, 136, 137–38
ceremonies and, 136
commerce and, 132–33
of Edirne, 131
empire and, 1–2, 2–3, 4–5, 130–42, 225–26
endowments and, 189
Hagia Sophia and, 135, 136, 141
Has Murad Pasha complex and, 124
historiography on, 9–10
Islamic city model and, 9–10, 124, 139, 161
Mahmud Pasha complex and, 117–19
Mehmed II and, 2–3, 133–34, 138
models of, 9–10, 131–35
monumentalization and, 130–42
multiplicity of, 70, 130–31, 141–42, 144, 225–26
neighborhoods and, 183–84, 189
New Complex and, 92–96, 135, 139, 141
New Mosque and, 140, 142
New Palace and, 59, 65–66, 133, 139
Old Palace and, 23–24, 133, 135, 139
Ottomans and, 1–2, 9–10, 13, 14–15, 130–42

Renaissance and, 1–2, 92, 133–35
representation and, 154–64, 208–9
streets and, 135–36, 217–18
views and visual relationships in, 70, 65, 120, 139–41, 252n. 29
Uruc, 12
Üsküdar
commerce and, 44
Mehmed II in, 119
neighborhoods of, 257n. 24
representation of, 207, 209, 211
Rum Mehmed Pasha complex at, 119–22, 139
Uzunçarşı, 186
baths of, 107–8
commerce and, 29, 31, 32, 33
neighborhood of, 184, 200
urban order and, 136

Valens, aqueduct of, 150, 153, 162, 208
Valturio, 159
Vavassore, Giovanni Andreas di
Barbari view compared with, 253n. 33
Buondelmonti view compared with, 156, 157, 161, 252n. 17
Byzantium sive Constantineopolis, xxvi–xxvii, 14, 148, 154–64, *155, 164*
Hippodrome image by, 136
Matrakcı Nasuh compared with, 209, 212
Old Palace view by, *22, 23*
Schedel compared with, 161, 166
Vefazade foundation, 99–101, *101, 102, 103,* 136, 186, 191, 224, 229n. 13

Velāyetnāme-i Otman Bābā (Küçük Abdal), 12, 43, 136, 140, 191, 194, 235n. 104, 235n. 105
Venetian colony
house of bailo in, 37, 205
loggia of, 37
urban fabric of, 30, 31–35, 37, 205
Venice, 144, 158, 159
Virgin Mary, 20

waqfs. *See* endowments
waqfiyyas. *See* endowment deeds, individual founders
waterways
baths and, 106, 107, 116
of Constantinople, generally, 116
construction and restoration of, 28, 34, 67, 106–7, 117, 150
endowments and, 190
Mahmud Pasha complex and, 116
neighborhoods and, 185, 190
New Mosque and, 67
representation of, 150, 153, 162–63
Wittek, Paul, 46–47, 48

Ya'kut, 89
Yavaşca Şahin masjid, 197. *See also* neighborhoods
Yavuzer Sinan masjid, 183, 197
Yazıcıoğlı Ahmed, 173
Yedikule. *See* Seven Towers
Yerasimos, Stéphane, 12, 47, 172, 185, 243n. 103

Zeyrek. *See* Mevlana Zeyrek

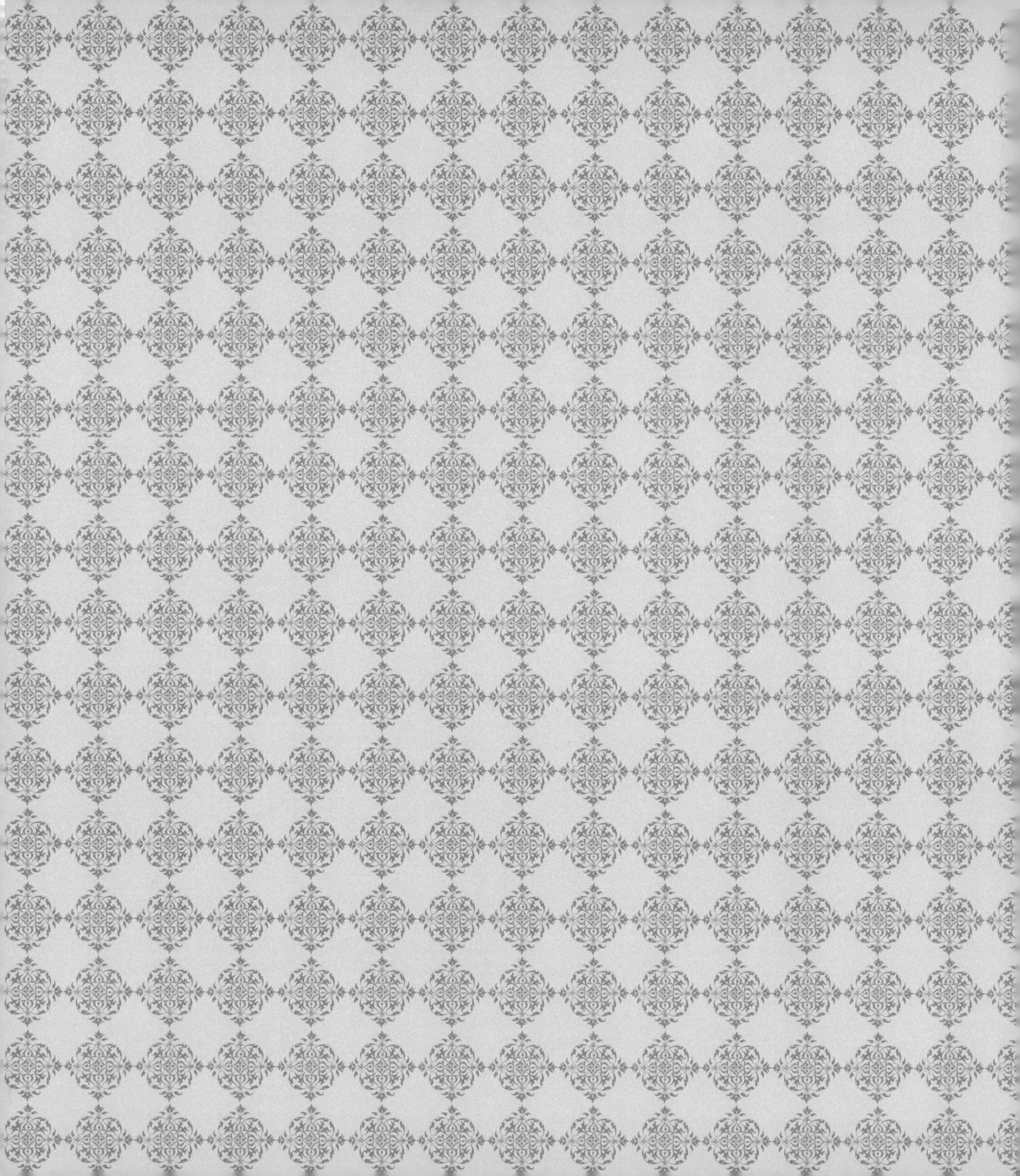